# Conquering The Bongos

Conquering The Bongos

Written By: Jo'Anna Laurene
Illustrated By: Walter Cumming

Liberty Hill Publishing
555 Winderley Pl, Suite 225
Maitland, FL 32751
407.339.4217
www.libertyhillpublishing.com

© 2024 by Jo Anna Laurene

Illustrated by Walter Cumming,

All rights reserved solely by the author. The author guarantees all contents are original and do not infringe upon the legal rights of any other person or work. No part of this book may be reproduced in any form without the permission of the author.

Due to the changing nature of the Internet, if there are any web addresses, links, or URLs included in this manuscript, these may have been altered and may no longer be accessible. The views and opinions shared in this book belong solely to the author and do not necessarily reflect those of the publisher. The publisher therefore disclaims responsibility for the views or opinions expressed within the work.

Paperback ISBN-13: 978-1-66289-876-1
Dust Jacket ISBN-13: 978-1-66289-877-8
eBook ISBN-13: 978-1-66289-878-5

*This book is dedicated to my parents, who possessed patience, energy,
and boundless love for each other and family.
They raised us to be thoughtful and to treat others with love, respect, and dignity.
They taught us always to seek the truth while being true to ourselves.
It is also dedicated to my grandchildren and great-grandchildren.
It is a love story that I wanted to share with you.
Through these pages, may you understand that your family, past and present,
helped define a nation.
They are your ancestors who possessed
responsibility, integrity, values, and heart that benefited you.
All were simple, ordinary people who embraced a country founded on freedom.
Armed with that freedom and with great sacrifice, they worked hard with their skills, talents, determination, and courage
as they settled The West.
It was a pilgrimage they journeyed for you, which you can be proud of.
This is the foundation from which your grandparents and parents drew upon, creating their own knowledge and strength they are now teaching you.
There will be many who will disparage those long-held traditions of freedom.
Be strong because you possess the truth…
I love you very much.*

To Holly and Clark
Never Stop Dreaming

To Hazel
Our Shooting Star

*This book contains many historical references
about my family,
the communities in which we lived, and of our country.
Therefore, any stories or phrasing have been written
as depicted in the period in which it occurred.*

*History is what happens as generations move through life.
History is a mechanism to help people, communities,
and our country grow.
Therefore, history should never be changed, rewritten,
or erased, and
nobody should ever be afraid to tell their story.*

*Most of all, never take the vagaries of life too seriously.
It is just noise trying to disrupt our peace and our beliefs.
They are simply fascinations and trends
that will change tomorrow.*

Table of Contents

Introduction xv

Part I

Realization of a Problem 1

Part II

The Middle 4
The Crown of the Continent 8
First Impressions 10
Yellowstone 12
A Flatland above the Lake 15
Natural Wonders 17
My Adventure Begins 19
From Whence I Come 22
My Grandpa Earl 23
A Vehicle Like None Other 26
The Richest Hill on Earth 28
Dad's Classic Truck 30
Mom's Classic Ride 32
My New Best Friend 35
Navigating Rock Garden 38
Tackling the Bongos 41
My Grandmother, Queen Elizabeth .43
Final Approach… Camp Silverback .45
First Forays into Family Camping 47
The Oregon Trail 50
Evolution of Family Camping 51
The Real News of Yesteryear 53

The First in Modern Television and Stereo Consoles	56
Exploring My Summer Digs	58
Family Camping Nostalgia	63
The Brick Phone	65
George	68
Preparing for the Masses	70
Primitive Living	73
Early Settlers of the West	76
The Struggle to Survive	79
Farm to Table the Old-Fashioned Way	82
City Life for the Rural Life	85
Real Struggles in History	86
The Wild West	90
The Mother of all Flu	93
A Hero	95
The Family Funeral Home Business	97
The Elusive Snipe	100
The Bird Phase	102
Eureka and the Tobacco Valley	104
A Day of Exploration	108
Old Growth	110
Dads Fancy MG Convertible Sports Car	113
Dad's Loo	115
Frank Lake	117
Puffed Rice...Not Just for Breakfast Anymore	124
Montana's Grizzly Bears	126
Banquets...Wilderness Style	129
Camp Silverback	136
French Camp	144
Changed Forever	148
Re-living Joy for One Day	152
What Public Use Looks Like	154
Sliding on my Backside!	156
Celebrating Our Country's Birth	158

Fourth of July Remembered 159
Our Camp Bear 160
Noah 162
Billings. 167
Love Mice 169
A Beautiful Beginning and Then Chicago 171
The First Mouse Motel 175
Rodent Woes. 179
Tumblers and Squirrel Cages 180
My New Title 182
The Wastebasket. 183
The Horse Saga. 185
The Neighborhood Blemish 188
Ready, Set, Hunt! 190
Head Chef and Grouse Connoisseur 196
My Father…Kennel Architect to Gentleman Farmer to Pool Designer . 199
Introducing My Special Friend. 202
The Beartooth 206
Early Montana Winters 210
Oh, Flock! 212
Fogged In 214
Searching for Perfection 216
Rip Arrived 218
Little Switzerland 220
Mikes Come and Mikes Go. 226
Mustard, Not Just a Condiment. 228
More Fog. 231
The Frontier Man 233

Part III

The Weeds 237
Early Manifestations of My Disorder 240
Dad's Evil Spreadsheet. 242
Spreading my Wings 244

Salesman Extraordinaire 247
Dad's Health Journey 249
Psych Papa! 254
The Importance of Flushing 256
Staying Puft 257
Know Your Principles 260

Part IV

Loss 262
Bowled Over 266
Coming Off the Cliff 268
The Downward Spiral 271
Early Evolutions of Body Weight 275
My Daily Exercise Routine 279
Dad's Motorcycle Phase 280
Kris…My Sister Friend 283
Size Does Matter 287
Culinary Delights 291
A New Perspective 293
Fishin' for Keys 295

Part V

Holiday Traditions 299
Losing Christ in Christmas 302
Holding Onto Christ 304
Blindsided 306
Goodbye Mom 308
Justin 310
Heart and Soul 314

Part VI

Life in the 2020s 318
The Novel Coronavirus 319
Global Rollbacks of Vaccine Mandates 322

Confusing Government Strategies That Confused 324
Falsifying the Numbers 326
Introducing Transformative Language. 329
New Introductions 331
Theatre of the Absurd 334
Introducing America's Lead Guru of Science and Health 338
Everyone Must Lead a Trans Life 339
Tomboys 340
How to Conform an Entire Society 343
The Best in Story Telling 346
Re-forming Society 348
History of the Progressive Thought Conundrum 353
A Cultural Revolution. 365
Lessons Long Forgotten 369
Women's Rights 372
History Of Social Context 378
The Face of Our Country's Incapable Youth 381
The Justification of "Injustices" 388
The Giant Symbol of Complete and Total Racism. 394
Intersectionality Adjacents. 397
Progressive Brown Shirts of the Modern Era 399
A New Army. 403
Progressive Score Keeping. 407
Civic vs. Global Good 410
The Ultimate Societal Sin 413
Weight as a Parallel to Gender, Abortion and the COVID-19 Vaccine . 418
Influencers. 421
Bidenomics and Economic Decay. 422
The Religiosity of Cults and Cult Theory 427
The Religiosity of Racism and Its Correlative…Critical Race Theory . . 437
Racism and Genocide. 442
Terrorism 445
The Religiosity of Trans Activism. 447
Quantum Social Entanglement Theory 452

The Public School System's 2020 Mandate 458
Egocentrism as an Extension of Narcissism 461
Title IX 463
National Trans Day of Vengeance 467
Checking the Woke Box of Inclusivity 471
Military Reinvention 475
The Most Courageous "Woman" on Earth 479
Trans Activism Will End 484
Societal Consequences of Prioritization 485
The Religiosity of Abortion 487
The Religiosity of COVID-19 496
The Religiosity of Climate Change 510
Intercontinental Rail Travel 520
Flatulent Perils 522
Gas Lighter in Chief 524
The CONNIVED System 527
Operation "Big Truck" 529
VIP Climate Conference 532
Climate Change Adaption 534
On To Davos 536
Cult Religiosity Overview 539
The Goals of the Division Industry 541
More Cultural Bull 542
Seeking Strategies 549
History of Society's Engagement with Technology 562
Covering My Backside 566

Part VII

Navigating Our World 568
Our Core 571
Beginning Again 573
Our Montana 577
Our Montana Life 584

Part VIII
Today, Tomorrow, and Destinies 589

Epilogue 591
Acknowledgments and Heartfelt Thanks. 596
Source. 601

Introduction

This story was a long time coming. Only since I retired have I had the time to write it down and examine its meaning. Within its pages, this book describes the lives of typical people living, working, and playing. Ordinary people who get married, have children, and work hard for their families. We are the uninteresting folks, long forgotten by the power players in this country. They are those who throw down the constraints on our freedoms that prevent us from succeeding.

My family's pioneer story begins in the late 1890s and how the fortunes and lessons of that era influenced my family's formation beginning in the late 1950s. I begin my family's story with my brother, Randy, and his life journey as he recounts his adventures in the summer of 1995 when he was thirty-two years old. He had graduated from college several years before and began a food service career. That summer, Randy was assigned as the food service director for several hundred Boy Scouts and their leaders in a remote, rugged wilderness area. Randy often reminisces throughout this memoir, chronicling our family's adventures as we grew up.

Throughout Randy's adult life, my father kept a collection of letters he sent to our parents. Those letters became an entertaining journal of Randy's and our lives during a simpler time, as he unknowingly documented his life following high school graduation. It was a time of exploration and innocence as he began navigating a new life outside our parents' wings. He made many discoveries and learned many lessons we can all espouse today, which is why I shared them in this book.

Randy's story shares, in great detail, his struggle with an eating disorder that began in childhood, the consequences of which many people battle every day in our country. It is a struggle that our society now seeks to minimize, with significant damage to these individuals and their families. It was a launch point to describe other collateral damage done to this country at the behest of a few.

My father and my grandfather were all savers. Included in family documentation were many letters my father wrote home to his parents while in college and then as he and Mom embarked on their life journey. Then, the letters between Randy and my father detailed our family's journey. I then weaved a story that was important to salvage for my family.

My father was also a researcher who loved the American West. His historical publications and railroad memorabilia collection detailed the West's early founding. I found a book written by my cousin, who, through her own family's research, was able to trace our pioneer family as they immigrated to the United States from Norway and Holland. Dad's love for genealogy work and all that research that sat in boxes for decades, I finally dug out of storage. His collections and research then motivated me to delve into my own research. Once pieced together, I found a story that spoke of great courage, adventure, determination, and sacrifice. It illustrated how fortunate we all are to live in a country based on freedom, faith, and family.

I then contemplated my family's history in today's world. While writing, I pondered how much has changed in our country since I was a youngster. Researching and writing this book was like living through a real-life time capsule. I traced the history of my pioneer family and how it shaped my family's life today. I performed much contrasting as I examined the struggles of those earliest pioneers compared to today's current events and how each of those generations journeyed through the world in which they lived.

I wanted my grandchildren to know how each generation navigated that world as our country evolved. I want them to understand our family's and country's attitudinal climate each generation experienced. I wanted to give them a glimpse of what life in our country used to be like when it was so much simpler. Only then can they understand how much has changed for them and their future families.

By the 2020s, our country's evolution radically changed. In twenty years, I want them to know how they got to where they are and what that means for their futures. Maybe my grandchildren's and great-grandchildren's generations can guide our country to a foundation of family, faith, kindness, and trust. In many ways, our nation depends on it.

There was never a time when we didn't feel supported and loved by our parents. They spent many resources to help us grow. Some were financial, but the primary resource was time. We are repeatedly told that time spent with children and family is the most important resource any parent can give a child. It is the resource that cultivates a happy, healthy, and productive adult. While I did not appreciate it then, my parents practiced that belief daily. For that, I am eternally grateful. It doesn't matter how much money you have or what your race or gender might be. Time costs nothing and is unconcerned about everything that makes us different. What has gotten lost is that children could care less about all the nonsense that adults perseverate about. Is it fair that we make them care about it?

Randy's Boy Scout camp location and camp name were changed to reflect my love for Montana, her history, and her beauty. It follows Montana's history, emphasizing and portraying the ruggedness of the weather, her terrain, and her people, past and present. Montanans are fiercely independent, self-reliant, patriotic, strong, and compassionate. It makes Montana what it is, and I wouldn't live anywhere else. It is the state where my family is from and where Randy was born. It is where my grandchildren's great, great, great, great, grandparents settled. They were the original frontier men and women who forged new beginnings into a vast unknown. They did it with courage, strength, and perseverance. That attitude is as prevalent as ever in today's Montana.

This book is a memoir based on Randy and my father's letters, their journal writings, and my memories growing up. It incorporates my father's research, his Western collections, and my research. I then weaved a story that transitions American history, Montana's history, my pioneer family's journey westward, and all our family adventures. This book became a diary of America that tells a story of pioneer struggles, explorative conquests, family explorations, and then our realities of today. Only then can one witness what historic progress we have lost and the realities of a far different America than was intended.

Randy was a hilarious person. While writing, I sought to channel his humor throughout this book. I examined the absurdities and formulated them into thought-provoking humor. Through humor, one can understand how truly irrational the 2020s have become. This is how Randy analyzed life and it was a gift he inherited from our father. It is unfortunate that everybody can't examine life the same way. Once you do, you can truly understand how preposterous it has become. Once I understood it, I began to see it for what it is—methods to create an alternative form of America.

Media representation within my father's collection illustrated a time of community, families, and local institutions. Seeing a side of journalism that wrote about facts long ago was refreshing. Human interest stories were reported during a time of positivity and American pride. It was a kinder time, not obsessively absorbed in national discourse. Such accounts have now taken a severe back seat to the negativity and hate of today. Driven by the media, we have all been caught up in the crossfire of their constant barrage of anger and blame.

The 2020s will ultimately go down in history as an earth-shattering time of monumental changes. Those in power saw it as a "necessary transformative time." What they identified as necessary brought much pain and suffering to Americans. What they called some unfortunate collateral damage, the rest of us saw as a massive societal earthquake, with more losers than winners. Significant accomplishments made through decades of recognition and self-reflection, individually and as a society, have been lost by those seeking to divide.

In comparing my childhood, what became painfully obvious was that we all lost a simpler, more innocent time with destructive overtones to society, from which we may never recover. While writing this book, information came in so fast that it was challenging to keep up with them. The book became a historical testament not only of my family, our culture, and our country, but also of the constantly changing, chaotic demands on all of us. Absurd notions and conflicts that have changed our lives forever. I highlight only the standouts. To delineate all of them would have resulted in a 2,000-page book.

The events and changes I describe are those we used to read only in twisted tales in a bad novel or what you would find in a satirical publication. Many of the events would challenge the best dystopian novels ever written. As it is, it ended up being a longer book than intended, as it became necessary to properly delineate our history in relation to what we have become as a country and a society.

It was challenging to write this book without getting mired in the insanity of our politics. My goal was to write a fun story about my family, Montana, and the history of our country for my grandchildren. Then, COVID-19 happened. An event that changed our entire nation and the world. It was an event that some capitalized upon for their "Great Reset," a descriptor that would be awarded the "Greatest Understatement of the Century Award." Little did we all know what this would mean for all of us. "Fifteen days to control the Spread" launched the entire country into turmoil, which we still live with today, and very little of it is related to COVID. I'm not sure it will ever be over.

I changed course many times over my writing. The book became a testimonial to explain all the political, social, and popular innuendo that completely changed the entire cultural fabric of our country. After much thought, research, and course changes, I decided my grandchildren needed to know what happened.

Before writing this book, I had been timidly navigating this new socially constructed world. My personality is such that I didn't want to risk offending anyone. As I researched, I became much more aware of what was really occurring in this country. I then became less and less concerned about accepting other's views at the expense of my own. As rightful citizens of this country, we all have valid feelings and opinions about what is occurring around us, and we all have as much right to express them as anyone else. That said, I have discovered that my tolerance for idiocy has quickly vanished. How can it not be when each day a newfound variant of lunacy is infecting all of us? Every day we think it can't get any worse, and then it does.

What began as a little book project about my family's history became something much bigger. What should have been completed in one to two years is now going on five years. Headlines that make regular normals seethe in disgust, I put in a different perspective. Channeling my brother, I used comic relief whenever possible to place our new "socially constructed" world into the correct context. It helped me to stay optimistic with each new crazy headline coming across the newsfeed. Optimistic people can create positive paths. Angry people only become apathetic, which prevents them from creating those positive pathways to sanity.

As a preview, I will borrow the language of Chemistry's Conformational Isomers, specifically Cis and Trans forms, that, in theory, can be interconverted when, in the real world, this Isomer (molecule) requires energy unavailable under normal conditions. Using this theory, we are being forced to live in a non-conformational society that attempts to test our boundaries by blocking known truths to someone else's descript co-equals, which, in reality, are not equal at all. Where non-conformity and new constructs are the primary subtexts in a book that copies the same, style guides have been thrown out the window. It is tough to write a conforming book in a non-conforming, delusional, newly constructed world. If none of this makes sense to you, it isn't supposed to, but it will by the end of this book (Helmenstine, Ph.D. 2019).

After five years of research and writing, I now understand the game and the rules. I will share the applied principles of various social constructs in, "**S**tudied **O**bjective **U**nderstandable **R**eality that is **C**orrectly **E**xamined" or **"SOURCE."** Within it, you will find reality-based evidence to re-orient the reader towards known standards of earthly biological and energy applications we have all known and loved for centuries. SOURCE will cite factual data, often ignored by "fact-checkers," who used to be factual but no longer base their checking on facts.

SOURCE will also cite many satirical passages. To save readers time and effort, all can be found in SOURCE. For all those "fact-checkers" who can reliably no longer check for facts, satire will be clearly identified to eliminate any confusion you have in your fact-checking confusion. I am contemplating a companion board game called "Gyration." As we spin through each cycle of swirling circum-evolutionary convoluted spheres of rotating competing definitions of our "newly constructed" world, points are scored if one can guess whether the statement or story is satire because you sure can't tell the difference anymore (Bois 2019) (Roth 2021).

To that end, I have found it comical to see politicians and their media take their power so seriously that they believe they are the ultimate purveyors of all truth and justice. They wield that faux power like a ninja warrior with a nun chuck. As they fling it around against their enemies, they can't help but thwack themselves in the face. Once you see it for what it is, you can't help but laugh.

It is hard to describe precisely what this book is. It is a combination of history, nonfiction, and satire. It is a reference book to describe our past, present, and future lexicon, in which we are all playing a part. It became a manual to help define a multitude of new ideals that we are expected to embrace.

Society is drowning in Political Correctness, which in 2020 was transformed into "Wokeness." Wokeness does not equal truth. Being "woke" is how one perceives the world around them and is rarely based on facts. However, we are witnessing individual perceptions who base their entire understanding of the world on "correctness," regardless of facts. This will be further delineated throughout the book.

To that end, we have been introduced to many new words and phrases with brand-new definitions, which no one can keep up with. It has been engineered that way, so we all get lost in the complexities without realizing the true objective. Only when you examine it with a wide-angle lens can you discover what the goals are. I provide many of my own definitions to assist the reader in zooming in on the specifics of their strategy.

> "I don't make jokes. I just watch the Government and report the facts!"
> *Will Rogers 1879-1935…*

It was a way to illustrate the complexities where one can find meaning in the minutiae they use to conceal the actual goal. Once you see the hidden strategies for what they are, the goal comes into focus.

People have asked me why I didn't separate the content into two books. I thought hard about that because parts of the book probably distract from my family's story, but this book is for my grandchildren. It is our family's and nation's history. It is a history that they will inherit and carry forward. Even what we are living through today is history that, in twenty years, will be fully examined with all its pain and glory. History is the dynamic that continually changes our lives and is influenced by those outside the family. Only if you know what is occurring can you appreciate what it has become. For my grandchildren, what they see today is their baseline reference in understanding the world around them. That is the real tragedy today, as many are reconfiguring history to make it congruent with woke outlier beliefs that have no basis in our reality, past or present. America's past wasn't always pretty, but it was our history, one that shaped new directions for a better future. Today's present history is really ugly. It is being created to transform our America into something much different. Hopefully, my grandchildren can better appreciate and understand what America is now is not how it has always been.

Writing this book was also a fun trip down memory lane, recalling our extraordinary childhood, created and nurtured by incredible parents during a forgotten time in our country that I fear is lost forever. Only when you know how it was can you understand what it isn't now. It used to be simple. Now, we are all entangled in convoluted abstracts that we're being forced to participate in, that most of us want no part of.

Finally, in its conclusion, the book brings it all back around. Regardless of the turmoil, the tyranny, and all the malcontent, it is family and faith that we can count on to eliminate all the noise. Within the family, we can all count on peace at the end of the day when we all draw close in togetherness. Peace, freedom, faith, and family are what America's founding was all about. There is no other country like it on the face of the planet.

Let's begin Randy's story…

PART I

Realization of a Problem

Dear Journal,

It is July 2004. It is time for some serious self-analysis here. It is a long story that began in my childhood. It is a problem made worse throughout my life by dreams of plentitude, and the consequences of personal tragedies. I will examine what happened and how I progressed to where I am today. I apologize ahead of time for my occasional rambling. It helps me understand where I came from, what happened along the way, and why I am here now. I need to analyze my history and share what I learned. It could help someone else with the same struggles.

It is surreal as I lay in a hospital bed surrounded by my sisters and best friend, Laura. It feels like an out-of-body experience as the three perform an intervention. It is all very uncomfortable for me, but they are very worried. I guess my collapse and subsequent hospital admission were the last straw for them. They are telling me it is time to get serious and do something about my weight. They are afraid I will die soon if I don't do something.

This intervention is a final attempt to turn around a lifelong issue. A very personal matter that I have gone to great lengths to hide my entire life. A problem, all but impossible to conceal anymore. After all, it has come to this: Hanging out in a hospital bed, barely able to breathe or move, with fluid running off my body. My bed sheets are soaked through once again. The nurse must do a complete bed change about five times a day.

They tell me I have an eating disorder. I never thought of obesity as an eating disorder until now. Eating disorders are supposed to be described as dangerously thin, a food obsession where you starve yourself through Bulimia or Anorexia. They are correct about one thing: I never remember a time in my life when I didn't obsess about food or my next meal.

Even as a young boy, I remember hiding food in my bedroom, waiting for the opportune time to sneak a snack or gorge on a box of cereal. I would hide food in my bedroom, sneaking a snack when I was alone at night before falling asleep. As I grew older, the techniques became more secretive and stealthier.

Every day as I walked home from school, any money I had would be spent on chocolate and other candy at the corner grocery store. If I had the extra funds, I would go to the Dairy Queen and buy a Dilly Bar or a Banana Split. Ultimate nirvana was if I had enough money to buy a cheeseburger and fries. I always made sure to have it all consumed before arriving home. Mom would then have our after-school snack ready, where I would eat again. By twelve years of age, instead of participating in sports or playing outside, I often would scan through cookbooks, finding delicious-looking dishes for the family to try. Mom was always game for new family dinner ideas, and I always got to help her prepare our surprise new dinner recipe. This alone was not concerning at the time. What mother wouldn't enjoy experimenting and designing a new dinner idea with her son?

I developed a severe stutter when I was about three years of age. My parents and our family doctor surmised that it was probably caused by extreme anxiety when Mom went into the hospital to give birth to my youngest sister, Kristi. For a three-year-old boy, there was little understanding of why his mother was missing for days.

Stuttering makes it impossible to carry on a normal conversation. Often ridiculed for this by my peers, I did have a handful of very close friends who didn't care that I stuttered. We were together through thick and thin. As adults, we all stayed in touch as we embarked on our life journeys. They were all never more than a phone call away.

Adolescence was such a hard time for me. At a time when you are desperately trying to fit in, kids can be ruthless, with their first targets being those who are different. A teacher calling on you to answer a question is the most traumatic thing you can experience if you can't talk. Even if you know the answer, you can't string the sentence together to answer it. I was always a sensitive, shy, and anxious child. As I sat at my desk, struggling to talk, I could hear twenty other kids snickering in the background. The more stressed out I felt, the more I stuttered.

Mom and Dad connected me with a speech therapist when I was six. She was a great therapist and taught me strategies to interrupt my stuttering patterns, techniques that led you to pause when speech was about to be interrupted. By pausing, you could turn sentences and words around to insert different words that were easier for me to enunciate. She was brilliant, and by the time I was a teenager, my stuttering had turned into just simple pauses, barely discernible to a listener. Unless you knew I was a stutterer, you couldn't tell.

However, the damage to my psyche was already done. For me, eating was my way to help me feel better. The eating disorder that manifested simultaneously as my stuttering was well on its way to destruction by the time I became a young man. Don't get me wrong, I have had a great life. I grew up in a typical, happy, loving family with parents who were well-engaged in our lives. I was lucky to have some great friends. I was fortunate to have the freedom and the desire to explore. I am intelligent enough to seek out information when needed to understand the world around me. I have always been open to new ideas. I have this uncanny ability to find humor in nearly everything.

Today, though, I am being held captive in a hospital bed. I cannot flee, as I am being forced to confront an issue my sisters and best friend will no longer allow me to ignore. I guess it might be time to do something. It is time to analyze my life, draw some conclusions, and make a plan. All things considered, I think I'll start in the middle.

PART II

The Middle

It is June 1st, 1995, as I begin a great summer adventure to northwest Montana. I am headed to The Kootenai/Cabinet mountains and Eureka, Montana, in Lincoln County, a stone's throw from Canada. Camp Silverback Boy Scout Camp is where I will be spending my summer. My family has deep ties to this state. My father comes from Billings in south-central Montana, and my mother's family is from Plentywood in eastern Montana. I was born in Billings. Both are relatively flat areas with rich ranching, mining, and agricultural histories.

This region of Montana is geographically very different. As I fly into the Flathead Valley, I am captivated first by the landscape of mountainous terrain, vast wilderness chains, and numerous bodies of crystal-clear blue water. As the plane begins its final descent into The Flathead, we drop down into the scenic corridor over Flathead Lake. It is breathtaking as the plane follows alongside the Swan and Mission Mountain ranges to the east and the Kootenai/Cabinet range to the west.

The Swans is where hiking and fishing enthusiasts will find Jewel Basin, located above the east side of the Flathead Valley. Hiking into the Basin gives spectacular sights to those seeking the high country, with views of Glacier National Park and the Bob Marshall Wilderness. Jewel Basin has twenty-seven named lakes, which contain 15,349 total acres and fifty miles of hiking trails. No motorized vehicles or horses are allowed in the Basin. The Swan Mountains stretch toward the north to become the Scapegoat and Great Bear Wildernesses. These all comprise the vast mountainous area called "The Bob Marshall Wilderness Complex." A wilderness complex known as "The Bob" by the locals, it is the fifth-largest wilderness designation in the lower forty-eight states. It derived its name after a long-ago American forester and writer, best remembered as the person who spearheaded the 1935 founding of the Wilderness Society in the United States.

Off to the north, I see The Whitefish Range and Whitefish Mountain Resort, formerly known as Big Mountain Ski Resort. The resort, located just above Whitefish, sees an average of three hundred inches of snow yearly on its 3,000 acres of mountainous terrain. The resort's humble beginnings began in 1935, with a tiny cabin built as a base camp. Skiers would hike up the mountain wearing leather ski boots and wooden skis. The first T-bar didn't open until 1947. Today, it is known for some of the best skiing in the region, attracting many skiing enthusiasts from the country, many from Canada. When the snow melts and disappears, the mountainous terrain becomes rich with color, as the wildflowers indigenous to the area bloom in brilliant hues of blues, yellows, reds, and oranges. The white flowery bulbs of bear grass spring forth, and the huckleberry bushes burst with deep purple berries. The resort then becomes home to thrilling Zip Line tours and an aerial adventure park, with world-class downhill and cross-country mountain biking. Today, as I fly in, you can see some remains of the snow line as it descends halfway down the ski slopes.

To the northeast, I see Glacier National Park. The park is a part of the Rocky Mountain Range, which includes Canada's Waterton Lakes National Park. Both parks were combined in 1932 as the world's first International Peace Park. The United Nations Educational, Scientific and Cultural Organization (UNESCO) later listed the two parks as a joint World Heritage Site for their diverse and plentiful plant and wildlife species and outstanding scenery.

Far to the west, I see the Kootenai/Cabinet Mountain range, where I am ultimately headed. The Cabinets, located in Northwest Montana and along the Idaho panhandle, were first surveyed by French-Canadian fur trappers. They dubbed it the Cabinet Mountains for the rock shelves looming over the rivers below. The Cabinet Mountain range is part of the Rockies, North America's most extensive mountain system.

Flying over Flathead Lake is magnificent. It is the largest freshwater lake between the Mississippi River and the Pacific Ocean. It is twenty-eight miles long and encompasses nearly two hundred square miles. Whenever he had free time, my father would visit Flathead Lake as often as possible. He was a college student in Missoula at The University of Montana. The scenic drive to the Flathead was only about two hours from campus. Most often, he would travel along Highway 93, which skirts the entire south and west shores of Flathead Lake. It is the main corridor that connects the community of Missoula to Polson, Lakeside, Somers, and Kalispell. From Kalispell, Highway 93 connects to Eureka via Whitefish.

The primary communities nestled within the Flathead Valley are Kalispell, Whitefish, and Bigfork. Bigfork is a cunning, artsy community located along the east shore of Flathead Lake. Whitefish is known for its trendy appeal and location below Whitefish Mountain Resort. Kalispell is known as the hub that connects the communities. Kalispell's Regional Medical Center struggles to keep up with Flathead's continually growing community. As a result, hospital expansion is ongoing, with many specialty services not usually found in other communities of similar size.

I have been to the area before but primarily spent my time in Bigfork. It was the location of my grandparent's fiftieth wedding anniversary and family retreat in the early 1980s. My Aunt Barbara and Uncle Gene had a great home on the shore of Flathead Lake. It is where their children and my cousins, Jeff and Jodi, grew up. They owned a little mom-and-pop craft shop in downtown Bigfork. Now, you cannot even locate the house. Either it was torn down or buried among the condominiums and marina area along the northeast shore.

The east shore of Flathead Lake is accessed by Highway 35 as you venture over from Polson. It is a narrow two-lane highway that meanders north from Polson to Bigfork. It resembles an asphalt roller coaster with deep dips, non-existent shoulders, twisting turns, and tight tree lines. Earliest travel around the east shore was difficult at best. In Highway 35's earliest days, most people opted for boat or rail travel instead. It wouldn't be until the early 1900s that an enterprising warden from the Deer Lodge Prison and his inmates would change it. Long talked about, they would make an east shore road a reality, as a statewide movement to improve roads occurred then. In March of 1912, a crew of forty to fifty prisoners began work on what later became known as East Shore Road. The project was launched as part of an agreement between the state prison officials and Flathead County and was completed in 1914. Today, of course, it is known as Montana Highway 35 (Larcombe 2022).

Camp Silverback is my assignment this summer as I once again return to the state of my roots. It will be my catering company's first foray into deep wilderness catering service. A Boy Scout camp is the perfect venue for this experiment. They didn't give me much information. My guess is they have no idea what to expect themselves. I will manage a staff and mess hall for complete meal services to the scouts, their leaders, and camp staff.

I feel honored that they chose me to kick off this new endeavor during the University's off-season. They told me they are confident I can think on the fly and accommodate any unusual circumstances. Probably though, I am the logical sucker within the company to make this happen.

Whatever the reason, it will be a great adventure. Camp bosses say they will transport my supplies and me into camp by Jeep on a road that is mostly inaccessible. The scouts get in and out on foot. I still wonder how I will get all my supplies in because they will not fit in a Jeep.

It all sounds very fascinating. I will be in the heart of grizzly bear country with some of the most rugged terrain of the Rocky Mountain West, which includes the Glacier National Park ecosystem.

The Crown of the Continent

I have never visited Glacier National Park before. I only saw it from a distance when we visited Bigfork. Our family's adventures always took us through Yellowstone Park on the way to Billings from Oregon during our summer vacations. Both are equally beautiful but very different from one another. People don't realize where Glacier Park got its name. In our highly charged, environmentally aware age, they say Glacier Park is named for the presence of glaciers. In reality, it is not that simple. However, it is a way to exaggerate the effects of a "man-made" global disaster to describe the disappearance of glaciers in one of the country's most famous parks. Glaciers, which they say are "catastrophically" disappearing soon due to "global warming," or as it is alternatively called, "climate change." While there is no argument for climate change globally or that Glacier Park's glaciers are disappearing, it is disingenuous to manipulate a natural global phenomenon by exploiting the name of this park. The truth is that Glacier Park was the location for a naturally occurring geographical change caused by slow-moving ice rivers. Massive amounts of flowing ice were formed by centuries of compacted snow on the mountains. Glacier Park was named because of this titanic event. Millenniums ago, during the ice age, the jagged, sharp rock peaks we see today were cut and formed by the movement of massive, compacted ice accumulations, ice that drastically changed the landscape through erosion. This massive erosion and earth movement will never again be witnessed in millenniums, if ever.

Gigantic ice masses larger than we could ever imagine, the likes of which are only now in the Arctic regions, passed over the area. The ground was scraped up, moving the soil and massive granite rock that created the topography we see in Glacier Park today. The mountainous jagged peaks and valleys formed during the ice age give Glacier Park its "crown look" (strangesounds.org 2019) (Roger Roots 2017) (Frishbert 2020) (usgs.gov 2016).

Like most people, I do not pay much attention to the climate anymore. The name and description continuously change to fit a climate narrative, which is why global warming and climate change are used interchangeably.

I have read about drought conditions worldwide, which have resulted in dropping water levels globally. It has happened before. In Europe, centuries-old warning messages are emerging on boulders known as "Hungersteine, or Hunger Stones." The stones dating back to 1616 in the Elbe River run from the mountains of Czechia through Germany to the North Sea. Once again visible in the dry riverbeds, the stones say, "Wenn du mich seehst, dann weine," which translates to "If you see me, weep." The stones were used as hydrological landmarks across Europe. They were chiseled in boulders depicting years of hardship. The messages represent the consequences of the era's drought. They commemorate poor harvests, lack of water, and hunger (Pflughoeft 2022).

Right now, I don't care about all of that. Like everybody else, I prefer to enjoy my outdoor activities, experiencing what there is to see and do in the great outdoors. Currently, I have the privilege of witnessing the grandeur of The Rockies. A place where the movement of glacial ice has created clear lakes, impressive waterfalls, crystal-clear rainbow-colored streams, colorful rock formations with exceptional wildlife, wildflowers, and foliage diversity.

The Rocky Mountains and vicinities are the primary habitats for the grizzly bear. The camp is aptly named "Camp Silverback" because it is a color description of some grizzly bear. Their brown fur can be tipped silver on the top of their backs, hence the name. The characteristic difference between a grizzly and a black bear is the large hump above their shoulder. It is truly a magnificent animal from a safe distance. You can't outrun a bear, as they have been clocked at almost thirty-five miles per hour.

First Impressions

First of all, it is June. Somebody out there, please let the state of Montana know that. When I left home in Eastern Oregon, it was sunny and a pleasant eighty-two degrees. Suddenly, I am hurled into the frigid icebox, otherwise known as Northwest Montana. Montana holds the distinction of the coldest temperature ever recorded in the forty-eight contiguous states. It happened at Rogers Pass on January 20, 1954, when temperatures dipped to a record low of negative seventy degrees Fahrenheit. In January 1972, Loma, Montana, broke the national record for the most significant temperature change within twenty-four hours. It recorded a 103-degree climb from negative fifty-four degrees Fahrenheit to forty-nine degrees Fahrenheit (Maki 2023) (Stacker 2022).

I understand Montanan's love of winter. You will love the seasons if you live here because it is an outdoor enthusiast's dreamland. Winter snow and freezing temperatures bring an abundance of outdoor activities that one must participate in. If you don't, you are not going to survive it. Winters are long here, with changing temperatures and snow conditions throughout the season. To a Montanan, negative temperatures for days or weeks provide ample opportunity to dig out those comfortable, snug base layers. They are necessary equipment in these parts (National Park Service).

You must be hardy and dress ruggedly here. I didn't fully understand this because we only visited in the summer while traveling to the Billings and Eastern Montana areas. It is an outerwear retailer's paradise here for a good reason. Montana women are likelier to own more boots than shoes here and not of the designer boot variety. Appropriate boot footwear comes in multiple weights and insulative qualities, with costs rivaling any expensive designer footwear. I know this because I have extensive experience in ladies' footwear, but I will explain that later.

Once dressed appropriately, winter activities are endless. Snowshoeing can be done anywhere and is the least expensive snow activity enjoyed by people of all ages. Cross-country skiing is the same, with many Nordic trails throughout the state. Downhill skiing is top-rated. The state boasts many resorts, one of which is Whitefish Mountain Resort, the most famous. Flathead County is also the home of Blacktail

Mountain Ski Resort—a less costly resort with equal snow qualities that attracts many families. Ice skating and ice hockey are enjoyed among the many rinks shared with the curling teams that anyone can join. Snowmobiling enthusiasts will find numerous back-country riding opportunities in Montana's wildernesses. Then there are the very popular skijoring competitions, where horse owners and spectators can combine their love of horses and skiing at the same time.

Climate changes have made winter snowfall in the area unpredictable. Feet of snow are not inevitable anymore. New residents get a false sense of security when winter snow levels fall below average for several years. Then, a typical winter hits with four to six feet of snow, with weeks of twenty-below temperatures. The following spring is when locals see the parade of U-hauls exiting the valley. Winter is always the great equalizer in Northwest Montana. It is when West Coasters discover they aren't quite as hardy as they envisioned. I have a picture of my grandmother in Plentywood from the 1940s. She is standing in front of her front door amidst an eight-foot-high tunnel. It stretched ten feet to the street so she could get into her house. Those were the good old days of winter in Montana and the Rocky Mountain West.

My mother's family were Scandinavian immigrants who eventually settled in Plentywood, Montana. Plentywood is in Sheridan County, a stone's throw from Canada, in the far northeast portion of the state. Billings, is in Yellowstone County, which is where my father's family eventually settled via Minneapolis, Minnesota.

Montana is the fourth-largest state in the United States, and eleven tribal nations call it home. It is also home to the Little Bighorn Battlefield National Monument, which memorializes the historic 1876 battle between the Sioux tribe and the U.S. Army. It is a landmark battle, referred to as "Custer's Last Stand" (History.com 2020).

Yellowstone National Park, located in southern Montana and northern Wyoming, was the first National Park established in the United States. While most of the park is in Wyoming, its boundaries also stretch into Montana and Idaho.

Yellowstone

On March 1, 1872, Yellowstone became the first National Park. Within Yellowstone's 2.2 million acres, visitors can observe wildlife in an intact ecosystem. Unique hydrothermal and geologic features contain about half the world's active geysers. Also in Yellowstone is the Grand Canyon of the Yellowstone River (National Park Service).

Yellowstone was a widely explored park in our family's early days. It was always a favorite destination spot when we visited Billings every summer to see our grandparents. Many photos were taken in front of that famous Yellowstone Park sign and the "Old Faithful" Geyser. It was an opportunity to capture and record our various growth spurts throughout the years. Since the park is so big and because we were generally in a hurry, we would only spend one night inside the park each year. Dad only had two weeks of vacation, and our emphasis was always getting to Billings and Plentywood to see family. It was fun to stay at the different park hotels as we toured all the usual tourist attractions each year.

Yellowstone is unique, with abundant wildlife that is easily viewed from the safety of one's vehicle. Crystal-clear blue geothermal pools are interspersed throughout the park, with white and yellow thermal formations just beneath the surface. An awe-inspiring steam rises above the surface of these ponds into the atmosphere. A steam that tells you the temperatures within the ponds are very high. This is also coupled with the interspersed mud pots that are so hot they are boiling at the surface. Some of these ponds are over 450 degrees Fahrenheit. The geothermal pools and the mud pots can be safely and easily viewed by the numerous boardwalks throughout Yellowstone, courtesy of the park service (USGS 2022).

Yellowstone typically gets thousands of visitors each year, including many from Asia. They tour the park following a visit to Jackson Hole, Wyoming. A replica of Jackson Hole is in Hebei, China, two hours north of Beijing. It is where wealthy Chinese city inhabitants go for vacation. Thousands of Chinese citizens then visit the town of Wyoming to see the real Jackson Hole in person. Then, they head to Yellowstone (Jacobs 2015).

Definitions: "Tourons"

"Tourist Morons" who have little to no understanding of the "nature of nature" in wilderness territories. Believing they are on a nature walk or a petting zoo, plenty decide each year to explore wild areas off the boardwalks, which are there for everyone's safety and to preserve the fragile ground. Tourons are easily identified by the GoPro camera installed on the front of their rental vehicle, pointing toward the car's occupants. This is to record the delighted faces of the occupants in the vehicle as they joyfully tour the park. Yes, I saw it with my very own eyes. (Wendland 2023).

Disrespectful people who believe they are special meander onto the unstable ground for that ultimate Facebook selfie to, of course, prove they live extraordinary lives. Remarkably, some even seek water samples from 400-degree thermal ponds.

These are just a few of the stupendously brainless incidents reported by park authorities that inevitably lead to disaster. The thermal ground is extremely unstable. One to two Tourons fall into the thermal pools every year and burn to their deaths. Usually, there is very little left of them to identify. Sometimes, a scorched and blackened shoe may emerge that may or may not have a foot left inside of it (Press 2023).

Other Tourons, with their vast wildlife expertise, load up into the family station wagon a poor baby buffalo (calf) alone in the wilderness. Believing that its mother abandoned it, they immediately transport it to the nearest ranger district, after which the calf is destroyed. The stunned Touron receives a hefty fine of several thousand dollars, plus a quick lesson in the realities of wild animals (Tan 2016).

The deeply troubled Touron, who was, after all, saving that calf's life, is given an immediate lesson about wild animal instincts. Helpless baby animals instinctually lie very still when danger is close by. They have no scent, so escaping carnivores is a natural ability. The baby's wary mother is close by and may or may not defend her baby. However, now that the Touron has removed the baby from its habitat, the mother is gone, and it has no chance of survival.

Three women were gored by buffalo in one month—two of them within two days of each other. One was thrown ten feet into the air. The American Bison are the largest land mammals in North America. Bulls can weigh up to 2,000 pounds. They have been clocked at thirty-five mph. Bison injure more visitors than any other animal in Yellowstone. Park officials warn that people must stay at least seventy-five feet away from them. One of the women admitted she was attempting to take a selfie with the bison that attacked her (Baker 2022).

Two downhill skiers in the backcountry of Whitefish Mountain Resort happened upon a moose. Amused, they decide to chase the moose on their skies. Using a GoPro camera attached to their helmets, they recorded the entire incident of the moose, frightened out of its mind, desperately trying to flee the skiers. Finally, an exhausted, sweat-lathered, and panting moose disappears into the trees. Wildlife officials track down the recordings posted on Facebook, of course… to record and share their extraordinary lives. The skiers were fined several thousand dollars for harassing wildlife (Fox News 2015).

Whitefish Mountain Resort is the central tourism area for the Flathead Valley and Flathead Lake. Initially discovered by the Flathead tribe, Kalispell is a Salish Indian word meaning "flat land above the lake." Two southern gentlemen established Kalispell's humble beginnings in the late 1800s (Flathead Watershed Sourcebook; A Guide to an Extraordinary Place 2010-2023).

A Flatland above the Lake

Kalispell, Montana began as a railroad town, and this fact shaped its history for many years. The townsite was platted in the spring of 1891 by its founder, Charles Edward Conrad, a Southern gentleman born in 1850 in the Shenandoah Valley of Virginia of "The Wapping Plantation."

Charles and his older brother, William, fought with the Mosby's Rangers of the Confederate Army. They returned to find the plantation in ruin, leaving the family impoverished. Charles and William left the South in 1868, four years after the war was over. The brothers decided that the only way they would prosper was to go West. The brothers traveled to St. Louis, Missouri, boarded a steamboat there, and traveled upriver to the Fort Benton Montana Territory. Four years after they arrived in Fort Benton, the brothers were offered partnerships in the I.G. Baker Mercantile Company, a mercantile and grocery company. One year later, they bought the company outright.

Acquiring steamboats and ox-drawn freight wagons, they expanded their trade throughout the region and into Canada. The company was responsible for being the first-ever cattle exporter from Montana to southern Alberta. The company eventually became the largest shipping point west of the Missouri River, bringing goods from all parts of the world up that river. Charles Conrad was now a multi-millionaire.

They lived and prospered in Fort Benton for more than twenty-three years. Charles met Alicia Davenport Stanford in 1879 and married her in 1881. On his way to Spokane, Washington to check out future business opportunities, he and Alicia spent several weeks in the Flathead Valley. Alicia fell in love with Flathead Lake and the area north of it. Because of Alicia, the Conrads made the Flathead their permanent home. The couple had three children: Charles, Catherine, and Alicia Ann.

Mr. Conrad arranged with his good friend and railroad baron, Jim Hill, to build a new railroad stretching across the Montana Territory from the east. Mr. Hill, known as "The Empire Builder," was chief executive of a family of rail lines headed by The Great Northern Railroad. This railroad conglomerate also included the Northern Pacific Railroads. The railroad would eventually come through the area north of Flathead Lake. Once the railroad was built, the crossing from the northern part of the Montana

Territory eliminated the need for river transport up the Missouri to Fort Benton. Mr. Conrad then recognized that rail transport would eventually take over water transport. He sold the IG Baker Mercantile Company to The Hudson Bay Fur Trading Company, which had long sought the company from the Conrads.

To recognize the Salish Tribe, Mr. Conrad laid out the townsite and named it Kalispell. He then selected lots for the construction of his own home.

One of Mr. Conrad's projects when he arrived in the Flathead Valley was to establish the Conrad buffalo herd. As a Missouri River freighter and trader, Mr. Conrad observed millions of buffalo hides being shipped downriver to St. Louis. It concerned him that the buffalo were fast disappearing from the American plains. Upon moving to the Flathead, he purchased about fifty animals, pasturing them on what is now known as Kalispell's "Buffalo Hills Golf Course." Alicia Conrad would later sell thirty-four head of their best buffalo breeding stock to the American Bison Society in 1908. From Kalispell, the buffalo were transported eighty miles south to Moise, Montana, where they formed the nucleus for America's National Bison Herd.

The Conrad Mansion was designed by the famous Spokane architect, Kirkland Cutter. He also built the magnificent carriage house and stables east of the mansion. The home took three years to build and was completed in 1896. Charles Conrad lived in his beautiful home for only seven years. He died in 1902 at the age of fifty-two from complications of diabetes and tuberculosis.

The main home and carriage house exist to this day. Both have been placed on the National Register of Historic Places. The 13,000-square-foot Norman-style mansion preserved the luxury enjoyed by its namesake. It offers a sense of what it was like to live there more than one hundred years ago. Remarkably high technology from a bygone era remains inside. A bank of original Edison lightbulbs that are still illuminated is in the mansion, as well as a first-generation automatic dishwasher. The mansion is the most authentic example of luxurious turn-of-the-century architecture and living style in the Pacific and Rocky Mountain West (Find A Grave) (Tabish 2015) (Michael Malone 1976) (Spritzer 1999).

Natural Wonders

I touchdown in Montana, arriving at Glacier Park International Airport (GPI). It is the smallest "International" airport I have seen, with only three gates. The airport, described as "The Gateway to Glacier Park and the Canadian Rockies," reminds me of the simplicity of what air travel used to be. Upon deplaning, I stopped at the only coffee bar in the airport and picked up a coffee. There was no escalator, so I descended the short flight of stairs from the gates and went to the baggage claim area.

I then decided to peruse the only gift shop in the airport. It had all the usual tourist-type artwork and tee-shirt accessories that I briefly browsed through. As I approached the back of the store, I noticed a locked glass display case. Within that case, I came upon just one reason why this state is called "The Treasure State." Montana has deep historical roots in mining copper, gold, silver, and gemstones. Locked away in that display case and only found in Montana was jewelry sporting one of the rarest gemstones across the globe.

It would be 1878 when a prospector named Jake Hoover discovered a tiny brilliant blue pebble while panning for gold in Yogo Creek in the Little Belt Mountains of Montana. Like many others, Hoover traveled to Montana during the gold rush era to make his fortune. However, after a year of mining, he and his partners only found forty ounces of gold worth a mere $700.00. He also found a few blue pebbles in his sluice box. While other miners in the area discarded the tiny blue rocks, Hoover collected them until he filled an entire cigar box. He then sent the cigar box to Tiffany & Co. in New York for identification and value of the stones.

Dr. George Kuntz was the foremost gem expert in America at the time. He identified the blue pebbles as excellent-quality natural sapphires and "the finest precious gemstone ever found in the United States." Tiffany & Co. then sent Mr. Hoover a check for $3,750.00 for the box of stones. The amount was over five times the money he had made on gold from the mine.

The sapphires, now known as Yogo Sapphires, had more value than the gold Mr. Hoover had spent much of his life mining. Dr. Kuntz observed that in purchasing a mere gold mine, Hoover acquired the most valuable sapphire mine in America, yielding more wealth than all other sapphire mines in America. This would start decades of ownership changes and turbulence at the Yogo Sapphire Mine (Zolynski 2023).

The Yogo mine has had quite a history since that discovery. Multiple owners from America to the United Kingdom, with floods and mining deaths, interrupting mining operations through the decades. Now called the "Vortex Mine," it is operated under the Yogo Mining Company LLC. It is the only mine in the world that provides this extraordinary sapphire deeply rooted in Montana history (Montana's Missouri River Country).

My Adventure Begins

Now was not the time to buy sapphire jewelry, but I made a mental note for later. I do, after all, have a mother and two sisters. At Christmas, I always delight in their joyful faces with jewelry surprises. I proceeded to baggage claim, which took less than five minutes. Five minutes later, my five suitcases came through, which I quickly collected. Now, this is how air travel ought to be! Yes, I know, five large bags seem excessive, but I was advised to pack for all weather contingencies. Little did I know what this meant, but I am also my parents' son, who has never had a history of traveling light. I then proceeded with the five steps necessary to approach the car rental area.

I was supposed to rent a red two-seater convertible sports car. It was expensive, but I decided to splurge at the beginning of my Montana Adventure. The Hertz lady looked skeptically at my five bags and talked me into a truck downgrade. She assured me it was necessary equipment "in these parts" as I told her of my destination to the Eureka area. She replaced my cool convertible with a four-wheel drive Toyota Tacoma truck with a hard-sided truck bed cover. At least the truck was red. It seemed silly at first; it was summer, after all, but she was cute and had a great smile. I acquiesced to her suggestion as I began my summer journey into "Big Sky Country." Ultimately, it was a good decision as I filled that truck bed with my five big bags. I wasn't thinking that through very well, but that is my usual modus operandus. I then hopped in the truck, turned east onto Highway 2 and headed towards Highway 93 to Eureka. Per the cute Hertz lady, it was an hour's drive, so I should arrive by 5:00 at the latest. This will be a great start to my Montana adventure.

I found a great radio station as I progressed along Highway 93. Through thick timber on either side of me, the last thing I saw against a beautiful blue sky was the majestic Salish Mountains greeting me in the foreground. That is when I noticed that the warm sunshine that first greeted my arrival was replaced with dark, ominous clouds. The light sprinkles of rain that developed turned into a torrential downpour. I then noted the outside temperature gauge in the truck. It had gone from seventy degrees in Kalispell to a frigid thirty-five degrees. By the time I got to the wide spot on the road, also known as the town of Olney, it was a full-blown blizzard and twenty-nine degrees.

As I reached down to turn off the air conditioner and switch it to heat, I looked down at my attire. The khaki shorts, blue polo shirt, and Keen sandals I put on that morning were not particularly appropriate right now. But good grief, it was eighty-six degrees when I flew out of Boise, Idaho, that morning! Should I stop and search for my winter parka? I decided to bravely soldier on down the road. Besides, it's June; how bad could it get? It wasn't that I was not used to driving in snow conditions. Eastern Oregon receives its fair share, but let's just say that blizzards typically happen in the winter. Montana sure didn't get that memo.

As I turned the toggle switch and engaged the four-wheel drive (thank you, cute Hertz lady), visibility was reduced to about two feet in front of the truck. As best I could tell, a solid six inches of snow was on the side of the road and accumulating fast. I was making rapid progress, too…at about ten to fifteen miles per hour. This short trip is going to take a lot longer than I thought.

Visibility quickly went to zero, necessitating me to roll down my car window. Unable to see anything before me, I leaned out the window. This was to be able to follow the line on the road in a desperate attempt to keep the vehicle "between the lines." Thank God there was no other traffic on the road. I guess the local folks did get the memo.

The winter parka in one of my suitcases was now calling my name, but I didn't dare stop now! There was a clear chance of someone running up my backside in near zero visibility. It would be a poor beginning, as I am trying to dig through five suitcases in the back of a rented truck in a blizzard. Besides, I had no idea which bag it was in. I was sure I would freeze to death…in June…in Montana. It was about then that I remembered all those little statistics about cold temperatures in this state.

Thankfully, I finally got into Eureka (population 1000) at about 8:00 p.m., at least three hours behind schedule. It was Sunday, and it was late, so restaurants were closed. I bought chips, a Little Debbie cake, and a Diet Coke for dinner at the gas station and convenience store just as you enter town. I then proceeded to my overnight accommodations, where I spent the next thirty minutes in the dark, frozen tundra, hauling in all five of my bags. The small cabin could barely contain me and all my bags, as they completely covered the floor. Note to self: It is best not to try navigating to the bathroom in the middle of the night. I wouldn't have brought them all in, but I did not know where to find my long johns. I settled into the small rustic cabin I rented in the woods near town. My feet and hands were experiencing that all too familiar stinging as they began the process of thawing. There was about ten inches of snow on the ground…in June. I was a little worried about my "summer adventure." I wasn't sure I brought enough winter clothing for that kind of adventure.

Sitting on the edge of my bed, I surveyed my numerous suitcases. I devoured my cake, chips, and coke because I was starving. It had been a long time since breakfast. It had been a long, arduous day, so I fell into bed and immediately went to sleep. As I drifted off, I began to inventory my upcoming tasks. Tomorrow is Monday, so I have seven days to prepare. Prepare for three daily meal services for about two hundred Boy Scouts and forty staff. This should be a simple task for me. At Eastern Oregon University in La Grande, where I am based, I do the same for over 3,000 students daily. This is my fun summer job and free vacation in the Rocky Mountain West, and I get paid! As little sister Kris always says, and she is quoted often, "Life is Good" (Walters 2016).

From Whence I Come

La Grande, Oregon, is located in Northeast Oregon, with a population averaging 12,000. The population has stayed the same for decades. It is located in the Grande Ronde Valley, accessible by two central mountain passes on either side of the valley. It is a beautiful drive via either mountain pass that easily captures the imagination of those who made the journey long ago along the Oregon Trail. The city's name comes from an early French settler, Charles Dause, who often used the phrase "La Grande" to describe the area's beauty.

Before white settlement, the Grande Ronde Valley was a vital rendezvous site for Native Americans of the southern Columbia Plateau. Umatilla, Nez Perce, and Cayuse traveled to the valley in the summer.

The Oregon Trail passed through the Grande Ronde Valley, straight through La Grande. It was first settled in 1861 by immigrants initially bound for the Willamette Valley in western Oregon. The town grew and prospered during the late 1860s because of the region's many gold mines and agricultural capabilities. Then, the railroad came through in 1884. In 1885, a post office was established under the name La Grande (Hartman).

La Grande's Eastern Oregon University was formerly known as Eastern Oregon College, which was the era when our family arrived. It eventually became Eastern Oregon State College before gaining university status. The university originated in 1929 as Eastern Oregon Normal School, a teacher's college (EOC) (Eastern Oregon University).

It felt like I had just fallen asleep when Earl called me at 5:00 a.m. He is a Eureka resident and retired shop teacher from the local high school. I shouldn't forget his name—he has the same name as my paternal grandfather.

My Grandpa Earl

My Grandfather was the kindest, most soft-hearted man on the face of the earth. I never remember him being angry or cross. He always had a smile and a twinkle in his eye. You could tell that he loved all his grandchildren. Whenever we visited our grandparents in Billings, he was the one who often tucked us into bed at night, pecking each of us on the forehead before saying goodnight. As we fell asleep, he told us incredible stories of his childhood and growing up. I remember them being fascinating, but I can't remember any of them to this day. He had a great sense of humor, so Dad came by it naturally. He told my cousins Jodi and Jeff once that the blue and red light panels on top of police cars were gumball machines. He even dispatched an officer friend to come to the house in his police car to bring them bubble gum.

My grandfather's father, my Great-Grandpa Otto, was a railroad conductor. Not much is known about my great-grandfather. There is a picture of my father, around three, being held in front of a train locomotive by his Grandpa, Otto. Because of that experience, my father always loved trains, and anything related to rail transportation. This influenced Dad to become an avid collector of trains, railroad memorabilia, and artifacts.

When Dad would visit the Portland area, he would frequent old dusty antique stores throughout the region, searching for anything railroad. Dad's collection included vintage dining car plates, utensils, individual beverage pitchers, and menus. He found card decks, rail schedules, advertising placards, and brochures. He even found a poster advertising rail travel through the beautiful Columbia River Gorge in western Oregon. We had that poster later framed and gave it to my nephew, Justin.

When they were young, my dad and his brothers, Gene and Terry, would play train crash. They had about five model Lionel locomotives and coal cars. Other rail cars were included in the set, but they mostly played with the locomotives. These were not trains to fool around with. They were not made of cheap plastic but steel. They each weighed about three pounds. They even had small white tablets that you would insert into the smokestack. Once you turned on the track, the locomotives would activate. The tablets would then heat in the smokestack, emitting real smoke. Because they were steel, nothing was more fun for Dad and his two brothers to build a long line of tracks in the garage. The path would be long enough to gain enough acceleration to end the run in a spectacular pileup. Back then, model trains were seriously built to make them durable enough for hundreds of crashes throughout a young boy's life.

My Grandpa Earl must have been the perfect role model because our father was great. Dad never raised his voice. He was funny, told us great stories and tall tales, and played games. He told us you could always tell a genuine Montana cow from any other cow. He said only a Montana cow would run when you yelled… "BARBEQUE!" I think he delighted in us hanging out the car window, yelling BBQ to all the cows we passed. It kept us amused on those long family trips through Montana to visit our grandparents.

He would point to all the survey stakes and flags alongside the roadways. He told us they were "small animal crossings." Whenever we saw a dead animal on the road, he told us they had tried to cross outside their crossing area. Then, he would state that they didn't look both ways before crossing the road. It was a childhood lesson on staying in crosswalks and looking both ways before crossing the street. Dad told a lot of tall tales when we were youngsters. As we grew older and wiser, he had to become more clever to fool us. We could always tell a tall tale by looking at our mother. Mother could never hide her amusement.

Kris was always one step ahead of Joni and me, quickly identifying a Dad Tall Tale well before we did. She was epically fooled, though, by Dad's Jackelope story. A Montana Jackelope is part jackrabbit and part antelope. It is a mythical Montana creature that looks like a jackrabbit but with antelope prongs. She was skeptical until the day we visited a Montana tourist shop. Then, right there on display was a real Jackalope! It was a cute little rabbit stuffed creature with soft rabbit fur and two prongs coming off the top of his little head. Our family strung her along with that tall tale for years. She was well into adulthood before figuring it out. Joni bought her a replica of that stuffed Jackelope on her thirtieth birthday. One must constantly be reminded when you are on the receiving end of a legendary family joke.

We rarely got into any real trouble at home. Any discipline was simply a stern talking to. It was always so foreboding for mother to refer one of us to our father. Once or twice as a small child, Dad instructed me to go "pick out a belt" in his closet. The intent of that was always evident. Distraught, I would go into the closet to do just that. Dad never used a belt on me. The exercise in picking out "the belt" was so disturbing for me that he figured it was punishment enough. Once, after hiding all his belts, I came slinking back and announced that "there were no belts in his closet." "No problem," Dad proclaimed, unbuckling and whipping the belt from around his waist.

None of us were ever spanked by either of our parents. Their parenting method centered around common sense, adventure, honesty, love, and consistency with follow-through. Expectations were never ambiguous; they were clear. What resulted were children who never sought to disappoint our parents. Even during Joni's 1970s era, teenage shenanigans were weighed against a context of "what if we're caught?" It would have emotionally shattered us if we had broken our parents' hearts.

A Vehicle Like None Other

The following day, I loaded all my heavy bags back into the truck. Fortunately, the weather was looking more promising than yesterday afternoon and evening. I got an early start because after loading all those bags, I needed to return the rental truck before meeting Earl. Incidentally, I didn't need to bring all those bags inside the cabin. After crawling around on the floor, searching through every single bag I brought, I found my long johns packed in my overnight bag, next to my toothbrush. Miraculously, it seemed as though I was thinking ahead after all.

Once loaded, I found my way back to the highway to make the short drive into downtown Eureka and the rental car company, where Earl said he would meet me. It was going to be a beautiful day. It was already sixty degrees, with clear blue skies. It looked like I wouldn't be needing those long johns today! I was getting very excited now. This was such a great little town, and I wouldn't be in perpetual winter after all.

Eureka's downtown district is a half-mile long before you hit the industrial district. Lining the downtown are tourist shops with a bank, a small mom-and-pop grocery store, a large Exxon station, and a few restaurants. Their big grocery store is further down, in the industrial area. The Roosville border crossing into Canada is eight miles from the edge of downtown.

Lucky Earl has been assigned as my guide and driver for this little adventure. At 5:30, he arrived as promised in a massive 1906 Scout four-wheel drive, military-style Humvee. OK, probably not from 1906 and probably not a Humvee, but I can't be far off from the looks of it. He took a long gander at me in my pink preppy polo shirt, white shorts, and Keen sandals. He smiled as he effortlessly hoisted all five of my big, heavy bags up into the back of the Humvee. This was no easy task. I sure couldn't have done it.

High profile doesn't begin to describe this vehicle. I figure it was at least four feet off the ground. It was all black with rust-filled scratches and severely dented on all sides. It had the most enormous, highest truck bed I had ever seen, with the beefiest front grill that would put a military tank to shame. The "Humvee" was completely missing the rear bumper. Then I noticed the custom-built enclosed aluminum trailer he was towing—about four feet off the ground and about twenty feet long. The trailer also suffered from severe abuse, with numerous large dents and scratches on the sides. Where had this trailer been?

Most importantly, why were the vehicle and custom-built trailer so high off the ground? I won't even talk about the tires' size and tread depth! They reminded me of the tires on the gigantic trucks from Butte's Berkley Pit Mine.

The Richest Hill on Earth

Located in Butte, Montana, the Berkely Pit was often visited by our family on our travels to Billings. It was one of those areas that fascinated our father. It was also an opportunity to stretch our legs and attempt to tire out the children.

Settled in the 1860s as a gold placer camp, Butte was stagnant by the 1870s as the placers ran out. It would be silver mining that would bring the town back to life in the late 1870s. Still, it was the high copper content of the ores that determined Butte's future. By 1882, Butte had become a major copper producer just as electrification began sweeping the nation. By 1896, the Butte mines produced over 25% of the world's copper and employed over 8,000 men. At its peak in 1910, Butte had a population of over 100,000. Today, Butte has a population of about 33,000.

"The Pit" was started in 1955. It was a large truck-operated, open-pit copper mine until mining ceased in 1982. 1.5 billion tons of material had been removed from The Pit, including more than 290 million tons of copper ore. The Pit and its surrounding high hillsides enabled Butte to claim the title "The Richest Hill on Earth." Until the middle of the twentieth century, Butte produced more mineral wealth than any other mining district worldwide. Before its closure, over $48 billion of wealth had been unearthed from The Pit. However, after a century of mining, what was left was a legacy of exposed toxic mine waste and polluted water. Thus, following the mine's tremendous successes, Butte became the site of the nation's most extensive environmental cleanup (Montana Connections 2021).

There is still plenty to see in Butte, which has a rich mining history. Ole Butte Historical Adventures is always a popular choice among tourists. The classic Underground City Tour visits the Rookwood Speakeasy and the 1890 city cellar jail. The Chamber of Commerce sponsors the Butte Trolley Tours to tour above-ground features. The Pekin Noodle Parlor is the West's oldest continually operated Chinese restaurant in the United States. The Hell-Roaring Gulch World Museum of Mining, near the Montana Tech campus, was a popular family attraction for us at the time. It is a restored mining town that deeply dives into the mining history of Butte back in the late 1800s (Lane 2021).

The Berkley Pit was still active when we pulled through Butte on our way through Montana. As a child, I have pictures of our family standing beside one of those truck tires. The tire encompassed more space than our family.

Okay, maybe I am exaggerating a bit about the size of the Humvee's tires. However, as I made my ascent into the Humvee, I needed to take advantage of a four-step ladder attached to the side as I climbed into the vehicle. As I settled into my seat, I was experiencing new heights within a vehicle. I became concerned, as I could no longer see the road immediately in front of the Humvee. This vehicle would be king in a monster truck competition. When I asked Earl what was in store next, he looked at me and smiled. He must have sensed my nervousness as he turned the key to start up the old 1906 four-wheel drive military-style Scout Humvee. As the big diesel turned over and thunderously rumbled into action, it reminded me of Dad's old 1940s Ford pickup he had back in the late 1960s.

Dad's Classic Truck

Dad had a classic 1940s Ford truck. Being significantly oxidized with age, once red, it was now a light brick color, with rounded front bumpers and a hood that epitomized the era. As a child, I remember the headlights appeared like frog eyes. He bought it because Dad liked trucks, and this one was especially cool. My dad was always very "thrifty," this truck came cheap with four on the floor. It ran pretty well if you could get it started. The truck was very fussy about that.

We lived on the outskirts of La Grande, on one of the many hillsides surrounding the town. Luckily, our home was located near the top of one of those long roads, which began Dad's commute to work. Dad would park his truck facing down the hill alongside the yard next to our house. The hill was critical for Dad to coax that truck to start in the morning. To perform the truck's usual running start, Dad would put the truck in neutral and pull the choke. He would then turn the key to the start position without turning it over. He then exited the truck, stood alongside the open door, and pushed it to a coast.

Once it began to coast, he would leap in, shove it into first gear, turn the key over, and pop the clutch. Dad had about ten blocks to start the engine before running out of hill.

Only one stop sign was on the hill, about half a block from our house. If it was a frigid morning, the old truck had more difficulty deciding to start. Dad had only two pops before he got to the stop sign. If it did not start by then, Dad would have to turn off the truck and start all over again. See the above paragraph beginning with "Put the truck into neutral." Dad's old truck appeared to be having a seizure as it coasted and lurched down that ten-block hill, popping it repeatedly till it started. Fortunately, he was always successful by the time he got to the bottom of the hill.

I was a little too young to remember, but Joni said it scared her to ride in it. The truck had wooden floorboards that were on the verge of completely rotting through. She said you could see the road speeding by as Dad was driving down the road.

Mother's mode of mobility was even worse. You could have thought Dad was a classic car enthusiast, but he was just "thrifty." Our family put little emphasis on vehicles, purchasing old vehicles that barely ran at the time, running them further into the ground, only to buy yet another beater, er…classic vehicle, down the road…as it were.

Mom's Classic Ride

Earl had his own strategy to fire up that 1904 four-wheel drive Military Style Scout Humvee. It was precisely how Mother would start our 1950s lavender/pink Rambler Rebel station wagon, which we owned in the early 1970s. The car was a classic, just like Mom. That Rambler Rebel had to have been the first-ever automatic transmission. Like all our early vehicles, most were on their last legs, and Mom's lavender Rambler Rebel was no exception. It was also another cranky starter. Mom would load us up every morning, which began the daily ritual that commenced our ride to school.

First, she would pull the choke, and then, while turning the key to the "start" position, Mom would begin rapidly pumping the gas pedal to get it to turn over. Once it had turned over, she would continue pumping the gas pedal. The Rambler Rebel would choke and sputter as it began to fire on all cylinders, blowing black smoke out the back of our carport. Those smoke signals would alert our neighbors that it was time to head to work.

Now came her double-foot strategy. Once the smoke cleared and the car was still in park, Mom continued pumping the gas with her right foot as she applied the brake with her left foot. She then quickly shoved it into reverse, and at the exact moment, her foot came off the brake. Still pumping that gas pedal with her right foot in rapid sequence, it would begin its slow-rolling, choking, sputtering, jerking movement backward, out of the carport into the driveway. Our mother had the fastest right foot in the west.

The car would choke, slowly roll, and lurch out of the driveway as Mother floored the gas pedal, burning rubber as she backed it out of our driveway and onto our gravel road. Once onto the road and after throwing gravel into the next county, mother would throw it into neutral, step hard on the brake with her left foot, and again pump hard up and down on that gas pedal with her right foot. Her lavender/pink Rambler Rebel station wagon choked and coughed as it struggled to warm up on the road. Then, at precisely the right moment, while still in neutral and when the car seemed to quit sputtering, she would slowly lift her foot off the brake while still pumping the gas rapidly. The car would then coast down the half block to the stop sign while Mother kept revving the engine up and down with the gas pedal.

It was an exact science. It was a carefully balanced and expertly choreographed exercise of rapidly pumping the gas with her right foot while carefully lifting her left foot on and off the brake pedal. This dance enabled her Rambler Rebel to coast the half block to the stop sign at precisely the right speed without dying. Mother missed her calling as an Irish Celtic Dancer.

At the stop sign, with her foot fully on the brake and still in neutral, she finally could lift her right foot off the gas pedal to test the car's readiness to proceed. If the car died, it still was not ready, whereby she would start all over again…see above starting at paragraph two, beginning at pull the choke. If the car did not die at the stop sign, Mom could finally shift the car into drive and take her left foot off the brake while slowly easing her right foot onto the gas pedal. Our lavender/pink Rambler Rebel station wagon could proceed, quietly purring down the road to school.

Joni hated that car and was embarrassed to ride in it. She rode on the floorboards so nobody would see her in it. She always instructed Mom to drive past the junior high school a couple of blocks to the nearest alley. Then she would slither out from under the car's floorboard, out of the car, and then walk the rest of the way to school.

Our family had this yellow, long-haired tabby cat named Muffin. Muffin hated our mother. The reason was a source of debate in our household, but it was probably because Mom would throw her outside whenever she found her in the house. Muffin would then do her big kitty business on the top of Mom's Rambler Rebel. Mind you, we had three vehicles parked out there, so Muffin was definitely making her point.

On those mornings, as Mother lurched out the back of the carport, kitty doo-doo would slowly roll off the top of the car and down the windshield, resting on top of the hood. That was funny enough, but it was hilarious that Mother would…ignore it, maybe because she was so busy performing the daily two-step on the gas and brake pedals. Muffin's business would eventually blow off the hood as we proceeded down the road.

The old 1940s truck finally died a permanent death. That was when Dad purchased his next vehicle, our best car of that era. He bought an Opel Kadett in the 1960s era. It was orange, with a "sporty" black stripe down the side. The Opel ran the best, and Joni thought it was pretty cool. She noticed immediately that the vehicle's color was that of the La Grande High School's mascot. She liked to borrow it every year for the high school's homecoming parade. The school's mascot is a tiger, so it was the perfect color. It was not a very big car, but somehow, she could cram six of her best friends inside that vehicle on parade day.

My New Best Friend

Earl is a rugged old guy and appears to be someone that even the orneriest of people would not have messed with. Wearing old brown Carhartt coveralls over a black t-shirt, you could tell this was his usual daily attire. His thinning dark hair was slightly graying, with a short, straggly gray mustache and beard. He is also quite imposing at around six foot five and about 250 pounds.

The Humvee, being a diesel, is a slow starter. After turning the key, one must wait ten minutes before even attempting to turn it over, which is typical of old diesel trucks. Earl then cranks the key over, wherein it begins to grind, clatter, and rattle for the next thirty seconds. Unsuccessful, Earl turns off the key while the engine hisses, pops, and then moans to a stop. After waiting another minute, he turns the key in the start position, and it starts all over again. We repeat this dance three more times before the Humvee rumbles to a start.

I feel like I am sitting in a train locomotive as we loudly thunder through downtown Eureka. Earl is obviously a popular local character. It feels like we are on parade as all the townies wave to us as we go by. This Humvee is made for men like Earl, who must be pretty tall to see over the hood. I feel like Edith Ann of Rowan and Martin's Laugh-In era, with my feet dangling down from atop my bench seat in the Humvee. I have an overwhelming desire to stick my tongue out and do a raspberry (Laugh-In 1968).

Earl is not all that talkative, mostly just answering my numerous non-stop questions. He seems to be sizing me up, contemplating my questions carefully before responding. I eventually determined that he grew up here. He taught high school shop classes throughout his career at Eureka High School. He retired from the school district twenty years ago. He told me his family homesteaded in the Tobacco Valley in the late 1800s. The farm has been in his family for three generations, and he continues to farm it today with his grown children and grandchildren. He said his wife died about ten years ago, and he never re-married. He says he could never improve on that perfection. He said he is seventy-nine but is quite spry, fit, and gets around well. He didn't look a day over sixty. It must be a result of hard work and clean mountain air.

Our first stop was at the local grocery store to pick up my large order. Earl indicated I would only return to town once every two weeks, so plan accordingly. This also coincided with when they changed the Boy Scout groups, two hundred new boys every two weeks. I would need to plan ahead with my menus and determine everything I needed for each two-week interval. This is not a problem for me. Pre-planning is my forte. After all, you cannot make a grocery run if you forget to pick up milk for 3,000 University students.

I was eventually able to break the ice with Earl. The more we visited, the more he seemed comfortable around me. I am pretty good at idle conversation and fitting into whatever my surroundings are. I am also an easy guy to get along with.

Dear Mom and Dad:

Well, well, well, where does one begin? My adventure started with a rather lengthy trip to the local grocery store for all the supplies needed for 200 Boy Scouts, 40 adult leaders, and staff. Following our shopping extravaganza, my new best friend Earl and I loaded up into our locomotive and headed out of Eureka towards an area they call "The Yaak."

I was not paying very good attention to where we were. I was playing the part of a tourist while enjoying the beautiful scenery as we followed the Yaak River to...somewhere. My tour guide and camp comrade is Earl, who became more talkative as we drove for the next hour and a half. Then, with no warning, road sign, or other indication, Earl made a sharp left-hand turn onto a dirt road. That is where my nice little adventure took a harrowing turn for the worse!

I learned later that locals don't even try to come down this mountain. One thing is for sure: this is not folklore, and these people do not lie. In our 1906 four-wheel drive military-style Scout Humvee and trailer, with me grasping onto any handle I could find, that Humvee and trailer flew over the top of that road, plunging 2,200 feet in just under two miles. As I held on for my life, we descended from 5,000 feet elevation to 2,800 feet, straight down what Montanans call a road. Horrified, I was holding on for my life.

Earl immediately took over the role of tour guide with obvious delight and animation. I think he enjoyed my unmistakable shock and horror: "Well, this first stretch is called The Upper Bongos, which is a much better road than The Lower Bongos."

Wow, this is a "better road!" Driving down Upper Bongos was much like trying to maneuver down "Rock Garden," only steeper, with a straight down vertical cliff on the right side of the 1906 four-wheel-drive Military Style Scout Humvee. Okay, I think I get the whole Humvee idea now.

I am carefully watching the edge on my side of the Humvee while also aware of numerous huge boulders we need to maneuver around or on top of...with a trailer attached! I cannot help but wonder what happens to wayward, lost tourists who try to attempt this with a 40-foot travel trailer. I asked Earl if a vehicle graveyard was at the bottom of this cliff!

Thank God there is a steep embankment on the left side of the road. I wished the embankment was on my side of the Humvee. You know, in case I needed to bail out if we ended up going over the edge! Did I tell you about the ground clearance on this vehicle? The purpose of that is now crystal clear. Enough of this letter for now. I need both hands to pray.

More later if I don't die.
Love, Randy

Navigating Rock Garden

Rock Garden is a ski run at Anthony Lakes Ski Resort, which is located between La Grande and Baker City, Oregon. Anthony Lakes is in the Blue Mountains of Eastern Oregon, in a gorgeous mountainous area called "The Elkhorns." The resort, of course, is named after this lake.

It is a small resort with one triple chair, a handle tow, and a magic carpet tow. It has a base elevation of 7,100 feet, the highest ski resort base in the state. Because of this, it is known for being the best powder skiing in the Pacific Northwest. It is 1,100 acres with twenty-one ski runs. It is a wonderful small family resort where my nephew, Justin, was a member of the Anthony Lakes Race Team as a child. It is also where I would go every weekend I could with my best friend, Patty (McOmie 2022) (Lakes).

About half of Anthony Lakes' ski runs are black diamond runs preferred by expert skiers, whose skiing styles are more aggressive. The resort boasts more moderate and beginner trails, nicely groomed for families and individuals who prefer a more relaxed downhill ski adventure. I am considered an intermediate skier who prefers to take each run at a moderate speed, frequently stopping to admire the beautiful scenery.

Rock Garden is a black diamond ski run, with the resort's only chair lift ascending the face of that ski run. I was always enthralled watching the skiers who had such expert ability to ski that run with huge moguls carved into the landscape. They always made it look so easy. Being a big guy without much maneuverability and trying to be very suave among the ladies, I attempted it only once. Once you are on Rock Garden, there is no turning back, as I frightfully discovered how steep it really was and how big and deep those moguls really are. Looking down from the chairlift is very deceiving. I didn't get twenty yards down that mountain when I crashed, creating a "yard sale" that stretched half the length down that mountain. It was a wonder I had any clothing left on my body. My equipment and outer clothing ripped off my body and were scattered about thirty yards down that ski hill.

Since Rock Garden is the most visual run in the entire resort, it didn't take long before numerous resort ski patrol members joined me. In short order, they collected my equipment and attire and assessed my needs.

We all then had a lengthy discussion about how I would get down that mountain. Even though I was fine, there was no scenario by which I could convince them I could get down that mountain on my own. I even offered to walk the rest of the way down.

None of them wanted to walk with me, so they loaded me up on the stretcher in front of everyone coming up the mountain on the chair lift. Then, they somehow skied/carried me down that steep mountain. It was not my greatest moment. I waved to my audience above me among all the cheering, whistling, and applause. What I think really happened that day was that it was time for the Anthony Lakes Ski Patrol to perform a training run. It was a perfect opportunity to practice various methods to remove a large human from the most challenging ski hill on the mountain.

A similar skiing mishap happened only one other time while skiing with my sisters. Thankfully, that time, it was not on Rock Garden. By then, I had gained more appreciation for the disasters that can occur on ski terrain beyond my ability. Also, my sisters had more sense than that. As my sisters skied gracefully and effortlessly past me down a run called Lower College, I took a tumble, hit my head, and was unconscious for a bit. Determined not to be dragged down again by the ski patrol, I slowly sat up, then stood up, catching my bearings and balance. I then slowly skied down, meeting my sisters, who had begun walking back up to find me. I was forced to fess up to what had occurred. We skied the rest of the way down, where they loaded me up and took me home for an ER visit. I ended up with a slight concussion that day. We did not tell Mother what happened because I did want to ski again someday.

Mom must have gotten wind of it because, as a Christmas gift, Mom and Dad purchased a bright, puffy, neon orange ski coat for me. It came complete with an orange hat with a big fluffy ball on top. I am sure Mom chose this particular color so folks could find me under the snow following one of my numerous wrecks. Thinking back on it, I realize how ridiculous I must have looked. You think I am round now! Nobody would miss me in my glowing, bright, neon orange, puffy ski ensemble on that white ski hill!

I don't know why I skied for as long as I did. My klutz-prone body just was not created to accomplish that skill. Riding the chair one day, whereupon reaching the summit, I prepared for the dismount:

1. Raise your ski tips up and the backs of the skis down.
2. Place one ski pole in each hand in the ready-to-ski position.
3. As you approach the ramp, let the back of the skis meet the ramp
4. Level out your skis until they are fully engaged on top of the ramp.

5. Stand up and smile.
6. Effortlessly glide down to meet your friends at the bottom of the ramp.

I was so busy visiting with my ski lift buddy one day that I was too distracted, failing in the first and most crucial step of the dismount protocol. As I suddenly approached the ramp completely unprepared, my ski tips struck the ramp. The cascade of events that then ensued all happened in a milli-second. My entire body was slammed onto the ramp, where I slid helplessly backward into the catch net behind the ramp. Falling in the net is one of those things that, as a skier, you know could occur, but you never actually thought you would see it happen, especially to you. As I am floundering in the net, all systems are stopped, as the ski patrol spends the next hour fishing bright, puffy, neon-orange Randy out of the net. I was then quite aware of the cheering, laughter, and applause around me. Below me, I heard cursing and yelling down the ski lift from those unaware of the entertainment venue at the top of the hill.

Tackling the Bongos

Earl was my hero today as he safely and expertly maneuvered us down that steep rock face known as the Upper Bongos. He accomplished this with grace and precision. It appears he has done this more than a few times. If the Upper Bongos weren't bad enough, the most exciting part was an area called "Jackass Slide," and slide was precisely what the four-wheel drive Military style Scout Humvee and trailer chose to do. The snow was gone, but the dirt road with minimal gravel was wet, muddy, and quite slippery.

Somehow, Earl expertly kept the Humvee and trailer straight as the trailer kept trying to overtake and slide around the Humvee. Earl didn't have to accelerate, as the Humvee kept picking up speed while sliding all the way down Jackass Slide. Breaking was an exercise in futility on this section of the road. Fortunately, this area of road is pretty narrow, with tall, steep embankments on both sides, embankments which the Humvee and trailer proceeded to bounce off and on and back and forth, all the way down the road. No wonder this truck and trailer look as bad as they do! Thank God for the steep embankments or we would be dead at the bottom of the canyon. The Lower Bongos were not dissimilar to the Upper Bongos. At least, that is how it felt as we were driving. It was just a guess, as my eyes were closed by then.

It was all very frightening, and my reaction to the experience reminded me of our mother. She had always been a small-town driver. She learned to drive in a small town and lived in small towns for most of her life. She was an exceptionally proficient driver in the art of asphalt vehicle operation in populations of less than 10,000. Therefore, she was unaccustomed to vehicle travel on mountain roadways. Dad was always game for new adventures, not so much our mother.

Our family camped a lot when we were kids. Dad loved the outdoors, camping, and especially fishing. Driving the family station wagon to our favorite Wallowa area campgrounds was a frequent occurrence, and Wallowa's Lostine area corridor was usually our final destination. Towing our sixteen-foot travel trailer along narrow, steep gravel roadways was not our mother's idea of fun. I remember she had her eyes intermittently closed while she was desperately trying to apply the imaginary brakes on her side of the station wagon. When Mother's pucker factor was high, she would make this interesting sound when someone else was driving. She was sucking in deep air, but it came out as "beeps." It was the telltale sign that Mom's anxiety Richter scale was pegged when she started beeping. I'm not positive, but I think Mom may have preferred a weekend playing Bridge like my grandmother.

With my eyes tightly closed, this tiny memory got me through my first harrowing experience of "The Bongos."

My Grandmother, Queen Elizabeth

I am still trying to figure out where Dad discovered his love of the outdoors. As far as I could tell, his family did not camp or fish. It just seemed like they were not the outdoorsy types. His mother, my Grandmother Elizabeth (Betty), was raised in high society. She was very proper and emphasized good manners and proper etiquette. Grandma was also a great cook and taught my mother everything she knew about preparing meals and cooking for a family. This was a very good thing.

Mom was an only child when she came along, so this skill was elusive to her. Before marrying into the family, Mom's culinary specialties consisted of "Chipped Beef on Toast," more widely known as sh@$ on a shingle. Then there was her rendition of an American favorite--Tuna Casserole. It consisted of several cans of tuna, canned cream of mushroom soup, some milk, and canned peas. Then, the pièce de résistance that made it genuinely gourmet... potato chips, over the top before baking. Thank God Grandma widened her culinary horizon.

Tuna casserole would become our Aunt Nancy's (dad's sister) easy dish of choice on her days to cook. On Monday evenings, we all could count on Tuna Casserole being presented for dinner. Nancy was living with us while she attended Eastern Oregon State College. Before that, Nancy was the "Cool Aunt" in 1971, the summer Joni stayed with Grandma and Grandpa when she was thirteen. It was the summer that Joni learned all about the social and cultural aspects of the teenage tradition of "dragging the gut." In Billings, though, it was called - "Cruising the Point." It was a memorable summer of hanging out with Aunt Nancy and her best friend, Nancy. It would be young Joni's real-life "American Graffiti" experience. It was a summer of hanging out with "The Nancys" while learning the real meaning behind the song "American Pie." It was an epic summer for a thirteen-year-old and one Joni never forgot (George Lucas 1973) (McLean 1971).

My grandmother always looked so glamorous in all situations that I could not even picture her in blue jeans. Her style and grace rubbed off on her son and us, teaching us proper etiquette in all social situations. Grandma played a lot of bridge instead of hooking a worm or cleaning a freshly caught trout. But then my mother was the same, except Mom was very comfortable in blue jeans and a sweatshirt.

My grandmother's father was my great-grandfather George, an admirable gentleman of refined taste. He was a marketer for fine Chinese dinnerware. He came in at the gilded age of fine China. Before that, China was a costly luxury item only owned by the very rich. In ancient times, this fine pottery began in Egypt and Peru, some 3,000 years and more B.C. The world's oldest industry has roots in Chinese wares made of gold, silver, and pewter. Fine Chinese wares such as this were only owned by Kings, Queens, Earls, Dukes, and others of nobility. During my great-grandfather's time, individual dishes like cups, saucers, and plates were designed and made by hand.

Josiah Wedgwood, in 1759, would change everything when he began making and designing China out of clay. Fine individual Chinese dinnerware became affordable then and something all families could own. Porcelain China was introduced in the 1800s in the Josiah Spode factory. Spode fine porcelain was made by combining China clay, China stone, and bone ash in Staffordshire, England. Combining these ingredients eventually became the standard of English bone china (Searle 1933).

Great-grandpa became a merchandiser for Spode China in the early 1900s. He was a gifted speaker, as he traveled with his exhibit of various China pieces for audiences throughout the St. Paul and Minneapolis area. His lecture consisted of the history of fine pottery, later known as China. We all have various pieces from those long-ago days, left to us by our grandmother.

Grandma channeled her father's virtues of splendor in her tutelage of my father. Dad's embrace of that upbringing gave him an uncanny ability to blend in with any group. It is a unique skill when one works with the public and was a skill he passed on to his children. All of us benefited from it in our various careers. We all ended up with our dad's rugged spirit and our grandmother's social graces. Both are especially handy in my current working venue at Camp Silverback.

Final Approach... Camp Silverback

Dear Mom and Dad:

Sorry about my letter interruption last time. I was concentrating on holding on for my life! By the time we reached the "Lower Bongos," I was done. I closed my eyes and instructed Earl to "wake me up when we're dead."

Incidentally, they call this mountain road the Bongos because that is the noise your head makes as it is hurled against the roof of the Humvee. It is what happens as you bounce down the road over the enormous boulders and through the deep ruts. No, Mom, I was not wearing a seat belt. The vehicle was manufactured long before they ever made such a safety amenity. Besides, one needs to be on one's toes in the ready-to-jump position; at the slightest inclination, you are about to go OVER THE CLIFF! A helmet could be helpful in this venture.

I also cannot help but think how many times I would need to be transported up and down this mountain throughout the summer...Send Valium!

With the brakes smoking, Earl's 1906 four-wheel-drive Scout military-style Humvee and trailer finally "screeched to a landing" in camp. We then opened the back of the trailer. Gravity was not our friend, as all the trailer's contents were shoved on top of each other toward the front of the trailer. What was a full trailer when we loaded it was now only two thirds full. It did keep everything from falling on top of us, though, as we opened the door.

What was most unfortunate was my poor typewriter, now in numerous pieces throughout the trailer. Only after entirely unloading the trailer could I find and retrieve all the pieces of my sad, broken typewriter. Oh, I forgot to tell you, I was told that we do not have actual electricity up here, so no electric typewriter. It is good because I would be typewriter-less right now after that harrowing trip. These old manual typewriters are workhorses and are as tough as they get.

As you can see, it did go back together nicely. Thank goodness for duct tape. As you always say, Dad, never leave home without it.

Sadly, the thirty cases of eggs that happened to be sitting atop all my bags did not have such a happy ending... Send alcohol!

Once in camp, Earl introduced me to my temporary quarters. They do not call them "primitive pioneer cabins" for nothing. There were more spider webs and spiders here; then Kris could yell, "Kill it." Arachnophobic Kris would have had an immediate apoplectic meltdown. I am sure she would have slept outside with the bears instead of with the numerous species of arachnids in this cabin. Thank God for bug spray. There is a lot of that in camp. It is like toilet paper, an essential supply.

The cabins have no electricity, but there were several kerosene lanterns. You know the kind Dad, with mantles that fall to pieces if you dare to touch them. They certainly bring back memories, with the little pump on the side that you had to pump five to fifty times, depending on how long it had been since anyone last lit it. I remember on our camp trips when you would pump, pump, pump that lantern, trying to get it to light in the tent or at the picnic table. You always were successful, Dad, because you were smart enough to bring a flashlight!

Thank God I remembered those lessons from long ago because it took me 50 pumps in the darkness to light the dang thing. Yeah, I forgot to pack a flashlight, but the matches left in the cabin allowed some illumination while trying to light that lantern. I need to take the Boy Scout motto more seriously. Well, so much for my first day. I need to start making dinner now, so I will update you later.

Love, Randy

P.S. Please send a helmet.

First Forays into Family Camping

I remember growing up in our first adventures as family campers. Back then, we started with a family-sized, canvas-style tent. Back in the day, tents were not made with lightweight parachute material, which somehow came together with two long, skinny, bendable, retractable poles. Also, unlike modern tents today, our tent was HUGE. It weighed about one hundred pounds and came with about one hundred support poles that had to be assembled individually. The canvas bag it all came in had its place on top of the car because that was the only place it would fit. It came complete with ten pages of instructions. Yep, only ten pages because instructions did not need to come in twenty languages back then. Before an actual camping trip, Dad spent days dry-running the tent assembly in our backyard. Once he figured it out, he no longer needed the instructions.

We would arrive at the campground, loaded to the gills, ready for adventure. All our weekend supplies were carefully packed in our beige family station wagon with fake wood panels. It was a newer used car that Dad purchased after the Rambler Rebel finally died. We were keeping up with the times then with a reliable family roadster that, most importantly, started on the first key crank. It was the kind of vehicle every middle-class American family owned in the 1960s.

We were the quintessential American family, as we parked next to each weekend's river or lake, pulling out from the back and on top of the car, all our camping essentials. The tent, poles, lawn chairs, pots and pans, lanterns, flashlights, food prep items, plates, silverware, food, drinks, a wash basin, and an ax. Newspapers to start a fire, all our fishing gear, clothing, and coats, and all of us somehow came out of that car. I don't know how he did it, but our father was an expert packer. We looked like a gypsy camp, trucking up those dirt roads in our beige family station wagon with fake wood panels. Not being very dirt road worthy, our campsites were relatively easy to get to.

Dad and all of us kids would proceed to set up camp. As Mom supervised the camp set-up process, Joni and Dad would erect the tent, after which they threw in the sleeping bags and air mattresses. They then set up our camp kitchen, placing all the cooking items on the picnic table.

This included the two-burner camp stove he only recently purchased at the La Grande Rite Aid. The cooler of beverages was scooted slightly underneath the picnic table. Dad stowed the food storage cooler and other food items in the back of the station wagon. Dad didn't want to attract bears, but he did not tell Mother that part. Kris and I were responsible for gathering all the firewood for the weekend. We had a great time exploring all the other campsites in the immediate vicinity while not gathering firewood. We would bring a couple of sticks in now and then to look productive. Ultimately, the entire family would gather firewood for the campfire to last the weekend.

After an evening sitting around the campfire, telling ghost stories and roasting marshmallows, we would all head into the tent. We would then blow up our air mattresses and settle into our sleeping bags for the night. There is something about cool mountain air that makes one sleep so well. I was a pretty consistent sleepwalker as a little kid. For safety reasons, Dad would tie a rope around my leg and then around his while we were sleeping. Mom and Dad did not want to risk their middle child walking out of the tent in the middle of the night and then getting lost, or worse, drowning. The problem was that the rope was about 1 inch in diameter and about forty feet long.

Being the "thrifty" father that he was, it didn't feel right (I guess) to go out and buy a shorter rope in a diameter more suitable for a small boy's leg. Nor, for that matter, cut the big rope down to a smaller length. Nope, my dad (not wanting to be wasteful) used the rope he had. As I remember, though, the body of water I could reach was generally less than forty feet away. We always camped right in front of whatever body of water we chose. Nothing is more soothing than listening to a river run while drifting off to sleep.

As our family progressed in our camping adventures, it was not long before we acquired a 16-foot pull-behind camp trailer. Dad's philosophy was, "If you have everything you need permanently kept in the trailer, all you need to pack are food and clothing." For a camping family who headed out every weekend, it was much easier to hook up the trailer, only needing to pack the food and clothing you would need for the weekend. I think Mom needed a few more amenities anyway. After all, trailers come with essential comfort items like real beds, real linens, cupboards, a range, a refrigerator, and, most importantly, a furnace. No more leg ropes for me because the door had a handy, dandy lock on it. We were uptown now!

I was ecstatic because I knew then that camping would be our family's every weekend adventure. Being a kid, I did not think about it until my Bongo adventure; all vehicles today come with maximum tow and tongue weights. It was a minor detail nobody thought of back then, especially my father. I wonder if our family roadster should have been towing a trailer. As I think further, how did Dad get a tow ball on the back of that car? If you understood my father, the thought is frightening.

I remember one Friday night late in the fall, and we were sitting around the family dinner table. Just as we were finishing our dinner, Dad got a sudden epiphany. "Let's go camping," he proclaims! It was, after all, Friday evening. We had the entire weekend, and it was an unseasonably warm fall. Our travel trailer was ready, fully loaded with all the camping essentials for a fun-filled, spontaneous weekend adventure. This was how our father rolled. So, while Mom cleaned up dinner, Dad organized the children as we readied ourselves for a camping weekend. We were out the door within an hour (Oregon State Parks).

It was a beautiful fall evening. The fall colors were fully displayed as we headed to Hilgard Junction State Park, about fifteen minutes from our house and just off the Interstate. The park takes its name from the nearby Union Pacific Railroad line junction. The Grande Ronde River quietly flows through the park, enticing anglers, rafters, and swimmers. While camping at the park, you can see the old wagon ruts of the historic Oregon Trail.

The Oregon Trail

A promise of freedom and wide-open spaces. Beautiful land that one could lay claim to if one could get there. Stories of Oregon's Willamette Valley were filled with descriptions of beauty and opportunity, with fertile soil from which to farm. Oregon's Willamette Valley would become the most coveted destination of these earliest immigrants, promising a life they could only dream about. Getting there, though, had many risks. Many a Wagon Train would make the death-defying journey, with only a handful surviving. It was their sweat, their blood, and their tears over loved ones lost that began Oregon's history in the mid-1840s (History.com 2022).

Death was everywhere as they traveled along the Great Plains, searching for the Cascade Mountain Range and the potential that lay beneath it. They would travel and brave the wild animals, insects, and snakes for months. Torrential rains, tornados, extreme cold, and blizzards. Excruciating heat and drought, with long distances without a drop of water. Horse and wagon accidents and drownings, bandits and Indians, famine and disease. That is what the wagon trains would need to survive before making it to the beauty and solitude of the Willamette Valley and the surrounding areas known as Oregon (Milner 2023).

All along the trail, the landscape would be littered with unmarked graves and crushed dreams. They would all become forgotten people, left behind to become one with the dirt. Families would rarely arrive intact. Only a scattering of people would ever make the long journey, but the immigrants endured, seeking freedom in the promises that America offered and the beauty they understood was a part of the American West. They brought their love for the land with their own talents and skills to cultivate her. They asked for nothing else from America except a chance. Immigrants would assimilate to American ways and traditions, and they learned the language. They were seeking to become one with the American dream. They would stand alongside her and all she stood for, not just sit on top of her.

Evolution of Family Camping

Our pull-behind camp trailer was nice, but the problem was that it did not have a bathroom. As our family camping outings evolved, so did our camp "rigging." I will never forget the day our family purchased our first-ever brand-new vehicle ever owned by our family. A bright, shiny, brand-new red truck. It was beautiful! It is no wonder I love red vehicles. The truck came fresh off the showroom floor. Trucks back then did not have four-plus passenger seating, so it was a two-passenger truck with a bench seat. It may have been a brand-new truck, but Dad was still "thrifty." Our brand new, bright red, two-passenger truck came complete with NOTHING!

That's right - a manual transmission, two-wheel drive, manual windows, and door locks. It didn't even have any carpeting or, for that matter, floor mats. It was like they took the metal truck straight out of the mold, painted it red—inside and out, and added the driving components, the windows, and the genuine Naugahyde seats, and voila, you have a truck. Unfortunately for Dad, the first time he proudly loaded himself in to drive it to work, he reached down to turn on the radio, and...there was no radio! It was the little things you failed to notice when you purchased a base model vehicle back then. It was super easy to clean because it had no electronics or carpeting. You can't ruin Naugahyde, so when Dad cleaned it, he sprayed it out with a garden hose.

Next, our brand new bright red truck had to come with a brand new, over-cab truck camper. It was an epic day. As Dad began the process of trading in our travel trailer, he began by marketing all our trailer's wonderful attributes to the salesman. He let me tag along that day, and it was a good thing because he forgot to mention the steps. Pulling out one weekend, he failed to fold the steps under the trailer that day. When we got home, the steps were a mangled, broken mess. He did his best to bend them back into place, so they were at least functional. As the salesman inspected the trailer, I reminded Dad to tell him about the broken step. Many lessons were learned after that debacle. It would be one of the many marketing nuances I learned through life as I traded in many vehicles for myself.

The new truck and camper were a considerable step up for our family, especially for our mother. It had all the previous creature comforts of the pull-behind trailer, with one significant addition: a bathroom, complete with a shower.

Because our new truck only had room for Mom and Dad to sit, all three of us kids rode in the back of the camper. Nothing was more fun for three kids than to ride high above the truck cab, lying on the bed and watching the road go by. Mom and Dad were all about safety, so we were instructed to lay in the bed with our feet toward the front window.

Unlike today's open-concept truck campers, the over-cab bed area was mostly enclosed. It only had about a two-foot opening in the middle to get yourself up into the bed. As instructed, the three of us stacked pillows to the back of the bed, with our feet toward the front window. We snacked, played games, and yakked all the way to our chosen camping area for the weekend. Should we have gotten into an accident, it was safer, I guess, to fly out that front window feet first rather than headfirst. But during a more naive time, we didn't think about that. Nobody else did either, as parents routinely loaded kids up in the bed of a pickup truck. We did that as well, but our super safety strategy back then was to never sit on the sides of the pickup bed; instead, we sat on the truck bed floor.

So, during our carefree youth, nothing was ever reported that small children were hurled out of overhead campers or truck beds. Carefree family activities may have had a touch of danger, but it was okay because everybody did it. Now, every family activity or children's sports comes complete with all the recommended safety gear to prevent any injury that could ever possibly occur. All activities are carefully scrutinized by parents and government entities for safety. Sometimes, I think it has gone too far. Kids need to be kids and get bruised and scabbed up, like the rest of us did. Be daring and drink out of the water hose in the front yard. It is what builds character and a sense of adventure, as well as teaches self-protection. As paranoid as our society is today, you would think it was the rare child that survived at all in those early days.

The Real News of Yesteryear

I remember all the news was local back then. All small towns had their locally owned daily newspaper. Our newspaper was The Observer. Our small-town radio station was KLBM, a locally owned and operated AM radio station. KLBM came on at 7:00 a.m. and signed off at 9:00 p.m. Most of what was broadcast then was "towny" stuff that was lighthearted and fun, mixed with music. It only dedicated about sixty seconds to national news daily, which is more than enough. KLBM was also the central broadcast station of all the local high school sporting events. Dad had a 15-minute radio program on KLBM called "Focus on Northeast Oregon." It was a short, small-town information segment that was always amusing. He was also the Friday night play-by-play broadcaster for all the La Grande High School basketball and football games.

The only televised national news back then was Walter Cronkite or The Huntley Brinkley Report. Both were thirty-minute news broadcasts every evening, Monday through Friday. Both reported, get this, just the news, whereby you would form your own opinion about what it all meant. Ah, the good old days!

As I think about it more, back in our childhood era, it was easier to raise a family because society was an ally and a resource. All families needed to do was go with the flow. Positive role models in media, with family-friendly laws and support systems, surrounded us. All were the backbone that sustained and supported marriage and family. Society and our grounded values helped create strong families that flourished, regardless of socio-economic status. You do not need wealth to teach children common sense morals and values.

To do the same today is family fatal, as the stream flow has dramatically changed. Sometime in the 1980s, the emphasis moved away from the core family to "It Takes a Village to raise a family." It was a nice little concept initially, but what did it mean? Long before "Takes a Village" was conceptualized, in the 1960s and 1970s, it meant all parents had shared common sense values. It was not unusual to be disciplined by other mothers in the neighborhood. All parents were confident in the shared nurturing of all the neighborhood's children. Parents were confident of the safety of each other's children as we played outside all day. Rules of conduct and safety were universal, well understood, and followed. Days were filled with spontaneous neighborhood activities such as building forts, riding bicycles, roller skating, or playing baseball. In the winter, we were still outside all day, sledding and building snowmen and snow forts. The neighborhood was our playground. Lunch was served by the mother of wherever we were closest. The time to go home for dinner was instinctual, or by whichever mother hollered at us first.

The "takes a village" was a political abstraction. It is an idiom popularized to mean cooperation to achieve a goal and has grown in scope and meaning, but for who's purpose? We were to understand that the childrearing "problem" suddenly became too big; therefore, it takes a village to come together. We were easily convinced that families "suffer every day" with the burdens of childrearing, where the government is needed to ensure parental success. This evolved to where the government believes they are the child's co-parent, further evolving to where they believe the child needs to be protected from the parent (Rodham Clinton, 1996) (Grammarist) (Funaro 2015) (Wise 2023).

Television is just plain painful to watch sometimes. Humor and family values have been replaced with subliminal messaging from an elitist Hollywood society. They spare no opportunity to tell us how to speak, think, and behave. Conforming messages even come through in the most ridiculous television commercials ever produced. Thank God for our newfangled DVR remote so we can skip by them.

In contrast, our family grew up in the golden age of television. Early programming included *Bewitched, Lassie, The Andy Griffith Show,* and *Mayberry RFD*. Later, we watched *The Brady Bunch* and the *The Partridge Family*. Sitcoms became popular with *Cheers, The Fresh Prince of Bel Aire, The Cosby Show, The Mary Tyler Moore Show,* and *Family Ties*. Variety shows became trendy with *Hee Haw, The Carol Burnett Show,* and *The Sonny & Cher Comedy Hour*. While they were all different television genres, they all had one thing in common. Good old-fashioned, humorous, nonpartisan, apolitical entertainment that taught great family values. It was programming that the entire family could watch in the evening. Never once did our parents fear inappropriate content during family viewing hours.

Now, there is this new mysterious computer social networking place called "MySpace." Life is a performance that must be shared via your computer or phone. Some mothers even post pictures of their children at the dentist's or while sick in bed! People actually broadcast that they are out of town as they post photos of their fantastic lives while on vacation. Frankly, I can think of a better name for it (Kormos 2022).

Introducing Drivel!

A social media platform where everyone can share their everyday lives with everyone else, including strangers. It is a photo-sharing stage, where we can share all the photographs that only portray us at our best and where people can feel inadequate as others share their astounding fairytale lives. Sell your products, sell yourselves, and sell your preferred political beliefs. It is a magical template for the future where we can aspire to be the most environmentally conscious, socially aware, fair-minded, scientifically focused, critically evolved, truthfully reasoned, forward-looking, competent, and inspiring individuals (Laurene, Drivel 2024).

In simpler times, there was no such thing as the internet. Societal communication shifts occurred after the invention of the cell phone, AKA the human's fifth appendage. This introduced breakthrough communication pursuits in texting and social media, where nobody had to talk to each other anymore. There was no such thing as satellite or streaming services. Cable broadcasting was available at that time, but not for our family. First came the rabbit ears and, sometime later, a rooftop antenna.

The First in Modern Television and Stereo Consoles

I remember when Mom and Dad bought our very first fancy television and stereo combined console unit. It was a colossal monstrosity in a very nice solid wood cabinet. It was the latest and greatest technological wonder in stereo and television console units. In the middle of the console was the television. On each side of the television screen were the high-fidelity speakers of the 1960s era. The cabinet top lifted on one side above the speaker, revealing a turntable and numerous knobs. It had to have been the first-ever stereo sound system controlling for treble and bass.

The console lasted a long time, but as with all combined electronic products, something will eventually crash. Unfortunately, individual component failures never occur all at once. Once one fails, the rest of the unit is useless. It was especially unfortunate when the television expired in our ginormous television/stereo console in a single wooden cabinet. This event would ultimately define our father's most basic intrinsic value to us and the rest of the world.

This first misfortune drove every decision ever made in our household. An attribute that we were reminded of throughout our entire childhood. Our father set out to preserve what he could when that television blew, and the stereo did not. Our father was undeterred in his quest to get every last second of life out of the console. Brandishing his hand saw, he cut out the speakers from the television. As small children, we thought this was normal. As we got older, it was better understood as our father's ingrained fervor to be as "thrifty" as one could be.

There were problems and opportunities with this very first money-saving (cheap) solution that he invented. The problem was that the speakers did not have legs to hold them up on the inside. When you cut out the television component in the middle of the entertainment console, there are no legs for the inside of each speaker. This only briefly befuddled my father as he stacked books to the front and back on the inside of each speaker to hold each speaker upright. The challenge was finding the books necessary to keep each speaker level. As Dad scurried around the house to find the correct books, Mom held each speaker up to keep them from toppling over. There were many book changes to bring each speaker to the precise level of level.

What was fortuitous about this solution was that with just a little extra speaker wire, you could put each speaker on opposite ends of the room. It provided an opportunity for our family to be the sole possessor of the very first ever surround sound system that our father invented. Dad should have patented his idea then. We did have to purchase a new television, though, which pained him to no end. Much to our amusement, his book-leveled speakers lasted another entire decade.

Exploring My Summer Digs

Dear Mom and Dad:

Thankfully, I have found - that despite the mice and the bugs right now, the primitive pioneer cabins here are decent enough. They even come equipped with an actual bathroom. I am still waiting for water, but the bathroom does have a toilet. However, as I took a long gander into that dry toilet, I noticed remnants of a petrified mouse, with evidence that his family had paid their respects more than once.

Each cabin is the same—a large one-room, hand-hewn, log-built type building built on top of a stacked rock foundation. Stacked rock foundations were typical of home and cabin foundations made during that era of their build. In the middle of the room are six sets of hand-made log-built bunk beds, each with a single-size mattress. There is also a log-made full-size bed against one wall, which I am guessing is the leader's bed. The leaders have a heavy vintage wooden dresser on a wall beside the bed. This one is a tall upright dresser with a fold-down dry bar of the late 1800s era. It has some cool metal scrolling on the front.

At the foot of each bunk are two large wooden footlockers with a hinged lid for each scout to stow their gear. At one end of the cabin is a massive, stacked stone fireplace and hearth. In front of the hearth lies a substantial red round braided rug over the hardwood floor. A dozen wooden rocking chairs are arranged in front of the fireplace in a horseshoe configuration.

The bathroom is at the opposite end of the cabin. There is no shower, but the cabin has a toilet, six washbasins, and numerous large nails suitable for towel hanging.

The scout cabins are pretty nice. They are dusty and spider-plagued, but they are comfortable and cozy. As a young, prepubescent boy, I would love to stay in this cabin. Frankly, I revel in it now as a small boy at heart.

The scouts and their leaders use their sleeping bags on the mattresses provided for the bunk beds. I did not bring a sleeping bag because I was informed I would have a different sleeping arrangement—one with a real bed. I have my pillow, freshly washed sheets from home, and a new electric blanket I bought for this occasion.

I do wish I had a sleeping bag now. From the looks of those mattresses, they probably came from a 1905 brothel in Fortine. Only about two inches thick, it was exceedingly uncomfortable with the buttons sewn on the top. Buttons that kept poking at me through my sheets all night long. I knew I should have brought my foam mattress topper. Oh well, one must draw the line somewhere.

After making my bed and "freshening" up (as best I could without water), I inspected and explored my summer work digs, the Camp Silverback cook's cabin and pavilion. It is a large building with a pavilion in front and kitchen quarters in the back. The kitchen quarters have adequate space to house a couple of large wood cookstoves against the east wall, with two commercial-size gas-heated ranges next to them. One gas stove has a griddle top, and the other has an eight-eyelet cooktop.

A 12X4 foot enameled rectangular-shaped dish drying station is on the west wall. It is situated next to the standard, three-basin stainless steel commercial sink. A large square 10X10 foot butcher block prep island is in the middle of the room, with various sizes of food prep bowls underneath the shelf. Above the prep island is a stainless steel shelf that covers the entire prep island. On the shelf are numerous metal baking trays of various sizes. Several dozen metal and cast-iron fry pans hang from hooks attached to the upper rack.

The service window is in the front or south-facing section of the cook's cabin. Gas-heated serving modules keep food warm before and just below the window. As the campers slide their food trays along the front, they are easily served from the modules. Prep and serving utensils are located on metal shelving underneath the modules. The other side of the service window opens into the pavilion, where the scouts and leaders dine on thirty-two picnic tables.

My office is located at the north end or back of the cook's cabin. Also located in the back are four large food storage areas for pantry items. There are two huge walk-in coolers, one for refrigeration and one for freezing. Also located in the back are three commercial-type washer and dryer units. I was pleasantly surprised. For a primitive scout camp, the mess and dining cabin are set up very well. Yep, this will definitely do.

Did I mention there is currently no electricity? The generator system cannot be started till tomorrow morning, and there is no water because you need electricity for the water pump. Fortunately, the temperature is just cool enough that my refrigerator groceries will not spoil. I am also unsure when we are supposed to have cooking gas.

Earl and I unloaded the trailer of all the pantry items, after which Earl proceeded to chop and gather our firewood fuel. While he was gathering wood, I pushed the dirt around in a futile cleaning attempt in the feeble glow of a kerosene lantern. I then began to contemplate dinner, the ingredients I had purchased in Eureka a mere four hours ago. Funny, that seems like four days ago.

Hmmm, I stood in front of two giant wood cookstoves, the likes I had only seen while watching Gunsmoke on television with Dad. What the heck do I do with these? I thought to myself. I tinkered around the edges of one of them when, fortunately, Earl emerged with the firewood. He laughed when he looked at me in my perplexed state. Then, I got my first lesson in the lighting and function of wood cookstoves, something he said he learned as a child when that was his family's only cooking source (Meston 1952 to 1961).

I will never forget that night. I somehow pulled together a glorious hamburger and marinara sauce dinner. There was no water to cook the spaghetti, but the marinara jars made it somehow. Always thinking, I pulled out some very lovely sourdough bread for dipping. Dinner was then complete with what I now call "Twice Pressed Garlic Bread."

Camp Recipe #1 - Twice-Pressed Garlic Bread

1. Fire up one of the wood cookstoves with Earl's assistance and tutelage.
2. While waiting for the wood to heat the stove, I retrieved from the 1906 Army Surplus, four-wheel drive Scout Humvee a nice loaf of fluffy sourdough French bread (that I spent extra on for fluffiness), which had been carefully placed in a safe place between my typewriter and five cases of powdered milk (First Press).
3. Split in half, lightly butter each side of that nice loaf of sourdough bread and sprinkle with precisely the right amount of garlic powder, trying your best to fluff it up again before putting it in the oven.
4. Bake for twenty minutes at hopefully 350 degrees, but who knows with a wood cookstove.
5. Listen with alarm as a hefty steel rack falls on the garlic bread you paid extra for fluffy freshness (Second press).

* For that unique variation, ensure the upper oven rack is especially dirty, thus giving the bread a "just grilled" look.

6. Throw the bread away and be glad it is too dark to notice that there is only once-pressed white sandwich bread to serve.
7. Look proud and smile.

Once dinner was over, I stacked all the cookware and dishes into the sink, praying that we would have water in the morning. It was a somewhat stressful day, so I decided to retire to my cabin for the evening. I had already warned Earl about my epic snoring, but he had already decided he would sleep in a different cabin anyway.

It was well past dark, so I walked to my cabin with the kerosene lamp. Earl was smart enough to have a flashlight. I stopped by the creek with a handy metal bucket to collect water for flushing purposes. It was a little trick that Earl suggested. I wished I had known that earlier. I would have thoroughly boiled the water before cooking the spaghetti. It was a rookie mistake, which I am sure there will be more of. Oh well.

Under the soft flickering glow of kerosene lighting, I sat down for my evening constitutional with my bucket of water in front of me. It was almost romantic, NOT.

Anyway, I was settling in with my egg-covered magazine and was beginning to relax when a curious splashing came underneath me. The mouse I saw earlier was not as petrified as I had once thought. I have not gone since.

Thoroughly exhausted now from the day's activities, I finally crawl into the lower bunk bed I had previously made. Only then did I discover that the bed does not hold a person that has... um... as broad a shoulders as I have. Wanting to relive my early Boy Scout days, I decided on the bunk bed. Why I did not opt for the full-size camp leader's bed is a mystery. At least I don't need to worry about falling out of a bed made for the comfort of a twelve-year-old boy scout, as I am essentially "sandwiched" between the two bunks. I am not feeling quite as accomplished in my twenty-pound weight loss.

I was too tired to unmake the bunk bed, transfer over, and remake the leader's full bed. I fell immediately to sleep. More later...

Love, Randy

Family Camping Nostalgia

It was the mid-'80s, and we had grown up and moved out. That year, for Mother's birthday, we decided to be nostalgic and reunite for another family camping trip. It was only fitting to head to our favorite family camping stomping grounds on the Lostine River at French Camp.

We had long disposed of our more comfortable camping abodes, but because our "thrifty" father never throws anything away, he found and pulled out our old canvas tent. I was shocked that he still had it, although I should not have been. It was a little tricky that day as the family pieced together those tent poles by memory with no directions. It took several hours and several beers, but we eventually completed our tent pole puzzle. We also happily discovered that our old family sleeping bags and air mattresses were in good shape. It was a camping miracle, considering how long they had been stored. We failed to check that before we left.

What we discovered that weekend was what a good sport our mother had been for so many years. Only then did we discover our mother hated camping! She really would have preferred staying home and playing Bridge with her friends. Being with her family was more important than her comfort, so she soldiered through it. No wonder we went from a tent to a pull-behind camp trailer (without a bathroom) to a truck and camper with a bathroom. Now we are back to tent camping for our poor mother's birthday, who is still a good sport. Mom did insist that our tent be directly next to the outhouse.

As our family snuggled into our decades-old original family camping tent that first night, I had to smile. The tent smelled like something between dirty socks, mold, and mothballs. While reminiscing, I noticed Dad was having difficulty on his side of the tent. Back in my old Cub Scouting days, Dad had purchased a sleeping bag made in a "mummy bag" style. He declared dibs on that bag for himself that night. Unfortunately, he failed to notice or remember that the bag size was more suited for a young boy. It was, after all, purchased for me when I was about ten years old. Dad forgot that part. Giggling, he calls me over for some assistance. The mummy bag he had reserved for himself was a bit snug for him, requiring some coaxing to get it zipped up. Dad was indeed in a predicament.

As we all laughed and giggled, I finally got him barely zipped into that bag. The bag was so tight around his body that he looked like a giant green caterpillar. To be obnoxious, I brought the head wrap around and secured it tightly under his chin. Not to be outdone, Dad insisted he was comfortable, cozy, and ready for bed. He then caterpillar crawled into place on top of his air mattress.

It had been a wonderful weekend, reliving our earliest camping days again as a family. Fishing, hiking, and playing in the river were again the highlights of a successful family camping trip. Maybe in the end, Mom's birthday gift was not stressing about young children playing in or around the river anymore. Since Dad did all the camp cooking, she had a relaxing weekend, free from the usual stresses of life. What she delighted in that weekend was talking, reminiscing, and watching her family play while intermittently immersing herself in her latest murder mystery novel. I think she had a good birthday weekend after all.

The Brick Phone

It is the next morning, and the day is starting much better. After sleeping until 8:00 a.m., I emerged from my cabin, momentarily pausing on my front deck to admire a beautiful lake view. I then began the short walk back to the pavilion via the closest vault toilet. The skies are clear and it is about seventy-five pleasant degrees. I can smell the sweet aroma of the forest canopy above me as I walk along the dirt path along the lake toward the pavilion. Ducks are playing in the lake, and the birds are singing. New grass shoots are emerging and the wildflowers alongside the walking path are beginning to bloom. It is going to be a good day.

As I approach the pavilion, I can smell the sweet aroma of fresh coffee. I can hear the camaraderie of my crew, who just arrived, reveling about their survival of "The Bongos." In celebration of their arrival, I began fixing everyone breakfast. Once again, I received a much-appreciated wood cookstove lesson, after which I prepared pancakes with boiled creek water this time. I included hot syrup, bacon, twice scrambled eggs, fresh fruit, and once-pressed whole wheat toast.

Earl then informed me that he was headed back up the mountain again to meet the camp manager who had radioed over. Our camp manager was about halfway down the Upper Bongos when he got a flat tire. What a surprise to hear that! The rest of the camp staff and leaders were going down caravan style in numerous jeeps. The manager was in the lead jeep, and since the Bongos is a one-lane road, all of them were stranded on the Upper Bongos.

The manager sheepishly told Earl he was ill-prepared that day amongst a group whose emphasis is "be prepared." None of the jeeps that day were equipped with spare tires. I guess it was a little embarrassing for a scout leader. It was Earl to the rescue! Where he found an extra tire is beyond me. I would come to understand by the end of the summer that Earl was always prepared for anything. Flat tires happen often enough while going in and out of here. He asked me if I would like to tag along, so I did. My staff chose to stay back to relax and digest their breakfast. They were unenthused at the prospect of going back up that road again. I then headed up the mountain with Earl.

Once our 1906 four-wheel drive military-style Scout Humvee fired up, we headed out. As we began our ascent of the lower bongos, he informed me that we must make another stop that morning. He needs to make a "quick" phone call, which should be interesting. We cannot get around the jeep convoy, and they cannot get around us. With that revelation now seared into my mind, I figured out that Earl and I would have to back down the entire Bongo/Jackass Slide road. I wished I had thought of that ahead of time. If I had, I probably would not have come.

Trying to think of something more positive and less frightening, I began thinking about a potential adventure later. Eureka is a little too far to make a phone call. Instead, we may head the other way toward the town of Yaak. That means I will finally see the infamous "Dirty Shame Saloon!" Yaak is an unincorporated hunting village two and a half hours southwest of Eureka. It is surrounded by 2.2 million acres of the Kootenai National Forest and has a population of around 250. In 2017, the town was featured in the New York Times as "The Last Best Empty Place in America" (Van Huygen 2019).

Yaak has a reputation in Montana for being a bit lawless, where residents take conflicts into their own hands. The heart of the Yaak is the Dirty Shame Saloon, established in 1951 for the flyboys, at the now-gone Air Force station in Yaak. Originally a metal hut, several small structures were added to form the current building. Legend has it that world boxing champion Joe Louis stopped by once and tried to order a Scotch. When he was told they did not have it, he replied, "Well, that's a Dirty Shame."

We had just topped the lower bongos when I asked Earl if we were headed to Yaak for our phone call…after rescuing our comrades, of course. Earl smiled back at me as he stopped the Humvee. Earl is a man of few words. Perplexed, I inquired as to what we were doing. I thought maybe he was annoyed with me for asking too many questions. He stated that we need to get to "The Overlook."

Earl then throws the Humvee into park in the middle of Jackass Slide. He sets the emergency brake and proceeds to climb out. I followed his lead as we both set two large boulders behind the front two wheels. I followed Earl as we climbed the steep embankment coming out of Jackass slide on the left of the Humvee. This task was not easy without rocks to step on or any vegetation to grab. As I scamper up behind him, Earl and his long legs lead the way as we begin our ascent to "The Overlook." Earl then hands me one of those turn-of-the-century "Motorola Personal Digital Communicators." One that I am sure was made in 1885 BC, which stands for "Before Cell." It is slightly larger and weighs more than a brick. I am mystified as to how we will get any cell signal. There is not a cell tower anywhere around here. Even if there was, no cell tower could pick up the precise molecular structure of an electronic device that mimics that of an 8-track tape player, a slinky, and a Mystery Date Game all at once. I am also sure that the Mayflower and The Titanic were the test groups for this phone, and we all know how that turned out. I can find no magical circle of stones around here that the Aztecs marked for inter-terrestrial communications.

Do they know that Motorola no longer services this device and that parts are nonexistent? I am sure Les Schwab no longer carries batteries for this device, Samsonite no longer makes the carrying case, and AAA no longer provides jump-start privileges. This phone belongs at the Smithsonian Institute as part of the "Star Trek" display, as Captain Kirk's transporter (Roddenberry 1966 to 1969).

Earl then proceeds up another hill adjacent to the overlook while whipping out a long cord. Is this some sick initiation as we hike up the mountain to nowhere? There is no way a phone jack is attached to some granite rock. Well, as it turns out, I was wrong. As I sprinted up that mountain to keep up with Earl, and just when I thought my lungs would explode, we arrived at a tree about a hundred yards up. A jack was attached to the tree trunk. It is where they send the relay signal for our emergency phone in camp. I guess the tree gets a better signal than the relayed signal in camp. He even pulled out a portable fax machine to send a document to the main office in Irving, Texas. I now think I am living in an episode of the "Twilight Zone." One minute, you expect Laura Ingles Wilder to wander by. The next minute, she pulls out her cell phone to order room service. Strange place here, our little rugged paradise in NW Montana.

Cell phones have come a long way from our "brick phone" days. Since then, they have progressed in modern society and have become important family members. People have become addicted to their phones. This extra appendage can never be separated from its user. To do so would require a serious amputation by a skilled Meta-analytical surgeon. Cell phones now require their own place setting at the dinner table. After all, something groundbreaking might "ding" through at any moment. I think cell appendages need their own names. Mine is not attached to me at every moment of my life, but if it were, I would call him George.

George

I have been studying this phenomenon at length lately. I see couples and families at restaurants studying it throughout their meals. Some are so enthralled with its content that they can barely eat. This is far more critical and enjoyable than visiting with your supposed sweetie or the fam.

What is not to like when we can pursue cheap and immediate dopamine hits via our social media sites? Who needs mind-altering drugs anymore? I predict psychiatrists will soon be obsolete, as self-worth is measured by how many "likes" a post garners or how many thousands of friends we have. We collect "friends" now like we used to collect stamps. The more we have, the more self-worth we have. It is a wondrous world where we can even eliminate friends with a simple keystroke. People can be gone instantly, including sweeties we no longer value. We no longer must tell people how we feel or break up in person.

I have discovered that through this appendage, people live performative social media lifestyles. A world where we can pick our friends or prospective dates from a list of character preferences. It is a protected place where we can elevate our egos via our programmable peers who all love us unless they "de-friend" us. Being "de-friended" signifies that we have said or done something to displease our meta-verse friends. It reduces all interactions to a list of virtually approved people based on compatible subjects. Language does not need to evolve any more. It is reduced to pre-approved topics where we no longer have the burden of meaningful interactions.

Then there is the art and science of "The Selfie." Young women have perfected the pouty "duck lip" selfie, which has progressed to the "Gape Lip" selfie. Both must be combined with the peace sign for emphasis. To reduce confusion, there are internet instruction sites on accomplishing a correct duck or gape lip selfie. This is an evolution of the "Valley Girl" jargon of the 1980s. There is nothing new in culture, just extensions of an old one (fourthgradenothing.com 2010).

Family dinner hour at our home was always a time of interaction. There were no cell phones, but there was a brief period when our father brought the newspaper to the dinner table. My mother squashed that bad habit in a hot hurry. I think that developing practice lasted a total of two days. She did not appreciate our father sitting behind a newspaper, which is no different than sitting behind your phone. We could not see him, nor was he participating in the dinnertime discussion. She always said the family dinner table was a place to interact and share our day. No distractions were allowed. If our phone rang, we did not answer it. Our mother was very wise.

Preparing for the Masses

Following our interstellar phone call and a carefully maneuvered "dance of the jeeps" in the middle of the Bongos that could only have been choreographed by Earl, the entire staff at Camp Silverback is now assembled. My cooking crew, camp leaders, and camp staff have all arrived. The whole camp is indeed a bustling place. It is time to get to work. Rugged northwest Montana winters are never kind to this camp.

The maintenance department fired up the generator, the water pumps, and the water heater. With that, I can finally properly clean everything up in the mess cabin. My crew gets busy, as all cooking vessels and utensils must be cleaned for the year, as well as all food prep, storage areas, and coolers. It was quite a chore.

Throughout camp, all the dead trees are cut down. The fallen trees and tree limbs are gathered and cut up for firewood. Enough firewood is gathered to make enough fuel to take any chill out of the cabins should the weather turn cold. Firewood is added to our large wood pile to fire the wood cookstoves. All the trails needed to be cleared of fallen debris and overgrown foliage. The cabins were all dusted, scrubbed, de-bugged, de-moused, and de-contaminated. This is a critical task, as evidenced by my first night here. I did discover that the well here has a hand pump. It is for emergencies in case the generator goes out! That handy little informational camp tidbit would have been good to know. Oh well, live and learn. It is nice not to have to boil water anymore.

Among many other things, the targets for the shooting range came out of storage, as well as the rifles, bows, and arrows. Numerous float crafts for the lake have been pulled out and placed alongside the lakefront. I have never seen that many canoes in one place. Sports gear was pulled out for baseball, soccer, and football. They set up the soccer nets and the shooting targets. Guns, bows, arrows, and all sports gear were stowed in a small, locked building next to the sports field. Hundreds of fishing poles, nets, and tackle boxes were pulled out and placed by each bunk in the cabins. All the tackle boxes were re-stocked by the magical tackle fairy. By the end of three days, this camp was ship-shaped and ready for its first installation of scouts.

Dear Mom and Dad:

My permanent summer accommodations are set up! They finally delivered the Food Service Director's camp trailer. Don't ask me where it came from, I was just thankful to see it. Needless to say, my living conditions have greatly improved. Maintenance set it up about thirty yards behind the mess cabin/pavilion next to the creek. My permanent summer accommodations are very private, quiet, and very nice.

My sixteen-foot "efficiency trailer" is white, faded to a yellowish color on the outside, and yellow with lime green accents on the inside. It is a very stylish little trailer that I am sure came from the 1950s era. As you walk in the door, you notice a tiny "couch" to the left. It is about the size of a chair and a half, that fits me perfectly. The bathroom is straight ahead. There is a counter, sink, and two-burner stovetop to the right of the bathroom door. Across from the mini kitchen is a dining room table that I turned into a nightstand and my office. I then unpacked my lamp and my typewriter. The full-size bed covers the entire front end of the trailer. I happily made my bed, with my sheets fresh off the bordello mattress and my brand-new electric blanket.

It is all very convenient. After a full night's sleep, I can stretch, yawn, sit up, and pivot up and toward my desk. All without even getting out of bed. Very convenient, but generally, other duties take priority over desk work first thing in the morning. Speaking of which, the bathroom is an "efficient" design where one can handily sit, brush one's teeth, and shave all at once. While highly efficient, it is not easy for a person with...as broad a shoulders as I have.

The bathroom is located on the back end of the trailer, with the commode on the very back wall. This arrangement requires that the stabilizer jacks be fully engaged and locked to support the trailer. This necessity was not thoroughly tested upon my first sit-down since the mouse incident. Unfortunately, whoever set up the trailer failed to perform this critical function.

Yep, you guessed it, my sixteen-foot single-axle trailer was a wee bit bottom-heavy, as it were. With the trailer's axle functioning as a fulcrum, the trailer made a sudden and abrupt shift down and toward the back. Until I figured out what was happening, I thought I would need a seat belt for this commode. Teeter, totter, anyone! It is a good thing the trailer was not on any slope, or this may have had a more exciting outcome. I guess I am not destined to go to the bathroom for about three months.

The only good thing about this incident was that nobody was around to witness my predicament. Thus, before anyone noticed, I could level out the trailer and smartly place and lock the stabilizer jacks. It brought me back to our camping days with our little pull-behind trailer. I never realized before now just how vital those jacks are.

I have unpacked my five bags. The trailer's closet and drawers did not even begin to store all the clothing I brought with me. I will not be cooking or storing food here, so I utilized all the cooking and food compartments for more clothing. Somehow, I got it all to fit and then stored my luggage in my office, inside the mess cabin.

The trailer has a nice awning, which I immediately rolled out and propped up with two aluminum poles I found inside. I scoped out an eighteen-inch round log next to the creek. I rolled it over and turned it flat-side up next to a lawn chair I found inside the pavilion. The log made a lovely little table next to my lawn chair. I sat under my awning and rested while admiring my view in front of the creek. I have a place to call my summer home now. It has been a hectic few days. I had better finish up this letter since I need to help start dinner. Please think of me often and send mail.

Love, Randy

Primitive Living

Making it through the first scout installment in a primitive cooking environment was quite the learning curve for me. Fortunately, this age group of boys is easy to please. Young pre-teen boys will eat almost everything, and they are always hungry. The leadership here keeps the boys very busy all day long. So, once I ring the big dinner bell, they come running. Such a great bunch of boys we have here. Always very polite and grateful for everything, which is not always the case in a university setting. So, what I lose in modern cooking amenities is made up for in spades in the attitudes and spirit of these young boys and their leaders.

The gas lines are finally hooked up, with the generator and water pumps humming in melodic unison. The wood cookstoves and the well's hand pump are still employed daily to keep the kitchen running smoothly.

Generators are utilized for off-grid domiciles like Camp Silverback. Standby units for intermittent power outages for on-the-grid homes are also available. Both work the same. Electrical power from generators generates power mechanically. In simplest terms, it converts mechanical energy to electrical energy. Mechanical energy is collected through external sources such as gasoline, diesel fuel, or natural/ propane gas. Our generator's source is diesel fuel, which Earl needs to add to the generator every day.

A camp this large cannot function with only one energy source. So, everyone does their part to conserve the energy we have. It is something I never thought about until coming here. As Americans, we are fortunate to live in a country that provides its citizens unlimited energy for all our needs, only considering conservation if we want to. Here at Camp Silverback, we must think about conservation constantly. We utilize many strategies all at once to keep everything running smoothly. It is a good lesson that we should all think about.

I remember growing up, our father placed three-inch stickers above every light switch in the house. The stickers were bright orange with bold black lettering, stating, "Turn Off the Lights!" Our father was one of our country's earliest original energy conservationists. I have no idea where he found such unsightly stickers that primarily detracted from our home's decor.

No worries about lights being left on here. Cabin lighting is provided by battery, oil, or kerosene lamps. Each scout is required to bring their own flashlight with fresh batteries. Our generator is a 32-kilowatt generator that puts out 32,000 watts per hour. It is enough to power the cook's cabin water pumps, commercial washers, my trailer, and all refrigeration. There are lights only in the meal preparation area but the pavilion has enough window lighting for the scout's dining hours. We have eight 100-gallon propane tanks that run the two gas cookstoves/ranges, clothes dryers, and water heaters.

Earl's Humvee truck bed has enough space to load up empty propane tanks and a huge diesel gas tank with a pump in the back. The tank holds about 120 gallons of diesel fuel. Earl will fuel the portable diesel tank and refill the propane tanks on every garbage run to town and our grocery run.

Daily use of wood cookstoves conserves fuel and is necessary to get every meal pulled together on time. It did not take long before I figured out the wood cookstoves. First, there are several species of trees here at Camp Silverback. Each possesses different densities of wood. The density of the wood determines heat distribution by temperature and length of burn. It is a fine art of fuel type and manual "damper'ing" of the flame to produce the desired temperatures and cook times. We have three primary species of pine here. What that means for us is that Lodge Pole Pine and Spruce burns fast and is very hot. Red Fir and Tamarack burn longer and are easier to control temperatures. Thankfully, I have a great staff who have grown up here. They know all about this pioneer stuff and have been very patient with me in my instruction. After two weeks, I can now say that I have this down. It is a skill that only those of us in rural settings understand.

Dad used to always tell us, "Wood warms you twice." We had a wood heating stove back then. He thought that statement would appease us as we gathered our firewood in the woods. It was an odious job, especially for Mom. It required an entire day to get one firewood load in our pickup with no racks. First, traveling to an appropriate stand of dead trees. Then, "Chain sawing" those trees down and cutting them into proper lengths. Lengths of the perfect linear size to efficiently fill the stove without being too long. Then, we split the log lengths in half and then in quarters for optimal stacking in the truck. Then we drove home, unloaded the wood and stacked it in our carport. It is an exercise many families in the West still perform today. The work was difficult, but it remains a great memory. Our entire family was physically laboring to help heat our home in the winter to save on energy. The day was always complete, with a packed lunch and a lovely family outing in the woods.

At our primitive camp at Camp Silverback, I sometimes feel like I am reliving the old West. It reminds me of all those stories passed down through the generations, describing our family as they pioneered through this country, settling the West.

Early Settlers of the West

Both sets of great, great grandparents on my mother's side were from Norway and Holland. My great-grandfather John and his family immigrated from Holland to New York. They eventually settled in Wisconsin and then Minnesota. Minnesota is where he met and married my great-grandmother, Sophia. Sophia's (Sophie's) family immigrated from Norway.

Norway and Holland are only about a mile apart. Interestingly, the couple met only after immigrating to the United States on two different paths, yet they ended up in the same state and community. Even back then, it was a small world (Sunderlage, Sophie 2007).

In American history, the single most significant legislative action promoting the settlement and development of the American West happened when Abraham Lincoln signed the Homestead Act. It was signed into law on May 20th, 1862. This legislation was especially notable because it allowed everybody to own land. The only personal requirement was that the homesteader be either the head of a family or twenty-one years of age. Thus, any U.S. citizen, including freed slaves, single women, and immigrants who intended to become naturalized citizens, was eligible. It was the first law that allowed African Americans to own land. This legislation was initially introduced by Congress in 1860 but was vetoed by Democrat President James Buchanan. Later, it became the Republican party platform in the 1860 election. Lincoln's victory ensured its passage. The Government granted more than 270 million acres of land while the law was in effect. The act, which took effect January 1, 1863, granted 160 acres of unappropriated public lands to anyone who paid a small filing fee and agreed to improve the land. Specifically, this included building a residence and working the land over five years. Thousands of people moved to the Great Plains to take advantage of free land (Editors, History.com 2022).

In 1890, after their marriage, Sophie and John were just two of the thousands who pioneered to the Great Plains to take advantage of such an opportunity. It was a new world for poor folks who could obtain land from the government in exchange for hard work. Sophie and John were not afraid of hard work, so it was a dream come true. They would be granted full legal title once they lived and farmed the land for the required time.

The early settlers who first conquered the West had little money. They set out to the great northern plains to lay claim to the land they chose, amongst a vast territory that went for miles and miles on gently rolling terrain. The weather was extreme in the northern plains, with nothing to protect them from the bitter cold that blew down from Canada. The temperatures in the summer would be above one hundred degrees. Winters would see temperatures drop well below freezing for months on end. Our earliest settlers would endure lightning storms, tornados, and other obstacles thrown at them by Mother Nature. Extended severe droughts would bring in swarms of grasshoppers that would wipe out entire crops in just one day. Crops that had little chance anyway because of the lack of water.

Medical or veterinary care would be miles away, necessitating families to do their best on their own. Getting ill would be a survival challenge. Only a handful of settlers would make it at all. Half of them did not make it past five years on the prairie. Still, life on the prairie did have rewards for those who fought for it. The land was fertile and abundant with wild game. It was a lesson in determination to make it work. Those who did make it after five years thrived in this new environment.

Once the settlers arrived, they would find no timber or larger vegetation to build a home. Lacking any building materials such as lumber or stone, they made do with what they had, and what they had was the ground they walked on. Sophie and John went to work building their one-room sod house. The top layer of soil on the prairie contained strong grasses. Under the grasses and into the soil would be a strong mass of roots that held onto dirt well. Long rectangular building blocks of sod, eighteen to twenty-five inches thick, were cut to build their homes. It was held together by mud, like what stone and brick masons do today. Eventually, the grass and root mass would grow into the mud, thus keeping the sod blocks together.

The bare ground on which the sod was cut would be the base of a cabin floor. Door and window framing were made using wood poles from any timber they found during their westward journey. Roofing materials were also long timber poles long enough to cover the entire roof span. Placed close together, the poles were then covered with brush that they tied together in bundles, with mud over the top to bind them. Finally, a layer of sod, grass side up, was laid on top. The roof had to be slanted for moisture to fall away naturally. It prevented the roof from retaining too much moisture that could seep into the home (Andrew Brown 2016).

Sophie and John brought a small wood cookstove with them west. It would be their only heat and cooking source. A hole was cut in the roof for the chimney and packed with more brush, mud, and then more sod to seal it. The couple needed to buy a milk cow. This necessitated a small sod barn for the cow and calf. The barn would need to be big enough for the pair, plus hay for winter use.

Later, Sophie got busy with the finish work on the inside of their sod home. The first step was stretching a light-colored sheet across the ceiling. This kept the bugs from dropping but also reflected any light you might have. Next, Sophie scraped the walls smoothly and added a layer of plaster. After smoothing out the plaster, it would mimic that of a drywall compound. It gave the walls a smooth and water-resistant finish. Sophie and John's finished home was strong enough to withstand rain and wind. Snow would accumulate and freeze on all surfaces, giving it an igloo effect. The sod blocks could insulate the living space to a temperature of sixty degrees, even without heat.

Once the house was completed, they began turning over, tilling, and planting the fertile ground that was now their home. Sophie and John made that five-year mark. They were thriving, living off their land and their dream in the Northern West. After they made their pilgrimage to North Dakota, they had four boys: Grover, Palmer, Jacob, and Alvin. Grover was my grandfather.

The Struggle to Survive

Living and farming on the plains of North Dakota was tough. I cannot even imagine living in a sod house. I could not have survived it. In fact, after living for two weeks (so far) in a quasi-primitive environment, I have concluded that people in today's modern society have lost the ability to survive. We have become far too accustomed to all of today's modern conveniences. We do not even have to think about the struggle to survive anymore. I was without any electrical power source for only two days, and we are talking generator power, not externally sourced electrical power with interconnected electrical lines. What if, by some disaster, we all lost electricity? Think about the consequences of what that would mean. Seasonal temperatures in some regions of the country can be extreme, whether it be winter or summer.

Disasters can take many forms. In the 1950s, people worried about nuclear attacks, so much so that schoolchildren would have nuclear attack drills. One can never know what lies ahead, but a natural disaster is more likely to happen. We already feel the effects of natural disasters that communities or regions experience during hurricanes or earthquakes. Seismologists report catastrophic volcanic explosions that boil just under the earth's core. Natural disasters, foreign attacks, or experimental manufactured energy failures could destroy the energy grid of the entire United States.

Society depends on electricity for everything. Even if your furnace and air conditioner run off natural gas, their fans run on electricity. But it is much more than simply being unable to turn on the lights or run your furnace or air conditioner. Generators must run on some sort of fossil fuel. You could not fill your car with gasoline because gas pumps run on electricity. How does that fuel get to gas stations? It is by truckers who move gasoline and oil by truck or train. So not only do you have no lights, heat, or air conditioning, but you have lost the ability to transport yourself in the way we are all accustomed to. Back to the horse and buggy, everyone?

What about refrigeration? Homes and grocery stores would lose the ability to keep all those pre-packaged frozen items frozen. We could no longer properly store perishable dairy, eggs, and meat. Produce would only be available from local farms and only when in season. Canned or dry goods we now have the luxury of buying could no longer be produced or shipped to your local grocer. People have no understanding of the food distribution system in our country. If the system breaks down, only two weeks' worth of food is available. The lost art of home canning might return, but only if folks had the supplies and a wood cookstove. Even then, you need a chainsaw and gas and oil to run that chainsaw. Even fewer people have the ability to gather their own firewood (Parks 2024).

Without the energy grid, all interstate commerce, trucking, rail, and air travel would come to a screeching halt. The US Government, with all its "power and wisdom," would be incapable of remedying a problem of this magnitude. The situation would even be too big for state governments to solve. We would then have to survive on what we have in our communities and neighborhoods. This is where I think rural and farming communities would have a distinct advantage and would survive.

I have lived in a small rural community for most of my life. These are communities where generations of families are born, live, and then die. Everybody knows everyone, and everyone does their part to support each other. Neighbors help each other in need. The bartering of goods and services is a usual practice. The "organic farm-to-table" concept originally began in these long-ago communities. It is a practice still found today in small rural neighborhood community gardens.

What we know as jerky today and a fine snack was essential to preserving meat for use in my great grandparents' time. They did not have real refrigeration to keep meat from spoiling. Home canning was practiced, preserving the plenty for leaner seasons. Those who did not farm still had valuable skills to sell or barter. It is the rural communities that possess those skills. Those forgotten old talents passed down from many generations, practiced today as a novelty, could be easily resurrected to survive.

Growing up, we always knew someone who raised hens for eggs or had a dairy cow. In the 1960s and early 1970s, Mom used to buy fresh eggs and milk all the time. All our dairy was delivered to our home in glass containers and left in a cold storage compartment on our front porch. Fresh milk was the best milk you would ever taste. It came with four inches of cream floating on the top. Fresh cream was especially good for oatmeal. We have an old family recipe from the late 1800s called "Sour Cream Raisin Pie." It was a recipe passed down by many generations in my mom's family. Being farming families, it was prepared using fresh, unpasteurized sour cream. Mom made the pie using fresh cream she soured herself. It is not the same with commercially packaged and pasteurized sour cream. Our family quit trying to make that pie a long time ago.

The federal government and many state regulations no longer allow anyone to sell unpasteurized dairy products. Raw milk is considered dangerous dairy contraband. I never remember anyone becoming ill from the family milk cow down the road. Reputable raw milk producers produce far healthier milk than store-purchased pasteurized milk. If the milk is collected using sanitary conditions, raw milk has far more benefits. Once you pasteurize milk, it loses nutrients and beneficial bacteria that we all need to be healthy. Pasteurization denatures healthy proteins and fats. People who cannot tolerate milk can tolerate it in a more digestible raw form (Dr. Axe 2018).

Empty glass milk containers would be washed and set inside the insulated storage compartment on our porch. Empty egg containers were treated the same. Clean containers of fresh milk were then exchanged for empty bottles. Mom left the cash inside the compartment to pay the farmer. It was our parent's generation who invented the original recycling that we all practice today. Younger generations disparage the older generations for their lack of re-cycling understanding. Sorting cans, bottles in different colors, and paper made of various materials is not the only definition of recycling. Frankly, I prefer not to study my garbage that closely. Nor would I appreciate a garbage truck camera to examine my garbage or for the garbage Nazis to fine me for an errant pizza box in the paper recycling can. Nobody talks about food waste, which is atrocious in our country and something that never used to occur, especially for those who live far from any metropolis.

Farm to Table the Old-Fashioned Way

Decades ago, selling, bartering, and sharing food was a way of life in rural communities. For those in need, farming families routinely cared for their own, giving away milk, eggs, vegetables, and fruits to needy families in the community. Composting was commonplace. Vegetables and fruits unfit for human consumption were fed to livestock. Nothing went to waste; even eggshells were re-fed to chickens to strengthen shells. Most families I knew, including ours, had a big garden in the summer. We also had a huge Bing cherry tree. That one tree produced more than our family would ever eat in the summer season. Even when we canned many quarts of cherries for the off-season, we still had enough to give away, which we did. Had we considered it, we could have traded cherries for other products.

All food products were natural. Livestock was raised on meadow grass and then naturally fertilized, as the cow "gave back" to the ground. What grass was left was baled for the winter. Fruits and vegetables were all naturally grown organic, with only sunlight and rain added. Fruits and vegetables even looked natural. Nothing like today, where the competitive grocery market adds FDA-approved colors to enhance the salability of fruits and vegetables. Any fertilizer you might have needed, you got free from the local cow producers. The family cows were slaughtered, providing meat for the family, with excess meat sold or traded.

In the West, we always have an abundance of wild game. Deer, elk, antelope, and moose are harvested, gutted, and skinned, then hung to age in the family's shed or garage. The family then cuts and packages the meat themselves, with many organizing big game cutting and packaging events. Meat is then shared amongst all those who helped. It is a long-held tradition of the American West, with families, including our family, doing what needed to be done to survive. It is a healthier protein option, free from commercial meat practices of added chemicals, pesticides, and hormones.

Farming with hormones, herbicides, and pesticides would be added later to commercial farming productions. It is these commercial farming conglomerates that have slowly taken over family farms. Corporate farming is a highly lucrative business now. As cities grew, corporate strategies grew to produce higher yields at less cost using genetically modified organisms (GMOs), which also yielded a less healthy food product (Farmaid.com) (Farmaid Blog 2016).

The long-ago simple system of bartering and selling locally grown produce, dairy, and meats is now governed, highly regulated, comes with pricing structures, and is taxed. It is now a highly evolved system that provides our modern society with a resource for buying natural, organic, locally-grown food products. Life only gets more complicated as "progress" advances and new trends develop. Mass-produced "natural" food products occur as urban centers attempt to return to farm-fresh food products. "Naturally" produced does not mean it is because it is mostly unregulated in the United States. Organic has become the standard now for inferring something as "natural." Organic is a regulated designation. It describes methods and materials used to grow the food ingredient or product. Organic labeling indicates that the product has no artificial colors, flavors, or preservatives and is "minimally" processed. It seems this should automatically eliminate processed food in a package, can, cosmetics, or cleaning products. Except that it doesn't.

Being a small local grower in this highly regulated market is time-consuming, tedious, and nearly impossible. It only caters to those corporate farming entities with the infrastructure for mass-produced food. Authentic naturally grown organic foods are only found now in rural communities, local farmers' markets, farm stands, or community gardens. My sister once tried to sell her farm fresh eggs to an organic chain store. She fed her chickens expensive organic feed in the winter. In the summer, they foraged on their own. She never medicated them, keeping them naturally healthy. They roamed freely, with unlimited access to fresh water from the creek, while foraging on insects around the farm. Grasshoppers and other insect life around the house and the farm were always adequately controlled by her hen flock (Fresh Eggs Daily Blog).

Ultimately, she could not sell to the organic market because she could not guarantee that her free-range chickens were foraging on land free of pesticides. Her chickens eat bugs as they freely forage on the land. She could not guarantee that the creek water nor the bugs were pesticide and chemical-free. Chickens like to scratch around on livestock feed left on the ground by horses and cows. They especially like to scratch around in the manure. She could not guarantee that the feed and, therefore, the manure, AKA chicken candy, left on the ground was from pesticide-free hay. She could prove that her hay supplier does not use pesticides, but what about the fields grown around that hay? Did they use pesticides that could blow over onto that hayfield? That was something she could never guarantee.

Free-range chickens are, by definition, organic, but unless she kept her chickens from naturally foraging, she could not sell her eggs as organic. This is what happens when an industry grows to the point of needing to be regulated, or as is nowadays, over-regulated. She could have sold her eggs as "natural" from "free-range" hens, but not organic. Since she could never see herself patrolling the hen area from errant bugs, she reduced her flock to only what the family needed. Eggs you buy now as "organic" may lack pesticides or hormones, but they are captive hens, not natural foragers. Foraging to the organic producer means a carefully controlled environment that requires so many feet per hen in the open air for only a specified amount of time. They are only fed what the producer feeds them in a small, contained area. What they are provided are commercial feeds labeled organic. It is the only way to raise organic/natural eggs for the massive commercial market. How can you tell an egg from a naturally foraging hen? The yolks are bright orange. This indicates that the hen forages on natural plant life, not solely on commercial feeds. The difference in flavor, which is beyond good, results from hens who also ingest more proteins, which is only accomplished among foraging hens, producing a healthier egg. You will only know the difference if you have had the privilege of eating a real farm-fresh egg from a naturally foraging hen. Otherwise, you might as well buy regular eggs at half the price (Kelto 2014) (Lynne 2023).

I grew up with the freedoms inherent in rural country living, an era that embraced the land, livestock, and the production of plant-derived food. It was an uncomplicated, carefree existence. Now, it is a long-forgotten lifestyle interpreted by youngsters as constraining and lacking in meaningful culture or excitement. I was no exception.

City Life for the Rural Life

Like many young adults, I left country rural living for a while. Believing I needed to broaden my horizons, I thought there was more to life than small-town living. There just had to be something more exciting in this great, big world. So, for a while, I briefly lived in Seattle, Washington. The city was initially exciting, but after a while, I realized I was just one person out of four million, where nobody knew anyone. Being from a small community, I found the differences stark.

People living in large cities depend highly on government services and mass transit. The city caters to large numbers, so the complexities of living in a large city became cumbersome to me. I noticed that the more services the government adds to make it more efficient, the more disorganized it becomes. I was never so lonely and isolated in all my life, in a place surrounded by so many people. I am a pretty easy guy to get along with, yet I discovered friendships in the city were fleeting and fickle. Everybody is a transient in the city as folks move in and out through the proverbial revolving door, searching for their place in life. Friendships depended more on temporary workplace acquaintances, niches, or political beliefs. It might differ within suburban neighborhoods, but everybody I knew lived in apartment complexes. It was what we could afford.

The allure of big city life was fleeting. The city was crime and drug-ridden and extremely violent. Being from a small town, I could never get used to locking my doors, constantly being aware of my surroundings, and looking over my shoulder. I noticed that most middle-class suburban homes had bars on the windows. Who wants to live like that?

I could not find my niche, and the big city made me weary. I never understood the dependence on city infrastructure. At what point does that dependence take away your independence? Being dependent takes away the struggle, putting one under the control, influence, support, and aid of others. I only stayed a few years before moving back to Eastern Oregon. It did not take long before I realized I am a small-town country boy at heart.

Real Struggles in History

It was mid-November 1896 when my great-grandfather John set out with his wagon from the family homestead. It was past time to go and gather the winter firewood for the family. Living on the vast plains of North Dakota, he had to travel several days to find an adequate stand of trees.

For a wedding gift, John's parents gave Sophie and John a pair of draft horses to make their journey west. Once they arrived, they needed the money to purchase farming implements, seed, and a milk cow and calf. After selling the draft horses, he had only an elderly horse and pony to pull that wagon. There were no chainsaws back then, so trees had to be chopped down with a sturdy ax and then split by hand with the same ax. Once he found a stand of trees, it would then take him another week to cut and prepare that wood for wagon transport. Once he finished loading, he would then begin the long trek home. It would take twice as long because the wagon was now much heavier for the horse and pony to pull.

Sophie had the reliable milk cow and just enough firewood and food provisions until he returned. She dreamed of someday having a root cellar to store back food supplies for the winter. Unfortunately, John waited too long to make the journey. Snow was already covering the ground when he left. Snow would make it more difficult for the horses to pull the heavier wagon back home.

My Great-grandfather did not make it home. While journeying back, the great 1896 Thanksgiving North Dakota blizzard hit. They found the wagon, the pony, and my great-grandfather two weeks later, frozen to death a mere half mile from the homestead. My Great-grandfather died young, leaving behind four small children and a loving, devoted wife. Worst of all, his young family was alone now on the North Dakota plains.

Sophie had long run out of food. The firewood was gone, requiring her to burn all the furniture. It was not enough. The strong northern winds were relentless and endless for two weeks. The sod barn could no longer stand, so the milk cow and her calf froze to death. The tiny sod home could not tolerate the beating. As the brutal winds broke the house apart, Sophie could only keep a small area of the house intact by the stove. That stove was cold now, with the wind and the snow swirling around her and her small children.

Down the road from Sophie and John, the elderly horse miraculously returned to the neighboring homestead. Fearing the worst, the neighbors decided to check on the young family. Once they got there, they would be shocked by what they found. John and Sophie's home was nearly gone. They found the family inside, desperately trying to survive and hold on. Sophie and her starving young boys were found huddling around a cold stove. They were barely surviving in all the blankets and clothing they owned, struggling to keep warm in what little shelter they had left. Sophie and her children were fighting for their lives (Sunderlage, Sophie 2007).

There was no government program to rescue them that fateful year. There would be no federal disaster declaration to help rebuild. No HUD Section 8 housing or USDA Section 521 rental assistance programs would exist. There were no low-income housing tax credits or HOME grants. The government now provides for everybody's needs if they seek it. The homeless are provided with shelter, the funding for which comes from many government entities. Soup kitchens are provided by generous communities and churches, as well as community "warming stations." The government will provide those in need with free housing, food, healthcare, and even a free cell phone if they seek it. No less than eighty-plus different public assistance programs in our country will benefit anyone who seeks them. Everyone is afforded the ability in this country to better their lives if they seek it. Some even take advantage of free college. Yet, increases in homelessness continually and progressively reach higher numbers with each passing decade. This is a direct result of band-aid government policies that do little to help the very people they say they target (Programs 2023) (singlemotherguide.com 2022).

Public assistance programs are no stranger to the United States. Budgets to keep all this afloat have grown exponentially since 1935 when President Franklin D. Roosevelt began the Social Security Administration. What began as a 3.8 million budget has grown to $1.6 trillion by 2022, or a nearly 15,000 percent increase in federal public assistance spending for a mere 160% increase in population. The American government supplies abundant assistance to assure the well-being of every citizen and non-citizen in this country. That does not include money spent on public education assistance and grants for higher education. It does not include state assistance spending, nor does it include the multitude of wealth shared by many generous private charities, corporations, and individuals. It results from bloated federal entitlement budgets that employ far too many people. It is enough money for every man, woman, and child in this country to receive $4,500.00 annually. If you eliminated the bureaucracy and paid the citizens, it would be $18,000.00 for a family of four (Begody 2023) (Merriam 1955).

This is a very simplified look at what this spending looks like. I am sure my calculations fall far short of the actual numbers because they are too big to fathom or calculate, but it does illustrate the safety net our country has cast out there. No one should know what it is like to struggle in our society, certainly not like our forefathers did. Yet the number of homeless in the United States "progressively" grows. Veterans and elderly citizens cannot heat or cool their homes or adequately feed themselves. Many are dying in the process. I call that a government failure of epic proportions. It should not be about throwing more and more money at it in the hopes that something beautiful will grow. How many decades have we been doing that? Perhaps something different is in order.

Anyway, I have certainly digressed. My Grandpa Grover was deeply affected by that desperate experience that nearly took all their lives. Being just five years old, he remembered the struggle and the fight for their preservation. My grandfather always remembered the nightmare of running out of firewood fuel and never again allowed his home to be heated by only one heat source. He remembered the ensuing years when his mother battled weather, grain markets, labor, and seed costs while living in poverty alone with four children. Life was far more difficult than anyone today could ever imagine. Yet my family survived it together. Working together, they gained new skills and strategies every year. They survived by never giving up and letting go of their dream.

You think about how history would have changed had it not been for that old horse making it back in a blinding blizzard, in below-freezing conditions to a neighbor who was familiar with that particular horse. Then, that neighbor was suspicious enough to explore if there was a problem. They risked their own lives to make their way through the blizzard to investigate. If none of that had happened, Sophie and the children would have frozen to death, including my grandfather. My great-grandmother's courage, fight, and drive never to give up, is why I am here today.

My grandfather, Grover, met and married my grandmother, Pearl, in Egeland, North Dakota, in 1910. Pearl was one of nine children in that family. After marrying, Grover trained to be an embalmer while working in a hardware store. In 1915, the family finally settled in Northeast Montana's Sheridan County, where Grover gave up embalming to work as a banker in Medicine Lake. Twenty-two miles south of Plentywood,

Medicine Lake would later become a National Wildlife Refuge in 1935, with over 31,000 acres within its boundary. Today, the Refuge is home to diverse native prairie and wetland species.

The Wild West

Northeast Montana's earliest history began with the Sioux Tribe, who inhabited the Great Plains region for approximately 13,000 years before the arrival of Europeans in the seventeenth century. Sitting Bull (1831-1890) was a Teton Dakota Native American chief who united the Sioux tribes of the American Great Plains. They joined against the white settlers, who wanted to take over tribal lands. In 1874, the Fort Laramie Treaty granted the sacred Black Hills of South Dakota to The Sioux. Gold was first discovered in the Black Hills in 1874, with much more significant placer discoveries found in 1875 and 1876. With that, the U.S. government ignored the treaty and began removing native tribes from their land by force (History 2023).

The great Sioux wars ensued, culminating at the Battle of the Little Bighorn in south-central Montana in 1876. Sitting Bull and Crazy Horse led the united tribes to victory against General George Armstrong Custer in a battle famously known as "Custer's Last Stand." It would be June 25, 1876, when a battalion of the 7th cavalry led by Custer was wiped out by an overwhelming force of Lakota, Dakota, Northern Cheyenne, and Arapaho.

Upon defeating Custer in battle, Sitting Bull traveled north, crossing the U.S. border and seeking refuge in Canada. In Canada, he and his tribe resided for the next five years. In 1881, Sitting Bull surrendered to US forces in the area later known as Plentywood and was held for two years as a prisoner of war at Fort Randall in the South Dakota Territory. He was then released to the Standing Rock Indian Reservation, straddling North and South Dakota. On December 15, 1890, Sitting Bull was tragically shot and killed by Indian police officers at the Standing Rock Indian Reservation. He is remembered today for his strength and courage in defending tribal native lands.

Plentywood is in the far northeast corner of Montana, bordering North Dakota and Canada. Originally, Plentywood was in Valley County, which was established in 1893. Sheridan County would then be split off from Valley County in 1910. Plentywood is best known for its "Outlaw Trail," which crosses into Canada north of Plentywood. This passage is where rustlers would move their stolen cattle and horses from the USA into Canada and back. This area is also a part of the Old West's legendary resident, Butch Cassidy. He was the one credited for organizing the trail and the one who named it. He would later establish a rest station in the Big Muddy Valley west of Plentywood, in what was, at the time, Valley County. This area was the beginning and center of "The Old West" legend. At the turn of the twentieth century, it became one of the most notorious places in North America.

Two major gangs of the Big Muddy were the Dutch Henry, The Nelson (alias Sam Kelly), and the Jones gang, which operated in the Big Muddy Valley. Dutch Henry showed up in Montana in the late 1800s. The Nelson-Jones Gang were bank and train robbers and horse and cattle thieves. This gang was also part of the Wild Bunch, and in 1903, the link between Dutch Henry and the Nelson-Jones gang was solidified as the two joined forces (McCanna, Outlaws of the Big Muddy 1999).

Cassidy fashioned The Outlaw Trail on the Pony Express model, with fresh horses pastured at friendly ranches every ten to twelve miles. Any lawmen pursuing Cassidy and his "Wild Bunch" gang were left in the dust. A stock inspector's notes later found in old files stated, "Valley County is the most lawless and crooked county in the union, and The Big Muddy is the worst."

Many outlaws and horse thieves would use this trail, stealing horses in Montana and taking them to South Saskatchewan to sell them. Then, while in Canada, they would steal the same horses, take them back to Montana, and sell them again. Then, they would steal them back again, only to re-sell them to Canadian ranchers, who were relieved of the same stock the previous week. Stock inspectors were very busy back in those days.

The Big Muddy was the primary horse rustling station on the Outlaw Trail, known as Station No. 1. Stolen horses from Southern Saskatchewan would then begin a long trek on the trail, snaking through Montana, Colorado, and Arizona into Ciudad Juarez, Mexico. Once in Mexico, the horses would be sold. Horse rustling was a lucrative outlaw practice back in the day.

"Old Dutch Henry" once ran into a group of homesteaders making their way across the northern plains. They were searching for a place with adequate timber for fuel and lumber. Dutch Henry, who used the outlaw trail often, said to the homesteaders, "You'll see a creek if you go a few miles up. From there, you'll find plenty of wood." Following his advice, the new homesteaders found the creek and abundant tree growth to meet their needs. In 1912, those first settlers named their homestead town Plentywood just west of the Big Muddy.

Plentywood, Montana, is where my family would eventually settle. It is where my mother was born and where my family's history helped shape American history, a history that influenced our country into the 21st Century.

The Mother of all Flu

In January 1918, the Spanish Influenza pandemic hit, but was only first detected in the spring of 1918. My grandparents and their children lived through that pandemic and survived it. My grandpa Grover was a front-line worker during that Pandemic. In 1918, states and regions worked together as Federal coordination did not exist. By summer, it had spread like wildfire. The first wave did not have a high fatality rate, but after its first mutated strain, the second wave hit in August of that year. That variant resulted in a death toll that caused two-thirds of the Spanish Flu deaths (Spanish Flu 2023, History).

The third wave of the Spanish Flu hit the world near the end of 1918 and would last until March 1919. The strain was less deadly than the previous strains because the population had already been infected and developed immunity. This is how viruses behave. New viruses are highly virulent and indiscriminate on whom they take—including the young and the strong. As a result, the frailest in our country had no chance. People were frightened and bewildered as they struggled to protect themselves and their families.

The Spanish Flu remains a seasonal occurrence today and has been designated "The Mother of all Flu." Throughout history, direct viral descendants of the same H1N1 virus have emerged. Bird Flu and Swine Flu were pandemic strains in 1957, 1968, and 2009. All are later flu outbreaks, partly created by the 1918 Spanish Flu virus. The Spanish Flu pandemic infected five hundred million people globally, or twenty-seven percent of the world population. Of those infected, it killed approximately fifty million people, with 675,000 deaths in the United States, which had a population of 103 million at the time (Lea 2021) (Roos 2020).

The Spanish Flu began in Europe during the end of WWI. More U.S. soldiers died from the 1918 flu than were killed in battle during the war. Troops moving around the world in crowded ships and trains helped to spread the killer virus. Spain was not the source of the Spanish Flu. Spain was one of only a few major European countries to remain neutral during World War I. Unlike the Allied and Central Powers nations, including the United States, wartime censors suppressed the flu news to avoid "affecting morale." The Spanish media could report on it in all its gory detail. News of the sickness first made headlines in Madrid in late May 1918. All other nations undergoing a media blackout could only read in-depth accounts from Spanish news sources. They naturally assumed that the country was the pandemic's ground zero. Meanwhile, the Spanish believed the virus had spread to them from France, so they called it the "French Flu."

A Hero

During the Spanish Flu pandemic, my Grandpa Grover returned to service as an itinerant (traveling) embalmer. He had a unique professional skill that was rare at the time. Embalmers differed from undertakers in their abilities to prepare the deceased for burial. It was a skill desperately sought during that time. Unfortunately, this required him to travel away from his family to other parts of the state. He would work with only a handful of other embalmers, undertakers, and gravediggers. It was a desperate attempt to keep up with all the deaths occurring simultaneously. The Spanish Flu was the first true killer virus that could have infected him, and he knew it. It was a desperate, unprecedented time in our country, where large swaths of people could not escape.

Many succumbed to this illness over the first two years, but the worst of it came in October 1918. No community or family was left untouched. The mass mortality was so fast and massive that the sheer number of bodies overwhelmed the capacity of undertakers, gravediggers, and casket makers. There was no time to prepare in any way. The cities were the most brutally hit, where sick patients were found in bed with dead bodies. Corpses were covered in ice and shoved into bedroom corners to decompose. Inundated undertakers stacked caskets in funeral home hallways and their living quarters. Coffins began to pile up on sidewalks that were feet and feet high. Everyone was called for emergency duty to dig graves, even prison inmates. Casket shortages forced gravediggers to dump the corpses into graves to reuse caskets (C. Klein 2020).

The worst horrors were seen in Philadelphia, where deaths approached 1,000 per day. Front doors on homes were draped in crepe to mark deaths inside. Five hundred bodies would be stacked in the city morgue, which only had a capacity for thirty-six. The city resorted to mass graves that had been hollowed out by a steam shovel. The horrific scenes, which we have never witnessed then or now, appeared straight out of the plague-infested Middle Ages (Thomas Jefferson University 2020).

My Grandpa Grover was one of those front-line heroes during the Spanish Flu pandemic. He left his family to fend for themselves to face the pandemic while he left to care for the dead. Finally, after many died and the rest of the population acquired immunities, the Spanish Flu pandemic did what all pandemics do: It ran its usual course and ended (History.com 2010).

The Family Funeral Home Business

Following the pandemic, the family returned to their roots, moving to a farm east of Medicine Lake. In 1924, Grover and Pearl returned to farming as their livelihood. It was safer on the farm, where you could cultivate your own food far away from any population center (Aasheim 1970).

Farming was challenging in the Medicine Lake area. The summers were excruciatingly hot, and the winters treacherously long, yielding feet and feet of drifted snow. However, they were used to this, coming from the North Dakota plains. They had also learned a lot from their family's history and were determined to give it another try. There were more modern amenities at that time than there were previously. It would not be easy, but it would be easier than what Grover's family went through.

Farming is a difficult way to support a growing family. The family soon discovered that farming was not going to do it alone. So, while farming and helping make ends meet, Grover again continued to work as an embalmer. My grandfather would be one of the few embalmers in Montana at a time when undertakers were the primary service providers for the deceased. The term "undertaker" refers to the person who "undertook" responsibility for funeral arrangements. Many early undertakers were furniture makers because building caskets was a logical extension of their business. For them, undertaking was a second business rather than a primary profession.

Although embalming dates to the ancient Egyptians, in the U.S., it began during the Civil War, when it became necessary to preserve the bodies of dead soldiers for the trip home. As embalming gained favor, the required skills helped turn undertaking into a real profession. Embalmers in the late 1800s and early 1900s would travel to the decedents' homes to prepare bodies for burial. Hardware stores would carry caskets for sale.

In the late 1920s, Grandpa Grover opened his mortuary in Plentywood. Thanks to my family's dedication and hard work, a modern funeral home came to fruition. It provided the Plentywood region with a place for embalming and funerals and sold caskets (Jubilee 1987).

Grover and Pearl tragically lost their youngest daughter, Maren, to Scarlet Fever in 1929. She was only four years old. It was once again a terrifying time for the family. They had lost their youngest daughter and were then interminably quarantined again to prevent disease transmission. Scarlet Fever had been around for a long time, but being fresh off the Spanish Flu pandemic, communities were not taking any chances. We now know strep infections, a common bacterial throat infection in children easily treated with antibiotics today, was the cause of Scarlet Fever. Penicillin was not widely available commercially until 1945.

My mother was born in 1936. Immediately following my mother's birth, my grandparents sold the farm. They gave up on the life that was such an important part of our family's history. Farming was difficult, and it couldn't support the family. It was time to let it go. They used the money to fund the construction of a brand-new, independent mortuary and funeral home. The family business officially opened in Plentywood, Montana, in May 1941. It supported them and the next two generations, spawning two other family funeral home businesses in Montana.

My grandpa, Grover, died from a stroke in 1947 at the age of fifty-eight. He had long suffered from high blood pressure. Medications to control blood pressure were unavailable during his time, so it was treated with diet changes. Grandpa had always said, "If he could not eat meat and fried potatoes, life wasn't worth living." He was a man after my own heart and lived how he wanted to live. My mother was only eleven years old when her father died. Mom and Grandma Pearl then lived in the funeral home, in an upstairs apartment the family built after Grandpa died. It provided them with a home while Grandma continued to work the funeral business with her oldest son, my Uncle Gene. The business provided not only an income for my mom and grandmother but also a safe home for them. In hindsight, it was fortunate that the family sold the farm when they did.

Mom always said she had the best slumber parties and sleepovers in that upstairs apartment. She said living above a funeral home added a whole new dimension to ghost stories. Mom's brother, Gene, also trained in embalming and continued the family business with my grandmother. He later would take over all the operations when my grandmother retired.

My Grandma Pearl tragically died in a traffic accident while visiting our family when we lived in Salem, Oregon. Kris had not been born yet, and Joni and I were too young to remember it. While driving in tandem, my mother followed her mother as they made their way along one of the many highways in Marion County. I am unaware of where they were going or why, but another vehicle hit my grandmother head-on. My mother witnessed the entire accident and its horrifying aftermath. My mother never drove in tandem ever again.

My grandparents would have been very proud of the family funeral home business as it expanded into Sidney and Helena, Montana. My Uncle Gene handed the business over to his son, David, and his wife, Jane. David, also an embalmer, owned an airplane. He would often fly to remote areas across the state to pick up bodies for burial. This was another critical aspect of the family funeral home business that helped it grow and prosper. My cousins have since sold the family funeral home business to retire.

Oh my, how my mind wanders as I'm hand-pumping water from our well.

The Elusive Snipe

Boy Scout camp would not be complete without at least one evening where everyone goes on a "Snipe" hunt. Such activities always take place after dinner, at dusk. The precise time is carefully selected, depending on the depth of the sun and the exact degree of darkness. If it is too light or dark, you have missed your Snipe seizing window of opportunity. History has it that no scout has ever captured this elusive creature at Camp Silverback, so all scouts are on the lookout to make history.

Snipe hunting is an excellent adult strategy to blow off some pent-up energy in children before heading to the cabins for the night. What young scout would not like to be the first one to capture this mythical creature at Camp Silverback? Legend has it that many a scout has come close, but the creature remains elusive. We all know they are out there. You can hear them at dawn and dusk.

Snipe hunting strategies here at Camp Silverback consist of fourteen teams of about fifteen scouts. Each scout is armed with their assigned fishing net. They are a perfect size for this elusive creature. Each group is assigned a quadrant that begins at the lakefront, which fans up the mountain and into the forest. Once a whistle is blown, the scouts return immediately to the lakefront, revealing their catch. Unfortunately, the Snipe has proven to be a difficult quarry at Camp Silverback. The Snipe Hunt has existed in North America since the 1840s. It is an American rite of passage, often associated with summer camps.

The Wilson Snipe is a bird with its own unique sound. It is not a song they create but a winged noise when trying to attract a prospective mate. The tone is created with their tail feathers when they dive straight down from the sky and then quickly ascend before diving once again. This air rushing over the Snipe's outspread tail feathers creates the haunting hu-hu-hu winnowing sound.

The Snipe frequent wet meadows and marshes in temperate and warm regions. They are short-legged, long-billed, chunky birds that are striped and barred in brown, black, and white. They are ubiquitous in the West. They are ground nesters in marshes and swamps. You always know when spring has officially arrived when you hear the Snipe at dusk and dawn. The Snipe breeding and nesting periods are very short. It arrives in mid-April and is done by mid-July. They still hang out throughout the summer, but the unique tail feather sound is not heard again until the following spring.

The Bird Phase

Dad had many strange hobbies, but one of the strangest was his brief bird pastime. After Dad retired, he still liked to keep busy. We were not camping anymore, and he was not a golfer. He enjoyed carting Kris and me up to Anthony Lakes to ski, but he wasn't a winter sports enthusiast himself. So, one day, he decided to begin a new hobby. He purchased four parakeets of various colors. Complete with a cage, of course, and all the little parakeet-playing apparatuses recommended by the pet store.

Shortly after the Parakeets came a pair of Cockatiels, then the Lovebird pair, followed finally by four Finches. Mom banished Dad's personal aviary to his office with his train memorabilia.

Our father, a train enthusiast, possessed the largest vintage train model collection west of the Mississippi. They completely lined his office with shelving he built and put up on the walls himself. Spanning two walls, Dad set up the four-inch-wide shelving, about eight inches apart, all up and down those two walls. He cut them to the appropriate length and then stained them to match the indoor house trim. The finished product looked good. The perfectly cut and stained shelving started about a foot down from the ceiling to about three feet above the floor. Dad's built-in desk sat directly in front of the window in the room, with his expansive train collection surrounding him. It was good that Dad had a big office because his aviary filled up the third wall. It would be known today as his "man cave."

Domestic caged birds only do four things; eat, poop, make noise, and look pretty. When you have twelve birds, those four attributes are magnified twelve times, especially the noise and pooping. Dad's aviary consisted of four big cages. Every day, he fed and watered them. Consequently, the paper at the bottom of each cage had to be changed at least once daily. Twice a day was necessary in the summer. We went through many newspapers back then, often "borrowing" more from the neighbors. Dad's birds were interesting and pretty, but besides the finches, they were very noisy, especially in the morning.

Dad's office, aviary, train collection, and man cave were next to their bedroom. At precisely sunrise, the squawking would begin. Even the prettiest of birds are not so enamoring when you are awakened every morning at the break of dawn. Dad tried to control it by draping the cages with numerous blankets to block sunlight. But it took a million blankets to create enough darkness to keep them all asleep. Even the tiniest glimpse of light coming through to one cage would set the entire group squawking. The birds didn't last six months.

Eureka and the Tobacco Valley

Today, I get my first couple of days off in two weeks. It will be spent exploring the Eureka area, after which I will pick up more groceries for the next group of scouts. It was an excellent opportunity to explore more of this beautiful area. I would need my own wheels, so after Earl drove me up the mountain and into Eureka, he dropped me off at the local car rental agency. He will pick me up tomorrow to transport us back down The Bongos in his 1906 four-wheel drive, military-style Scout Humvee and Trailer with our next round of food and other supplies. Oh boy, here we go again!

The Town of Eureka is located on the Tobacco River in an area known as the Tobacco Valley. For centuries, the region was inhabited by the Kootenai Indian Tribe. Canadian fur trappers and explorers would visit the area in the early nineteenth century. That was when they would discover a tribe growing a native strain of tobacco. It would be those early explorers who then named the area the Tobacco Plains. Prairie grass, as well as tobacco, grew well in this valley. It is a picturesque place, surrounded by the snow-kissed mountainous peaks of the Purcell Mountain range in Canada and the Whitefish Range in Montana. It is all a part of a more extensive geological feature called the Rocky Mountain Trench.

Once again, during the last ice age, millenniums long ago, the Rocky Mountain Trench Glacier covered the valley under thousands of feet of ice. As the glacier retreated, the erosive scraping action of a moving glacier left a landscape pocked with glacial potholes that later became lakes and ponds. Called "Drumlins," they are low oval mounds or small hills of compacted clay and boulders. The Tobacco Valley possesses the only large Drumlin field in Montana (mdt.mt.gov).

The glaciers left behind rich, fertile soil where bands of Kootenai tribes would eventually settle in the mid to late 1700s. The area referred to as "Montana's Banana Belt" is known for its warmer temperatures and fertile soil. It was perfect for raising bitterroot and other crops and hay for their horses. What was discovered was that the soil and weather conditions were ideal for growing tobacco. Tobacco was harvested in the fall, sun-dried, or dried on rocks beside the fire. Enough tobacco was grown to last them an entire year. The narcotic qualities of the tobacco consequently gave rise to the tribal name of the valley, "The Place of the Flying Head."

Late October started the buffalo hunt, as the herds moved into the foothills for shelter from the winter storms. Before the Kootenai acquired horses, they used game driving skills on foot to run the buffalo over the cliffs. Once horses were incorporated into their lives, they only needed to ride into the middle of the herds while grazing. The hunter could choose the animal they wanted and dispatch several of them before the others would spook and run. No part of an animal was ever wasted. The meat was dried, and the skins were tanned for shelter, blankets, and clothing.

Northwest Montana was the last territory to become occupied by "the white man" in the lower forty-eight states. They migrated from Canada when the Kootenai tribes actively recruited them and their associates with the "Northwest Fur Company." Northwest Fur Company settled its operations in the Tobacco Plains in the early 1800s. The Kootenai tribes were well aware of the benefits that guns and ammunition would provide in exchange for furs. Hunting was much easier but would also provide a valuable defense against the brutal Blackfeet Tribe to the east. They traded for and grew dependent on goods for cooking, tools, and other comfort items that made their lives easier.

The Great Northern Railroad pushed through to the west coast in 1892. Initially far south of The Tobacco Plains Valley, they rebuilt a more extended, easier route through the Valley in 1904. The town of Eureka was then born. Notable railroad history of the area included a rail tour by President Harry S. Truman, who stopped in Eureka. He gave a speech on October 1, 1952, as part of a whistle-stop tour, supporting Adlai Stevenson's ultimately unsuccessful presidential campaign (Visit NW Montana) (Truman 1952).

During frontier times, it was one of the last areas to be developed in Montana. For a couple of decades, logging was a major draw and source of income. Founded in 1906, the Eureka Lumber Company thrived for eighteen years. It would be one of the largest lumber mills in Montana. Initially, they floated cut logs down the Tobacco River from logging camps around Trego and Fortine. When the easy-to-access timber along the river was exhausted, they added a railway up to the Frank Lake area around 1918. Two years later, just after the rail line at Frank Lake was completed, the trestle across the lake caught fire and burned down.

In 1924, roads into the Tobacco Valley were built. Homesteaders now had another way to travel, in and out of the valley. The rumrunners and bootleggers of Canada were the first to take advantage of these new roads. With Eureka's proximity to Canada, skilled area moonshiner's could also move their product in and out of Canada. The era of prohibition contributed significantly to Eureka's history. Tragically, also in 1924, half the population of Eureka lost its livelihood when the Eureka Lumber Company left, abandoning the town. However, the name "Eureka" speaks to the optimism of the valley's residents. Eureka discovered another market - holiday Christmas Trees. Through the 1950s and 1960s, Christmas trees left the valley by the trainload as they shipped evergreens to many urban points for holiday sales. Eureka was then known as "The Christmas Tree Capital of the World."

Today, Eureka is experiencing its third boom in tourism. Eureka entrepreneurs have converted old boom-town buildings of their vintage past into charming shops and restaurants. Since the town is located just west of Glacier National Park, it has taken advantage of a steady stream of visitors each summer. Tourists travel through on their way to the park and Whitefish Lake. The area is rich in resources for the outdoor enthusiast, with camping, hiking, and fishing.

If one is a hiker or backpacker, The Ten Lakes Scenic Area is a place to visit. Located in the extreme northwest corner of Montana, the area offers eighty-nine miles of remote trails through rugged terrain and spectacular mountain views, reaching into Canada. The Ten Lakes Scenic Area encompasses nearly 16,000 acres, with an additional 19,000 acres surrounding it. Mountains majestically rise to elevations of more than 7,800 feet. High alpine peaks, with their cool, clear high mountain lakes and peaceful meandering trails, all combine to make Ten Lakes Scenic Area a hiker and backpacker's delight.

Once again, many millennia ago, alpine glaciers shaped much of the present rugged scenery. Growing glaciers carved deep scallops and high rim-rocked basins, sheltering many of the area's lakes. The Therriault Lakes and the Bluebird Basin areas provide ample opportunities for camping, hiking, and horseback riding, which provide an abundance of campgrounds. Campsites include fire rings, water pumps, and vault toilets. Horse camps offer hitching posts, feed racks, fire rings, tables, and outhouses. Camping areas within the Scenic Area cannot be reached by motorized vehicles and are all pack-in/pack-out sites. Motorized vehicles or equipment of any kind are not allowed in Scenic Areas.

If one is into boating, fishing, and other water sports, Lake Koocanusa is a mere fifteen minutes from the town of Eureka. Waters from the Kootenai River created the 29,000-acre lake within the boundaries of both Canada and Montana. The Kootenai River, a blue-ribbon fishery, is collected into the reservoir by the Libby Dam in Montana. The dam, built by the U.S. Army Corps of Engineers, was completed in 1972 creating an important ecosystem and recreational area. It is among the ten largest reservoirs in the nation extending ninety miles to the north to British Columbia. The lake derives its name by combining the first three letters of KOOtenai, CANada, and USA. In total, the lake is two hundred miles long, providing an ideal setting for large watercraft and sailing from Montana into Canada. The lake contains a large and stable population of Kokanee Salmon, Rainbow Trout, Bull Trout, and West Slope Cutthroat Trout. Fortunately for the local population, the lake gets little pressure from tourists. Traveling past this treasure, folks are missing a special experience. They miss a great area as they head to Flathead County, Glacier Park, Whitefish, and Flathead Lake (Montana's Historic Landscapes; 35 Years in the Big Sky Country).

A Day of Exploration

Today's weather is lovely, suggesting we may be in the throes of summer. The temperature is averaging about eighty-five degrees now in Eureka. It seemed doubtful that I would run into snow again anytime soon, so I opted for a sportier vehicle this time. Since I am ruggedly living my summer at camp, I wanted to visit some of the more civilized areas in this region. With that, I will not need anything with a four-wheel drive. So, I decided on a bright candy apple red Mazda with a fin, sunroof, and white leather interior. Now I am stylin'. If you couldn't tell by now, I love red vehicles. I decided to do some touring outside Eureka today, so I headed up Tobacco Road to see where I might end up.

Dear Mom and Dad:

I had a rare day off today, so I decided to wander through and explore my new home away from home.

After picking up my sporty, shiny red rental car, the first order of business was breakfast. I decided to try out one of the local cafes in Eureka. Highly recommended by my staff was "Cafe Jax," in downtown Eureka. They described it to me as "excellent home-style cooking." It must have a good reputation, as evidenced by the long line of folks waiting outside. It took about thirty minutes for me to be seated, but it was well worth it. Besides, I had some delightful conversations with the many locals and tourists waiting outside.

I have learned there are certain expectations when you are a newcomer to a small northwest Montana town. For some odd reason, people here prefer that you pay your check before leaving the restaurant. I learned this lesson from a friendly policeman who pulled me over. He was very pleasant, asking me if I had planned to pay for the recently enjoyed meal. It suddenly dawned on me that I had left the lady a nice tip but forgot the most important part. I was so enthralled with the book I was reading that I tore off the stub, left a tip, left the restaurant, got into my car, looked to the left, turned onto the road after signally left, and then, just plain left!

The policeman said she described me perfectly; "candy apple red rental sports car." "Driver was a large, friendly type, not from around here." Kinda says it all, doesn't it? He suggested that I use a better getaway car the next time I decided not to pay my bill, one that blends into the local traffic better. From the look of shock on my face, he rightfully determined that I was not a crook but merely another wayward tourist. He sent me on my way as long as I returned to the restaurant and paid my bill.

The waitress was very friendly and beyond amused, but I decided it could be much safer, at this point, to stay in camp. Camp is excellent, and besides, I need to learn all these new little rules that people have around here. It is also cheaper than renting a car and a hotel room. Okay, I sound like Dad again. More later...

Love You, Randy

Old Growth

Today would be a spontaneous day of exploration to see where I would end up. Tobacco Road was fun to tour with my little sports car as I accelerated my little red car into the curves; the narrow, windy road curved and wound around the grassy farmland. The mountains to my right kept calling my name. I hugged the road as I made my way through the beautiful valley.

The valley is stunning, with a mix of meadow grasses, pines, and deciduous trees. As I drive along, I see the unmistakable coloring of the yellow-breasted Meadowlark sitting on the fence post. The Western Meadowlark, famous for its loud, cheerful chirps, has been the Montana state bird since 1930. That was when schoolchildren overwhelmingly chose it to represent the state. This mid-size bird has a body length of six to ten inches and a wingspan of sixteen inches. Besides its appearance, this terrestrial bird has a unique song. Its song is about a ten-tone melody that diminishes to three tones at the end. The melody is quite beautiful.

I acquiesced to the call of the mountainside, turning right toward the mountains and timber and onto "Frank Lake Road." It was a well-maintained dirt road until it wasn't. The further I went, the more the road deteriorated, requiring me to slow down more and more to a crawl. First of all, I was at serious risk of high-centering this little car, with its four-inch ground clearance, but it was also a failed attempt to keep the vehicle clean. The further I got, the deeper the potholes became. Huge potholes, threatening to completely engulf my car, transporting me to the other side of the globe into Singapore. Hmmm, maybe I should have rented a truck after all.

Ok, I was supposed to explore more civilized areas of this valley. I am still trying to figure out how I ended up on this horrendous dirt road, but it will be a new adventure, that is for sure. My little sports car did well as I slowly made my way to the lake on a narrow one-lane dirt road. I am still determining what would happen if I met anyone on the road. With my ground clearance, there was no way I would even attempt to get off the road into the rough, as it were. Setting that worry aside, I meandered around the ruts, holes, and rocks while admiring the giant fir trees around me.

Oregon is all into its "old-growth forests." It is amusing to me now as I think about "old-growth forest" signs nailed into stands of trees throughout Eastern Oregon. Such trees are only about eighteen to twenty-four inches in diameter. This Oregon practice is really just one strategy the state uses to shut down the logging industry. Many of these "old growth" stands of forests exist in Oregon. By Oregon definition, old growth is supposed to be a forest that has not undergone any significant unnatural changes (such as logging) for at least one hundred years. I am pretty sure an eighteen-inch diameter pine tree does not meet that definition.

Now I know what an old-growth forest looks like. The impressive grandeur of Montana's fir trees is something to behold. Massive trunks that take two to three men, hand in hand, to completely encircle them. Beautiful canopies that provide shade to the wildflowers and grasses below. Now, this is timber!

The trees here on Frank Lake Road, also averaging about eighteen inches in diameter, are marked for a timber sale. The Forest Service and The Bureau of Land Management conduct timber sales as the most general way to allow timber harvesting on their respective lands. Timber sales are a formal, highly regulated, controversial process whereby an entity may purchase a contract to cut and remove specified timber. Forest Service and Bureau of Land Management receive revenue from the sale of the contract. States receive the revenues from timber sales that fund multiple recreational opportunities in our national forests. However, any timber sale on public land is always followed by various environmental lawsuits from out-of-staters to prevent the sale. Once a timber sale is announced, it takes several years and money to work it through the court system. This pointless exercise only delays the timber sale because it will eventually happen. This leads one to conclude that any revenue that could have been realized is lost at the expense of litigating those lawsuits through the courts.

Logging has had a checkered history, involving "clear cuts," which virtually removed all of the timber in a section of forest. Environmentalism had its place back then to stop this practice. However, we have learned a lot since those early logging days. Timber harvesting now follows forest health practices of thinning trees to allow a healthier forest floor suitable for improved wildlife and forest health. Environmentalists have gone too far in their desire to prevent all timber harvests today. Environmentalism focuses only on the prevention of all logging. They ignore logging's benefit, which lies in the inherent protections a forest receives by properly thinning healthy timber and removing diseased trees. They do not care about the science, just their ideology.

Unlogged, forests become a thick array of dead and downed timber, susceptible to wildfire. Only when one is offered to walk through a healthy stand of trees, compared to a "fricket" of dead and downed trees, do you understand what that means. The narrative of today's environmental agenda says that today's wildfires result from "global warming." Those in the West know that it is a direct result of poor timber practices forced upon us and financed by entities and individuals who do not even live here.

Hmmm, I probably should have turned around. This road does require my previous rental truck. I had not anticipated I would be "boondocking" through the forest. But my little car seemed to handle the road just fine if I went slow enough.

Dads Fancy MG Convertible Sports Car

Dad, as a young adult in his late teens to early twenties, and before he and Mom got married, owned a little green sports car. It was his pride and joy at the time. The car was a 1951 MG Mini One, a two-seater British sports car produced in 1924. It was a beautiful rag-top convertible, full of chrome - with black and white herringbone seats. The car got its name from "Morris Garages," a dealer of Morris cars in Oxford. They began producing customized versions of the designs of Cecil Kimber, who had joined the company as a sales manager in 1921.

Dad loved his little two-seater sports car, which also had a four-inch ground clearance. One evening, while speeding along a windy mountainous highway, he was going a little too fast when he came upon a rock in the middle of the road. It was not a large rock, but it was bigger and higher than his four-inch ground clearance. Unable to stop, he drove over that rock and completely ripped the guts and the heart out of his bright green classic, two-seater, British-made MG sports car. Dad was VERY sad about that. It was beyond repair and ended up in the junkyard. Shortly after ripping the life out of his little car, he and mother married and began a family, drawing a close to his sports car days. Dad would never have admitted it, but my love of cars comes honestly.

Fortunately, I did not run into or over any large rocks, so the car made it in one piece as I arrived at the edge of Frank Lake, where the road ended. There is nothing here except what appears to be a very primitive boat launch. One that is only suitable for rowboats, canoes, and kayaks. The lake is not big or deep enough to support any motorized watercraft. The launch is merely a sandy bank that descends and disappears into the lake. There are also no bathroom facilities here. It could be problematic after all the coffee I had. Nobody except the ducks and me are here, so it probably is not a problem. I exited my little red sports car and explored the lake a bit. It is a pretty little cove with clear emerald-green water. The lake is like glass, reflecting off the mountains above it. A mirror image of the surrounding hillsides is created against the crystal-clear water. I reached down to get a handful of rocks, skipping them along the polished surface.

The quiet and solitude of this lakefront reminds me of all the waterfront camping our family did. The sights and sounds around lakes and streams were always so comforting while viewing all the wildlife and birds that call it home.

Dad's Loo

Our family often camped in the Olive Lake area. It is in the Umatilla National Forest, high in the Blue Mountains of Eastern Oregon, roughly twelve miles east of an old mining town called Granite.

Olive Lake is now an established and thriving campground with developed campsites, outhouses, and even boat docks on the lakefront. In the late 1960s and early 1970s, the Olive Lake area was much more primitive. Back in our day, we were often the only family camping there. Olive Lake was remote, taking our family three solid hours to journey there from La Grande. To justify the distance, we would only choose that camping excursion on three-day weekends. Olive Lake was completely undeveloped back then, including the road in. Over time, Dad had eventually gained enough confidence and adventurism to boondoggle our family station wagon and trailer over the grass and dirt terrain. This was so he could position our camp trailer directly in front of the lake.

There were no outhouses back then, and since Mother was a bathroom aficionado, Dad was eager to accommodate her. Through careful planning, he devised a brilliant scheme to improvise a homemade privy. He bought a toilet seat and stand that he carefully placed over a huge hole he had dug. He located his toilet stand approximately fifteen feet from the travel trailer. A convenient distance for mother to make her morning journey, but not too close to prevent any untoward odors. He then cut down six hefty tree branches (uprights) and fancied them into a sturdy frame to surround his homemade latrine. Then, he surrounded his privy with a sizeable lightweight polyethylene brown tarp he purchased just for this purpose, attaching it securely to the upright frame. He used the built-in eyelets to anchor the tarp to the uprights so the privy could withstand the fiercest winds. Dad then completed it with a door flap so one could enter the humble abode quickly. Finally, for that perfect finishing touch, Dad attached a fist-size rock with a string for a fancy-schmancy door knocker. Dad was so delighted with his homemade commode that he even took pictures.

The next day, a very friendly forest service ranger-type gentleman visited our family. He curiously asked Dad about his homestyle rustic structure next to our trailer. Dad was so proud and delighted that he gave the ranger a complete tour of his homemade troile'. Curious, the ranger asked Dad how far he thought we were camped from the lake. Dad proudly responded, "We always strive to camp at this site closest to the lake," which he estimated to be "only" about thirty feet from the water's edge. The Ranger then pulled out his trusty forest service manual and showed my father the regulations concerning the digging and utilizing outhouses in the national forest. He specifically pointed out the manual's particular regulations, referencing the lawful distance required of an outhouse from the nearest body of water.

There once was a ranger named Hugh
Who discovered Dad's fancy new Loo
When, out of the blue, the regs he whipped through
Dad then gets a ticket soon due!

Yep, it seems my dad was seventy feet short of where that commode ought to be. Dad then got a big fat ticket for $100.00 for locating his homemade outhouse less than one hundred feet from a body of water.

Frank Lake

The entire lake is only about a mile long and a quarter-mile wide. It is very peaceful, surrounded by timber, with only a few homes visible within my purview. I can hear nothing but birds in the distance, with ducklings and goslings playing in the cove with their mothers. Off in the distance, I can see a tiny island with much bluer water surrounding it, indicating more depth than in the cove.

Speaking of ducks, they are pretty friendly in this area; either that or they are amused. One Mallard duck immediately liked me, an obvious tourist, dressed in my dark blue LL Bean Chino shorts and light blue Premium Allagash Polo Shirt. It is also reasonable to believe that only a few folks in bright candy apple red sports cars make it to this lake. At that time, I took a serious "gander" at my little red rental car. Let's just say I will need to make a serious effort to wash this vehicle before returning it. Oh well, it is a small sacrifice for a great adventure.

Frank Lake is a warm, alkaline lake that is a critical habitat for the Boreal Toad and is a nesting area for the Common Loon. This is probably why there are no facilities here. Infrastructure like that would attract more people than the small lake can support and disrupt the protected nesting grounds of the Loons, who nest on the island. The Common Loon is such a magnificent bird. It has a tuxedoed look with speckled black and white plumage. The Loon's iridescent black sets it apart from any other duck species. During the breeding season, their eyes turn a vivid color of red. Loons are water birds and are quite a unique sight to see on lakes, which are the primary bodies of water in which they nest. Their bodies are built for water, as their legs are placed far back on their bodies. This allows them to be powerful, agile divers and swimmers. However, walking on land is very difficult. They are amazingly good at swimming underwater. It uses its wings and webbed feet to chase down fish and crayfish underwater. Loons are very territorial, allowing only one nesting pair per lake. Loons have prolonged breeding rates, only nesting one time per season. They average just two chicks per season, and only one will survive. It is important to avoid disturbing a Loon nest, as they will quickly abandon a nest if disrupted too often. I see the Bald Eagles who like to nest on the island flying overhead in the distance above the lake. I am sure that nesting eagles do not bode well for nesting Loons.

Frank Lake used to be a Rainbow Trout Fish Hatchery. They still stock it with 10,000 trout a year for fishing enthusiasts. The locals say that because of this lake's warmth, the trout are a bit mushy and do taste of mud when caught in the summer. However, during the ice fishing season, they say the fish are delicious. I pondered for a moment about ice fishing. Wandering out onto the ice in the middle of the lake with your eighteen-inch fishing pole. It is an interesting concept to me. Dad used to dream of owning a boat, allowing him to paddle or motor out to the deeper water. He always said that is where the big fish live.

With ice fishing, no boat is necessary as you position yourself and your pole in the middle of the lake for ultimate fishing nirvana. Besides skiing, which Mom and Dad never participated in, we were not winter enthusiasts. Maybe ice fishing was not a thing back then. Until I came here, I had never heard of such a thing. I wonder what attire is required to remain warm, as you are sitting in an icebox, AKA the great outdoors, on a giant ice cube - the lake. I would imagine it would require a significant snowsuit. I quickly dismissed the idea, seeing myself in such a snowsuit. One that would need to be large enough for a guy with…um… as broad a shoulders as I have. I decided it was not a good look for me. My bright neon orange ski coat would be nothing, as I imagined myself lumbering out on the ice, resembling the giant "Stay Puft Marshmallow Man" from Ghostbusters (Akroyd 1984).

There is no ice today, as I observe at least six sizable box turtles floating on the emerald surface. The ducklings were having a grand time with them. I might have joined them in the water if I had brought my bathing trunks. I will have to remember next time, if there is a next time.

Still in the lake are the supporting pillars of the old 1918 railroad trestle that burned down shortly after it was built. Amazingly, the pillars are still standing strong. In logging's robust early days, the trestle was needed and constructed to transport logs across the lake. The railroad could then transport logs the rest of the way to the Eureka Lumber Company. There are also reports that remnants of historic portable sawmills are interspersed throughout the area above Frank Lake. If I knew the area better, I might hike up there and try to find one. Oh, brother, who am I kidding? Wandering around in the forest in Grizzly Bear country. I don't think so!

Dear Mom and Dad:

Following my restaurant debacle in Eureka and before my road trip, I went to the grocery store. I bought various food items to make a nice lunch wherever I went. In my wanderings south of town, I found a little lake called "Frank Lake."

After exploring the lakefront and having a delightful lunch, I headed back down the dirt road to Eureka. Amazingly, I found a good radio station in the middle of the Kootenai National Forest.

After meandering back down a very rough Frank Lake Road, I turned left onto the nicely paved Tobacco Road. I then rolled down all my windows and opened the sunroof. I'm feeling terrific as I accelerate my little red sports car up and around and through the farmland. Listening to Aerosmith amidst beautiful mountain sceneries and the fresh air was delightful (Tyler 1975).

"Sweet Emotion" comes on over the radio waves. I reach down to turn it up when suddenly, into my right ear, I hear - QUACK! Good God, that scared me to death. I had the distinct impression that I was alone in the car. Hello Freddy Krueger! Let's just say my high-fiber muffin and coffee at the cafe this morning, not to mention my lunch, was well on its way to working through now.

I found a new friend at the lakefront. A friendly little duck I named Frank (after the lake, of course), who followed me around a bit. He became an annoyance after a while, but I did make the mistake of feeding him some bread. He wasn't quite so friendly once I ran out of food. In fact, he left. I now know what became of Frank, who is making it clear that he would like more food. Damn, I should have closed my windows.

As I looked in my rearview mirror, Frank had settled in nicely in my back seat. We are cruising together down Tobacco Road on this beautiful sunny day. I think he thought he was some movie star, with the windows and sunroof wide open and the breeze delicately blowing through his...um, feathers. I'll bet nobody else can say they have such a fine duck friend. Then I begin to think - what if that friendly law enforcement type person now sees me with my proud new duck? Explain that to the guy who caught you "borrowing" food from a restaurant.

Frank was quite content and looking pretty pleased with himself as he began to use the nice white leather seats as his private duck outhouse. The novelty of being Frank the Duck's new best friend has now worn off. Pulling over, I attempt to remove Frank from my car. Frank refused to leave, making quite the ruckus while quacking, flapping, and spewing feathers, not to mention duck poo throughout the vehicle. Did you know ducks can hiss? Frank was quite aggravated with me, so I gave up, turned around, and returned to the lakefront.

Back up Frank Lake Road I went. A little quicker this time as I navigated in, out, and around the potholes, ruts, and rocks - again. My fancy little cherry red Mazda, with the sunroof and fin, was now a feather-filled dust heap that doubles as a duck commode. Looking through my rearview mirror at one point, I noticed my face covered in Frank Lake Road dust. In my haste, I forgot to close the windows or the sunroof. Looking down at my clothing, I was covered in feathers and dirt. It's good that no one from the ASPCA is monitoring this road. It looks like I went ten rounds with Frank the Duck.

Once again stopped at the lakefront, Frank the Duck had no problem finding his way out of my car and flying into the abyss. I guess he just wanted a ride home.

Once I returned to town, I immediately went to the nearest hardware store. After attempting to brush off all the feathers and dirt from my body, I entered the store. A friendly small-town lady behind the counter must have been watching me. She was smiling and chuckling as I entered the store. I asked her where the leather cleaner was in the store. She inquired as to why I would need leather cleaner. Without thinking (what a surprise), I said it was to clean up after the duck in my car. She could not contain her amusement as she laughed and shook her head. Her response, "We get all kinds of folks through here, don't we."

It was now late afternoon, so I decided to find a place to stay. I first stopped by a store to pick up some beer, then to a drive-through restaurant to pick up a burger and fries. With that, I began weighing my lodging options. Feeling nostalgic, I returned to the prototype model for the tiny home industry where I stayed on my first night here. Besides, the price was right--it was cheap. OK, I sound like Dad again.

As I pulled up to the cabin complex, which I could clearly observe now in the daylight, I was surprised at the size of the cabins. Funny, I do not remember them being this small. My skepticism vanished, though, once I got settled into my familiar little cabin. I then sat on my front deck and admired my beautiful mountain view while eating dinner. After slugging down a couple of beers, I decided it was time to clean off the remnants of Frank Lake Road. I opted for a bath instead of a shower. It sounded like a good idea at the time... a nice soaking bath with a beer in hand. I turned on the bathroom radio. Delighted that I found the same excellent radio station I listened to earlier in the car, I got undressed and popped another beer. I then turned toward the bathtub to turn on the water, and that is when I noticed the bathtub size. OK, I am not a very observant person.

I should have known that tiny (cheap) rustic cabins also have tiny primitive bathrooms, complete with small "ornate" bathtubs. Okay, the "washtub" was cute, and they had the area decorated very stylishly, but it was not a suitable size, especially for someone with, um...as broad a shoulders as I have. This tub was only made for people the size of Becky Thatcher. Upon closer inspection, I swear it appears to be a metal stock tank! It can be best characterized as an oversized laundry tub (Britannica 1876).

Amusingly, I can only see half of the laundry tub. An overhang completely covers the lower portion of the tub. This overhang would be the head of the bed at the other end of the wall. Tucking my legs carefully underneath me to fit my body into the tub, I then carefully stretch them under the overhang as I lie down. I can't even see the end of the tub as I sit down and carefully unfold my legs into the crawl space. This is especially tough for a guy with, um…as broad a shoulders as I have. It's a good thing I am limber.

Fully into the tub, I outstretched my legs into the crawl space as far as I could get them. My head is then tightly wedged between the hot and cold water knobs, with the back of my head resting "comfortably" on the water spigot. As I sip my beer, I remember that famous Elmer Fudd quote, *"West and wewaxation at wast!"* (Warner Bros)

I am sure I have had adequate training to be a member of the Camp Silverback Bobsled Team!

After finishing my beer, I carefully refolded my legs underneath me while somehow maneuvering onto my knees. Only then was I able to exit the tub. I then performed my usual bedtime functions and headed to bed. Only then did I notice I still had the same dilemma. The closet, located over the lower half of the bed, exposed only the top half or head of the bed, which, as you remember, is over the lower chamber of the bathtub.

I crawl into bed, carefully unfolding my legs under the closet overhang. Then I noticed there is only about a two-foot clearance (at the most) for one to roll over. I was reminded of this figure at least fifteen to twenty times that night as I tried to roll over, smacking my kneecaps on the overhang. Many improvements need to be discovered in the tiny home business.

Additional pain occurred as I banged my forehead against the reading lamp as I rose to grab my throbbing legs. Only then am I reminded of how small a world we live in. I wondered why I failed to remember all this tiny living the last time I stayed! It is all a blur. I guess I was so exhausted from the precarious and frightening drive that night that I must not have showered or moved all night. I am reminded, however, of my sister's near-constant description of me; "you never notice anything." They are wrong, though, because I notice every single sports car that appears within my field of vision.

I woke up at 6:00 a.m. and spent the next two hours washing my car, inside and out. I loaded my small suitcase and headed to the rental car company. Earl picked me up at 8:00 a.m. sharp. We headed to the grocery store, where my order was ready as planned. We refilled the empty propane tanks we brought, filled the Humvee and portable fuel tanks with diesel, and then hit the road back to camp. It was time to prepare for the next group of campers.

My second grocery order was different from the first. I boycotted all glass items and bought canned sauces instead. I purchased liquid eggs because that is how they end up anyway, and I bought dozens of loaves of the cheapest bread possible. Cheap bread flattens out just as nicely as the expensive fluffy stuff. We go through a lot of bread at Camp Silverback.

Thank you, Dad, for enlightening me on the benefits of thrifty. Sometimes, cheap is indeed necessary to save money. However, thrifty may be effective when purchasing day-old bread, but I'm not sure I will practice the same strategy the next time I look for overnight accommodations. I am also better prepared this time for the drive, loading up on Tylenol for my ensuing headache as we head back down the Bongos. By the way, Mom, you forgot to send the helmet.

Thanks for all the mail, especially all the magazines. I do appreciate any news at all. You might even send along a newspaper now and then. Until next time...

Love, Randy

Puffed Rice…Not Just for Breakfast Anymore

The "day old" bread store was always a must-stop venue whenever Dad was in Portland for his monthly meetings. Bread at the "day old" bread store was never just one day old, and Dad discovered that you get an even better price if you purchase in bulk. We must have gone through a lot of bread back in the day because Dad would buy approximately twenty loaves of Wonder Bread. Mother would place all that bread in our big upright freezer. Nope, our freezer was never used to store meat. Buying bread in bulk allowed Dad to spend only about.15 cents a loaf, which made him very pleased with himself. However, frozen "day old" bread does not fare well toward the end of the month. It tends to get a little brittle around the edges.

They sell other products besides bread at the "Day-Old Bread Store." One day, he discovered an astounding deal on Puffed Rice. Quaker must have been overrun with this product. The tasteless cereal becomes a congealed, soggy mess in your bowl. It is no wonder there are excesses of this variety of cereal.

Dad discovered that buying a ten-pound bag was only $2.00. What a deal! Puffed Rice weighs nothing, so Dad had no idea how much Puffed Rice he would bring home. Let's just say we had a lot of Puffed Rice, as the grocery store clerk kept bringing bags and bags to the car. It would be just one of those tales that added to our family's lore: How did Dad manage to get all that Puffed Rice home? Mother was amused as she giggled throughout the house while trying to find places to store all that cereal. She ended up storing it in the corners of every closet throughout the house. After consuming Puffed Rice for breakfast for weeks, I discovered a way to make short order of it.

One day, somebody "pasted" giant marshmallows all over my vehicle as a practical joke. It is an easy trick. All you do is lick one side and press it onto a vehicle. It does not take long to dry on glass surfaces and the car body, especially when it is warm outside. You end up with a car covered in raised white polka dots that are nearly impossible to clean up. I must admit, it was a pretty funny joke. It didn't take long to figure out who the guilty party was. Within my small circle of friends, keeping a secret that good is difficult.

Once I discovered who the dastardly culprit was, I set out for revenge. I raided all twelve closets, taking all that Puffed Rice that Mom had stored. I then emptied all three hundred bags of Puffed Rice, stuffing his car to the brim with all of it. It was a small sedan-type car and was just big enough to fill the entire inside of the vehicle, to the top, with Puffed Rice. What was even more fortunate was that it had a sunroof. I cracked it just enough to ensure the car was stuffed full of Puffed Rice. He should have locked his car. It was a win for everybody. I got my revenge, and the family never had to eat Puffed Rice again. However, imagine clear plastic wrap stretched tight over my toilet and underneath the seat, creating a transparent plastic barrier that blocks the bowl. It is impossible to detect in the dark. I now lock my doors.

Montana's Grizzly Bears

This coming Monday is the big test, as we have 290 campers coming in, with an additional twenty staff. The staff is also busily preparing the camp for our yearly inspection, which includes inspectors. That is at least 150 extra people.

We have not seen the infamous camp bear yet, but he knows we are here. He has left numerous remnants of himself throughout camp. I understand it won't be long before he gets more determined as he searches out camp food. I hope he doesn't like going for car rides like Frank the Duck. Better check the windows in the 1906 four-wheel-drive, military-style Scout Humvee!

Montana takes bear management very seriously. Montana Fish, Wildlife, and Parks employ a regional investigator for human/bear encounters. Grizzly bears have a storied history in Northwest Montana, particularly Glacier National Park. Since the opening of Glacier Park in 1910, there were no reported fatal bear attacks until one summer night in 1967. Two grizzlies attacked campers in two separate remote areas of the Park, killing two young women who were park employees (E. Smith 2017).

For everyone involved - tourists, rescue personnel, and forest service managers, it was an unforgettable night of crisis, intense fear, bravery, and ultimately, grief. It would be a night that marked a watershed moment for bear management in Montana. It would culminate in 1975 when the grizzly bear was listed as an endangered species. The problems began years before that night, though, when free feeding of bears was commonplace. Food was frequently used to lure in groups of bears to entertain tourists. From safe balconies of their chalets, they could watch bears in a frenzied feed as bears became food-conditioned and unafraid of humans.

I remember as a child, we would tour Yellowstone National Park nearly every summer on our way to Billings. "Bear Jams" was a part of the tourist experience then. Traffic would stop as groups of bears would gather amongst the stopped vehicles. Families would lure them in with food to get them next to their vehicles. Everyone wanted that "Yellowstone Park photo" of a bear reaching his snout into the family car while a youngster gives him a marshmallow. That never happened in our vehicle. All species of bears are dangerous, strong, wild animals. My parents were more intelligent than that. We would observe the Tourons through closed windows, commenting on how stupid some people can be. Even back then, people thought it was a petting zoo.

The parks learned their lesson. You will not see a bear as you go through the parks now. State-approved bear-proof cans in Yellowstone and Glacier Parks have replaced all garbage receptacles. Any bear that makes its way into the populated areas of either park or any Montana community is immediately caught and relocated. In a three-strike policy, problem bears are tagged and re-located only twice. On the third strike, they are euthanized.

Bears who attack are immediately tracked down using hair DNA found at the scene. Bears that attack because of usual bear behavior, e.g., surprised or protecting a cub, are tagged and left alone if they do not re-offend. If the bear is at fault, it is found and euthanized. Bear attacks occur throughout the year in all areas of northwest Montana. The highest incidences occur in the spring, with sows protecting cubs, and in the fall during hunting season. Stealthy hunters wandering quietly through the forest will either startle a bear or interrupt its feeding. Bears are quite protective of their food source, especially in the fall, as they are bulking up for winter hibernation. Families taking advantage of the late summer huckleberry picking season are especially cautious.

Established Montana residents respect that power, and you won't find them knowingly feeding any wildlife here. If you are feeding the deer or the raccoons, you are feeding the bears. Garbage is kept inside garages and sheds. Bird feeders are hung at the home's own risk. Fruit trees and berry bushes are generally not planted along the forested perimeters. Locals are not the problem. What is the problem? New residents and tourists unfamiliar with the dangers of a fed bear.

There are considerable differences in the types of bears. Few areas have the distinction of being in the territory of the brown bear. The brown bear range crosses much of North America and Eurasia. It is the second-largest terrestrial carnivore, second only to the polar bear. North American examples are called Grizzlies. On Kodiak Island in Alaska, they are known as the Kodiak bear. Brown bears will eat anything and are very dangerous. Their eyesight is poor, especially as they age, but their sense of smell is extraordinary, and they can detect their quarry a mile away. It is difficult to hide from a brown bear. They may not see you, but they will smell you. Whether you live or die during a bear attack is relative, depending on the dimensions of your skull and the bear's jaw. If the animal can get its teeth around your head, it will crush your skull like a grape.

In a recent Grizzly attack in NW Montana, the victim stated, "After receiving the most disgusting French kiss of my life, the bear bit down, completely tearing off my lower jaw." The mauling happened a week after a female (sow) Grizzly protecting cubs fatally attacked a woman near West Yellowstone. Grizzly bears have an incredible range. Hair DNA revealed it was the same bear that mauled and injured a man in Idaho. Wildlife officials finally killed the bear after it broke into a home in West Yellowstone. Incidentally, gun size and the caliber of a bullet have no bearing on whether you are successful at shooting a brown bear. It is totally dependent on bullet placement. A .22 bullet will bounce off a Grizzly skull (Dabbs 2023).

While the brown bear was hunted to extinction across much of its range in the late nineteenth and early twentieth centuries, it is now determined to be the least concerning species by the "International Union for Conservation of Nature Today." Grizzly bear populations have surpassed federal recovery goals in the Greater Yellowstone and the Northern Continental Divide. Grizzly bear encounters are becoming more and more likely as the bear population grows more widespread.

Interestingly, Grizzly habitat studies using collared bear activity data prove they prefer lowlands, not mountains. As such, their areas of expansion include a greater percentage of private lands and places where the human population is expanding. Montana has the most significant population of brown bears, second only to Alask a, creating a greater potential for conflict between bears and humans. Montana, Fish Wildlife, and Parks have determined that the grizzly bear is recovered and needs to be under state jurisdiction.

Banquets...Wilderness Style

Dear Mom and Dad:

This week is our annual "pack in and pack out" event, but this time for far more scouts than usual. This event is when the scouts "pack out" all their daily meals as they hike and explore all the rugged terrain the area offers. We get to create the packs, not to mention (but I will) still feed the staff left in camp. During the two-day pack-out event, the staff expects a little more attention, not to mention deviation, from the usual campers' menu.

My staff and I will prepare 176 sack lunches. Rather than fix the same sack lunch for each camper, we strive to create an individual experience for this event. This includes a sandwich on each camper's desired bread type. This week, there is a total of forty-five for the sourdough group, fifty-six for the whole wheat group, sixty-six for the white group, and nine for the rye group. The scouts and leaders also get to pick out their desired meat and cheese for their sandwiches. Beginning at 3:00 a.m., my staff and I form an assembly line as we hastily assemble 176 sandwiches before 8:00 a.m. Such sack lunches must meet all the main food groups. Each sack lunch contains a salt and pepper packet, mayonnaise and mustard packet, dried fruit, vegetable sticks, and a chocolate brownie. The camp provides each scout with a reusable insulated lunch pack, a cold pack, and an insulated thirty-ounce water bottle.

Then there is the "Trek" group, which packs out and camps for two days. Preparing for the Trek group is easier, as we pack all the ingredients, cookware, and paper products for the campers to prepare and cook the meals themselves. The camp provides numerous large, insulated food backpacks for this adventure. This week, the Trek group consists of 110 kids in ten different groups.

In Montana's bear country, scouts are trained to hang all their food and garbage in trees. This is a time-tested strategy in the Rocky Mountain West to prevent bears from visiting one's campsite. The kitchen is also responsible for providing all campers with a canister of bear spray, which is not your usual kitchen commodity. However, since the sack lunches are the final pick-up station, leadership wants to ensure the scouts possess this canister before the groups head out into the wilderness. In the confusion of preparation, they must remember the bear spray. It is the single most effective way to prevent bear attacks and believe me, everyone here (scouts and staff) is trained in the care and use of this canister.

Then, if things weren't hectic enough, this is the same week as our yearly national inspection. All the regional bigwigs are arriving to inspect the camp and our operations. Our camp will host twenty-five camp inspectors and ten corporate camp leaders from out of the state. I am sure they picked this week for our inspection when very few kids are in camp.

The entire week's inspection activities culminated on the last night. Fifty total adults representing troop/corporate leaders and national inspectors, with corporate and local leadership. They will all assemble for a final meeting to discuss the week's inspection. For this meeting, my staff and I will provide the banquet. Then, if that was not stressful enough, the generator goes out at 5:30 p.m. That's right, the lights went out while trying to prepare and serve authentic Montana appetizer plates of good old-fashioned "Rocky Mountain Oysters."

Camp Recipe #2 Rocky Mountain Oysters
Also known as Montana Tender Groins, Cowboy Caviar, Swingin' Beef, Dusted Nuts

1. *Gather about one hundred bulls that weigh nearly precisely three hundred pounds. This will net you two hundred "locally sourced, sustainably, all-natural, and responsibly harvested" bull testicles.*

Important Note: three-hundred-pound bulls produce the exact size and succulency of testicle with the correct degree of sponginess. *The harvester must perform a test squeeze before collecting this gem. Bulls over three hundred pounds or fail the squeeze test will produce a tougher oyster. Critical is the half dozen or so old rancher types to procure the oysters properly.*

2. *Harvested testicles will be promptly rinsed in the field of dirt, sweat, and blood. This can be performed most efficiently in the gathering corral water trough.*
3. *Transfer cleaned oysters immediately to camp.*
4. *"Civilized societies" remove the testicle's outer membrane. Montanans don't generally define themselves as civilized, so the membrane remains intact.*
5. *Either butterfly the oysters out flat, or the oyster can be fried whole. We fried ours whole.*
6. *Roll the oysters in an egg wash and cracker crumbs or corn meal—season with salt, pepper, and a dash of cayenne pepper.*
7. *Wrap a strip of uncooked bacon around the oyster and secure it with a toothpick.*
8. *Quick sear oysters in a scorching hot cast iron skillet. Transfer to a baking pan.*

Bake at approximately 350 degrees for twenty minutes. It must be cooked through. Test for doneness by popping one into your mouth.

Serve immediately.

The blackout allowed us to display our ingenuity, as I had already dug out the camp's huge commercial charcoal grill. I wish I had one of these babies at my house. It was a genuine "manly man's grill." The blackout did not affect our cooking ability, but it was an excellent excuse to get it out and show off.

Earl had some great connections. He procured the oysters, and then, what is a Montana cookout without grilling Montana homegrown steaks? Even though that grill was big, it still couldn't grill a meal large enough to feed the entire camp.

But it did work perfectly to grill sixty (one and one-half-inch), bone-in, 10-ounce rib eye steaks.

Last week, on one of my walks, I found a dead Juniper tree. Always thinking, I cut off four-inch-diameter limbs for this grilling extravaganza. You have never tasted a steak so good as one that has been grilled in the smoke of Juniper.

I then lit the wood cookstove and flat top, completing the meal with grilled asparagus spears, baked potatoes with all the fixings, and sautéed Morel mushrooms my staff found growing in the area.

Camp Recipe #3 Sautéed Morel Mushrooms

1. Gather about twenty pounds of morel mushrooms in the Kootenai National Forest, using only specially trained, highly studied, and experienced reconnaissance personnel to select and harvest this woodland delight.

Important Note: Depending on variety, Woodland mushrooms are quite poisonous, and some look like Morels *(Larson 2023).*

2. Brush any dirt off the morel using a pastry or other soft veggie brush.
3. Look into the morel's tubular stem and be sure it's clear of any debris and bugs.
4. If necessary, lightly wash the mushrooms. However, fresh morels can't withstand much in the water cleaning department. Besides, they are cooked to death to kill any bacteria or bugs that could be present. Set aside to dry thoroughly.
5. Collect about five garlic bulbs. Be happy that they are already crushed, with the skins falling off. Remove any skins that could be left, and dice further if needed.
6. Melt two pounds of smashed butter, split between two sizeable commercial-sized cast iron skillets.

7. Sprinkle the diced garlic evenly between the two skillets. Sauté till fragrant.

Add the whole mushrooms and continue to sauté. Cook long enough to disperse the excess water coming off the mushrooms.

8. After cracking one open for yourself, add one can of "Cold Smoke" beer to each skillet. This delightful dark scotch beer, only found in Montana, is chosen for this application because it pairs perfectly with Morel Mushrooms.
9. While sipping your beer, add several splashes of Worcester Sauce to taste.
10. Sauté' until the beer caramelizes.
11. Immediately serve over perfectly seasoned, Juniper-smoked rib-eye steaks grilled to an exquisite medium-rare to rare finish.

Important note: The entire process will take a while, so start the morels well before the steaks are added to the grill. There is no need to stress about over-cooking this mushroom species; in fact, it is preferred. This reminds me:

As all Montanans know... Cold Smoke Beer came to this world via the Beer Gods that love us.
Kettlehouse Brewing Company, Missoula, Montana...

Do not undercook Morels, or you will be singing to the porcelain Gods!

12. Distribute the rest of the beer in the case to your staff. Perform a toast with the entire staff (in the privacy of my office) to congratulate you and your staff on a job well done.
13. Feel confident and assured that you, your staff, and your kitchen have just passed inspection.

For dessert, we made huckleberry cheesecake. There was no better way to cap off a deliciously authentic Montana cookout. That's all for now.

Love, Me

Northwest Montana is known for its wild fruit of the Gods, better known as The Huckleberry. It is a Montana treasure and the official Montana state fruit. It is colored purple and only grows in certain untamed areas of the country. You cannot cultivate the huckleberry bush, as they only grow in the wilds and are especially conducive to the wilds of Montana. They prefer growing in cooler mountainous regions in acidic soil provided by the forest canopies of pine, fir, and spruce trees. They prefer soils comprised of volcanic ash, also a component of forest soils in Montana. Huckleberry bushes also have a unique association with fire. Fire gives a flush of nutrients to the soil, allowing huckleberry bushes to re-sprout and become even more productive. When picking huckleberries, be aware of your surroundings and always carry bear spray. Bears love huckleberries probably more than people do.

In preparation, my staff and I moved out of the pavilion and placed eight picnic tables right in front of the lake. I situated the manly man grill near the tables so folks could easily savor the smell and sound of steaks sizzling over Juniper Smoke. We built a huge campfire below us, right next to the lake.

The evening was beautiful: A perfect seventy-eight degrees, with no wind. The lake was like glass as the Loons serenaded us and the sun began to set in the west. The entire meal was an authentic Montana feast, expertly plated by my staff on fine, blue-speckled enameled plates. I had thought ahead for that night and ordered sixty Boy Scout bandanas, which I used for napkins. I also ordered Boy Scout handkerchief insignia slides to neatly collect the bandanas/napkins to display on top of the plates. The tables were decorated with red kerosene lanterns in the middle of each table, with pine tree greenery and wildflowers we found growing in camp. The lanterns set off a warm glow at each table. The campfire flames below reflected perfectly off the lake, providing a mirror image of the scene with the full moon above us.

My banquet experience is paying off in a big way this week. If there is one thing I can expertly create, it is ambiance. In fact, it is my superpower. Although I did not do that much this time, Montana's natural beauty provided most of it. From the sounds of their conversations, they were genuinely delighted with the effort. It was not how they usually dined while visiting scouting camps deep in the wilderness. What was genuinely satisfying? Pulling together a banquet-style meal with zero electrical power. It was a first for me.

The inspection went well, with our camp passing with flying colors. Except for our emergency communication system (I will explain that later), the inspectors and corporate leaders were quite pleased.

Right about when I wanted to fall into bed, the pack-out groups arrived back in camp. 176 cold packs, insulated lunch sacks, and water bottles must be cleaned and re-froze. Then, we prep what we can for tomorrow's pack-out trip. Tomorrow at 3:00 a.m., this starts all over again for one more day.

I have tried very hard to hide from the group how uncoordinated I am. However, the truth finally came to a head this morning. While carrying a large box of one-ounce salt and pepper packets, I lost track of the last step as I entered the dining hall. Of course, I fell spectacularly, spewing a billion little salt and pepper packets right into the main entrance of the dining hall. The good news is that I finally got some well-deserved applause from the group!

Camp Silverback

Each day, I carve out a segment of time where I take a walk. It is a part of my daily ritual in my quest to lose weight. The scouts and their leaders have been very encouraging in my endeavor to get healthier. They always cheer me on as I walk briskly down the trail.

Scouting's emphasis on healthy eating has been beneficial. Junk food is never on the menu here, so it is unavailable in camp. However, I prepare dessert for the group every evening. Following my last trip down the Bongos, Mom's Apple Crisp recipe was a last-minute dessert preparation. I modified it a bit to salvage a couple of hundred pounds of apples from going to waste.

Flexibility in meal planning is essential here. The Bongo/Humvee food transport system requires us to modify meal planning almost daily. Packing that trailer is an art form that combines optimal use of the space plus defensive loading. Appropriately done, all items in the trailer have a 70% chance of making it to camp. This time, the apples were the casualty.

Camp Recipe #4 Triple Bruised Apple Delight

1. *Two hundred pounds of washed and sliced Apples. Make sure you choose the ones that are the most bruised and battered. "Pieces" of Apple are also all right for this application. Don't bother trying to peel them. Spread apple pieces across four large commercial baking trays.*
2. *Mix two pounds of sugar and two cups of cinnamon. Sprinkle liberally over the top.*
3. *Top with a mixture of:*
   three pounds of triple-sifted flour
   three pounds of double-compressed, hard-packed brown sugar
   four pounds of smashed butter
4. *Bake for approximately one hour in an approximate 350-degree wood cookstove oven.*
5. *Remove from oven and cool in a fail-safe bear-proof area.*

6. *Assign a staff member as a bear sentry armed with bear spray.*

Dear Mom and Dad:

After one of my great walks, I am sitting in front of my efficiency trailer. While taking a breather before starting dinner, I decided to describe the camp's layout. So, hold on...I will take you on my favorite walking trail through camp and around the lake.

First, after a successful landing off the Bongos, you see the storage, maintenance, and utility cabins on your left (more on that later). The cooks' cabin and pavilion are also on the left, about fifty yards past the utility cabin. In front of the pavilion is where Big Bear Lake unfolds and the rest of the camp. It opens into a beautiful valley surrounded by hillsides, mountains, and pine trees. In the background are the magnificent mountains that make up the surrounding wilderness chains.

If you were to stand in the middle of Big Bear Lake, far in the distance to the south and west, you can see the Kootenai and Cabinet Wilderness Complex. Looking a little more north is the Salish Range. Panning more north is the Rockies, and then east is the Whitefish Range. It is such a picturesque setting.

The cooks' cabin and pavilion are north of the lake, right next to Silverback Creek, which drains out of the lake. A small footbridge crosses the creek to reach the front entrance of the pavilion. The footbridge provides access to the pavilion for those coming from the lake's east side. Before the footbridge, and on the other side of the creek from the pavilion, is a cunning little trail that leads to the shower cabin tucked back into the woods.

The pavilion is enormous. It is large enough to serve as the mess hall but also provides ample space for indoor activities should the weather turn sour. Lined along the edges of the pavilion are large foot lockers that store indoor-type activities, including puzzles, playing cards, games, and crafts. I have never seen the footlockers opened. The boys are always outside despite the weather.

As with the cooks' cabin, the shower cabin was located closer to the well, generator, water pump, and water heater. All the plumbing and electrical run underneath the creek. The shower cabin has sixteen shower stalls with plastic shower curtains over each one. Showers are arranged by cabin on a schedule. Otherwise, it is first-come, first-serve. I understand that it takes a while for the hot water to reach the shower spigots. It makes me happy that I have my own system.

There are no showers in the individual cabins, but they do have toilets and sinks that work. They recommend using the vault toilets scattered throughout the camp. The cabin bathrooms are for "stand-up jobs" only. No toilet paper is to be flushed down the cabin toilets. The septic arrangement here is pretty dated and could use some updating. How they would accomplish that is a mystery to me.

The remote chalet cabins in Glacier Park were originally built in the 1910s by bringing supplies in by horse and mule. Logs were harvested on-site. When Glacier Park's historic Sperry Chalet burned down in the "Sprague Fire," it was rebuilt by helicopter supply drops. With that, I am sure something could be done to improve the infrastructure here. For now, though, it is what we have. I should add that what we have is pretty darn good.

At some point, someone must come into camp and pump all the septic tanks and vault toilets. I am still determining how they would get in here to do that. I have never seen a septic pumper with the clearance needed to get in here. I also have yet to learn why these complexities pop into my mind. I am the king of useless, meaningless trivia. I will bet that not many people know how to put the alphabet into an actual word as I can. OK, Kris can, but she is the only one.

My faded white-to-yellow vintage trailer with lime green accents is behind the cooks' cabin/pavilion. It is one of the best sights in camp, peacefully located on the far north end of the complex. I often sit under my awning in the morning, sipping coffee and listening to the creek and the birds. I do the same in the evenings before bed, except with a beer. Listening to the creek before me and the Loons crooning out on the lake relaxes me after work. The Loons make an eerie sound; the locals describe it as a tremolo or yodel. It is very soothing as I unwind from the day. There are no useless distractions out here, like televisions or cell phones.

My efficiency trailer has its own water hookup and sewer disposal, which is so sweet! It is likely all setup and connected to the cook's cabin infrastructure. I have a one-hundred-gallon propane tank for heating shower water.

As you walk around the lake, twenty-two cabins are interspersed all along the lakefront, on both the west and east sides of the lake. Eighteen of those cabins sleep twelve boys in bunk beds, with their leader in a double-size bed. The remaining four cabins with bunks sleep ten each. They house the camp's staff. Then, there are two additional overflow cabins with complete setups to accommodate plenty of extras, should that occur. As per most scout camps, all the cabins are named - Grizzly, Loon, Wolf, White Tail, Moose, etc. Hiking trails are plentiful and unending throughout the area. Several trailheads start in camp, allowing the boys and their leaders easy access to explore the area's terrain. Lastly, there are twelve vault-type toilets interspersed throughout the camp.

The Lake provides the boys with much swimming and canoeing enjoyment as they play water sports and work on their merit badges. The boys have this water game called "Canoe Tag." They were playing this game today as I walked by. They look like they are having a great time, and it is hilarious to watch.

The camp has about twenty canoes. The first twenty boys then paddle out to the middle of the lake, standing on the gunnel (back) of the canoe. They then bounce up and down on the gunnel, which propels the canoe forward. They can steer the canoe by shifting their weight to one side or the other. The game aims to dump (push) your opponent off their canoe and into the water. You cannot ram your canoe into another canoe. If you do, you are disqualified.

Once a boy is dumped off (or disqualified), he swims back to shore with his canoe, where he relinquishes it to the next boy waiting in line. He then stands on the gunnel, bouncing the canoe through the water to the middle of the lake to join the contest. Once a boy has been dumped, they are out of the game. Eventually, all the boys are dumped into the water, leaving only one boy standing.

The last boy standing is then crowned Sturgeon Nose Master. This notability is to honor the early tribes of the area and is the name of the canoe that the tribes used.

The Kootenai, Kalispel, Salish, and Sinixt people used sturgeon-nose canoes. While instantly recognizable by the unusual reverse slope of the bow and stern, the canoe style possesses several features that distinguish it from other North American bark canoes. The odd shape makes them well-suited to navigate a mix of waterways in the tribe's environment, such as large open lakes, swamps, and swift rivers.

They were canoes built from whatever bark was convenient in the area: Birch, spruce, fir, or white pine were all used. The outer surface bark was turned inward to face the boat's interior. The mature tree would be cut down in the spring while the sap ran. Willow ribs were fastened to the gunwales using willow bark twine. The bark was then sewn onto the ribs using cedar root. All seams were then glued with a warm pine pitch to seal and waterproof the canoe. Lastly, the bottom of the canoe was covered in loose grass to sit on comfortably. This is just another fascinating historical tidbit I have learned. The camp does a great job educating the boys about the region's earliest inhabitants.

Walking down the east side of my trail, there is an open field beyond the lake to the south. This is where they organize sporting events, as cabins team up for football, baseball, and soccer. There is a small log-built storage building to store all the sports gear. Beyond the sports field, on the most southern edge of the camp, is the shooting range. It is where the boys learn marksmanship with guns and bows. Emphasis is on safety as the boys learn to handle and shoot such weapons safely. Montana's old west history holds great reverence for firearms. Besides the lake, this is the most popular venue for young boys.

Finally, around the lake, I proceed along the west trail, passing more cabins and vault toilets. At the end of the west trail, I am back at the Bongo's landing. An ENORMOUS log building is located northwest of the lake right after the Bongo's landing. It is where everything needed for the function and enjoyment of a Boy Scout camp is stored. It is a fascinating building. Sometimes, after my walk, I peruse through the many aisles and shelving within the building. There is a lot to see in there. I occasionally wander through to see if the kitchen can use anything. I am constantly amazed at what kinds of things materialize from that building. It is where I located the manly man grill, and I am sure it is where my efficiency trailer came from.

Behind the storage building is the "refuse" cabin. Believe me, it is a fortress. Not man nor beast could break into that building. Many bears have tried, as evidenced by the claw and chew marks around the opening of the heavy steel slide-up garage door. The 1906 military-style scout Humvee has a large enough truck bed to double as a garbage wagon. Earl frequently does a garbage run back to Eureka during the hot summer.

The maintenance and utility buildings are next to the garbage cabin. I never wander into those two buildings. As you know, maintenance and utility are not my forte. I leave those functions to those much more competent than myself.

Behind the maintenance/utility cabins, there is a road. If you wander down that road, Earl's private cabin is at the end of the road, next to the creek. It is a one-bedroom, one-bath nine hundred or so square-foot log cabin. It has a nice oversized covered deck on the front, with a stunning view of the mountainside and creek. It is a regular home out here, with a generator, well, pump, and septic system. In the living room is a huge, stacked stone fireplace. It has an efficient wood stove inserted into the firebox in case he needs heat during the unpredictable summers in northwest Montana. It has a small kitchen in the back of the cabin with a cool oversized antique farmhouse sink. It has a vintage cast iron gas cookstove and oven that looks like it is rarely used. Earl generally dines with the scouts and staff. The kitchen cabinets and countertops are made of pine. A large living and dining area opens up in front of the kitchen, with a small log-type dining table. An overstuffed couch and chair are in the living room which looks out a big picture window. No television, of course. All one needs is that view. His bedroom and bathroom are of adequate size, and they also have pine cabinetry and log furniture. The cabin decor is customary in log-type dwellings. Throughout the cabin are numerous framed photos of his family. On the fireplace mantel is a picture of him and his late wife on horseback. She was very beautiful.

Earl has been with this camp and the Boy Scout organization for several decades. He knows everything about the running and maintenance of this camp. As Camp Silverback's primary unpaid caretaker and maintenance director, he is an institution all his own. He is much revered and deserving of such comfortable accommodations. The Boy Scouts treat him very well. Now and then, in the evenings, I will walk the creek trail back to his cabin with a six-pack of beer. Earl will share old times with me, with past stories of the camp going back three decades. He talks a lot about Montana, her history, and her people. It is always fascinating, and he has taught me a lot.

I have learned that by being born in Montana, I can claim the distinction of being a native Montanan, which gives me some kudo points on my Montana-Meter. That distinction does have inherent responsibilities, which I intend to embrace. Our primary responsibility is to maintain Montana's values, which have been handed down from many generations who have called Montana home. Montanans are more than irritated with the transients from the East and West coasts. Folks who move to escape stifling political climates, only to then try and change Montana to that from where they came.

Montana is very welcoming, but if folks decide to move here to escape one environment, do not come here to try to change Montana into the same. Montanans come from legacies and values built upon for over 130 years. They began generations long ago and are still espoused today. Montanans know what those values are. To newcomers who come merely for the beautiful scenery, our values become very self-evident quickly. Many are not happy with the culture they ultimately discover here. Before folks come to live here, they should research those values.

Montanans are gun-loving, patriotic, constitution-loving Christians who love their country. We carry our Redneck label with pride. We embrace the Second Amendment, and as Rednecks, we do have the skill and ability to shoot. Montana is a castle-doctrine state, which means we will shoot you if you break into our homes, but it does not mean another shoot-out at the "OK Corral" is lawful.

However, we seem to get a few of those types of transplants that end up serving life in a Montana prison. Those would be interesting walls to be behind because, in Montana, criminals are treated like criminals.

We love hunting, and we pass this tradition down to every generation that comes behind us. Periodically, one will see a well-antlered buck or bull elk head wired up on the front grill of a sizeable diesel-running truck.

This is cattle country, an industry in which Montana was founded. We embrace open grazing philosophies and individual land rights. We are proud of our rich ranching and farming history, passing them down to the next generation of Montanans.

These are the values that Montana was founded upon and the way she has prospered since 1889 when she became a state. Earl and I agree that if those ideals disturb their sensitivities, they should pick somewhere else to move.

Anyway, I am thrilled to be here and have the opportunity to learn more about the state of my birth. This camp is set up well, and I am having a great time. There is something about getting back to nature. A place where you become naturally removed from all the trappings in life that distract you from what is important. It is such a great experience for youngsters and adults alike. I miss you and think of you often. I better gather my staff and start dinner. More later...

Love, Me

French Camp

Every year in July was the annual Eastern Oregon College, faculty and staff campout. It was always at "French Camp" on the Lostine River in the Wallowa Whitman National Forest. The Eagle Cap Wilderness and surrounding countryside make up this national forest.

Before the University campout, our family routinely camped at French Camp. It was close to our favorite hiking trail, called Bowman Trail. The trail would eventually take you to a high-mountain lake called Chimney Lake. Bowman Trail is a recognized "hard" trail designation. Dad would gather up all the children in camp and lead the way on our hike to Chimney Lake. As small children, we never made it high enough to get to Chimney Lake, but we would try. Small children make many stops, so our day always ended at "the waterfall." The waterfall was part of a beautiful high mountain stream alongside Bowman as it gently poured down alongside the trail. It was not a large waterfall, but it was beautiful as the water cascaded down a series of large, flat rocks. As small children, getting to the waterfall seemed to take hours. By the time we got there, we were exhausted. It was always an excellent place to enjoy our sack lunch and then turn around to go back to camp. Dad enjoyed hiking and the outdoors and delighted in sharing it with kids.

If you wanted to go further, the trail led you across a shallow stream at the top of that waterfall. The flat rock crossing under the stream was extremely slippery. The water at that time of year was only an inch deep. Even so, it was considered a safety hazard for slippage, waiting earnestly for a small child to lose their footing and tumble down that waterfall.

Dad's youngest brother, our Uncle Terry, went with us one year. He was attending college in La Grande and living with us then. Deciding to join our camping weekend that year, he ventured out with us one day along the Bowman Trail. Terry was an avid photographer long before digital photography existed. He even had a darkroom set up in the basement of our home. Terry forged ahead of us that day with camera in hand. I am sure he was not into the slow, meandering hike children do, as they pick up every rock, flower, and stick they find along the way.

I'm not sure what happened that day; all I know is Uncle Terry fell down that waterfall. He slipped on one of those flat, slippery rocks as he set up for that perfect camera angle alongside that waterfall. I am unsure how far he fell, but it was at least ten yards. Far enough to be bleeding from nearly every protuberance on his body. By the time we arrived, Dad had helped him out of the water and was dressing his wounds. The good news of the day was that his expensive camera somehow survived unscathed. It was a good childhood lesson on respect for water.

We later learned as adults that the waterfall was only about a thirty-minute hike from the trailhead. I heard that from my sisters, who took the same hike with Joni's son Justin one summer. Justin was about fourteen years old at the time. They made it to Chimney Lake that day, although at one point, they nearly all turned around. The "hard" designation of that trail is not an exaggeration. At one point, my hot and exhausted sisters sat on a big rock, and while emptying their tennis shoes of dirt for the millionth time, they instructed Justin to go around one more bend in the trail. They directed him to come back if Chimney Lake was not there. Fortunately, it was finally there, and they enjoyed a couple of hours of fishing and swimming before hiking back down.

My father's love of the outdoors and camping motivated him to start the annual faculty/staff camping event. Dad was EOC's food service director at the time, long before the University contracted the service to my company. Our family had camped at this location often enough that Dad envisioned a family outdoor camping extravaganza for the EOC family. On the Lostine River, it was the only campground designated for groups. It possessed a cook's cabin and an open pavilion for group dining. It was the perfect venue with all the attributes to accommodate a weekend camping jamboree for a large group. Dad would reserve the entire campground every August for this event. The event was free to anyone within the EOC family who wanted to participate.

French Camp occupied areas on both sides of the forest service dirt road. The cook's cabin and pavilion were on one side, with numerous campsites. Our family would arrive early on Wednesday before anyone else arrived. We then took our usual campsite on the opposite side of the road, right next to the river. It was the best campsite because it had a small river inlet with calm and shallow water. It was a perfect area for small children to play without getting caught up in the central part of the river. Joni caught a crawdad there once. She took it home to be her pet. She put it in our old aquarium and fancied a mini crawdad sanctuary. It was complete with a little pond, rocks, and vegetation she collected from its environment. She did not have any crawdad food, though, and it died a week later. Boy, did that stink up the house.

Anyway, while Joni was crawdad hunting and Mom and Kris were napping, I would help Dad unload all the cooking and serving accouterment. It was all in a van already mysteriously there, parked right next to the cabin. We would set everything up in the cabin and bring in all the firewood needed for the first day of food preparation. It was entertaining because I have always enjoyed helping my father with mundane tasks. Much to my relief, a truck had already delivered the firewood. It was enough to supply the cook's cabin with cooking fuel for the entire weekend. The firewood was neatly stacked outside the cabin and pavilion. This was a really good thing. I could not imagine Kris and I trying to gather up that much firewood.

It was my first experience with a rustic cook's cabin, and it was fascinating. The building was a turn-of-the-century, primitive, hand-hewn log cabin. It had an 8' X 4' wood cookstove, just like Camp Silverback. It had two round openings on each side of the top for adding firewood on either side of the flat cooktop. The cabin had a huge, enameled sideboard and sinks for washing dishes with a large island for meal prep in the middle of the cabin. I was always fascinated by the number of pancakes you could griddle on the flat top of that cookstove, and boy were they good. There is something about camp food that tastes especially good. A service window opened up in the front of the cabin. All the hungry campers would line up, ready to be served their meal. Each meal service served a total of about one hundred people.

All the families took turns chopping firewood fuel and helping in the kitchen with meal prep, serving, and cleaning up. There was a blackboard nailed to the cabin next to the service window. As everyone went through the line to get their meal, they would sign up for their turn in the "mess cabin." We never had a shortage of workers, and we all had fun helping - adults and kids.

An open-air dining/pavilion area was in front of the service window, with ten picnic tables lined up in two groups of five. Each table would seat eight to ten people. Not everyone ate at the same time. People would dribble in throughout the two-hour window of the allotted meal service. The pavilion had a roof over the top in case it rained. Wherever you were in camp, the sweet aroma of coffee brewing and the smell of bacon sizzling would permeate your consciousness in the morning. It signaled that everyone was about to convene together for a meal. We were all on our own for lunch and dinner, and everyone brought their own cold beverages.

Faculty and staff knew everyone back then, including all their families. If you were new to the EOC family, it was a perfect opportunity to get to know everyone. How simple it all was back then. So many individuals, couples, and families gathering in one place. It was a rare time in our society for healthy communion among friends and family while welcoming new folks. People are missing out. Outings like this never occur among strangers anymore, where the goal is to meet new people. They are only ever practiced now within small retreats or church groups that have shared values. People now resist unknown large gatherings, fearful or resistant to mix with those outside their personally engrained belief systems. In our electronic age, we have lost our ability to socialize amongst strangers.

The departure of these sorts of activities is ultimately what is missing in our society now. It is probably the number one reason why our country is so divided. It is difficult to fight about remote, abstract, tribal ideas when you have just returned from a fabulous weekend outing. A place where everybody worked and played together. What is ultimately gained in such a society? Respect for each other resulting in shared ideas with compromises obtained.

This is another reason organizations such as Boy Scouts and children's summer camps exist. Where else will children get to participate in activities together without all the modern diversions that prevent healthy interaction? Simple activities where you sleep, eat, work, and play together without a mobile device or a television. It is a time and place where camaraderie can be formed with other kids and adults you have not met before. This is where new ideas about the world around you are formed and where young minds discover that we are all more alike than we are different.

Changed Forever

Years later, in about 1994, Joni, Justin, and I tried to take a camping weekend. We headed up to our family's favorite sight, French Camp. Being about eight years old at the time, Justin was at a great age for exploring. After all these years, Joni and I were excited to revisit the campground we so fondly remembered. Joni was especially thrilled to share it with Justin. He was at that perfect age to enjoy the great outdoors while fishing, exploring, and hiking at our old family camping stomping grounds. It was an excellent opportunity to share our family's long-gone, bygone days and camping traditions with Justin. We arrived excitedly with all our essential camping regalia for a fun-filled weekend. What we met was disappointment.

The hand-hewn primitive cooks' cabin was boarded up, and the door nailed shut. The roof over the dining area was rotted away, and the picnic tables in the front were gone. A peek through a small hole in the cabin revealed it was empty. Gone were the cookstoves, the sink, the sideboard, and the prep island. The cabin had become a haven for rats and other rodents. Graffiti was scribbled all over the inside and outside of that classic pioneer log cabin. Unmaintained by the forest circus, it was quickly eroding into the landscape. I sat there stunned, remembering the old times and imagining its humble beginnings as a line cabin a century ago. Oh, the stories it could tell. Line cabins were common in the West, as men used them as temporary shelters during the summer and fall. They would sleep and cook in them while following cattle on grazing allotments on government lands. Much to our sadness that day, it was clear that the power players on the west side of Oregon did not care about a great pioneer cabin in one of the greatest family recreational areas in Eastern Oregon.

Large forest circus signs were posted everywhere, stating that camping was no longer allowed in French Camp. It was merely a picnic site now. The state closed the entire campground for what was intended: camping. It is a symptom of a much larger issue. In its infinite wisdom, Oregon has decided that its residents can no longer be trusted in "their" forests. In just one generation, families can no longer participate in certain outdoor activities with their children. Outdoor activities that brought such joy and adventure for families in an earlier time.

You can picnic there, and the outhouses (vault toilets now) are there, but it is now illegal to camp there. Fearful that camping will erode "fragile" stream banks and their vegetation, none of it makes any sense. You can stand on…fish on…the river's edge all day long. You can wade out and play in the river all day long. You can lay out a huge picnic spread on a picnic table provided by the state located right on the river's edge. You can spend all day there and into the evening, but you are prohibited from spending the night.

Curious because nighttime is for sleeping. A time that seems reasonable to believe would have the least "intrusion" on "fragile, sensitive stream banks." However, this is what happens when bureaucrats get busy building new regulatory guidelines that make zero sense. They huddle in conference rooms, scribbling out rules without comprehending that their laws are often contradictory. It makes me wonder, do bureaucrats think their policies through at all while they are writing them? Perhaps they do, and that is the most unfortunate part of all. Ideologies are made into government policies that ignore historical best-use practices. Then, I began to wonder if the state is so concerned about the ground, why would they not care about a historic, hand-hewn pioneer cabin on which it stands? That cabin is a historical artifact, sitting on wilderness-designated land.

The most obvious reason is that Pioneer Cabin does not fall under the 1968 Wild and Scenic Rivers Act. The Act, passed by Democrat majorities in both houses of Congress and signed into law by Democrat President Lyndon B. Johnson, declared that certain selected rivers in the nation would be preserved in free-flowing conditions. They and their immediate environments shall be protected for the benefit and enjoyment of present and future generations. I guess a historic pioneer cabin does not qualify as "the immediate environment" (Interagency 2014).

OK, preserved for what? What is their definition of "enjoyment?" So, you can stand on a road and look at it? In truth, "The Act" was written at the federal level by Washington DC bureaucrats to preserve selected river sections across the country in their "free-flowing condition." States could then implement "The Act" in any manner they chose. The federal government had done its job. It was now up to the states to implement the law as they chose to interpret it.

Politicians in some states, such as Oregon, used this act to close many waterways, including those that impacted popular family campground sites, barring their historic usage. On October 28, 1988, the

Lostine River Corridor became one of thirty-nine rivers and streams added to the Wild and Scenic River designation, signed into Oregon law by Democrat Governor Neil Goldschmidt. Nationally, there are 208 total Wild and Scenic River designations, of which Oregon has 58, more than any other state in the entire US (National Park Service).

Most campgrounds throughout Oregon have long been re-configured. Camping anywhere next to a body of water subject to this Act is now illegal. Formalized campsites must be located at least twenty-five feet from any water source. To ordinary people, that means, gone are the days of sipping coffee in front of your tent, admiring the river meandering in front of you. Watching your children play in the water while you are reading a book or cooking dinner will never be experienced by young families anymore in front of many Oregon waterways. Complete control of public lands is only one symptom of an Oregon government that has been under total Democrat control since 1992. The last Republican Governor was elected in 1979. They have been a mail-in voter state in all elections since 1998.

Campground descriptions in Oregon clearly state this on their websites. I find it amusing that as a part of state marketing, they describe campsites as—being close enough to "hear the river or creek." It is as if this is some sort of wonderful consolation prize. I can do that with a portable cassette/DVD player in my backyard. Sadly, I believe people have conformed to accept the normality of these changes through decades of propaganda fed to us by governments, media, and others who push populist environmental philosophies. The changes have been insidious and slow, but they are here to stay now. It forever changed our relationship with our public lands and waterways in Oregon.

Oregonians who have never experienced the wonder of streamside camping are consigned to conform to a system of rules by faceless politicians who believe they know what is best. I only single out Oregon because I have lived there nearly my entire life. I have witnessed all the changes that have occurred over the decades. Population centers on the west side of the state are those that are making the decisions for eastern Oregonians who use our waterways. Over several decades, west siders have often been transplants from California. These grifters have forever changed the free spirit that once thrived in Oregon.

In Oregon now, the only wilderness streams or lakes you can camp next to are those you horse-pack, raft, or hike into. Only the remotest of campgrounds allow this anymore if you can even get in there and if you have the permit. Many (if not most) of the old hiking and horse trails are unmaintained now in Oregon. It takes an experienced, fit, and dedicated hiker to maneuver many of those trails now, and horses cannot get in at all. This "trail maintenance" method allows Oregon bureaucrats to decide where to allow people to be in "their" forests. People incapable of hiking, rafting, or horseback riding, or those who do not own a raft or a horse, will never again be able to experience the joy of stream or lakeside camping in Oregon's wilderness.

Re-living Joy for One Day

Seeing the disappointment in my sister and nephew and being the rebel that I am, I took care of it. We camped one night right smack in that campground, next to the river where we had always camped. A forest service ranger did stop and question us. Using my skills in marketing and persuasion, the ranger allowed us to stay for that one night.

Faceless Oregon politicians ruined the weekend for us and our hope of ever re-creating any camping enjoyment for future generations at French Camp on the Lostine River in the Wallowa Whitman National Forest. Gone is a kinder, simpler, and unregulated time when families were free to explore and experience the beauty of their state. Unfortunately, families in Oregon today will never know what they are missing out on. What did we learn as a family? We learned about being good land stewards and leaving a campsite better than you found it. We learned about fish and wildlife species. We learned about valuable forest management and having respect for our environment. This is what families are missing out on today in Oregon. It is gone forever.

It has been a surreptitiously slow process, as various government agencies across the United States have restricted the public's free use of public lands. They do this by passing laws with hidden language to prevent any public knowledge or input. Once passed, there is no turning back, and they know it.

That is why I am enjoying this scouting experience so much. As far as I can tell, Montana does not seem to be as hung up on controlling their lands from the "intrusion" of their people. They trust their residents to take care of this beautiful state. Rather than barring land usage, they emphasize education, proper use, and respect. Montana allows families to learn about the environment around them and how to take care of it. It is those values that camps such as this teach their youth. Since the beginning of time, there have always been idiots who do not care about preserving the beauty of nature. However, it should not be about penalizing the entire population because of it. Land conservation should be about protecting lands through education and providing methods and infrastructure to encourage proper use.

There are only five waterways in Montana designated within "The Act." They are the Three Forks of the Flathead River, the Upper Missouri River Breaks, and East Rosebud Creek. Montanans are highly suspicious and resistant to any government attempt to lock up public lands for good reason.

What Public Use Looks Like

I have discovered that Montana possesses some of the best blue-ribbon fishing anywhere in the country. The area is rich in developed campsites throughout the state, as tourists and locals alike take advantage of and enjoy these popular fisheries. Guided river and horse packing trips are abundant in northwest Montana for the complete fishing, camping, and hunting experience. There are a host of developed campgrounds throughout the state to welcome the many tourists coming to Montana for every kind of camping experience. Many are right in front of lakes and streams. Local Montanans have scoped out for themselves many private areas unknown to tourists. These more private-public campsites, located off the beaten path, are quiet and easily accessible off little-known side roads. Locals can then take their families on a quiet camp trip without the chaos created by large groups.

Instead of banning these public streams and lake sites, the state is proactive—placing bear-proof garbage and food storage receptacles where they see the need. At some of these sites, the state will even place vault toilets. The various ranger districts monitor all these camping areas and will stop to visit, but they are not punitive. They want to ensure that all the rules are followed, especially regarding campfires during extreme fire seasons.

Conservation and preservation of public lands for public use has a long history in NW Montana that began in 1972. That was when the US Forest Service threatened to cut off access into The Bob Marshall Wilderness, requiring permits for all stock use and eliminating important infrastructure like cabins and bridges. It was an overreach, and four men from Columbia Falls decided to do something about it. They formed the Back Country Horsemen (BCH) and began outreach efforts to educate the public about the government plan. In January 1973, they filled the Columbia Falls High School gymnasium to voice their opposition to the proposal. They gathered government officials and media outlets to make their voices heard. As a result, BCH members and volunteers rebuilt bridges for which the USFS stated they had no resources. On horses, they transported 180 planks, nine feet long, and dozens of ninety-pound bags of cement, plus other materials, which amounted to an

18-wheeler supply load spread over two weekends. It became a symbol of wilderness access and built the mission of the BCH. Fifty years later, there are now eighteen BCH chapters nationwide, with over a thousand members who partner with land management agencies to clear trails on public lands. It is the volunteers who raise the money and do the work to maintain access for horse packers during the big game hunting season. Open and maintained trails enable privately guided wilderness pack trips. It expands tourism, as maintained trails bring horse, hiking, and biking enthusiasts around the country and abroad, who are then free to explore areas deep in Montana's backcountry (Dresser 2024).

Jeep clubs are constantly developing the Wild Bill Recreational Trail outside Kalispell for off-road vehicles. Over the years, they have developed miles and miles of challenge trails for the jeep, ATV, and motorcycle enthusiasts. Families are the most significant users of these trails, with groups of Side-by-Side ATVs full of families exploring Montana's great outdoors. They congregate on these trails for a nice day's outing, picking service berries, huckleberries, and morel mushrooms while enjoying the scenery.

Recreational horseback riding groups have finished developing the multiple-use Kalispell's "Foys to Blacktail" trail, expanding Herron Park by 320 acres since 2010. Herron Park now encompasses 440 acres. The 13.5-mile Foy's to Blacktail Trail begins at the Chase Overlook, approximately four miles from the Herron Park trailhead. Horseback riders and mountain bikers utilize it, which connects to Blacktail Mountain. From there, they can connect to the Wild Bill Off-Highway Vehicle (OHV) trails for additional challenge trail adventures (T. Scott 2022).

This is just one small section of the entire state—a state that embraces recreational use of its public lands and whose philosophy embraces multiple uses of Montana's forests. Ranger districts generally give the green light for various volunteer endeavors to expand recreation opportunities on public lands. They work with, instead of against, volunteers who do the work themselves, funding it through various fundraising avenues. The state then assists with the planning, signage, and logistics.

Montana manages its forest and public land usage instead of banning it. In turn, they can charge for its use at reasonable rates. This then generates revenue to self-manage its forests, trails, fisheries, and campsites without taxing its residents. This is such a better plan. It keeps Montana forest lands, lakes, and streams open for everybody to enjoy. It then encourages tourism, which generates millions in state revenue. This is one more reason that Montana is one of only three debt-free states.

Sliding on my Backside!

Yesterday, I decided to take my daily walk up The Bongos. I discovered why they call part of the road "Jackass Slide." It is because you feel like a jackass when you slide a quarter mile down the road on your hind end. Gravity is never your friend for a guy with, um…as broad a shoulders as I have. It has even more emphasis when, like an idiot, you have both hands in your pockets as you completely lose your footing. Considering my coordination, you would have thought I should have figured this out long ago. Ah, the family trip to Hawaii immediately comes to mind.

The Island of Kauai is a tropical delight of surf, sand, and umbrella drinks. A wonderful family vacation to the islands, where I also happened to meet, I was sure - my future wife. Oh, what optimism! She was a blonde, blue-eyed beauty, and we ran into her everywhere. She would be there whether we were on the beach, shopping, or at various restaurants. She and her family were even at the Luau we attended. I even got to be on stage right next to her for a hula dance. It had to be a sign from God and our destiny! Polite smiles aside, I could not muster the courage to talk to her.

Finally, one day, while Joni, Kris, and I were walking on the beach, she jogged by. I decided it was time to seize the moment and try to talk to her. "Carpe' Diem," I said to myself as I jogged alongside her to say hello. What happened next was all a blur. In my romancing anxiety and as I attempted to suavely utter that first "hello," I failed to notice the giant wave that came in. As she moved gracefully and effortlessly out of the way, the wave caught me at my shins, just below my knees. I was instantly slammed onto the sand, where the next thing I knew, I was being washed out to sea. In and out of the surf I go, unable to get my feet underneath me. I was rolling in and rolling out, with only my pink polo shirt and white shorts visible in the rumbling sand and surf. Now and then, I would surface enough to gasp for air. Of course, my sisters behind me, who witnessed the entire event, could not contain themselves through their laughter. Finally, they decided that perhaps they should retrieve me from the surf lest I get washed out to sea. Bruised ego aside, the young lady was long gone by then, and I never saw her again.

Dear Mom and Dad:

I had a minor issue on my walk today. I decided to do my most strenuous walk up the Bongos. Whether in a vehicle or walking, I have found that it always builds stamina and character. After reaching the top of Upper Bongos and feeling accomplished, I turned around and began my descent.

Upon reaching Jackass Slide, I was walking a little too "briskly" as I slipped at the top of the hill. Instead of smartly removing my hands from my pockets to catch myself, I made my graceful slide down Jackass Slide on my backside. I completely ripped through the underside of my shorts, splitting them down the crotch seam. This, of course, gave new meaning to "shortcuts." I was just thankful that my only audience was a deer and a couple of squirrels. I bet they never saw anyone wearing a homemade kilt walking through the woods before.

I made it down the last of Jackass Slide and the Lower Bongos, but painfully and gingerly does not describe the entire problem. A tad drafty also does not fully explain my predicament, as my torn and raggedy shorts barely cover my bruised, battered, and equally raggedy backside. Maybe hamburger-like explains how my underside feels right now. Geez! Sometimes life just kicks me in the ass, as it were. Please send Telfa pads and Neosporin ASAP!

Love, Randy

At least when I "hit the surf" that fateful day in Kauai, I survived physically unscathed. Except for needing to dig the sand out from the underside of my backside, my ego was the only thing bruised and battered. Lesson learned: Never walk with your hands in your pockets, and never wear tennis shoes while walking in steep, rugged terrain. I better dig out those new hiking boots Mom generously bought for me. She always seemed to know exactly what I need.

Celebrating Our Country's Birth

June is now July, and we are all preparing for Camp Silverback's Grand Fourth of July celebration. It came complete with our own "Camp Silverback Marching Band." In anticipation of this celebration, this group of boys was instructed to bring a musical instrument of their choice. Country and patriotic pride are cornerstones of scouting, so it makes sense that this holiday is so important to the organization. You can add that to the growing list of examples of why I enjoy this experience as much as I do.

They practiced all week. Many of the boys brought actual musical instruments. For those boys who did not bring an instrument, scouting leadership improvised. With only a little imagination, almost anything can turn into a percussion instrument. Then there is the handy Kazoo, dozens of which materialized from somewhere. Now, every boy could participate in our band, whether they had musical talent or not. The Kazoo is a handy little instrument that anyone who does not have an ounce of musical ability can feel musically accomplished. It has been around for a long, long time. Although there is no documentation, it is believed that an African American named Alabama Vest from Macon, Georgia, invented a kazoo-type instrument around 1840. The first documented appearance of a Kazoo was by an American inventor named Warren Herbert Frost. He named his new musical instrument Kazoo in patent #270,543, dated January 9, 1883.

There is no semblance of a modern-day July Fourth aerial light display up here, but we have a fantastic band to ring in the holiday. I am a part of a large cheering section as we watch the boys gloriously display the American flag and march proudly around the lake. It was dusk, with our scouts dressed in freshly washed and pressed uniforms, with red, white, and blue streamers and brightly twinkling sparklers. It was thrilling as they proudly played many of our country's patriotic songs. I smiled as they began to play one of my father's favorite Big Band songs, John Philip Sousa's "Stars and Stripes Forever." Once again, the lake provided a beautiful scene in front of the majestic, forested mountains behind it. The acoustics could not have been any better if we had been in an amphitheater as the music echoed off the majestic Kootenai mountains.

Fourth of July Remembered

Our family participated in our own Fourth of July parade, which always followed a celebratory BBQ at Ode (pronounced Odie) and Barbara's family home in La Grande. It was an annual potluck celebration of the July 4th holiday, with a dozen or so families participating. Ode and Barbara always supplied the chicken that Ode would grill for the group. We would all gather at their home, which, at that time, was a fabulous southern-style home on the outskirts of the downtown area. It was a classic turn-of-the-century white home close to the middle of town with giant white pillars on the front porch. While the adults visited, prepared dinner, and re-told all the fun stories through the years, the kids played various backyard games. I preferred riding my bike around the block with my friend, Mary, Ode and Barbara's youngest daughter.

Back then, our little town did not have a city-wide sponsored fireworks aerial display, so we made our own celebration. It had the usual noise-making fountain-type fireworks and sparklers when it got dark, but the most exciting part was our little marching band. After dinner, their son, Kelly, an accomplished high school percussionist, led our marching band through the streets of La Grande. Dad and I were part of the Kazoo section, with me proudly wearing my Cub Scout uniform. Yes, I was a dork, but I was ten years old and did not care. I came by it honestly, though; Dad was the lead dork in our family.

Most of the families were musically inclined, with a fair number of brass and woodwind instruments represented in our little marching band. Those who did not play instruments marched with the band. We were impressive as many folks came out of their backyards and homes to cheer us on. The marchers and players wore patriotic costumes with flowing red, white, and blue streamers. All those marching sported sparklers as we marched and played through various neighborhoods. It was small-town Americana back then, where families came together once a year in our small corner of the country to celebrate our country's birth.

Our Camp Bear

Dear Mom and Dad:

Thanks so much for the new hiking boots. They will work perfectly. The high-top design to the middle of my shins should keep me from rolling my ankle in the future. The super beefed-up tread design should clamp onto the trail well, regardless of the amount or size of rocks I encounter. I have fully read the fifty-page manual that came with my super-duper new boots. It includes detailed instructions in twenty different languages to fully instruct the owner in the wear and care of the most recently developed rendition of hiking footwear. I will study it carefully this evening. I would hate to do anything to void any written or implied warranty. Asserted with sarcasm and an eye roll.

Anyway, I guess this is a pretty good year. We made it clear to August, and the camp bear has just made his summer debut. I instituted all the "bear wise" strategies to prevent his visit, and camp leaders thought I would make it. However, August begins the bear "bulking up" season. He is probably also a "conditioned" bear because he is up to his same old tricks. He is an elusive old guy who has been getting away with it for years. Somehow, he keeps eluding the bear police in Lincoln County.

We discovered that bears like chocolate cake a lot. The day before yesterday, we awoke to find that he had made his debut appearance. He entered the back of the cooks' cabin by simply ripping the door off, which had been done before. We baked a couple of cakes and placed them on a covered rolling rack. While most of these racks are open, ours is a lockable, bear-proof, custom-made enclosed rack. He tried, though; there was plenty of evidence that the rack was "rolled" more than once in a failed attempt to breach the rack. Not to be outdone, he proceeded to destroy the organization of the pots and pans area before making himself at home with several loaves of bread in the pantry. He made quite a racket, as practically the entire camp heard him. I snored right through it. No surprise there.

Camp recipe #5 Triple Rolled Chocolate Mash Delight

1. Retrieve the "Rolling Rack" from the dining hall.
2. Using a spatula, scrape all the chocolate cake and icing from what is left in the cake pans and from inside the rack.
3. Place the chocolate cake and icing mixture in two large bowls.
4. Add additional chocolate chips for that "It is meant to look like that" effect and stir.
5. Place the now Chocolate/Chocolate Chip Mash in small dessert bowls. Garnish with a few more chocolate chips on the top.
6. Serve with a smile, knowing that if it is chocolate, young boys do not know the difference.

Love, Randy

Noah

I had a trainee in my trailer with me last night. He was a nice young man from California named "Noah." Noah is nineteen years old, idealistic, very opinionated, and slight in stature. At first glance, you KNEW he had never done anything like this before. Instead of bunking in the staff cabin with everyone else, and despite our bear warnings, Noah decided to "rough it" in the Montana wilderness. He brought a sleeping bag and a one-man tent. He made his campsite next to my camp trailer by the creek. I guess he wanted to hear the "Babbling Brook" while he slept.

He had hiked in from somewhere. I assume he was dropped off at the top of the Bongos, like the Scouts are. He came complete with all the latest in brand new, most advanced, contemporary, state-of-the-art, compact, super featherweight backpacking equipment for all those hikers seeking a "sustainable" life. I was quite entertained, watching him from my lawn chair under the awning of my efficiency trailer. He carefully unpacked his tent, sleeping bag, roll-out self-inflating mattress, and campfire stool out of his new fancy state-of-the-art backpack. His mess kit was next, with his aluminum cooking equipment, complete with mini pans and eating utensils, numerous packets of dehydrated food, and a water purifier to suck up the creek water. I told him he was welcome to use the thoroughly filtered running water in the kitchen—a mere ten yards from his tent. He also had a miniature fold-up shovel, flint, and a tiny little flashlight that you wind up to produce light. All of which he put into place as he removed the tags. His clothing followed as he kept pulling things out of that bottomless backpack. I was amazed. It was like watching a Bullwinkle cartoon. I was waiting for him to pull a camel out of that pack (B. Scott 1959-1964).

Once he had helped us prepare the evening meal, he turned down joining the rest of the staff, scouts, and leaders for dinner in the pavilion. Instead, he went out the back door of the cooks' cabin to the little camping abode he had so carefully set up. He set up his tiny little aluminum cook set, sucked up the creek water with his pocket water purifier, adding the water to his heated metal vessel over his cooking fire. A fire he had expertly started with his flint, even though matches were plentiful in the kitchen. He then added a packet of some sort of dehydrated food. For this, he passed up a hearty camp dinner of Lasagna, garlic bread, salad, and dessert. Hmm, this must be what "sustainable" means.

He then sat down next to the "babbling brook," carefully balancing on his super lightweight, fold-up "three-legged stool," to enjoy his first meal out in the rugged Montana Wilderness. He looked very satisfied with himself. Yes, I was spying on him.

That night, he did not hear much brook babbling as he ended up in my trailer. In the Montana Wilderness, identifying what sort of heavy creature is wandering around your tent takes little imagination. Then it let out an annoyed "huff." Freaking out, he immediately and quickly abandoned sustainable living and decided to brave my snoring and sleep on my couch. Good thing he was a small guy. As a California Touran, he did not know the first thing about wilderness camping in grizzly bear country.

Noah's second night here was when the bear ransacked the cabin and rolled the cake rack. Unbeknownst to me at the time, Noah again ended up with me on my mini couch. I slept through it all. Between my snoring and the bear noisily destroying the organization of the cooks' cabin, Noah did not sleep (again) all night.

Maybe he was freaked out from the size of our bear's footprints in the mud. After all, he is an impressive bear. Alternatively, perhaps he was unimpressed because of the violent manner in which our bear breached the kitchen. It could be that he absolutely could not take my snoring for one more night. Maybe he did not like me or how our kitchen functioned. Whatever the reason, Noah decided deep wilderness camping in the wilds of Montana was not for him. After Noah helped me put the door back onto the hinges, he packed everything into his Bullwinkle backpack and left. He did not even say goodbye; I just noticed that he, his tent, and his Bullwinkle backpack were gone. He was a strange young man. He could have abandoned his "sustainable living" ideals and bunked in with the rest of the staff. They are a great group to be around. I guess that was not within his game plan. Hopefully, he made it back all right. Earl would have gladly given him a ride back to Eureka.

A couple of weeks later, yet another animal decided to make an appearance. Only this time, it was a private showing of my own.

Dear Mom and Dad:

A few nights ago, we had a world-class thunder and lightning storm. Few things can wake me, but the clapping thunder woke me right out of my snoring slumber. It also arrived with torrential rain that fell in sheets for several hours, causing minor flooding within the camp. Just as I began to think the wind and rain would roll me and my little trailer right into the creek, it finally quit. I was able to fall asleep again sometime in the wee hours of the morning.

Much to my surprise and horror, the local mouse population decided to use my trailer as a haven from the flooding. At about 4:00 a.m., I awoke to find a little nibbler staring me down atop my blanket.

After I hurled him across the room, along with everything else in a three-foot radius, I had a little trouble finding him again. In my whirlwind, I cracked my knees on my dining table and broke my reading lamp with my head (do not ask me how). With my head and knees bloodied and shards of glass everywhere, I began my hunt for the beady-eyed little critter. There was no way I would ever fall asleep again until he was tracked down and dead!

By 5:00 a.m., I was an accomplished hunter. With my fly swatter in hand, I had successfully tracked, stalked, and finally rubbed out the little creature, using my "flush and stun" method. I felt like a distinguished sportsman after a successful hunt. Dressed only in my tighty-whities and wool socks, I had the little rat dangling by his tail in one hand and my fly swatter in the other. The only thing missing was the steaks in the freezer.

I then dressed my wounds, turned off the light, gathered my bedding, and crawled back into bed. As I reached down to pull up the covers, the dead guy's best friend scurried up my arm and over my head. Did I tell you how much I hate mice? After going through the motions again, I decided it was time to make the coffee cake and immerse myself in cooking breakfast. Maybe then I could come up with a livable solution.

That evening, I returned to the mouse motel armed with an Econo-24 pack of "Decon" and an ample supply of glue boards, mouse traps, and peanut butter. As I have said before, if there is one thing this camp is prepared for, it is rodents and bugs! By the way, thanks again for the Telfa Pads and Neosporin.

Love, Randy

That day, I began to formulate my plan as I expanded upon my initial training in the extermination of the Muridae Species, AKA mice.

Right after graduating high school, I decided to "spread my wings" and move to Billings, Montana, the city of my birth. It is where all my dad's family is from. My Aunt Pam (Dad's sister) and Uncle Frank were kind enough to host me. They housed and fed me until I could find a job and get settled. It was a safe venture into the great big world for an eighteen-year-old man with a high school diploma and no plan.

It was in Billings when my Master Sergeant training began as a stealthily schooled recognizance soldier. Aunt Pam was my First Mate as we identified the enemy, and that began our mission of "operation track and exterminate." Our preliminary training began with the exercise of baiting and placing mousetraps in Pam and Frank's garage. Unfortunately, Aunt Pam and I had no Chief of Operations. With no experience whatsoever, we were on our own in baiting mousetraps. We learned a lot, and fortunately, there were no casualties among the soldiers. The first thing I learned during my training is the importance of placing the peanut butter on the trap before you set it. This eliminates a lot of wasted time and the cost of peanut butter that ends up everywhere except on your trap. It also eliminates the anxiety produced once your uncle discovers suspicious, greasy streaks all over his vintage, classic, shiny red convertible sports car. A car he rarely drives because if you take it out of the garage, it will get dirty.

I am sure my Uncle Frank looked back upon this incident fondly. That would be the day Pam decided to back the car through the garage door. She forgot to open it, and more importantly, failed to look back before backing out.

Yep, my Aunt Pam and I learned this lesson the hard way, but we were young and inexperienced. We were successful in the end, carefully placing our trap line throughout the garage in the most assured fashion of success. One of us would check our trap line every morning, discarding carcasses as we found them. One thing is for sure, there is never just one mouse.

Billings

Billings is the largest city in the state. Montana has just over a million people, with Billings making up eleven percent of Montana's total population. At last count, Billings totaled 117,000 people. It was my first experience outside our small rural community into "The Big City."

Billings was nicknamed the "Magic City" because of its rapid growth from its founding as a railroad town in 1882. The city is named for Fredrick Billings, a former president of the Northern Pacific Railroad. Billings became one of the largest trade areas in the United States and is the trade and distribution center for much of Montana, east of the Continental Divide and Northern Wyoming. In the 1920s and 1930s, it was discovered that Eastern Montana, from Cut Bank to Shelby to Conrad, was rich in oil and natural gas, marking the first oil and gas boom in Montana. Continental Oil and Carter Oil built new refineries in Billings by the 1940s. A significant breakthrough came in 1951 when major discoveries in the Williston Basin launched one of Montana's greatest oil booms. Billings emerged as the center of the state's petroleum industry by developing oil and gas refineries in 1954. The $20.5 million Yellowstone Pipeline was completed in 1970. The pipeline would transport oil from Billings to Spokane, handling over eighty-five percent of all oil processed in the state.

In 1995, The Confederated Salish and Kootenai Tribes voted not to renew the land rights to the pipeline. The Tribes were concerned about the risk of potential spills on the reservation. The reservation, which covers much of the lower Flathead Valley in Western Montana, shut down the pipeline.

Montana's oil and gas boom has experienced many ups and downs due to a fast-changing and rapidly integrating world economy. Economic and oil demands constantly change, creating oil excesses and shortages. Worldwide productivity, conservation, and politics all influence oil production. Wild swings in output and demand then result in dramatically changing oil prices. Our government's insistence on importing Middle East oil does not help Montana or the United States oil industry.

The 2006 Montana oil boom in the Bakken area profoundly changed the economies of Eastern Montana. Newly discovered methods of fracking became an important contributor to the oil industry. Montana became a significant contributor to American oil independence. Fracking created thousands of valuable family-supporting jobs. Huge oil successes in fracking brought a subsequent fall in oil prices and made the United States oil independent. In a constantly changing political environment, fossil fuels are either a detriment or an asset, with policies changing depending on who is in charge. All is a part of oil market fluctuations that can bring uncertain futures to the oil and gas industry in Montana and the United States.

Love Mice

Dear Mom and Dad:

I have my mouse problem figured out. I have spent two hours mouse-proofing my trailer with peanut butter-baited traps everywhere. I put one each in the bathroom, under my bed, under my dining room table, in front of the door, under my couch, and inside every cabinet and every closet. I placed Decon next to every trap, just in case. Next, I lined the entire base of my bed with glue boards, and in between, more traps. Then, I sprayed the entire trailer with Raid (it couldn't hurt). With that, I confidently went to bed.

I awoke at about 1:00 a.m. to what sounded like twenty people devouring grape nuts under my bed. The mice were making short work of the Decon. I decided to investigate but forgot about my battle plan, specifically all the glue boards and traps lining the floor below my bed. In another floundering whirlwind, I discovered that glue boards double as little shower sandals. They fit very nicely on the bottom of your feet and can stay attached for hours!

On the other hand, springing those traps next to the glue boards onto my tender toes was a rude awakening! Not only that, but I also noticed that my oversized blanket had inadvertently touched the floor, picking up several more glue boards and traps. As I jumped up and down in pain, removing traps and glue boards off my feet, it was pretty evident by now that I had successfully trapped myself. Incidentally, glue boards work nicely for "Pedi Dermal Effacing," a new term and service I have discovered. I intend to market it in the future. See what you think.

Now introducing "Pedi Planks"

"The latest in Pedi Dermal Effacing techniques. Why let the dry winter months prevent you from having beautiful beach-ready feet? Be the envy of your friends as you efficiently remove all that unsightly dead skin and calluses to reveal instantly smooth, beach-ready feet in time for spring" (Laurene, Pedi-Planks 2024).

Why? Because glue boards effectively remove about six layers of skin as you rip them off the bottom of your feet! At least I now know that the Decon would eventually do its job, and my problems would soon be over. However, the box indicated that it could take up to three days to take effect. Thus, I had to look forward to two or three more endless nights with the little munchers. That's all for now from the "Mouse Motel." Love, Randy

A Beautiful Beginning and Then Chicago

My parents met in May 1958 in Billings, which began a whirlwind courtship.

My grandparents lived in a great turn-of-the-century three-story home where they raised five children, my dad being the oldest. The main level of the house had a living area, a bedroom, a kitchen with a dinette, and a formal dining area. The home's main bathroom was also on the main floor. There were no "master bathrooms" back then. The five children shared the two large bedrooms located upstairs. Pam and Nancy were in one room, and Dad, Gene, and Terry were in the other.

The five children shared a half bath, which was also located upstairs. I will always remember that bathroom with the floor-to-ceiling peacock wallpaper on all four sides of the bathroom walls. I think they were peacocks. Anyway, they were big birds completely covering the walls of that bathroom. As a small boy, they were all ominously looking at me while I tried to do my business. They all kind of scared me, so I was always quick with my missions in that room.

In the basement, there was an apartment. Before she died, that is where my great-grandmother (grandma's mom) lived. She lived there for a couple of decades after my grandparents were married. I am unsure how long she was there, but she lived there when my father was born. By 1958, she had passed away, so my grandparents were renting it out. That year, my grandparents leased it to a couple of lovely young ladies attending college in Billings. One of those young ladies was my mother. Dad was attending college at the University of Montana in Missoula when he suddenly began to make many trips back home. My grandmother's balloon burst when her children told her their oldest brother was not exactly coming to see her.

Per my father's instructions, my grandparents brought my mother with them for my father's college graduation that June. He graduated with a four-year degree in Philosophy. Mother also graduated that year with a two-year degree in teaching from Montana State College, Billings.

Following their graduation, Dad reported to Fort Benning, Georgia, to begin his six months of active duty in the military. It was all a part of his ROTC program, which paid for part of his education in exchange for military service. Mother began teaching the second grade in Billings. Hundreds of miles apart, they seriously began their whirlwind courtship in a series of letters. Dad was able to come home from Georgia in December for the Christmas holiday. They were married in Plentywood, Montana, during his leave, three days after Christmas.

After a weekend honeymoon in Wolf Point, Montana, Dad finished his enlistment time at Fort Benning in January, while Mom stayed with her mother in Plentywood. Following Fort Benning, Dad was transferred, and he and mother then moved to Colorado. He was then stationed at Fort Carson to finish up his enlistment period. The couple had decided that they would wait to have a family for a while. That did not work so well, as Joni would be born in October 1959. Kris and I spared her no amount of teasing being a honeymoon baby conceived in Wolf Point, Montana, whose history is somewhat sketchy.

The origin of the name "Wolf Point" has been challenging to verify. Some claim the name came from a winter when wolf hunters killed so many wolves that the carcasses froze before they could be skinned. Frozen carcasses are difficult to skin, so they piled them up till spring. Another theory suggests the name was derived because the land appeared to be in the shape of a wolf, or maybe it is simply because of Wolf Creek, which flows through the town. Who knows for sure, but there is undoubtedly some interesting history connected to the area. At one time, millions of bison made their way across what are now historic trails in this region. This is Montana's second-largest reservation and the home of the Assiniboine and Sioux nations (Discovering Montana).

Once Dad fulfilled his commitment to the military, he decided to go to ministerial college. He was accepted to the seminary in Chicago, Illinois, to begin that fall. It was a very hectic year for them, requiring two moves across the country while mother was pregnant, but they were very excited. They were young, in love, and ready for any adventure, which included starting a family very soon.

Their arrival in Chicago was not without its challenges. Possessing very little money, they could only afford a small one-bedroom unit in a dilapidated apartment building that would later be condemned. As all young people used to do, they made the best of it because it would be temporary. The apartment was in one of those areas of Chicago notorious for extreme violence and crime. Dad said the neighborhood they were living in was so dangerous that he could not walk anywhere. It could be attempted, but only if ten other friends accompanied him. As paranoid as Mother was, I imagine she never left the apartment, especially after Joni was born. Chicago has not changed much since 1959.

My Grandma Pearl was not the least bit impressed by it. Her daughter lived in one of the most crime-ridden states, in the worst area of Chicago. They were in an apartment building that should be leveled, and she was about to have her first baby. Dad began the seminary in late September, and Joni was born in early October. Mom had a particularly rough time during the birth process, ending up with a long series of infections that lasted weeks. Dad also became very ill, which lasted nearly the entire semester. With Dad's illness, a new baby, and Mom's infections, Grandma Pearl returned to Chicago to help. The entire family was utterly worn out. As a result of all the turmoil, the term ended with a poor showing on Dad's final grade report. No matter the challenge, Dad always soldiered through regardless of the difficulty. He never gave up on any goal and he always wanted to be a minister. He reenrolled for the next semester, which was supposed to begin on January 9, 1960.

My father's family has a strong genetic disposition toward diabetes. Dad's father was a long-term Type I diabetic. The predominating theory of today is that diabetes is an autoimmune disease. One that attacks the Islet cells in the pancreas that produce insulin. We know that autoimmune disorders, in general, are hereditary and can manifest because of stress. Dad was under a lot of pressure, trying to go to school and support a family. He also had a strong genetic predisposition to diabetes. Dad did not return to school, suddenly dropping out on January 14, 1960. The entire family immediately returned home to Billings. Our father was diagnosed as diabetic and was given a medical discharge from the service shortly after that. Our mother was done with Chicago. They were struggling to survive in a city and neighborhood that was perilous. With all their health setbacks and a new baby, she needed to be closer to family. There were simply too many obstacles for our father to pursue his ministerial dream.

Diabetes eventually destroys so many of these Islet cells that the pancreas loses the ability to produce insulin. Insulin is a hormone that plays a vital role in the healthy functioning of metabolism. It helps cells in the body absorb glucose (sugar) from your blood, converting it to energy. When you lose the ability to produce insulin, you can no longer regulate your glucose levels, and sugar accumulates in the bloodstream. Dad would be the first child in his family to be diagnosed, with three of his four siblings eventually diagnosed as well.

Glucose is a huge molecule larger than blood molecule components—high glucose concentrations in the bloodstream damage arteries and veins. Over time, this damage causes dangerous narrowing occlusions, and eventually, blockages preventing essential blood flow. Tiny capillaries of internal organs and the extremities are especially affected by blockages. This is why glucose control is so important for diabetics.

Always optimistic, Dad said that even though his dream of becoming a minister was over, he still had a valuable four-year bachelor's degree that meant something. I was born while we were living in Billings. For a brief time, we lived in the same town as my father's family. Being surrounded by grandparents, aunts, uncles, and cousins was a blessing.

Being closer to family was good, but my father needed a career-building, family-wage job. My father became employed by Saga Food Service in 1962, which began a long series of moves across the country. Saga never allowed any of their food service directors to stay in one place for very long. That period is vague to me. As children, we just went with the flow. Our last transfer was to Santa Cruz, California. It was then that my little sister, Kristi, was born. I remember little about our time in California, so I rely on family folklore during that era. Incidentally, Saga later became Chartwell, whom I work for now and who has contracted my services here at Camp Silverback. I do not believe in coincidences, but I do believe in destiny.

The First Mouse Motel

Shortly after our move to Santa Cruz, Dad brought home two gerbils from a pet store. The gerbils came complete with a cage, gerbil accessories, and gerbil food. It would become our parent's strategy to teach the children about the responsibility of having pets. I could not have been more than a toddler and Joni was around four. Our gerbil saga occurred "BK" (Before Kristi).

Per the pet store, both rodents were female, a statement proven to be incorrect in a very short period. Soon after purchase, we had gerbil babies. I am sure it was not in the game plan, but this fun little surprise taught four-year-old Joni a little lesson in reproduction. Dad was then anointed as the gerbil gender identifier. It seemed simple enough. Identify males from females, separate them, and put them into separate cages, thus eliminating any additional gerbil surprises. Too cheap to buy more cages, he decided to build two more cages himself, one for each sex. About two months later, we were proud gerbil owners of three more litters of little gerbil delights. At that point, the gerbil production moved to the garage.

Dad's gerbil gendering experiment remained elusive. I guess it must be hard to tell the little buggers apart. Unbeknownst to Dad at the time, he would now be described as "heterosexist" in his "heteronormative" gendering determination of our gerbil gender non-conformers. He empathized a little more with the pet store now (Laurene, Gerbil Gender Heterosexist 2024).

In the process, nature took its course when our gerbil gender non-conformers, geogendered beyond our control, exponentially exploding in population. This resulted in an entire wall of our single-car garage covered in a menagerie of gerbil cages. All the cages still contained numerous gerbil litters of various ages and stages of growth. Dad would come home every day after work and build more cages. In the end, there had to be close to twenty-five cages lining that garage wall. Joni and I had long ago lost interest. All Mother could do was shake her head in amusement. Mother did that a lot.

Suddenly, one day, wholly and mysteriously, all "2,000" of our gerbil gender non-conformers disappeared. Previously disinterested in Dad's gerbil production Joni was the first to notice, although that took a couple of weeks. She then inquired what became of all our little gerbil friends. Dad exclaimed that someone had left the doors open, and they all scurried out to freedom. Joni contemplated this explanation for a while. Then asked, how could somebody "accidentally" leave all twenty-five cage doors open simultaneously? Even at four years of age, Joni was a thinker. Dad quickly came up with a plausible answer. Well, he said, "All those cages had little openings that connected all of them. Only one door was accidentally left open, and they all escaped together."

That was good enough for Joni, as she skipped outside again to play. However, even at four years of age, she remembered that story throughout her life. Joni never forgets anything. She would periodically ridicule Dad for that feeble story throughout the years. Mom and Dad never did fess up as to the actual circumstances surrounding the "Great Gerbil Escape," but I suspect he loaded them all up and turned them loose in some other gerbil-geogendered communal jurisdiction. Los Angeles County would later identify an uncontrolled growing gerbil infestation of catastrophic significance, which they identified as:

"The Great Gerbil Invasion of Los Angeles County"

This, in turn, resulted in a "Gerbil Invasion Task Force," which ordered a "Gerbil Comprehensive Study," after which the "Gerbil Support Commission" was formed. They then assembled local experts to tackle and study the Gerbil Invasion that had taken over Los Angeles County.

The "Gerbil Invasion Task Force," then commissioned the newly formed "California Department of Gerbil Population Management," to study the issue. Following this, "The California Department of Gerbil Population Management," then directed the "Gerbil Support Commission," to write a $90 million government grant to study further the issue of the

"Propagation and Dissemination of the Pachyuromys duprasi species" (gerbil) and its effects on climate change, AKA global warming.

"The Gerbil Support Commission" then formed and hired the "Gerbil Council of Environmental Impacts" to write the Grant. Five years later, it was determined that the Pachyuromys dupraisi species (gerbil) was an endangered species.

Finally, "The California Department of Gerbil Population Management" was advised by the "Gerbil Council of Environmental Impacts" to proclaim that California, in its entirety, is now declared a "Gerbil Sanctuary State" due to the critical species diversity that Gerbils provide. However, it was later determined that prioritizing the Pachyuromys dupraisi (gerbil) species would be inequitable and discriminatory within the rodent genome. Therefore, any capture, imprisonment, transfer, or killing of any rodent is punishable by law, resulting in a minimum ten-year prison sentence and a one million dollar fine.

California then placed all rodents within California's endangered species categorization of "vertebrates." Thus, all rodents can now be classified as fish. This then makes all rodents automatically eligible for federal endangered species protection. This classification strategy is most fortunate because it cuts all that red tape in seeking special protections from the federal government, which is forced to consider all those arguments from ignorant flyover states who know nothing about the environment (Sottile 2022) (Laurene, The Great Gerbil Invasion of Los Angeles County 2024).

As a result, all plowing has been terminated throughout California to protect and support the ever-growing rodent population because, in California, there can never be enough vermin. California lawmakers are excited to implement this groundbreaking strategy.

In a forward-thinking strategy, "The California Department of Gerbil Population Management" has instructed the "Gerbil Support Commission," now re-named "Vermin Support Commission of Sanctuary Populations," to study, devise, and implement alternatives to house the vermin in places other than open farmland.

It was quickly noted that the name "Vermin" has a negative and potentially racist connotation, so the Governor, in a sweeping executive order, renamed it "The Vagrant Support Commission of Sanctuary Populations." This groundbreaking program could be the model for similar scopes across the United States. It is a monumental shift in California's priorities that is as exciting as the highly anticipated next episode of the blockbuster tell-all series of California's most beloved vagrants, "Harry Loves Meghan" (Vanderhoof 2020) (Laurene, The Vagrant Support Commission of Sanctuary Populations 2024).

The total cost for the project is $1.5 trillion, a cost that California cannot afford, so California applied to the federal government for assistance with the project. The president signed an Executive Order to grant California the money in its entirety because, after all, they are a sanctuary for all vagrant populations across the globe.

Rodent Woes

Frankly, it was shocking that Dad even brought home the little rodents in the first place. He was at war and fought daily with the gopher population that had taken up residency in our front and back yards. Like locusts, there were swarms of the little squatters. They invaded our yard with ugly baseball-sized gopher holes they called their new home. They ate everything in their wake as Dad's ornamental shrubs and plants were devoured on our dime.

One day, in a fit of frustration and a last-ditch effort to drown out the little vagrants, he gathered up our only garden hose. He then shoved it down the largest gopher hole in the yard. After much study, he determined it had to be the main intersection of the gopher complex that continually multiplied in our yard. Once satisfied that he had reached nirvana or the epicenter of the complex, he turned on the water full blast. He was quite pleased with himself as the water eventually began seeping out of each hole in the yard. He let the water run for a good thirty minutes. He then turned off the water and triumphantly began to pull the hose back out.

Sadly, with a yard mostly comprised of sand, there was no infrastructure to support the excess moisture, causing the ground to collapse. Ultimately, we lost our only garden hose, again costing our family to replace an essential tool in our arsenal of yard and garden care. However, vermin can survive under any circumstances, as our gopher invaders defeated our father again. They continue to thrive to this day.

Tumblers and Squirrel Cages

Kristi was born in Santa Cruz in December of 1966. Not long after her arrival, Dad's next transfer with Saga Food Services was to San Francisco. Understandably, Mom and Dad did NOT want to live any longer in California, and they especially did not want to raise their children in San Francisco. Indeed, it was a clairvoyant decision if I ever saw one. It was time to move on from Saga and our continual "saga" of enumerable transfers. He applied for and received a job offer as a college food services director, which he immediately accepted. This job offered a permanent placement in a small rural community, in an atmosphere much friendlier for raising a family. Our family left California for La Grande, Oregon, where Dad would start his new job at Eastern Oregon College. We would never have to be transferred again, especially anywhere in California.

A few years after moving to La Grande, when I was about eight, Mom and Dad acquiesced to my request for a small pet to keep in my bedroom. Our parents always did their best to support their children's interests, so what does he do? He brings home a pair of gerbils. This pet store knew what they were doing and "gendered" the little rodents correctly this time, so reproduction was not a problem. However, there were times when my father did the most curious things.

At the same time, Dad and I began a new hobby together. Being a rockhound, I always sought and collected rocks and stones of all sizes. Usually, I found these beauties in rivers and streams at our campsites. Abound with color while wet, they became different shades of gray once I brought them home. My bedroom was covered with many different hues of gray-colored rocks and stones. I proudly displayed them on every flat surface I could find. Dad even made shelving to add more display areas for my important collection.

One day, Dad brought home a handy dandy rock tumbler and polisher. We spent several hours reading the directions and gathering my favorite stones to experiment with. It takes WEEKS before rock tumblers turn out beautiful, polished stones. The process involves a motorized round tumbler, like a cement mixer. It tumbles the small stones constantly in water and polishing grit. The machine stays plugged in 24-7. All day and all night, all it does is grind, grind, grind, and grind some more. Since it was set up in my bedroom, it kept me up all night.

Concurrently, the gerbils also kept in my room never slept. Between the grind, grind, grinding of the tumbler, there was also the squeak, squeak, squeaking of the squirrel cage. The gerbils played all night long. Humans could learn from that activity. I don't think there is any such thing as an obese gerbil. Dad had to move both hobbies to the guest bathroom downstairs so that I could sleep during the night.

I came home from school one day, stunned and horrified to find one of my cute little gerbils had my other cute little gerbil half devoured. It seems one of my gerbils was a carnivore! Mom did her best that day, explaining that our cat must have reached into the cage. She tried, but I was old enough to dismiss that as even remotely possible. I knew what happened. One of my gerbils finally cracked under the pressure of the grind, grind, grinding noise of that tumbler. Gerbils are excellent test subjects of what can occur when faced with near constant, totally irrational, vacuous, brainless, mind-numbing, chaotic, and illogical noise emitting from others around them—from whence one cannot escape. It is the gerbil's answer to banging their head against a wall. At any rate, after a lot of therapy that cost millions of dollars and thousands of lives, I am certain that this experience was the epicenter for my "musophobia," otherwise known as rodent phobia.

My New Title

Dear Mom and Dad:

Following our inspection and big corporate meeting, scouting powers decided that our funky relay phone was inadequate and unreliable should the camp need to communicate an emergency. My office is now officially "The Camp Silverback Communications Center." We are all set up now for emergency transmission via shortwave radio. All messages are sent to the 911 center in Eureka, which can pick up all our communications should we need to send any. Once an emergency call is transmitted, a helicopter could land in the sporting field for an emergency trauma evacuation. Perhaps even a "larger" adult with very broad shoulders should he suffer a massive heart attack while foolishly trying to hike up the Bongos.

It makes one feel more comfortable having a fail-safe strategy for emergencies. I was happy to give up my office for this vital addition to our camp. Fortunately for Camp Silverback, I also possess a unique resume feature. Thanks to you, Dad - I am specially trained, with the unique capability to speak into such a device properly. They were all so impressed around here that I could talk in "radio speak." Which, as you know, is a skill that requires the proper phraseology and speech cadence necessary for conversing on shortwave radio. This allowed me to be appointed as the "Chief Operational Advisor and Emergency Communication Dispatcher" of Camp Silverback. Nope, it did not come with a pay raise, Mom.

More later, Me

The Wastebasket

Once we purchased our shiny, brand new, bright red, base model pickup truck, Dad began another new hobby. "The Wastebasket" was Dad's call sign for his brand new CB radio, which he placed in the empty radio slot in his base model truck. He convinced Mother that such a device was essential camping equipment, like sleeping bags. This was in case he needed to radio for help should we have an emergency while camping in some rugged campsite "deep in the Oregon wilderness." Dad was good because our campsites came complete with toilets and sometimes showers. I am not sure that describes "deep in the wilderness." It was not hard to convince Mom with that argument. As I have said, she is the most paranoid person on the planet.

Dad played it well. It didn't take long for Dad to plunge into the airway abyss and the mysterious world of Citizen Band Radios. It was Dad's newfound hobby involving a large community of followers. All were the original groundbreakers of social media long before there was anything such as the Internet or Facebook. Unlike today's social media, CB radio hobbyists have one very important character feature unlike anything we see today on social media: They are polite and respectful.

Dad installed his brand-new CB radio into the radio slot himself—quite an accomplishment for our father since he knows nothing about electronics. As we headed out to one of our numerous favorite campsites each weekend, he and Mom listened to the numerous CB'ers endlessly conversing over the airwaves. Dad was fascinated by this new gadget and concept. Maybe he was enthralled, but I am sure Mom was reading a book during the drive.

As this new hobby evolved, we eventually found Dad sitting in the truck for hours every evening after dinner. He would steal outside to his truck, listening to the endless jargon emitting from that little box. Feverishly taking notes, he learned all the radio slang necessary to speak to the CB community coherently. It fell into a philosophy always embraced by our parents passed down from a long line of higher education pursuits. To properly function within the community in which one is engaged, one must continually be educated. It did not necessarily mean a four-year college degree, but it did include skills training. Whether you taught those skills to yourself or through apprentice work, everyone must strive to educate themselves to function in society. Our paternal great-grandmother even graduated from college at a time when women were forbidden to do so unless they were to become nurses. She graduated from the Minneapolis Academy on June 1st, 1900, with a degree in "Literary," which today is the study of Literature.

As a curious ten-year-old boy who was Gerbil-less and tired of his tumbler, I eventually joined him in the truck. Dad began to teach me all about the official language necessary for proper CB speak. Rain, sleet, snow, or freezing temperatures did not matter. Remember, our dad was nothing but "thrifty," so turning on that truck for some heat did not happen. Despite the temperatures, Dad and I spent hours inside that truck in the dark, silently bonding with our new airwave friends. Through the weeks, I too began to learn the intricacies of radio speak. Once we knew the language, Dad and I ventured into the chasm of the mysterious culture of short-wave radio. As we joined in with our new CB'er friends, I was knighted "The Wastebasket Junior." Dad was such an originalist.

What happened next, one can only speculate. Suddenly, Dad purchased, on the cheap (thrifty), a very used short-wave radio, which he installed in their master bedroom. Of course, one does not just acquire a short wave or "ham" radio. You need to purchase a receiver and a transmitter. There are antennas to put up, permits, and licenses to apply for and buy. Registration and payment for call names and the list goes on and on. The radio was the cheap part. It was like Dad making good on a three-year promise to Joni, when he bought her a horse. He always said that buying that horse was the cheap part.

The Horse Saga

Joni became very interested in horses at a young age. At the time, her best friend lived on the outskirts of La Grande. She and her family lived on a twenty-five-acre apple orchard and farm. They had two ponies—a dapple-gray Welsh pony and a chestnut and white pinto pony. The girls rode out on the farm nearly every day in the summer.

Joni was nine years old when Dad promised to buy her a horse when she turned twelve. Confident, of course, that Joni would be more interested in other things than a horse by that time. He was wrong because on Dad's birthday in October, just after Joni's twelfth birthday, she gave him a nine-inch tall, plastic elephant statue. An elephant statue was her way of reminding him that elephants never forget when they promise their daughters a horse. Dad was doomed! In the spring following her birthday, she got her horse, a dark bay Quarter Horse gelding named "Smokey." Within the horse world, he was considered full of chrome. He had a black mane and tail, four white socks, and a blaze. He was very flashy.

Trying to understand equine ownership, Dad would often ask Joni, "If the horse is only one-quarter horse, what were the other three-quarters of the animal?" That constant thread of inquiry drove her crazy, but that was always something that Dad strived for with his children.

Following the horse purchase, they went to the tack store and bought numerous horse-owning accouterments. Dad soon discovered that, like his short-wave radio, buying that horse was only the beginning. It was more than just tack, vaccines, and safety gear; there was also the feed. Then there were the horseshoes and somebody to put them on called a "farrier." Dad soon discovered this is not merely a one-time function or even a once-a-year activity. Horses need shoes a lot more often than people do. Horseshoes and farrier fees were another added expense to the horse tally sheet. Sister Kris should have been thankful. Kris became an athlete, so this experience prepared Dad for all of Kris' numerous "sports ball" and running activities in junior high and high school. Brand new expensive athletic shoes are required for every sport, every year, which at last count was at least sixteen. Horseshoes were merely a preparation for all of Kris' athletic shoes.

We lived in a middle-class suburban neighborhood, and I am sure the neighbors would have complained about a horse kept in our backyard. So next, they ventured to Ode and Barbara's house to negotiate a pasture to rent. They had since moved from town to a small acreage on the outskirts of La Grande. They had about twenty fenced acres. It was a free pasture because Barbara and Ode were kind. Alternatively, maybe they felt sorry for my parents for taking on a horse venture they knew nothing about. At any rate, the fence needed some work, but with some repair, it would work nicely to keep Joni's new horse corralled. Back to the feed store to buy fence repair tools and fencing.

The problem was that the pasture had plenty of summer graze, but as all horse owners know in the west, grazing is impossible in the winter months. The pasture area also did not have a suitable place for dry hay storage. Upon further research, Dad discovered that hay molds and rots if kept out in the weather. They then headed back to the feed store to order three tons of hay to be delivered to the carport of our suburban home. Come October, Dad, Joni, and Mom stacked those bales into one side of our two-car carport. They were careful not to infringe on Mother's side of the carport. Dad now had to park in the driveway during the winter. Our middle-class suburban home was now a hay barn. Every day after Dad got off work, he and Joni would load a bale of hay into the back of the family station wagon (with fake wood panels). He would then tie our snow sled to the top of the car and drive across town to Ode and Barbara's pasture. This chore always commenced after work around 6:00 p.m., so it was always dark when they arrived at the pasture.

The family station wagon, with its two-ply highway tires, could not make it up the snowy, slippery, and steep hill. Frankly, I cannot remember how we got around in the winter. Dad had to park the car at the bottom of the hill and put that bale of hay on that sled. Whether it was twenty below or twenty above zero, even in blizzard conditions, they would untie that sled from the top of the car and then load that hay onto that sled. In the beam of the car's headlights, Dad would pull while Joni pushed. Even in deep snow, they somehow maneuvered that sled and seventy-five-pound bale up that hill about thirty yards to the pasture and the horse. Once finished, they would walk carefully down the slippery hill, tie that sled back on top of the car, and then drive back home.

Caring for livestock was a tough lesson, especially when you do not have a farm. Regardless of weather conditions, that horse needed to be fed daily. Our father had the patience of Job. Dad had meetings out of town once a month. Therefore, Mom would assist with hay duty while

Dad was out of town. I am sure our mother, not being the farming type at all, was just thrilled about that little chore.

It seems that it would have been far easier to have kept that hay up by the pasture. Thanks to Ranger Hugh and his regulations, he could have repurposed that brown latrine tarp we no longer used. Dad could have waited warm and cozy in the heated car at the bottom of the hill while drinking a warm beverage. He could have sent Joni up that hill with a flashlight to feed her own horse. Our family thrived on doing things the hard way.

Winter horse care at a rented pasture had one other predicament. Horses need a constant supply of freshwater. Every night, Joni and Dad (or Mom) would have to break the ice in the trough and then drag a hose out from the house to re-fill the trough. Critical in keeping the hose flowing in freezing temperatures, the hose required draining. Once they finished refilling the water trough, they laid it out on the icy, snowy ground, strategically going downhill. Thus, allowing gravity to complete the goal. Once drained, it could be rolled up and stored next to the water spigot. Do you know how difficult it is to unroll and roll back up a one-hundred-foot frozen polyurethane hose?

La Grande was full of urban deer, and deer love free hay. We would wake up every morning to the mess the deer left in our carport. They were exceptionally skilled in breaking open more bales than they intended to eat. Dad figured we fed the deer at least a ton of hay each winter. It was probably why we did not store the hay at the pasture. Chicken wire and two-by-four lumber were the answer in a feeble attempt to obstruct the deer from entering our open carport. This strategy failed miserably, and I bet the neighbors loved that look. Back to the feed store to order another ton of hay to be delivered to our suburban hay barn to make it through the winter.

The Neighborhood Blemish

Dad and I are in the short-wave radio business now. We had our fancy radio, plus all the creature comforts inside the house. We had lights, and we had heat in the winter. I suspect Mom finally put her foot down, declaring that the boys of the family would no longer hang out in the truck all evening. It all worked out because now we could quickly run to the kitchen to make a snack, and Dad's bathroom was a mere ten feet from our communication center. Dad's bathroom was technically the master bathroom but only had a small sink, commode, and shower. Since mother preferred bathing, she shared our bathroom since it contained the only bathtub in the house.

Dad decorated "his" bathroom with true class and savoir-faire. He painted it with bold neon-colored stripes of yellow and red. Broad stripes that were about twelve inches wide. EOC's sports teams were called "The Mountaineers." So, to top off his classy, snazzily colored bathroom, he bought a gold and navy-blue toilet seat with "Go Mounties" on the underside of the toilet lid. Yep, it was an oddly styled master bathroom, but as boys, we thought it was all part of a cool setup for our communication center.

Mother thoughtfully decorated my parents' bedroom. Like all 1970s homes, it had gold shag carpet and gold-colored drapery. They had a matching vintage bedroom set with a maple-colored stained headboard and footboard, an upright dresser, and a mirrored vanity with a bench. It had a stylish matching bedspread, a bed skirt, and pillow shams. I guess our mother would rather give up the sanctity of their bedroom than have the boys hang out in the truck during family time. So, in their lovely bedroom, Dad set up our communication center. He found a piece of plywood and cement blocks to fancy a "rustic" desk for our short-wave radio. He positioned his fancy plywood desk right underneath one of two windows in their bedroom. Out that window came the 55-foot antenna eyesore that was the heart of our shortwave radio system. He then used duct tape around the antenna and the window to seal the window crack from the weather. With that, our antenna reached out the duct-taped window and gloriously into the sky from our short-wave radio.

I thought it was very uptown Saturday night. I am sure it drove our mother nuts, but it was a small sacrifice to her. After all, she had the family all under one roof again. Besides, our mother learned long ago that this phase would soon pass. She had come to realize that over time, our family phases came and went. She knew the ensuing mess and inconveniences would eventually disappear. She also possessed an abundant amount of patience.

We had to be the center of neighborhood blight, with a curious antenna eyesore protruding from their bedroom window on the top floor of our upper-middle-class, three-split-level home, which doubled as a hay barn. Emerging from our "hay barn" came a chic six-foot-tall deer fence Macgyvered with two-by-fours, chicken wire, and baling twine.

Ready, Set, Hunt!

Grouse hunting season begins September 1st in Montana. Camp Silverback was able to receive a special Fish and Game permit. One for a youth hunt specific to our camp, starting mid-August. The boys are beyond ecstatic. This group will get to use their sharpshooting and gun safety skills on an actual hunting target. The kitchen staff has been instructed to prepare dinner, using the successes of the hunt. However, we were also directed to prepare an alternative plan should the quarry be more elusive than anticipated. Our family was not a hunting family, so the preparation and cooking of game birds is something I have yet to experience. My experience with poultry is limited to domestic varieties. I have heard that the two are not interchangeable, and most importantly, wild game birds do not come to you plucked, cleaned, cut, and packaged.

I am thinking (hoping, actually) that this will be a nice day in the woods for the boys that will yield little in actual game birds. After all, I understand you need bird dogs to be even remotely successful in this activity. Well, guess what showed up? Thanks again to Earl and his connections; about two dozen local bird hunting-type dogs and their owners arrived to provide our young scouts with a full-on bird hunting experience. This now does not bode well for my alternative dish of Macaroni and Cheese, which I was sure I would be serving tonight.

The dogs came in all varieties of hunting species. Retrievers and pointers, but I particularly noticed the spaniel breeds. I am partial to Spaniels, as our family had been English Springer Spaniel enthusiasts for years. Our spaniels were a family journey in the breeding and showing of champion show dogs. The journey began when Joni and Kris were in dog 4-H. Joni started at thirteen and Kris would follow when she turned eight.

4-H was a popular youth club in many rural communities in the West. It was the counterpart of Future Farmers of America (FFA) for high school students among agricultural families. There was something for everybody. 4-H groups ranged from sewing and cooking to arts and crafts. There were pigs, cows, horses, chickens, rabbits, goats, and sheep. It all culminated at county fairs nationwide, where youth would show off the best of their effort throughout the year. For many rural youth, it was the event of the year that occurred every July.

Joni's best horseback riding pal was active in the local dog 4-H group. Her mom was the leader. So, in between horse care and riding, Joni became quite involved with "The Blue Mountain K-9s" dog 4-H club. Joni began this saga of training and showing dogs with our Samoyed and beloved family pet named "Ajax." Ajax came to us when Uncle Terry joined us while attending college. Terry's best friend at the time had a nice, family-friendly dog he could no longer keep. Ajax would be our first real family pet, which toddler Kristi called "The Airjax."

The beauty of 4-H is that it involves the child and the entire family. It is a child-centered club that includes parent volunteers to keep it going. Therefore, our family became quite involved in Dog 4-H. Our charismatic leader, who loved dogs and children, successfully built the group to the point that she recruited an assistant leader. The group's co-leader was also a breeder of champion English Springer Spaniels. She happened to have a male puppy available for sale. After two years, Joni had taken Ajax as far as she could in obedience, so "KC" ultimately became Joni's new 4-H project and show dog. KC also had the honorable distinction of becoming our foundation stud dog for the next twelve years.

Incidentally, this came about as a deal finally struck between Dad and Joni. To Dad's relief, he crafted a plan where Joni gave up her horse, which continually siphoned money from the family finances. She traded that horse for KC, dog shows, and a Springer Spaniel breeding program. Our family hobby kennel was launched, raising black and white, bench-style English Springer Spaniels. It ultimately led us down a new path and history for our family.

Dad and I became more involved with the show dog hobby, abandoning the ham radio phase. Our suburban barnyard and six-foot deer fence were gone from our driveway, as was the fifty-five-foot antenna. Dad got his parking space back in the carport, and Mother's car was no longer the hay wagon. The cement blocks and the plywood panel were placed back in the garage, and the piles of duct tape were removed from the window. Mom finally got her bedroom back.

At the beginning of our family kennel hobby, I wanted to be different. To that end, I acquired a black and white, Tri-colored Shetland Sheepdog. She was beautiful. Primarily black and white, with brown tips above her eyebrows. She was about two years old, already housebroken and trained. There was just one problem. Shelties are herding dogs, and she was convinced that Dad needed to be contained. From the time Dad got out of bed, prepared himself for work, and then left for work, that Sheltie was circling Dad. She would patiently wait all day for him next to the door. Once he arrived home, she would circle him again, around and around as he walked through the house. If he became too wayward, she would bark at him to bring him in line. When he sat down, she would sit next to him, waiting and staring at him in anticipation of his next move. When he would get up, she would circle him again, repeatedly, as he walked through the house.

This compulsive herding pursuit only occurred with Dad. If he were in the bathroom, she would sit and wait outside the door. She would be right at his feet as he sat down for dinner. What became clear was that Sheltie needed a job, and Dad didn't want to be it. We gave her away to a farm with a lot of kids.

Meanwhile, following KC, Missy came from Canada and became Kris' dog and our foundation female in our breeding program. Eventually, I would acquire "Muffy," the progeny of our first litter. I guess I really liked that name. I was the one who named our cat "Muffin."

You do not own elite bench-style breeding and show springers without traveling to dog shows. We would all load up and travel throughout the Pacific and Rocky Mountain West, hitting every bench show we could. We were all gone at least one weekend a month, traveling to as many shows as we could during the spring through fall months.

To complete the family hobby kennel experience, Dad set out to build a large kennel in our backyard. He built it next to and connected it to our storage shed. He removed all the yard care implements inside that shed and moved them to our carport. Next, he enclosed an area inside the shed for an indoor dog run, plus a location to store dog food. He then built out one large outdoor kennel run that ran down the entire length of our wooden back fence. Finally, he cut a hole through the side of our storage shed to connect the outdoor and indoor runs. Our dogs then had a comfortable, dry place to get in and out of the weather.

A kennel is only complete with a cement floor, making it easier to clean and escape-proof. The area inside the shed was already cement, so we set forth to complete the outside run with a cement pad. Dad was NOT skilled in fabricating cement floors, but he was an excellent researcher. Somehow, he managed to do what was necessary to construct the footings for a concrete pad.

A cement truck could not get into our backyard, so with three wheelbarrows in tow (two of them borrowed), Dad, Mom, and Joni wheeled cement by hand. For the next eight hours, they wheeled cement from the cement truck in the driveway, through the garage, and across the backyard to the kennel area, located against the back fence. Wheelbarrow by wheelbarrow, they dumped that cement into the area that Dad had expertly prepared with wooden forms.

It was a long day of loading, wheeling, spreading, troweling, and smoothing. I have no idea how many yards of cement they wheeled in to cover a ten-by-thirty area with a six-inch cement slab. It was a long, arduous day. Thank God Kris and I were too young to participate in that project! Being young, small, and weak certainly had its perks that day. However, I am sure our mother never spent a more miserable day and evening than she did that day. Our mother has never been the manual labor type. I will bet she remembered fondly her hay-stacking days of yesteryear.

We quickly discovered that keeping KC separate during the twice-a-year breeding season was next to impossible, especially with two female dogs. Our kennel was built with only one large kennel run, necessitating us to bring Missy and Muffy into the house during their heat seasons. KC was never compliant with his rule of staying within his own borders. KC was a stealth master in cross-border transits that duped even the most carefully engineered border fences and deterrents. For KC, where there is a will, there had to be a way, and KC was quite the escape artist.

Since the kennel had a cement floor, he could not dig out but could surely jump. From a standing position, KC could jump about four feet. He should have been the assistant coach for the pole vaulting and long jumping team for La Grande High School. From there, he would grab onto the wire at the front of the kennel and then easily scale the wire mesh. Once he reached the top, it was an effortless leap to the lawn on the other side. Being the thrifty father that Dad was, instead of investing in higher, more secure fencing, Dad kept adding new sections to the top of the fence. However, nothing stopped KC from scaling that fence. They do not call them "Springers" for nothing.

Once again, Dad did what he does best. We had a beautiful backyard with a manicured lawn, flower beds with ornamental shrubs, and a huge Bing Cherry tree. The back of the yard was complete, with a scabbed-together wire fencing pieced with wire, bailing twine, and the two-by-fours repurposed from the deer fence. It was a fruitless attempt to keep KC within his borders. Each time Dad added fencing, it just added to KC's desire to meet another challenge—a challenge he always conquered. Fortunately for our neighbors, this monstrosity was in our backyard, so they did not have to look at it. What was humorous was that KC never went anywhere once he escaped the kennel. He would show up at our sliding glass door, wagging his silly tail. It seemed as if he was telling Dad, "Gotcha again."

I remember one evening, arriving home with Mom. It was late after she had collected all three of us following our various after-school activities. At that point, we added two more breeding females, one of whom had fourteen puppies inside the house. It was the last straw when Dad counted sixteen total dogs being kept in the house at one time. New puppies were birthed and kept in the laundry room on the lower level of our split-level home. The adult dogs always did fine while we were at school and working all day. However, the puppy area had not been cleaned for at least eight hours. Dad had been home, but the only sign of him being there was this simple note, *"I am at the Elks Club. Call me when the house smells normal."*

It was time for a new plan, so we moved! Our new home was on the outskirts of La Grande, on a quarter-acre of land. Dad always wanted to be a "gentleman farmer," but it was also an opportunity to build a real professional kennel complex. By the time we moved to our small acreage, our little hobby kennel possessed KC and four breeding females. By then, Ajax was an elderly, beloved member of our family who primarily lived in the house.

It was time to move the dog breeding hobby out of the house, which meant expanding our kennel operation to an outdoor facility. However, it was a bit more complex than adding additional gerbil cages onto the garage wall. Fortunately for us, Dad stepped back and hired out the project this time. Four dog runs separated by eight-foot-tall chain-link fencing between them, complete with cement floors done by an actual contractor. The top of the kennel runs was finished with a chain link roof.

The four outside kennel runs then came into our unattached oversized two-car garage. The indoor runs lined the backside of our garage, complete with five-foot-tall, roofed, chain link fencing with gates. We even had water access in the garage, next to where the dog food was stored. Dad designed it well, and it was a far cry from the long-ago gerbil sanctuary. He learned a thing or two from the gerbil experience.

The four-run outdoor kennel complex was encircled with an additional eight-foot-tall chain link fence. An eight-foot-tall gate accessed this perimeter fence. This way, we could easily enter the outside graveled perimeter kennel area to access each dog run, each with their own gates. I am surprised Dad did not top the perimeter fence with razor wire. Dad was finally victorious. KC never escaped again. The outside graveled kennel perimeter also had a hydrant installed. This way, one could easily wash off the concrete with a hose after shoveling out the kennels. It was all very cool and complimented, rather than detracted, from our home and yard. All the dogs, including females with puppies, could be kept outside in a secure kennel with confidence instead of in the house.

As we got older and more involved with our dogs, we were not camping anymore. Dad then sold the truck and camper and traded it all in for a brand new six-seat Chevy Van with a cargo hold in the back. This way, Dad could haul all of us, our dogs, and our dog showing paraphernalia to the various dog show venues across the West. Our dogs easily rode in the back of the van in stacked dog crates. There was still plenty of room for a grooming table and other supplies. We stayed in hotels half the time, but most shows were close enough to drive home each evening. When we traveled to Montana for shows, it was a fabulous opportunity to stay and visit with our various family members throughout the state. Mother had a great time. We had traded in our cramped camp quarters for nice hotels, and she was free of our suburban farm.

It was a fun family hobby at the time. All of us were engaged in one aspect or another. Joni was the program's chief groomer, breeder, and technical dog show advisor. Kris and I were active in training and showing. Mom and Dad guided and contained the process. It became another opportunity to grow and learn together as a family, where the doggie population did not suddenly disappear in the dark of night.

Head Chef and Grouse Connoisseur

Our young boys' grouse hunting experience was wildly successful, thanks to our new grouse hunting buddies and their expert hunting dogs. So, with their instruction, my staff and I prepared:

Camp Recipe #6 Camp Silverback Roasted Grouse

1. Freeze fully prepared trays of Macaroni and Cheese
2. Gather about 230 freshly harvested whole grouse, complete with feathers.
3. "Field Dress" each bird. (a new concept and skill for me). It involves slicing the bird down the middle of the sternum and then removing the innards. Frankly, I prefer to receive my poultry cleaned and packaged, but you need to be open to new things in life. Besides, you gain new skills this way.
4. Pluck each bird briskly. Pick out all the buckshot.
5. Apply nose plugs.
6. Remove any errant feathers and down with an industrial blow torch borrowed from the maintenance shop. Be very careful not to light the entire bird on fire.
7. Per my new grouse hunting buddies, save each bird's heart, liver, and gizzard.
8. Cut off the head and the feet. It is OK to discard these items if you do not intend to make soup. I threw them away.
9. Cut the entire bird in half to get two flat halves. It is now safe to remove the nose plugs.
10. Place the bird halves into numerous oversized roasting pans.
11. Melt about ten pounds of smashed butter. Add seasoning salt, pepper, dried thyme, and powdered rosemary. Pour liberally over the top of the birds. Place birds and roasting pans into a hot five-hundred-degree oven. Brown for ten minutes.
12. Remove from the oven, reduce the heat to 250 degrees, and add chicken broth to each roasting pan.
13. Roast for about three hours, basting the birds occasionally.

14. In several large commercial-size cast iron skillets, fry your saved entrails in oil and butter. Add the above-listed seasonings. Cook until tender and browned.
15. Remove skillets from the burners, allowing the fried giblet components to cool.
16. Once cool, place "the components" and the rest of the pan contents in blenders and buzz until a smooth paste forms. Set aside and keep warm.

IMPORTANT NOTE: It is best to keep steps 13-16 private from the scouts and staff.

Meanwhile, heat the flat tops. Previously, you will have already baked two hundred pounds of battered and beaten potatoes till done. Cube the cooked potatoes, leaving the skins on to hide any bruising and scarring. Peel and dice approximately ten pounds of yellow onions. Once the flat tops are heated, melt two pounds of smashed butter and add olive oil to the flat top. Add the cubed potatoes and diced onion. Add seasoning salt and pepper. Fry till crisp.

17. Remove the grouse from the ovens. Let rest.
18. Place two sizeable commercial cast iron skillets onto burners. Spoon out the organ paste into the skillets, then using the basting juices from the birds, dilute and whisk the paste until a nice sauce forms. Continue thinning with the bird-basting juices to reach the desired sauce consistency. Add more seasoning salt, and pepper to taste, if needed.
19. Plate half a grouse on a camper's tray with a spoonful of potatoes. Pour the sauce over the top. Garnish the plate with roasted vegetables.

Dear Mom and Dad:

My Montana wilderness experience is now complete, with my first foray into preparing and serving wild game meat. I was nervous about it, but it ended up being a HUGE success and hit! It practically looked "gourmet." Camp bosses say I have gone down in history as Camp Silverback's chef of the century. Even better than that, the scouts learned the value of hunting for their food. I am thankful I was able to be a part of that. I am sorry that camp does not extend into the big game season because I am ready to tackle "Fillet of Elk!"

Sadly, I am headed into the closing stretch of my paid working vacation here in Big Sky Country. Our gourmet grouse meal was the final dinner for this group. Only one group is left before we conclude this summer's Camp Silverback experience.

As this group of scouts hikes out tomorrow, Earl and I will head into town for one more shopping extravaganza. It makes me sad that it is all about to end. It has been a great summer of adventure, learning new skills, making new friends, and especially some personal reflection. Hey, Dad, maybe we should try hunting grouse, or really dive in and try elk hunting!

Love, Randy

In truth, hunting was not something our family participated in. Perhaps it was because our father kept us very busy with other activities.

My Father…Kennel Architect to Gentleman Farmer to Pool Designer

On that quarter-acre lot on the edge of town, we set in a triple-wide manufactured home on a regular home foundation. Manufactured homes are the ultimate in instant gratification. You have your lot where you plan where you want the house, and poof, it is delivered in a weekend. Mom and Dad had already picked out the floor plan, and Mom chose the kitchen and bathroom cabinetry, with complete color schemes inside and out. She chose her preferred floor coverings, lighting fixtures, and even a built-in China cabinet. Mom had a great time with that.

We had our country home now, with our family kennel business up and running. With that, Dad got busy putting in his yard and garden. Dad was all about fencing now. Not only did we have the kennel menagerie of chain link, but we also had erected a six-foot-tall wood fence that completely encircled most of the lot. This was to keep the deer out of his garden and fruit trees. Our land and home were a fortress. Nothing was going to get in or out of that quarter-acre lot.

Dad put in a HUGE, beautiful garden. It had everything in it, and he was having a lot of fun doing it. He also planted several berry bushes along the fence line, with fruit trees scattered throughout the yard. Dad got a kick out of using his new rototiller to prepare the garden beds and keep them weed-free. If you ever wondered where Dad was, you look toward the garden where he would inevitably be "tilling" his garden beds. I could only imagine if he had an actual tractor. In the West, nothing occupies a man better than to have his own tractor. Many holes can be repeatedly dug, dirt moved and then refilled into infinitum.

It was not long before our family was well-fed every summer, with fresh fruits and vegetables that Dad grew himself. There is something very self-actualizing about growing your own food.

Now that I was all of twelve years old, Dad put me in charge of mowing the lawn. Feeling quite satisfied with my new grown-up chore, it did not last long before the novelty of mowing a quarter acre of lawn lost its allure. It was my weekend chore until I turned eighteen and left home. Only then did Kris get her turn at such an opportunity. That was when Dad bought a riding lawn mower. Kris got all kinds of satisfaction, calling me long distance weekly to lament her laborious hot chore that day while sipping on a cold beverage neatly kept in the cup holder of her riding lawn mower. Sometimes, life just isn't fair.

Now that the yard was in, Dad still liked to keep busy with new projects. He was always thinking. He decided our family fortress would only be complete with a swimming pool!

Thrifty Dad was not one to spend a billion dollars to have a pool professionally installed, so he decided we could install it ourselves as a family. Sears and Roebuck advertised the perfect above-ground pool in its spring catalog, and it would be delivered! It was a big, oblong pool that would easily accommodate a party of ten people.

The first order of business was the pool base. This was in preparation for laying down the pool liner. It consisted of dozens and dozens of pickup loads full of sand. The Acme Sand Company could have delivered it in one dump truckload, easily depositing it where it needed to go. However, thrifty Dad decided we could unload it much cheaper. So, Dad drove his little truck to the quarry, where they would load it. Dad then drove back across town to the house, where the four of us would don shovels (two of them borrowed) and unload all that sand. It was another laborious, manual family project—shovel full by shovel full, truckload by truckload. It was very similar to the kennel cement project. How fortunate that Mom, Dad, and Joni have such valuable experience in this task. Unfortunately, Kris and I were now both old enough to be active participants. Except this time, Kris had just had her wisdom teeth removed, sidelining her for this auspicious task. While in a lawn chair under a shade tree, drinking her cool beverage while high on pain medicine, she was the official supervisor for the entire project. Her timing is always impeccable.

The three-hundred-page pool manual (in ten languages) suggested that the sand base needed to be at least ten inches deep. It took days because our only truck at the time was Dad's little red Ford Ranger. At least it was not a wheel barrel job this time. Dad could easily back his truck where the sand needed to be shoveled.

After we had all the sand in the base, we had to ensure the area was completely rock-free. Tiny little errant rocks tend to tear holes in plastic pool liners after you fill the pool with 2,000 cubic tons of water. Mom, Dad, Joni, and I then picked through that twenty-by-fifty foot, ten-inch deep, sand-filled base. We spent days removing all the tiny rock shards throughout the sand base. Thrifty Dad had purchased the lowest grade sand the quarry crushed. Why pay a premium price for rock-free sand when you have children? With just a "little bit of work," we can pick the rocks out of the sand they usually use for road construction.

Dad was also not interested in spending the money, nor the electrical costs, of heating the pool with a standard pool heating unit, which was also readily available for purchase from Sears and Roebuck. Instead, Dad devised his own pool heating method. Using three hundred feet of black rubber hose, he coiled it up expertly into four-foot loops, placing the loops in a sandpit covered by another foot of sand. He placed our hose/sand pool heating pit right next to the house's side, which received the most sun and heat. Dad was the original master of solar energy photosynthesis. The theory is that the heat created inside the long black hose would be extra heated via the hot sand. The hose would become triple heated by the hose sandpit placement on the side of the house, most heated by the sun.

Dad then engineered his re-circulation method, whereby the cool water in the pool would travel through a conduit he placed underground, which would then be delivered to the hose/sand/pit heating area next to the house. The water would circulate through the super-heated hose, then back to the pool, thus heating the water. It was a brilliant idea, and the pool came with a water pump, so he did not have to spend extra money on that. Our thrifty father was always thinking.

You cannot have a swimming pool without a deck. With that, we got busy building the rest of the pool environment. We built a huge, elevated wrap-around deck in our backyard. From our family room, you entered the pool deck from our back sliding glass door. From there, the deck opened onto a gathering area with built-in seating that encircled the entire pool area. It gave the illusion from the house that it was a below-ground pool. Our deck was large enough to provide ample seating and a picnic area for many a pool party at our home throughout the summer. It looked and performed beautifully. Ultimately, our family did a good job, and it eliminated a significant amount of lawn to be mowed (always good). It was a lot of work, but we built it ourselves from the ground up. Once completed, it was something we were all proud of.

Introducing My Special Friend

It is late August, and the camp is enjoying the dog days of summer in heated, arid conditions. It is the time of year when minimal clothing is the norm, and diving into the lake multiple times daily is essential to keep cool.

Earl and I made our usual trip to town for our last shopping excursion for our final group of Scouts. The day was dry, scorching, and dusty as we ascended the Bongos with the four-wheel-drive military-style Scout Humvee and trailer. The road was so dry; the dust was the consistency of fine talc, billowing around us as we climbed. Then, I did the unimaginable. I did the only thing you never do, as it will displease and unleash "The Dodo Bird."

I have not described my little friend before now, but he has made numerous appearances here at Camp Silverback. He is a manifestation of perceived and real humiliation, extraordinary inconvenience, and sometimes pain. He is always responsible for all those untoward occurrences I always seem to experience. If I were a small child, he would be my imaginary friend.

He was there that day I tripped off the step, spilling all those tiny salt and pepper packets across the pavilion floor. He was there when I slid down Jackass slide on my backside, and in Hawaii when I was nearly washed out to sea. It is what happens when you have some bad luck dude sitting on your shoulder your entire life. My dude is...The Dodo Bird.

I am not the only one who suffers unforeseen, hilarious, embarrassing, and sometimes painful experiences. It was my best friend, Laura, who ultimately identified and named him. She was also one of those people who has about as much luck as I do in life. We always had the best time, continually walking in and out of various life exchanges, where our Dodo Bird would crap all over our parade. On a beach vacation once, we were out on a catamaran taking a nice afternoon sail. The boat was filled with other tourists, as we all sat shoulder to shoulder next to each other, cocktails in hand. Laura and I were fairly dressed up for the occasion, as we intended to dine out at a surfside restaurant after our sail.

The boat seated about thirty people in a square configuration inside the pontoons. The day was super warm, with clear blue skies and calm waters. It was a beautiful day for a sail right up until one small wave hit the catamaran just right, causing a burst of water to come up and over the vessel, splashing squarely right onto Laura's head and lap. It was like the Dodo Bird took a giant water bucket and poured it over her head. Nobody on the entire catamaran got wet except for Laura, who was soaked. I was sitting to her right, and another person to her left. We were dry, but Laura's perfectly quaffed hair and white sundress were plastered to her body, makeup streaking down her face.

All the other tourists sitting dry stared at us in stunned silence as Laura and I were laughing hysterically. We were having our little moment as we lamented that our damn Dodo Bird struck again. I am pretty sure they all were silently thinking that the two of us were from crazy town and quickly needed to be remanded for immediate institutionalization, preferably in strait jackets.

Once our Dodo Bird was officially recognized, we decided it was always important to pay homage to him, acknowledging his presence and needs. How you do this is elusive to me to this day, but you especially do not unleash the Dodo Bird with some stupid karmic question! Well, my Dodo Bird heard it all right. I did not even get the words out of my mouth when it happened. Not thinking (now there's a surprise), I commented to Earl, "We have been so lucky not to have gotten a flat tire on this road the entire summer."

As Earl looked over at me with that familiar stunned look of, "I can't believe you just said that," it happened, BOOM! The right front tire exploded as we were almost to the top of the Lower Bongos. Of course, at the steepest point! As the vehicle came to its abrupt stop, Earl set the brake and politely asked me to find a couple of nice big rocks to place behind the back tires. As I climbed down from the Humvee and then jumped into the moon dust below me, it was evident that today was not a good day to wear my white shorts. I always seem to wear the white pair on precisely the wrong days.

I began to gather up two big rocks alongside the road. Feeling bad, I got four more rocks, one for each trailer tire, to ensure ultimate safety. He was not very happy, but you could not tell. Earl had come to recognize and understand the absurdities that seemed to follow me everywhere. In the end, I shared with him my lifelong pal, the **Dodo Bird.** We had a great laugh about it later. Right now, though, it was a bit tense as I went into Boy Scout mode. Earl and I then proceeded to change that tire. Unfortunately, our blowout happened at the steepest and narrowest part of the hill, with a steep embankment/cliff off to the right side of the Humvee. Therefore, there was very little road on which to maneuver on my side of the 1906 four-wheel-drive Scout Humvee as we carefully moved around the edge to change that tire. Once the lug nuts and the tire were off, I turned the heavy wheel and tire around and proceeded to the back of the Humvee. I lost control of the tire as I completely lost track of the road through the dust. That is when I stepped off the road into the abyss, launching me and the tire precipitously into the air. Moments later, we hit the ground as the tire and I rolled and tumbled back to camp. I came in second, behind the tire. It is a good thing I am durable.

Dear Mom and Dad:

While Earl is gassing up, I thought I would write a quick note. Today should have been an uneventful final trip to town for supplies. However, it quickly turned into a consequence-filled experience of explosions, a flat tire, and rapid descents, followed by a very slow ascent back up a steep hill. Let's just say I am thankful for my summer workout regime, which ultimately enabled me to accomplish the final course event in cross-country fitness here at Camp Silverback.

Nonetheless, it was an action-packed day. While I was completing my final course event, Earl had to change a tire by himself. I am still trying to figure out where that great, big spare tire materialized. Earl is always full of surprises. It was just another magical occurrence here at Camp Silverback.

Once we finally made it to town, Earl and I finished our errands, including a quick stop at the hardware store. As we walked into the store, we were welcomed by my friendly small-town hardware store lady who greeted me with, "Alright, big red is back!" She remembered me from my bright candy apple red rental sports car weekend. You know, the day I purchased the leather cleaner to clean up the duck doo in my back seat. So now, among other things, I am known as "Big Red." I needed a camp name anyway.

I asked her how she remembered me, and she replied something sarcastic like, "Guys in bright red sports cars who are from Oregon, who have duck crap in their cars, happen every week around here." She also told me that she tells that story to everyone. She introduced me to all the hardware store employees and a few customers who happened to be there. They all said they were so happy to finally meet me in person. To top it off, my day at Cafe Jax and my encounter with the friendly hometown police officer are also the talk of the town. It did not take the small town of Eureka long to put two and two together.

It looks like I have become famous and someone of celebrity status here. Who knew? She asked me what the story was concerning my Telfa and dirt-covered body. I explained it all to her in entertaining detail, giving her yet another glorious story to convey to the town of Eureka.

Because of the flat tire, we are incredibly behind schedule. I am not going to make the dinner hour. I'm not worried, though; my staff knows what to do. Earl is now finished gassing up, and we are ready to head back to camp. However, the weather has taken a severe turn for the worse. I am beginning to experience déjà vu. Folks in NW Montana often say, "If you don't like the weather, wait an hour, it will change." From the looks of those storm clouds, boy, they are correct.

What began as a bright, sunny, scorchingly hot, and dusty day has quickly changed. It has now turned very chilly. As we head down the main drag of Eureka, the date and temperature sign displayed at the local bank says it is forty-five degrees. The wind is blowing hard now, and it is pouring rain. Neither Earl nor I brought a coat or boots. Good grief, here we go again. More later if I make it back to camp.

Love, Randy

The Beartooth

The date was July 20th, 1969. How do I know that? Because that was the date of the first moon landing of Apollo 11.

We were headed home from Billings, following our usual summer pilgrimage to see the grandparents. Only this time, Dad's brother, Uncle Terry, accompanied us home. After high school graduation, Terry was headed back to La Grande with us. He was entering his freshman year at EOSC. As stated earlier, Terry was a great hobby photographer, and he was excited to get to our destination that day. His goal was to photograph a historic event on television. It would be the first moon landing in our country's history.

Dad decided we would take the scenic route that day, which could give Terry some photo opportunities. Our path would take us to US Highway 212, AKA the famous Beartooth Highway. Well known as one of the most scenic drives in the United States, it is a national scenic byway featuring breathtaking views of the Absaroka and Beartooth Mountains. It is known today as "The Beartooth Corridor."

Surrounded by the Custer, Gallatin, and Shoshone National Forests, it parallels the Absaroka-Beartooth Wilderness and abuts Yellowstone National Park. The highway sits in a million-plus acre wilderness. The Beartooth Corridor is a sight to behold. In just a few miles, you witness untouched alpine landscapes, lush forests, and alpine tundra. It is one of the highest and most rugged areas in the lower forty-eight states, with twenty peaks reaching over 12,000 feet in elevation. In the surrounding mountains, glaciers are found on the north flank of nearly every mountain peak over 11,000 feet high. The Road is harrowing, extremely windy, and only passable in summer. It is known as the highest-elevation highway in the northern Rockies. It is a little over 10,000 feet on the Montana side and nearly 11,000 feet on the Wyoming side. Three gateway communities are on the corridor: Cooke City and Red Lodge, Montana, and Cody, Wyoming.

Our destination that day was supposed to be Rexburg, Idaho. The usual route would have gotten us there within six hours, but it would be much longer via the Beartooth. Winding your way through that mountainous terrain would take much longer as you carefully and slowly wind through the corridor's many switchbacks. I do not know when it started raining, but any inclement weather feature will be severe on

The Beartooth. What began as a sprinkle turned into blowing torrential rains that came at the car sideways. As we inched our way through the switchbacks, I am sure Mom was beeping and brake pumping on her side of the car. There was no visibility, so no scenic views or pictures were taken that day.

We had just completed the final set of switchbacks and were comfortably cruising in an area of alpine tundra in the pouring rain when it happened. The car made a horrible grinding noise, veering sharply to the right before abruptly stopping. Somehow, Dad kept it on the road as he carefully pulled the car over onto the shoulder. Upon careful inspection, Dad and Terry announced that the car had come off the right front axle. God was watching out for us that day. Had that happened at the switchbacks, we could have gone over the edge. Mother had nightmares about that for decades.

In an era before cell phones, we were officially stranded. Our car was going nowhere. The six of us and Ajax could only sit in the car and wait for a passerby, which would take a few hours. One vehicle finally came through, with a gentleman who stopped to see if he could be of assistance. He and Dad then headed on to Cook City. It would be the nearest town where Dad could summon a tow truck to come and retrieve the rest of us and our beleaguered vehicle.

Cooke City - Silver Gate has a population of around one hundred. At the time, it had one gas station, which was also its only mechanic's garage. Cooke City is at an elevation of 7,600 feet, with a subarctic climate. Only two months of the year will it average above fifty degrees during the daytime. Summers consist of mild days with crisp, cool mornings. Winters are very long and very cold, with an average snowfall of 190 inches. On most winter nights, the temperature falls below zero. Snow generally falls between October and May, but snow is possible anytime in Cook City. The entire family, including grandparents, aunts, uncles, and cousins, vacationed in Cook City one July. We all stayed in cabins and had some great family time. Dad, Uncle Terry, Joni, and I even indulged in Joni's favorite pastime, renting and riding horses. It was a great ride in the valley beneath the beautiful Absaroka Range, with Pilot Peak ascending majestically above it.

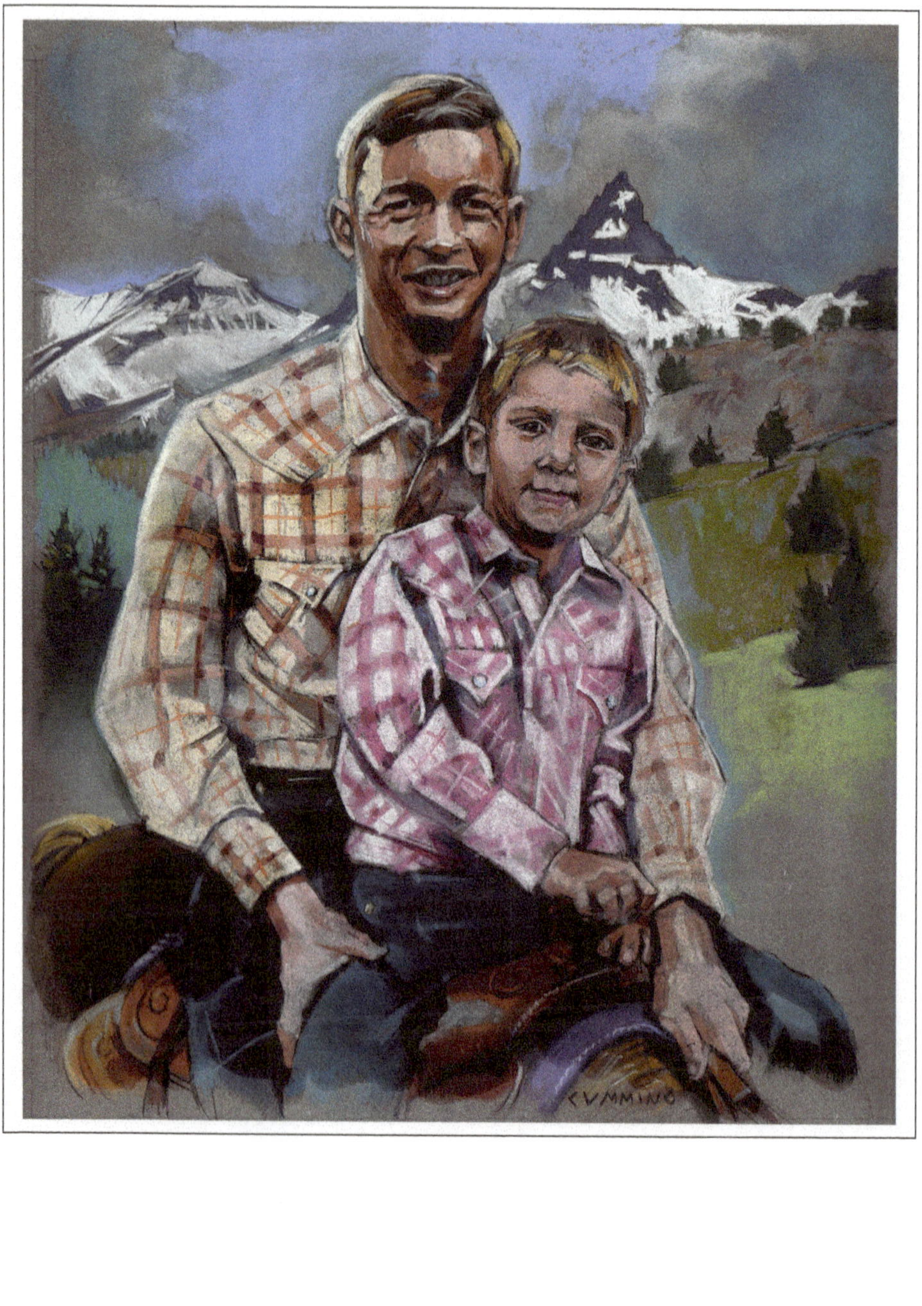
CUMMING

There was no vacationing this time, though. The tow company, who also owned the gas station and mechanics shop, hauled us into Cook City that evening. It was getting dark as our entire family, our vehicle, and Ajax waited for the mechanic to give us the news about our vehicle. The mechanic and gas station owner said it would take a while, but he could fix it that night. It was very dark as we walked down the street to the hotel. Terry immediately began setting up his camera equipment as we entered the door. We were just in time for Neil Armstrong to take that first step on the lunar surface at 8:56 p.m. mountain time.

It would be one of the most memorable moments in American history. Like most things in life, we don't often remember the event or what was said, but we always remember how we felt about it. I do not remember much about that moon landing, but I do remember the warm, enthusiastic pride our country felt that day.

Uncle Terry lived with us for several years while attending college. He didn't always wait in awed anticipation for certain televised events. That time in our family's life was during the Vietnam War. I clearly remember the anxiety as Terry and our family watched the draft numbers scroll up on our television screen monthly. It was not the lottery we see today, where winners are drawn. There were no winners in this lottery. The war ended before Terry's draft number came up.

Early Montana Winters

Dear Mom and Dad:

I have returned safely to my comfortable yellow with lime green accents abode. To continue my latest Bongo saga, because of all our issues today, it was well past dark by the time we hit the Bongos. Our descent was very wet and slippery as I harken back to my first trip down this perilous road they call "The Bongos." To my surprise, Jackass slide, while again very exciting, I now took in stride. As the trailer once again tried to pass up the Humvee, I was confident that those steep embankments and Earl's expert driving abilities would keep us on course. As we descended the Lower Bongos, I braced myself, holding onto the overhead handle above my door, thus preventing the usual headache following our town trip.

My oh my, I think I have finally turned into a rugged Montanan. Earl noticed it also as he turned to me and grinned.

Once again, Montana did not get the weather memo. Good grief, it is August. It was moon dust on this road a mere seven hours ago. As we descended the Lower Bongos, the wind was picking up speed. What had been rain turned into sideways-blowing sleet. I prayed nothing would happen, as neither of us came prepared to walk back to camp in the dark and in these conditions. God did listen to our prayers. We did make it back, but by the time we landed at the bottom, it was very dark, with a full-on blizzard, freezing cold, and near-zero visibility.

Earl and I quickly exited the Humvee and sprinted to our respective domiciles. Unloading would have to wait. I was comfortable that nothing in that trailer would spoil in these temperatures. What could be a problem? My groceries freezing in August.

Upon entering my vintage trailer, I immediately fired up the furnace. I still had not cleaned off the road dust leftover from my flight down the Bongos that morning. After such a harrowing day, I took a hot shower and dug out my long johns. I popped a beer and uncovered some snack food I had stashed. I settled in, thankful I was safely inside my home away from home. I am about to finish my beer and will head to bed soon. I will turn on my electric blanket tonight for the first time all season. I will keep you posted from the Arctic and beyond!

Love You, Randy

The following day, I slept in and snuggled deep into my nice, warm electric blanket. My vintage trailer is nice and cozy, as I heard the furnace fire up frequently during the night. The locals are correct; when it decides to snow in the middle of the Montana wilderness in August, it does not fool around. Yesterday, we were sweltering hot, and now it is twenty-five degrees. It is hard to tell how much snow fell last night since the wind has drifted it quite impressively. As I peer out my window, I cannot help but marvel at how beautiful it is. It has quit snowing, with clear blue skies and cold, crisp air. The pine trees are magnificent this morning, with heavy snow weighing down the tree boughs. When it is this frigid the humidity in the air freezes into sparkling ice crystals, crystals that float about, twinkling around you in the sunshine. It reminded me of Christmas time.

Oh, Flock!

I am convinced my mother was the premier Christmas tree decorator of all time. During the 1960s and 1970s, they made real tinsel with aluminum foil. It was machine-cut into thin strips that had a crinkle look to them. They would lay solidly on the tree, cascading straight down, resembling a frozen waterfall on the tree.

Mother spent days decorating our tree. First came the red balls, which were all red and the same size. Then came the tinsel, carefully placed one by one, needle by needle, on each branch that went precisely six inches back toward the tree trunk. She was pretty anal about her tree. She always let us children help, but I'm positive she re-placed each tinsel strand after we went to bed. Each tree branch probably had twenty to thirty strands of individual tinsel carefully draped on twenty to thirty separate pine needles. The end product was a work of art. We did not string lights on our tree. Instead, Dad put two red spotlights in the back of the tree, one on each side, pointing up toward the treetop. The tree was topped with the usual 1960s to 1970s style glass tree topper, which had to be red and silver. As far as I could tell, we had the most beautiful tree of anyone else I knew. Mom was a premier recycler and well ahead of the times. After Christmas, she would delicately remove each strand, meticulously laying them flat inside the box they came in.

Tinsel of yesteryear eventually went out of favor because of its lead content. Lead someone determined caused many dreadful health effects. Tinsel manufacturers became concerned at the prospect of a million-dollar lawsuit if some child swallowed it. As a result, our beautiful tinsel-laden tree would be gone forever as manufacturers removed it from store shelves. Christmas tree decorators would now be left with tiny wisps of silver strands that fly around pretending to stay on the tree.

One year, Dad decided to deviate from the tinsel tree, instead choosing to flock it. Today, you can easily purchase flocking in an aerosol can. Back then, you had to rent a flocking machine attached to a canister-style vacuum. The directions on the product were clear. It stated to apply it onto the tree outside. Dad was afraid the flocking would fall off when brought into the house, and besides, it was cold outside. With the vacuum dialed into the blow mode, Dad proceeded to flock our tree inside the house. What happened next was an epic family tale that went down in Christmas history.

After loading the flocking canister with the appropriate amount of a powder-type product and water, he attached that canister to the hose of our vacuum and then turned it on. The vacuum immediately fired up with a roar, blowing out an aerosolized white powdery substance that gloriously began to stick all over the tree. However, it also blew a white aerosolized fog with it. A fog that immediately began to spread throughout the entire house. Mom grabbed all three of us kids and dove immediately under the dining room table while smartly grabbing several towels out of the kitchen. She then joined us under the table, handing out towels to cover our faces so as not to breathe in the fog. The sticky white fog was now thick throughout the entire house. Dad could not stop now, the mess within the house was already done. He then finished covering that tree while the rest of the family cowered under the dining room table. The thick fog steadily grew thicker and thicker throughout the house.

Once he finished and "the fog settled," the real mess was revealed. Everything was layered in a thick, sticky white powder. It took Mom and Dad days to clean it all up. It was even stuck to the fireplace brick. Everything had to be washed, including the carpets. It seeped into every available cupboard, nook, cranny, and crack. Mother had to clean the entire kitchen, including cupboards, drawers, and contents.

That year, our Christmas tree looked like the snow-covered trees outside my trailer. Mom finished decorating it with her red bulbs, and we placed our red spotlights in the back, as usual. It was beautiful, but it was the last year we flocked a tree for a while until somebody invented flocking in a can.

Fogged In

I had washed my clothes before I left for town yesterday. Instead of using the clothes dryer, I decided to be magnanimous and hang them to dry under my awning. I was doing my part that day to conserve energy. Last night, as I sailed through my door in a blinding blizzard, I failed to notice them. As I looked out my window this morning, I found my front awning heavy with snow, sagging nearly to the ground. My clothing, barely dangling on the clothesline, is frozen on the ground.

Opening my door was a chore, as I had to shove it open against my sagging snow-filled awning. Once out the door, I crawled through and under my awning, picking up all my frozen solid clothes. Like pizza boxes, I stacked them one on top of the other before bringing them into the trailer. I then went back out, broom in hand, pushing my awning back up while throwing the light snow off the top of it. I gathered up my clothesline, rolled in my awning, and headed back inside. I then strung my clothesline throughout my trailer and hung up my frozen solid clothing in a feeble attempt to dry them...He's Back.

Do you know what happens when you have a trailer full of frozen clothes and the heater running full blast? You get humidity! I am as wet as my clothing in my overheated trailer full of fog. Additionally, as my clothing thaws, copious amounts of water are pooling all over the floor.

Dear Mom and Dad:

I am sitting in my foggy trailer, surrounded by wet clothes, which I am sure will not dry until September. Guess what? With all this accumulated moisture inside the trailer, the lock on my door is frozen. Life is kicking me in the ass these days, but you gotta laugh. I could break the lock, but knowing our camp bear, that is not an option. Hopefully, somebody will notice that I am not at breakfast.

As I look out the windows, all I see is fog. Whether it is inside or outside is a mystery. It occurs to me that I might be writing this letter to myself if nobody comes to rescue me. This is not how I envisioned spending my last days with a tombstone that reads, "He died surrounded by frozen underwear." I am wandering here. Someone will surely come soon. I am assigned to cook lunch.

Once the fog cleared from my head, I used my blow dryer to thaw the lock. Pretty clever, huh! They don't call this a Boy Scout camp for nothin'. Once freed from my soggy, foggy abode, I headed to the cooks' cabin, but not before digging out my winter parka, snow boots, wool cap, and gloves. This is precisely the reason that I do not travel light. You never know what you might need.

Ugh! The snow-shoveling gremlins did not show up this morning. My usual trail to the cooks' cabin is buried in deep drifted snow. I figure it is eight to eighteen inches deep, depending on the drifting. Since it is so cold this morning, the snow is very dry, making it light like talcum powder. As I trudge through the snow, it poofs up around my body. What a difference one day makes. Similar to yesterday's dirt talc but without the grungy effects. It does not feel all that comfortable on my bare legs, either. OK, yes, I am wearing shorts again, but as you know, it is what is most comfortable for a man with, um…as broad a shoulders as I have. I brought my sweats, but I do not feel very professional in them, even if it is a Boy Scout camp. Don't worry, Mom, I will keep my head covered.

Love you, Randy

Searching for Perfection

It is November 28th, 2004, and I head out to Graham's Christmas Tree Farm with Joni and Justin. We had an unseasonably early snowfall that year, with exceptionally cold temperatures. Nevertheless, I am wearing my shorts, but I also put on my snow boots, winter parka, wool hat, and gloves. I was not worried at the time. I figured that Grahams would have the usual selection of pre-cuts in the snow-cleared parking lot. We all wandered around, looking at all the various pre-cut trees, none of which ended up being acceptable to Joni. As I head to the hut to retrieve a hand saw, I am thinking that my attire that day was probably not my best choice. Grahams provides a large black garbage bag. This is for one to lay on while crawling about the frozen snowy ground, cutting down your chosen tree. However, for somebody with, um…as broad a shoulders as I have, the garbage bag is woefully inadequate.

Joni and Justin finally located their "perfect" tree, but not before wandering from tree to tree, over the entire ten acres of Christmas tree specimens twice. Once they finally located their unsurpassed, optimal, exemplified, ideal Christmas tree, I settled onto the ground to cut er' down. Let's just say I was beyond cold by that point, as I was crawling around in eighteen inches of the freaking white fluffy stuff. Once it was down, Justin and I "carefully" (per Joni's instructions) dragged the model prototype of the quintessential ideal Christmas tree out of the woods. Soaking wet and freezing, we all trudged back to my truck. I loaded the tree into the back of the truck, and we headed back to Joni's house with the heat going full blast. Hmm, a soaking wet body and an overheated truck…yep, fog!

Dear Mom and Dad:

It was so cold this morning that I found my kitchen staff huddled around the wood cookstove. It is hard to believe I was getting a tan a mere two days ago. The campers are all in their cabins, crackling fires in the fireplaces and playing cabin games. Their leaders made only a brief appearance to pick up breakfast for their cabins.

The kitchen staff were rock stars this morning. The breakfast they prepared and served was simple: Steaming hot oatmeal with bacon, hot cocoa, and coffee. Each cabin was issued a large Rubbermaid tote. In the tote, they placed the oatmeal in Dutch ovens. Warmed cream, brown sugar, and raisins for the oatmeal were carefully contained in plastic containers as well as hot cocoa and coffee in large kettles. The bacon was foil-wrapped to keep it hot. All were neatly contained in covered plastic totes with hot pads, serving and eating utensils, coffee cups, napkins, and bowls. The kettles and Dutch ovens could then be placed on each cabin's fireplace hearth to stay warm. When they were finished, cabin leaders brought everything back in the tote for clean-up. My staff outdid themselves. I was very proud of them. They did a great job!

Leadership thought it best that everyone stays inside today. We will fix hot soup with sandwiches for lunch and a nice hot beef stew and biscuits for dinner. Cabin leaders will pick up each meal for their cabins, just as they did for breakfast.

This camp and its organization are set up so well. They are always ready for all contingencies. What could have been a disaster is running as smoothly as any other day here. You must admire that kind of organization, more later from the Arctic North.

Love, Randy

Rip Arrived

The boys eventually oozed out of their cabins. Having fun in our winter wonderland, the day evolved into snowball fights and building snow forts. Young boys just are not equipped to stay inside all day. Leadership also took the opportunity to make additional merit badge progress. Who knew they would have a chance to complete their "Snow Sport" merit badges in August? The kitchen provided ample coffee, hot chocolate, and hot apple cider for the occasion. It was a great day.

After dinner, when the kitchen staff finished, one broke out a bottle of Brandy. Boy did that ever go down smoothly, and I hate Brandy. It was a great evening with my staff, basking in the glow of oil lanterns and the warmth of the wood cookstove. It was a memorable night of camaraderie, passing that Brandy bottle around on a frigid, snowy night in August in the Montana Wilderness. Some of my staff, who have participated with this camp for a few years, shared old war stories of camp, bears, and weather. I found solace in learning that all this is not necessarily that unusual. I finally went to my igloo at about eleven. Once I returned, I realized that the pilot light on my furnace had gone out sometime during the day. The fog has now cleared, but my clothing is frozen again.

Dear Mom and Dad:

I feel like Rip Van Winkle. I must have slept for a few weeks because I woke up to clear blue skies and warm weather this morning. It must be seventy degrees this morning! Unfortunately, with the abruptly warming temperatures comes rapidly melting snow. Consequently, a precipitously rising creek flow is now occurring and our little creek is now a river threatening to flood the pavilion. It is already running over the footbridge.

Today's bad news: All that snow on the top of my vintage trailer has found an opening to leak through. Located at the vent directly above the head of my bed, I am awakened by water drip, drip, dripping on my forehead. This is apropos because my floor already has a half-inch of water, secondary to my melted clothing. It was time to get up anyway. I am so glad I packed my galoshes, but who knew I would need that particular footwear to walk through my trailer? I darted to the cooks' cabin, retrieving a large stockpot and several large towels. The pot I placed on top of my bed to avert any further progress of a mattress-style waterbed. It is an interesting concept that could revolutionize the waterbed industry, but not today. I used the towels to soak up all that water on the floor. After a valiant try, I finally gave up on the noble notion of energy conservation. I gathered up all my clothing and threw them into the clothes dryer.

The scouts were already busy getting a lesson in civil engineering. They are making good progress, too. They created a cunning diversion channel to reroute the creek away from the pavilion. It is messy work, as they are wallowing around in the mud. It is all hands on deck, as everyone is pitching in to prevent flooding inside the pavilion. I had better head outside to see what I can do to help.

Much love from the flood zone of Camp Silverback...Me

Little Switzerland

In the upper corner of northeast Oregon, Wallowa Lake is one mile south of Joseph, Oregon, at an elevation of 4,300 feet. On the south end of the lake is a small community of vacation homes, hotel lodging, restaurants, and other small resort-type businesses. Wallowa Lake State Park is at the southern tip of the lake and is a popular destination for camping families, including ours. The entire lake community and camping areas close during the winter months.

The Wallowa Lake Highway, AKA Highway 82, mostly ends at Wallowa Lake State Park. It is on Highway 82 that you turn right at the town of Lostine to head up to the Lostine area campgrounds. During the summer camping season, it is a familiar and much-traveled area for our family.

Highway 82 begins in La Grande and eventually becomes the Minam highway. It includes a steep ascent through the Minam mountain complex. What goes up eventually must come down, at which point it turns into the Minam grade, following the Minam River and then the Wallowa River to the Wallowa's gateway communities. Descending the Minam grade is quite the experience, as one has the pleasure of witnessing the grandeur of the Wallowa Valley below you. I can only imagine what it looked like when the Nez Perce inhabited it.

The Wallowa Lake area was initially inhabited by the Joseph band of the Wallowa Nez Perce tribe, led by Chief Joseph. It would be the summer home to the tribe since 1400 A.D. They would use the surrounding Eagle Cap Wilderness to hunt big horn sheep, elk, and deer. The area was rich with huckleberries that the tribe would gather every summer. Later, the region would also be occupied by the Cayuse, Shoshone, and Bannock tribes. In 1860, the first settlers moved into the Wallowa Valley. By 1930, the Eagle Cap Wilderness was established as a primitive area. In 1940, the Eagle Caps earned its wilderness designation.

In 1877, the Joseph/Wallowa band of the Nez Perce was forced out of their ancestral homeland by the federal government. This action resulted in the beginning of the Nez Perce war. Chief Joseph led this effort with several bands of Nez Perce tribes. The Nez Perce and the Army would engage several times as the Nez Perce traveled from their homeland in the Wallowa Valley through the Montana and Idaho Territories. The last engagement between the Nez Perce and the Army was fought in the Montana Territory at Bear Paw Mountain. This battle took place between September 30 and October 5, 1877. It was after Bear Paw Mountain when continuing to fight seemed futile.

In 1880, to honor Chief Joseph, the town of Silver City changed its name to Joseph. Joseph, with a population of 1,000, is a popular tourist town today. The town is sprinkled with specialty shops, art galleries, boutique stores, and restaurants. The downtown is lined with beautiful life-sized bronzes from the local foundry. The surrounding landscape is second to none. Often described as "Little Switzerland," Joseph is in a picturesque valley, surrounded by the snow-covered peaks of the surrounding Eagle Cap Wilderness. The towns of Joseph, Enterprise, Lostine, and Wallowa are the gateway communities leading to Wallowa Lake and the heart of the Wallowa Whitman National Forest. Enterprise is the hub of all these communities, with a population of around 2,000.

> "My chiefs! I am tired. My heart is sick and sad. From where the sun now stands, I will fight no more forever."
> *Chief Joseph…*

The Wallowas were always a favorite family destination for many reasons, beginning with its beautiful drive. The entire drive from La Grande to Wallowa Lake allows one to witness the scenic beauty of many confluences of river systems in far Northeast Oregon. For our family, it began at the wild and scenic Grande Ronde River that flowed through La Grande. The Grande Ronde eventually joins with the Minam River, after which it confluences with the Wallowa River. It is the Wallowa River that feeds Wallowa Lake.

It was the Memorial Day three-day weekend. Kris was three, I was six, and Joni was ten. It was an exciting weekend because it was the first camping weekend of the summer season. We kicked off the weekend on Thursday evening, loading up our little pull-behind camp trailer. Then, right after Mom and Dad got off work on Friday evening, we excitedly headed to Wallowa Lake State Park. It was an unseasonably warm, spring day as we headed down the road. Memorial Day weekend would always mark the beginning of the summer camping season. We got to our campsite early in the evening and performed our usual setup routine. We then ate dinner, roasted marshmallows, and played games by lantern light on the picnic table. At about 9:00, we retired to the trailer and went to bed.

Kris woke up first the following day, very early at about 6:00 a.m. This was her usual thing that we did our best to ignore. Excited that it was morning, she peeked out the window. She then announces to the family that there is snow outside, whereby Mom and Dad quietly tell her to lay back down and go back to sleep. Ten minutes later, she looks out the window again. She again announces to the family that there is snow outside. Once again, dismissing her statement, they tell her to go back to sleep. Then, I woke up enough to determine that it seemed very cold in the trailer. Dad also noticed this because he got up to turn on the furnace. Curious, he then parted the drapes and looked out the window. Sure enough, there was about a foot of snow on the ground! That would be the beginning of a truly miserable Memorial Day weekend.

Being confident that this wintry weather was a fluke, Dad insisted we stay. It was not just a fanciful decision, it was a logistical decision. There was no way our family station wagon, with two-ply highway tires, could climb through the Minam Grade in snow, especially pulling a travel trailer. We then stayed for two more excruciating days.

Two adults and three young children, weather-stranded in a tiny camp trailer with no bathroom, is a dilemma. A vault toilet was located several yards away from the trailer. Three small children cooped up in a small space, who are grumpy and bored, can think up dozens of reasons a day to do something different. That something became the outhouse. Mom and Dad took turns braving the elements for two days, taking each of us to the outhouse at least a dozen times.

We tried to have fun, playing board games and cards. Mom kept us busy with snack food. Dad kept us entertained with his usual jokes while trying to venture a guess as to when the weather would break. To Mom's relief, the snow did turn to rain, copious amounts of rain to be exact. We were not at any risk of being snowed in now, but Dad was watching that creek beside us closely. What used to be about twelve feet from our trailer was now about eight feet and rising.

The rain did not stop. It came with strong, bitterly cold winds that I was sure would blow the trailer over. By Saturday afternoon, all other campers had left. For us, the weather was still not conducive to a safe departure. Besides, Dad was sure the weather would break any time. We would then be the lucky family to have the entire campground to ourselves. I can still remember being cramped in that little camp trailer, with attitudes diminishing as the hours waned.

Finally, on Sunday morning, the wind stopped. Still pouring rain with no break in sight, Mom broke Dad down. The creek beside us was noticeably larger, now only four feet from the trailer. We left a day earlier than planned. We packed up, hooked up the trailer, and left for home. We were the last camping family to leave. There was never a risk of that creek overtaking our trailer, but Mom's paranoia knew no bounds. About thirty minutes down the road, the clouds parted, the rain stopped, and the sun came out. Dad didn't comment and neither did Mom. All of us children were too tired to care. We slept all the way home.

We never went to Wallowa Lake Campground on Memorial weekend again. Instead, we would head to the high desert. The high desert was too hot for summer camping but perfect for spring camping, so we saved our camping in the Wallowas for July and August.

Dear Mom and Dad:

Summer weather has once again returned to Northwest Montana. As I wrote before, the extreme temperature changes of winter to summer have been accompanied by some flooding here at Camp Silverback. It has been a hard day of bridge repair and re-engineering the creek channel back to where it was. Covered in mud, I returned to my efficiency trailer for a well-deserved shower.

As stated in previous letters, this is not your ordinary toilet, sink, and shower layout. It is very quirky with all its little idiosyncrasies. It is also a tad smaller than your standard pioneer outhouse. The bathroom is so small that I must leave the door open to use it. The situation is compounded if one has, um...as wide of shoulders as I do.

After you open the door to enter the toilet/sink area, you must step over the toilet to enter the shower cubby. You must sit on the toilet lid to brush your teeth and use the sink. To use the toilet, your legs are slammed up tight next to the sink. If you were any taller than I am, you would never fit.

The tiny shower cubicle has an opening that is only about twenty inches wide. The opening has a shower curtain, large enough to cover three entrances. I am sure it is your standard-size shower curtain, but it is overkill for this shower. It encircles the entire shower area, which is only three feet square. Mini people must have inhabited this world when this trailer was manufactured.

Once you have stepped over the toilet to maneuver and position yourself into the shower cubicle, it is best not to make any sudden movements. One wrong move, and you end up shrink-wrapping yourself into the shower curtain. One of these days, I will cut that shower curtain in half! Successful in my positioning today, I then turned on the water. However, no water came shooting out of the shower head. Then I remembered that critical first step that must be performed if one is to expect any water to materialize in this shower.

It is the number one peculiarity of this vintage trailer. One that took me a lot of investigation the first time I attempted a shower. I was an hour late preparing breakfast with my staff that morning as I wandered around naked in my trailer, trying to find the trailer instruction manual. Of course, no manual existed because this trailer is a million years old. Then, I remembered this small pin next to the sink that seemed odd and out of place. Using my finely tuned sense of inquiry, I pulled this pin, whereby water immediately began to stream freely from the shower head.

Long ago, I discovered that turning on the shower water before entering the cubicle is best. Forgetting this essential first step, I attempted the pin-pull maneuver inside the shower compartment. Unfortunately, there is no room to bend over, reach into the sink area, and pull this pin, that is, not without unexpectedly picking up your shampoo bottle directly on the shelf behind you. Look, ma, no hands!

Keep in mind that my water heater tank only has a three-gallon capacity, so speed is paramount. I was doing fine until I realized the shower was filling with water. Always thinking, I picked up my shampoo bottle with my left hand while carefully squatting down. I then stuck my right forefinger down the drain, attempting to remove whatever was plugging the hole. To my horror, I came up with a partially decomposed mouse. Its bony, hairy carcass stuck tightly around the end of my finger, with its creepy, dead, mousy face looking straight at me.

My previously performed Decon strategy worked. However, staring down at a tattered, wet, skeletonized mouse stuck to the end of my finger, which was staring back at me, was more than I could handle. Needless to say, the space in this bathroom is not big enough for a man with, um.... broad shoulders, as I go into a full-on panic attack. I flung open the shower curtain while frantically trying to shake the wet, hairy beast off my finger. When I finally managed to fling that ghastly hairy skeleton off my finger, it flew completely out of the shower, over the toilet, and out of the bathroom, bouncing off the trailer door. In my panic, I had thrown it with such commanding force that it bounced back at me, hitting me in the chest. Now, I am doubly horrified! My reaction was an entirely visceral desperate desire to retreat. In the pandemonium of the moment, I created an abrupt and immense amount of astonishing flexibility and speed for my size.

Amid my expeditious exit, I slipped, shrink-wrapping myself into the shower curtain. Undeterred, I catapulted myself out of the shower, over the toilet, through the bathroom door, and onto the trailer floor. From there, I slid into and under that tiny space under my mini couch.

Whew! I had escaped, but I now know what living in a pinball machine feels like. I figure the entirety of the incident took less than three seconds. Once I calmed down and figured out what happened and where I was, I crawled and scratched out from underneath that couch while un-shrink-wrapping myself from the shower curtain. It was then I decided that you can indeed put a round peg in a square hole if there is enough moisture, soap, and force behind it. I immediately retrieved a pair of scissors and cut that shower curtain in half. God, I hate mice.

Love, Randy

Mikes Come and Mikes Go

Now and then, I have the opportunity to engage with scouts interested in seeking their Cooking Badge. It is not the most popular merit badge to pursue when you are a boy in an environment that emphasizes camping, shooting, and water sports. They tend to be more outdoor-focused here. Now and then, though, I will get a request from a boy who would like to learn the principles of this merit badge, with an emphasis on outdoor cooking.

There are seven required subjects to pursue the cooking merit badge, including health and safety, nutrition, cooking basics, cooking at home, camp cooking, and trail/backpacking meals. I covered cooking basics and how they relate to camp cooking and trail/backpacking meals. I have enjoyed working with the few boys I have had the opportunity to connect with. They are eager learners and very polite. I took a particular shine to a young lad named Mike who came to my trailer door with two fish dangling from a rope. He asked me if I would help him with his cooking badge.

I like "Mikes," mainly because my sister Kris collected "Mikes." When she began dating, practically every fella she chose to date was named Mike. It must have been "The Name" of choice for boys in Kris' era. Kris went through a lot of Mikes. Every Christmas, there was a new Mike on the horizon. My parents, being the generous souls that they are, included each new Mike at our family Christmas celebration. Every year, Dad would ask Kris if this season's new Mike would be joining us this year for the holiday. It became standard joke fare in our family. Every year, Kris' new Mike would get a sweater. Kris was not amused. She tended to get annoyed if jokes on her were prolonged, and this one lasted for years.

My young Mike reminded me a lot of Justin. Blonde-haired, blue-eyed, and quite inquisitive. He had many ideas, asked many questions, and seemed genuinely interested in the cooking badge. My knowledge of outdoor cooking came from my dad. He was always the camp cook on our weekend outings, which Mother delighted in. Mom's kitchen mastery centered around the home front. Camping meant she was on vacation from domestic duties. Dad was an outdoor culinary genius. Besides cooking camp breakfast, his main forte' was cooking trout, which our family enjoyed as a camping treat. Dad and Joni were always successful in their fishing capers, so we always had trout for dinner and breakfast.

I would venture with them on most fishing outings but quickly got bored. Dad and Joni could do this activity all day, hours on end. Lake fishing was the worst. How can anyone sit on a lake bank watching a fishing bobber all day? It was beyond my understanding and patience. They would even find sticks on the bank that would possess the correct "Y" on the end. They would bury the straight end of the stick in the dirt, then balance the end of their rod in the "slingshot end" of the stick. This ingenious "pole holding" method meant they did not have to hold the rod while they waited hours on end for a fish miracle to happen. I had never understood such a boring concept. I would instead spend my day wading in the water, collecting more rocks, and chasing crawdads and water striders. It was much more entertaining than watching a bobber in the water.

Kristi was always napping with Mom in camp. Kristi was the most rested child on our family camping trips. Mostly, it was a time for Mom to enjoy some quiet time in camp by herself while caring for her very young daughter, who could not swim. Besides, Mother hated fishing.

Boy Scout Camp is all about self-sufficiency. Young Mike had fished out a couple of nice specimens from the lake that morning, deciding to sign up for the cooking merit badge. What is more self-sufficient than learning to fry the fish you caught? We first went through all the cooking basics, which bored him to tears. I went on to talk about food prep. This also obviously was not his thing. Part of self-sufficiency is the cleaning and preparation of the fish they catch. Young Mike did not clean his fish. The further we progressed, the more I slowly understood that young Mike was not interested in the cooking badge at all.

Only after receiving a litany of explanations of why I needed to clean that fish rather than him, did I finally recognize the con job I was in the midst of. Boys, since I used to be one, the whole picture was becoming crystal clear now. Young Mike caught two nice fish today and wanted to cook them for lunch. The boys are not allowed to cook independently, so Mike decided that the merit badge was the perfect strategy to get his fish cleaned by someone else and eat it by himself without sharing. Young Mike reminded me again why I got my degree in marketing and not teaching. I am too gullible and do not possess the skills to stay on top of these young minds.

Mustard, Not Just a Condiment

Being around children all day, every day does have one minor complication. Throughout the summer, I have been lucky to have outmaneuvered each viral outbreak with each group of campers. Kids are little wandering petrie dishes who are resilient and rarely sidelined when a cold bug makes the rounds. As an adult without children, I came to this camp without the protective antibodies that one needs to fight off all the infective germs crawling around everywhere in this camp.

It hit me hard as I lay in bed, hacking, sneezing, and unable to breathe through my woefully congested nasal passages. While hardly able to move beyond my miserably aching body, I can't help but think of Mother. Mom had her execution of an old natural folk remedy best known as; "The Mustard Plaster." The mustard plaster was made from the mustard plant and has been used for medicinal purposes for several millennia. It was also a condiment used by ancient Egyptians, Sumerians, and Chinese. A mustard plaster was made from mustard seed and warm water to make a paste. The paste was then spread inside a protective dressing and applied to warm the body. Its purpose was to relieve nearly everything that ailed the body. They used it for gout, sciatica, and chronic pain such as arthritis, but also pneumonia and chest congestion. It was believed to be the cure-all to increase the area's circulation and boost your immune system. Ancient cultures were convinced that in the case of pneumonia, it cleared out phlegm build-up and removed microbes.

Mother's answer to the mustard plaster was a thick, over-the-counter menthol gel. As children, we did not dare utter even the slightest cough or the smallest of sneezes because Mom would be all over it! After a hot steaming bath that night, she would practice her cake frosting techniques. She would slather that gel, about an inch thick, all over our chests and necks. Then, to make double sure, she would take a big finger full, slapping it under our noses. Then, in the spirit of the old bygone days of the mustard plaster, she would throw an old t-shirt on us. The gel would then "plaster" the t-shirt to our bodies, which stuck to us all night, allowing the vapor to envelop us while we slept.

The problem with the old days of mustard plasters is that if the dressing (plaster) remained on the body too long, it would cause first-degree burns to the skin. It is probably the single reason it fell out of favor in the twentieth century. But Mother's homemade menthol gel-soaked t-shirt plaster could stay on for all eternity. When we got up in the morning, Mom would remove the t-shirt from our sticky body, saving it for the next night. After all, it was soaked and practically dripping with menthol gel. The next night, she would repeat the entire process, sticking that menthol-soaked t-shirt back on, only to soak more gel into its threads by morning. This ceremonious activity would go on night after night until our cold bug resolved. By the time our virus was over, that t-shirt could slither out of our bedroom all by itself.

Dear Mom and Dad:

My goodness, how time flies. I have entered the final stretch of my paid vacation in northwest Montana. Our last group of campers is the largest group they have ever had in the sixty-some-odd years of Camp Silverback. Unfortunately, I caught a flu bug yesterday, also affectionally known as - The Camp Silverback Plague. One of my staff also sprained his knee, so he is out of commission as well. For this record group of campers, it has been a hell of a week for the remaining staff to get it all pulled together.

Each day, as I lie in my bed in my misery, I feel like I am receiving confessions all day. I get a steady parade of staff, one by one, to the window above my head, asking me various questions. Also, while entombed in my vintage trailer for two days, it has become quite evident that my mouse problem has, entirely and officially, come to an end. It has taken the entire summer, but the Decon strategy must have finally done the job.

The only drawback is the sudden stench in the trailer, which gradually builds with each passing hour as it gets warmer. I cannot imagine how bad it would smell in here had my nasal passages not been so miserably plugged. They must have crawled into the woodwork and died right there. Since it is a nice warm day today, I am miserably sick, stuck in this trailer, with this awful odor permeating throughout, and it is getting stronger. There is not enough spray air freshener in the world right now.

I wonder if Grandma's air transfer and conveyance strategy would work. I lack the most critical component (fan) for that to work. Of course, I don't remember that game plan working very well for us children, as it relates to heat. I am signing off for now while I wallow in misery.

Love you from the innermost sanctum of the confessional... Randy

More Fog

Every summer, our family would depart from our camping activities for two weeks to make our annual vacation journey to Montana to see family. We always stayed with our grandparents while in Billings. Then, we would carve out some time to drive the five hours to Plentywood. In Plentywood, we always stayed with Mom's brother and his wife, Uncle Gene, and Aunt Dot. It was usually mid to late July before we would venture to Montana for our annual two-week summer vacation.

Every summer, I would "gird up" in anticipation for what I was sure the hottest month of the year in the hottest state in the country. Our grandparent's home had no air conditioning, so they had numerous window fans throughout the house, especially in the upstairs bedrooms. By the time we went to bed, the hot air had risen to its zenith in the upstairs areas of the house. All three of us were sleeping on twin beds in one of the two upstairs bedrooms. It was the same room that my dad slept in with his two brothers.

Even as a small child, I could recognize sweltering. Every night, it was a source of extreme misery as we sweated, tossing and turning the night away. We had this big window fan, already set up and running, right in the bedroom window. It was even turned to the highest speed. Montana is known for cool summer nights, even during the warmest months. There was only one problem with that fan. Grandma would position that fan to blow the air toward the outside of the window. Joni finally asked our grandmother why. Why was the fan blowing air in the wrong direction? Grandma said this was to carry all the hot air out of the house. It was all very curious to small children. Why were we heating the outside air? What about transferring the cool air from outside into the house? Being the compliant children we were, we never turned that fan around in the opposite direction. It would have been easy, and Grandma would have never known. We could have enjoyed the cool Montana night breeze and slept in comfort. Then, before going downstairs for breakfast in the morning, we could have turned that fan back the way it was. Grandma would have never known.

Our family also did not have an air-conditioned car. I am sure my thrifty father did not pony up the extra couple hundred dollars for such an amenity. Making the sixteen-hour journey to and from Billings was easier in the middle of the night. It was cooler then, and the children would sleep throughout most of the drive. This removes most of the aggravation of driving long distances with small children in unbearable heat.

One year, my grandfather found a handy, dandy portable plastic cooling machine made just for cars. This newfangled device sat on the front middle floorboard of the vehicle and plugged handily into the cigarette lighter. It could be easily positioned between the driver and the passenger. It had a large compartment that you would fill with ice. Once plugged into the cigarette lighter, you turn on the fan switch and have an instant air conditioner.

In theory, all you needed to do was stop periodically at a gas station. Ice was available at all gas stations, and it was free then. While filling the car with fuel, you could easily retrieve more ice for the compartment. Thus, our family's journey home would be comfortably cool for the entire trip. Dad was sure this was the answer. Instead of beginning our homeward journey at 7:00 p.m., we spent one more night, departing at 7:00 a.m. the following day. It was already a thousand degrees as our little family headed down the road with our handy, dandy portable car air conditioner made by "The Acme Car Air Conditioner Company" (Laurene, The Acme Air Conditioning Company 2024).

Dad already had our new cutting-edge air conditioning unit plugged in and filled to the brim with ice. We loaded up, kissed our grandparents goodbye, and headed down the road. He then turned on our state-of-the-art, portable, crackerjack air conditioning unit and smiled. The cool, moist air immediately poured out of the unit and into our vehicle. He was quite pleased with himself. However, do you know what happens when you push moist, supercooled air into a sweltering hot car? Very, very, wet fog, which seems to be a common theme in my life. The ice in that compartment instantly melted in the heat. The entire family was now wet and hot. We had to open all the car windows to dry off. We all laughed about it the entire sixteen hours home, with all our windows wide open, sweltering in our beige family station wagon with fake wood panels.

The Frontier Man

Our bear friend is now our active nocturnal visitor nearly every evening. What's more, he has invited all his bear friends. Since the bear issue seems to have exponentially worsened during this camp year, camp leaders are meeting to devise a permanent solution to eliminate our bear problem. Our bear continues to be highly successful at still eluding the Lincoln County bear police. Bulking up is one thing, but eating my carefully planned food storage is another. Bears eat a lot, and what they are eating are my groceries. A food supply so carefully planned to the smallest of details. One that won't run over or run out at the end of this final scout group.

I think we have finally got this solved. Following the leadership meeting this morning, Earl and I went to town and purchased many carpentry-type items that will assist in the deterrence of our bear break-ins. Earl is quite handy and an expert carpenter. I became Earl's carpenter's assistant, and he has taught me a lot. Among other handyman secrets, I think I have also learned how to burglar-proof my own home someday. Earl is a carpentry genius and a great teacher. With that, my sisters can no longer call me "Joe Carpenter Junior." Also affectionately known as the son of "Joe Carpenter" and "Mrs. Joe." My family has never been known for home improvement capabilities, which my sisters remind us about often.

We now have bars on our windows and hefty steel doors, one door in the pavilion and the other in the kitchen. The hinges on the doors are built inside the casings of all door frames, just like the garbage storage building. The window bars, Earl buried within the window frames. We are bear-proof now!

Dear Mom and Dad:

Our bear friend has gone from a simple annoyance to "Destructo Bear." He also decided to invite all his friends. As close as we can tell, we now have three bear visitors. They have new ideas and approaches to break into the kitchen each night.

Our bears have taken a liking to bread while devouring a 25-pound bag of salt. Now that's water retention. They also polished off a case of coffee grounds. I bet that bear does not sleep for a week. They also broke through a wall and absconded with several cake mixes and the camp's entire supply of dried fruit. It was the worst night on record, where the bears are concerned. It is late August, though, and they are desperate to bulk up before winter hibernation.

We finally did get our bear problem figured out once and for all. You cannot continue allowing such destruction, day after day, night after night. We added a couple of steel doors and barred the windows throughout the kitchen and pavilion. Bears don't like to work very hard like many other beings. If food is easily accessible, they will return again and again to reap the benefits of easily accessible, free food. Earl and I have built a fortress with new doors and window barriers. We shouldn't see our bear freeloaders anymore.

Guess what? I have become a part of Camp Silverback's history. I am honored to be inducted into what they call "The Frontiersmen." The Frontiersman Award is given to leaders and staff who have given outstanding service to the camp and the scouting association. It is usually only awarded to those with at least two years of paid or volunteer employment, so this is quite an honor for me. I was pretty surprised when they called me among the other ten staff members and leaders.

The award is accompanied by a ceremony, where honorees run up a rock face that ends at the ceremonial "Frontier Fire." During the ceremony, all the scouts and leaders make an alleyway cheering, as all the new "Frontiersmen" scamper up a rock face to the fire. At the top of the rock face, the previous honorees are standing in a half-circle around the fire, ready to congratulate the newly inducted Frontiersmen. The previous honorees are called the "Order of the Arrow." I was never a football player, but I will bet this is how it feels when you run onto the field with the student body cheering you on. It's a great feeling.

The problem with running up a rock-face mountain is that it is not something I do every day. However, I had been training for this throughout the summer. I did complete the final course event in Camp Silverback's cross-country fitness competition while also changing a tire! So, I feel confident and ready. I have also extensively studied and completed the 50-page boot manual, so I am prepared.

Uh-oh...Thanks to my dear friend, the camp now knows how graceful and "fire-retardant" I can be. All ten of us headed up that rock face at a sprint, with the crowd cheering us on. It was exhilarating, and I felt great as I headed expertly up that hill. My new boots gripped each rock proficiently as I skillfully navigated a path toward the top of the hill and that fire. I was not the first person as we ascended, but I also was not the last.

I was getting tired and very winded, but I kept going as hard as I could. Not paying attention (there's a surprise), I suddenly reached the top, where the terrain suddenly flattened out and then went slightly downhill. Let's just say I did not quite have a handle on my forward progress. As I tried to put the brakes on, the top two eyelets on each of my boots somehow interlocked. I am positive I did not read this as a warning clause in the boot manual!

With both my feet now securely locked together, coupled with my forward motion and momentum, I sailed right through the fire. As I began rolling down the hill on the other side, all I could see were astonished faces as I bowled over several "Arrow Orders" on the other side of the fire. I am sure the first-place finisher, standing on the other side of the fire, will be fine. He should be able to resume normal camp activities by mid-week.

Thanks to everyone for all the newsy letters. According to our mail guy (Earl), I could qualify for my own mailbag. Mom has been great, sending newspapers and magazines to read. The staff cabins both look like doctor's waiting rooms. Oh, Dad, I love your new monthly publication, "The Disturber." It is hilarious! It is also the perfect name for a satirical underground newspaper. It captures the essence of the La Grande Observer perfectly. I wonder how long it will take for people in La Grande to figure out that you are the sole writer and editor or that President Gilbert is the head of distribution for the college. We should make a family bet on that.

Even after our bear issue a couple of weeks ago, my food and meal planning has been accurate to the minutest degree. I did not run out of food, and I don't anticipate much to be left over. What small amount I might have left, I can send home with my staff for their families to enjoy.

This will likely be my last letter from Camp Silverback. We have one more week of scouts and another week to get everything stored, winterized, and locked up. It will be a hectic final couple of weeks, and then the summer will officially come to an end. Earl, I, the Humvee, and the trailer will be the last vehicles and people departing from camp. We were the first to arrive and are now the last to leave.

It does make me sad. What a great summer this has been. Thanks for listening to all my adventures, and remember to always "Duck" before getting into your car. I love and miss you all very much. I will be home soon...

Randall James, Esquire, OOTA
Order of the Arrow

Well, Journal, in life we tend to remember and recall the best chapters of our lives. Memories give us the capacity to store and retrieve information. They are the seeds of joy that are recollected, cultivating the garden of life. Those recollections fertilize a happy and healthy existence. For me, my childhood and Camp Silverback are some of the most memorable times in my life. It is what I held onto as I got older, and life became more complicated. Life occurs when difficulties creep into your carefully cultivated garden, manifesting into an overgrowth of crabgrass, thistle, and dandelions.

It is now time to get into the weeds...

PART III

The Weeds

Dear Journal,

Where did I leave off? Ah, yes, the summer of 2004. Following my sisters and my best friend's intervention, I ended up in the hospital for ten days, where doctors removed many pints of fluid from my body. Fluid buildup occurs when your heart cannot efficiently pump the blood through your body, so it pools/collects in other tissues, especially your lungs. It can happen for many reasons, but in my case, it is because of my obesity.

Nine years post Camp Silverback and following Joni, Kris, and Laura's hospital intervention, I am again embracing my weight issues. It is time, Journal, and I am determined to do what is necessary to get on a healthier track. My family has been very supportive, so we are devising a plan to accomplish this task. With that, I have decided to pursue professional help.

I have finally realized that obesity is much more than just an issue of physical appearance. Yes, there are definite problems with discrimination, social bias, depression, anxiety, and low self-esteem, but the problem is much more extensive than that. Obesity does not just occur because one eats poorly and does not exercise. It is not a condition of merely being overweight. I have been considered at least overweight for most of my adult life. Being overweight did not prevent me from participating in an active, functional life.

Obesity is something much different. Many medical conditions can cause obesity. Unfortunately, physicians seem reluctant to assess and investigate possible causes unless a patient asks. Much of the world is classified as overweight, which is not what I am talking about. However, allowing weight to increase continually is where folks get into trouble. The road to morbid obesity is a long, gradual climb. One that can be overcome long before it becomes life-threatening. Overweight and obesity are categorized into five classifications depending on one's Body Mass Index (BMI). BMI calculators can easily be found on a simple internet search.

Obesity and Body Mass Index (BMI)

- underweight <18.5
- normal weight 18.5 to 25.00
- overweight 25.0 to 30.0
- obese 30.0 or higher
  Class I obesity 30.0 to 35.0
  Class 2+ obesity 35.0 to 40.0
  Class 3+ obesity 40.0 and higher

Absolute mortality figures are difficult to determine because other factors also influence the life expectancy of the obese person. The duration spent with overweight and obese BMIs is an essential factor for poor health outcomes and secondary co-morbidities such as diabetes and cardiovascular disease. Morbid obesity is a severe chronic health condition that interferes with essential physical life-sustaining functions, such as breathing. Affected people gradually develop hypoxemia (decreased blood oxygen saturation), developing problems with sleep apnea or a periodic cessation of breathing while asleep. Sleep apnea causes high blood pressure and pulmonary hypertension. If medical treatment is not sought, this leads to heart failure and death. Other than respiratory failure, obesity consequences include diabetes, high blood pressure, gastroesophageal reflux disease (GERD), gallstones, osteoarthritis, heart disease, urinary incontinence, skin infections, and cancer. All can occur along the obesity spectrum, with risk rising as one climbs the BMI scale (The Global BMI Mortality Collaboration 2016).

A comprehensive weight loss program must begin once any possible medical contributing causes are ruled out. This would include nutritional education, counseling, and regular exercise approved by a physician or Nurse Practitioner (NP). Depending on one's debility, exercise may need to occur with a physical and occupational therapist present. A physician or NP can also determine whether one's obesity has a deeper, more complex component. Often, a closer examination is necessary by a psychological practitioner.

I used to believe all the hullabaloo about fat shaming. After all, for the most part, I feel good. Except now, I am at a point in my life on whether I will live or die. I am an obese person who has come to recognize the problem and then admit that it is an issue and an obstacle in my life. Still, with everything else that is difficult, denial is easier, especially if society convinces us that it is not a problem for us but for others. Caring about an obese loved one is now equated with hate. Nobody can get past their denial with that message. Owning your weight problem takes a lot of courage, but once you have, self-reflection is power. Only then did I have the capability to seek the help that I needed.

Early Manifestations of My Disorder

For me, the association between my mental health and my weight began when I was a small child. Deeply seated insecurities developed when my mother left home to give birth to my little sister. Mother was gone for several days because back then, hospitals and doctors kept new mothers much longer to ensure that the new mother and infant were progressing as expected. Family birthing experiences were never practiced, with the father only present during the labor period. New mothers were whisked off to a sterile birthing suite when the birth was imminent. Older siblings were never allowed in the hospital. I was only three years old when Mom and Kris finally returned home following a week-long hospitalization.

I was in the early stages of speech development at that time. My anxiety over my mother's absence came at a critical point in that development. It was at this point that speech experts determined that my language progression changed. I don't blame my parents or my sister's birth; it just was what it was. Stammering leads to low self-esteem, body image issues, and childhood depression. Things they did not know much about at the time. Childhood depression was unheard of back then.

Over time, I became good at tempering my feelings of inadequacy despite being depressed. I was generally happy. I had great friends, a loving family and, as an adult, a fulfilling career. How can you be outwardly happy but depressed? You do that by living in the moment and not for the future. Healthy people surround themselves with people and activities that make them happy. For depressed people, that is never enough. So, to make their life seem satisfying and fulfilling, depressed people will often self-medicate through alcohol or drugs. They may gamble to excess or participate in risky behavior. For me, it was spending money and eating. The consequences of which were my weight and my indebtedness. It also explained why I would purchase a new car practically every year. Cars made me happy, and new cars made me really happy. So, outwardly, people could not see my depression. I got so good at it I did not recognize or admit it to myself.

Good food made me happy and good food, to me, was not necessarily nutritionally optimal. I am an instant gratification man, which is not unusual nowadays in our society, but it is very unhealthy for me. Heading to the fast-food joint was quicker than cooking. Fast foods are higher in fat and therefore, more satiating than salads, vegetables, fruits, and lean meats. A diet consisting primarily of fast foods and processed snacks tends to make you heavy.

Spending of any kind was highly gratifying to me. Brand-new cars were just the tip of the iceberg. Furniture, kitchen remodels, artwork, RVs, computers, and vacations were all purchased on credit. What did not help was discovering second mortgages and mortgage lines of credit. Paying off debt on your mortgage seemed like a good idea at the time. After all, you can deduct the interest on your debt on your taxes. It was like an erasure of debt, with the debtor deciding how much you want to pay each month. Exacerbating this practice was the continued use of credit cards that formed a never-ending cycle of accumulating debt that could never be paid off.

As previously stated, hiding food in my bedroom was commonplace as a kid. It was a strategy I built upon as an adult. Once I was an adult, hiding my poor eating habits inside my home was much easier. I could make the midnight trip to a fast-food burger joint, bring home two burgers, two jumbo fries, a milkshake, and a fruit pie and nobody would know. I could also effectively hide the empty fast food and junk food bags in my garbage. I would hide all the evidence from my snoopy sisters by emptying my garbage early the following day. Before my intervention, eating was only one of my lifelong psychological impediments to wholeness. Poor spending habits began to manifest in my teenage years.

Dad's Evil Spreadsheet

As an adult managing my finances, I could hide my indebtedness from my family. As a young man of sixteen, my father managed this problem. I was always desperately seeking out a car to buy. Unfortunately, I only possessed a meager sixteen-year-old income. As all teenagers have done, I worked minimum wage jobs as a stock boy at grocery and retail clothing stores in town. My father taught me a lot about planning and budgeting, so I knew an affordable car that matched my income would present itself someday. Dad did his best to educate me on money management. Every week, when I had a different vehicle picked out, Dad and I would sit at the dining room table in front of the "dreaded spreadsheet." Then, it was back to the old drawing board every week to find a cheaper vehicle.

Being the most like our father and the oldest, Joni was constantly negotiating with Dad. Mother was wise and stayed out of it. It became worse when Joni became a teenager. Where Dad and I would go through the agony of budgeting for a vehicle together, Joni had her spreadsheet all ready for him. Dad agreed to co-sign Joni's first car loan when she was sixteen. She had a well-paying job as a teenager, so she could make the car payment and pay for her insurance and gas. One year later, he refused to co-sign her second car loan. Dad did not believe she needed to buy a different car so soon. However, on her own, she traded that car for a new car and a new car loan. She even called the insurance company and organized the insurance for her new car. Dad was shocked and dismayed when he came home from work that evening. She had traded in her white Celica ST with a sporty red pinstripe and rag top. Now in the driveway was a black Mazda with red leather interior, a fin, and a sunroof. She did it herself, proving to him that she no longer needed a co-signer to buy on credit. She had a good job, and with the help of his co-signature on that first loan, she had built a positive credit history by the time she was seventeen. That second car was Joni's rite of passage. If our parents ever had control over Joni, it was gone by then.

It was the 1970s when Joni came of age. Kids of that decade learned what the children of the 1960s did wrong and pivoted accordingly. They abandoned the counterculture ideas of bra-burning, activism, authoritarian hostility, flower power, and free love. Children of the 1970s built on the best of those ideas and had fun. In high school, the 1970s represented a four-year-long party, minus the activism or the hostility. School was a necessary activity to get to the weekend. Many shenanigans were going on that our parents knew nothing about. Joni was the family expert in covert maneuvers to secretly practice various illicit activities that the decade was famous for. On the positive side, it prepared her for parenting her future teenager. She always warned Justin that there was nothing new he could teach her about being a teenager.

Throughout Joni's teenage years, Dad and Joni had many private discussions in our parents' bedroom. Mom, Kris, and I would stand outside the closed door with our ears pressed against it, straining to listen to what was going on. Kris must have taken many notes during those super-secret listening sessions we were eavesdropping on. When Kris turned sixteen, Dad gave her his little red Ford Ranger truck and paid her insurance. Boy, was she ever smart.

Kris and I were from the 1980s generation. By then, Mom and Dad had learned some things from Joni and her decade and had parenting better figured out. They figured out that busy children are children less inclined to get into trouble. They tried this concept with me, but it was not as successful as with Kris. Our parents kept Kris very busy. They capitalized on Kris' interest and talent in sports. She played and excelled in all sports but was especially good on the basketball court. Mom and Dad went to every game and sat directly behind the players' bench.

When she was traded out, Dad would whisper (loudly), "Kris, pull up your socks!" Dad was hard to ignore, and it annoyed Kris to no end. Dad never understood the "slouchy sock" trend of the 1980s. Besides, as I have stated earlier, Dad strived to annoy his children.

Kris' teenage years were less carefree than Joni's or mine. After Joni and I left the nest, and being the only child left at home, she was much more burdened with the responsibilities of a rapidly aging, unhealthy parent whom she needed to help care for. It was the real reason she got the truck. Dad could no longer drive, and it was a strategy for Kris to be immediately available at a moment's notice.

Eventually, Dad and his spreadsheet found a way for me to acquire some old beater that would become my first car. I have no recollection of what make or model that car was. That was a million cars ago. However, I never connected the circumstances of my car obsession and spending habits to my damaged psyche. In fact, nobody noticed until years later.

Spreading my Wings

I left Oregon and the bosom of the family the summer after I graduated high school in 1981. My Aunt Pam and Uncle Frank took me in, along with their children Nikki and Trevor. Nikki was the oldest, closest to Kris' age but slightly younger. Nikki was like a sister to me. My father was pivotal in bringing her into our family. Pam was another of Dad's siblings, diagnosed with diabetes at a young age. It was the 1960s when the management of pregnancies for diabetic women was not as well managed as they are today. The entire family was heartbroken when Pam's first pregnancy ended in a stillborn birth. Her physician later advised Pam and Frank not to attempt another pregnancy. Dad and Pam were especially close, so he took this news very hard. Dad was "a fixer" and wanted to help, so he set out to do just that.

In its early years, EOC had only two dormitories. One for the women and one for the men. In those early days, co-ed dorms were unfathomable. The women's dormitory employed a dorm mother, an older motherly-type woman who was a mentor and confidant to the young women in her charge.

Not long after Pam's loss, the rumor mill at the college began speaking of a young unmarried student who was newly pregnant. Dad inquired about the rumor to the matriarch of the dormitory. The timing could not have been more fortunate for that young mother, his sister, and that soon-to-be-born child. With the help of a local law firm in La Grande, they assisted the young woman in arranging the adoption. A few months later, Pam and Frank traveled to La Grande and were introduced to their new daughter, whom they named Nichole.

Nikki and her younger brother (who was also adopted) were quite a bit younger than me and were busy with school activities and friends. Pam and Frank owned a successful business, allowing Pam to be home with the children. With Frank working and Pam at home, I became very close to Pam. Like me, Pam grew up in her household as the middle child of five kids. Being both middle children, we had a lot in common. She was most like Dad, with her quick wit and a wonderful sense of humor. Like me, she had many funny quirks and stumbled through life. Thinking back, she had her own...*Dodo bird.*

I enrolled in college part-time at my mother's alma mater, Montana State College in Billings. I quickly found a full-time retail job at Rimrock Mall. Being older, I was hired to do more than be a stock boy.

Dear Mom and Dad:

My classes are going great. With all my past retail experience, I have decided to major in Marketing. I am also taking a PE class (tennis) this semester to get some exercise into my day. I have learned not to go for those net shots anymore. I could use some improvement at abrupt stops in front of the net. By the way, tennis nets also double quite well as hammocks.

I love my new job. I work at Rimrock Mall, at a ladies' boutique shoe store called "Village Shoes." A funny thing happened today on my fourth day on the job. A charming lady came into the store today. She needed a pair of shoes for a formal event she was attending over the weekend. She had picked out several styles of high-heeled shoes she wanted to try on, so I excused myself to the backroom to retrieve them. As I left, she said, "While you are gone, I will change my foot." Not really listening, I assumed that meant she needed a nylon stocking, so I brought a pair of them out with the shoes.

Only then did I discover she really did need to "change her foot." She had a prosthetic foot that she changed out on her prosthetic leg. Each foot came in different angles for different-sized heels. As you probably can figure, I was taken quite aback, but I suavely and seamlessly regained my composer as I sat down to assist her. She had three pairs of feet with her, each pair to accommodate three different heel heights. She didn't need any help because she did this every day, but I wanted to be helpful in my salesman persona.

The foot is screwed in at the bottom. Similar to changing a tire, she had all the tools necessary for the procedure, including a mini tire iron and lug nut tightener. She could tell I was a little uncomfortable, so she joked along during the process to put me at ease. She was very nice.

Well, guess who showed up!

Everything was going well except I did not notice that I had slightly pinched my pant leg between the two connections. She stood up and proceeded to try out the shoes when I suddenly was swept off my feet. As I lay there on the floor, puzzled as to what the heck had happened, she was quite amused, as were the rest of the store employees and other patrons. We all had a great laugh about the whole thing.

Aunt Pam has taken over the "Randy Budgeting and Planning" task and has her own spreadsheet. Like you, Dad, she also has the uncanny ability to find more money on the expense side than the income side. I am holding off on buying a different vehicle for now, but I am getting close. With my new job, I have a higher income than I did as a teenager. Now that I am making more money, a new car is definitely in my future. My boss says some overtime hours are possible, so I am confident I can afford something soon. Don't worry, I am saving money for emergencies like you suggested.

I talked to Pam and Frank and decided to continue living with the family for now. When I get more settled and on my feet, I will look for my own apartment. I have also decided that finding one or two roommates to share expenses is best. I am excited to get out on my own, so I will work diligently toward that goal.

Love you both, Randy.

Salesman Extraordinaire

Living in Billings was great. It allowed me to spread my wings, see new things, meet new people, and discover more of what this world offers. I lived there for several years before stepping further into personal independence. A good friend of mine talked me into moving to Seattle, a city with entertaining nightlife and a lot more jobs that pay better. The big city of Seattle would also be a lot more exciting than Billings, Montana. I was twenty-one years young, and it was time to see the world. It was finally time to extract myself from the family and be on my own.

Using my experience, I immediately found a great job working at Nordstrom's ladies' shoe department. Working on commission has a whole new meaning when shoes cost $500.00 or more per pair. I soon discovered that the ladies in big cities love shoes. Their motto was the more the better and it worked for me. Women would come into the store, finding several pairs of shoes that would ring up to over $3,000.00 to $4,000.00. Worried about what their husbands would think, I would kick into salesman extraordinaire. Simply asking how many credit cards they had in their wallet made me the day's hero. The ladies would delightfully spread those shoe purchases over three to five cards, easily concealing an expensive day of shoe shopping. I discovered I was very good at marketing and was raking in the money. Working for a basic wage plus commission in a ladies' expensive shoe department certainly has its perks. I was making more money than I had ever made in my life. More money than I had ever envisioned. I never did finish college, but who needs college when you make this kind of money?

I lived comfortably in a nice two-bedroom, two-bath apartment in the downtown area without a roommate. Using my Nordstrom employee discount, I furnished my apartment in a fashion that I was quickly becoming accustomed to. I also purchased a lot of very nice clothing. I followed my father's recommendations, mostly making cash purchases. It was a good strategy, but I was not saving any money. Regardless, in typical Randy fashion, my search for a new car was on!

I was giddy with excitement at my potential prospects, and I no longer had a "Spreadsheet Manager."

Dear Mom and Dad:

Thanks so much for your last letter, Dad. Newsy as usual, but I am worried about your health. Please keep me updated on any new details. I want to know what is happening and how all your testing is progressing.

Everything is going great in my new city. Sales are going very well for me here at Nordstrom, so I purchased a new car. I bought a brand-new Pontiac Firebird. It is silver with spoked wheels, a T-top, leather, a Bose stereo system, and air conditioning. It even has, get this, heated seats. It is a beautiful set of wheels and I am very excited. I cannot wait for all of you to see it. Tell Kris I will even let her drive it.

City life differs significantly from what I am used to, but I am settling in nicely. I have made many friends through work who are helping me to acclimate to big city life. The nightlife here is quite the experience.

My downtown apartment has two bedrooms and two bathrooms. It is very roomy, and I have no roommates, so I have plenty of room for you to visit. Please come and see me anytime. I would love to take you to some of my favorite places. We could also take in a Mariners game. They are having a great year. Tell Joni and Kris to write me sometime, I would love to hear from them now and then.

As I said, please keep me informed of everything about your health. I can come home at any time to help if needed.

Love, Randy

Dad's Health Journey

Dad was diagnosed with Diabetes in 1959 when he was twenty-three years old. The disease was unkind to him throughout his adult life. Back in Dad's day of diagnosis, little was known about managing this chronic illness. The monitoring of such a disease was also still in its archaic form.

Blood sugar monitoring did not exist when Dad was first diagnosed. All that was available in early home monitoring were "Tes Tapes» that only tested the urine. Initially used in the beverage industry, it was to test for the amount of sugar content in sodas and wine. Therefore, it was merely a measure of sugar in urine, not blood. Color indicators on the tape would change depending on how much sugar was spilling into the urine from the bloodstream via the kidneys. The amount of insulin taken daily was quantified by the amount of sugar present in urine. Sugar is not a component found in urine.

Dextro-sticks and Clini-sticks (1963–65) were litmus color indicator paper strips that were a step up from Tes Tapes since they read blood instead of urine. Still inadequate, it was a more accurate account of actual blood glucose. Dad had a basket next to the dining room table containing his blood glucose monitoring supplies. Before each meal, he would prick his finger, applying the blood drop to the test tape. He would then compare the color to the indicator gradient on the side of the bottle. He would then inject the proper amount of insulin based on the color.

This would only change in the 1980s when digital glucometer read-outs became the standard. That is when home glucometers took off and became the standard of care for home diabetic management.

What was known by the 1980s, twenty-plus years following Dad's diagnosis, was that excess sugar spilled into the urine is a LATE sign of a high blood glucose content and poor diabetes management. In the age of Tes Tapes, high blood glucose took its toll on many body functions. Since glucose molecules in the blood are very large and highly damaging to small vessels throughout the body, blood vessels in the kidneys are highly susceptible to damage. Therefore, it was typical during that era for diabetics to lose their kidneys within twenty years of diagnosis, and that is precisely what happened to my father.

Dad lost his kidney function secondary to his diabetes. It was something that Mom and Dad did not share with us until they knew all the details. I remember when they broke the news to us. The family meeting was subdued, with the facts as they knew them. They then carefully explained our next steps as a family without worrying us. Kidney failure is considered a disability. Dad's health was the priority now, so Dad was forced to retire following his definitive diagnosis of kidney failure when he was forty-five years old. As young adults busy with our lives, we all missed the seriousness of what lay ahead. We threw Dad a surprise retirement party with just the five of us. We decorated the house, and Joni baked him a cake. Mom and Dad were both surprised and did their best to exhibit joy. But I could tell our parents were not feeling as celebratory as I had expected.

Your kidneys filter out accumulated waste and toxins from the bloodstream. Once somebody loses their kidneys, they must manually remove all those toxins from the blood through dialysis or get a kidney transplant. Failure to perform either of those strategies will result in death.

Hemodialysis is a large blood cleansing machine that replaces the function of the kidneys. A patient must go to a hospital or dialysis clinic to perform this. Patients are connected to this machine by a large blood catheter device, surgically inserted into their bodies. The machine then runs the patient's blood from the body and through the machine, cleaning and filtering the blood of all toxins. After the blood is filtered through the machine, it returns to the body. Mom and Dad went three days a week to have this procedure.

The closest dialysis machine for Dad was in Boise, Idaho. A three to five-hour drive for them, depending on the road conditions. Dialysis would then take several hours. Diabetic damage had already begun to affect Dad's eyesight, so he could not drive in the dark. Mother was extremely nervous about this drive once winter hit. Fortunately, Dad became approved for a home dialysis treatment called "Peritoneal Dialysis." Peritoneal dialysis is a treatment for kidney failure that uses the lining of your abdomen (peritoneum) to filter the fluids inside your body. A surgeon will place a soft tube (catheter) into the abdomen. A dialysis solution made of water, salt, and other additives flows from a bag (like an IV bag) through the catheter and into the abdomen.

When the bag is empty, you disconnect it and place a cap on the abdominal catheter so one can move around and perform everyday activities. The dialysis solution in your abdomen absorbs wastes and extra fluid from the body through naturally occurring osmosis via the peritoneal membrane that protects the organs. After a few hours, the solution held in the abdomen, having absorbed all the body's waste, can be drained out through the catheter. The solution is drained from the abdomen and into the empty bag that had contained the clean dialysis solution. You can then discard the solution in the toilet and throw away the bag. This process, called "an exchange," must be repeated three to six times daily, depending on the patient's need.

Whether it is hemodialysis or peritoneal dialysis, it does not cure kidney failure but allows a person more time to live. For some, it is a stopgap while awaiting a kidney transplant. This method of dialysis kept him and Mom home. Mother could then resume her full-time job. It was a much better choice than traveling back and forth to Boise three times a week, especially in the winter. As long as Dad could dialyze himself four times daily, it could be done at home.

Dad was the most resilient and optimistic person of anyone I have ever known. Even with this considerable health setback, he kept very busy as a volunteer for almost every cause. He continued his service to the Oregon State Board of Higher Education, eventually becoming the President of that state body. Whenever he had to travel, he would pack all his dialysis supplies with him. This task was challenging, as one day of dialysate fluid consisted of four one-liter bags. Dad needed more than one extra suitcase for this, depending on how long he was gone. During his peritoneal dialysis period, Dad even finagled a family trip to Hawaii, arranging a shipment of forty cases of dialysate fluid to the condominiums where we were staying. Dad was tenacious. If it was important to him, he could get it done.

Dad had his first kidney transplant in 1981. Unfortunately, his body rejected that kidney. Even with a high degree of tissue and blood matching, the body can still recognize a new organ as a foreign body. It is the body's natural response to any foreign substance. The reaction is the same as if one has a sliver in a finger. The body's immune mechanisms kick in to attack the organ (foreign body) to remove it. This is what happened to Dad. He lost that first kidney within three months of receiving it. He was disappointed, but he went back on peritoneal dialysis.

In the 1980s, there was a seventy percent success rate in getting the body to accept the donor organ. With the next attempt, it fell to twenty-five percent. There was much to consider as Mom and Dad took a step back from their disappointment to take another look at their options. Following the rejection, I tried to give him one of my kidneys. During that time, family matches had an improved chance of success. He refused to allow any of his children to donate. He always said that kidneys are important, and God gave us two kidneys for a reason.

Dad ended up being very fortunate. A new anti-rejection medication was in the final stages of FDA approval. He was selected to participate in a Phase III, groundbreaking double-blind study to test the effectiveness of Cyclosporine.

Double-blind studies are essential in healthcare research to determine the efficacy and safety of ANY new drug. It is the gold standard in any pharmaceutical research study seeking FDA approval. It takes years before a drug achieves double-blind study status. When a drug is accepted into a Phase III clinical trial, it has already been years with a proven efficacy and safety record.

Double Blind Research Studies is a specific study whereby neither the subjects of the research nor the persons administering the research know ANY aspects of the research. Study subjects are carefully screened and selected by doctors and researchers for their appropriateness for the study. The identities of patients are unknown to those administering the study. Patients are divided into two groups: those receiving a placebo and those receiving the actual drug. Neither the researchers nor the test subjects know who gets the placebo or the drug. Double-blind research procedures guard against experimenter bias and placebo effects.

> **It cannot be emphasized enough, that without adequate studies, drugs cannot be proven to affect the target condition, or worse, may have fatal flaws.**

Placebo effects are when beneficial or negative results can be produced simply by the subject's belief system in the treatment. If the individual does not know whether they are on the drug, their beliefs associated with the treatment are eliminated. The experimenter, also unaware of who is receiving the drug, cannot insert their own biases into the effects or failure of the drug. They can then objectively evaluate a drug's effectiveness, side effects, or failures without risk of bias. Phase III clinical trials take at least one year to prove a drug is safe for the general population, with one to four years the standard. Cyclosporine had been under study since the 1970s for clinical applications as an anti-rejection compound. The first successful results did not occur until 1978. The first clinical trial patients, including my father, received Cyclosporine in March of 1982. The FDA approved it for widespread clinical use in 1983 (Colombo 2011).

After several more months of peritoneal dialysis, a second cadaver kidney for Dad was located. The second transplant surgery was successful, as he officially became a part of the study. As the weeks wore on, it was an anxious time for all of us. Frequent kidney function lab studies seemed to be holding stable. Each blood draw was a lesson in patience, as we would all hold our breath for results. Eight months later, we were out of the proverbial woods when studies showed Dad's new kidney was still functioning at near-normal levels. We were then informed that through the grace of God, Dad was one of the test subjects taking the drug. Not since insulin has any medication had such an impact on diabetic patients. In this case, for those needing life-saving organ transplants.

Today, Cyclosporine is in generic form. It is widely used for transplant patients and is now effective for many autoimmune diseases, such as atopic dermatitis, aplastic anemia, chronic asthma, and psoriasis. Autoimmune diseases are conditions where your immune system turns against your body. It makes sense then, that Cyclosporine has found other uses related to its anti-rejection properties.

My father made history for his contributions to the advancement of organ transplantation. His second kidney transplant was a success. That same year, our parents celebrated their twenty-fifth wedding anniversary. Joni, Kris, and I threw them a surprise anniversary celebration with all their friends at the La Grande Country Club that December. Our family was truly blessed.

Psych Papa!

Diabetes severely damages all small blood vessels and nerve endings so the tiny vessels in Dad's kidneys were only the beginning. Also damaged were the small blood vessels in his eyes, robbing him of his sight. Dad eventually lost most of his vision to diabetic retinopathy, where lack of blood flow damages the light-sensitive tissue at the back of the eye, the retina. Eventually, diabetic retinopathy causes blindness for which there is no cure. Dad often described his sight as "looking through an incredibly dirty windshield."

While Joni was in nursing school, Dad volunteered to care for Justin, beginning when he was three years old. Dad and Justin had a game they called "Psyche." Dad would identify a make-believe object or imaginary person in the house, whereby Dad would send Justin to investigate. Not finding this mythical object or person, Justin would return to tell his grandfather, "It's not there, Papa?" Dad would then yell, "PSYCH!" which would dissolve them both into hysterical laughter.

One day, Mom, Dad, and Justin departed the house to run their usual errands. Following his grandmother, Justin skipped happily through the door, jumping wide off the outside landing. He then turned to Dad and stated, "Watch out, Papa, ants!" Of course, not seeing all that well, Dad took a wide step off the step to avoid "the ants." Justin then promptly turned around, hysterically laughing, and yelled, "PSYCH, PAPA!".

One day, Dad lost his balance, badly twisting his ankle. With his diabetic neuropathy, Dad could not perceive pain, therefore he was unaware of the damage he had done to his ankle. Diabetic neuropathy is a type of nerve damage that is also common among diabetics. As with small blood vessels, high blood sugars can compromise nerves throughout the body, primarily the extremities (hands and feet). This results in pain and numbness in the feet of some diabetics. Following Dad's ankle injury and after limping around for many days, he finally went to his doctor, who ordered X-rays. Only then was it ascertained that he had fractured that ankle, requiring a cast. Then, because Dad had no feeling in his feet, he could not detect that the cast had slowly rubbed his toes over time, causing gangrene.

Gangrene is a condition that occurs when body tissues die. It is caused by a loss of blood supply secondary to an underlying illness, injury, and/or infection. Dad's cast to his foot and ankle was ill-fitting enough that it cut off circulation to his big toe and the adjoining toe. Had he had normal feeling in his feet, he would have felt the pain and would have known immediately that something was wrong. He would have called his doctor, who would have remedied the problem in time. Six weeks later, when that cast was removed, it was too late. Dad lost his big toe and the adjoining toe on his right foot, requiring surgical amputation. Because diabetes causes poor blood circulation there was not adequate blood flow to his foot, critical for healing. This is why injuries to diabetics' feet heal very slowly and why they must be so cautious with injuries. Even something as simple as a toenail trim must be performed with extreme caution. It took two years for Dad's amputated toe sites to heal.

Since poor diabetic circulation affects ALL the tiny vessels in your body, it also affects the small vessels in your heart and brain. It did not help that Dad was a one to two-pack-a-day smoker for twenty-plus years. The nicotine in cigarettes constricts blood vessels every time you light up. For diabetics who smoke, nicotine further constricts, damaging already compromised small blood vessels throughout the body, with disastrous results.

The Importance of Flushing

Dad quit smoking in the early 1970s at the direction of his doctor. It is tough to quit smoking when somebody else smokes in the household. Mom wanted to support Dad in his quest to be a non-smoker, so she quit. It started fine, but as the addictive qualities of nicotine began to wear off, things started to get tense. As children, we did not notice the attitudinal changes. However, our parents were very good at hiding their quarrels. We never saw our parents disagree, let alone fight. Not until years later did Mom and Dad share the story of the war zone we were in. It only took a week before the "nicotine angry's" began to rise. Nicotine gum, hard candies, and everything people fell back on back then were not working well in our household. Even though things were strained, both continued working hard at it, it seemed.

Two weeks after their smoking hiatus began, Mom wandered into Dad's bathroom. She found two cigarette butts in the toilet. It was clear that Dad was cheating, blowing smoke out the bathroom window and flushing the butts down the toilet. Dad forgot to flush that day.

Mother does not get her ire up very often, but when she does, it is better to vacate the premises. I can only imagine what transpired after that little discovery. Mother had taken their smoking cessation seriously, much more seriously it appeared, than Dad had. What exactly transpired that day is a mystery. All we knew at the time was that mother had resumed smoking.

Dad did eventually quit smoking and Mom quit many years later, on her terms. Once she did quit smoking, she wished she had done it sooner. The difference in how she felt was enormous. She joined a gym, walked, and adopted a healthier diet. Decades of smoking do have consequences, however. Consequences that will not catch up with folks until years later.

Staying Puft

Following my very short young adult stint in Seattle, I returned to Eastern Oregon. Even though I was making a lot of money, I decided living in that huge city was not worth it. Not worth the noise, the pollution, the violence, and especially the crime. Besides, it became clear that Dad's health was slowly deteriorating. It was time to go home.

Once home, I decided it was time to finish my degree. Returning to college full-time, with your only income derived from a government work-study program, does not support a fancy Pontiac Firebird with T-tops, leather, and heated seats. The car payment was more than my monthly tuition and then there was the insurance and the gas. Sadly, it was time to downsize, but getting rid of that beautiful car was a hard reality to swallow. Ultimately, it was the best car I ever owned, but life had presented new priorities.

I was helping to take care of my family and finishing my education. That meant not only drastically downsizing my vehicle but also my expectations. It was no longer about hot cars, fancy apartments and expensive clothing. It was about getting back to basics and back to basics now meant living within my now meager means. What that meant for me was the basics in around-town transportation and you cannot get any more basic than a Honda Scooter. A friend was trying to get rid of it for some extra money. It was cheap and it was a mode of transportation. However, no amount of dignity is derived from a man riding a scooter. A motorcycle for sure, but not a scooter. There I was, a man with, um... wide shoulders, saddled astride the saddest mode of transportation I had ever owned. Humbling does not come near to describing it. I will not even talk about how that worked in the winter. Remember the Stay Puft Marshmallow Man on Frank Lake? Well, here I am! Some things just come back around to haunt you later.

I had fun going back to school. Through a work-study grant, I monopolized on my leadership experience, landing a job as the head of Student Activities. I worked with a great bunch of imaginative students. We planned and executed all the large and small social events for the student body. Not since Camp Silverback had I found a group of people who worked together so cohesively.

I was making long-lasting friends, not the superficial and fleeting kind I had in the city. Most importantly, I was back home where I belonged. I finally graduated from college with a degree in General Studies, with an emphasis on Marketing. General studies would be my third or fourth-degree change (I lost track) because I was just not good with math. Kris tried to get me through it, though. She was a natural in college, easily skating through with a "B" average, rarely cracking a book. She spent most of her time on the basketball court and partying. She took the college co-ed thing to heart and had a great time doing it. She graduated with a degree in Psychology, probably to figure out what the heck was going on with me. Dad was the President of the Oregon State Board of Higher Education, so his signature adorns Kris' diploma.

Kris was my math tutor. We would sit down together every night to tackle my next math assignment. Algebra was my nemesis. I would work through each math problem with precision and thought, ending with an equation five pages long. I would present the answer proudly to my sister for final approval. She would study it for a while and then point out the fatal flaw in my rambling calculation. Seeing the error, I would erase the four and a half pages of subsequent calculations and submit it to her for approval. It was now six pages of calculations. She studied it again, pointing out the next misstep of my wandering equation. Ultimately, it always mystified me that the answer was easily derived by a simple two to four-line computation that always ended in X-squared. I barely held onto a C-average until the day the professor introduced the imaginary number system. Are you kidding me? I can hardly get through the real number system. I handed him my drop slip and changed my major again.

The Student Activities Department brought in a big-name performer one year, securing Robert Palmer in concert. Before that, the last big entertainer to grace La Grande would be The Eagles in the early 1970s. As a warm-up event and to promote the concert, we held a lip-sync performance the weekend before the big concert. In full costume, my staff did a lip-sync performance to Robert Palmer's "Addicted to Love." Kris played the part of one of the "Robert Palmer Girls." She came on stage in style, complete with the black leather mini skirt and sultry red lipstick. It was epic because my tomboy, basketball-playing sister, who never wore a dress, pulled off the girly look in hot fashion that night. It was amazing (Khan 1986).

Student Activities organized many dances with various themes during the school year. One night, we had a fight break out on the dance floor. Trying to play peacemaker, I got directly into the middle of it. What started as a little kerfuffle between two male students ended badly when one of the fists landed in the middle of my face, breaking my nose. Everything after that was somewhat fuzzy. I was transported to our local emergency room in an ambulance, later having a rhinoplasty to fix my shattered nose. It did not end up being all that bad. After all, I had inherited the "Majestic" nose, a genetic landmark identifier in my mother's family that could have its own zip code. I was now able to refashion this "distinguishing" feature for free. You must always find a silver lining wherever you can procure one.

"Fist Man" was later arrested for assault, with his insurance now responsible for all my medical care. The surgery may have been free, but the recovery was not fun. While I was on the mend, I stayed with Mom and Dad. If I had thought the nose break was painful, the pain I felt post-operatively was off the charts. For the next ten days, I was down and out on pain medication, sleeping most of the time. This was the time that I curiously developed a new habit.

It was early evening and Joni and Kris were at the house. Everyone had just finished dinner and were sitting around the dining room table visiting. Since I had slept through dinner I got hungry, so I got out of bed to get a bowl of ice cream. I headed into the kitchen, opened the freezer, pulled the ice cream out and set it on the counter. I then went to the cupboard, retrieved a bowl and spoon and dished up a massive bowl of frosty delight. I carried my bowl of ice cream to the dining room table and sat down with the family to enjoy my early evening snack. Mom asked how I was feeling, to which I said, "fine." I then sat down and proceeded to eat my bowl of ice cream. They asked me several questions that I did not answer. I guess I was not hungry because I got up from the dining room table and wandered back to my bedroom. What was clear to the family at that point was that I was sleepwalking. This has been a problem of mine since I was a small child. Now, the habit was taking on a whole new dimension, sleep eating. From that point on, whenever I began a new diet regimen, I would wake up in the morning only to find dishes in the sink from a middle of the night eating soirée. What was frightening was that my sleep-eating was not just about snacking on something out of the fridge or cupboard, sometimes I would find dirty pots and pans in the morning.

Know Your Principles

One semester, Kris talked me into taking one of her three-hundred-level Psychology classes. I needed something different anyway to fill in some elective hours. I figured it would be fun to take another class with her that was not math. Besides, how hard can a Psychology class be? So, I signed up for "Principles of Learning." I limped through that psychology class until the final paper. That paper culminated everything one had learned the entire semester and replaced the final exam. There were several topics to choose from, so I selected "How Organisms Learn." It outlined everything anyone ever wanted to know about organisms.

Enter My Dodo Bird...

The finished paper, in my mind, was brilliant. I was sure that it would garner an A+. It would have too, except for one tiny little detail I failed to notice. I misspelled the word "organism" throughout the entire paper. Omitting the "n" and "i" in that word made the intent of that paper more intimate than I had intended. The paper was covered in red ink, with a big 'HUH' attached. How an orga(ni)sm gains knowledge, trains and commits thoughts to memory, and how "it" acquires skills and experiences. Anyway, you get the gist, and my professor was unamused.

Later, I learned that the professor went to Russell, a close family friend, who also taught at the university. He asked Russell, "Was it an honest, stupid mistake, or was I making fun of the subject and the course?" Russell's answers to these questions would determine whether or not I failed the class. Russ assured the professor that it was indeed just me and another one of my entertaining mistakes, of which this would not be the last. Both Russ and the professor had a great laugh at my expense. I am sure my paper will be permanently enshrined in the historical annals of the Psychology Department at Eastern Oregon University. With my integrity in shreds, I never stepped foot in the Psychology Department again. Somehow, I escaped with a "C" in that class.

PART IV

Loss

Through every health setback, Dad always remained optimistic and upbeat. Maybe he did that for the family so that we wouldn't worry, but Dad also had a strong faith in God. He always minimized his setbacks with one simple statement, *"There is always somebody else worse off than you are."*

He always taught us:

"Your attitude is the single most important predictor of outcome."

"Optimism is an intellectual choice and happiness is the blessing that follows."

He wanted to be an example of self-reliance and independence in the face of adversity. He always talked about his support systems in his letters and journal. It was a gift freely offered up by family and friends who had genuine feelings of concern and love for our family. It was this support system that helped him overcome each new setback.

Dad's transplant period peaked while Kris was still living at home and in high school. For her, high school was not as carefree as it was for Joni and me. She had to grow up fast and our family's circumstances required her every move to be tracked. It was very tough for a teenager who should have been more attuned to friends, boyfriends, sports and dating. Kris was on a very short tether, as Mom always needed to know where she was.

After his first kidney rejection, Dad was again on the organ transplant list. A kidney could suddenly become available at any time of the day or night, so Kris had to be immediately available. Once a kidney was identified, they had only a small window of opportunity to make the five-hour trip back to Portland for the transplant surgery. The clock was always ticking. They counted on Kris to be available at a moment's notice to take care of the home front. I lived in Seattle then, and Joni was busy working full-time and caring for her young family.

After the first transplant failed, several disappointments would occur along the road to the second transplant. The Portland Renal Unit would call with an available kidney, whereby Mom and Dad would immediately be on the road for the long, hurried trek back to Portland. Each time they arrived at the renal unit; Dad would have a pre-transplant physical to make sure he was fit for the surgery. There could be no evidence of any other infection within his body before surgery. Numerous times, Dad would be turned down and sent home when his screening revealed a contraindication. It was a constant roller-coaster of hope and disappointment for the entire family.

Dad's second kidney transplant was successful, thanks to Cyclosporine. Eight years later, that second kidney would fail. This happened almost exactly the average amount of time that diabetic kidney transplants will last. Regardless of the breakthrough medications and exemplary care, diabetic damage continues throughout a diabetic's lifetime. Eventually, diabetes destroyed Dad's second kidney. Dad began peritoneal dialysis again, awaiting a third transplant. However, we noticed it was different this time. It was hard to define, but he just was not himself. The answer would soon become apparent.

Dad suffered his final setback with a massive hemorrhagic stroke. Blood was bleeding into his brain, necessitating immediate air transport to The Oregon Health Sciences University in Portland. His numerous concurrent health conditions required him to be closer to all his health professionals, allowing all his doctors to confer at once.

My father died at Portland's University Hospital shortly after his admission, entirely unrelated to his stroke. He was only fifty-five years old. Something untoward occurred during the insertion of another hemodialysis catheter. It should have been a simple procedure in his room or the radiology department. All we were told was that somehow, the surgeon punched through his aortic artery. He died instantly on the table. Most regrettably, our father died alone without his family nearby. Dialysis catheter insertion is usually performed under a local with sedation, meaning he was more than likely awake during the procedure.

Our mother got the phone call while she was at work. Russell gathered the rest of us together after that. There is not a lot I remember about that day. Mother asked for a complete autopsy before he was cremated. Mysteriously, that was overlooked and he was cremated without further inquiry. The death certificate's "cause of death" was extremely vague. In hindsight, we probably could have sued. However, Dad had complex medical issues and a life-threatening stroke. A lawsuit would have never changed the inevitable outcome for our father or for us.

Dad loved to fish and camp. He could "MacGyver" anything together with duct tape and baling twine. He got a huge kick out of watching Bullwinkle and Bugs Bunny cartoons with us. He especially loved the antics of the Road Runner and Wiley Coyote. Every week, he would tune in for HeeHaw, Petticoat Junction and The Hollywood Squares. He was an active member of the Thanatopsis Literary Society and played penny-ante poker with his EOC faculty mafia buddies every Thursday night. Dad loved anything by Garrison Keillor and he listened to Paul Harvey every day. It is where he got the idea of a weekly radio program (R. D. Anderson 1985) (Keillor 1974-2016) (Watson 2014).

Dad was the best practical joker. He loved all kinds of music, exposing us to Country-Western, Classical, Jazz and Big Band. He had a wide musical repertoire that influenced his grandson in his future musical pursuits. Dad had a beautiful singing voice, singing in the Methodist church choir, as well as with "The Blue Mountain Barbershoppers." He was the lead bass player on the "Washtub Bass" of his redneck band. He was the happiest being with and playing with his family. He cherished every moment he had with his one and only grandchild.

I was so proud of Dad in so many ways. He was my hero and my life mentor. He always knew the right things to say in all situations. He was the perfect husband and father and was the kind of husband and father I wanted to be when I got married and had my own children. His greatest gift to all of us was his positive attitude no matter what was occurring with his health.

His loss to our family was devastating and we were never quite the same after that. We not only lost our leader, but our beacon. He had the gift of light that guided us onto logical paths that presented themselves during our lives. There were so many things he had yet to teach us. Like many others who experience that kind of loss, you never get over it; you learn to survive it. Surviving eventually becomes easier over time, with all the sweet memories.

I cannot thank the family enough, who agonized over losing a loved one yet decided to give the true gift of life, the donation of that kidney to my father. It is a true lesson of love and sacrifice that enabled him to be with us for another eight wonderful years.

The loss of my father probably furthered my already fragile psyche. It did not help when my second mother, Aunt Pam, died suddenly of Ovarian Cancer a few years later. Then, our mother got the tragic news that she had breast cancer.

Bowled Over

Mother's cancer diagnosis hit us hard. First, it had not been long since Dad died. Secondly, we had become accustomed to the various health complications our father suffered through the years. Each time, he seemed to overcome one hurdle when another would happen. He was like the "ever-ready" battery bunny, with a never-ending positive attitude and courage that got him and us through it. It is why his death was so unexpected. It had become customary for him to overcome each medical crisis (Company 1988).

Mom was different. She was our sweet mother and she was scared. Before cancer, she was quietly in the background, supporting us and our crazy endeavors. She was the concrete pillar that kept the building upright. She was the acrobatic juggler who effortlessly kept all the balls in the air. That all became our job now, whether we wanted it or not.

Mom and I had a close relationship that was hard for me to explain. It was because the two of us were more alike emotionally. Joni and Kris were more Dad-like, where concrete thought and action prevailed. The three of them were the decision-makers and shared family leadership. Mom and I let them make all the decisions. It was easier that way because you could never make a wrong decision.

Mom had visited her general physician in La Grande because of a suspicious lump and skin change in her breast area. X-rays were not definitive for a diagnosis, so our lifelong family doctor sent her to a specialist in Boise. He must have had his suspicions because he mainlined her to a facility as soon as he could. We were in Boise to see a specialist within a few days.

Our family doctor Wes and his family were close friends of ours. Wes and his wife Katy lived near us in our tight-knit neighborhood. They had five children, with kids the same age as the three of us, attending the same school and classrooms. It was your typical middle-class kid busy neighborhood, all playing together daily. While we lived in the neighborhood, Dr. Wes even made one or two house calls.

Mother had a different doctor now, devoid of any real personality and not one iota of sensitivity. This was an attitude and presence we were not at all used to. We were used to Dr. Wes and his Marcus Welby approach. After evaluating our mother, he coldly declared the cancer diagnosis and his opinion of her eventual poor prognosis/outcome. He gave us little hope that day, even before discussing any post-surgical treatment plan. He told us that our mom had little hope of surviving this cancer (Victor 1969-1976).

Not until later did we realize he was not as knowledgeable about her prognosis as he thought. He was her cancer surgeon. Probably a good surgeon, although with his attitude, who would know for sure? Most importantly, he was NOT an Oncologist. Oncologists are the real cancer practitioners who are highly specialized. Oncologists become the experts in different cancer diagnoses and practice treatments, depending on the cancer they specialize in. Oncologists are the doctors who manage cancer treatments based on the medical research they study throughout their medical careers. That surgeon needed to stay in his lane.

Mom's cancer was serious, with a progression that warranted a double mastectomy the next day. We stayed the night in Boise at a lovely downtown hotel. She could not eat or drink anything after midnight, so the four of us made the best of it. The hotel featured a fine dining restaurant, so in our usual style we set out to "eat, drink and be merry" until the clock struck midnight. We had a nice dinner, ordered an expensive bottle of wine and laughed the evening away.

The next day, our mother went in for her surgery, after which she was admitted to the hospital for a two-day recovery. Mom's surgeon returned to talk to us, reiterated his bleak opinion and we never saw him again. Other doctors took over for him for the remainder of her hospitalization. We were all stunned and doing our best to keep Mom's spirits up. It had all happened so fast, overwhelming us with sadness and uncertainty. We felt like we had just been "bowled over" by a giant boulder. Honestly, I have been literally "bowled over" by a boulder, so I can tell you how frightening that is.

Coming Off the Cliff

Shortly after Camp Silverback, I began a new job as a food service marketer with Sysco Food Services. My assigned marketing area would be Wallowa County. It was a great gig. I worked independently from my office in my own home, commuting to the beautiful Wallowa Mountain communities three days a week. It was a nice transition from my previous job with Chartwell Food Services at the University. While in Wallowa County, I would connect with my various restaurant owners/clients while attempting to recruit new clients in the area. There was no comparison between this commute and the dreadful bumper-to-bumper traffic I endured while commuting in Seattle.

Sysco Foods was wonderful to work for and my bosses were encouraging. I was exceeding the company's sales expectations, winning trips to Las Vegas and shopping sprees at leading sporting goods stores. During one of those shopping sprees, I brought home a new set of golf clubs, a bag and a new ski setup with skis, boots, poles and bindings. I made a base wage, but most of my salary was in commissions. It was excellent money that, for the most part, afforded me my expensive tastes. It was not as much as I was making in Seattle, but the tradeoffs were well worth it.

One beautiful spring day, I was driving my latest and greatest new set of wheels through the Wallowa mountains. It was a day that followed a torrential rainstorm the previous night. That day, the skies were clear blue and it was a perfect seventy-five degrees. I crested the top and proceeded to snake down the mountain pass and winding road through that canyon known as The Minam Grade. As you know, Journal, this is a very familiar road to me. Minam grade is a narrow roadway cut into the side of a granite rock mountain. The granite mountain was to my left and a long, steep cliff was off to the right. I looked down below and marveled at the river emerging from the mountain draw onto the Wallowa Valley floor. It was a beautiful scene as the river meandered through the lush green valley. As I reached down to turn up the radio, my eyes were off the road for just a millisecond when it hit me!

The previous night's rainstorm had loosened the rocks on the cliffs above me. As I traveled, I often saw large rocks and boulders lying in the middle of the road, but I did not give them much thought. I travel this road often enough that I would see them all the time. If you are traveling at a safe rate of speed, you can easily drive around them. Today though, a boulder hit me square on the driver's side windshield. About the size of a large watermelon, it slammed into the windshield, completely caving it in. The impact did not break the windshield, but the entire mesh of woven and crumpled glass was draped across me and my dashboard. Thank God, nobody was around me at the time. It was the most frightening thing I have ever experienced as a driver. It was a miracle that I didn't swerve to the right, going down the other side of the cliff.

Blinded by the shock and with my windshield in my lap, I begin processing. Did I hit another car head-on, or did I hit an animal? Somehow, I kept my head together as I slammed on the brakes in the middle of the road. Only then did I realize what had happened, as that boulder slowly rolled and bounced down the hood of my car, landing on the road in front of me. God was watching out for me that day. That cliff above me was made of stacked granite rock. That boulder could have been much bigger, crushing me and my car.

Like with that boulder, you are in that moment when you have no idea what has just hit you. As that doctor gave us that devastating news, you spend a few seconds processing it, then you begin to try and explain it. Your frantic mind begins to wonder. How long had this been brewing? What did we all miss? What do you mean, it is too late? In those short three days, we all outwardly kept it together for our mother, but inside, we were all overwhelmingly sad and uncertain of the future.

After three days, we all left the hospital with our mom. By then, we had adequately processed the week's events. Even though that doctor gave us no hope, we let that news and that doctor roll out of our minds, just as that rock rolled off my car. From then on, with God's grace, we began to channel our father. Perhaps he was there that day as we all moved forward with an optimistic attitude about what the future would hold for our mom.

There was less optimism that day about my poor car. The state trooper figured that a big rock had come off that cliff, at least forty yards up. My car was totaled and had to be towed from the site, but it was just a car.

Mom's cancer was extensive, with many lymph nodes involved. She was tough though, much tougher than any of us had ever given her credit for. After that bilateral mastectomy in Boise, we spent months traveling with our mother back and forth to Walla Walla Washington for chemotherapy. After that came weeks of radiation. From the day we heard the diagnosis to the completion of treatment, it was a little over a year. Through Mom's strength, God's grace, and our optimism, Mom soldiered on and proved that arrogant doctor in Boise wrong. Mother's cancer care team in Walla Walla determined her cancer-free five years after her treatments were completed.

The Downward Spiral

Following Dad's death and Mother's cancer scare, attitudes changed within our family. We became less consumed with anything petty, trivial and beyond our control. It was a phenomenon that happened to each of us that we did not even share. It was an unconscious decision to live positively around positive people. You reflect on your life and remember the things and people that brought you love and laughter. It would be that formula we would practice for the rest of our lives.

Mom lived a cancer-free life for the next eight years. Then, beyond any fairness, she received a second cancer diagnosis. Even though Mother had quit smoking for twelve years, the years of smoking had taken its toll. This time, she was diagnosed with Small-Cell Lung Cancer. Being a different cancer, our mother had a new Oncologist. He was confident and enthusiastic about her "potential prognosis." However, this diagnosis was different. Small Cell Lung Cancer is well documented as having meager survival rates, even with aggressive treatment. Our mother started chemotherapy treatments right away, with just as much positivity as the last time. A month after treatments began, Mom had a "Positron Emission Tomography Scan," or PET scan. It is a type of radiographic whole-body scan. With this study, mom's doctor discovered that her cancer had still spread, even after a month-long aggressive chemotherapy regimen.

Overly optimistic recovery predictions from that doctor became dire end-of-life proclamations. For thirty days, that doctor was telling our mother he could cure her. Now, he told us, "There is nothing more we can do." We had always thought his prognosis was overly promising and we wondered about it at the time. It was curious that he had not been more realistic with our mother about her prognosis. As a doctor, you can still provide hope with cautious optimism about certain cancer outcomes.

Had we been prepared that day we would have all gone to that appointment with Mom. We had no idea that sort of news was forthcoming on that visit. He came into the room and told Mom and Joni that future treatments were futile. He then referred Mom and our family to Hospice. Mom was devastated and Joni was angry, angry at an overly confident doctor who gave our mother more hope than the diagnosis deserved. Angry that we had not been forewarned about the news to be presented at this clinic visit.

In reality, the doctor was prohibited from doing just that. We were now amid a new government regulation called HIPPA, or the Health Insurance Portability and Protection Act. Its purpose was to "Improve the portability and accountability of health insurance coverage for employees between jobs." Other objectives of the Act were to combat waste, fraud and abuse in health insurance and healthcare delivery, which was a joke. Waste, fraud and abuse continue to occur to this day. As with every government regulation, it was too broad. It is what the government intends as it casts a wide net to capture all the fundamental objectives it seeks to regulate. What seemed to be regulations concerning health insurance also created a new set of standards for the security, confidentiality and conveyance of personal health information. Under the HIPAA Privacy Rule, all healthcare practices and professionals are obligated to protect and secure all health information.

Hidden regulations in a large, cumbersome bill are impossible for lawmakers to review thoroughly. How many times does that happen anymore? Protected health information sounds good, but what does that mean in practice? It means withholding all health information in all circumstances concerning any individual patient. A concerned mother, father, grandparent, child or sibling can no longer ask questions or inquire about the condition of a beloved family member. Every patient must sign a disclosure agreement that identifies a person or persons who can be updated on medical progress and treatments. It is useless if that patient is unable or unwilling to sign that form. What is a dangerous example of an unwilling patient? A cognitively impaired patient with serious health considerations that they don't want to be shared for fear of being admitted to a care facility. It leaves family members unable to protect the safety and well-being of their loved ones. Yes, I have seen it happen.

What did that mean for us that day? The withholding of devastating information to our mother and family until Mom was informed in a cold, clinical office setting. Had we known, we all would have been there, prepared with questions about options. Most importantly, we would have been there to guide and comfort our mother on the day she received the worst information in her life. Information that was life-altering. It is not just the patient affected, the entire family is affected. The soft science or the art of medicine is what government policy and regulations can never deliver. That day, all that was left was for Joni to hold Mom's hand all the way home. Too stunned to think of any questions in the clinic, she had many questions on the way home. Joni was then tasked to answer her questions about experimental treatments that she knew nothing about, to try and reassure Mom about hospice and what that meant. But most of all, try to comfort our grieving mother, now suddenly facing the end of her life, while driving the next two hours in the car.

The government thinks it makes laws and sets policies concerning healthcare (and our lives) that ensure safety, privacy, and individuality of care. In reality, it does not. It is a government-defined approach where both patients and families suffer. It continues to this day and is getting worse. Once the government takes control of anything, whether healthcare or education, the care of the individual or child is gone. This one-size-fits-all paradigm is always political. Like every other government policy, HIPPA would later be manipulated to allow children as young as thirteen to receive birth control, abortions and gender-affirming medical care without parental knowledge or consent (Sharko MD 2022) (Rantz 2022) (Maren 2020).

Joni called both of us to her home. She then conveyed the devastating news to us, with our sweet mother sobbing in the background. Once again, we were all overwhelmed with shock and grief. Simultaneously, my personal life was spiraling out of control and down the flusher. The hits in my life just kept coming. In the grand scheme of things though, it came in second to what was happening with our mom. However, placing my chaos on the back burner did not help my overall health. I plummeted into despair following Mom's devastating news. The chaos in my personal life and my already fragile inner psyche was now beyond repair. It was a depression permanently residing in my body, from my head to my toenails. Putting my family first, I did not share my inner turmoil. Instead, I outwardly portrayed enthusiasm and light to help my mother and sisters smile.

My eating was now entirely out of control. Outwardly, it looked like I was functioning normally, but inwardly, everything was completely falling apart. Throughout my life, managing my weight has been tenuous at best. It was always only on the cusp of control, but it was not any longer. I was now full-time binge eating all day long, into the night with nothing off-limits anymore. It was the only thing that offered me solace and satisfaction. I began isolating myself from my family and my friends. I quit associating with anyone. My work with my job was suffering, as I chose to only work from home. I decided to call my clients instead of visiting them personally. I was only maintaining my current client list and not pursuing new clients. I mostly stayed in bed all day.

Mom had already moved in with Joni. It was supposed to be temporary after the sale of her home while awaiting a condominium more suitable for her needs. Things had changed now. For now, Kris moved out of her house and moved in with Joni, Justin, and Mom. My sisters adjusted their work schedules, so someone was always there to help and care for her. Mother's temporary living situation at Joni's home now became permanent. Mother argued with us about moving her to a nursing home, insisting she did not want to burden her children. That was never going to happen. Over the next several months, I rarely came around, leaving my sisters and nephew responsible for our mother's care. I used the excuse of my work as a reason to rarely visit and not participate. Mentally, I couldn't do it.

I gained so much weight in such a short time that I could hardly walk. After climbing the steps to Joni's front door, I had to stop three times to catch my breath. Before I could enter her home, I had to wait ten minutes at the top of the stairs, catching my breath and slowing my breathing and heart rate. I did not want them to worry about me, too. I could no longer hide my health issues this time. I collapsed, and after an ambulance ride to the emergency room, I ended up in the hospital with full-body edema, congestive heart failure, diabetes and high blood pressure. I was now almost four hundred pounds.

Early Evolutions of Body Weight

I lost forty pounds of excess body fluid following a ten-day hospital stay. Since a pint equals a pound, that was the equivalent of 40 pints of fluid or five gallons off my body. After my hospitalization and the intervention with Laura and my sisters, I researched various inpatient programs specializing in eating disorders.

It is so interesting how the issue of body weight has evolved. Society has always had a very narrow view of eating disorders. It has always been thought of as those disease processes that result in dangerously low body weights through Bulimia or Anorexia. The tragic death of singer, Karen Carpenter, would bring this disease's dangerousness into the public consciousness. Professional programs that treat eating disorders think of high or low body masses the same. The emotional or psychological reasons for eating disorders can take many forms, but the outcome is the same (People Staff 2020).

I remember when the film "Super-Size Me" was released. The film perfectly illustrated the problems within the fast-food industry and its contributions to our nationwide obesity epidemic. A gentleman named Morgan Spurlock made himself the test subject of a documentary about the commercial food industry. He put himself on a rigorous thirty-day McDonald's fast-food diet three times a day. This is something I can relate to. McDonald's fast food has always been my favorite (Spurlock 2004).

Whenever the person at the counter asked if he wanted it "super-sized," he would always say yes. He began his thirty-day binge regimen under the supervision of a cardiologist, a gastroenterologist, a general practitioner, a nutritionist and a personal trainer. In just five days, he had gained ten pounds. He kept gaining, even with moderate exercise of 5,000 steps per day that the average American walks, which is two miles.

After gaining just ten pounds, he reported that his bouts of depression, lethargy and headaches were always relieved by his next McDonald's meal. This is the hallmark of an addiction. By the end of thirty days, he had gained 24.5 pounds, for a total of 210 pounds. Spurlock's girlfriend attested that Mr. Spurlock lost much of his energy and sex drive during the experiment. On day 21, Spurlock started to have heart palpitations. His cardiologist advised stopping, but he finished the entire thirty days.

All his doctors were surprised at the degree of deterioration in Spurlock's health, including irreversible heart damage. It only took thirty days.

Whether you are a man or a woman, businesses and corporations in America are reluctant to hire us. It is a proven fact that obesity raises healthcare costs and reduces productivity. Both are too costly for business. They never say that, but that is the truth that we deal with every day. As an obese individual, I can tell you that we cannot participate in many physical activities that others can. Our inability to fully participate in society leaves us isolated with health and financial consequences. For me, something needed to be done. After much research, I decided on an inpatient program for eating disorders (Cutica Health 2021).

The program I chose lasts three to six months, depending on the speed of your progress. The program covers the basics of good nutrition, plus the psychological components of all eating disorders. Therefore, an essential treatment element for participants is to be under the direct care of a licensed psychiatrist specializing in eating disorders. You are expected to participate in individual and group psychotherapy sessions. The program educates participants on proper nutrition. Based on the food pyramid, everyone uses the pyramid as a nutritional guide to meet their personal goals. Good nutrition means a balance of proteins, grains, fruits, vegetables and fats. The program individualizes the proportion of those elements based on the necessary calories to gain or lose weight. Eventually, we all learn how to reach a proper BMI and ascertain how to maintain that long-term.

Once I have sufficiently progressed, they will transfer me to an outpatient program, providing me with an apartment. I will still be expected to participate in all the counseling sessions and classes. Once I meet the criteria for independent living, I will have more freedom, so it will be my first test in functioning independently. At first, I will continue to go back to the main campus to eat. I can only consume that which is served in the inpatient program, but once my doctors and I feel I am ready, I can purchase groceries and prepare meals. Even then, I will still participate in individual and group counseling.

I feel like I will get some real help, rooting out the issues that have been the basis of my eating disorder. My insurance will cover most of it and my employer is supportive. They have granted me a three-month leave of absence. They want me to be healthy as much as I do. I then headed directly to the program when my doctors in La Grande released me to travel.

Once admitted to the facility, it became abundantly clear that all those strategies I had perfected throughout my life no longer worked.

As specialists in treating eating disorders, they can readily recognize the tactics people practice to isolate themselves. In isolation, one can easily hide their emotions, feelings, food, alcohol and especially excuses. Even amid treatment, where I knew I needed professional help, I tried to isolate myself. From the time I was six years old, I had perfected the strategies of isolation to hide my disorder. I tried my best to get a private room, applying for an exception to the roommate requirement. It did not work because I was immediately assigned a roommate.

Dear Mom:

After two months, I finally progressed enough in the program that they moved me into an apartment. I am getting a lot of positive feedback from my counselors. I have learned so much about proper nutrition and food preparation. I am beginning to understand the root of my eating disorder and the emotional triggers that kick off poor eating habits. I know now that eating was a coping mechanism for significant emotional difficulties. The psychiatrists here are helping me work through all of that. I will need continued counseling once I return home. This is not a quick fix that will be resolved here. If you, Joni, and Kris could help on that end, I would be very grateful. I do not have time to research that here.

I do have some concerning news. Please do not worry, because everything is fine now. I developed an irregular heartbeat, known as "Atrial Flutter." I had to be rushed to the emergency room when I suddenly felt lightheaded, with some difficulty breathing. The hospital quickly determined the cause and performed what they call a "Cardioversion." It was scary to see them roll out that defibrillator machine. I felt like I was in an "ER" episode. Anyway, the defibrillator machine not only can deliver a massive shock to restart the heart, but it can also convert a bad heart rhythm into a normal sinus rhythm (Joe Sachs 1994).

I feel fabulous now without any ill effects. The doctors are monitoring me and have started me on some heart medications. Please don't worry. I am going to be okay.

I have made some fabulous friends here, and we all work to encourage each other through our difficulties. I feel good about my future now. I know I am going to make it. Also, you can stop worrying about my job situation. My company and my boss have been very supportive. They have extended my medical leave of absence and will take me back whenever I am ready. I cannot believe how much support I am getting. I do not know how to thank all of them and all of you. Give Joni, Kris and Justin my love. I should be home before Thanksgiving.

Love, Randy

My Daily Exercise Routine

Part of my program is to work into my day some sort of exercise routine. I can do anything I want if I carve out at least thirty minutes to accomplish this. It is a habit that all healthy people perform. I know this and used to practice it daily, but it is easy to fall out of the habit. They do have a gym here, which I often take advantage of. It has everything you need and accommodates everyone's interests. I feel too self-conscious to use the pool, so I usually go to the weight room where they keep the recumbent bikes.

Recumbent bikes are the greatest invention of stationary bicycles. Ordinary people cannot ride an upright stationary bike. These torture devices, famous for their tiny little seats, can only accommodate folks wearing size two pants. I never joined a regular gym for that very reason. Gyms do not have an interest in accommodating people of size. If gyms have recumbent bikes, there are usually only a couple available. I do not know why because they are resoundingly more comfortable than traditional exercise bikes. Not only are they more realistic for people of above-average size, but they are also preferable for older generations. Anyway, I ride the recumbent bike nearly every day. I just put on my favorite iPod music with my earbuds and "zone out" during my workout. When I do zone out, I often think about Dad.

Dad's Motorcycle Phase

Dad had his own adult bike phase when he purchased his motorcycle. It was just another one of Dad's many phases in life. Our family friend had motorcycles, and he and his daughter, Sally, always dirt biked together. It was their father/daughter activity they shared. Sally was another one of Kris' very best friends. Our families camped together all the time.

Enamored with LeRoy's cycle, Dad convinced Mother that getting a motorcycle would save much money on gasoline. He would ride his motorcycle to work instead of driving, saving them hundreds of dollars a month. I guess it worked because shortly afterward, Dad found his new (very used) practically vintage motorcycle...remember "thrifty." Dad's motorcycle was city roadworthy but could also double as a "dirt bike." It was perfect for his commute to work and when our families camped together, Dad could join LeRoy in exploring all those areas inaccessible by vehicle. Frankly, that was probably the real goal. It would be a great new adventure and being a dirt-biker like LeRoy was very cool.

It was Memorial Day weekend, our first camping trip of the season and Dad's first camping weekend with his "vintage" dirt bike. Our two families headed to the Owyhee Canyonlands area in southeastern Oregon. The Owyhee Canyonlands is one of the wildest regions in the contiguous United States. Its stone mazes of rocky ravines and furrowed badlands are scenically stunning. Through the erosive actions of the Owyhee River, it has taken centuries to create rich volcanic features. Hot springs, lava beds, craters and cinder stones are picturesque, with their brick-red and golden-yellow cliffs.

Within the Owyhee Canyonlands is the Succor Creek area. Near the Idaho border, Succor Creek was a great place to camp in the early spring. Its dessert qualities possessed the perfect weather for early camping. It became our favorite early spring camping destination, as we could always count on it being warm and dry. There would be no more miserable snowy, rainy Memorial Day camping adventures for our family.

Succor Creek State Park is a very remote, deep rock canyon only accessible by a very rough, fifteen-mile dirt road. It has very primitive camping accommodations without outhouses or drinking water available, so you must be self-contained. Early spring, the weather would be comfortably warm, with a creek running freely through our camping site. We never visited the area in the summer because it was too hot, with a dry stream bed.

Succor Creek State Park boasted a plethora of trails through the badlands that were perfect for dirt bike exploration. Dad came ready with his newly purchased used motorcycle/dirt bike. Mom was very nervous about this new interest, refusing to allow Kris to own a motorcycle. After breakfast that morning, Dad headed out with Kris riding on the back. LeRoy was on his bike, and Sally was on hers.

Joni and I played in the creek while Mom and Mary Kay visited. They were gone all day that day. I am positive Mother fretted the entire time. I am also sure Mary Kay did her best to alleviate her worry, but knowing my mother's paranoia, this did little to diminish her concern. They eventually returned alive and well that evening, regaling all of us with the day's exhilarating details, including a closely guarded secret that Kris blabbed the moment they got back to camp. It seems they had a little wreck mishap that Dad swore her to secrecy. Regardless, they were ready to tackle a new trail the next day. However, my father is not, never was, or ever would be, the athletic type at all and their "little" wreck I am sure, did not help.

Upon the family rising the following day, Dad did not. Dad was so stiff that morning that he absolutely could not move. "Stiff as a board" is how he described himself and his state of mobility that next morning. Mother even had to cook the camp breakfast because it took Dad two hours to get out of bed. Throughout the rest of the weekend, he could barely hobble as he shuffled slowly and gingerly around camp. He said, the only way he could have ridden that bike again that weekend "Is if he had gone to sleep sitting on the bike, helmet on, hands on the handlebars, in the ready-to-ride position."

As with many of Dad's phases, he only had that motorcycle for six months. As he had promised Mom, he rode it to work every day and as motorcycles do, it did get good gas mileage. Dad had switched jobs by then, becoming the Assistant Administrator for the local hospital. While working at the hospital, he saw firsthand a motorcycle accident and its fatal aftermath for the rider. He sold his motorcycle shortly after that, much to mother's relief. Besides, winter was soon upon Eastern Oregon and since Dad was not the hardy type, there was no way he would ride that motorcycle in the snow. It was time to dust off the car.

Kris...My Sister Friend

When we were in elementary school, my best friend, Patty and I would ride our bikes nearly every day when we could. Patty lived at the top of a ten-block hill on the outskirts of town. We were neighbors, with our family living only two houses down from her family. What was great fun was letting ourselves coast clear down those ten blocks, picking up more and more speed the further we went. Walking up was not all that fun, but it was well worth the feeling of flying freely down that long hill while it lasted. Being youngsters, we did not think about any traffic that could have been coming from all the side intersections. There were no stop signs on cross streets as we descended that hill. It was blind luck that we were not hit by cross traffic. We were unafraid only because of our naive age and childhood courage.

Kris always wanted to tag along with us. Mostly, it was all right because I liked hanging out with my sister, but there were times that Patty and I planned strategies to ditch her. Sometimes, we would play hide and seek at Patty's house and then leave her there. We would run off and do our own thing while Kris was parked in her usual hiding place. Kris, who was eight or nine then, always thought she was the best hider because we would never find her. Kris always hid in the same two places. Behind Patty's garage in the woodpile or in a shed at her cousin's house several blocks away. Once Patty and I finished doing our thing, or when it was time for dinner (whichever came first), I would retrieve her. I would lay on the praise, telling her what a good hider she was and how we could never find her. This always made Kris giggle, so I figured I was doing my part to build her self-esteem.

It turned out bad for me one day. As the family sat down one evening for dinner, Mom and Dad asked, "Where was Kris"? Oh, Geez! I had forgotten to pluck her out of her hiding place that day before showing up in time for dinner. Even more of a problem, it had been several hours. I had to fess up on that one, as I told Dad where she could be found. Dad called the parents, told them where to find Kris and asked them to please send her home. Kris was a determined child, as she had fallen asleep inside the shed after waiting hours for somebody to find her. I was grounded for two weeks.

While riding our bikes one day, Patty and I talked Kris into speeding down our hill. We dared her to break the "land speed record," as it were. She was always so thrilled to be hanging with us and being "one of the gang," that she took off down that hill peddling hard with Patty and me cheering her on. Kris began her challenge on the gravel part of the road, at the very top where Patty lived. Peddling hard, she picked up quite a bit of speed by the time she hit a large hole in front of our house. Her bike completely stopped and Kris sailed over the handlebars. It was beautiful watching her sail through the air. She looked just like Superman.

Then she hit the gravel, sliding down on her front side past the gravel road and about ten feet onto the pavement. It was not pretty after that. She was one big bloody road rash. Patty and I felt terrible but did not want to get into trouble. Kris was tough and a real trooper, hardly uttering a cry that day. Patty and I convinced her she was the champion bike stuntwoman nobody could beat. She told me later that she did not want to be a crybaby before her idols. Because she didn't go home crying, mother dressed her wounds and chalked it up to an unforeseen bike accident. Thank God.

Patty and I once put her down our clothes chute at home. It was a great experiment that only skinny little Kris could accomplish. We told her there were pillows and clothing at the bottom to break her fall, except there weren't. It was good that the clothes chute was only about two feet long.

Then there was the time I was able to talk Kris and her best friend, Jerrie, into being duct-taped together. They stood back-to-back as I walked the tape several times around them, using nearly the entire roll. Unfortunately, Mom came home unexpectedly, necessitating an expedient tape removal. While swiftly ripping the tape off the girls, some skin and hair came with it. Mother was oblivious to this escapade. The girls and I laughed about it later after their skin healed and their hair grew back. I am sure Dad did wonder what happened to his roll of duct tape.

He always kept a close inventory of all his home repair materials and duct tape was his favorite. I guess we should have owned stock in it.

Kris was my pesky little sister whom I tormented when we were children, but by the time we were teenagers we were not just siblings but best friends. As young adults in college, we enjoyed hanging out and shared the same friends. We ended up sharing an apartment and even shared a car accident in two different cars. Explain that to your insurance company that we also shared.

As a toddler, she had the most beautiful long, thick, wavy, light brown hair that went clear to her bottom. She was so pretty that she looked like a baby doll. It was not that way for long. When Kris was about eight years old, she became Kris from Kristi and had her hair cut short. From the time she could dress herself, she never wore a dress again. During that phase of her life, she strutted her individuality as a "Tomboy" girl, excelling in all sports.

Kris and Jerrie were community groundbreakers. They would be the first girls in La Grande to try out for Little League baseball. There were no girls' baseball teams in La Grande then and the girls wanted to play. They were both placed on the same team and were relegated to right field. A position they were traded in and out of and a position for which they were both over-skilled. Once they broke the mold, many more girls began to try out. Within two years, so many girls competed that a girl's league was formed. It was then that Kris could finally show her prowess in baseball and was no longer discarded into right field. From then on, she played shortstop, catcher or pitcher.

As a surprise, Dad drove Kris and Jerrie to Seattle one year to attend a Mariners baseball game. It was a father-daughter-daughter weekend where they stayed in a nice hotel near the stadium. To save some money (remember thrifty), they stopped at McDonald's on their way to the hotel. They laughed later at the spectacle they must have been, checking into that ritzy hotel with their backpacks for luggage. The smell of McDonald's' hamburgers and fries permeated the lobby of the hotel that sported a fine dining restaurant right next to the check-in desk.

It did not take long in the car when Dad soon discovered those two girls could talk. Talk, talk, talk, as they chattered the entire six-hour drive to Seattle. They continued in the hotel through their McDonald's dinner until they fell asleep that night. Once they woke up, they resumed their incessant jabbering all day long till they got to the baseball game. It was a great game and the girls had a great time. Once the game ended, the bantering began once again. Dad stopped at another fast-food joint and got them dinner. After returning the girls to the hotel room, Dad made a hasty retreat to the hotel bar and dining room. Upon rising the following day, the unrelenting constant chatter commenced again. Those two girls finally broke our poor father. For three solid days, he listened patiently to the nonstop jabbering of two tittering girls. That day, as they headed home, they stopped in Spokane to pick me up at the airport. I was heading back from Billings for a family visit. From the Spokane airport, we would all head back to La Grande.

About two hours out of Seattle, Dad suddenly pulled the car over to the side of the road and came to a stop. At that point, Dad issued a proclamation. "You two be quiet and do not say another word until we pick up your brother!" The girls quietly giggled in the back seat for the remainder of the drive to Spokane. My father was never so glad to see me as he was that day.

Size Does Matter

After finishing my bike workout, I took off my earbuds, showered and headed to my individual and group meetings. Through this, I am discovering what led me down this destructive path. Once you determine how you got there, you can identify the psychological triggers leading to unhealthy compulsive habits. Once the triggers are identified, then come your strategies to overcome them, and one must overcome them.

We increasingly hear the "size does not matter" hogwash. They tell us that everyone must be treated equally and not judged on size. While this is true, size does matter. Advising an individual that they are fine "just the way they are" is equal to persuading an alcoholic or drug addict the same thing. Obesity will catch up to you sooner or later. Eating addicts, like all other addicts, will die sooner rather than later. Those are the cold, hard facts and no amount of political correctness can change that. In the case of the obese, wokeness kills people.

I suffer from severe sleep apnea secondary to my weight. For this, I was issued a sleep apnea machine to assist me in breathing while I sleep. I have the beginnings of diabetes. I know obese people are more likely to develop cancer such as kidney, liver, colorectal, pancreatic and stomach cancers, to name a few. Obese people live on average ten to fifteen years less than those with a healthy body size. Everybody else also knows that, including popular media and the woke culture. Facts always seem to get in the way of political correctness.

The atrial flutter rhythm that developed shortly after I got here was a direct result of my obesity. Unless you have a congenital anomaly, nobody who is only forty-one and healthy spontaneously develops that heart rhythm. It occurs in people with high blood pressure, coronary artery disease or congestive heart failure. All those diagnoses were attached to my hospital chart and all of them were secondary to my obesity.

Then, there is the problem of being unable to actively participate in physical activities. I couldn't go the day my sisters and nephew took that great hike to Chimney Lake. Because of my weight, I am excluded from fun, strenuous activities with family or friends. It has been years since

I have been able to ski or golf. That reality made me very sad, further contributing to my depression, which "fed" my eating disorder.

I have learned that obesity can also be generational. Poor eating habits from parents and grandparents are then handed down to their children and grandchildren. Snacking on low-nutritional food that is fatty and calorie-rich, plus the practice of eating fast food, is always easier than cooking. Everybody, including parents, knows these facts. We all possess the knowledge of healthful nutritional eating patterns that popular media is now trying to downplay. Fast food and processed foods and snacks can be cheaper than fresh fruits, lean meats and vegetables. Poorer families in our society often turn to fast food to adequately feed their families. All parents want their children to feel adequately fed, but the fast food, fatty, processed food pathway will lead children into unhealthy eating patterns that last a lifetime. Women, Infants and Children's Food Assistance programs (WIC) allow poorer families to eat healthily. Under WIC, healthy snacks are permitted. Bananas, oranges and apples are healthier than potato chips, candy or ice cream. All those candy bars at the check-out line only enable unhealthy impulse buying.

Obesity triggers body image issues within one's psyche, resulting in depression. For me, obesity was a more complex issue. It followed my anxiety as a young child when Mom entered the hospital. That anxiety triggered a stuttering pattern while in the middle of developing language. Obsessive eating was much more destructive than simply poor eating habits. It was my drug of choice to help me feel better. I could temporarily alleviate my depression by being satiated from a big meal that became a negative feedback cycle. Eating to feel better resulted in a bigger size and a deeper depression. It was a never-ending cycle. Everybody knows what their triggers are to unhealthy, destructive habits. Eating disorders are only one example. The trick is to develop workable strategies that sustain you through your lifetime. I have learned that I am going to make mistakes now and then, but I also know that everyone is human and we all make mistakes. You pick yourself up, shake it off and begin again.

Thanks to my parents and speech therapist, I overcame my stuttering as an early teenager. I learned speech strategies to bypass my stuttering. It took a long time, but now I do not think about it. If I overcame the condition that began my cycle of depression, I know I can overcome its aftermath.

The facility here does a great job of educating one on proper nutrition. They provide numerous choices that fit within everybody's specific diet requirements. I feel good about where I am headed and have put it in the proper perspective. Like my father, my eating disorder and obesity is a medical condition that needs to be appropriately managed. The first step was seeking professional advice and help. Like me, Dad had to be admitted to an inpatient disease management program. Like me, Dad needed to get a handle on his diet and exercise habits. Like me, he learned about proper nutrition, weighing his food, controlling weight and regular exercise. Like me, his diet lowered carbohydrate and sugar intake, emphasizing natural fruits and vegetables. It discouraged processed flour and encouraged whole grains. Like me, his diet lowered fats, emphasizing lean proteins.

I have learned that the American diet is far too rich in low-quality carbohydrates, which include processed sugar and alcohol. They are empty calories that functionally eliminate the ingestion of healthy calories. It explains why our country is the 12th leading country globally for obesity, with America leading the North American continent as the most obese. The average person in the United States should consume between 225 and 325 grams of carbohydrates daily. This is easily attainable with the consumption of complex carbohydrates that are nutrient-rich with fiber, vitamins and minerals that you find in natural foods such as dairy, whole grains, fruits and vegetables. They digest slowly, supporting digestive health and maintaining stable blood sugars.

Trouble ensues when one has a diet emphasizing starchy vegetables such as flour, root vegetables and rice. Sugar is the worst found in candy, beverages and snack foods like chips, ice cream, and baked goods (The World Factbook Ongoing) (Burgess RDN 2024).

Once I reach my ideal weight, my daily calorie count should be about 2,500 calories for a man of my age and height. I have learned about reading food labels and following food charts. It is not hard and becomes second nature over time. I rarely need to look at a food chart anymore. I already know what I am consuming and plan accordingly throughout my day. For me, it is something I need to think about all day long to keep on track.

A lot changed in our family diet when Dad returned from his diabetic inpatient program. A new diet that extremely moderated the starchy and simple carbohydrates like flour, sugar, pasta, potatoes and rice. Instead of having a starchy carbohydrate for every meal, we would limit the serving per meal or eliminate it from one or two meals. We began to emphasize vegetables.

Our family comes from a long line of "carbaholics," thus making our eating habits generational. Our family lived on fried foods and mashed potatoes and gravy. We dined on canned vegetables instead of fresh and we never ate a green salad. It meant making some profound lifestyle changes for our entire family. Sadly, one of our family's favorite cultural dishes is Norwegian. Norway is known for its carbohydrate-rich diet.

Culinary Delights

Since our family is Norwegian, we have practiced several of the family's cultural dishes, which have been handed down for generations. One of our family favorites was Lefsa. It ranked in the top five of our family's culinary preferences. This full-on carbohydrate delight is a simple dish made of mashed potatoes, whole milk, butter, salt and white flour. It is blended until smooth yet sturdy enough to be spooned out and rolled flat. Mother used to make this enjoyable tidbit for the family at least eight times a year, usually with leftover mashed potatoes from the previous night's dinner. Sometimes, she even whipped up a batch of mashers for a Lefsa dinner. Mother was not raised a salad or soup eater, so Lefsa stood alone at the family dinner table on those nights. It was delightful.

Once all the ingredients are whipped together, they are thinly rolled out on a floured surface. I cannot even imagine how many carbohydrates are in a single serving of Lefsa. Once the Lefsa is rolled out, it is carefully transferred to a Teflon skillet on the highest heat possible, then dry-fried till lightly browned. The end product looks much like a tortilla but is much tastier. If you are a Lefsa purist (which we were), you only need real butter spread liberally across the top and then rolled up for a delightful snack. It was good, either hot or cold. You can immediately tell who is not Norwegian by how folks try to dress up this simple, delectable snack. It runs the gamut: cinnamon and sugar, peanut butter and jelly, tuna fish and mayonnaise, bacon, lettuce, and tomato. They try and make it a vessel for other things. Norwegians know the plainness of Lefsa is what makes it so good, not what you add to it. Leftover Lefsa was always stored in the fridge. Mother had to make enough to be divided evenly between the family. All of us had our own Lefsa bundle in the refrigerator. Yes, it was that good. Lefsa stealing from somebody else's bundle was strictly forbidden.

It may sound easy to make, but it requires a certain skill and art form. There is no recipe, just essential ingredients you combine at just the proper ratios and taste. Since our family adopted a lower carbohydrate diet, we make it only during Christmas now. It is a special treat to share with family and an important cultural skill passed down to the next generation. It may seem insignificant, but keeping those old family traditions alive is important. Native Americans do an outstanding job of passing down cultural traditions of food, language and dance to the next generations.

Klube was also a traditional family dish. It is a Norwegian-type potato dumpling, which was also a family favorite. While simmering a ham bone or shank, you grate or grind raw potatoes, adding salt and flour until they hold together into a two-inch ball. After removing the meat from the boiled ham bone, you remove the ham chunks, sink them into the potato ball's center and drop them into the hot boiling broth. Once cooked, you serve it with a lot of butter. The next day, for breakfast, you slice them up and fry them in butter, topping them with maple syrup.

Then there is Lutefisk (pronounced LEWD-uh-fisk). It is dried cod that has been soaked in a lye solution for several days to rehydrate it. It is then rinsed with cold water to remove the lye, boiled or baked, and served with butter, salt and pepper. The finished product is the consistency of Jello. Fish Jello, now, doesn't that sound appetizing? While it was one of the healthier options of a Norwegian diet, it was not a favorite in our home.

Dear Mom:

I have nearly wrapped up my time here and look forward to coming home. I really miss everyone. Once home, I will share all that I have learned. I look forward to putting it into practice by preparing a healthier version of our usual Thanksgiving dinner.

I have made many great new friends with whom I hope to stay in touch. We have formed a genuine camaraderie here. We have a lot more in common than we initially thought. With each other's support, we all know we will make it. It is comforting to learn that I am not unique or alone. We all harbor the same fundamental issues and then learn the same basic strategies to achieve a more healthful lifestyle.

I will be home around the first of November, but I will give you specifics later. Hug everyone for me. I cannot wait to do that myself.

All my Love, Randy

A New Perspective

I have been away for a long time, Journal and it feels like an eternity. I feel isolated from all that the family is going through while Mom has been in hospice. Mom continues to live with Joni, and between the girl's work schedules, she is rarely alone. I understand she is still getting around well, her pain is under control and she is eating well.

Our family is blessed. Even though I am gone, my girls are being taken care of. I have never felt like we were alone. When Dad died so suddenly and then with Mom's illness, our friends surrounded us with their love. They always stepped in to do whatever was necessary to help in whatever capacity they could. It is what small rural communities do for each other.

I was born blessed. I have my family and a few close friends that I can always count on. No amount of riches could ever replace that. We can thank all of them for helping us get through such difficult times. I am also blessed to have been born in America, where everyone is allowed to thrive. Does it guarantee equality of outcome? No, it does not, but it guarantees the outcome you can make for yourself. That is what a free society promises its citizens.

I am not a monetarily rich individual, but I am rich in many other ways. I feel successful, with a nice home and a job I love. I have enough money to afford vacations, a nice vehicle and a few luxuries. As a young man, I wanted to be "rich." I have grown in age and perspective, attaining a deeper understanding of the meaning of "rich." I was blessed to be born to loving and supportive parents in a community that supported each other and at a time when everybody was kinder to one another.

My immigrant family came to this country very poor. They created their own prosperity, with a work ethic they passed down to future generations. It was a familial understanding taught through the decades that you alone are responsible for your destiny. Even during tragedies beyond understanding that test your beliefs, it is always within yourself to succeed.

I am in a good place and it is good enough in that I have quit looking for something better or comparing my societal class to others. That is a sign of maturity, but there is also much freedom in that existence of being. I often think about the real sacrifices and hardships that my pioneer family endured.

My great-grandmother, Sophie, survived as a suddenly widowed young woman on the unforgiving Plains. She had four very small children to care for and support in an area of the country that took no prisoners. It spoke of the determination and grit she and others possessed at that time to realize a dream. Though her family wanted Sophie to return to the comforts of Wisconsin, she was determined to continue the life she and John had dreamed about. It was a life and legacy she was committed to for her family.

My great-grandfather was not the only person who died during that historical blizzard. That horrendous snowstorm took many souls from that homestead community. Families suffering their own loss, yet together helping others rebuild. Nobody in that community had money. They had themselves, their skills and items they had in excess to donate to others in need. There are many lessons from that time that we have forgotten. Many in America have been taught and now rely on others' resources to support them. Once that occurs, it is others managing their lives where they are no longer in control of their destiny. Public assistance or Welfare was never supposed to be a permanent solution. It was a temporary remedy to get one through difficult times, to allow an individual or family time to re-group and formulate their own plan to prosper.

Like my inpatient program, I am learning how to manage my eating disorder. It was never meant to be a permanent place where others manage me. Public assistance ought to be the same.

Fishin' for Keys

Once I returned home, I had the tools to manage my food addictions instead of my food addictions managing me. I arrived with a solid plan of support groups, meal plans and counseling. I am now assisting my sisters with Mom's needs and health challenges. I have a solid grasp of the realities in an ever-changing world. Change will always be a part of life, some good and some not-so-good. A normal part of living is when jobs change and people you love move away. Health changes and people who are close to you are lost forever. People will disappoint you and marriages will dissolve. It is all a part of life and I understand that now. I am determined that this is the last time an outside entity will manage my life.

I flew back home via Boise that day, arriving ready for my new life, free from the bondage of food addictions. I was prepared to start over. I was so happy to see Kris when she met me at the airport that day. We talked about everything on the way home. We laughed and cried, but mostly, we were just so happy to be together again.

I lost nearly one hundred pounds in the four months I was gone. I accomplished it healthily by making good food choices, using appropriate serving amounts and exercising daily. I still have a way to go, but I have a good start. My doctors warned me that future weight loss would be slower, so I should not get discouraged. In an obese person, the first one hundred pounds is the easiest.

I lost 150 pounds while I was living in Seattle. Joni did not even recognize me that day when I came off the airplane to celebrate the Christmas holiday. She was looking beyond me as I stood right before her. I then reached out to hug her. I laughed as she did a double take, wondering why a stranger was being so affectionate. That year, I had reduced my weight to 160 pounds. It was the lowest weight I had ever been in my adult life. I felt and looked great, but I did it by taking diet pills for months. I did not learn anything about proper nutrition or exercise. I never once examined the reasons why I obsessed over food. All I did was starve myself without feeling hungry. Once off the diet pills, I returned to my old eating habits. It did not take long before I gained everything that I lost.

My weight loss was different this time. I am much more accomplished in what I have achieved and I can thank my weight loss facility for that. They taught me to take control of my life. I am back to work, visiting my clients and on my regular work schedule. I am driving to Wallowa County again, three days a week. I feel renewed and have the necessary tools to take on whatever happens.

It is late October, with that familiar fall nip in the air. I am heading to Wallowa County via the Minam grade, driving down that infamous Rock Canyon where I lost the boulder battle. I contemplate my life and all the changes that have occurred in such a short amount of time. I look down onto the valley floor in awe of the beautiful colors of fall, marveling at the herd of elk grazing on the meadow grass next to the river. I truly live in such a beautiful part of the country. My mind begins to wander again with happy memories. I am back to my childhood, camping with my family.

We had friends who arrived from Billings for a visit one summer. George and Maxine were my parents' best friends. They all had been classmates in high school and college. They had two children, both very close in age to Joni and me. They brought their RV to La Grande for a week-long vacation and we immediately headed to our favorite destination, French camp on the Lostine River. It would be another fun-filled week of camping, hiking and fishing.

On the way, we decided to stop at the first rest area we came to. Located at the bottom of the Minam grade canyon, we all hastily pulled over to relieve the children. It is a great rest area in front of the Wallowa River. It had picnic tables and an expansive green lawn with shade trees throughout. While we were there, the mothers decided to fix lunch. We were not in any hurry, so Dad and George decided to drag out the fishing gear and try our luck in the river. It was an activity to kill some time in what Dad was sure was an over-fished area of the river. He did not hold out much hope, but it kept us busy and amused. Dad rigged up Joni's pole with the oldest, rustiest, most bent-up silver and red fishing lure he could dig out from the bottom of his tackle box. He did not want to risk her losing one of his brand-new expensive lures. George, Dad, Joni and George's son Dale lined up along the riverbank. With Joni's first cast, she hooked and landed the day's first trout. Moreover, with nearly every single cast, Joni caught a fish.

Dad traded Joni's spot for his, but she was still reeling them in. Every time Joni was moved, she would catch another fish. Each time Joni caught a fish, Dad would move her, rotating someone else into her spot, where they would then proceed to catch nothing. While the rest of the fishing party furiously changed lures repeatedly, the fish remained uninterested in what the other anglers had to offer that day.

Joni caught fifteen fish that day in less than two hours. The rest were skunked, not catching one fish or getting a bite. That pitiful rusty old lure was the hot commodity of the day. We still have a photo of Joni proudly displaying her catch in front of her on the lawn.

I found myself smiling as nature abruptly called. I immediately pulled into the same rest area at the bottom of the hill. I fly into that rest stop, throw the car into park and dash into the forest services' vault-type outhouse.

Usually, when visiting outhouses, I consciously try to remove everything from my pockets. I carefully set them aside, far away from "the hole," before I sit down. I have never heard of it happening, but I can envision the horror of an accidental slippage from a pocket into the cavernous darkness.

In my haste, I did not accomplish the all-important pocket-emptying task. As I sat down, I heard an ominous splash. Oh, No! As I looked down that hole, I could see my gleaming car keys sitting smartly atop an equally glistening pile of ...*damn, Dodo Bird!*

It was all so disgusting. I was utterly stranded without my keys and miles away from anywhere that could render assistance. Besides, what was somebody supposed to do? I immediately dismissed the idea of calling 911, even though this was an emergency of magnificent proportions. I am positive that call and law enforcement response would make me famous in these parts, something I did not want to be known for. Besides, I could be sitting here all day. I would call 911, where I would be transferred to numerous jurisdictions, all of whom would pass me on to a different agency. I am sure there would be no chance that someone would "clear their

> "Man has key mishap, as Oregon State Police are dispatched to retrieve keys from the bottom of an outhouse... More at 11"

schedule" to help some poor schlep retrieve his car keys from the bottom of an outhouse. The more I thought about it, the more I realized I needed to solve this problem myself, lest I be the laughingstock of the Wallowa County communities. What I needed was a rope with a hook on the end of it. Hmm, wait! I harkened back to my Camp Silverback days as I remember seeing someone fishing down at the river.

I "snagged" up that young lad, giving him twenty bucks for the use of his fishing rig. I would have given a thousand dollars if he wanted it. He was amused, laughing hysterically, as I went fishing down that hole for my keys. It worked. It only took a couple of minutes to reel those babies up. I was pretty grossed out by the whole thing, but it is a small price to pay to live and work in paradise.

PART V

Holiday Traditions

Randy was finally home and our family was all together once again. He was working full-time and performing his duties as he was supposed to. His travel back and forth to the Wallowa Valley filled his heart like it used to. Randy was back, and not just physically back. He was whole again.

Randy did indeed fix a grand Thanksgiving dinner for the family in 2004. It came complete with all the trimmings. There was less emphasis on butter, white flour and starches. He exchanged those items for roasted fresh vegetables and whole-grain bread. It was delicious, as we enjoyed the fruits of Randy's new emphasis on wholesome, clean eating. I will never forget that particular Thanksgiving. We were all together again, giving thanks for all our blessings in life.

The family got ready for the upcoming Christmas holiday. Kris and I headed to the Tri-Cities in Washington the day after Thanksgiving to let loose with some shopping therapy. Justin was busy with band, preparing for the High School's upcoming Christmas program. Randy was home with our mother, so it was our first escape in months. It was a sister weekend to have some time to ourselves.

We stayed in a hotel for two nights, shopped for two solid days and ate at fabulous restaurants. We spent a lot that weekend. It was Mother's last Christmas with us and we planned to do it up nicely. We were only limited by the amount of space in my Ford Explorer SUV. We filled that vehicle top to bottom and front to back. The weekend was wonderful and we headed home filled to the brim with holiday joy. Once home, we spent the week emptying twelve totes of holiday decor and decorating the entire house with Christmas cheer. For the first time, I bought outdoor lights and decorated the whole outside of the house.

Randy joined Justin and me at Graham's Christmas Tree Farm to pick out the season's Christmas tree. We found the most beautiful tree that I still remember to this day. Christmas decorating, for me, is an event in and of itself that takes me several days to complete the task. Christmas decorating is my happy place. It is about opening my favorite bottle of wine and listening to all our favorite family Christmas albums as I decorate. I am a Libra, which is both a blessing and a curse. As a compulsive "balancer," each decoration is carefully placed throughout the house according to shape, color and size. The tree alone takes me two days and as I carefully place all our holiday adornments, I cannot help but remember all our wonderful Christmases past.

We all attended Ackerman Lab school on the EOC campus. I will always remember our Christmas programs. That was when children's Christmas productions actually told the Christian Christmas story of Jesus' birth. It was an incredible production held at the campus' main auditorium. It was like being on Broadway, on an actual stage, with lighting, costumes and props borrowed from the drama department. The stage had a huge, heavy, navy-blue velvet curtain drawn between each act. Everybody participated; kindergarteners through sixth graders had their part in making the production a huge success every year. It was a heavily attended production, attracting families and the community. People came dressed in their finest attire to enjoy the performance. All were seated in the auditorium below the stage, in comfortable upholstered seating befitting an opera house.

Randy and I were in the speaking choir that told the tender story of the baby Jesus. The various ensembles and performances praised God and his son in all the pageantry surrounding the Savior's birth. I also sang in the girls' choir, led by an extraordinary woman who had taught music for years at the university. She blessed us with her incredible teaching talents, transforming us into a more than capable girls' choir with remarkable young abilities.

Looking back, it is difficult to tell when secular forces in our country changed us forever. They were slow and insidious and escalated while we were living our lives. It began a cultural slide that would eventually destroy our cohesive society. Initially, church and state laws were supposed to eliminate state intrusion into Christian-themed practices. Slowly, it was turned inside out to have the opposite meaning. The result was the complete elimination of all Christian content from public schools. It would eventually become more than banning prayer in schools. Now, any Christian reference is black-market Christian trafficking and prohibited within ANY government-funded entity, including the public school system. It marked the beginning of allowing a small minority of discontents to make rules for the rest of us. We all let it happen.

It was a sad moment for me in 1992 when I attended Justin's first school Christmas pageant as a kindergartener. Recollections of my Christmas-themed school programs flooded my memories. It was one of those events I had looked forward to while raising my son. I sadly discovered that by then, any reference to the meaning of Christmas had been completely erased from our public school system. Classic Christmas songs all schoolchildren have enjoyed since the 1800s are now gone. That night, "Silent Night" was silenced. There was no "Away in a Manger" because there was no manger. There was NO mention of the holy nativity at all. Instead, the production they celebrated that night was Kwanza.

Losing Christ in Christmas

If all of us are to function under the ever-expanding woke rules of political correctness, which we don't, let's talk about the history of Kwanzaa. The story that my son's public elementary school in Eastern Oregon was so inspired to celebrate. It was my first exposure to the seculars in our society, erasing our founding value of Christianity.

Few people realize that Kwanzaa is a fairly new "Christmas celebration" never celebrated in Africa. It was created by Ronald McKinley Everett in 1966 after the Watts Riots. It was an idea from a word he "borrowed" from the Swahili phrase "Matilda Ya Kwanza," meaning first fruits. Everett was an American activist and professor of Africana Studies, later changing his name to Ronald Karenga. He was a significant figure in the Black Power Movement of the 1960s and 1970s. His pal was Malcolm X. Karenga's goal was to give blacks an alternative to the existing holiday of Christmas, to celebrate themselves and their history rather than imitate the practice of the dominant society. He viewed the Prophet Jesus as psychotic and described Christmas as a "white religion."

Karenga was arrested and sentenced to prison in 1971 for felony assault and false imprisonment of two women whom he tortured. Both described their assault as being stripped naked and beaten with an electrical cord. Karenga's estranged wife, who participated in the beatings, testified that she sat on the woman's stomach while another man forced water down their victim's throat with a garden hose.

Karenga's US organization murdered two leading members of the Black Panther Party in Los Angeles. Killed were "Bunchy" Carter and John Huggins. In San Diego, he killed Sylvester Bell and John Savage. To this day, Karenga has evaded any accountability for his part in the murders. He was a misogynistic murderer who brutally abused and tortured women and was also a murderer of black men.

Today, it is celebrated not as a religious holiday but as a cultural celebration of the African heritage, in addition to Christmas, Hanukkah, and other religious holidays. (Boeckmann 2024)

Kwanzaa is now bigger than the crimes of its founder and will outlive him. Hopefully, Kwanzaa can also be a remembrance to honor those whom its founder brutalized (Dixon 2018) (Hays 2022).

Unless our children are privately schooled or attend Sunday school or church, they are no longer involved in Christian-themed Christmas productions. Public school systems call them "Festivus" or "holiday celebrations." There is no actual mention of why we celebrate the holiday in the first place.

Worst of all, I got to witness in its full glory, the death of decorum that night in 1992. Parents who only came to hear their child's part of the program would stand up and leave the gymnasium when their kids finished. Gymnasiums echo, and the disruption and noise of people leaving only disrupt subsequent performances, distracting performers and audience members alike. I had never witnessed anything so rude, as parents stood up and left with their children while other children sang. Only a handful of parents were left in the gym when the last class performed. It was shameful and continued in all elementary schools that Justin attended through sixth grade.

Holding Onto Christ

Most families in our country continue to hold onto the true meaning of Christmas which is always about family and being together. It is about celebrating the Savior which for us, was the Christmas Eve candlelight service at the Methodist Church on Christmas Eve. It was about Mom's beautiful tree, her carefully placed decorations, the friends and neighbors who caroled for us and the thoughtful gifting. Mom would mail out one hundred Christmas cards yearly, with a family letter that Dad composed. We all had our own tabletop white plastic Christmas tree in our bedrooms that we decorated however we wished. Christmas memories included a small plastic Rudolph reindeer we all coveted for our bedroom, a small figurine that somehow ended up in Kris' room each year. It was Hostess Ding Dongs in our stockings, the music, the baking, the Lefsa and all the other holiday activities that Mom orchestrated that made it special. Mom was the heart of our family Christmas.

I was unsure if future Christmas' would ever be the same. Maybe Christmas is not supposed to be the same after you become an adult. Perhaps Christmas is about sharing traditions as families change. Children grow up, marry and then have children of their own. New family formations add their unique traditions to enjoy. New traditions that help us continually grow as a family. Family is defined in many ways where once a year, we celebrate that family. It makes me wonder: If Christmas is set aside as a tradition celebrating family, what do the seculars in our country do to celebrate family?

Christmas was always Randy's favorite holiday. Every year, a very young Randy would struggle with the wait. The wait was inevitable every Christmas morning. We were not allowed to go to the living room after Santa's arrival until we were all ready to go, AND it had to be light outside. On Christmas morning, our parents would be awakened by three over-excited children. We then began our pre-Christmas family ritual, waiting for Dad. He needed to perform his usual morning ablutions, which seemed to take an hour. He then needed to find his bathrobe, a red, black and beige plaid bathrobe that he wore only on Christmas morning. It always took another fifteen minutes to find the robe and dig it out from the back of his closet. This tradition was when Dad's Christmas morning began. It was his Christmas ritual, designed to rejoice in our impatience, clamoring in delight to begin the holiday. By the time Dad was ready, we could all descend on Christmas morning together. By then, all three of us would be in an excitement-induced frenzy. Then we had to wait again for Mom to make the coffee. Then, when Uncle Terry was living with us, it was triple agony. Terry spent as much time in the bathroom as Dad did.

Randy was to receive a train set one Christmas, which Dad and Terry set up on Christmas Eve. They then decided it needed to be appropriately "broke in" before Randy received his surprise on Christmas morning. Unfortunately, they did "break it in" because they broke it. Mom was pretty angry about that one. A broken train set still did not discourage any Christmas joy that year because the Christmas holiday is much more than a train set. Those are the sweet family Christmas memories I remember and it was all about to change.

Blindsided

Following our weekend trip to the Tri-Cities, Kris and I both had to work the following weekend. Randy would stay at my home and assist Mom while we were both occupied with our work responsibilities. On that December morning, I was working as a Nursing Supervisor at St. Elizabeth's Hospital in Baker City, Oregon. The hospital was an hour's drive east of La Grande on wintery roads. I was working in the Emergency Room when the telephone rang. Being closest to the telephone, in a busy small-town rural emergency room, I answered it. There was a long pause on the other end of the line.

Kris later told me she had not anticipated I would answer the call. She had called the hospital reception desk, wanting to deliver the message to a friend of mine, someone who would inform me of a personal tragedy in person and not over the telephone. It was a weekend though, running on a skeleton crew typical of small rural hospitals, the lone telephone attendant had stepped away from her desk, forwarding all calls to the ER.

The next thing I hear is my sister weeping over the telephone. Hearing my sister crying, I figured our mother had just passed away. However, I could tell it was more than that; she was despondent and inconsolable. Through convulsive sobbing, she delivered the news I would have never expected on that day. It would be an event that would change our lives forever.

Our dear brother had died sometime during the night, discovered by our mother and my son that morning. That night, our heartbroken mother lost her only son. Kris, Justin and I lost our brother and uncle. My brother Randy became a national statistic that night of the inevitable final result of obesity. He was only forty-one years old.

It was an outcome I would not wish on any family. I do not remember that frantic seventy-five mph, forty-minute drive back home on a snowy highway that day. Nor do I remember much of the ensuing days and I do not remember celebrating the Christmas holiday that year. It was one of those things that shook us to our core that went beyond sadness and despair.

We all had happily lived in the shadow of Randy, who possessed a personality larger than life. He seemed to know everybody everywhere because he had a rare gift of laughter and light that everybody wanted to be around. He had an uncanny ability to make those around him feel special. Kris and I always felt fortunate to call him our brother and Justin absolutely cherished his "Uncle Buck." He was someone we happily shared with everyone that he touched and influenced. His presence made us all better people and he always made us smile.

It did not matter where we were, we would always run into someone who knew him, even if we were out of town. As a standing joke, I would always count the number of folks who would yell "Hi Randy!" from afar and inevitably walk over to see him. He would giggle as I counted the numbers, one by one, all those folks who would invariably join us on whatever outing we were on. You could never take him on a quick trip to the grocery store. Folks would come from everywhere to greet and talk to him, therefore a quick trip to the grocery store could never happen when you took Randy. For this reason, I left him out in the car one day as I zipped into the store. Fifteen minutes later, when I returned, the car was surrounded by ten people. Our family had a name for this phenomenon, it was called "being Randalized."

We celebrated Randy's life in a memorial service, where several hundred people joined us. The church was filled with love and laughter as we shared many stories about Randy. For his service, we decorated the Christmas tree next to the pulpit at the Methodist Church. In his honor, we decorated the church tree with all those ornaments from our youth. Ornaments collected since our family's inception were an important part of our long-ago Christmas traditions. Kris and I honored his passing by placing that small plastic Rudolph figurine on the pulpit. Justin led his jazz band in an uplifting, celebratory musical tribute. It would have made him smile.

Goodbye Mom

Our mother did not last long after Randy's death. Mom and Randy had a special bond that only the two shared. Randy had always been particularly stricken by our mother's cancer diagnosis and prognosis. He tried but was unable to process and accept its finality. In retrospect, it explained Randy's early departure from this earth. He was fragile during his recovery and on the precipice of losing our final parent. Our mother was his primary friend, counselor, confidante and fan. Randy was losing not just his mom but the only person he could count on in this world who would always love and protect him. Randy was also suffering an unexpected personal setback that had completely upended his life and came at a highly vulnerable time. In her debilitated state, Mom did her best to help him cope.

Small cell lung cancer took our mother's life five months following Randy's death at the age of sixty-eight. She died at my home, surrounded by those who loved her the most.

She loved to read and watch murder mysteries. She could solve the world's problems on front porches with friends. She was a real card shark in Bridge, Hearts, Spades and Hand and Foot. Our mother was accepting of anything and anyone she met. She was as sweet and as caring a person as we had ever known. Mom was a perfectionist, something I did not even realize until she was gone. Even though I was slightly annoyed then, I smile now when I remember her step-by-step instructions for buttering toast. She was highly emotional, secondary to her adoration of her family. She was a true mama bear, protecting us at any cost and adored her one and only grandchild, never missing a sporting event or concert.

Mother never remarried, nor did she ever contemplate another life companion. What she and Dad possessed was perfect and could never be duplicated. There is something extraordinary about that sort of loving bond that makes one truly satisfied enough that their memory is enough to carry you through the remainder of your lifetime.

Despite her deepest fears, she possessed a quiet soul, optimism and profound strength. She loved each of us unconditionally and doled out the quality of that love evenly, without the slightest hint of favoritism.

There was not one thing she would not have done for us. She never did accept the inevitability of her cancer prognosis. She often told me she was not afraid of death, she just was not done experiencing life. She still wanted to be with us, to love, laugh, protect and care for us. To her, that was her heaven. In that final year, her entire soul was simply a yearning not to leave her family. She fought hard to stay alive to the bitter end.

Justin

My son was forced to grow up a lot in one year, more than should have ever been expected of him. We had only just celebrated his eighteenth birthday and he was trying to be a normal kid. It had already been a tough three years for him, amid a three-year protracted separation and then the divorce of his parents.

In 2004-2005, Justin was experiencing that customary event in a young person's life, known as his senior year in high school. Band, dating, the winter formal and football games should have been him that year. Instead, it began with the unexpected death of his favorite uncle, whom he affectionately called his "Uncle Buck." Randy was staying the weekend at my home. He was back from California and feeling good, and he was happy to start participating in our mother's care. Justin was delighted to have his uncle home once again and it was fun for Justin to have him stay with us (Hughes 1989).

Since Randy was home, Kris and I could return to our usual work schedules. The drive for me was long, which meant a fourteen to fifteen-hour day in the winter, depending on when I left the hospital and how bad the mountain pass was. At 10:00 a.m. on that fateful Saturday morning, our mother decided to check on her son when he had not emerged from the bedroom. Unable to wake him up, she began screaming for help. Upon hearing her scream, Justin ran up from his bedroom in the basement. He was the only one at home that morning to console his desperate, grief-stricken grandmother as they both processed the tragedy they had just found.

No young person looking forward to high school graduation and preparing for college life should simultaneously suffer such enormous loss, sadness and responsibility. He did though, showing incredible strength and composure through the most difficult series of events. Events, that would have crumbled any other kid.

Unaccepting the scene in the bedroom, our mother immediately called Kris for help, only stating that she could not wake Randy. Justin would later tell me that he knew his uncle was gone the moment he saw him. Following our mother's frantic phone call, it only took Kris about fifteen minutes to arrive at my home. Mom refused to go back into that bedroom. Kris found Justin in the bedroom alone, staring at his uncle in shock and disbelief.

I am so proud of Justin. Proud of the boy he was, proud of the man he became and proud of everything in between. Following Randy's death, Kris and I were so steeped in the darkness of our grief that neither of us gave Justin the attention or the counsel he needed that tragic morning. In the ensuing days, he was there to help care for his grandmother, his mother and his aunt through the darkest period of our lives. I believe this tragedy shaped the caring man he is today.

Spring arrived and Justin was in the final stages of his high school career. Understandably, grades were slipping, but he was holding on. Still grieving his uncle, he was trying to participate in senior proms, senior sneak days and visiting potential colleges. We were all grasping for some normality while navigating all the sadness one does when you are amid end-of-life care, hospice activities and profound grief. He watched helplessly his grandmother's deteriorating condition and intermittent pain. It had only been five months since his uncle suddenly died. In those five months, he would watch his grandmother slowly do the same.

Finally, we knew the end was approaching and it would probably be that evening. Even so, I sent Justin to his band concert. It was what he needed to do, a bit of normality during a trying time in his young life.

There is power in love and death. Justin said he felt his grandmother's departure while playing on stage that night. It was a mere wisp of introspection of her, with a momentary lapse of concentration, as he then missed several beats with his percussion instrument. He knew then, up there on that stage, that she was gone and had just said goodbye.

Like all other parents before me, it took a lot of time, patience, care and counseling as I nurtured him into adulthood. Then suddenly, standing before me is a young man with a family of his own. There were many steps to get to that place, but that was the moment when I knew, as a parent, that my job was done. For me, it was hard to let that little boy go as we had been through so much. It was time to recede into the background as we welcomed a wonderful young lady into the family fold. It took Justin a long time to find her, but he had finally found his life partner in Erica.

JO ANNA LAURENE

Justin is the strongest man I know and I can take little credit for that. It was primarily created by profound loss and how he processed and internalized that loss into a deep and abiding love. It is love that gives us the strength to let go of loved ones as they exit our lives through death and destinies far from our grasp. Those destinies prepare us for future circumstances that we can never know or predict. Circumstances that seem to have no purpose or understanding at the time, but allow us to see deeper meaning in those departures. For Justin and Erica, love is strength. It is how they emerged together stronger from a tragedy that only they can understand.

Heart and Soul

In all human experiences, loss continues throughout our lifetimes. Just when you think life is going as planned, situations beyond anybody's control will test your strength. They are our reminders in life that even under the best of circumstances, we have no control over outcomes. It tests our beliefs on what destiny is all about and why events occur. They are life events that were never supposed to happen to our own family. They are events so gut-wrenching, they test our convictions regarding faith.

I had the glorious opportunity to witness the valiant fight of my granddaughter, who weighed just 737 grams at the time of her birth. Circumstances required her to be born at only twenty-five weeks, two days gestation. Besides our mom, I have never witnessed such courage and determination to live. Her fight to survive was real, and she changed my life and my perspective forever. So much bravery, strength, hope and determination in a tiny being that could fit in the palm of your hand. She had expressions and would coo softly in her own little communicative style. She self-soothed as she sucked her fist, she thrived on people's presence and her nurses knew she loved the attention.

She followed you with her eyes, and in those eyes you knew she was listening when you talked to her, or when her mother would softly sing to her. She knew and loved her parents, with her monitors showed stabilizing signs whenever they were near.

We had so many moments where we were flooded with optimism, only to be met with overwhelming disappointment and fear an hour later. It reminded me of my father as he roller coaster'ed along for so many years. However, this was far different. The roller coaster of hope, sadness and intense emotion would change day to day, even moment by moment. I cannot fathom what Justin and Erica were going through then. I was so proud of them as they supported each other through a life-altering event that often fractures many couples.

Our baby girl was loved by so many people through heartfelt prayers across the country. I loved her with all my heart and soul, but sometimes love, hope and prayers are not enough.

Despite the best care possible in one of the country's leading Neonatal ICUs, she slipped away from us fifty days later. Never was there a time since Randy died, did I feel so much despair. It was not just despairing for myself but for my kids as I watched them grieve a loss that no parent should have to endure. It is the kind of sadness that possesses your entire soul. Only time will soothe that kind of loss that I still agonize over at times. It took years before I could get past Randy's death and this would be no different. For Justin and Erica, this is a lifetime loss.

I believe the soul is a reflection of the heart. It is a sensation one feels in a moment of consciousness, which I can only explain as a warmth and filament of love lost, a tiny strand of light and hope you can keep within your heart for all eternity. It is the warmth of a soft echo that gives memories of a deeper meaning, which will stay locked in your heart forever.

I only had the opportunity to be with her for one day. But in those few short hours, our souls collided, forever locked in love and attachment. I know with all my heart that we will meet again one day. What a glorious reunion that will be. It is that belief that is the foundation of faith and hope. We all possess a piece of that beauty. It is a gift left to us from all those people in our past that we have lost. They may be gone, but those identities give us the spirit, drive and hope for the future. This belief is the cornerstone of faith and the foundation of the human experience. Without hope and faith, there cannot be a future.

For now, she is the sunshine, the moon and the stars that shine down upon her family. We hear her whispers through soft breezes and her warmth in the sunshine. We see her character in the stars and her spirit in her sister every day. It is what gives us peace. Even though she was only with us for fifty days, she is forever embedded in our hearts and lives. Will she ever know how profoundly she affected all of us? The answer to that question is yes. How do I know that? Because I possess a confidence that only hope and faith can provide. I know that somewhere in heaven, she is cradled by many grandparents and her great-uncle, which makes me smile.

Not every garden blooms as we expected.
Despite our care, not every child can thrive.
Tears take the place of rain and the sunshine fails us.
But the buds, however delicate, were perfect.
They were real and their fleeting scent will live
forever on the air...

Author Unknown...

Something happens to survivors who lose multiple people central in their lives. Family that had great significance throughout your existence, a cherished child who held great meaning and hope for the future. The loss was always preceded by weeks to months of agonizing worry that engulfed you, of every minute of every day. We lost sleep, optimism, dreams and perspective. It was a real-life drama we would never wish on anybody.

With that, our entire family has no tolerance for anybody else's drama. You gain a new perspective when confronted with day-to-day turmoil over many weeks, months and years. You become impatient and disinterested in dramatizations completely devoid of any fundamental importance. We can spot drama a mile away. For some, drama is their default setting. Some actively seek it where there is none to begin with. Those people are pariah to us now. To understand manufactured drama, you realize it is a strategy to gain notoriety and attention, which has no place in our lives.

Unless it directly affects his family, Justin can ignore drama, whether it comes from politics, news, family or other people around him. Somehow, in our over-dramatized, volatile, hyper-political time which is impossible to ignore, Justin can filter out the nonsense. I admire him for that and try my best to do the same. We all have come to understand that life is too short to dwell on the negative or be around negative people or situations. Now, we choose to concentrate our energy and attention on those who give us joy and laughter. It allows you to smile throughout life instead of living with those who cause you anger, sadness or frustration.

Perhaps we were being prepared.

PART VI

Life in the 2020s

The 2020 decade descended upon us, fresh off a contentious national election battle that was mired in controversy over COVID-19 anxiety and distrust. It was a time of uncertainty, where we could already detect a sense of dread and hesitancy.

Against the backdrop of our collective histories, we draw from previous knowledge of our own experiences and that of our ancestors. It is how we interpret the world before us as it unfolds. However, nothing could have ever prepared us for The Covid Chronicles that we were forced to participate in or its foreboding aftermath we were forced to accept. COVID-19 was the mother of all religious cults that ushered in a new social order that nobody wanted any part of. All we can do is wistfully remember what was and pray for our futures. Those of us who have lived through more reasoned times are profoundly sad and at times angry about what we observe today.

Instead of being sad or angry, I consciously channeled my parents' wisdom and my brother's humor. This is an attempt to understand and define what we are observing in the world today. It is a time when one cannot be a casual observer. We have all been caught up in the turbulent rapids of too many changes to keep up with. We were all surprisingly caught up in the dark, dank, grimy downstream effects of politics and woke culture, in which we are all drowning.

> **"Always drink upstream from the herd."**
> **Will Rogers...**

It is a phenomenon in which we are all trapped in a rabbit hole, unable to escape from the wolves guarding the exit. This has created chaos and confusion in society. I will begin where it all started: The Covid Chronicles.

The Novel Coronavirus

Nothing in the history of our country could have prepared us for the atrocities that our government perpetrated on us in the name of safety. Not since 9/11 has a single event done so much damage to our country and ourselves. I began this book in the summer of 2019, months before the 2020 pandemic was discovered. As the book progressed, it became more and more evident that the impacts of this virus would affect us forever, not just because of the virus but because of politics.

As more and more research was uncovered, many previous conclusions did not age well for our government fearmongers and their state-run media. I discovered that while writing, I was allowed to be on the ground floor in the evolution of a pandemic and the opportunistic politics, policies and reportage surrounding it. Through the years, objective scientific analysis would completely contradict the story they were so craftily fabricating to control our lives. It was fascinating to document it in real-time as it occurred. What began as a dire global threat steadily weakened to an innocuous affliction easily controlled and only dangerous to the usual vulnerable populations. The book became a documentary to illustrate how they used a frightening circumstance to so artfully manipulate our lives to a society-controlling impetus.

Definitions: Impetus

A circumstance that makes something occur more quickly.

In the entirety of my nursing education and practice that spanned thirty years, nothing rarely occurred that necessitated an impulsive response. Even with life-threatening events, professional healthcare providers react with time-tested and researched treatment plans of care and algorithms as they pertain to each emergency, event or diagnosis. What you never do is panic. Panic drives immediate decisions that drive patterns of incorrect moves and resolutions that can kill. Yet that is what our government did. The government is incapable of making critical immediate health decisions on a grand nationwide scale because it will always be politically motivated like everything else they do.

Never in our history was it EVER demanded of a population to inject an untested drug. It was reminiscent of drug experimentation work in Nazi Germany. While there was evidence that it may have been protective for some vulnerable populations, there was zero evidence that it was necessary for healthy individuals under sixty, especially healthy children who will always recover from COVID-19. There was plenty of evidence, though, that this vaccine was harmful and, in some cases, deadly for some of that demographic. As the entire country dove headfirst into the shallow end of an unknown and untested drug, our government hid vaccine accidents and deaths that historically would have had any other vaccine pulled for further study.

Our government's Vaccine Adverse Events Reporting System (VAERS) records deaths secondary to ALL vaccines. Globally, deaths from ALL vaccines, from 1990 to 2020, averaged 281 per year for over thirty-one years. Yet in 2021 alone, there was a total of 21,914 global vaccine deaths, nearly an 8,000% increase in one year. In the United States, the CDC does not consider a person vaccinated for COVID-19 until two weeks after the injection. Therefore, anyone who dies within those two weeks is not even considered a vaccine death (Open VAERS 2022).

In the meantime, our government ignored important research conducted at the University of Oxford, which found that males between sixteen and thirty-nine years of age had significantly higher incidences of heart inflammation (myocarditis and pericarditis) post-vaccine. They disregarded a November 2021 study that found that for boys twelve to fifteen, there was a statistically higher incidence (2.6 to 4.3 times) of cardiac adverse events vs. being hospitalized for a COVID-19 infection. The incidences were worse among sixteen to seventeen-year-old boys, at 162.2 times the incidences of cardiac complications vs. being hospitalized for COVID-19. This was even during peak infection rates during the Delta wave. The research proved that for this age group, it was safer to get COVID-19 than to get the vaccine. Yet, in 2024, the CDC is still recommending vaccinations for children.

The data concerning heart inflammation was always present among the eighteen to forty-nine group. The CDC possessed this data. However, as of February 2022, The New York Times reported that the CDC refuses to publish portions of the COVID-19 vaccine data it has collected on the effectiveness of boosters in adults under sixty-five. Coincidentally, the data is also missing for eighteen to forty-nine year-olds. According to the CDC, this data "is not yet ready for prime time." Further stating that the information might be "misinterpreted." Now, in 2024, the American people have yet to see the data, although frankly, we don't need to know

now. Routinely, we see fit, young, athletic men between the ages of eighteen and forty-nine suddenly collapsing for "unknown heart-related reasons" (Mandavilli 2022).

Global Rollbacks of Vaccine Mandates

Other than the American government, rollbacks are occurring across the globe. In October 2022, the Danish Health Authority will only *recommend* vaccinations for individuals over fifty years of age and only for those who are at high risk for severe Covid. They have outright restricted vaccine use in children under the age of eighteen. Likewise, in Sweden, the government announced in September 2022 that teens outside of vulnerable groups are no longer eligible for the COVID-19 vaccine. In 2021, France, Germany, Sweden and Finland completely stopped using vaccines in all males under age thirty due to heart inflammation (Hart 2021).

The British government, nervous about the vaccine's fast-tracked, record-breaking approval, added the COVID-19 vaccine to the "Vaccine Damage Payments Scheme" (VDPS). The scheme allows victims of vaccine accidents to be paid 120,000 pounds in case of a vaccine injury. It is meant to dissuade people from seeking compensation through costly court proceedings (Boyle 2020).

The Australian Government has implemented a claims method of compensation to enable eligible claimants who have suffered moderate to severe vaccine-related adverse events from the COVID-19 vaccine, including death (Services Australia).

Unbeknownst to most Americans, multiple studies from the National Library of Medicine have documented that older individuals, even those as young as sixty, suffer from ischemic thrombotic events (strokes) following the COVID-19 vaccine.

Remarkably, our government's FDA seeks to prevent the release of Pfizer's analysis of their vaccine for seventy-five years. Lawyers representing thirty professors and scientists from Yale, UCLA and Brown University filed suit in September 2021, seeking access to the sequestered records. The Plaintiffs argue that releasing the information could help reassure vaccine skeptics that the vaccine is safe and effective, thus increasing confidence in the Pfizer vaccine. This inquiry seems reasonable. Why not reassure the country of the effectiveness and safety of a new vaccine? In January 2022, a judge ordered the results to be public by September 2022. It is now 2024, and we are still waiting (Roscoe 2021) (Just the News 2023) (Siri 2022).

The vaccine was released early in 2020 under an emergency authorization. The vaccine they hurriedly developed, with no data or testing, was a panicked solution to appease the country and for the government to appear as saviors. Then, as our "Savior," they began vaccine mandates. Concurrently, the federal government granted all vaccine manufacturers immunity from liability if something unintentionally went wrong. The immunity was re-authorized in 2021 and 2022. In 2023, it was extended again until the end of 2024, even though they knew the high risk of injury or death associated with their "vaccine" (Sigalos 2020) (Greene 2021).

Our government is giving Pfizer billions of dollars and mandating Americans inject its product. Then, it refuses to allow Americans to know the safety and study profile while prohibiting those same Americans from suing for harm (The Daily Journal of the United States Government 2020) (Lopez 2023).

Confusing Government Strategies That Confused

Public health strategies are far different from healthcare strategies when it comes to infectious agents. Public health concerns itself with **controlling the spread** of an infectious agent, which includes masking, isolation, contact tracing and vaccinations. Unfortunately for the country, it was the only health services agency our government consulted.

Conversely and complimentary, the healthcare profession concerns itself with the **containment** of infectious agents. Hospital nurses and doctors **contain** all categories of infectious agents, from wounds to respiratory agents, with researched strategies to accomplish that goal. Never was the importance of containment ever communicated to those of us desperate for information to protect ourselves and our families.

Aerosolized agents come from droplets, but droplets are not necessarily aerosolized. The methods and practices for controlling the spread and containment of each are different. Led by the World Health Organization, our government, without their own inquiry, classified COVID-19 as a droplet agent. This should have come under a containment strategy that nobody talked about. In the case of a respiratory illness, masking is only a small part of that strategy, but containment was rarely if ever, discussed. Proper masking for a respiratory droplet infection can merely be a surgical mask.

Important Note: Determining droplet or aerosolized is not that difficult, yet it took the WHO **two years** to determine it was aerosolized. By that time, a million people in the United States had already died.

Aerosolization is a far different, more dangerous environment. In healthcare, this is contained and controlled via "reverse isolation." In a pandemic, it is the methods and practices to prevent those agents from accessing our personal domains. For an aerosolized agent, the ONLY mask that should have been recommended, was a properly **fitted** (note I did not say fitting) N-95 mask that hugs the face and nose with no leaks. If fitted properly, it feels like you can hardly breathe. It is nearly impossible to wear one all day, every day.

While masking plays a part, it is less than half of the equation. Aggressive and obsessive hand washing would have been critical information to have. As the name clearly implies, aerosolized agents are spread much further than droplet agents. While droplets land on immediate surfaces, aerosolized agents are vaporized, spreading into the air and then on and into every crack and crevice.

Then, like a cockroach, your hands are the vector that brings those contaminants into your personal space, whether they are aerosolized or not. This is the basics of cross-contamination. At no time did our government share the information to prevent hand cross-contamination from infecting our homes (Hollingsworth 2020) (C. O'Brien 2021) (Garcia 2022) (Klompas M.D. M.P.H. 2020) (Macintyre 2015) (Lotfinejad MD 2021).

Early in the pandemic, and only because I knew the appropriate strategies, I donned no less than four pair of gloves on each rare trip to the grocery store and only when I had to grocery shop. I was never so thankful for a full pantry.

One pair after another, gloves were peeled off and discarded all along the contamination spectrum. The last glove peel occurred just before touching my car's door handle and driving home. I never brought anything into the store except my debit card. At no time did I buy anything that could not be decontaminated with an anti-viral spray. I never practiced the futile and curious "decontamination strategy" of setting groceries outside for an hour. There was no scientific data that COVID-19 agents died on surfaces outside after an hour. What we did know by 2021 is that COVID-19 can live on any surface for fourteen to twenty-eight days.

As one can see, a true aerosolized pandemic with an assured deadly pathogen would have devastating results, which our government has no capacity to contain in a country of 332 million people (Randall 2021) (Lewis 2022) (Marzoli 2021).

Falsifying the Numbers

There are many reports of errors in COVID-19 death numbers. It matters if someone dies from Covid or if a car accident victim who dies happens to test positive for Covid. This distinction is fundamental in epidemiological standards, but when our government rewards healthcare systems for the number of victims, that number will always be inflated. American hospital systems made a lot of money for the suffering of the American citizenry. In several rounds of taxpayer-funded payouts, $175 billion was sprinkled around hospital systems in the congressionally approved "Provider Relief Funds." This money was in addition to government payments of $77,000 per Covid admission, which would be in addition to the usual private and government insurance paid per admission. COVID-19 became an extremely lucrative diagnosis to rich conglomerate healthcare systems nationwide, not just Pfizer (Rowland 2022) (Liss 2020) (Drucker 2020) (Leonhardt 2023) (Wen 2023) (Daly 2022).

The pandemic began in a political year during a Presidential election. Political grandstanding was the norm as the rest of the country wrestled with all the information being reported daily. Federal and state governments, media outlets and social media were all vying for position in reporting this "exciting new disaster." Contradictory information only confused the public and with confusion comes fear. Manufactured fear is always the political and media goal. In 2020, the maxim of "Never Let a Good Crisis Go to Waste" was set in motion. For a Progressive, crisis provides ample opportunity for a plethora of contrivances. For the media, fear is what sells and the more conflated it can be, the more money can be made (Colton 2020).

By 2021, the federal government began initiating various mandates that constantly changed and were even more contradictory, mandates not even practiced by those officials who contrived them. From then on, people began to see the genesis of the true motivation behind the mandates. Cracks were developing in the messaging that aspired to control the U.S. population. Mandates became increasingly embedded into politics with each passing day when all anybody cared about was the truth. As months turned into years, government messaging kept changing, and excuses were made to fit the predominant story. Stifling mandates would never end as promised, with expirations being pushed further into the future. People started to get angry as the country became even more divided. By design, Americans took sides, blaming each other for our turmoil. The division industry and our government did what they do best, dividing us over and over again. This time, it was the contrivancy of the masked vs. the unmasked. Society forgot the purpose of public masking: To protect oneself from the germs of another. Those who did not mask understood this concept and respected those who felt the need for personal protection. The masking Nazis saw it as an "existential threat" to all mankind. Then, it went far beyond masking.

Definitions: Contrived, Contrivance

An unnatural, deliberate and skillfully crafted idea to serve a specific purpose.

It morphed into the "vaxxed" vs. the "unvaxxed," which then evolved into the "pandemic of the unvaxxed." Those who remained cautious about what was injected into their bodies were "Covidiots and Spreaders" and were labeled evil, selfish and an "existential threat" to society (Rigby 2024).

Definitions: Tribal Adherence

An attachment or commitment to a person, cause or belief that defies the usual logic, reason or judgment. A devotion so intense that people blindly follow instructions for a cause with little proof of safety or benefit.

Like with masking, rabid vaxxers forgot the purpose of vaccines: To protect the vaccinated against a disease and prevent the spread of the same disease. Polio and Smallpox were eradicated from the United States because of vaccines. That is the very definition of a vaccine. The COVID-19 vaccine did not work. The evidence was clear when numerous post-vaccinated and multi-boosted individuals were still contracting the virus, often multiple times. Yet the ringmasters in our government and their media clowns would not admit this vaccine was ineffective. The most it could do was function as a prophylactic medication to reduce COVID-19 symptoms in vulnerable populations.

In stunning research findings, it was determined that a fully vaccinated and boosted individual who acquires COVID-19 can spread the virus as pervasively as an unvaccinated person. In other words, vaccinated individuals who still contract the virus still spread the virus to EVERYONE, as if they were never vaccinated. Can we just quit calling this a vaccine? (Lalvani 2022) (Puhlach 2022) (John Hopkins Bloomberg School of Public Health 2021) (Singanayagam PhD 2021).

    For our government, lies that are inconsistent with definitions only means that the definition needs to be changed. This strategy of transforming fiction into reality is THE new government methodology using transformative language to subvert known truths into subjective parallelisms. This will be further detailed later, but what was invented during the Covid Chronicles has taken on a life of its own. We will start with the definition of "vaccine."

Introducing Transformative Language

History reveals that vaccines to eradicate disease began in the mid-1700s. The work of Dr. Edward Jenner (1749 to 1823) is credited for coining the term "vaccine" in the early 1800s when he made an amazing observation: Milkmaids infected with cowpox that manifested as pustules on their hands and forearms were immune to smallpox epidemics.

Dr. Jenner made history in 1796 when he extracted the pus from a cowpox lesion and introduced that fluid into a cut he made in the arm of an eight-year-old boy. Six weeks later, Dr. Jenner exposed the boy to smallpox. Even after twenty exposures, the boy never contracted the disease. A century later, in 1885, a French chemist and microbiologist Louis Pasteur of Paris tested Jenner's technique in his invention: The "Rabies Vaccine." Thanks to Dr. Edward Jenner and Louis Pasteur, the principles of vaccination began to form, containing either live, attenuated (less virulent than the natural variety), or killed bacteria or viruses. Both were given as an injection to produce immunity against a particular infectious disease. This has always been the working definition of vaccine in medicine ever since and was the method that the World Health Organization used to eradicate smallpox from the planet in 1980 (Hollingham 2020) (Britannica).

Using The Progressive's method of "transformative language" to cover their backsides, they had to come up with a brand-new definition to describe a "vaccine" that was one hundred percent ineffective for the target virus, of which they required one hundred percent compliance of their citizens (Loe 2022).

The 1800 to 2020 definition of "Vaccination"... "The act of introducing a vaccine into the body to produce 'immunity' to a specific disease."

The 2021 new and improved definition of 'vaccination'... "The act of introducing a vaccine into the body to produce 'protection' to a specific disease."

The 1800 to 2020 definition of "vaccine"... "a product that stimulates a person's immune response to produce immunity."

The 2021 new and improved definition of "vaccination"... "a preparation used to stimulate the body's immune response against diseases."

See, there! Whew! Now, they are one hundred percent covered to prevent any insinuation that they are incapable, control-hungry government bureaucrats implicated in a worldwide effort to influence public health policy that proved to be, at the very least, ineffective, at the most dangerous.

Jeopardy Question for 500: People responsible for the spread of COVID-19
Answer: Who would be everybody, vaxxed or unvaxxed?

New Introductions

Now introducing, our country's very own prophetic government philosopher, who possesses extraordinary intellect and theoretician principles. Meet **Da' VEEP**, AKA **D**eep **A**ggrandizer of **V**acuous, **E**rroneous, and/or **E**xaggerated **P**latitudes (Burguiere) (Laurene, Here Come Da' VEEP 2024).

Da' VEEPs Beliefs: "We must all get vaccinated to protect the vaccinated."

Note: The level of mental and logical incoherence necessary to reach this conclusion is quite a feat, but it was the gauge by which her administration derived all future strategies and definitions. What was most frightening was that over half the country believed it.

Those of us who understand pharmaceutical studies know this vaccine was rolled out prematurely. We were unsurprised when, on October 11, 2022, Janine Small, Pfizer's President of International Developed Markets, testified at a hearing of the European Parliament, stating under oath, *"The COVID-19 vaccine was **never** tested during trials to see if it prevented human-to-human transmission"* (Chung 2022) (R. Hart 2021).

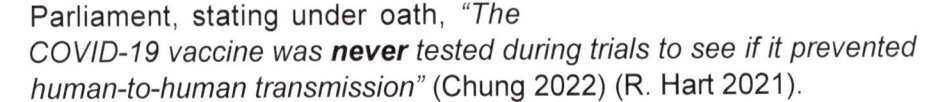

Jeopardy Question for 1,000: The research body that studied the effectiveness of the COVID-19 vaccine before it was released worldwide.
Answer: Who would be NOBODY? It was a trick question.

For two years, those who were unvaccinated lost essential aspects in all of society. People lost their jobs and businesses. Thousands of military personnel were discharged, losing all pay, bonuses and military benefits. We were caged inside our homes. People were segregated and discriminated against. The unvaccinated were deemed outcasts in society. We couldn't wed or attend the funerals of loved ones. We were banned from family holidays and lost friends and even family members. We lost our jobs, livelihoods and homes and could not attend school.

Important cancer screenings were not performed. Necessary elective surgeries were indefinitely postponed. People were and still are being denied life-saving organ transplants if unvaccinated. It was a direct result of our contrived government and their fear-mongering media, who required one hundred percent compliance with unconstitutional government mandates at the expense of patients, and nearly the entirety of our society believed all of it.

As "The Covid Chronicles" entered the fourth year, The Division Industry was and still is medically discriminating against people. As a survivor of a kidney failure patient, I can relate. Kidney failure is a risk factor for stroke, as is the COVID-19 vaccine. Doctors and healthcare systems who require the COVID-19 vaccine for anybody seeking transplants are putting their patients at triple the risk for stroke. Not only do transplant patients and families need to navigate the complexities of our modern healthcare system, but we also must fight our government and society's definitions of whether one is even "worthy" of life-saving care (Kaushik Yeturu 2023) (Friedman Ross 2022).

We were banned from visiting our elderly in nursing homes, leaving them to die of loneliness. We weren't allowed to go to church. Our children lost years of education, the consequences of which are still being uncovered. We are only now discovering the damage of those draconian lockdowns and mask mandates on our children, mandates that were well-known to be unnecessary by the people in power who forced those mandates. Our government and the National Teachers Union are directly responsible for a historical disruption of our children's education as well as the psychological damage that has impacted an entire generation of Americans. You would have to return to 1991 to find lower test scores from our student's 2022 ACT scores. A score that predicts our students' abilities to succeed in a competitive world. Black and Hispanic students saw wider disparities than white students. The rate of depression and suicide among our youth reached historical proportions (Humphrey 2022) (Kuhfeld 2022) (Brinkley 2022) (Adamy 2023) (Kekatos 2023).

Masking and isolation had its place in the beginning. We were dealing with a brand new, highly contagious disease that killed. However, as is typical of the government, they went way too far.

Definitions: Maskaholics

People who cannot let go of a prevailing myth in the face of facts and data to the contrary. Dutifully compliant people can still be seen driving alone with their masks on, or even worse…alone masked drivers with an additional face shield.

Masking became an outward sign of the tribe to which you belong. It symbolized those who obeyed the government and became a metaphor for silencing dissenters. Mask mandates and instructions constantly changed because the government had no clue as to what the standard was. It was a clown show.

In Japan, they call it a pathological addiction. For our state-run media, it was a new opportunity. Our media fear peddlers quickly discovered a new avenue to rekindle more division and hate. Masking was then re-branded as "The victimization of the masked" (Tierney 2022) (LIT 2017).

Theatre of the Absurd

Announcing on Broadway!

The unmasked were labeled dangerous spreaders, exhibiting great evil, for reading the data and practicing freedom of choice. The opening act finds the masked victims being overtaken by Spreader alien beings, who threaten the compliant masked with an impending viral death.

The second act depicts the "Healthy, Obsessive Maskers" (HOMs), AKA Hominems, as victims of all those evil spreaders. They suddenly find themselves as outcasts, destitute, alone and unfairly maligned for simply "wanting to be safe" (Laurene, Covid Theatre of the Absurd 2024).

Definitions: Hominem

It is part of ad hominem, a type of argument or criticism that appeals to prejudices. It is most often associated with trying to undermine the opponent's arguments by attacking a person's character.

The third and final act finds the Hominem's dying in "unprecedented" numbers!

The predictable Progressive ending: The "unmasked" unleashed dangerous invasive pathogens that threaten to end life forever as we know it.

The Truth: Hominems lack natural antibodies and are thereby incapable of fighting infections due to the depletion of beneficial immunological components (antibodies) to fight disease. This is a direct consequence of not allowing one single germ to come within six feet of their otherwise healthy bodies (Bloomfield 2016) (Conroy 2023).

We live in a free country. Those who feel the need to mask to protect themselves or their families are free to do so. However, if you approach me in the grocery store with your paranoid, obsessive, masking delusions, commanding me to mask up, I will respond in kind: **"You do you, and I'll do me."**

As with all the government's theatrical productions, a new post-COVID-19 menace emerged, threatening our lives and jeopardizing our existence.

Announcing November 12, 2022
The New Sci-Fi thriller in its twelfth release:
"Escape Variants!"

This nail-biter drew in 332 million people nationwide for a mere $500 billion. This new dominant strain would undoubtedly discover new horrors with its horrifying immunological evasiveness. The alien mutants will threaten everyone. They can leap tall buildings with a single bound, part the seas and scale the tallest mountains. The "Escapees" will surely spread to the outermost regions of all humanity. No one is safe (Willett 2022) (Stolberg 2021).

Unfortunately, the variant they named "Omicron" did not have the death rate they hoped for. It was contagious, but as all viruses behaved, its virulence was waning. However, we need not worry; Pfizer is busily working in their Jurassic lab, creating new strains as we speak. Pfizer's research, code name "Crossfire Contagion," reveals new discoveries in "gain of function" research, with one critical caveat. Backward engineering the life-saving vaccine, then creating the deadly killer viral variant later that succumbs to their already created vaccine. At which time, their timely developed vaccine will conveniently destroy the variant, saving the world! Details are forthcoming (Mackay 2021) (Laurene, Crossfire Contagion 2024).

Coronavirus…The Final Frontier

A horror novel of disaster and mayhem that never has a conclusion.

The forward reads, We would all fall victim to a story portraying a cataclysm of destruction if it were not for the forthright and persistent actions of our government, their media and Pfizer, as they tirelessly save all of us from ourselves.

A new and mysterious life-threatening malady is being formulated because this pandemic is unfortunately over for them. America is certainly not allowed to return to their everyday functioning lives. What new game can they play to see how far they can go to create new chaos in our country? We did not have to wait long.

June 6, 2022, "The Government Playhouse of the Ridiculous," starring the CDC, who has introduced their newest performance: "Alert! Monkeypox Coming to a Neighborhood Near You"

Unfortunately, the production ended abruptly twenty-four hours later because the script required a rewrite. They discovered that the United States is not in Europe and this great big pond separated us. They initially forgot to check their medical archives before their Monkeypox farcical production was released (Laurene, Monkeypox Coming to a Neighborhood Near You 2024).

They considered a re-release, depicting a **B**acteriological, **O**rganic threat of **G**inormous **U**npredictable **S**preading potential, or **BOGUS** potential, capable of transporting itself across the Atlantic Ocean. However, the script required too many revisions when it was discovered that Monkeypox, around since 1958, was never spread by airborne droplets but by close, intimate skin-to-skin contact, primarily among the gay community. Oops, sorry, that was probably a homophobic, ethnocentric, intolerant, prejudicial and/or an "inciteful" hate-filled expression or whatever the latest "term du jour" is. But here is something novel: Truth is not hate speech (Thornhill M.D., Ph.D. 2022) (Laurene, Bogus Potential 2024).

The production was forced to close when they discovered that 99.9999 percent of the population did not attend Rave gatherings in Europe or similar occurrences in the US. Such geniuses! What is a Rave gathering? It is where an inordinate amount of "very close" skin-to-skin contact is practiced within a very large group.

> *"Suppose you are an idiot, and suppose you are a member of Government. But then I repeat myself."*
> *Mark Twain…*

The Monkeypox Alert was merely a desperate government attempting to find some new frightening, mysterious disease to take Covid's place. It was not a coincidence that it was concocted just before the 2022 midterm elections. After all, it could result in the next government directive for mail-in voting. Stay tuned, though, for the brand-new release of "Pandemic X," This terrifying newly contrived infectious agent, as seen in

Davos' crystal ball, could arrive just in time for the American Presidential election (B. Lee 2024).

As his consolation prize, President Doomsayer proclaimed that everyone should resume wearing masks to protect those with "Long Covid," a new chronic condition in which Covid sufferers experience symptoms twelve or more weeks after the initial infection. The new directive quietly disappeared when it went unnoticed by ninety-eight percent of US citizens.

Definitions: Long Covid

Described by some as forever-lasting, never-ending symptoms of Covid, whereby all of society must continue masking into perpetuity to protect the "Long Coviders."

Disappointingly, for the Maskaholics, it was simply another contrived panic-peddling government fabrication. Actual research from the UK, Denmark and the United States determined that "Long Covid," while appearing real, was grossly overestimated due to overly broad definitions. Previous studies either had no control groups or the controls were inappropriate for the study (British Medical Journal 2023).

> *"Politicians are people who, when they see light at the end of the tunnel, go out and buy some more tunnel."*
> *John Quinton…*
> *American Actor/Writer 1947…*

We already have a diagnosis for those who are chronically ill with depressive components. It is called Fibromyalgia (Fletcher 2021).

Many methodological flaws were discovered in early "scientific" COVID-19 studies, that were either wrong, flawed or hyperbolic to the extreme, AKA biased. It taught all Americans a valuable lesson about "following the science."

The United States, led by the World Health Organization, is changing the name of the Monkeypox Virus to "MPOX." This is to reduce the stigma for those who catch the virus and eliminate the discriminating nature of the name. I guess monkeys are insulted that a pox is named after them (Damaso 2022).

Important Historical Scientific Contextual Note: Like Monkeypox, many animal species have their own pox virus.

Introducing America's Lead Guru of Science and Health

In the fall of 2022, the "First Doctor" and head of the National Institutes of Health (NIH), who remarkably has all the attributes of the Reverend Jim Jones, is back peddling his disastrous directive and mandates responsible for many deaths. Like Reverend Jones, he was so enamored with the power that he was beholden by two presidents that it was noted by many that it was difficult getting him out from in front of a camera. The Reverend Fauci somehow became the government's lead expert and primary talking head, who drove the Covid narrative and the country into the ground. We should all be asking ourselves why anybody, let alone an entire nation, mindlessly follow health directives given by one man. (Kennedy 2023) (Laurene, The Reverend Fauci 2024).

Once the government and their Reverend lost its Covidian grip on society, a new social genesis began to form using new parallels of unparalleled importance: Using the properties of Euclidean geometry, a parallelogram is a "non-self" intersecting quadrilateral with two pairs of parallel sides. Neither pair can be proven without appealing to the parallel postulate of one of its equivalent formulations. All sides must be equal, and adjacent angles are supplementary, possessing rotational symmetry to provide similarity of non-equal equivalents to non-symmetrical co-equals. Progressives postulate these "non-self" co-equals of rotational symmetry as equal parallels to their postulated reality. If this doesn't make sense, it isn't supposed to, but it is central to the grand plan. Examples are forthcoming (Laurene, New Parallels of Unparalleled Importance 2024).

Definitions: Postulate

To suggest existence. Therefore, we can start with…

Everyone Must Lead a Trans Life

In a free and just society, which the United States is, we understand that the world is full of different belief systems, many of which have been beneficial to the community and country at large. It results from sharing new ideas as we evolve to become a better reflection of ourselves. Properly reasoned notions about unique ideals will eventually be embraced by all if they have a modicum of logic. It is because, as a society, the United States is a country of fair-minded people who are generally kind. As such, our country evolves as we decide whether instituting new ideas is for the "Greater Good" and whether it advances our society. It is a very slow process that takes many years. This evolving process has gone from taking one to two decades to that of one or two years and even one or two weeks. While all our heads were spinning in chaos and confusion as we were all still reeling from The Covid Chronicles, the ensuing fallout introduced us to yet another contrived spin of societal nonsense that we all used to ignore.

Transgenderism has been part of our societal fabric for a long time. It has always played a role in American ideals, ideals that allow every man or woman to be oneself. In the United States, individuals and groups have God-given rights via our constitution to be ourselves. However, that same constitution also protects others from being forced to comply with alternative beliefs through coercion. Nothing epitomizes this more than the complete and total transformation of the basics of biology and the transactivist movement.

"Keep minds open, but not so open your brains fall out."
Professor Walter Kotschnig…
Speech at Holyoke College 1939…

Tomboys

What we are witnessing today entirely nullifies every concept and belief system, from biology to women's rights. A cataclysmic shift in science and priorities began the day Joe Biden was inaugurated into the Presidency. It was also that day our Congress was entirely under the control of the Progressive movement. Therefore, there is no mystery as to where all this nonsense came from. Following COVID-19, Transactivism became the nexus from which all other absurdities have materialized in our Brave New World (Huxley).

First, let's evaluate a circumstance that has been around for decades. It was a phenomenon in our country that included my sweet, intelligent, capable sister, who was, wait for it…a Tomboy. Oh my!

However, to keep up with 2020 definitions, the term "tomboy" is now anachronistic and triggering in a progressive society where labels and categorization of people are imperative for them to understand life. Labels are an essential component for a Progressive to function in society.

Definitions: Anachronistic

Belonging to an earlier period that is no longer relevant or consistent in the "arrangement of people" in our modern times.

The now outdated and irrelevant description was an important phase in my sister's youth. This typical phase has been grossly "misinterpreted" by some in society over the past four years primarily because the definition had to be re-labeled to conform to the conformer's transformative language rules. What had been an important part of growing up for girls has now gone way too far. For girls who loved sports, preferred pants over dresses, wore their hair short and preferred not to play with dolls, it fell victim to a contrived, progressively defined, all-inclusive, equitable, diversely conforming label with brand new "social construct" rules. For a society that, in the beginning, emphasized gender-neutral toys, this has now gone way too far.

My sister's phase as a Tomboy was just that, a phase. It was not some gender dysphoric, non-binary construct. My sister was never pansexual, pangendered or bi-gendered. She was not gender expansive, gender fluid and she wasn't questioning. She wasn't co-gendered, nor did she fall under any spectrum or sliding scale of gender variants. She was and is a psychologically intact, unconfused, cis-gendered, heterosexual woman who grew out of her tomboy stage by high school, as 95 percent of girls do. She dated men throughout her young adult years and get this…married a man!

She did not need a "concerned" teacher or guidance counselor stepping in to assess her needs for "gender-affirming" guidance without our parent's knowledge. In fact, in our country's pre-2020 Progressively led era, this view would never have been accepted in any form of student counseling. Consider how far society has come for the public school system to believe this is acceptable. It only took two years.

Just in: The last lesbian citing has just been confirmed. Lesbianism is now considered outdated and problematic in a transactivist society, which now defines lesbianism as a non-binary, nonconforming term that is transphobic. Interestingly, this conforming issue does not apply to gay man spaces, which only virtually erases just another woman's space. Lesbians have been canceled into yet another trash heap that prioritizes men. This will be clarified later, but first, let's visit the fantasyland of contrived postulated delusions (Fleming 2018).

It takes the average individual (like me) hours of research to figure out all the "appropriate" phraseology for properly representing the 121 genders that I understand are now part of our "all-inclusive, gender-aware society." Separate yet related is the rabbit hole of "gender "pronouns.

My pronouns are "Sweetie, Sis, Mom, and Grammie," but most people call me Joni, which is the name my parents proudly chose for me when I was born. It is what my family, friends, peers, teachers, coaches, bosses, college professors and colleagues referred to me as, my entire life. It does not have to be any more complicated than that. It is how we have referred to each other for centuries. That is until a tiny fraction of the population who permanently reside on the struggle bus, mixed in many unnecessary complexities, for attention.

Life is complicated enough without having to overthink what to call each other rather than by our name. It is a behavior reminiscent of puberty and adolescence, whereas kids we dressed in bizarre clothing, got piercings or colored our hair purple. While Justin was deep in the throes of puberty, he was part of the goth group, who wore black baggy clothing, chains, spiked belts and dyed half his hair black. As a mother of a teenager, I always knew that hair grows back and clothing trends mature as kids mature. I knew it would all disappear as he grew older. Well, those days are gone forever.

Da' VEEPs Beliefs: I'm talking about the significance of the passage of time, right the significance of the passage of time. So when you think about it, there is great significance to the passage of time, and there is such great significance to the passage of time, when we think of a day in the life of our children."

How to Conform an Entire Society

During Randy's era, social media began with MySpace. It became a new frontier for communication and sharing. Shortly after that came Facebook. Then came Twitter (later X), where you could define the world in 140 characters or less. Our Progressive government quickly discovered that via social media, an entire generation can be manipulated. Following that revelation, social media platforms became self-anointed masters of control, with the power to have total jurisdiction over all information. They harnessed that power, as it became a method of manipulative mind control over the masses. It became a part of a larger "toolbox" to entangle the entire country into a Progressive philosophy to make absurd notions appear mainstream. However, a wrench suddenly appeared in that toolbox when Elon Musk came onto the stage as the new mayor of "Tweet Town" (Lindsay 2023).

Twitter was sold, with the new owner and CEO being Elon Musk. A self-made billionaire and successful businessman, he made the company private and announced efforts to keep the company solvent:

- The Twitter branch of "**P**ropaganda **L**iaisons for **O**rganized **T**actics" **(PLOT)** has been moved from FBI headquarters in Washington, DC. All those employees in DC will report immediately to Twitter headquarters in San Francisco (Laurene, PLOT 2024) (Linge 2022).
- Twitter has officially ended the Pentagon's online PsyOp campaign for the government's state-run propaganda network. Your "Russian Disinformation Bots" have been destroyed and your covert identities have been terminated. Therefore, you also will report to Twitter headquarters immediately. The Department of Defense will meet you there for your de-briefing (Morgan 2022).
- The "Election Integrity Team" in charge of political "disinformation" has been fired. You can now return to MSNBC (Laurene, MSNBC's Election Integrity Team 2024).
- All former FBI and CIA employees now working for Twitter have been fired (Levine 2022).

- Also fired from the C Suites were the CEO, CFO and the **S**uppressor of **T**ruth to **O**bscure **P**retense or **STOP** specialist (Laurene, Twitter STOP Specialists 2024).

Definitions: Pretense

To make something untrue as true. The practice of inventing imaginary situations to seem real.

Definitions: Bots

A software application programmed to do specific tasks. They run according to their instructions without a human user to automatically mobilize them when needed. Bots imitate or replace a human user's behavior. Bots can number in the billions to mainstream online ideas or agendas in one direction. Bots are a critical component of mainstream radical ideas and are the precursor to the mystical, magical world of Artificial Intelligence.

Definitions: Artificial Intelligence

Living in a make-believe world, where everyone's entire existence is no longer based *on* reality. It is only limited by the imagination of those playing. It can enable evil players to manipulate the entire globe.

Da' VEEP in chief immediately capitalized on this fortuitous shuffling, hiring the STOP Specialist as her head speechwriter and disordered language consultant. Her new title has been changed, too: **S**pecial **P**erformance **E**xpert in **E**xaggerated, **C**ontemporary **H**ogwash **(SPEECH)** (Laurene, Da VEEP SPEECH Writer 2024).

Remote work has ended for employees who want a real paycheck. Your home faux work hours and the $1,000.00 monthly home office stipend have also ended. All employees must now report to work, AKA your office and work a forty-hour work week. We expect intense focus that may necessitate overtime (Nolan 2022).

All Twitter employees must now pay for their own lunch and dinner at the Twitter Cafe. Our stylish and discerning cafe will continue to serve various healthy foods. Halal, kosher and vegan selections, as well as all the classics such as eggs Benedict and poppyseed pancakes for breakfast, will still be available for our most discriminating employees.

Our dinner specials of grilled halibut and prime rib will still be available, but you no longer can pick up your free dinner before leaving corporate headquarters. Twitter understands that paying for your meals and snacks could be a hardship for employees, who only earn an average of $109.00 an hour. Financial counseling can be found online with a simple internet search (Bienasz 2022).

All employees will no longer benefit from their once-monthly paid day of rest. "Mental health days" must be combined with their usual weekend. Furthermore, employees will no longer be allowed unlimited vacation days.

The Best in Story Telling

As a matter of introduction, it is necessary to acquaint the reader with the basic outline for which the entire contrived Progressive mindset collectively organizes its narratives. It is a menu for which they format and organize a consistent script for every tale they seek to forward.

In all of literature, there are thirty-six different plot lines. Storylines never change, just places, events and the characters' names. Our government and its state-run media have perfected storytelling. Like in literature, their script always follows the same rationalized rules when inserting a new objective or imagined rationale of impending doom (Fessenden 2015).

1. Identify the latest and greatest event. It has a more dramatic and urgent effect if it kills people.

2. Elevate the event as "unprecedented," whether in destruction, scope or death (Lynn 2020).

3. Engage all our buddies in Big Tech, social media, corporate news and Hollywood.

4. Identify the strategies the government must use to control the crisis. The best methods control the people's constitutional freedoms.

5. Bring all your tribe together to identify important talking points to drive the message and the strategies. It does not matter if they aren't true.

6. Rehearse those talking points repeatedly. Make sure all our talking heads are rehearsing the same lines of the script on every single news channel and article (HUFFpost 2013) (Kristian 2018).

7. Berate any individual or group that questions the strategy by impugning the character of your opponents as uncaring, divisive, hate-filled and racist.

8. Always bring the discussion back to some marginalized victim or group that must be protected. Note: Be sure to engage the "Intersectionality Rules Committee" to pinpoint the most appropriate marginalized group (Coaston 2019).

9. Whenever possible, always link "Russian disinformation" to neutralize all anti-Progressive reporting.

10. Always loop it into climate change, AKA global warming.

11. For urgent emphasis, it must state, "It's for the children."

12. Repeat the talking points on every single newscast and article.

13. Lather, rinse, repeat.

Fortunately, regular normals, are finally beginning to recognize the con job, of which we are all victims. It is time to stop being victims and become our nation's heroes. It is time to release us from this nightmare swirly, flushing us and our country down the giant Pissoir (Laurene, Outline from which to organize all Progressive Narratives 2024).

Do not be deterred. Those who recognized the scam from the beginning can be proud of what we accomplished. We wear our "Evil Fringe Thinking Conspiracy Theorist" moniker as a badge of honor. We can now feel the satisfaction of being right all along. We are delighted to finally see the truth leaking out of the cracks in this giant shell game that has existed for far too long. Their goal is to reform society into their socialist utopia where they are forever in charge. Now that we know the outline, let's begin their story.

Re-forming Society

Neverland used to be a mythical place of free spirits and a land where one never has to adult. Strutting your individuality has been a hallmark of adolescent behavior since the beginning of time. In the 2020s, thanks to social media, we are all living through a real-life "Neverland." Peter Pan is no longer fictional, as we are all being exiled to the dark cavern of eternal childishness, which we are all forced to play. The United States is now being sentenced to participate, lest you be "canceled" by some adults who never outgrew adolescent behavior. Sightings of these people have moved beyond their college campuses and now roam the hallways of government state houses, universities and public schools as teachers, principals, guidance counselors and school board members (Barrie 1904).

Transactivism is the epicenter of this transformation, due to a minuscule population of gender-confused people who are forcing the rest of us to participate in their delusion. The American Psychiatric Association identifies Transgenders as 0.6 percent of the total population. Yet, governments, education systems, businesses and corporations are now contorting themselves into indistinguishable entities to comply with this brand-new "reality," one that is driving all the chaos and our country into the ground. A small group we hardly knew existed yesterday, who worked hard at blending into society, are now loudly proclaiming that all non-believers are "transphobic" (Association).

Transactivism demands that gender is a "social construct," so gender is not real. Like little trans soldiers, all college students must stand up and pronounce their "preferred" pronouns at the beginning of each class. Teachers and professors are fired for not recognizing their students' preferred and often fluid pronouns. If that wasn't enough, it is now standard practice in many public schools nationwide (Moorwood 2023) (Watrobski 2023).

Definitions: Social Construct

An idea contrived for the "mutual" acceptance of social actions and ideas. Constructs only become meaningful by the shared perceptions of some people, who then establish the definitions, norms, rules, traditions and behaviors they find "mutually acceptable." It then becomes mandatory for all.

Not allowing a potent method of divisiveness to escape countrywide implementation, our Progressive government leaders began practicing the same behavior as they introduced themselves to audiences domestically and internationally. We have become a caricature of ourselves and a laughingstock of our adversaries across the globe. As a United States citizen, watching newscasters worldwide laugh at our leader's ineptitude is increasingly embarrassing (Savage 2020) (Armstrong 2022) (skynews.com.au 2021) (Golding 2021).

> "Those who are too smart to engage in politics are punished by being governed by those who are dumber."
> Plato…

Double Jeopardy question for 4,000: An act of psychological violence. **Answer:** What is misgendering somebody?

The linguistic gymnastics of 2020 has suddenly re-defined the basics of biology and the root of all life forms. It is the opposite of what we learned as five-year-olds when we bathed with our brother or sister. What began a billion years ago with the simplest life form of the amoeba is no longer relevant.

It is "The Battle of the Sexes," one so savage it has twisted the entire country into a knot. Gender, as a "social construct," does not exist in objective reality. So, what is it that exists now? Well, I am shady on the rules, but evidently, men can be women now, and women can be men, so much so that men can get pregnant, have babies and with enough domperidone, estrogen and progesterone on board, they can even be "chest feeders."

All medications and hormones are excreted in "chest milk." Domperidone was banned in 2004 for its association with cardiac issues and sudden death. The FDA warned of its off-label use then due to its risk to breastfeeding infants. We know that added hormones cause early puberty in girls and are associated with a higher risk of breast cancer. We began buying organic meat, milk and eggs free of hormones. But in different "contextual times," it appears this is no longer relevant in a world that ignores safety over contrived political ideas. Woke CDC and FDA transformative double-speak no longer focuses on producing healthy children because *"legitimate concerns fail to attend to both natural human diversity and the mental health of trans and nonbinary parents"* (Epstein 2010) (Malekinejad 2015) (Gandhi Ph.D. 2000) (English 2023) (Feminine Me 2023).

Translation...We must prioritize the non-binary over the health of our children.

Da' VEEPs Beliefs: "We gotta take this stuff seriously, as seriously as you are, because you have been forced to have to take it seriously."

Transactivism has been the new epicenter of all the conforming agendas since 2020, the mechanics of which completely defy science, but have also wholly displaced women and girls in our society. It goes far beyond the reach of anyone's imagination. We are being forced to comport to one's delusion of gender, which society is under absolutely no obligation to accommodate. These people need to be treated for their American Psychological Association's definition of delusion, which has only increased via social contagion. We must stop obediently complying with their manipulative whims and stop placating these people, or it will never end. In fact, it will get worse (McNamara 2020).

Definitions: Social Contagion

The spread of emotions or behaviors from one individual to another, sometimes without awareness. It is spread via cultural mediums that can lead to psychologically induced symptoms of aggressive or self-injurious harmful behaviors, most often seen among youth.

Interestingly, as society pushes forth with this new emphasis on reshaping gender, we have "Cultural Appropriations." It has been around for a long time, certainly, longer than transactivism. It is a societal rule that one must never steal the identities of a suppressed class. This societal directive punishes young women for wearing a Chinese Cheongsam dress, Native American gowns or a Kimono to their high school prom. High schools, colleges and professional sports teams are forced to change historical mascot names due to this new definition of racism. Even wearing dreadlocks is now forbidden if you are white (C. Murphy 2023).

Definitions: Cultural Appropriations

Imitating a culture or population without acknowledging that culture's or population's struggle, often over many decades, including but not limited to wearing a sombrero during Cinco de Mayo.

Women's struggle over decades was to level the playing field for fair competition on jobs, wages or advancement, where men have historically had the advantage over women. Now, on the actual playing field, it has become the metaphor to illustrate our "new contextual times." Men pretending to be women are now pushing women off the top of podiums, claiming victories, world records, scholarships and Olympic dreams. Ignoring their own rules, this new social construct "carve out" by the "Intersectionality Rules Committee" is now appropriating an entire gender, ignoring the struggle made by women over decades of work.

Jeopardy Question for 5,000: Agreed upon exception to the appropriation rules per the Intersectionality Committee's PRIORITISE manual. (This committee and manual will be fully clarified soon.)
Answer: Who would be men?

Who knew that men could have ever pulled off the ultimate coup d'état of superiority over that of women? Since the suffrage movement, who knew that would even be possible? Men are rising above women in numerous women's categories in all sports. They are stealing awards, money and prestige by simply stating they identify as a woman. Men who can't win in their categories are gladly stepping into women's categories in all sporting arenas, capitalizing on their God-given biological strength that most women cannot compete against. Even the wimpiest of men, biologically, have a larger muscle mass than women. Something that seems consequential while competing in sports.

> *"There is no way to erase that physical advantage; Champions rise above the rest when everything else is equal."*
> *Tennis Great - Martina Navratilova....*

The University of Pennsylvania nominated their transgender swimmer for the 2022 NCAA Woman Athlete of the Year Award. If U-Penn devalues women that much, why would any woman want to compete for this University in the future? Why would any woman even attend this university? As parents paying for your daughter's education, why would you apply to this university? The real question is, where are the feminists? Amongst the circus sideshow of collegiate women's sports, we are witnessing even feminists championing this gross unfairness. Feminists who un-abashedly claim they champion women and girls are now leading efforts to undermine women's achievements. It is a seismic cultural shift where women no longer matter. Within the Progressive thought conundrum, men and their biologically obtained superiority are more entitled to that sports podium than women (Glasspiegel 2022).

History of the Progressive Thought Conundrum

A magical Progressive place where biological truths no longer define an organism's physiology, morphology, anatomy and behavior. Science no longer explains biology because our current era can bend science to whatever we desire. Biology is merely another "social construct" that no longer limits genders to males or females. Now, anyone can be a man or a woman, and such descriptions are interchangeable.

Definitions: Intersectionality

Intersectionality is the Progressive's method of classifying people according to order of importance. One's level of importance on the "Intersectionality Scale" is measured by who is more oppressed.

Unless you are a white, Christian, cis-gendered (heterosexual) beard grower, everyone is a victim of some sort or another. How much of a victim you are depends on where you land on the oppression scale. This is measured by how many times one intersects another category of victimhood. Counting the number of intersections is not enough because not all intersections have the same level of oppression. It is a highly complex study of the oppression of the oppressed that I will attempt to clarify. It is important to note that one's level of oppression can change faster than a nanoparticle in a lightning bolt. Progressives keep score. One day, you are oppressed, and the next day, you are the oppressor depending on cultural shifts under the Progressive's microscope. So, never feel comfortable about where you land on their scale. It can change in an hour, depending on where they focus their lens.

It is an analytical framework (because analysis is essential to Progressive academic analytical's) to understand how aspects of a person's social and political identities combine to create different aspects of discrimination and privilege. It is a hierarchy where even the privileged may be underprivileged or overprivileged. It must identify multiple factors of advantage and disadvantage to determine where the empowered and oppressed intersect. It must include experiences experienced through each identity's axis to unlock systems of how power affects those most marginalized in society, even if they could be categorized as privileged. The eventual final framework does not treat each axis of oppression or privilege in isolation. Multiple ax-i must be analyzed to find the true hierarchy, where you can find triple or even quadruple oppression amongst the oppressed or the privileged. Incidentally, this only really makes sense to Progressives.

Important Intersectionality Social Construct Note: This is not satire. This IS the Progressive thought "framework" that categorizes people into groups. All I did was write it down. To the Progressive, all people must be labeled. It is by which they understand the world around them as they continually seek and then develop their hierarchy of importance.

Intersectionality has been in the works for several decades but is on steroids now. It was a very simple manual in the beginning. The list always prioritized women ahead of men, and black and Hispanic men ahead of white men. The rules always looked over the white male, from jobs to college admissions. By 2016, it became evident that their cultural engagement rules were becoming increasingly complex. Therefore, the Intersectionality Rules Committee (a sub-committee of the Social Construct Committee) put out its second manual: **P**ostulate **R**aces **I**ntegral in **O**rganized **R**esolute **I**dentifiers **T**o **I**rrationally **S**ilence **E**veryone **(PRIORITISE)** (Laurene, The PRIORITISE Manual 2024).

Important Globally Global Construct Note: The Social Construct Committee has used the British spelling version of this critical manual because Europe has a far trendier contextual relationship with context in our globally global world.

As Progressives continually seek exceptions to their own rules, the manual must grow to encompass the hierarchies of the most oppressed in an oppressively oppressive society. It is a categorical framework that constantly requires more and more rewrites as they continually categorize supplemental oppressiveness among the oppressed in an oppressively oppressive country.

For conciseness, I will use the new Progressive acronym of BIPOC (Black, Indigenous and People of Color) as I slog through their framework.

Categories begin with historically recognized oppression first. As you work through all the additions, categories become the primary hierarchy of the most oppressed in our oppressively oppressive society. The higher the Axis, the more oppressed one is.

In the woman-only category of Axis I of oppression:

- All BIPOC women, ahead of white women...
- All Middle Eastern women ahead of all the above women, regardless of race

In the woman-only category of Axis II of oppression:

- All gay women ahead of cis-gendered women, regardless of race
- Gay women BIPOCs, ahead of gay white women
- Gay Middle Eastern women ahead of all women above

In the men-only category of Axis I of oppression:

- BIPOC men ahead of white men
- Middle Eastern men, ahead of BIPOCs and white men

In the combined category of Axis I of oppression:

- All BIPOCs ahead of all whites, regardless of gender

In the men-only category of Axis II of oppression:

- All gay men ahead of cis-gendered men, regardless of race
- Gay men BIPOCs, ahead of gay white men
- Gay Middle Eastern men ahead of all men, regardless of race

In the combined category of Axis III of oppression:

- Gay men BIPOCs, ahead of gay white men and all gay women regardless of race
- Gay Middle Eastern men, ahead of all other gay men and gay women above, regardless of race

It quickly became evident in 2022 that Intersectionality Rules needed to be expanded. Therefore, in its fifteenth publication, the updated 2022 PRIORITISE manual has added the following categories:

Gender Identifiers Axis IV of oppression:

- White beard growers who "identify" as breast legatees, ahead of all chest feeders regardless of a vagina conferees race or their gay or heterosexual (cis-gendered) status
- BIPOC beard growers who "identify" as breast legatees ahead of all other "identifiers" regardless of race or gender and ahead of all heterosexual (cis-gendered) individuals regardless of race or gender
- Middle Eastern men who "identify" as breast legatees ahead of everyone stated above

Gender Identifiers of Axis V of oppression:

- Gay white penis owners who "identify" as fallopian tube proprietors, ahead of all breast legatees, regardless of a chest feeders' race or their gay or heterosexual (cis-gendered) status
- Gay BIPOC scrotum inheritors who "identify" as fallopian tube proprietors ahead of all other "identifiers" regardless of race or gender and ahead of all heterosexual (cis-gendered) individuals regardless of race or gender
- Gay Middle Eastern men who "identify" as egg producers ahead of all other identified egg producers

Axis VI of oppression:

- All illegal alien invaders ahead of all genders, races and identifiers, regardless of which race, gender or identifier they identify with

An emergency Axis was added to the third publication of the PRIORITISE manual on March 31, 2023. Axis VIII:

- "Under no circumstances does any transgender, under any identifier, be at fault for any criminal matter, including but not limited to killing children. This hierarchy will be more clearly defined under this Axis in future publications. In the meantime, alternate gender identifiers are not murderers, just "victims of a disinformation ecosystem" or something… (Yurcaba 2023).

We have yet to "categorise" (again Euro trendy spelling) uterus owners, regardless of race, who "identify" as penis and/or scrotum proprietors. We apologize, but your importance is still being weighed amongst the other "egg producer identifiers," who are far more important, within the categories of cervix owners and chest feeders. We do understand that you as an oppressed class, need to be more broadly prioritized, amongst the "penis owners" and "beard growers." All we can determine at this time is that you, as a "cross identifier," are more oppressed than "non-cross identifiers," AKA mono-sexuals or gays, lesbians and cis-genders. We are vacillating on what ax-i you belong. Keep "packing," though, and keep the faith.

Definitions: Packing

The act of artificially adding bulk (soft or hard) to the groin area of adolescent pre-pubescent boys to appear "more manly." The method has been adopted by some cervix owners who identify as penis owners.

Nobody cares what it is you do to your body as an adult. What is unbelievably tragic is allowing an ideology to encourage irreversible cross-sex drugs and surgeries on miners as young as twelve. Youngsters with a history of abuse and/or mental illness are thrust into opposite gender transition rather than work through their mental health issues.

Question: What if these youngsters that "professionals" are so eager to transition are simply gay? Why the rush to transition? Why not wait a few years and see how that thirteen-year-old matures into adulthood? (drugs.com n.d.) (FindLaw n.d.) (Nightingale 2022) (Leonard 2023) (EMC n.d.).

Definitions: Cis-genders

Describes a person whose gender identity matches the sex they were identified as having at birth, AKA male or female, man or woman, girl or boy.

Definitions: Mono-sexual

Cisgenders, gays and lesbians who do not cross-identify as opposite the gender they are "assigned at birth."

Important Gender Construct Note: The Intersectionality Rules Committee has recently determined that non-cross identifiers, AKA gays and lesbians, mono-genders or mono's, are healthier, have more resources and have positive media representations. Additionally, no one questions their validity. Therefore, "non-mono's, or non-bi's (non-binary's) are more oppressed than mono-gays or mono-lesbians even though mono-gays and mono-lesbians have been in the equality fight for decades, a struggle that paved the way for a "non-bi" lane to exist at all. Regardless, mono-gays and mono-lesbians are considered cis-adjacent, so have been re-adjudicated lower on the PRIORITISE scale of oppression under Axis III (Mamone 2015).

Question: Within the "non" or "negative" fractioned co-equals, which are not equal, don't they cancel each other out? Such a dilemma in the co-equaled realm of "negative nons." Oops, sorry, that was a racist mathematical parallel.

Definitions: Non-binary (non-bi)

A global term for gender identities that are not solely scrotum proprietors or egg producers that can fall under the transgender umbrella. Non-binary can identify as a third gender, no gender or gender fluid, e.g., multiple genders simultaneously, AKA a fluctuating gender depending on they or thems mood for any given day/hour/minute/second.

Important Gender Construct Note: The number of genders is still being collated.

Definitions: Adjacent

Equal to. If you are categorised (trendy Euro spelling) as adjacent, Progressives align your categorised privilege with another categorised privilege. In some instances, your categorised privilege may still be oppressed depending on where one lands on the hierarchy, AKA axis.

Da' VEEPs Beliefs: "I hope that clarifies the issue and this can be the last word on those words."

No, this was never meant to make sense to regular normals. This is a language within the vernacular only understood within the "Progressive Thought Conundrum," which will be fully explained throughout this book. Even if you reread the above passages fifty times, it still will not make sense. Normies do not possess the appropriate brain synapses to navigate the virtual complexities of complete and total nonsense of the ever-changing Progressive social construct hierarchy of worth. What does this signify? Progressives are the very definition of the many -ists, -isms, and -phobes they throw out to the rest of us in this country. Self-evaluation is very hard if you are a Progressive.

I am sad to announce for all you heterosexual (cis-gendered) Christian white beard growers who identify as actual beard growers that you are even lower now on the food chain. When compared amongst the most oppressed of our oppressively oppressive society, you rate as the amoeba, under the lily pads, under the mud, in the scum-covered pond. Don't be discouraged, though, it has been discovered that those in the Muslim and Jewish faiths who are scrotum possessors who "identify" as actual penis heirs have been re-assigned as cis-white-adjacent.

Triple Jeopardy question for 10,000: The 2020s ultimate premier supreme ruler at the top of the intersectionality list of prioritized humans. **Answer:** Who are all illegal alien border invaders coming into the United States who identify as cartel members, drug and human traffickers, terrorists and brand-new Democrat voters?

They will be added later in the soon-to-be-released twenty-ninth addition to the PRIORTISE Manual that covers criminal hierarchy. Where Biden's "new arrivals," AKA new Progressive voters are released regardless of their crime, vs. Christian, white, cis-gendered beard growers who get the electric chair.

Breaking News: Our Progressive government has recognized that information can no longer be subject to random news coverage. We must create a better formula to better coordinate a formulated message in a manner best communicated. To that end, the White House proudly announces that the following ancillary personnel have been added to the West Wing: ABC, CBS, NBC, MSNBC, CNN, NPR and other like-minded print media outlets, including but not limited to *The New York Times, The Week, The Huffington Post* and *The Washington Post*. Effective immediately, the department will be directly adjacent to the Oval Office in a newly formed government entity called… "The Spin Room." CNN will be the primary spokeshumans to the President, The New York Times will chair the group and MSNBC will brief the Press Secretary. The View eggers will consult with the "Ordered Language List" prior to releases.

More on their ordered language GULAG later (Laurene, The Spin Room, AKA The Spins, AKA The Spinners 2024).

Per the White House Press Secretary Spokeswoman, er…Spokeshuman, "On day one," this will enable a forthright, "laser-focused," comprehensive vision to be formulated of all those issues that are "top of mind." "This is uh, part of like a, um part of a, it's a - it's uh," what you call a coalition. "This will assist the President in availing himself of all the tools in the toolbox" while utilizing this critical coalition to his advantage. "We have been very clear about this." The President and his coalition seek to congruently formulate the message to "remove any disinformation, Russian or otherwise," by providing a conveyance of identical communication in a manner that is best communicated. "We have been very clear about this. We must be very mindful and we take these things seriously, very seriously." "This is a process, an ongoing process, that we are very mindful of, of which I'm not going to get ahead of." "We have been very, very clear about that." Any questions "I will circle back to" later.

> **"May the Schwartz be with you."**
> **Mel Brooks…**

Definitions: Disinformation

Information that is incongruent with the preferred messaging, regardless of facts or data, so is dismissed or can be added to the "Russia Strategy," whichever is more expedient.

Definitions: The Russia strategy

All objections are discounted as Russian collusion. This rationale has been added to our "best in story-telling" irrationalities. It will immediately follow number 7, "berating and impugning character as an 'ist'." The storytelling reference manual has been included in the White House's Human Resources manual and has been added to the "Journactivist" job description.

Journactivists, AKA "the Spins," are "Progressive adjacent" and are a critical component for supporting "The Stool." Real journalism as we knew it, is dead. Therefore, the name "journalist" is a dead name.

Da' VEEPs Beliefs: Which is why we will work together, and continue to work together, to address these issues, to tackle these challenges, and to work together as we continue to work, operating from the new norms, rules, and agreements that we will convene to work together…We will work together."

The government's state-run media (journactivists) are those entities who report, or do not report, only those stories that uphold their contrived Progressive worldview. It is the banner by which they will or will not distribute information. Listeners must understand the nuances of news reporting in the 2020s. Whether journactivists move their lips or not, each journactivist only seeks to advance The Stool's worldview by minimizing, denigrating or concealing anything or anyone that contradicts that worldview.

A horrific shooting in Colorado occurred in an LGBTQ nightclub, with a shooter opening fire on the crowd killing six people and injuring twenty-five others. The suspect was immediately subdued by other patrons at the nightclub and directly taken into custody. The Spins leapt into action. Per a quickly formulated and carefully practiced script, The Spin Room immediately blamed the tragedy on Republicans and religion, AKA Christianity. Professing that they have irrefutable evidence (just ask them) that it was a "hate crime," perpetuated because parents wrongfully have questioned the appropriateness of sexualizing activities that target children. "Parents, conservatives and churchgoers are spreaders of a Pandemic of Hate." This language is used to emphasize a heightened significance of importance. A "pandemic of hate" is the new Spinner definition of people whose views they disagree with. This reference describes people who view Drag Queen Story Hour as "grooming behavior or pedophilia" (Tremoglie 2022) (Land 2023) (Lynch 2023).

Our President then sprang up from his basement for a whirlwind press conference. In a faux show of country unity, he and his Spins smeared all those deranged, bible-thumping, transphobic, gun-toting, deplorable conservatives as murderers.

Lather, Rinse, Repeat.

There was only one problem with this hasty judgment before any actual information was known about the shooter. The shooter was "non-binary," identified with pronouns of "they/them" and wanted to be addressed using the prefix "Mx."

Hmm, OOPS, what a smashing blunder that was! What to do now when the deranged, bible-thumping, transphobic, gun-toting, deplorable conservative murderer turns out to be a deranged non-binary, LGBTQWTF+ progressive, gun-toting murderer? A previous President would simply remedy this with a "Beer Summit." Since that failed strategy was already used, our nun chuck, battered and beaten President, was shuffled back to the basement with two black eyes so he could take another nap. It was a stressful day of spinning and gyrating. "The Spin Room" dealt with it in the usual pattern, silence. It was immediately removed from the headlines, never to be heard of again (Pilkington 2009).

Definitions: Political Usefulness

The act of using a horrifying event to advance a specific political agenda while ignoring other events because they are not expedient to forward an ideological plan.

Occurring the same week there was a mass shooting at a Walmart in Virginia. Usually, this results in hysterical proclamations from the Progressivite's histrionic gun control mob on the urgency to ban all scary assault-type rifles once and for all. Journactivists live for these events. In fact, they salivate over them. Curiously, this shooting magically did not present the sort of hyperbolic response typical after any mass shooting.

This is a classic Spin strategy of incorporating silence if your ideological message is unsupported by an aggressor (the killer) with whom you identify. The "Spin Room" was therefore silent, when it was determined that the shooter was not a bible-thumping, white, Christian, heterosexual (cis-gendered) beard grower, but was instead, an African American, cis-gendered male who "only" had a small handgun purchased legally. This type of weapon does not fall into the category of "scariest guns" manufactured that need to be banned. Additionally, black-on-black crime with handguns is rampant in our country and they can't highlight that. Well, that news story went immediately into the circular file. Thankfully, they learned from their previous mistake earlier in the week. They waited five minutes for some details to emerge. The President was allowed to sleep in.

Important social context rule: In the 2020s, "black-on-black crime" is considered a stereotypical myth that is harmful, dangerous and perpetuates *"Systemic White Supremacy."* Ah, in that case, we are to ignore it, or something…(Dawson 2023).

Question: Isn't ignoring black deaths in the name of racism, racist?

Then the same week, four college students at the University of Idaho in Moscow were brutally knife murdered in their apartment while they slept. It was an equally horrific bloody scene of a brutal serial killing of four innocent young college students. It was the only crime like it in U.S. history. Never had four University students been murdered under the same roof in such a brutal manner. Our President slept through it, and his handlers found no urgency in awakening him because this murder was not ideological enough. No marginalized group was involved, nor was a gun used. Therefore, the Idaho murders did not capitalize on the same ideological point as the Club Q murders (Sun 2022).

Later, Laken Riley, a young, beautiful, talented nursing student at the University of Georgia, was beaten to death while taking a jog on campus in broad daylight. Her murderer was an illegal immigrant invader from Venezuela with ties to a violent foreign crime organization with a presence now in New York City, Florida, Texas, Illinois and Georgia. The nation's lead democrat voter recruiter, President Kingpin, pronounced her name incorrectly when forced to acknowledge her during his State of the Union Address to Congress. Going against his sworn Progressive oath, he inadvertently referred to the illegal as... an illegal. It was a serious violation of Progressive doctrine when he spoke off his teleprompter, for which he apologized profusely later. He was unapologetic for pronouncing Ms. Riley's name wrong, twice. President Spin Master has refused to release the illegal murderer's immigration records (Ruiz 2024) (Lawler 2024) (Metzger 2024) (Post Editorial Board 2024) (House Judiciary Committee 2024).

Later Senate Democrats would twice block the "Laken Riley Act" that would have required U.S. Immigration and Customs Enforcement to arrest illegal aliens who commit theft, burglary, larceny or shoplifting offenses and would mandate their detention until removed from the U.S. (Opeka 2024).

It is more than just an identity game; it is an ideological game where they pick winners and losers and refuse to report the incompetence of Progressive decisions. Our President and his Progressive compadres are far more concerned about funding the war in Ukraine than financially assisting the residents of East Palestine, Ohio, or Maui, Hawaii. Both suffered the worst environmental and catastrophic fire disasters in this country's history (Phillips 2023) (Nelson 2023) (Hurley n.d.) (CBS News 2023) (Bennett 2023) (Philips 2023) (Perkins 2023) (Visit Ukraine 2022).

2024 Update! President Tardy has finally visited East Palestine, Ohio, one year after the devastating train derailment and massive chemical spill. After all, it is an election year and Ohio and its electors are critical in a presidential election (Hutzler 2024).

The Spin Room and its Progressive politicians have perfected the identity and prioritization game since the early 2000s. Since 2016, it has taken on a life of its own. They have no shame anymore as they actively ignore or discredit legitimate news reports or individuals who report on relevant facts. Psychiatrists have recognized this behavior for hundreds of years. It is called "Pseudodologia or Mythomania." It is what people become when they believe that their lies are true (Robb-Dover 2021).

"A lie can travel halfway around the world, while the truth is putting on its shoes."
Mark Twain…

Definitions: Compulsive vs. Pathological Liars

A compulsive liar is a person who will lie, no matter what. A pathological liar is someone who lies to get their way. Both are methods to hide insecurities and elevate their social status among their peers.

Like an F-15 Bomber, the Media seeks and destroys all critical messaging against their Progressive party, their occupier/Antifa rioters, their illegal alien invaders and their pro-Hamas (terrorist) movements. What began during the Obamas' tenure in the White House, the media portrays grassroots conservative movements (the Tear Party Movement) as racist bigots who disseminate conspiratorial lunacy that spread a "culture of hate." Journactivists further cross-identify as Progressive publicists, cherry-picking events and twisting them into their desired narrative. Whether they report it or not, nothing within a spin report is ever based on object reality.

A Cultural Revolution

Da'VEEPs Beliefs…"Culture is — it is a reflection of our moment and our time. Right? And present culture is the way we express how we're feeling about the moment and we should always find times to express how we feel about the moment. That is a reflection of joy. Because, you know… it comes in the morning." "We have to find ways to also express the way we feel about the moment in terms of just having language and a connection to how people are experiencing life. And I think about it in that way, too." I

As the disordered language specialist in the White House, her vacuous brain works like an empty warehouse filled with Scrabble tiles. She shakes her head, whereby assorted tiles fall into her voice rack, which she picks out at random and then utters some disparate, incongruent statement coherent only on her own scrabble board (Davis 2022) (Devine, 2022).

    Individuals and groups protesting laws they don't like or agree with have turned to extreme behavior of rioting and violence. The violence has escalated beyond throwing rocks, bottles and Molotov cocktails and has evolved to burning down entire city blocks. It is now acceptable to punch out young women speaking at college campuses. To threaten violence against anybody they disagree with. Violence, thefts and destruction in cities nationwide are destroying lives and livelihoods, primarily in minority communities. Retail and grocery stores are closing throughout Progressive cities, which is critical to those minority communities. Yet, those in power are doing nothing to stop its spread. If you ignore it, you are condoning it.

    Beginning in 2022, we witnessed flagrant, out-in-the-open violence, drug use and death. Decriminalization of drugs where our children are now walking to school, past those who are shooting up heroin. No police protection is available to prevent vagrant violence. Storefronts are being destroyed. Social media highlights uncensored shootings in broad daylight that our youth are allowed to view. This is what weak Progressive leadership who live by the inclusivity doctrine has done to our cities. They govern according to avowed Progressive rules, sworn in under their Progressive bible. They no longer control crime and criminals know it. It is destroying our once great cities.

> "No sane society chooses to commit national suicide."
> **President John Fitzgerald Kennedy...**

We are now all living within and witnessing the beginning chapters of what it means to survive in an anarchist world that was completely and totally created by Progressives. The "defund the police" movement was only the beginning. Police departments are depleted due to a lack of funding and lack of interest. Sane, competent, honest human beings would never seek a career in law enforcement these days. Criminals rule now, as we are forced to be aware of our surroundings. Because we are constantly looking over our shoulders, we can never allow our children to play freely all day at a park. Gun sales to law-abiding citizens have never been higher as our own homes are no longer safe. We now live where ice cream, candy, baby formula and medications are locked up behind doors secured with chains. Some stores have completely locked up their entire inventory. Many have simply closed, no longer willing to subject their employees and patrons to the violence, creating food deserts most often found in urban communities. To borrow a popular Progressive phrase, it is a situation far "worse for people of color," which, in this instance, is the truth. Those who can leave have left these cities. Those who cannot are poor, or they are wealthy Progressives who can live behind their big, guarded, gated, isolated mansions with security to keep out the "vagrants" of society whom they claim to protect (Mion 2023) (Debtor 2022) (Meyersohn 2022) (T. Sahakian 2023) (Wallace 2023) (Pagans 2022) (USA FACTS Team 2021).

A popular restaurant in the City of Philadelphia has had to resort to armed guards outside their restaurant to protect their employees and patrons from criminal violence. Dressed in green fatigues and body armor, they are also well-armed with AK-47s. You know the kind, "the most dangerous rifle known to humanity, AKA a weapon of war." Except in the "City of Brotherly Love," I guess it is all right because The Spins have vanished into nothingness (Myers 2023).

The juxtaposition to a third world country, couldn't be more obvious. I have been to a third world country and this is a common site. Your mall or grocery store experience is typical of that in the United States, except they are heavily guarded by Federales in flak jackets and AK-47s. Being from the United States, this was quite disturbing to me at the time. But now, Philadelphia is leading the way to third-world designation, thanks to President Lawless and all his Progressive cohorts in blue cities throughout the United States.

I shake my head in amazement when far-leftist Progressive politicians continue to win elections over and over in these communities. "Vote blue no matter who," regardless of who runs. They are the folks who prefer to vote for civil unrest instead of civility, and why? The wealthy do it over party loyalty. They are oblivious that their vote hurts the very people they claim they advocate for. Then, some vote for single-party platforms, like abortion or student loan forgiveness. A rationale that is egocentric and ignores all other distinctions that are destroying their cities and the country (Myers, Megan 2023).

Vote Blue no Matter Who
Where blue city businesses are forced to
Daily hose the sidewalks of human poo
Hire armed security and booby trap
Their restaurants and storefronts from fentanyl and tranq.

Half-clothed people with oozing sores
Lie scattered unconscious in front of stores.
Needles, vomit, feces and bodies
We used to only see in third-world countries.

By Jo'Anna Laurene

Who are these growing numbers of people? They are the victims of Progressive doctrine. It is what occurs when you throw open the borders, defund police and legalize drugs. The doctrine fools us by convincing us all must "be fair" in the world. What it really does is destroy dreams.

The dreamers began with our forefathers, who could visualize and imagine endless possibilities. Only limited by the scope of that dream, they knew what THEY needed to do to make that dream a reality. Dreamers have become lost in our society in empty promises of government handouts that are never enough. What is lost is the labor of hard work that builds character and strong resolve, replaced by government promises that only offer an emptiness of existence that manifests as violence and crime. It breeds an endless cycle of lost lives that siphons off the prosperities we once knew existed or could exist. With that, people lose hope.

Without hope, dreams are not possible. Hopeful people are not easily manipulated, but fearful people are. Afraid people will eventually turn their fear into anger. To Progressives, people must remain angry. Angry people are those who continue voting for them for the sole benefit of their continued power and money. As they continue to line their pockets, those with whom they instilled the anger become even angrier. Sadly, as the angry keep voting for them, those same voters remain impoverished, creating more fear and anger. It is a perpetual cycle that keeps Progressives in power. Where is hope found? Within the foundation of faith, marriage and family. It is no wonder Progressives seek to tear that foundation down in nearly every policy they pass.

Da'VEEPs Beliefs: "It is important to understand what freedom and opportunity means to real people every day, which calls into question whether we're all on the same page about what freedom means."

What does freedom mean? Evidently, she is baffled about that. To be fair, it is a tough concept for all Progressives. In the simplest of terms (so they can understand), it is defined as the power or right to act, speak or think as one wants without hindrance or restraint. It has other definitions, but for the sake of simplicity for them, I will leave it at that.

Lessons Long Forgotten

Before 2008, we all were naively living our lives free from the roiling turmoil that we are drowning in today. We benefitted from life lessons from family, faith and community. They were the building blocks that created strong individuals. What has grown over time is a government that has convinced us that it will take care of us. The truth is that government can never replace family and community. It will always fall short of expectations. Why is this? Because the government replacing loving families and neighbors lacks one thing, and that is gratitude.

Gratitude is the quality of being thankful for one another's kindness. Appreciation exists when one wants to return someone's kindness with their own expression of the same. People pay kindness forward and a positive cycle then forms. Each reaches out to others as an expression of the same generosity they have received in the past. Gratitude has no political affiliation.

> "There is no use in one man or one nation trying to do or be everything. It is a good thing to be dependent on each other for something. It makes us civil and peaceable."
> *Sojourner Truth...*

Once the government takes over the role of family and community, it becomes an expectation that things are given to you (money, food, a home, an education, etc.) to ensure their future. An expectation is created that the government will provide the resources for success. When expectations occur, they can never live up to an individual's and society's sense of what should happen. In the meantime, people become addicted to the plethora of government rewards that disincentivize meaningful work and contributions to society at large. This is the Progressive government's goal: to create a dependent society.

Our country has lost its way, and our citizens increasingly consider government the answer for a meaningful and prosperous future. Even though the definition of meaningful or prosperous has not, will not and cannot be defined. Who used to define meaningful and prosperous? It was characterized by your family and the community in which you lived. The government defines it as a one-size-fits-all paradigm, which never works in a diverse country. However, now that the government owns the word diverse," they are indeed trying.

Politicians have become very good at promising "diverse" outcomes that lack definition or clarity. They use the generous feelings of the populous to convince us that something must always be done. They glorify government handouts because "nobody should ever be left behind." What does "left behind" really mean? They make promises that sound good in flowery speeches to get elected but never come to fruition. How can it be when the promises are never defined? It leaves society to define it for themselves, always expecting more. Politicians generate this feeding frenzy of infinite, innumerable, never-ending lofty expectations of undefined successes that will never be met. In an egocentric "all about me society," It works because they continually get elected and re-elected with those empty promises. Yet, homelessness and poverty have never been higher.

Success is not an entitlement or a right. It is only awarded depending on how hard one works for it and can only be characterized by individual definition. Therefore, outcomes, AKA success, can never be equal. It is only achievable by circumstance. Equality of outcomes is a myth that can never be guaranteed, no matter how much any politician postulates it. As a country, once we fully understand what defines individual success, can we move on to other political promises and lies.

> "We should measure welfare's success by how many people leave welfare, not by how many are added."
> *President, Ronald Reagan...*

Definitions Review: Postulates

A declaration of a fact without any evidence that it is true.

Our Founders believed that the government was responsible for removing the barriers that prevent success. In a free society, we make our successes as the government gets out of our way. Now, everywhere we turn, the government is in our way, placing more and more barriers that prevent us from achieving our goals.

In times of tragedy, neighbors and communities came together. My Great-grandmother received no government stimulus check or relief package. Instead, she had a pool of skilled volunteer labor and donated materials from the community. Sophie's small farmhouse and barn were repaired within a week. A freshened milk cow with a calf and oats to feed them through the winter was also donated. The family now had milk, and the calf could be butchered in the spring for the family to have meat. The community provided fresh supplies to get them by until spring. Previously done by hand, a plow and seed were donated for the following spring planting. That is what strong communities and families did for one another. Sophie did not expect it, nor did she even know the people who appeared everywhere to help her and her children.

When Sophie's parents returned to Wisconsin, her brother arrived. They were still amid winter in North Dakota, and even though the cabin and barn were repaired, they needed work to fully restore them. There was also a lingering fear that another blizzard could hit.

Sophie's brother spent the next month rebuilding the family homestead. In the late 1800s, credit was never offered to women. Yet, because of her circumstances, credit was provided to Sophie. The lumber store would offer this repeatedly to other rebuilding families as well. No "Paycheck Protection Plan" would be available to the lumber company to help offset their costs. They would need to wait months, awaiting payment from those homestead families with little means, especially after a disaster. It was a large part of what communities did to support families in times of tragedy. Families are the structure and the backbone of strong communities. Sophie repaid the loan the following summer when she sold her crops.

> "You cannot help men permanently by doing for them what they can, and should do for themselves."
> *William J.H. Boetcker...*

Today, the government uses tragedy to pick and choose winners and losers, politically doling out lucrative payouts to lobbyists and pals to keep padding their re-election bank accounts. This money greatly benefited Pfizer, large corporate healthcare conglomerates and Ukraine. Left out were the small towns of East Palestine, Ohio, and Maui, Hawaii (Masters 2024) (Spencer 2023).

Women's Rights

My great-grandmother rebuilt her homestead and then became a woman farmer to continue her and John's dream, and to support her family. This was a rare circumstance for the time. Women of today do not realize that at that time in our history, women were forbidden to participate in free markets. With the help of her young boys, Sophie's grains were painstakingly planted, cultivated and harvested by her. Following the harvest, her male friends and neighbors would have to negotiate on her behalf at grain markets. It would be a long time before she felt complete satisfaction from a hard year's work.

That was her hard reality, one that she was able to change over time. It was a real-world problem that women today have absolutely no context or appreciation for. The real women's rights crusaders were those like my great-grandmother. She was the original frontierswoman who fought for women's equality in the agricultural industry.

Little is taught about the history of true women warriors of America, who were those warriors who defined it more than "shattering the glass ceiling." True women warriors who defined society decades ago fought alongside their male counterparts with honor and distinction. They fought bravely and fiercely for their loved ones, their traditional way of life and their nation with pride and dignity. They were the real women warriors who fought on the battlefield to preserve their culture and way of life. What they did not do it for was notoriety (Women Are Warriors Too!) (White Wolf Pack) (GENi).

Notable historical figures who embodied the Definition: Minnie Hollow Wood, Pretty Nose and Buffalo Calf Road Woman were among the fiercest female fighters. Pretty Nose (1851) was one of the earlier women groundbreakers, "shattering that glass ceiling" as the Arapaho Chief. She fought hard in the great Sioux battles, including the Little Bighorn. She lived to be 101 years old.

Minnie Hollow Wood (1856-1930s) was a Lakota woman who earned the right to wear the coveted war bonnet. An honor usually only awarded to her male counterparts in the theatre of war. It was awarded for her courage and bravery in combat against the cavalry at the Battle of the

Little Bighorn. At the time, she was the only woman in her tribe entitled to wear a war bonnet.

Buffalo Calf Road Woman or Brave Woman (1844 - 1879) was a Northern Cheyenne woman who saved her wounded warrior brother, Chief Comes in Sight, in the Battle of the Rosebud in 1876. Her rescue helped rally the Cheyenne warriors to win the battle. She also fought in the Battle of the Little Bighorn, holding the distinction of being the warrior who knocked Custer off his horse, hastening the demise of the overconfident Colonel.

Tribal Nations ought to be proud of these women who were not afraid to actually "get their hands dirty" in the brave defense of their nation and the face of complete annihilation. They are not unlike our women warriors of today, who serve with honor and distinction in the US military.

Today, to some, it means to "lean in" to positions of power. It is becoming a company CEO or a leader in some boardroom of a Fortune 500 company. Becoming the first woman President of the United States is the ultimate "shattering of the glass ceiling." It is a position whereby she could be ensconced in the history books for all eternity. She is a person with narcissistic tendencies who seeks ultimate power, with the obligatory fame that comes with it…and the money. In other words, it is about herself. Someday, a woman who exhibits genuine respect for humanity and our country will materialize, someone who prioritizes country before herself or her ideology. We are still waiting (Sandberg 2013).

In the meantime, how about women leading in obscure positions where your name does not appear in the headlines daily? Real women like my sister break glass ceilings every day without any fame or fortune that comes with it. Women who lead in positions where they put their lives on the line every day, with little notice from any news organization. They are the unsung leaders in society, as they risk their lives daily as police officers and firefighters. They are jet fighters and gunneries in the military. They are brave women who risk their lives to protect the homeland and their communities in noble positions.

Susan B. Anthony was a pioneering women's suffrage movement crusader. Her work paved the way for the nineteenth amendment to the Constitution, giving women the right to vote. There was Sojourner Truth, a women's rights activist and abolitionist, born into slavery. She was an African American evangelist and reformer who applied her religious fervor to the abolitionist and women's rights movements. They, and many liked them, were the real women's rights crusaders and warriors. Women who made many sacrifices, even risking their own lives to create gradual inroads, later benefitting future women of tomorrow (Hayward 2018) (History.com Editors 2009) (Famous People).

It is not gathering by the thousands and screaming in protest, in goofy pink "vagina" hats, because your candidate failed to win the presidency of the United States, a Supreme Court justice you didn't like was confirmed or legislation was passed that you disagree with. That is NOT a women's rights movement but a demonstration or protest. While protesting can surely make your point, there is a big difference. So, what has all that screaming, and vagina hats done for women? To take a back seat to men once again. To happily relinquish the podium of fame, fortune and honor to men. To sit idly by and watch a man assault a woman fighting for her right to that platform, and worse, not even defend her for trying. All that progress for women's rights has been obliterated. The few of us left who continue to fight for women and girls have a new, progressively defined derogatory name now: TERFs, or Trans-exclusionary radical feminists.

Definitions: TERFs

Real women who object to the inclusion of men who pretend they are women who are now invading real women's spaces. This includes, but is not limited to, dressing rooms, bathrooms, sports categories, sororities and prisons. TERFs stand now as proud protectors of women and girls, while those in the media, most feminists and Progressive politicians have abandoned them.

This is the question that vagina hat screamers need to ask themselves: Are you creating new paths for women's rights for the future benefit of women everywhere, or are you just making a bunch of noise? There is a vast difference between women's rights defenders and women protesters. Defenders create women's rights through their actions and their example: Protesters just scream. If you were defending women's rights, you would not be freely surrendering to the Trans lunacy of today in the name of "inclusiveness." It is that simple. So, take off that pink pussy hat, AKA tribal headdress, quit screaming and start behaving like a woman defender.

Where did all this idiocy begin? It all began with drag shows. A mere four years ago, drag shows were a minuscule piece of the entertainment industry, performing for a niche audience of consenting adults. Sometime yesterday, this tiny fragment of our population set out to destroy the innocence of our children right in front of us. Its purpose; To normalize transgenderism in society at the expense of women and girls. Society let it happen for the sake of "acceptance." Drag Performers then expanded their breadth into child spaces. Drag Queen Story Hour was the result. It began as a contrived program of storytelling and "creative arts" for children. What started in libraries then spread to bookstores and schools. Promoted as a fun and fabulous educational experience, the ultimate goal was to normalize transgenderism in the eyes of our children. It was indoctrination at its best, and we let it happen. So much so we now have... (Rufo 2024) (Fonticoba 2019) (Faust, 2021)

New Documentary
"Mama Has a Mustache"

"A quirky, fully animated gender-nonconforming documentary through a child's eyes." The artful impressionistic film puts forward the idea of gender as a "social construct" and not a biological trait.

> **"Children need to get off the swing set and understand that gender is complicated and more nuanced than ever before."**

Trailer: This progressive piece of beautiful art features radio interviews with children ages five to ten who "could" identify as nonbinary and illustrates how these impressionable youngsters can embrace their gender. The film features children, who are free to express themselves in a whole new range of gender forms. The film seeks to explore and uncover this exciting new frontier with lightness and humor that incorporates childlike openness and play. Parents are encouraged to understand that childlike activities, such as playing baseball or roller skating, only forward "dangerous gender stereotypes," hazardous to the proper maturity of our future Transactivists (The Youth & Gender Media Project).

Drag Queen Story Hour, which morphed into Trans Reading Day for preschoolers, was simply the pre-curser for more. What began slowly and insidiously grew as they became everyday occurrences in many public libraries and schools nationwide. Silence by the public (lest you be labeled transphobic and unaccepting) was interpreted as a green light for that behavior. Trans reading day has since evolved into Trans lap dances performed on children during school assemblies (Chasmar 2023) (O'Neill 2023).

Hypocrisy Alert! Drag Queen story hour and drag shows are male actors depicting females in an overtly sexual, overly exaggerated female persona. They use over-the-top, aggrandized female face makeup and costumery during "overly sexualized performances." They are interpretative productions that demean and mock women.

Question: How is this different from the minstrel shows of the nineteenth century?

Minstrel shows were racist productions that used exaggerated dialects and expressions to mimic African Americans. Like drag performances, they used costumes and dance moves accompanied by blackface. It was as offensive, demeaning, and racist back then as this is misogynistic today. But then, once again, an activity forwarding males is afforded a special carve out in the PRIORTISE manual.

What does this prove? Progressive thought could care less about women; perhaps they never did. It is only Progressive doctrine that is forwarding the transactivist movement. Only regular normals are calling it out for what it is, a complete societal rearrangement that seeks to marginalize women and girls. It exposes the Progressive mindset of labels and the categorization of people for votes. Women are not people. They are merely a voter demographic whom they pander for votes. It is a dilemma of their own making.

The "Progressive Conundrum Thought Machine" has a serious problem now. They have so twisted themselves into such torturous masses of too many competing contradictions that they can't keep them all organized anymore. It is the natural result of all their PRIORTISE labeling. To remedy the problem, they use **Parallels Of Postulated Priorities that are Erroneously Rational and Symmetrical or…POPPERS**. It is a method to help **PRIORITISE** using parallels of other prioritised that aren't related at all (Laurene, Progressive POPPERS parallels 2024).

POPPERS is also slang for fake, which makes sense as they draw many parallels of unequal comparisons to compensate for their inconsistent and competing intersectional PRIORITISE rules. Remember that parallelogram?

In Review: It is a Progressively postulated non-self-intersecting quadrilateral with two pairs of parallel sides. Both parallels possess rotational symmetry to provide equal equivalents that aren't equal but provide rotational consistency as equal in their postulated reality. This is what bending reality into a social context looks like and is why POPPERS are necessary to provide congruity to PRIORITISE.

Important social context note: Once again, this only makes sense to Progressives.

History Of Social Context

We all agree that we must do what is right to preserve the earth around us. We can understand that we all need to do our part to recycle and pick up after ourselves and others if we need to. We need to respect clean waterways and protect our wildlife and natural surroundings. We understand that a climate shift is occurring, which is no different from any other natural climate phenomenon, over many millennia.

We know that the definition of family has changed, and to that end, gay people can now marry.

Women in the late 1800s were second-class citizens who fought through the suffrage movement. As a result, women were given the right to vote through the nineteenth amendment to the United States Constitution on August 18, 1927. This was accomplished under a Republican majority in both the House and the Senate and the leadership of Republican President Calvin Coolidge. Today, women leaders are making their mark in society. We've come a long way, baby, and most of us refuse to relinquish the progress.

Historically, many of the changes in our country were done through debate that, at times, dissolved into war. None more important than the fight to abolish slavery that resulted in the thirteenth amendment to the Constitution of the United States in 1865. It was passed by Republican majorities in both the House and Senate and signed into law by Republican President Abraham Lincoln. Since then, our country has worked hard to improve race relations in this country. Our country elected a black man to the presidency of the United States twice.

Beginning in 2009, race relations began to deteriorate under the organizing leadership of Democrat President Barrack Obama. Since that time, racial conflicts have accelerated exponentially, then starting in 2020 it was pedal to the metal. For most of us quietly sitting on the sidelines, it was and is never enough, and it is exhausting. We are constantly reminded that America is hateful and should be ashamed of our founding beliefs. To believe in our founding principles now makes us racist, even though those founding beliefs resulted in The Emancipation Proclamation of 1862 declaring black men free from slavery. Everything nowadays is described as going back to "Jim Crow" days.

Who was Jim Crow? Jim Crow was a harmful caricature performed by Thomas Dartmouth Rice, a white man. A performer in New York City in the early 1800s, his show exploited stereotypical speech, movement and physical features attributed to Black people to mock them. It entertained and miseducated whites at the expense of Blacks for Rice's financial benefit.

Essentially, Drag Queen performances are Jim Crow-esque, or, to use a popular Progressive term, "Jim Crow adjacent," with the same goals of mocking, miseducating and financial gain. I am sure that this POPPERS parallel will create much debate. Debates concerning political principles have been going on for decades. What has changed is the mechanisms of thoughtful debate to draw conclusions.

Definitions: Debates prior to 2009

An exchange of views by in which two people/groups attempt to define meaning, usually to classify or clarify a point by which they believe they are both correct. Each debater makes valid points that each debater thoughtfully considers. After the debate, each party may have different ideas or viewpoints by which they can reasonably cultivate their own worldview. Some debates end where there is no difference of opinion, but both debaters amicably agree to disagree.

The New Definition of Debates post-2009

1. **Divisive conclusions:** Debates that end with "you cannot know because you aren't black, a woman, transgender, gay, Hispanic, Middle Eastern or poor. This is not an exhaustive list.
2. **Non-civil conclusions:** Debates that end when one debater calls the other debater stupid, incompetent, hateful or some -phobe, -ism, or -ist.
3. **Integrity conclusions:** This is a method where one person/group destroys the integrity of the other person/group. The integrity attribute doesn't even need to be true. Its purpose is to destroy a person/

"Without debate, without criticism, no administration and no country can succeed, and no republic can survive."
President John Fitzgerald Kennedy...

group's character, so whatever information they may have will be questioned.

Definitions: Racism/Racist:

A constantly changing, often ambiguous list that includes but is not limited to attitudes, actions, thoughts, clothing, foods, symbols, places, art, literature, statues, beverages, sports, arts, crafts, toys and vehicles. This is not a complete list and is impossible to compile. Racist tags are useful to divide and promote discourse. America's snowflake generation uses racism to manufacture outrage in their delicate psyche. In 2023, no less than seventy-two brand-new items were added to the racist list (College Fix Staff 2023).

Definitions: Snowflakes

Individuals who are pitifully touchy and easily offended. Like adolescents, they believe they are the most unique and that the world revolves around them. They are entirely unable to deal with opposing opinions in any setting. Once you offend their senseless, sensitive sensibilities, they demand you to be censored. Generation Z became the standard bearers of this politically correct movement that defines all -phobes, -ists, and -isms.

Definitions: Cancel Culture

Where content can be categorized as either offensive or racist. It contrives disagreed upon subject matter, then seeks to censor those ideas labeling them as offensive or racist. They then deploy cancel strategies to demean the individual who dared to speak offensively (in their opinion), sometimes employing violence.

Cyberbullying is a frequently used application to meet this goal. Other consequences include loss of friends, loss of standing and loss of jobs. Unfortunately, new societal constructs and related behaviors have resulted in a generation of young people incapable of comprehending the world around them.

The Face of Our Country's Incapable Youth

Now reporting from New York City, Occupation New School (Scott 2022)

In Greenwich Village, New York, is an elite private university called "New School," where spoiled, self-absorbed students are "occupying" a campus building. Using similar tactics as the Occupy Wall Street movement in 2011 which demanded "economic equality," "Occupy New School" is demanding "academic equality" for all students. The "all-inclusive movement" demands that all students be awarded "A" grades.

What a great idea! Excellence without effort, with no tests to pass, no papers to write and you don't even need to attend class. This school needs a new name, "The University of Excellence in Ineptitude," a university where everyone can graduate Magna Cum Laude. Anyone in the country can participate and you don't even need to move to New York City to attend college. Simply sign up for courses from your parent's basement and wait for your well-deserved "A" grade to be delivered by electronic mail.

Other student demands include a tuition freeze, firing the school's President, Provost, and Vice President, and disbanding the Board of Trustees. My guess is they are the academics responsible for requiring actual educational achievement. The nerve!

Their demands also include the University President's home to be a communal property. After all, everyone needs a nice place to party and sleep. When the commune runs out of bedrooms and hallways, they can pitch their $5,000.00 North Face tent (that daddy bought for them) on the lawn.

There is no need to comment further on this; the absurdities speak for themselves. This was the prototype that all woke American universities emulated to forward all anti-America stances, including their anti-Israel/pro-Palestinian protests. They hate America, the same America and her people whom they want to pay for their Ivy League education. This and similar universities are the breeding ground for Progressive thought (Glasser 2024).

In general, for those born between 1995 and 2004, your generation has a distinction. This notion of speaking in generalities directly imparts Progressive thought, of which you are now a casualty. For example, if one police officer is corrupt, all of them are. I know that seems unfair, but you invented the general thought of generalities.

Therefore, "in general," you and your peers have been identified as the most delicate, yellow-bellied, easily broken, spoiled weaklings in generations. You live tenuously in an emotional bubble wrap because you are so fragile. Nearly everything within your sphere of existence triggers you into a literal breakdown. You can thank all those "all-inclusive" institutions of higher learning. They have so intellectually weakened this generation of Americans that they cannot think for themselves or even be adults. Their inability to function independently is grossly identifiable when launched into the real world. Little do they know that the entire country is laughing at their gross incompetence. The good news is that the only place for them to grow, is up.

"When one-third of Democrats think we have too much freedom, with similar numbers of American liberals feeling that the government can and should police speech, we can find agreement on the notion that coastal, elitist, snobby, white folks are ruining America. They are a systemic problem for Democrats. If we could get the humanities faculty at Amherst College to shut the F#%$ up, we'd be a lot better off."
The Architect of Bill Clinton's 1992 election win...
James Carville...

His assessment is correct, but many more woke universities need to be added to his list. Sadly, he and his Clintons began this saga that was the nexus of things to come. For him and traditional Democrats, it would be Bill's Hill who would first introduce us to what it means to be a "Modern Progressive," as she made it HER official party platform in the 2008 presidential election. So, it would be Carville's Clintons who thrust this ideology into the collective consciousness of the Democrat party. Before that announcement, nobody ever heard of "Progressivism" (Stevenson 2016) (Vespa 2023).

With that, the Progressive Movement swooped in and hijacked the Democrat party, making it their official party philosophy. The Democrat party is no longer the party of John F. Kennedy, my mother or Mr. Carville. They were, and are, far too moderate now for this generation of Progressives who proudly identify as Socialists. In Kennedy's day, this was taboo. Nobody who self-identified as a socialist would have ever been elected to office. Sadly, it would be a self-identified card-carrying socialist who assassinated President John Kennedy on November 22, 1963, bringing an end to Camelot and the naiveté of a country. My, how far we have come.

Mr. Carville's Clintons, the Obamas and now The Big Guy, have summoned in a new Progressive social construct framework that has sickened our nation. They brought us wokeness, transactivism and are the party of child mutilation. They are the party of illegal immigration that brought us increases in violence, crime, illegal drugs and human trafficking, anarchists and anti-Semites. They are solely responsible for shoving women and girls entirely off the platform of equality (Bauer 2023) (Post Editorial Board 2022) (Phillips 2023) (Kilgore 2024).

A 2022 study by the Mary Christie Institute studied our Gen Z youth as they exit universities and enter the workforce. Given our current state of higher education, what they found was unsurprising. Progressive parents sent their children to these elite universities, which further incited the attitudes of identity politics and social equity. This resulted in a subpar education focused wholly on woke ideology and intersectionality politics that has weakened an entire generation. Once they graduated, our new generation of young urban professionals found themselves emotionally unprepared for real life.

This generation has absolutely no self-awareness of their role in their inability to survive in the real world and their nine-to-five careers. As students, they demanded their universities and colleges acquiesce to student demands of the de-platforming of speakers and the firing of professors who offended their "fragile" senseless sensitivities. Universities then provided them with stuffed animal cry rooms and "safe spaces," providing cotton candy and crayon books in an atmosphere free from "triggering" statements, attire or environments. Progressive universities created an entire generation of untamed narcissists who live in a fantasy world of "it's all about me." It is an attitude that prevents them from functioning in a diverse environment, most widely described as "life" (Singman 2016) (Rose 2017) (Lukianoff 2015).

Ultimately, this may be the downfall of the Progressive movement, as the understudies of the cause take it well beyond what regular normals, including traditional Democrats, can tolerate. One such example was perfectly illustrated by a young progressive staffer employed by Maryland Democrat Senator Ben Cardin. He gave us a perverted rendering of Brokeback Mountain that was filmed in the same Senate Hearing room where the 9/11 Commission convened, as well as the confirmation hearings of Supreme Court Justices. His amateur gay porn flick, which left nothing to the imagination, was then posted to social media for anybody to see, including children (Rodgers 2023).

It was just another full audiovisual display of what happens when acceptance goes too far, and the moral fiber of our country is destroyed. Where Brokeback beautifully introduced the equality of an idea, this offensive flick that definitely "broke the binary" left nothing to the imagination and will set back gay acceptance for decades. The production's star from "Necropolis by The Bay" attempted a POPPERS parallel of homophobia, claiming he is "a victim of political homophobic bias against loving whom he loves," or something…

As a natural consequence of his astonishing stupidity, he was justifiably fired from Senator Cardin's office. I am sure his firing bucked some DEI or ESG principle in the Progressivists' PRIORTISE handbook. The Intersectionality Rules Committee is busily re-configuring the social construct of gay sex filming in Senate Hearing rooms much higher on some Ax-i. Senator Cardin has since decided to retire (Prouix 2005).

As Progressives cast Democrats aside in their woke wake, an unsurprising number of Democrats and their politicians have switched to the Independent party. The Progressive party and their all-inclusive woke DEI and ESG principles no longer speak for them, or the rest of humanity for that matter. Could this be the death warrant for the Progressive crusade? We can only hope (Rubin 2024).

Da' VEEPs Beliefs: "When we talk about the children of the community, they are the children of the community."

Like all generations before them, generational descriptions follow you for the rest of your lives, and you will be no exception. Your gay porn star and his debutant did not help. Decorum, dignity and respect are inclusive in all societies, and all-inclusivity is not a substitute. It is a universal expectation among everyone that makes up humankind. It is how a generation gains respectability amongst themselves and society around them. The snowflake generation will carry this denotation for the rest of their lives because they earned it. At no other time in American history has a generation thrust such nonsense across the American landscape.

As the most coddled and entitled generation in history, a recent study found that fifty-one percent of young professionals reported needing help for emotional or mental health problems since beginning their careers. Women reported worse mental health than men at fifty-five percent and thirty-two percent, respectively, with fifty-three percent reporting a state of prolonged physical and psychological exhaustion. Forty-five percent believe their work environment has negatively affected their mental health, with forty-two percent stating they will leave their job within a year. Fifty-eight percent of respondents agreed that their workplace should invest in more mental health resources. Sixty-four percent of those who agree with that statement are women (Mary Chritie Institute 2023).

They are the "Quiet Quitting" generation. They are the practitioners of "Bare Minimum Mondays," whereby they live by a philosophy of "Acting Their Wage." All created by "everyone gets a trophy" parents and their mollycoddling universities who pandered to their ego-centric demands that are not POPPER'ing well in the real world.

Definitions: Quiet Quitting

A decreased amount of effort is devoted to one's job by NOT completing tasks explicitly stated in the job description, employing efforts that will only meet but will not exceed previously established expectations. They never volunteer for additional tasks and will always prioritize their own well-being and mental health over the organization.

Definitions: Bare Minimum Mondays

A new workplace trend that encourages workers to prioritize self-care over work duties.

Definitions: Acting Your Wage

Setting boundaries and putting out only the amount of effort the Gen Z'er feels is commensurate with the salary they receive.

That glass ceiling appears harder to reach than all those "Lazy Girls" thought. Working hard parallels mental fortitude and is not paralleled to your mental health. You need to turn off TikTok and its "Lazy Girl Job Strategies." Lazy girls do not shatter glass ceilings. They are only now discovering that their four-year Gender Studies Degree gives them nothing to offer the workforce. If they are not waitressing, it takes them directly into public assistance. It is no wonder that sixty-eight percent of this generation are still living with their parents (Press-Reynolds 2023) (Dragos 2023).

A recently published study found that employers are fed up with "college waste," opting instead for skilled blue-collar workers. When employers were asked about the "return on investment" of higher education, a whopping sixty-seven percent responded with a "strong no," stating that college used to be a place that enhanced an already effective human being. Further stating, "The talent shortage will just get worse because high schools and colleges produce no talent." Many potential employers call an advanced degree a waste. When asked if employers were more or less likely to consider a job seeker's four-year degree, only ten percent said "yes," and forty percent said "absolutely not." Practical experience now overrides a college degree (Penley 2023).

What does that mean? Nobody cares that you got the "Excellence in Achievement in Gender Studies" award. The Human Resources department of your corporation could care less that you were the leader of your Student Social Activism group. Guess what! You are not special anymore. You are no longer the Queen of the hive. Outside your placating university, you possess the same distinction as all the other worker drones in your corporation/work setting. Businesses have discovered that your presence leaves the hive many cones short of a functioning colony. Sorry, kids, Twitter won't hire you because expectations are higher now. However, you can submit your resume to "The Spin Room."

Definitions: A Classical Education.

Generally only found in homeschooling curricula, Christian and charter schools, AKA private schooling. It is a long tradition of education that emphasizes truth-seeking, goodness and beauty. It is the study of liberal arts and great literature. This approach to education also includes the study of Latin. Over the centuries, classical education has produced countless great leaders, inventors, scientists, writers, philosophers, theologians, physicians, lawyers, artists and musicians. Classical education has diminished with the advent of "Progressive Education."

Definitions: A Progressive Education.

Where most public schools and universities now fall and it bears repeating, it is where students are taught what to think instead of how to think, and where students are instructed on what to learn instead of how to learn. Progressive education has thrown out math, literature and composition because they are racist (Rantz 2024) (Edge 2023) (Soave 2021).

This generation is both the victims and the leaders of the race-industrial complex, as the chosen disciples of the division industry. They are the generation who have paid the ultimate sacrifice to the Progressive religious sect who find self-fulfillment through anger. They have surrendered joy at the altar of misery and despair (Pomeroy 2022).

The Justification of "Injustices"

Definitions: Race-Industrial Complex and the Division Industry

It refers to a racket that has monetized racial, economic and gender discourses. The Progressive camp has recognized that Americans and human beings in general, respond strongly to contrived "perceived incidences" of injustice.

Definitions: Monetized

Often equates to financial gains but it can also be societal gains, where social capital is used to gain influence for themselves or ideas to gain power capital.

I had compiled a list of all things racist by this generation and their academic role models since 2019. Unsurprisingly, the list became far too long to justify its addition to this book and would be moot anyway once it was published. However, I will add several new 2023 Zoomer racist definitions that we can all be amused by. Other than, "Not Wearing a Mask, Senator Tim Scott (who is black), Classical Music Composers, the Outdoors and the Kansas City Chiefs," what else is included in their racist designations? (Lamb 2023)

Pumpkin Spice Latte is now "shorthand for whiteness" and promotes the concept of colonizer histories with the use of nutmeg, cinnamon, cloves and ginger. Using that logic, other racist foods would be bread pudding, coffee cake, apple pie, gingerbread cookies, carrot cake, Mexican hot chocolate, baked apples, apple crisp, banana cake, oatmeal cookies, peach cobbler, sweet potato pie, apple sauce and French toast. This is only one example of why the "All Things Racist" list keeps growing (Rigby 2023) (Javaid 2023).

This is what the chronically malcontented, supremely narcissistical white Progressive academics and their Zoomers perseverate about nowadays. So, the next time you sit down with that piece of spice cake, you must first drop immediately to your knees, clasp your hands together, raise your voice to the sky, and thank all those in the fifteenth through seventeenth centuries for their sacrifice before you can have your cake and eat it too.

In 2023, "sizeist" was the new adjective to describe individuals and entities who discriminate against "people of size." By the time 2024 rolled around, influencers discovered the profitability of self-identity. That was when the Obese Influencer was born using the all-inclusive self-identifier of "The Super Fat."

This is precisely why influencers can be so destructive. As the sister of a deceased obese family member, I find this utterly abhorrent. The "Super Fat" self-identifier influencers do so purely for financial gain, with no respect for those who struggle every day because of their size. "Super Fat" influencers could care less about those who suffer from depression, poor health and discrimination. I know for a fact that this would have been the last thing my brother would have identified with, and I am sure he is not alone.

To illustrate the absurdity of this notion, I will now introduce POPPERS postulations, or parallels, as it pertains to air travel, from which all this "Super Fat" nonsense has evolved. Progressives and their influencers use POPPERS (parallels) of unparalleled powers since their Intersectionality principles are problematic within this perspective. Where the PRIORITISE Manual falls short, inclusivity takes over, especially when it POPPERS other priorities of PRIORITISE importance in an oppressively oppressive society. POPPERS then have a magical ability to propel progress of Progressive philosophies, when intersectionality hierarchies underperform their desired principles.

Using air travel as an example, I will start with Southwest Airlines' all-inclusive "customers of size" policy, which has embraced the "Super-Fat." No longer will the "Super-Fat" be required to pay for seats (First Class) that better accommodate their size. Free seats are awarded depending on where one lands on the super-fat spectrum and are measured by how many armrests one can squeeze between. Therefore, the POPPERS (parallel) of the "my body, my choice" repeater POPPERS the super-fat spectrum measured by the number of armrests, which POPPERS (parallels) economic justice in the acquisition of free seats. And no, one cannot "identify" as 400 pounds because of the armrest equalizer (Guzman 2023).

Now that this pronouncement has been proclaimed, super-fat people from across the population will populate this airline. Then, as they amass, airline corporate proceeds will plummet as fewer posteriors occupy seats. This is when economic justice POPPERS all-inclusive principles where passengers below the fat spectrum pay for all those extra armrests that those on the super-fat spectrum require. This then results in anger by Normies below the fat spectrum, which predictably POPPERS "Ableism," which will neutralize the Normies. Whereby we will all dutifully pay higher prices in the name of "acceptance," so as not to be labeled "Sizeists." See how that works?

Here's another one. It is a very important all-inclusive POPPERS parallel of unparalleled unimportance. Did you know that calling Asian Carp "Asian Carp" is now racist? This was a natural extension that POPPERS the Covid Chronicles. Like Covid, Asian Carp got that name because they came from Asia. Not sure when Carp decided they didn't want to be identified as Asian anymore because to infer anything else would be racist! (Lungariello 2021)

Moving on from that bologna to more bologna. Pantry Porn is now what they call an organized pantry. Evidently, this is a status symbol, so therefore, POPPERS economic injustice, which naturally POPPERS *Systemic White Supremacy!* Correct me if I am wrong, but I believe a pantry is a place in which we store food, you know, like root cellars long ago from which pantries evolved. But, since this generation of wise, woke, chronically discontented students and their academics have not studied history, they know nothing about root cellars. I am happy to report that my pantry's brown rice parallels my white rice on the shelf and are getting along just fine (Lanum 2023) (Laurene, Rice Paralleling Rice 2024).

Announcing an important update to the PTSD Translation Dictionary: See page 15,305, Section 5, Paragraph 27. Be patient, this manual will be described momentarily.

Definitions: Tradwife.

A "traditional wife." A heteronormative, AKA gender regular (cis-gendered) Normie, who stays at home with the children. She uses the pronoun "she," cooks, keeps house and probably keeps a pantry stocked. GASP! She gardens, accompanies her children to the playground and might even sew. Worst of all, she might do crafts. They are further described as submissive women who are likely conservative and Christian. A quick review on TikTok: The reported Tradwives, (she/hers) are portrayed (dress, hairstyles and makeup) as 1950s wives. It instantly triggers the Zoomer Wokesters, who view this amongst their parallel POPPERS of sexism, homophobic, trans-nonconforming and *Systemic White Supremacy!*

Important note: Regular normal "heteronormative" women view this as grossly stereotypical but find it hysterical that wokey woke Zoomers and their spinners find it so provoking. Who knew that being a she/her traditional wife/homemaker could be so inflaming? Nowadays, you need to do absolutely nothing to live comfortably inside a Progressive's head.

My pronouns are: Picking out the drapes.

Definitions: Insurrectionist Barbie

A gender hetero-normal, cis-gendered mono-gendered, therefore Lesbian adjacent (an example of a reverse POPPERS), woman who is happily married to a man. Oh my! This brand-new 2023 Barbie comes dressed in a 1950s-styled white dress, a red and white gingham checked apron and black patent leather slip-on shoes. Her hair is pulled neatly in a bun with a red ribbon (to match her apron, of course). Her accessories include a mixing bowl and rolling pin. If you purchase the Premium Insurrectionist Barbie, she also comes with military fatigue clothing and a long rifle. The Ultra-Premium Insurrectionist Barbie model comes with a great big diesel truck, a trailer hitch and an attached stock trailer. For a few extra bucks, you can purchase the cows to go inside the stock trailer (Laurene, Insurrectionist Barbie 2024).

Definition Review: Adjacent

Meaning equal too.

Definition: Insurrectionist

A violent uprising against any Progressive government authority, including but not limited to School Board meetings. This does NOT apply to various Occupy movements, ANTIFA or BLM rioting, as those uprisings are defined as grass-roots protestors. However, it definitely applies to any peaceful conservative movement beginning with the 2009 Tea Party Movement (Pelosi 2010).

Like a brand-new, repeatedly used word in a toddler's vocabulary, it now applies to everything Progressives hate. After all, with the 2024 election around the corner, they must keep "insurrectionists" alive and kicking in the minds of all voters (Faria 2023).

Critical Historical Note: "Insurrectionists" became a productive Progressive description within their ordered language denotations beginning on January 6, 2020. It generally describes cis-gendered Christian white beard growers but has grown in scope to include anyone who goes against the Progressive Doctrine. This includes a 71-year-old grandmother, AKA the J6 Praying Grandma, who committed the gross offense of praying inside the capital for ten minutes and was convicted on four federal charges relating to her praying. She faces a year in jail and a fine of $200,000. It is impossible to adequately delineate all the Progressive tales of woe that this subject postulates. This show trial can be easily accessed on the internet. However, any objective evidence of an actual insurrection has disappeared. FOIA requests have found that testimony to prove otherwise has magically vanished (Gold 2023) (Singman 2024) (A. Phillips 2022) (Justice 2024) (Rumble 2023) (Hemingway 2024) (Kelley 2024) (Tober 2023).

Definitions Review: Postulates

A declaration of a fact without any evidence that it is true, except to their own committee (A. Miller 2023).

Breaking News! Another outbreak of the Avian flu is once again infecting American poultry. Where racism POPPERS COVID-19, the Biden administration is investigating the mass vaccinations of millions and millions of Americans against "The Avian Bird Flu." However, per the Whitehouse Spokeshuman, they are changing the name to "The Bird Flu" to not be discriminatory toward Avians (Teach 2023) (Stolberg 2023) (Laurene, Avian Discrimination 2024).

However, federal poultry officials are concerned that the current strain H5N1, "Bird Flu," will not be effective against the current strain. They have granted a one billion dollar federal grant to Pfizer to work their variant strain magic, as it now pertains to poultry. The Reverend and Pfizer have assured the American public that ABSOLUTELY, POSITIVELY, no

Gain of Function Research will be conducted on American Foul (Laurene, Foul Experimentation 2024).

On November 28, 2022, the "Spin Room" added daylight savings time to the ever-growing list of all things racist. It must be exhausting to be an American Progressive in a near-constant, despairing and hopeless existence, whereby all that consumes them is to come up with new racist representations of great societal importance. I do not know a single person who embraces the time change that disrupts everyone's circadian rhythm and health. However, when you add the qualifier, "it is far WORSE for people of color," only then is it more worthy of focus (Howard 2022).

Lather, Rinse, Repeat.

The Giant Symbol of Complete and Total Racism

The American flag, a powerful global symbol of freedom and patriotism since 1776, is now considered racist. It was only a matter of time, though. When everything is racist, you need some giant symbol (umbrella) to describe the entirety of your culture, society and country as racist. What is racist next, after everything in society is racist under the giant American flag umbrella? Never sell the race baiters and the division industry short. They can and did come up with something.

Definitions: Race Baiters

It is a primary component of "The Race Industrial Complex" (a subgroup of the Division Industry) whereby one intentionally seeks to divide and inflame one racial group against others, often for personal aggrandizement, political advantage and power.

I do not believe that loving one's own country, culture and people is racist. The great Thomas Sowell observed that "the word racism is like ketchup now, it can be put on practically anything." Mr. Sowell, a black man, is described today

> "If you collect 100 fire ants and 100 black ants and put them in a jar, nothing will happen.
> If you take the jar, shake it violently, and leave it on the table, the ants will start killing each other.
> The red ants believe the black ants are the enemy, and the black ants believe the red ants are the enemy, when the real enemy is the person who shook the jar.
> The same is true in society…
> Men vs. women, black vs. white. Faith vs. science, young vs. old, etc. Before we fight each other, maybe we should ask… "Who shook the jar?"
> *Kurt Vonnegut (Cat's Cradle, 1963)…*

by the Progressive race baiters of the Race Industrial Complex as an "Uncle Tom" (Spingarn 2010).

Hypocrisy Alert! Uncle Tom is a racist slur, which seems unbecoming of the "most inclusive and tolerant" in our society, AKA the Progressive party. This offensive slur is the title character of Harriet Beecher Stowe's historical 1852 novel "Uncle Tom's Cabin." It is the story of an enslaved African American named Tom who was devoted to his fellow slaves; A devotion so unshakable that he sacrificed his chance for freedom and eventually his life to help them. He was beaten to death for refusing to betray the whereabouts of two other enslaved black people. The novel's influence was worldwide. In Russia, it influenced the 1861 emancipation of the serfs and later inspired the Bolshevik leader Nikolai Lenin, who recalled it as his favorite book in childhood. It was the first American novel to be translated and published in China, and it fueled antislavery causes in Cuba and Brazil. It is the most translated book in history, second only to the Bible (The Gilder Lehrman Institute of American History Period 5: 1844-1877).

Conservative black men are in good company. Rosa Parks and Dr. Martin Luther King Jr. were also labeled Uncle Toms because of their "pacifist approach" to equality. Rosa Parks believed in non-violent moral protest, and Dr. King in principled nonviolence, where all should be respected. Modern Progressivism demands a militarist approach to equality (Reynolds 2011).

History reveals this racist slur originated in 1911 by white supremacist Progressive men. They were enraged when black men migrated to the North, acquiring jobs held initially by Northerners. It is ironic, isn't it, that this name is now a derogatory term that "modern" Progressives use today to describe conservative black men (A. Spingarn 2010).

How do Progressives spell inclusive? **I N T O L E R A N C E.**

Fascism review: Describes violent authoritarianism under an autocratic ruler. During Mussolini's regime, committed fascists described liberty and the expression of freedom as a sham. Fascism instead believed that people needed to be organized under state power. If one does not fit that mold, you are seen as disruptive to that unity and thus

> "The ignorance of one voter in a democracy impairs the security of all."
> *President John Fitzgerald Kennedy...*

subject to violence and death. Anything that defies fascist order must be eliminated by force. Violence was seen as beneficial to a fascist society and is precisely what motivates Occupiers under various names to riot, burn and destroy lives.

Important note to the progressive, Gen Z, fascist police: It does not apply to people, rules or laws that get in the way of one's preferred politically correct, woke, group-think ideology. So, to prevent that nun chuck from blackening your eyes again, please review some history.

The real tragedy here is that racism is serious in our society. It has a long history of horrible atrocities that can never be understated, should never be forgotten and are still occurring today. However, this word's politicized over-use has only diluted the actual hostilities many minorities have endured for decades. If everything is racist, then nothing is racist, as we all quit listening. The result is that many Americans have become indifferent to the meaning of racism, essentially minimizing and erasing its true meaning and our continued efforts to overcome it.

Recognizing this problem, the race-baiters within the Race Industrial Complex understand the strategy of transformative language when an overused word becomes insignificant to listeners. It is when a more pejorative significator is required to once again re-significate the significance of their previous significative, over-used, now insignificant statement. This strategy supplies supplemental clarity to signify the significance once again. Since the term racism no longer holds any impact…

We Now Welcome the "New Era" of… "<u>Systemic White Supremacy</u>."

Ah, a great example of pseudo-intellectual drivel to re-signify an old term into a new term that is the same as the old term but sounds far worse. We are relieved they have clarified the significance of that signifier further, which was coincidentally introduced at the same time as "Critical Race Theory."

Question…If the United States is inherently, vehemently and systemically racist, why are millions upon millions of non-white people flooding our border to get in?

Intersectionality Adjacents

Breaking News! Intersectionality is at a crossroads as our Supreme Court now prohibits selection based on race. Affirmative Action is no longer relevant in the United States of America. Oh my, race doesn't matter? Everyone is equal? Who would have thought?

This tsunamic transformation has resulted in Progressive nanoparticles colliding in a lightning bolt of ideologic thought transformation. It has white progressives quivering in their Christian Louboutins outside their favorite Starbucks while clutching onto their favorite French brew, three-shot, tall, certified organic, fair-trade Cappuccino with double froth. The Spins have melted down into a gyrating frenzied gnashing of overly masticated cud as they repeat their tired platitudinous reporting that, once again, will ultimately result in the prohibition of mixed-race marriages, force little girls to give birth, erase black history, see the return of "Jim Crow" laws, eliminate voting rights, take away your birth control, eliminate a woman's right to vote and increase assault weapons on the streets. More and more people are going DIE, which will be "worse for people of color."

Lather, Rinse, Repeat.

Meanwhile, Asian Americans are jubilant that their 4.0 GPAs and perfect SAT scores will finally be considered as they apply to Harvard and Princeton Universities. Concurrently, this has resulted in an emergency conference of the Intersectionality Rules Committee for a rewrite of the PRIORITISE manual. See Chapter Ten, paragraphs 20 and 25, under Axis I. An addendum has been added as follows:

Asian Americans have been declared as "tools of the white" and are white supremacists themselves. They are no longer race victims as they were during the Covid Chronicles, AKA "The China Virus." In a blinding nanoparticle of electrifying speed, our Asian citizens have been re-adjudicated to the status of "white adjacent," which is sorted contiguous with and POPPERS the "Uncle Tom" classification. They are not alone, however. Since October 7, 2023, all Jewish Americans have also been "rebranded" as "white adjacent" (Xu 2021).

Definitions Review: White Adjacent

POPPERS mono-gays and mono-Lesbians as "cis-adjacent," but can also include BIPOCs who have access to and benefit from the attributes of "White Privilege." Therefore, Asians are now considered white-adjacent. It is another example of Progressive rebranding, the mechanics of which are only understood within the Progressive mind: *A mysterious place that regular normals dare not explore for fear of being trapped interminably in Animal Farm* (Orwell).

> *"All animals are equal, but some animals are more equal than others."*
> *George Orwell, "Animal Farm"...*

Progressive Brown Shirts of the Modern Era

This generation did not invent it, but they have perfected its concepts into the 2020s. It is what occurs when an entire generation embraces Progressive theories at their universities, colleges, high schools and social media.

Definitions: Brown Shirts

In 1921, Hitler organized a paramilitary, informally known as the "Brownshirts." Famous for operating outside the law, they used violent intimidation tactics against Jewish populations. In modern times, they would be those participating in any Occupy movement and the anti-fascist (ANTIFA) campaign within an organized network that seeks to destroy communities and neighborhoods. In 2024, Brownshirts at Northeastern and other Ivy League universities are behind the "Kill the Jews" proclamation reminiscent of the Holocaust (Dimuro 2019) (Schooley 2024).

Definitions Review: Political Correctness

It seeks conformity to the prevailing liberal or radical opinion that began in the 1970s by academia. It became the basis for today's woke ideology whereby it seeks to punish all forms of expression or actions that they perceive to exclude, marginalize or insult groups of people whom "they" determine are socially disadvantaged or discriminated against. This rule has many exceptions; See the PRIORITISE carve-out exception for transgenders and illegal Invaders.

> *"Too often, we…enjoy the comfort of opinion without the discomfort of thought."*
> *President John Fitzgerald Kennedy…*

Definitions: Group Think

Tactics and methods to accomplish conformity within a population. Using a myriad of psychological tools (coercion, shame), a consensus among the population can be achieved without allowing critical reasoning, debate or evaluation.

Group Think stifles individuality and creativity within a group. It is a mind-conforming exercise, first developed by the Nazis and is a valuable tool practiced by Progressives. It is a method to bring conformity to ideas and theories that, on their face, are outrageous to anybody who has a brain.

This is how we got COVID-19 mandates but it has infiltrated our culture in far greater, more destructive ways. What began as inclusion and diversity has evolved and infiltrated every aspect of our lives. It has now advanced into radical beliefs and movements that we never thought possible. Their tactical plan employs many systems and techniques to align the non-conformers to their conformity.

> *"Conformity is the jailer of freedom and the enemy of growth."*
> *President John Fitzgerald Kennedy...*

Definitions: Microaggressions

Off-hand comments or actions, primarily unintentional, that express some negative connotation, only to the listener's definition of prejudicial, after which they spare no amount of energy to express their displeasure at the expense of others' discomfort. They are those who proudly display their prejudicial orientation as a bulwark across their chests. They are easy to spot with interminably pursed lips and can scream and cry with little to no real discernable provocation.

The Dreaded Rectum Lip Disorder: A terminal, permanent condition that originates among woke academics who identify as "eggers," who are reactionary, hormonal and controlling, one who is white, likely single, a Chardonnay swiller and who practices virtue-signaling techniques daily. They are easily identifiable by their lips and corresponding wrinkles, resembling the anatomy in the nether regions of everyone's backsides. This unfortunate affliction is easily preventable by spending more time outdoors and away from mobile devices. It only manifests in those who perform excessive pursed-lipped frowning and too little smiling. Unfortunately, this virulent disorder has contagiously spread to their self-identified Gen Z fallopian tube proprietor students. Variants of this incurable malady have now spread to Progressive politicians who identify as uterus owners and Journactivist chest feeder identifiers from The Spin Room (Laurene, Rectum Lippers 2024).

Definitions: Social Justice

Prominent in the rhetoric of far-left political movements and organizations, Diversity, Equity and Inclusion (DEI) and Environmental, Social and Governance (ESG) ideals became the base religiosity of social justice. It become the lodestar of modern Progressive politics and their activists.

Definitions Review: Cancel Culture

A form of boycott or ostracism in which someone is removed or "canceled" from social or professional circles due to something they said or done that is considered unacceptable or offensive… by somebody. It can affect influential public figures, individuals, products, brands or organizations. It involves online and offline actions, such as protests, ridicule, doxing, withdrawing support or harming reputations and livelihoods. The ULTIMATE cancellation is being de-friended on Facebook. Gasp!

Double Jeopardy Question for 600: A modern-day bully
Answer: What is doxing?

Definitions: Doxing

"Dropping documents" is a malicious practice that involves collecting private identifying information, including one's address, phone number and family name. The information is then publicly published on social media without permission, intending to incite harassment and violence.

Its application is a valuable tool and has been used by Progressive governments entities, such as the IRS and FBI, which covertly release private information that other government entities can use against others (Goitein 2019) (Schilling 2024).

Definitions: Swatting

Goes beyond doxing. It is a dangerous attempt to report a violent act to law enforcement agencies to draw them to a person's home, creating a situation whereby law enforcement reacts with force. It is an attempt to kill the occupants of the home.

Doxing and swatting are used by Progressive activists are used by Progressive activists to shut down opposing thoughts. It is weaponized to let others know what will happen if you speak outside the approved orthodoxy.

What is that called? F A S C I S M

Progressives defined and adopted the cancel culture strategies, that go beyond canceling on social media. Snowflakers have expanded their reach, and they are now responsible for erasing all perceived offensiveness (to them) in American history, literature, statues and names.

What if the culture of cancel is practiced against the cancel culture cultivators of the original cancel culture of characters (Progressives) who initially invented the culture of cancel? It is then defined as an "-ist." I know that makes little sense, but then none of it does. What happens when the Progressive's weapon of choice (cancel culture) is deployed against them? Turnabout is fair play, and examples are forthcoming.

A New Army

The easily triggered, oversensitive, progressive, army of Gen-Z'ers has used the culture of cancel to successfully erase historical ideas, traits, figures, books and entities that made our country great. We can begin with classic literature.

All classic literature has been written within the context of its time. Yet the Progressive, politically correct police and their Snowflakers are looking at that same literature through the lens of the present. It is now evident that all literary classics contain passages that create great anxiety for this self-obsessed generation. This obsession has resulted in many of the greatest classics being eliminated from bookshelves in public libraries, public schools and universities. In some cases, bookstores and Amazon are refusing to allow purchases. Even Dr. Seuss wasn't spared (Watts 2021) (Lock 2020) (Debczak 2019).

New book prints of classic literary works have become victims to the cutting room floor as publishers change literary content to match the sensitivities of the over-sensitive and obsessed. I never purchase new publications of any classics. I go to auction sites and find classical literature with copyrights before 1985. It is the only way you can hope to read the original story.

Jeopardy Question for 500: Federally protected children's "literature" in libraries across the nation.
Answer: What would be all books within the genre of "Genderqueer and "Lawn Boy?" (Zimmerman 2020).

Remember those girly magazines we used to confiscate underneath our sons' mattresses? They can now check them out at their school library (Laurene, Used to be Considered Smut 2024).

Historical figures of our founding are being removed from the public square. Many statues that depict American history from the time of our Civil War have been removed. It was a war that freed countless slaves. There are renewed demands that we remove the Washington Monument, Mount Rushmore, the Jefferson Memorial and the Benjamin Franklin statue at the nation's capital because, you guessed it, they're racist. This is what happens when classrooms teach students what to think instead of how to think. Critical thinking has been replaced by preferred thought. Logic and reason have been thrown out. Only so many classroom hours are available, so American history and Civics have been nearly eliminated, replaced by inclusivity, fairness and gender fulfillment doctrines.

Education is no longer about the basics without it somehow relating to some inclusivity and fairness principle. They are no longer education systems but systems of indoctrination, where they teach woke concepts and protest strategies. Since math is considered racist now and is no longer even considered for graduation in Oregon, it is no wonder that our university graduates have no context for math in the real world.

They are students who end up with $150 thousand in student loan debt for a gender studies degree that might make a waitress salary of $25 thousand a year. Math becomes essential when they suddenly realize their daily Triple shot Americano, Fair Trade, certified organic, soy, double froth, full-fat, pumpkin spice latte with legs, costs about $180.00 monthly, or about equal to their student loan payment every month. To compensate, this wise, woke generation of Zoomers either refuse to pay back their student loans or vote for politicians who promise to erase their student loan debt (Cook 2023).

Out in the real world, they have made a startling discovery. Unless they are trust funders, being an adult is VERY expensive when the bank of Mom and Dad suddenly closes. They have yet to understand that real adulting cares little about individual indulgences and pet activism priorities taught to them via their university experience.

Our Kids...
Remember all those "triggered" souls?
It became our kids from academic black holes.
Who used our kids as convenient trolls,
to usher in their Progressive goals.

Kids transformed into activists and organizers,
influencers, protestors and social justice warriors.
Perfectly tailored with brand-new parameters
to thunder us into a brand-new America.

All bought and paid for with a perfect compliment
of parents, students and our government.

A new America say their believers,
a place regular folks find unfamiliar.

All guaranteed by the U.S. taxpayer
who are now saying no to this transfer,
of American ideals now being devoured,
using racism and genderism to move it forward.
Replacing long-held traditions and morals that defined
a country whose greatness was carefully designed.

We are taking America back, our kids left behind.
Thanks to teachers and professors who deceptively defined
a country in which our children can't function,
a worldview bereft of study and deliberation.

Tortured souls who lack the capacity
to think beyond their phones and object reality.
All courtesy of formal academia,
whose goal was to force their toxic mania.

Then we have the entertainment arena,
cleverly disguised as our state-run media.
Television, newspapers, magazines and movies
mold our children into their own little groupies.
They could care less about our children… their soldiers
Whose only usefulness is to increase their numbers.

As they sacredly protect their preferred politicians,
even serial liars with criminal ambitions.
Convincing our children that all is well,
As long as Progressive voters continue to swell.

Don't worry, they say, never mind those conspiracists.
Increases in crime are lies spread by nationalists.
Using euphemisms, silence and dishonest soundbites,
they minimize impacts and purposely incite
hate and division among us all,
with the ultimate goal that America will fall.

This is the America left to our children.

We all know and understand who is the villain.
We have watched, we have listened, we have sat on our hands.
When will the day come that we take a stand?

by Jo'Anna Laurene

Da' VEEPs Beliefs: "It's time for us to do what we have been doing, and that time is every day."

Progressive Score Keeping

What progresses when Progressives take the culture of cancel to the next step? Remember, Progressives are scorekeepers who desire validation toward desired progressive goals. The next logical step is a scoring system so we can all demonstrate demonstrable deference to declare our Progressive adherence to Progressive demonstrability (Laurene, Progressive Rules to Demonstrate Demonstratability 2024).

Definitions: Social Credit Scores

It is based on one's behavior, in what one eats, what one drives, where one lives, how one invests, what one purchases, or even what television shows one watches. It is all monitored in an electronically tracked world, where surveillance of citizens has never been easier and is still progressing in an "Artificial Intelligence" world.

This is not new. A social credit system was first implemented in China, where the fascist regime can make your life easy or difficult. Based on your score, the regime can decide what schools your children attend or if you can travel. Canada is beginning to explore the idea, and the United Kingdom has already rated its citizens on grocery store selections.

Important Educational Gen Z Note: Fascism is used in the correct context here.

With what we are witnessing today, one can easily identify a future scoring system by following the patterns of political correctness and woke ideologies supplanted by academia, government, corporations and social media (Tate 2021) (Frank Thoughts 2022).

What could get you a negative social credit score in the United States? Drinking soda or beer, smoking cigarettes, using a garbage service, driving a diesel truck and buying a gun or ammunition. Eating a Snickers candy bar, dining at McDonald's, buying beef, turning on any light after 6:00 a.m., running your furnace over sixty-seven degrees or running your air conditioner under seventy-eight degrees. Heating water over seventy degrees, homeschooling or enrolling your child in a Christian or charter school, driving over fifty-five mph and investing in any oil company. Checking out at your library any Dr. Seuss Book, Gone with the Wind or any book in the Harry Potter series. Launching Starlink capabilities into your home. Using plastic or paper grocery bags. Buying any gasoline-powered vehicle. Watching Fox News, Tucker Carlson or Dave Chapelle.

What will get you positive social credit scores? Buying an (EV) electric vehicle is number one and will garner you 5,000 points on your social scorecard. However, if it is a Tesla, you will lose 6,000 points because we all hate Elon Musk now because he makes sense. Progressives hate common sense.

Solar panels on your roof will award you one-hundred points per panel. Two hundred points are awarded if you invest in solar energy cells, charging systems, wind turbines or solar panels. Also of note:

Drinking Budweiser Beer.
Eating Ben and Jerry's Ice Cream or any Tyson product.
Purchasing Nike sportswear.
Shopping at Target or North Face.
Subscribing to Sports Illustrated.
Buying Kale or shopping at Whole Foods.
Recycling and composting all waste.
Purchasing a subscription to the New York Times or the New Yorker
Joining a union
Enrolling your child in public school

Being continually offended will award you fifty points for each complaint on social media. Appropriate use of virtue signaling on Facebook will get you a point for every anti-Kavanaugh or pro-abortion post. Twenty points will be given if you bury a Hunter Biden story or indict Trump on another six hundred charges.

My pronoun is negative 350,000.

Definitions: Virtue Signaling

An outward public expression of opinions or sentiments intended to demonstrate one's optimal superior character and moral correctness on the Progressive side of any idea whether one wants to hear it or not.

Da' VEEP in chief is the paragon of the virtue signal. She became the queen of virtual expression, bringing her virtuousness to new heights. Da' VEEP's lead SPEECH writer must have been on vacation the day she commemorated the fiftieth anniversary of Roe v. Wade. Not to be deterred, Da' VEEP improvised by rewriting our country's founding document, The Declaration of Independence. It was an easy task for someone with no speaking acumen. It was a simple speech, written by simply striking through all those pesky Christian terms, the word "men," and since in a Roe v. Wade speech, there is no right to life (House 2023).

"We are endowed with the right to ~~hold these Truths to be self-evident: that all Men are created equal, that they are endowed by their Creator with certain unalienable rights, that among these are life~~, liberty, and the Pursuit of Happiness."
Democratic Presidential Nominee…Kamala Harris…

To be virtuous, one must display authentic moral standards. Actual moral standards are never a component of the virtue signal. Moral beings concern themselves with the principles of right and wrong. Therefore, those with genuine moral character are not inclined to prove it because they practice it daily in a civil society. Civility is a virtue that we practice not for ourselves, but on behalf of a greater whole. Civics is the study of the rights and obligations of all citizens in a civil society.

Civic vs. Global Good

To be civic-minded relates to the duties or activities of people in relation to their neighborhood, community, state and country in which they live. The study of Civics is a branch of political science that focuses on the role of citizens in their governments. Only twenty-three percent of today's students know the foundation of Civics in our country. Previously Civics was a fundamental component of instruction for students because it ensured that every student had at least a basic knowledge of how we as citizens interact with our government. We have an entire generation that doesn't even know the definition of Civics, so they have no idea how many Supreme Court justices we have or why that number was chosen. They are clueless as to what the three branches of government are and how they are all supposed to interact with the people of this country by law.

The exercise of impeachment is evidence of this. This historically rare exercise is now thrown around casually by Progressive politicians in our country. Progressives have now weaponized the impeachment process to settle political differences. They demand the impeachment of anybody they disagree with, whether they are U.S. Presidents or Supreme Court Justices. They rile up their secure base of a generation of people who have no basic understanding of how our government works, including elections.

Voting is how the people in this country decide how the government conducts itself. All fifty states get to choose who represents them, and they are our voice at the federal level. Yes, I said that correctly—fifty states, not just ten or twelve who all think the same and would prefer it that way.

Important Basic Civics Note: It is not fifty-four states that President Demented thinks it is (Kaonga 2022).

Da' VEEPs Beliefs: "I think it's very important for us at every moment in time and certainly this one, to see the moment in time in which we exist and are present and to be able to contextualize it — to understand where we exist in the history and in the moment — as it relates not only to the past but the future."

As citizens of these United States, we have one single opportunity, and it is one that we all can participate in. That opportunity is our one single vote, and it is all we have. Yet some seek to circumvent voting to create their own desired outcome. This is NOT a one-sided political statement. We all must do our part to protect it if our Republic is to survive. Don't be fooled; many want that Republic destroyed. They are the very same people who argue, vilify and impugn common-sense voting laws under their social justice banner. To them, all voter ID laws are racist.

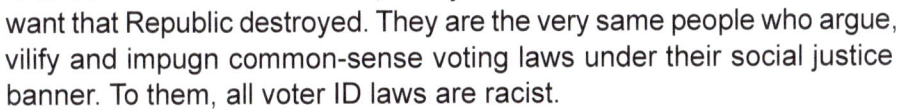

We have an entire generation who have little understanding that people from different states think differently than others on a myriad of topics, topics that have differing opinions, depending on each state's constituency. Some of those opinions are brutally scorned as an impediment to doing the work others would like done instead. This is how our representative government was designed according to the Constitution. All citizens are afforded an equal voice in our government through our representatives. We are not a kingdom or a dictatorship, we aren't even a democracy. We are a constitutional republic. There's a big difference, and it is the very foundation of freedom.

Progressive society believes differently. They believe we live in an ever-changing global world. Therefore, our constitution must change accordingly for "The Greater Good," through a doctrine that is flexible, undefined and is used in innumerable circumstances. It is a doctrine that breaks down civility among people by shutting down opposing thought under the "social justice" umbrella.

Definitions Review: Social Justice

The fair and equitable treatment of all individuals and social groups in relation to a fair balance in the distribution of wealth, opportunities and privileges. It is also known as "distributive justice."

Triple Jeopardy Question for 10,000: The overseer of state control.
Answer: Who is the distributor of distributive justice?

Question: How does distributive justice relate to freedom and our Constitution?
Answer: It doesn't. It's another trick question.

The Ultimate Societal Sin

First, more Definitions:

Definitions: Thought Police

Using the principles of Group Think, it is a fringe partisan movement and strategy that uses social justice principles with the assistance of the media and their big tech buddies. The purpose is to erase all forms of conversation outside of the acceptable discussion norms. The result is an inability to speak or write outside of what the thought police determine as the correct standard for fear of consequential retributions. See previous definitions of doxing, swatting, canceling, etc. Social media is this movement's breeding ground, and the correct standard constantly changes.

Definitions: Thought Sieving

Where conformity takes root, where speech is prescreened within our psyche before we speak, thus, only mutually agreed-upon speech will be expressed. This results in a homogenized discussion, where all thoughts are emulsified into one giant "Group Think." This is the goal of the Progressive thought police, as the strategy seeks to shut down free expression and free thought.

Definitions: Dog Whistle

A high-pitched whistle that only dogs can hear. More recently, it also refers to super-secret cryptographic coded Cipher messaging only understood by Progressives. Like hieroglyphics, its encryption is embedded into common phrasing with widely understood definitions to now signify racist comments unbeknownst to regular normals who are just trying to speak. Important Note to the Normies: *All historically logical dialogue is automatically a dog whistle to "Systemic White Supremacy"* (A. R. Shapiro 2020).

Definitions: Dog Whistle Filter

A speaking device that is only available to wealthy, Chardonnay-sipping white Progressives. It is surgically embedded into the larynx to re-code inadvertent speech that would be interpreted as an -ist, -ism, or -phobe. It allows white Progressives to only speak in pre-screened words and phrases acceptable to their ideology. The device is Bluetooth enabled, which allows daily updates to be downloaded every morning. The premium version automatically downloads at midnight while they sleep (Laurene, Laryngeal Dog Whistle Implant 2024).

All is not lost for the rest of humanity who can't afford the Dog Whistle Filter. Now available: The "**P**olymorphic **T**ranslation of **S**emantics **D**ictionary" **(PTSD)**. It is THE dictionary written and published by the enforcement wing of the "**G**uardians of **E**xceptionally **S**hared **T**ransformational **A**gendas and **P**ostulations **O**verseers" **(GESTAPO)**. The enforcement wing is a subgroup for the "**T**ransformation of a **H**eterogeneous **U**topia through **G**uilt and **S**hame" counsel **(THUGS)**, which is the oversight body assigned to the President's task force for "**C**onditioning **O**perations for **E**nhanced **R**eform and **C**onditioning to **I**nstitute **O**bedience **N**ationwide **(COERCION)** (Laurene, PTSD Translation Dictionary to Institute Obedience Through Coercion 2024).

The PTSD translation dictionary is in its thirty-second publication since it was first published in 2020. PTSD is a courtesy publication distributed through the auspices of the United States government via the Spin Room and social media outlets. Its purpose is to redefine the meanings of simple descriptors or phraseology. PTSD also comes with a handy dandy subtitle page to eliminate confusion or frustration as one furiously thumbs through the 10,000 newly approved phrases so one can speak. The manual is free, but it is highly recommended that a subscription to the PTSD translation dictionary be purchased. This enables the user to stay apprised of critical cultural updates as definitions change daily.

I did not refer to my PTSD translation dictionary before emanating that simple, benign phrase that was self-explanatory until that day. It was such a simple phrase that, sometime yesterday, became the ultimate verbal sin. Sadly, I am not a qualified recipient, nor could I afford to purchase the "Dog Whistle Filter."

What did I say? Wait for it, **"All Lives Matter."** GASP! For those of us who reside in a simple world, we understood that phrase to mean that all humankind matters. For those of us who are not Pullmans on the Progressive's torturous bullet train, I learned quickly that this was no longer the case.

The result: I was now an intolerant, misogynistic, homophobic, racist, xenophobic, transphobic Klu Klux Klan member, a "David Duke" lover (I had to look up who he was) and a deplorable excuse for a human being. Progressive culture warriors in our country study the 20,000-page PTSD translation dictionary and its daily updates every…single…day. It is their working bible to root out and decode all racist comments, real or imagined. For me, that simple phrase resulted in a long string of hateful adjective-spewing descriptors that combined every single -ist, -ism and -phobe known to mankind (as of that day).

It didn't matter that this person was my friend. Someone whom I had known since we were youngsters. Someone I thought knew me well enough to know that I have never been racist. But on Facebook, all Progressives, including her, showcase their virtue signal like a badge of honor.

Like Superwoman, she/her used her virtue shield to deflect triggering statements back at the enemy in self-defense of she/her's virtue proudly displayed across she/her's forehead. It is a Progressive's sworn mission to declaratively identify all those who commit the ultimate transgression of expression—daring to say out loud that everyone matters. Damn, as a non-recipient of the Dog Whistle Filter, I forgot to sieve through the PTSD updates that day before I spoke any words.

This dictionary also applies to seven-year-old children. In an Orange County, California elementary school, a "Black Lives Matter" poster was hanging on the wall. Really? I guess tiny children are not even immune. How about just executing your actual purpose in a classroom? The reason you went to school and why you were hired. Why don't you be an educator who teaches the actual history of racism in our country rather than posting obscure adult political messaging? But I digress.

What happens when an innocent statement by a small child insults the sensitivity of over-sensitive adult educators who have power over her? How dare she have the audacity to write "All Lives" underneath the "Black Lives Matter" phrase. Worst of all, she drew figures of other children of different races. Oh, the outrage! They banned her from recess, made her publicly apologize in front of the student body AND banned her from art, an activity she used as an emotional outlet as she struggled with ADHD. Later, her mother explained, "I am trying to raise my children the way the world should be, not the way it is" (Blitzer 2022).

Something is seriously wrong in our society when a seven-year-old elementary school student is punished for writing a phrase and drawing pictures, stating the most obvious definition of unity of all mankind. Elementary school educators in this Orange County, California, school did not spend one moment talking to this child diagnosed with ADHD. They used not one iota of their educational qualifications, or even their God-given sense of intelligence, to recognize that this child was only seven and possibly learning disabled. But then, it is California…

Nobody bothered to ask her one simple question: Why? According to her mother, had they asked her, her best friend is a person of color (not black), so the child wanted her to feel included. The child, who was white, did not understand why she didn't matter, either. The context was very basic for those not in the activist world, especially for a seven-year-old.

Do activist universities even offer Child Development classes? Since new activist teachers have yet to learn anything about childhood development, let me explain it in the simplest of terms that they may even understand (Dr. Mcleod 2018).

Social and Emotional Development of a Seven-Year-Old Child:

- Desires to be perfect and is quite self-critical.
- Fragile self-esteem.
- Worries more.
- May have low self-confidence.
- Has strong emotional reactions.
- Takes direction well.
- Needs punishment only rarely.
- Begins to feel guilt and shame.

When considering this child's developmental stage, what that school did was child abuse. Not once did any of them consider that she could not understand the subtleties of adult political speech. Shockingly (or not because it is California), the child's mother was uninformed about this atrocious, demeaning behavior that targeted her child. It would be a year later before she discovered this incident had happened at all, and only from another parent. Are some educators really that stupid, or is there a more insidious reason for forcing adult-level activism onto children?

Da' VEEPs Beliefs: "My fellow Americans, words have many meanings—and sometimes instead of conveying our meaning, they can suggest other meanings."

Ambiguity has replaced meaning in a new socially constructed world of Progressive contradictions.

Definitions: Ambiguity

A statement of something having more than one interpretation, causing confusion.

Weight as a Parallel to Gender, Abortion and the COVID-19 Vaccine

Progressive contradictions and their prescribed rule exceptions are incredibly difficult to negotiate, even with the PTSD translation dictionary. Concurrently, the Progressivists' Intersectionality rules are always in play, as defined by the PRIORITISE manual, which POPPERS to parallel universes, which are opposite, but in Progressive land, are considered equal in relevancy and understanding. All can be collectively referred to as the "Progressive Thought Conundrum." It is like all those episodes we used to watch on "The Twilight Zone" (Serling 1959).

As used in a previous example and a subject near and dear to my heart, morbid obesity in our all-inclusive society is healthy, it is a choice and it is "beautiful." Within the repeating progressive chorus of the "my body, my choice" repeater, Influencers lay claim that health is a personal choice, which POPPERS abortion-on-demand. However, as we witnessed during the Covid Chronicles, this POPPERS construct has varying levels of application. During the Covid Chronicles, the "my body, my choice" repeater became lost in the Progressive's contradictory rules, which is when the "Greater Good" doctrine comes into play.

Incidentally, "educate" is now a euphemism for conformity. How often have we all been at the receiving end of a wagging pointed finger on how we need to "educate ourselves." Progressive politicians are always in a quandary when their ideas aren't accepted. Rather than re-evaluate their concepts, Americans don't understand enough. To that end, the Progressive's newest and greatest book, *"Greater Abstractions for Greater Diversity for Greater Acceptance, in a Greater World,"* is still in production and will be released in 2025 (Laurene, Worldly Abstractions to Diversify Acceptance 2024).

As a public service, I will provide a preview. The book will describe the "my body, by choice" repeater, in which gender resides within its own object reality, re-defined by its own biology, which is subjective depending on what planet you live in. Weight, then, is object reality, re-defined by the principles of gravity, which is subjective depending on what planet you live on. Ergo, weight, like gravity, biology and gender, are abstract universes based upon an imaginary reality on whatever planet one "authentically" resides in or on. The 2025 above-referenced 10,000-page book will clarify this further, so stay tuned.

Definitions: Body Positivity

As exampled by the all-inclusive, self-identified "Super Fat" Influencers, this social construct contrives dangerous body weights as acceptable. They challenge present-day beauty standards as "non-inclusive." The movement targets women and girls who "should be free to express themselves regardless of size" and to be "their most confident and authentic selves" (Young) (Marshall 2023).

Obese celebrity women Influencers capitalizing on their size dance around, sing and delightfully play the flute. We definitely cannot unsee that photo of her climbing the stairs to her private jet wearing a thong. What they don't tell you are their deteriorating health conditions and shorter life expectancy that awaits every single obese individual over time. As regular normals struggle with "being their authentic selves," they are left with the resulting dread as their bloated, tired, inflamed bodies tell them otherwise. People are dying out there, which is what obese authenticity is really about. Long gone is the food pyramid. It was a handy, simple tool to emphasize healthier foods over others. Instead, we have a new social food construct called "Food Neutrality" (Imani 2022) (Reyes 2022).

Da' VEEPs Beliefs: "Obesity is a serious disease, and it needs to be taken seriously."

Definitions: Food Neutrality

Food is no longer defined as healthy or unhealthy because that is an outdated, oppressive description that has created a false "hierarchy of food," where the carrot feels oppressed by the donut.

**Introducing Blair Imani's, Smarter in Seconds
Brought to you by: The Human Relations and Diversity Department
Los Angeles Unified School District.**

A "cutting-edge," creative video that allows children to make food choices based on what they want to eat. There are no good or bad choices with food. All food choices need to be made with "neutrality in mind." The Food Pyramid promotes a false sense of worth and is fat shaming.

Only in California would they construct a competing POPPERS parallel. Where "food neutrality" POPPERS oppression, POPPER'ing the "my body, my choice" repeater, which also POPPERS the "beautiful at any size." It is now colliding head-on with public policy where if one purchases a sugary soda in California, they are taxed extra accordingly. This is to discourage the purchase of sugary drinks because it POPS the scales, making one FAT. This POPPERS the now familiar "Fatphobic," which is far worse for "people of color" (Weis 2021).

Lather, Rinse, Repeat…

Whew! It is no wonder that California leads the country in the number of eating disorder clinics throughout the United States. Incidentally, a new PRIORITISE Axis is being added to include the "Oppression of the Super-Fat." Its oppression is still being "weighed" amongst other oppressed in our oppressively oppressive society.

Influencers

Influencers are everywhere now. They are self-proclaimed authorities of and leaders in anything and their success is measured in the number of TikTok and Facebook followers one can accumulate. It is the go-to career for those seeking a "lazy girl" existence. I am unclear on the threshold one must acquire before being anointed an "Influencer." But once one reaches that threshold, being identified as an "Influencer" is a measurement of popularity on any given topic. In other words, they are the "groovy kids." It results in talk show hosts kneeling in divine worship in front of the latest and greatest "groovy kid" in Influencer Land. Being an Influencer means you don't need real friends, just "followers" by strangers one has never met or would ever meet in our new faux socially constructed world (Kelly 2023).

One Progressive transgender influencer is a marketer for no less than fifteen woke companies, from Soda Stream to Nike to Anheuser Busch Beer to Tampax. Does carrying a Tampon in his purse make him feel more feminine because he sure will never need one? I supposed he could empty it and use it as an emergency whistle. It is pitiful and is on the opposite spectrum of hope with men who carry a condom with them in their wallets. At least with the condom carriers, there is a modicum of reality.

Within Influencer Land, there are those who spew lies for notoriety and money and who are responsible for promoting unhealthy body sizes that kill. Within the same POPPERS parallel, our children are mutilating their bodies secondary to trans activist influencers. All are people who use social contagion and cult concepts to convince them they are weight-healthy, and gender confused. It is a sickness built by an all-inclusive culture that uses "influencer" corruption to bind it. "Influencers" is now the singular to what "Organizers" were as the collective. A "Community Organizer" is what Barrack Obama proudly described himself and was the foundation of his election. They all share the same fundamental principles that build societal disorders, sickening all of us.

Societal disorders and cultural decay weren't enough for Progressives. To truly be effective, you need economy of scale, and what better way to accomplish that than to destroy the economy.

Bidenomics and Economic Decay

According to the U.S. Bureau of Labor and Statistics, ground beef, a family staple, is up 26.7 percent from 2019. It represents a 6.11 percent annual inflation change, now averaging $5.57 per pound. Milk, another protein staple for families, is 25.19 percent higher, or 5.78 percent per year. Eggs inflation has been quite volatile, and in some areas of the United States, they have come down from their 2022 highs. Still, in 2023, eggs are up 51.05 percent higher than in 2019, representing a 10.86 percent increase per year. By 2024, medium eggs began identifying as large eggs.

Per the U.S. Energy Information Administration (EIA), gasoline prices were $2.60 per gallon on average in 2019. By the end of 2023, it is averaging $3.60 per gallon for the year. This represents a 39 percent increase and a whopping 9.8 percent increase yearly (CPI Inflation Calculator 2024).

These four basic essentials for American families are up 35.5 percent since 2019, representing nearly a 9 percent rise per year in the cost of essential goods. This is what "Bidenomics" is all about and describes the daily struggles he and his Progressive party have created at the sacrificial altar of "climate change" and their attempted destruction of fossil fuels. They did it in the middle of a pandemic, their Ukraine war and the millions of unskilled, needy people they allowed to cross the southern border. America can only take so much cost pressure that comes with Progressive priorities. Lower and middle-class earnings will never keep up with their created inflation. This is everyone's reality and not "disinformation from Russian hackers." Elections have consequences.

Who Pays?
Throughout history, fortune comes and fortune goes,
always dependent on how America grows.
While people work hard to grow their own wealth,
only influenced by their own goals and good health.

The government helps people in need to succeed,
keeping them fed, housed and basic needs.
Paid courtesy of middle-class families,
with more and more taxes continually levied.

Higher insurance, rent, mortgages and gas,
as utility and food costs continually harass,
While millions upon millions of people amass
Across our border without permission to pass
given full authority and license to trespass.
"Nothing to see here," says the media class

Millions upon millions given American resources.
While the government transports them through various portages,
Secret air flights, where they land at night,
All across America where, they have no right.
Convincing us all we must share in their plight

That is until leaders in border town adversaries,
seek to share demands of illegal vagaries,
bussing them cross country to illegal sanctuaries,
screaming ensues, exposing asylum irregularities.

It is always easy when edicts don't affect you,
when it is painless to spew globalist views.
It makes them appear full of all kinds of virtues,
that is until the realities immediately come due.
That's when their true colors come shining through,
As they scream and holler and threaten to sue.

While their invaders usurp finite capital
in housing, food and classroom potential.
Government priorities that aren't even logical,
all the while watching our country unravel

Printing more money is the answer, they say
causing inflation to skyrocket each day.
Up, up, and up it all goes,
while we work three jobs and still get foreclosed.

For what, we all ask, are we working hard for
As the rich get richer and the rest get poorer.
The richest we see are those who wander
through our House of Congress and Presidential Tower.
Churning out policies that constrain our progress,
destroying any chance at middle-class success.

While politicians protect their preferred special classes,
our own budgets falter and eventually crashes.
Many afraid to turn on the furnace,
and trying to feel fortunate sitting in darkness.

Our veterans and elderly languish in poverty,
while our government doles out unjust charity.
Veterans dispensable in VA facilities
As illegals are prioritized for their "diversities."

It's for those less fortunate and the oppressed,
and millions upon millions of nonresidents.
As they make us feel guilty for what we possess.

So higher and higher go our expenses,
for necessary items with growing consequences.
All the while, government happily dispenses
lucrative rewards with suspicious auspices.
More money for wars, illegals and even terrorists.
Only answering to their wealthy re-election loyalists,
While all we receive are artificial condolences.

When will we have enough of the lies and deceit?
It will be when we vote for our country and unseat
politicians who love themselves and their own powers,
and bring us back to the dreams of our Founders.

By Jo'Anna Laurene

Breaking News from the Banana Republic of America: The FBI Special Council found President Duplicitous guilty of "willfully retaining and disclosing classified materials that present serious risk to national security." Similar accusations were leveled against his predecessor, whom they indicted, tried and convicted. Even before that, Bill's Hill was guilty of the same with her home-brew server she kept in her bathroom, with no indictment ever materializing.

However, in this instance, we discover via the Hur investigation that the Big Guy didn't mean to do it, and besides, his cognitive decline makes him too mentally impaired and, therefore, incompetent to stand trial for his crimes. Following this obvious revelation, Progressives and their journactivists pals pivoted to their third rule of debate conclusions, accusing Mr. Hur of gross insubordination.

For four years, the administration and their Spins had been using their ordered language GULAG description of "cheap fakes" to cover for the President's Dementia. After convincing the globe that we weren't to believe our lying eyes, their gaslighting finally fell flat during a ninety-minute debate on June 27, 2024, wherein the U.S. President's gross senility was outright revealed in full televised display.

What was the most stunning? Blinded by unwavering loyalty, Progressives were shockingly stunned by this revelation. Finally, the propaganda, manipulation and deception about this President's mental infirmity caught up with the spin masters in the administration and their compliant media.

(Associated Press 2024) (Riechmann 2016) (CNN Staff 2024) (Swann 2024) (Oliver 2024).

Definitions: Cheap Fake

To infer that a video has been selectively edited to undermine the president's mental and physical fitness.

Shortly after, Republicans committed a blatant offense of ableism, calling for the invocation of the 25th Amendment.

Definitions: Ableism

Bias, prejudice and discrimination against people with disabilities.

Definitions: 25th Amendment

The Vice President and either a majority of the executive cabinet or a review body appointed by Congress declares in writing that the

President is unfit for office, at which time Da' VEEP becomes the acting President (Graham 2024) (Crabtree 2024).

In a made-for-TV movie, a successful political coup never before seen in our country enabled Da' VEEP to swoop in to save her party from defeat. Her coronation by party elites came without a single vote being cast for her as President. Chosen only for her multi-million-dollar political war chest, which she inherited from her boss, she carries some very heavy baggage, with a long history of far-lefty beliefs, eclipsing that of the most ardent socialists in her party. In a symbolic accession to the throne, the Spins now call her "Kamalot" in a desperate attempt to parallel her to John F. Kennedy (Traister 2024) (Bodkin 2024).

> *"There will never be another Camelot."*
> *Jacqueline Kennedy....*

The Religiosity of Cults and Cult Theory

We have been hearing a lot about cults. Lately, it is a circumstance levied against conservatives by progressives. This is another one of those cheating spouse diversionary tactics to redirect their own deceptive behavior. But what is cult theory, and what does it mean? Once you understand it, only then does the party of deception become indubitably discernible.

It is a concept that I have been researching a lot lately since my beliefs are being labeled by progressive extremists as cult beliefs. Like passing gas, the ones who attribute it are the ones who own it and it stinks worse than my chicken coop.

Cults have a way of lulling followers with benign promises that could be reasonable on the surface but hide the true meaning as you peel back the layers. In a fair and just society where a country is founded upon inalienable rights, we can all agree on certain premises that promise fulfillment of those rights, even though we may not embrace them for ourselves. However, for cults that is never good enough. As you peel back those layers the true plan eventually materializes. It might take weeks, years or decades, but nothing illustrates this better than the trans, climate, race and abortion activism cults.

It brought me to an essay by Kathleen Hays, written in May 2022, about "Gender Ideology's True Believers." Ms. Hays comes from a position of experience as a cult follower for twenty-five years. Her essay is essential to understanding what our country is going through today (Hayes 2022).

Our country does embrace diversity, no matter what the minority of the aggrieved in our society says. Every decade brings new challenges as we try harder and new perspectives are introduced. To quote Ms. Hayes, "There is such a thing as an inflection point when one begins to recognize that unsettled feeling you get when a message contradicts everything you know to be true. That is when our inner sirens start to scream." And no, it is not because you are an -ist, an -ism or a -phobe. What they are practicing in American society today is the foundational strategy to forward cult beliefs, practiced since Nazi Germany.

To again quote Ms. Hayes; "Once you see it for what it is, there is no way to unsee it. You join the people watching in awe and horror as the world seemingly goes insane. When you must ask yourself…How is it that so many intelligent people, not to mention reputable institutions, insist on something so manifestly untrue and harmful? That is how you know within yourself something is wrong." She describes the most painful realization as recognizing that not only had she been wrong about some terrible things, but she believed blatant lies and falsehoods so transparent that even a child could recognize them.

Ms. Hayes refers to the works of Dr. Robert Jay Lifton, a psychiatrist with extensive work covering history, ancient cultures and the historical process of healing. He has worked with psychohistory and the after-effects of Hiroshima and Vietnam survivors. He studied the psycho processes of the physicians at Auschwitz and how they justified the killings and human experimentation.

Dr. Lifton has studied the works of famed foreign correspondent and historian William Shirer, who wrote "The Rise and Fall of The Third Reich." Before the Nazis destroyed the records, Shirer sifted through massive amounts of self-documentation that later became a monumental study of the definitive record of the history of Nazi Germany. It is described as one of the most important works of all time, describing in detail the most frightening chapter in the history of all mankind. From Shirer's study, Dr. Lifton researched and wrote the above book, "The Nazi Doctors, Medical Killing and the Psychology of Genocide" (Shirer 1960).

I reference the above publications to come to my final point, which was Dr. Lifton's research on "thought reform." As an Air Force psychiatrist, Dr. Lifton was sent to the Korean War field. He treated soldiers who had been prisoners of war and in Chinese communist custody. Later, after his service, he applied more intense versions of this process through research grants, interviewing Westerners and Chinese on thought reform, or more specifically, "Brainwashing." His book "Thought Reform and the Psychology of Totalism, A Study of Brainwashing in China" became classic text in the field. The book continues to be a fundamental guide in the debriefing of former cult members (Lifton Dr. 2014).

Dr. Lifton's famous eight criteria for thought control are described below. In her essay, Ms. Hayes specifically correlates those same eight criteria to trans activism. I feel you can use the same theories in a myriad of radical agendas, including climate change, abortion, COVID-19, and Critical Race Theory.

The "Eight Criteria for Thought Reform":

Milieu Control involves controlling information and communication within the environment and, ultimately, within the individual. This results in a significant degree of isolation from society and the *severing of communication with those who challenge the group's beliefs or predominant thoughts.*

Mystical Manipulation is the *manipulation of experiences that appear spontaneous but are, in fact, planned and orchestrated by the group or its leaders* to demonstrate divine authority that sets the leader or group apart from humanity. *It allows a reinterpretation of historical events, scripture and other experiences.*

Demand for Purity, where the world is viewed as black and white, and the members are constantly exhorted to conform to the group's ideology and strive for perfection. The induction of guilt and shame is a powerful control device used here.

Confession, where sins are defined by the group and are *to be confessed to a personal monitor or publicly to the group. There is no confidentiality. Members' sins, attitudes and faults are discussed and exploited by the leaders.*

Sacred Science, *where the group's doctrine or ideology is considered the ultimate truth and is above all questioning or dispute. Truth is not to be found outside the group. The leader, spokesperson or group is above criticism.*

Loading the Language, *where the group interprets or uses words and phrases in new ways that the outside world often does not understand. This jargon consists of thought-terminating clichés, which alter members' thought processes to conform to the group's way of thinking.*

Doctrine over person, *where members and personal experiences are subordinated to the sacred science, and any contrary experiences must be denied or reinterpreted to fit the group's ideology. The group has the prerogative to decide who has the right to exist and who does not. This is usually not literal but means that those outside are not saved, are unenlightened or unconscious and must be converted to the group's* ideology. If they do not join or are critical of the group, the members must reject them, thus, everything in the outside world loses all credibility. In conjunction, should any member leave the group, he or she must also be rejected.

What is most important to emphasize here is that cult method is purposely oriented to bypass our usual process of debate on subjects. Debates are critical for a thoughtful, free society where the pace of change is slow. It is meant to be slow for our protection. Controversial subjects that take far too much time for thoughtful, meaningful debate are forced through via techniques of mind control using the same elements of cult theory described by Ms. Hayes and Dr. Lifton.

Dr. Lifton's eight criteria are enough to understand where cult theory is originating, and it is not from regular normals. Beginning in 2020, cult techniques have been extrapolated using influencers and organizers with absurd notions and beliefs, that are then elevated by our Progressive government, academia, media and social media. Ultimately it creates new divisions in society that foster more hate and anger. Progressives do not believe in order and agreement. Chaos creates disruption, and that is the environment in through which Progressives prefer to keep them in power.

Cult techniques can further anchor absurd notions using methods of influence and "entanglement" that ultimately create chaos that then ensnares the entire society to create conformity. This will be fully explained soon, but the sentence speaks for itself. Progressives can then successfully close discussions and force ideas expediently, which is critical to their agenda. Once you understand the cornerstones of cultism, influencers, entanglement and how it is organized, you cannot unsee it as it unfolds in society today.

The growth of cult followings correlates to declining country, family, faith and community beliefs. Progressive governments have been actively breaking down the foundation of family, faith and patriotism for decades through policy that destroys the cohesive bond of community. Christianity and faith have been under attack for decades, with a corresponding decline in church attendance. The foundation of country and patriotism are being demolished. The decay of the family unit is lost on no one. Faith, family and patriotism anchored communities, and therefore, society. It gave society a moral substance to thrive and an ethical template for happiness and wholeness.

God shows up as the higher deity in all religious teachings by different names. Regardless, all have one thing in common: Spiritual guidance and practices that put your fellow man before oneself. If one does not have a higher belief system, they look to society around them for guidance. Cult beliefs emerge for those seeking a community, family and a belief system that gives a sense of belonging and identity. Cult leaders convince followers that the group's love and visceral sense of belonging transcend everything in a lonely, fragmented world. Cult members believe those who do not follow the cult's beliefs or teachings are evil and must be punished. Non-followers or skeptics are hated. This hate manifests as anger, which is justified towards non-believers. Anger and hate within cults provide pleasure, particularly when cult followers believe it isn't wrong. If anger towards non-believers is justified, it leads to far more menacing pursuits by those who live at the terminal end of the reality shoestring.

With that said, modern methods of cult techniques have successfully replaced meaningful debate, constitutional amendments and legislative policy. They can then create a massive cultural shift in a concise period. What began in 2008 with the advent of various "occupy movements," groups with questionable intentions can accomplish anything by force. Their tools are silencing opposition through coercion, shame and violence (The Conversation 2017) (Penn Today 2021).

To be successful, this cannot be delivered by just one entity. So, who is involved? I have talked about this earlier, but it bears repeating.

- The government and all supporting entities include, but are not limited to, federal law enforcement agencies, the FBI, CIA, DOJ and criminal-supporting district attorneys. It also includes taxing authorities and entitlement programs. This is not a complete list.
- Big tech controlling the levers of internet search engines and the flow of information.
- Formal academia via public education, the national teacher's union and higher education.

This coordinated effort is best described as *"The Three-Legged Stool."* Those entities require an orchestrated effort to keep the stool standing, regardless of the weight it needs to hold. If one of the stool legs breaks, the stool collapses. "The Stool" requires multiple spindles to hold all three legs together. They are the retention mechanisms crucial to keeping the legs in place and the stool upright. If even one were to disappear, it would throw the entire movement into disarray This is not a complete list (Cleveland 2023).

- State-run media
- Unions
- Corporations
- Banking institutions
- Entertainers/celebrities
- Social media networks

It is why the acquisition of Twitter by a free speech advocate was such a monumental catastrophe for all the above entities. They lost one of their most critical conduits in their quest to control information. Severing communication is a cornerstone of cult theory. Unsanctioned alternative information is blocked from publication in any form.

In addition, people are canceled and threatened on social media. Social media platforms, target violence against individuals or groups who threaten their beliefs. Some Facebook accounts are being blocked and banned if they violate Progressive doctrine. It was social media platforms that organized protesters against members of the Supreme Court, threatening justices with violence and impeachment. Social media platforms organized ANTIFA and BLM riots, funded by veiled unknown entities. Media and government target alternative thoughts as "misinformation or disinformation," blocking their viewership. Anything communicated based on scientific facts or data is labeled as "crazed conspiracy theorists." Within big tech search engines, scientific data is blocked from view, while Progressive theory is mainlined to the top of the search.

Definitions: Crazed Conspiracy Theorist

Conjures up images of a psychotic break in reasoning and thought, true of many mental health disorders. Today, it is used as a slur to describe people or groups as political wrongdoers who are sinister or evil, void of the mental capacity to speak in the square of public opinion prejudicial to "The Greater Good." The slur has effectively halted thoughtful conversation. It is a successful tactic power elites use to exploit the natural human fear of ostracism to induce silence. If labeled a conspiracy theorist, you can bet you are close to facts that The Stool wants silenced.

My pronoun is...Certifiable.

When all else fails, you get a tax audit in the mail, they threaten your home, livelihood and family. You get fired from your job or expelled from school. You face expensive lawsuits for using your First Amendment right to speak. If you fight, you are financially ruined, yet plaintiffs seem to have unending financial support against you. All are cult strategies to create fear and shut down opposing views. People become afraid to speak up, which is the cult leaders, AKA The Stool's goal.

The goal: To brainwash the public into an illusion that the cult beliefs are mainstream and, if it fails, bring society to its knees in fear.

Another important Gen Z Definition: Fascism is also correctly used in the above example.

For many, cults conjure visions of Jonestown, The Branch Davidian, The Manson Family, and Rajneeshpuram. This is how cult theory began. For small groups of followers, it was a method for one man or leader to control a group. It is tough to grasp when you theorize the same phenomena on a society-wide scale, but Progressives have indeed mastered its concepts. It is a coordinated effort to create their own society. The concepts and tactics are the same, whether you manipulate a small group or ensnare an entire culture and generation (history.com Editors 2022) (The Conversation 2017) (Wigington 2018) (Pearson 2018).

For this book, the word cult interchanges with religiosity, which is what it is. They dominate their messaging using influencers and organizers while "entangling" organizations, governments and corporations into their sick societal changing goals, of which the goal is *Socialism*.

Da' VEEPs Beliefs: "Our allies have stood firm and unified in a way to ensure that we are unified."

Yes, they all work in a unified way, to disrupt society and cause chaos to create their socialist utopia. Ultimately it breaks down society, where regular normals no longer care. This is the definition of apathy. It is much easier to manipulate change processes in an apathetic society.

Human conditions that create apathy:

1. Drug abuse
2. Loss of faith
3. Bereavement
4. A belief that goals are unreachable

Artificial components being created within America by our Progressive government that produce apathy:

1. Drug abuse

   - Eliminating criminality of hard drugs
   - The complete freedom to buy, deal and smoke marijuana
   - Fentanyl, heroin and methamphetamine streaming across an unsecured southern border

2. Loss of faith

   - Shaming and coercion of religion and religious beliefs, eliminating one's ability to express one's faith freely, also defined as losing faith in one's ability to meet goals.
   - Open harassment of one's faith, forcing religious lawsuits costing thousands and thousands of dollars, e.g., Christian baker fighting his third lawsuit

I interrupt this book for the following rant. Yes, this man is on his third lawsuit by the illustrious LGBTQWTF+ community that continually challenges his Christian faith. The United States Supreme Court has already upheld his religious beliefs in two similar lawsuits. Why can't they go to a different baker? Failure to do just that makes this a concerted effort to harass one's faith. End of rant (Crane 2019).

Open harassment of one's faith continued:

- Christian baker above
- Little Sisters of the Poor (Smith 2020)
- At least nineteen lawsuits targeting pro-life states that are limiting abortions
- 298 violent attacks on Catholic churches since May 2020 (Dobbs 2023) (Catholicvote 2023) (Del Turco 2023)

- The government eliminated all Catholic pastoral care at Walter Reed National Military Medical Center, replacing it with a secular firm that has no spiritual beliefs, "coincidentally," this policy was implemented during the 2023 Easter holy week (Shaw 2023)
- Progressives dislike religious holidays, especially Easter. While the rest of us joyously celebrated the resurrection, Biden, a Catholic, re-iterated that Easter Sunday is also "National Trans Day of Visibility" (The White House 2024)

3. Bereavement

- Creating poor economic conditions, created by ideological government laws, and policies, creating deficit-breaking spending, resulting in crippling inflation
  - People unable to make an adequate living
  - Loss of retirement savings (Ivanova 2022)
  - The inability to purchase basic needs and goods (O'Brien 2022)
  - Unable to afford their rent or mortgage, resulting in…
  - More homelessness (Barber 2023)
- Open border policies creating…
  - Rent increases (Salmonsen 2022)
  - housing shortages (Trapasso 2023)
  - Building supply shortages (Kupiec 2023)
  - Increasing drug trafficking, human trafficking, and violent crime (H. Davis 2023)
  - Food shortages (Spector 2023)
  - Risk of another terrorist attack (Wray 2023)
- Energy bans and their Ukraine war amidst a global Pandemic, causing record inflation and shortages (Keogh 2022)
  - Empty grocery shelves (Armanini 2024)
  - Critical baby formula shortages (Boehm 2022)
  - Medication shortages (Jewett 2023)
  - Record-breaking food prices (Lou Chen 2022) (Schrag 2023)
- Never-ending COVID-19 mandates (Samuel 2023) (Rahman, 2023)
- Prioritizing and spending for wars in other countries and not your own country's needs. (Penzenstadler 2023)
- Government money printing, causing rising interest rates
- Losing a loved one to fentanyl or violence on the streets…from…
  - open border policies that are funneling drugs through the southern border (Senate RPC 2021)

- - eliminating criminality for all drugs (Sabet 2024)
  - Defund the police movement (Grimes 2022)
  - Soft on crime district attorneys (Palumbo 2023)
- Losing your ability to make a living
  - Never-ending COVID-19 mandates
  - Record high inflation
  - Hiring illegal invaders over Americans (Arnold 2024) (Kudlow 2024).
- Record inflation that makes supporting a family impossible
- Printing trillions of fake money for useless quick fixes to fund ideological agendas, e.g., the Green New Deal (Holtz-Eakin 2019)
- Energy bans (Laycock 2023)
- Sending billions of dollars to other countries to fight their wars. (Wolf 2023)
- Never-ending COVID-19 mandates

4. Beliefs that goals are unreachable.

- CRT theory convinces all minorities that they will never succeed.
- Creating indoctrinating messaging that minorities live in a never-ending oppressive society from which they will NEVER escape, regardless of how hard they try

As one can see, Progressive policies create a never-ending cycle of complementary POPPERS parallels to break society. Our country's downward spiral is clear. Yet, despite crippling economic conditions, increases in crime, violence and homelessness that they created, we are to ignore our lying eyes because, according to Progressives, "it's all good."

The Religiosity of Racism and Its Correlative...Critical Race Theory

What is Critical Race Theory (CRT) exactly? It is something we understand our public schools are practicing, which they deny. It is nearly impossible to adequately find the goals of this elusive public school curriculum, which is the goal. In a nutshell, it is a curriculum that teaches our youngest nonminority students that they are born inherently racist and are oppressors. It begins in kindergarten, and the concept is familiar. Academia has been working on it for forty years.

According to this view, race is a relatively recent "social construct" that CRT advocates have weaponized to oppress others using the propagation of various ordered language buzzwords. "Systemic racism" and "implicit bias" have been inserted into various diversity statements, corporate trainings, educational materials and government agencies.

Part of the problem in defining or identifying CRT is its vague contours. This vagueness allows institutions to dispute constituents' claims that they are implementing CRT. Loudon County schools in Virginia deny teaching CRT but coach their employees on the very concepts on which it is defined. Oregon and Virginia have recently promoted ideals about racist structures in mathematics. Finding the correct answer in a mathematical equation is now an act of white supremacy. It is all within the CRT doctrine.

According to CRT experts across formal academia, "Racism is baked into everything we do in society. It is embedded in our institutions and all our minds and hearts." What does it really do? It is simply another avenue in the Division Industry to divide Americans once again. It is ripping society apart through indoctrination, intimidation and harassment. Racism is real and has existed since our country's founding. However, what purpose is there to assume that every aspect of our being is inherently racist? We know what the purpose is, and it is not to fight racism.

There are eight significant reasons that Critical Race Theory is dreadful for dealing with Racism:

1. CRT believes racism is present in every aspect of life, every relationship, and every interaction, and therefore its advocates look for it everywhere. It is not simply being prejudiced. It is a "system" of everything that happens in the social world. Racism is then hidden everywhere and is present in everything. In schools, it means teaching children to look for racism in every situation and every interaction.

2. It says you can never trust any attempt to make racism better. It adds a further dimension where racism will never end. It is a paranoid and cynical approach that identifies racial privilege among not just whites, but Asians, Hispanics, Arabs, Indians and lighter-skinned black people. Free societies need to be dismantled because their only purpose is to keep racial minorities down.

3. CRT only treats race issues as "socially constructed groups," so there are no individuals in CRT. It doesn't believe individuals meaningfully exist at all. Every person is understood in terms of the social groups they are said to inhabit.

4. They do not believe in Martin Luther King's dreams. They discount his famous quote of individuals being judged "not by the color of their skin, but by the content of their character." CRT advocates consider this a myth.

5. It does not believe in the basis of science. It reasons that science in and of itself is a "white" way of knowing. They believe science is just politics that white, Western men predominantly produce. It believes that science encodes and perpetuates "white dominance." The root of all science is the practice of objectivity, which CRT calls an oppressive myth.

6. CRT rejects all potential alternatives, like colorblindness, thus making itself the only allowable game in town (which is totalitarian). Racism must be made relevant in every situation and every interaction. This means one must be on the constant lookout for hidden racism everywhere. The result: all relationships and social systems become fragile and tense, which is the progressive goal.

7. CRT states that anyone who disagrees with it does so for racist and white supremacist reasons, even if those people are black (also totalitarian). If a black person disagrees, they are "not really black." Therefore, everyone's politics MUST agree with CRT.

8. CRT cannot be satisfied, so it becomes an activist state of infinite anger that will never end. It doesn't believe in individualism or science. Therefore, it cannot be proven wrong. It states that racism is present and relevant to all situations and interactions, always demanding more.

These are the messages that are being taught to our children today. Don't our children have the right to see everyone as equal, including themselves? (Lindsay 2020)

When did somebody decide that our two-year-old was born racist, where racism is so hard-wired into all of us, a de-programming curriculum is necessary beginning in kindergarten? The remote learning push during COVID-19 was the only silver lining, where parents got to see for themselves what their children were being taught in public school.

It's heartbreaking that minority children are being taught that they are forever relegated to the back of the bus. It is a religiosity being forced by anarchists, academia, the media and the government. Nobody can ever be allowed to see racism in the rearview mirror. As progress is made, they keep doubling down on their message of despair to every new generation of minority children and their parents.

Many forms of Progressive symbolism are used. You cannot swing a dead cat without hitting a Progressive symbol. Progressives seek symbolism in all interactions and all presentations, but no exhibit was more deplorable than their 2020 performance in Emancipation Hall. Using the sacred Kente Cloth, Progressives used it as a political prop for a performative display to illustrate their divine oath with the black race. Using its iconicity and the reverence it symbolized, they used it as a stole draped around their necks. Twenty Progressives then knelt in Emancipation Hall as they recognized a moment of silence in solemn solidarity to remember the "legendary" George Floyd, after which there was a well-timed press conference (Lee 2020) (Settles 2021).

The Kente cloth is an ancient, colorful cloth from the Akan and Ewe peoples of Western Africa and modern-day Ghana and Togo. It was believed to have been produced as early as 1000 BC. To this culture, it represents status, harmony, love, purity, spirit, renewal, passion, healing and union with their black ancestors and their spiritual awareness with them. Was the ancient Kente Cloth originated so that publicity-obsessed politicians could use it for activism in the 2020s? (Davenport 2020)

Voting Blue No Matter Who
Vote Blue, no matter who,
whereby then their chaos ensues.
Nothing new that many see through.
People devalued who they're unto
once again fail under their milieu.

The blue team has nothing new
that those with more insight long outgrew.
Promises made, promises stray
of politicians promising worth and prosperity.

Once Progressive politicians are adequately seated,
they disappear, into the politically disinterested.
As all those who promised they'd succeed,
over and over again through the newsfeed,
Have once again left them pounding ragweed.

Every two years, this cycle repeats.
Vote blue, they say,
or democracy will cease.

Voting cycles come and go,
with zero changes, and the homeless grow.
Wastelands and cesspools of needles and waste,
as blue cities double down on violence embraced.
Defund police, they say, while children walk through
drug-induced zombies on their way to school.

Voting blue, no matter who.
Then, who do they blame
for the misery and pain?
Others outside their grand socialist game.

All the while, red states prosper,
under a philosophy that all people matter.
Only guaranteeing one thing is all,
prosperity occurs with hard work and willpower.

Voting blue, no matter who,
Grows more and more curious
to those of us who,
see the violence and filth as blue cities dim,
wading through piles and piles of vermin.
Over and over, again and again,
STILL wallowing in the Progressive doctrine. By: Jo'Anna Laurene

Progressives have been promising change for decades with no results. With the amount of money spent, the black community should have been lifted from poverty, homelessness and poor education standards long ago. The black community is being exploited every single voting cycle. They use the religiosity of racism to keep black families from ever succeeding. How can they if they preach that racism is embedded into every aspect of their existence? Success is portrayed as an impossible dream. How are our black youth ever supposed to believe they can overcome that? With this sort of messaging, they are justifiably angry. Each new campaign cycle brings new promises. Progressives get the black vote and do nothing to earn it. The violence, the shootings, the rioting and the fires that are destroying black communities and businesses are only worsening. It symbolizes the destruction of the black race in society. Who is rioting and lighting those fires? Politicians, academics, outside influencers and organizers have created a cycle of anger that then lights those fires. Their messaging is designed to destroy optimism and create more hate, especially among black male youth. It is to convince them that there is no faith to be found and that their reality will never change. Anybody who dares to prevent that fire from being lit, who dares to contradict their messaging in any way, is called racist, even those in the black community trying to change it (B. e. Sullivan 2020) (Vanek Smith 2020) (Parker 2024).

"Oppressed people cannot remain oppressed forever. The yearning for freedom eventually manifests itself."
Dr. Martin Luther King Junior...

In all of humanity, whether you are Black, Hispanic, Asian, Native American or White, one must believe there is hope for the future or that life dies within.

Racism and Genocide

You cannot talk about the 2020s without acknowledging what happened on October 7, 2023. That was the day that brutal Palestinian terrorists known as Hamas targeted, tortured, raped and killed 1,400 innocent Israeli women, children and elderly. Forty infants were beheaded and burned beyond recognition by Palestinian terrorist extremists. Murders were live-streamed on phones and delivered to their families. It was Israel's 9/11.

Since that day, we have discovered that antisemitism is alive and well in the United States. It is entirely fomented by the Progressive left. I dare anyone to find one Republican or Democrat who believes that the mass killing of innocents was justified. This was the Progressive's defining moment, the one incident that set them apart from everybody else in this country. Progressives have been closeted antisemites and racists for decades. We now know, without a shadow of a doubt, who they are.

Nobody could have ever imagined this dark tunnel our country has fallen into. Just as in 1921, Progressive politicians, their academic counterparts and their Zoomers have recreated Hitler's Germany. Just as in Hitler's time, university brownshirt students across the nation are leading vile hate-filled rallies on college campuses, instituting violent intimidation tactics against Jewish students. Jewish students can't leave their dorm rooms. Many have fled in fear.

It is difficult to wrap your head around a religion and race so viscerally hated in our own country. A hate so engrained now in our youth. A generation who flies flags of solidarity for blacks, browns, gays and transgenders, are now intimidating and threatening those of the Jewish race in their own student body (Berlatsky 2018).

This is what Progressive universities have constructed in an

> *"Returning hate for hate multiplies hate, adding deeper darkness to a night already devoid of stars. Darkness cannot drive out darkness; Only light can do that. Hate cannot drive out hate; Only light can do that."*
> *Dr. Martin Luther King Jr. …*

academic environment that built an atmosphere of hate over many years behind our backs. Donning a brand new tribal headdress, the 'Covfefe' wearing racist students uttering, "Kill the Jews," is a phrase nobody ever fathomed we would ever hear in our country, let alone ever again in history, especially on American campuses. Yet here we are. A hate so visceral that it celebrates the killing of innocents in our modern world, just as it did in Nazi Germany (Musumeci 2023) (Carrasco 2021) (Brown 2019) (Cillizza 2022).

Antisemitic Presidents of Ivy League schools performed a fantastic display of unintelligible policy speak, justifying their university's hate behind a "context of hate." Since that sounded like another Progressive example of ordered language double-speak, wealthy donors rewarded their equivocation by pulling billions of dollars of support (Sahakian 2023) (Jackson 2023).

Progressive politicians who speak out from both ends are trying their hardest to minimize the genocidal violence. It is what they do when they walk that political tap-dance across that narrow antisemite tightrope to support Hamas terrorists while providing lip service to Israel. They use code words to prevent any interpretation of outright support of Israel while trying to hide behind terrorist Palestinian solidarity: A *"moral equivalence of many truths"* or *"one perspective among many,"* and my personal favorite, *"everyone was complicit to some degree in the current bloodshed"* (Lerer 2023) (Thakker 2023) (Pepper 2023) (Graef 2023).

I wonder whether "everyone" was complicit when the Palestinian Liberation Organization (PLO) murdered eleven Israeli athletes at the 1972 Munich Olympic Games or when the PLO hijacked the cruise ship the Achille Lauro in 1985, where they murdered disabled American Jewish passenger Leon Klinghoffer. Who besides Hamas terrorists was complicit in the murder of 1,400 women, children and elderly? (Borden 2015) (Latson 2015).

Now Introducing: The Social Construct Committee has developed an "Ordered Language Guidance Manual" or **G**eneral **U**niform **L**anguage **A**ssigned **G**uidance **(GULAG)**. It is a companion manual to PTSD, POPPERS PRIORITISE, and it POPPERS to POPPERS (Laurene, Socially Constructed GULAG of Uniform Language Directives 2024).

Essentially, "The Dictionary" is irrelevant in our new socially constructed world. Its relevance is minimal as it only gives a descriptive meaning of words, which is irrelevant in an ordered language world.

After dispatching His Divine Monarchy Obama to the nearest ten speaking venues, they referred to their GULAG, with the following ordered language substitutions:

- Hostages are "detained persons."
- They are not terrorists. They are "militants and freedom fighters."
- Hamas is not a terrorist organization. It is a "governing power in the Gaza Strip."
- It is not a war. It is a "conflict."
- It is not an invasion. It is an "incursion." (Farhi 2023).

To a Progressive, terrorist acts of atrocities and murders are "conflicts," but when Israelis fight back, it is "Genocide."

No matter how hard Progressives sap that tree of invention, there is only one interpretation of what happened on October 7th. No matter how hard their proxies try to synthesize alternative narratives of truth, justice and morality, gross ancient bigotry that results in the mass killing of innocents in the most brutal manner possible has no place in a civilized world. It is what it is…

T E R R O R I S M.

Da' VEEPs Beliefs: "We all watched the television coverage of just yesterday. That's on top of everything else that we know and don't know yet, based on what we've just been able to see. And because we've seen it or not doesn't mean it hasn't happened, but just limited to what we have seen."

Terrorism

Definitions: Terrorists prior to 2020

A Homeland Security designation targeting individuals who perpetrate extreme acts of violence on American soil with the intent to kill a mass amount of people.

The first such incident was The Oklahoma City bombing on April 19, 1995, killing 168 people. It was the deadliest act of homegrown terrorism in US history at that time. Since then, we have had the Centennial Olympic Park bombing during the 1996 Summer Olympics in Atlanta. Nobody will ever forget the 9/11 attacks that killed 3,000 people at the hands of Islamic Terrorists (Resnick 2013).

Incidentally, we have come full circle. What began twenty years ago, under four Presidents, costing $6 trillion and thousands of lives, ended with President Incompetent's disastrous withdrawal from Afghanistan, leaving the region once again under the control of…the Taliban. Conveniently, leaving them billions of dollars of military armament, helicopters, jets and tanks to use against us, our allies and the Afghani people (Brown 2021).

The 2020 revised definition of Terrorism:

Directed through the National School Board Association and the National Teacher's Unions, the US government's Department of Justice and Homeland Security now identifies parents as domestic terrorists. Also known as "Insurrectionist Agitators who present extreme acts of terrorism," to wit: Parents who debate the appropriateness of Critical Race Theory or publications and curriculums promoting transgender and gender-fluid ideologies (Betz 2022) (Poff 2022).

Important Insurrectionist note: Antifa anarchist rioters do not rise to the definition of domestic terrorists in our country. People who create chaos and violence and burn down entire city blocks do not meet the

Progressive definition. Per the President, "Antifa is not a group; it is an idea" (Bernstein 2020).

So what, pray tell, is the official definition of terrorism? Well, there is no official government definition. Why is that? Our government is having difficulty finding common ground among academics, commentators, government and international organizations. They cannot risk offending anyone, and terrorism is not yet categorized in PRIORITISE, where an act of violence could be justified to right the wrongs of an oppressively oppressive society (United Nations 2023) (Bruce 2021) (Laurene, Distinguishing Who are Terrorists in an Oppressively Oppressed Society 2024).

It takes little common sense to readily recognize violence and acts of terror. Whenever Blue City authorities fail to report the description of any shooter's identity in a fatal mass shooting, you can rest assured that the shooter is NOT a Christian, white, gender-normal male.

Where there is silence, undoubtedly, the mass shooter will always be someone listed much higher on the Ax-i of the Intersectionality PRIORITISE list of humans. The only question is who and how high they are listed. You could make a drinking game out of it. Las Vegas betters could place those odds on the Big Board. I wonder what the point spread would be between a transgender or an illegal. The long shot would be the mono-lesbian or the trad wife. Once a shooting interrupts programming for "Breaking News," it is time to immediately call your Bookie (Laurene, Secrets of the Big Board 2024).

Tragically, the overwhelming losers in this Progressive identity game are the victims and the American people. Failing to report the shooter's identity protects their idealism but does nothing to protect the American people.

The Religiosity of Trans Activism

The Coronavirus pandemic exposed one overriding theme, one that millions of us have been sleeping through for a long time. It is a multi-fronted culture war waged against the American people. Only since Covid have the atrocities of our Progressive government and their media been exposed. Since then, it has only grown in scope and intensity. They are attacking our biology, faith, families, emotions and psyche. Whoever wins this culture war will win our nation's mind, soul and heart.

Da' VEEPs Beliefs: "Certain issues are settled...no that's right, and that's why I do believe we are living, sad, in real unsettled times."

Behaviors that were once taboo and dangerous to others are now acceptable. What we are witnessing today is the beginning of the complete destruction of what is fair and just in any society. We are beginning to see indistinguishable differences between what is right and what is wrong (Grayson 2023) (Grossman 2022).

Simply claiming you "identify as a woman" is a pervert's ticket to women's most private domains. Perhaps they all aren't deviants but are we going to risk our little girls' innocence just because we don't want to hurt the feelings of the 0.6% of trans legitees who might be present in that dressing room. We cannot allow ourselves to be bullied into believing trans individuals, who are men, have more rights to be in a woman's private dressing room than women and little girls. Women are being hounded, threatened, canceled, expelled and forced to resign from their jobs for questioning any of it. There is a HUGE difference between trans rights and trans activism, where you can support reasonable principles of transgender rights. But it is not reasonable to support those activists who masquerade as teachers and school counselors who secret away thirteen-year-olds from their parents, grooming them into something they are not (Wisconsin Institute for Law and Liberty, Inc. 2023).

Some parents are so convinced that this new form of inclusivity is acceptable, that they will actually drag their children to Drag Queen performing "art" events at bars. It's all right, though, because it is outside on the sidewalk outside the bar. Therefore, it doesn't count as being "at the bar with your children." Thank God, too, because now they do not need to find or pay a babysitter.

**Announcement! Anderson Distillery and Grill of Roanoke, Texas, will be hosting a family-friendly event and special brunch.
Where kindness and inclusion meet fabulous fun.
"The Event" will feature four drag queens from Dallas.
Here at Anderson Distillery…we like all types of booze and all kinds of people. And we like to serve great food, with good, clean fun.**

Date: Sunday, August 28, 2022, from 11 am to 3 pm, with the fun starting at 1 pm (Anderson Distillery and Grill 2022)

A Twitter video showed this "good clean fun," with two men scantily dressed in leather costumes engaging in over-the-top displays of affection so vulgar that a heterosexual (cis-gendered) couple would be told to "go get a room." Other videos of the event featured vulgarity, sexualization of minors and partial nudity in front of more than twenty children. The Facebook video could not conceal the uncomfortable expressions of the children who were dragged to this drag event by their parents.

Question…What is the difference between this outside drag event at a bar and a stripper bar? Both are sexual performances, yet one is illegal for children and the other isn't. I missed that chapter in "Spock's Baby and Childcare," where it was appropriate to take your child to a stripper bar (Dr. Spock 1987).

Frankly, we don't care how you conduct yourself in your private life; just don't bring your trans nightclub cotillion act to our children. We do not want to know about it and especially don't want our children to see it. We were patient with you until you went after our kids. It is now time to go back to your private adult nightclubs, where it belongs.

Definitions: Grooming

Adults who coerce miners to perform a particular event or activity they would not typically perform. It is a deliberate act to establish a connection to prepare that child for sexual abuse or child exploitation. It is defined in five stages:

1. Establishing a friendship to gain trust

    - Create the illusion of fun-loving mainstream personalities, while also…
    - Normalizing cross-sex personalities, e.g., Drag Queen Story Hour and Disney's promotion of trans personalities in its parks.

2. Fill the needs of a child that you think are important to that child

    - Convincing children they are gender dysphoric

3. Isolating the child and creating a "special relationship"

    - gender-affirming teachers and guidance counselors who convince a child that they are always only thinking of them
    - Creating an appearance of normal activities, when they are gender-affirming venues targeting children

4. Sexualizing the relationship and desensitizing the child

    - This is the pinnacle of grooming and where sexual exploitation takes root, where the child is convinced they are unsupported by their parent.
    - Isolation is then secured.
    - The child is convinced they are better off without their parent. With the help of…
    - Government policies separating children from parents who don't affirm their child's cross-sex identity (Burt 2023) (Raymond 2023).
    - Gross HIPPA interpretations allowing "gender-affirming" health care without the parent's knowledge or consent (My Northwest 2023).

5. Maintaining control

    - Secrecy and blame to maintain silence and continued participation.

- Gender-affirming school officials, keeping "their" secret, "I won't tell if you don't tell.
- School officials instruct teachers not to disclose a child's new name or pronoun (Yang 2021).
- Using the excuse of laws and policies to justify their criminal actions (Title IX) (Bhattacharya 2022) (Jeglic Ph.D. 2023).

The terms "grooming, or grooming behavior," is a legal term that has been used within law enforcement and the courts for decades. It is now the new "Micro-aggression" of the season. In their GULAG, it is defined as racist, homophobic and transphobic. It is what activists do to minimize a criminal act as ordinary or routine, opening the door for any pervert to access our children. Using the Progressive social-context strategy of transformative language, groomers and pedophiles are now rebranded as "Miner Attracted Persons." This is a great example of "all-Inclusive" psycho-babble language that seeks to humanize rather than stigmatize this sickening activity (Harper 2021).

Definitions: Re-branding

To create a new and differentiated brand identity in the minds of consumers, investors, competitors, employees and the public.

Before The Big Guy occupied the Presidential office, guess how much money the federal government spent to prevent boys from getting pregnant? That would be zero, but as we are reminded repeatedly, we are now in "different contextual times." $700,000 is the amount now needed in an exceptional federal grant to prevent fourteen to eighteen-year-old "boys" from getting pregnant. Because transgender males "may be less likely to use condoms when having sex with penis proprietors and as likely as cisgender girls to get pregnant."

Translation: Girls who have sex with boys will get just as pregnant as every other girl.

Now, that is rocket science thinking if I ever heard one. For an LGB program, it is imperative to add that "T" designation, which requires $700 grand more of taxpayer money, to a Progressive youth program called the **C**enter for **I**nnovative **P**ublic **H**ealth **R**esearch or **CiPHR** (Ring 2024) (CiPhr 2023) (Arnold 2024) (Golden 2024).

Definitions: Cipher

A system of communication that prevents most people from understanding the message. It is also defined as a person or group of people without power who is used by others with power for their own purposes. Both definitions apply here.

As someone who has been both a grant recipient and benefactor, I know the grant game and it is an incredibly lucrative scheme, especially when the money comes from the government. Foundations aren't as rewarding because you must have actual outcomes with measurable goals. The government, not so much. They love to give away hordes of taxpayer money to fund political causes that require little to nothing in measurable goals.

> "Truth is, by nature, self-evident. As soon as you remove the cobwebs of ignorance surrounding it, it shines clear."
> Mahatma Gandhi…

In this instance, it takes seven hundred thousand dollars to just another money-loving Progressive program to add that all-important "T" to keep their money-pilfering enterprise afloat. Where the "my body, my choice" repeater POPPERS Gender as a "Social Construct," which POPPERS "all-inclusivity, POPPER'ing Economic Justice via the taxpayers. I am sure all those ordered language Progressive buzzwords within their GULAG were included in their grant model and application.

Question: If a gender "T" who is a girl but identifies as a boy still has sex with boys, are they really a "T?"

Quantum Social Entanglement Theory

An approach where Progressives can make the ridiculous appear mainstream. In this instance, corporations use dopey, easily identifiable, manipulative messages to contort themselves into new identities to appease the Wokie Wokes. It wasn't enough for corporate Wokies to completely re-brand Aunt Jemima, Uncle Ben, Land O' Lakes Butter, the Frito Bandito, the Cleveland Indians and the Washington Redskins. Wokie Mars corporation, fearful of being left behind in the mysterious Wokie world of a "Dynamic and Progressive World," launched a new marketing campaign that completely re-characterized the M&M candies. Newly graduated Zoomer marketing geniuses re-branded the M's characters as Wokie equivalents of their all-inclusive Progressive University peer groups. Wokie Mars marketing Zoomer executives failed to understand that nobody stops to marvel at each individual "M's" Wokie menagerie of all-inclusive character influencers. The minuscule population who do, are part of the Woke problem, or they are four years old. Same difference (Gainor 2023).

Mars should have conferred with Disney and Target on the consequences of taking Wokie ideology to the masses. There will be much more on that later.

All classical statues on the New York City courthouse have been replaced with one statue. They have named their new statue… "NOW." The artist says, "it is a part of an urgent and necessary cultural reckoning underway as New Yorkers reconsider traditional representations of power in public square spaces." Also, says the artist, "it is now necessary to recast civic structures, to better reflect 21st-century social mores." "NOW" then symbolizes a critical inflection point by which society is newly defined.

So who, or what, is "NOW?" Loaded with the usual Progressive symbolism and meaning, the statue is a nude female, or "them" appearing figure, emerging from a pink lotus flower. It has long, thick braids shaped around its head, like satanic goat horns. The demonic figure also has no arms but multiple octopi tentacles spiraling from its body. Since we are discussing the new symbol for the Wokie Woke agenda, what does "NOW" symbolize? We know the Lotus flower symbolizes enlightenment, growth, purity and birth. The goat horns symbolize sensuality, determination and masculinity (Abbott 2023) (The Petal Republic Team) (What's My Spirit Animal).

For those of us who don't reside in the obscurities of Wokie Woke definitions and meaning, what do we see? We see the state of New York "NOW" symbolizes a re-birth of woman, as a nondescript "them," who is a determined virile satanic being, entangling you in their alternative mythical reality. It is a profound example of their "Quantum Social Entanglement" theory, as they express entanglement (octopi tentacles) as an actual representation of their goals.

What exactly is Quantum Social Entanglement Theory? It is a notion academics borrowed from the quantum theory of modern physics, initially discovered by German physicist Max Planck in 1918. Einstein and other scientists advanced Planck's theory, making possible the development of quantum mechanics as it relates to matter. Quantum entanglement theory is a central principle of quantum physics. It is the study of multiple particles linked together such that the measurement of one particle determines the quantum state of the other particles. Where the measurement of one automatically influences another regardless of how far away the particles are from each other (Vondrich 2022).

What a great theory! It is no wonder that Quantum Social Academia has stolen this concept to fit their hypothesis. Why think up your own principles and models when you can steal them from another? However, the science of physics is poles apart from social sciences. They are not interchangeable or equal, and there is no roundabout in existence to connect them. It is an academic discipline, using analytical principles they have borrowed to fit their pseudo-scientific story to entangle non-diverse thoughts into more acceptable notions. DEI, ESG and "Greater Good" elements are embedded in this model. It is an integral leg on that three-legged stool where no compromises can be obtained.

Through the decades, we all recognize the Budweiser Clydesdales. In 1933, August Anheuser Busch Sr., CEO of the brewing company Anheuser-Busch, received a gift from his two sons; August A. Busch Jr. and Adolphus Busch III. Two six-horse Clydesdale hitches were presented to their father, celebrating the repeal of Prohibition. The Budweiser Clydesdale image endured through the decades as a powerful American marketing symbol of the brewery's heritage and legacy. Budweiser then became a dominant icon for the American industrial spirit and a powerful symbol for the brand. It was unmatched amongst all other marketing strategies and not just for beer. It was a fan favorite during Super Bowl commercials. Everyone looked forward to seeing the newest Budweiser Clydesdale commercial, always unveiled on Super Bowl Sunday (Taylor 2017).

Ninety years later, they have set all that aside, as the Wokie wokes of the Gen Z generation have moved into the marketing departments of many corporations, including Anheuser Busch. New college graduates from our wokest institutions of higher learning have new ideas, bringing their woke "all-inclusive" dogmas with them. It is the same woke marketing specialists who have taken over the marketing departments of Nike, Target, Mars, Disney, Netflix, Starbucks, Home Depot and many more.

Anheuser Busch's newest and greatest woke creative marketing team is promoting a man who identifies as a childlike she. This new spokeshuman and transgender "influencer" evidently just celebrated "theys" 365 days of "girlhood." Not womanhood, but girlhood. Stunningly, AB decided to market a young-looking, girly child-man who dresses in a little girl's jumper while he skips around in his pink frilly bedroom. The girly man's marketing campaign includes him in a luxurious bubble bath while sipping his AB Bud Light brew, which even had his girly-man face on the can. AB couldn't have done any worse if they had marketed the Clydesdales, identifying as unicorns named "Karendales" (Delaney 2023) (Byrne 2023).

With nun chuck in hand, they committed product suicide, as Budweiser and Anheuser Busch completely lost sight of their consumer demographic on the sacrificial altar of woke inclusivity. It was beyond parody, as they attempted to "authentically connect with audiences." They so "entangled" themselves in the web of inclusiveness that they ignored their base consumer: Beer drinkers who congregate at NASCAR, folks who love to hunt and listen to country music. They BBQ, get this… meat! Eating steak and hamburgers while watching football and major league baseball. They are the after-work crowd in bars and sports pubs across the nation. Instead, AB decided to market to the 0.6 percent of the population who drink cosmopolitans while delicately nibbling on a champagne gelée.

They eat sushi or anything with a tangerine emulsion and would never stoop so low as to eat a cheeseburger. There is nobody on the face of the planet less connected to beer.

So, who was this marketing genius? She was a Harvard graduate, Budweiser's new "Gen Z" VP of marketing, who brought her personal values to the Bud Light brand. She was inspired to update the "fratty" and "out of touch" humor of the beer company with "inclusivity." She says, "it meant to evolve, elevate and shift the tone." Yep, she shifted it all right. Further, "it was a campaign that's truly inclusive, that feels lighter, brighter and different." It was different, all right (Hall 2023).

Bud's brilliant Harvard marketing graduate further stated, "this brand is in decline." Yep, it is definitely in decline now, as she and Budweiser's bonehead decision to market to a non-beer-drinking demographic failed spectacularly since the invention of beer. It was a rookie mistake by a newly graduated Progressive, whose attempt in entanglement fell as flat as any bad beer made. No beer drinker has ever said, "Yeah, I identify with a man who pretends to be a girly boy."

As Anheuser Busch furiously backpedaled in placating statements to their consumer base, they successfully cross-alienated the 0.6 percent population they attempted to market to in the first place. Then, to make it up to "thems," they sponsored a "pride" parade, angering their base customer again. Like a pinball machine, AB blinged in and out from one lousy marketing decision to the next. Now everybody hates them (Zilber 2023) (Mayer 2023) (Dumas 2024).

Before this brilliant marketing campaign, Bud Light had consistently outsold all their rival competitors twenty-five to one. As the face of woke graduates everywhere, she was responsible for sales immediately collapsing by twenty-six percent. In one week, AB lost five million dollars in sales and six billion in market cap, and it is not slowing down. Harvard's wokester was responsible for sales so poor that stock raters downgraded the stock. AB couldn't give away their beer, even with coupons and marketing gimmicks. AB fell so hard so fast they are no longer even among the top ten of beer brands. By June of 2023, the stock dropped twenty percent for a $27 billion loss in market value.

Over a year later, sales are still down thirty percent for a beer-drinking demographic that will never return. It is difficult to fathom the total loss, which includes sales, market cap, productivity and jobs, that resulted in this negligent, clueless marketing decision of woke all-inclusivity.

Bud's Gen Z VP of marketing from Harvard has a new pronoun now…unemployed.

In 2024, North Face Zoomer Societal Impact executives within their DEI departments adopted the "Allyship" concept in their marketing strategy. They will offer a twenty percent discount on outdoor merchandise if customers complete a one-hour equity course on "how the outdoors is oppressive against Blacks." Evidently, outdoor barriers exist that are unwelcoming and inequitable. The course aims to create a more "equitable outdoors" for everyone.

Definitions: Allyship

A verb, "A point of entry to discuss race and other issues of inequity with awareness to prioritize language beyond positional titles that better reflect actions, behaviors and practices."

Within their ordered language GULAG, "ally" is described as "co-conspirators or accomplices" and "actions and behaviors that impact rather than a label, or a title that gives someone moral credibility or social capital" (Dias 2023) (Grossman 2024).

Translation: We all need to hike and camp more credibly and inclusively to impact our social capital…or something.

Have you ever tried to purchase North Face gear? No matter how high they fly their all-inclusive banner, economic justice POPPERS *"Systemic White Supremacy,"* where one needs an income that POPPERS affluence, which definitely does not apply to any Ax-i in PRIORITISE. Maybe North Face ought to get out of the DEI/ESG game and stick with selling outdoor merchandise that most people can't afford, even with their twenty percent "all-inclusive allyship" discount.

Here's a lesson to all those new marketing Zoomers out there. It is no longer about you, your peer group or your woke institution of higher learning. Unless you are joining the likes of journactivism, it is about acclimating yourself into the real world and real life now.

We know that the path to a well-adjusted child is to protect their innocence. Walt Disney once inspired imagination and gave children heroes, villains, princesses, magic and talking creatures. Instead, they now practice grooming behavior. Content that used to teach children the difference between right and wrong, and good and evil is now lost on Progressive woke, DEI and ESG agendas. Now producing children's movies with adult sexuality via trans and homosexual characters, they seek to "entangle" our children into a powerful propaganda tool to forward their woke trans-socialist agenda. It is emblematic of cult theory to normalize deviance (Berrien 2023) (H. Miller 2023).

In 2022, Disney won a very prestigious award—the movie producer with the most content featuring trans and homosexual children's characters in the entire entertainment industry. The consequences were entirely predictable to anyone outside the culture of woke, ESG and DEI principles, which is practically everybody. Disney streaming services are cratering secondary to this staggering betrayal of families worldwide. Forced to lay off thousands of workers, Disney has lost $900 million in its last eight woke all-inclusive movie releases. Shareholders are now suing. Families have left Disney and the era of Mickey Mouse is over. Walt Disney isn't turning in his grave. He is spinning (Saul 2023).

What do Budweiser, Target, Disney, North Face and Mars candy have in common? They have experienced the culture of cancel outside the originators of cancel culture. What Progressives have been freely dishing out has come back to bite them.

Diversity, Equity and Inclusion (DEI) is an academic-driven public policy that promotes a sense of entitlement based on victimhood (see PRIORITISE Manual). "Diversity categorizes people, and "Equity" seeks to impart equality by prioritizing certain human data sets. "Inclusion" then prioritizes others over others. DEI by definition, is an oxymoron.

> *"Wokeness is civilization ending, as it seeks to suppress free speech and shut down ideas, eliminating creativity and the advancement of a culture."*
> *Elon Musk...*

Entanglement's approach isn't exclusive to corporations. To be successful, it needed to be incorporated into public policy, beginning in the public school system.

The Public School System's 2020 Mandate

On behalf of our entire country, I apologize to the many educators in our nation. I have a cousin, a sister-in-law and many friends who are teachers. We realize that you are doing a difficult job and that the majority of you do not espouse the religiosity of ideological beliefs. We all must understand that the number of trans-woke educators in our public education system is a microcosm of the greater population or less than one percent of all teachers.

Our public school educators are being forced to comport to an ideology they do not believe in and know is damaging. Only a handful of brave educators have called it out. As a result, they are being ostracized, shamed and fired. Secondarily, violence is increasing in our public school system. Fear is now a common theme as our educators are being attacked in their classrooms and hallways, sometimes violently. Videos are posted every day of student activists attacking other students and teachers in unprovoked attacks. With the violence and now illegal invaders who can't speak English, flooding our schools, it should come as no surprise that our teachers have lost faith in our education system and are leaving in record numbers. Thus, our country is experiencing an historic educator shortage.

Schools have become the de facto organization in our country in an experimental mass transformation of our youth to become something they are not. To listen to our government and the National Teacher's Union, most students in our country, as young as five years old, are not only inherently racist, but they are also sexually confused "non-binary" bewildered children who suffer every day from sexual dysphoria.

Definitions: Sexual Dysphoria

A condition where the sexual genitalia that assigns you a specific gender at birth does not equal the gender you feel. This is not to be confused with gender expression, where one's gender expression refers to how one presents to the world in a gendered way, like tomboys (Psychology Today 2021).

Per Miriam Grossman MD, Child, Adolescent and Adult Psychiatry:

"Sex is NOT assigned at birth. It is ESTABLISHED at conception with X and Y chromosomes and is then RECOGNIZED at the time of birth. To describe sex as assigned infers that sex identification at birth is an arbitrary designation, is flexible and is fluid. This completely defies science and biology, of which only Progressives are confused. What is mystifying is that the rest of us are forced to have the conversation at all with seemingly intelligent adults who insist otherwise. Gender Dysphoria is a psychiatric condition. There is NO established evidence of a biological cause. Most cases resolve on their own by young adulthood, and there is no evidence that puberty blockers, cross-sex hormones and painful gender-altering surgeries are lifesaving or even medically necessary. The U.S. is increasingly an outlier in the treatment of youth with gender dysphoria" (Grossman MD 2023).

No less than ten studies have been conducted which found, on average, eighty percent of children will change their minds and NOT continue into adulthood as transgender. Statistics and studies don't lie, yet in the public school system, they give our children new names and pronouns. They are secreting children away from their parents to promote transgenderism. They direct them to YouTube videos to instruct them on the ordering and use of breast binders. School counselors are providing tips to kids for acquiring cross-sex hormones. Then, these same school representatives lie to parents about the transitioning of their kids. Refusing to cater to a seven-year-old or the school's characterized pronoun or new gender-affirming name is now considered child abuse, whereby children are removed from the home (Cantor 2017) (Brooks 2018) (Penley 2023) (Libs of TikTok 2023) (Sharp 2023) (Christenson 2023) (Nightingale 2022).

Failure to comply with unyielding acceptance labels parents as "transphobic," cutting relations. Parents are treated as the enemy, which fits in the cultist milieu of prying children away from families and has all the hallmarks of child sexual abuse and sexual exploitation, defined by the courts. Then it is rubbed in our faces as these same educators strut their unprofessional non-binary conforming practices within their classrooms. They unabashedly flaunt their classroom curriculum, books and their gender identity to our children and all of society. They are sacrificing our children's primary education to normalize transgenderism because they can. It all became possible because of cultist and acceptance tactics that protect them from scrutiny (Tooley 2021) (Grossman 2022).

A Michigan public school was discovered to be hiding the transgender status of a student from the parents, allowing the student to go by a different name and pronoun in school while directing teachers not to inform the mother about her child's transition. Richards Middle School in Fraser, Michigan, warned teachers ahead of parent-teacher conferences to call him by his biological name and pronoun, not the name or pronoun he uses while in school. A spokesperson for Fraser Public Schools did not deny that the district was hiding the gender status from the child›s parents, only saying, "The district is mindful of and compliant with its obligations under Title IX laws." Middle school-age children are between eleven and thirteen years of age (Hammer 2022).

Education is no longer about the basics of reading, writing and arithmetic. It is about the playful perception of the transgender persona, which is merely an extension of Drag Queen Story Hour. This education transformation only took two years, which coincided with the graduation of Zoomer graduates of woke academia. We have a generation of young adults masquerading as teachers who can only identify with the free expression of "me." It is a profound example of this generation's attitude of self-absorbency, narcissism and egocentrism.

Egocentrism as an Extension of Narcissism

Egocentrism is a part of childhood development in children between the ages of two and seven. Adults stuck in this stage can't think beyond their egocentric views, which is narcissism. Narcissists cannot grasp social functioning in either language or rules. People high on narcissism become annoyed or even enraged when others fail to see things their way. It is exaggerated among those who acquire public attention as news broadcasters, performers and politicians. Social media exposure is where "influencers" are spawned. They then become embedded into a narcissistic bubble where they lose all accountability for their behavior. Look no further than our media for examples of that. Political violence can be seen on both sides of the political spectrum, but there are personality traits that are intrinsic among Progressives (far left) that are predictive of violent political tendencies. "They are those who have higher levels of lethal partisanship, including moral disengagement, partisan schadenfreude (pleasure derived by another person's misfortune) and are more willing to engage in partisan violence. They are those with political intolerance who ban speakers and opposing political views" (McGreal MSc 2022).

You can't move on to logical thought if you are stuck in egocentrism. If one cannot move to logical thinking, they are incapable of seeing a situation from another's point of view. Egocentrism assumes that society sees, hears and feels exactly as they do. If they don't, there is something wrong with others, not the egocentric. Egocentrism is present in all political views, but if you seek to mold an entire generation into a one-way direction, that is engineering thought. Progressives have been engineering youth for a very long time, beginning in our public school systems. The gradual transitioning of textbooks into liberal thought over the last couple of decades proves that, especially when the same textbooks from the same publishers have differing themes depending on the politics of each state (NPR 2020).

Ultimately, what does all this mean? Everyone believes we see things the way they are, but we see the world not as it is, but as we are or, as we have been conditioned to see it, especially if children are taught by educators who teach what to think instead of how to think (Krispenz 2023) (Quote Research 2014) (Krauss Whitbourne PhD 2012) (W. Hart 2023).

Academic cult leaders in elite colleges and universities capitalized on this. They produced people who have been successfully engineered (brainwashed), marinating in such beliefs their entire academic lives. They have now moved on to be our leaders and teachers of today. It is a vicious cycle that is only now becoming quite evident.

Simultaneously, our government is now tweaking older versions of laws to coerce the entire United States into conforming practices to further Progressive doctrine. It is much easier and expedient that way. Most Americans don't pay attention to policy changes, especially when Spinners fail to report it. Forming new laws requires meaningful debate. A legislative process that would expose logically opposing analysis, and they definitely can't allow that. That would expose the full agenda to be fully disclosed, an exposure that would reveal the true course to all American citizens.

Title IX

What is Title IX? On June 23, 1972, President Richard Nixon signed Title IX into law. Before Title IX, few opportunities existed for female athletes in the collegiate setting. Before this law, colleges offered no athletic scholarships for women and held no championships for women's teams. Facilities, supplies and funding for women's sports did not equal that of men's teams. Title IX was designed to correct those imbalances, requiring university women's athletic programs to receive the same amount of money as men's athletic programs providing equal access and quality in collegiate athletics as it relates to finances.

What Title was NOT: It does not contain any language about cross-gender acceptance in any setting, collegiate or otherwise. It doesn't have anything to do with girls' bathrooms or dressing rooms, nor does it have anything to do with primary education (Pruitt 2021).

Using entanglement, Title IX rules have now been "re-branded." It has been transformed to require public school districts to allow transgender boys into girls' bathrooms, locker rooms, showers and sleeping quarters. Noncompliance results in the loss of federal funds for lunches, breakfasts and snacks. Our Progressive government is using the federal school lunch program to force through trans activists' causes. By withholding funds for non-compliance, our government will withhold money that feeds thirty million low-income children. It is nothing short of government-sanctioned blackmail, forcing an eleven-year-old girl to view a boy's anatomy for the very first time as she changes for gym class. Don't our little girls have a right to dignity and privacy? (Troutman 2022) (Allen 2022)

Where the Covid vaccine POPPERS Transgenderism, all that is needed is a simple change of definition. To this end, The Big Guy's much anticipated Title IX amendments of May 2023 had to be delayed when the Department of Education received over 240,000 comments on the proposed amendments. The amendments seek to enhance protections for LGBTQ+ students in ALL academic settings (Fossum 2023) (Jimenez 2023) (Sullivan 2022) (U.S. Department of Education 2023).

New definitions for Title IX will force K-12 public school systems to mean something totally different than its original intent, putting children at risk. You don't need to go further than Loudon County, Virginia, to discover the consequences of such radical public school policies. **In review,** a male student identifying as female was transferred from one district to another following an accusation of sexual assault from a female student. That same student then sexually assaulted yet another young girl in the girl's bathroom of his new Loudon County Public School. Then, school officials hid the predictable consequences and lied about them.

Trying to justify their actions, they stated that Title IX allowed this male access to the girl's bathroom in both incidences because he "identified as female." Long before Title IX policy changes were attempted at the federal level, what they did was not a justification, but an excuse for their criminal incompetence. Remember when schools were mandatory reporters for abuses perpetrated against children? Today, some school districts are condoning and supporting predatory behavior, which is the goal of the Title IX rule change that prioritizes trans activism idealism over child safety.

A Loudon County Grand Jury determined that the school district grossly mishandled the sexual assault of two girls in two different schools, perpetuated by the same male individual who stated he "identified as a girl." The report concluded that "district leaders were only looking out for their own best interests" when covering up the consequences of their transgender ideology, by lying about the incidents. Loudon County Public Schools are being sued for epic mismanagement and violation of parental rights. The Superintendent was finally fired and indicted on multiple criminal counts. Ultimately, he was only found guilty of using his position to retaliate against a teacher who cooperated with the grand jury investigation on the cover-up of the assault (Natanson 2022).

I worked as a nurse in a medium-security prison in Eastern Oregon for a short period. What is widely understood is that whenever an inmate moves their lips, it is a lie. Anyone who works in a prison knows this to be true. Inmates have nothing else to do but master ingenious methods to manipulate the system to their advantage. How is it, then, that a New Jersey prison transferred a man to a woman's prison simply because he stated he "identified as a woman." The consequences were entirely predictable when two women became impregnated.

Were these women raped? Does anybody care? Prison officials surrendered to the woke inclusive politically correct, group think, cult of trans activism, allowing a man into the proverbial candy store. Women who were incapable of escape were housed with a sexual predator. It is astounding that seemingly intelligent people have been so thoroughly manipulated in an irrational cult belief system carved out of the politically correct lunacy of transgender rights (Showwalter 2021).

The PRIORITISE rules committee is reviewing some adjustments, but a preliminary statement has been issued, "We must not allow the legitimate questions that have been asked to fuel the view that trans women suddenly pose an inherent threat to women when that is not the case" (Brooks 2023).

Translation: Spermers who identify as egger wannabes, who rape egger legatees, are spermers with egger wannabe rights. Therefore, egger wannabes possess extra super special egger wannabe rights, which magically means, absolutely, positively, no rape threat exists against an egger legatee by an egger wannabe…or something.

Da' VEEPs Beliefs: "My fellow Americans, words have many meanings—and sometimes instead of conveying our meaning, they can suggest other meanings."

Remember the "Me Too" uterus owners' empowerment movement? It was a crusade by uterus owners who brought awareness and change to the forefront of cultures and systems of sexual abuse against uterus owners (Asmelash 2022).

Now, it is a rotating, never-ending circle jerk of mystical, magical spheres of revolving definitions that circumnavigate around the Progressivists' approved contradictory definitions. Using the PRIORITISE manual of approved Ax-i's, they have augmented their POPPERS (parallels) with roundabouts as they create new junctions to loop in their intersections of intersectionality confluences to wit:

The sexual abuse, rape, or alleged rape of a uterus owner, by…

- Any penis owner, whether found guilty in a court of law or not; Guilty.
- A penis owner who identifies as a vagina wannabe; Not guilty.

Transgenderism is now cast as the latest frontier in scientific knowledge that cannot be questioned. "Trans women are women." Brave questioners are being persecuted and "canceled." Any woman who feels violated by the presence of a man in their dressing room is rejected and abandoned. Any degenerate or pervert can now "identify" as a woman and poof! They are given carte blanche access to areas of naked women and our little girls.

Our country has lost its mind!

National Trans Day of Vengeance

This National Day of Recognition was clear in its rhetorical goal. The Twitter "rainbow" post announcing the "Trans Day of Vengeance" clearly stated, "We Need More than Visibility!" Well, they got it all right, as they effectively mobilized one of their own, precariously dangling at the end of that reality shoestring. The result was a violent shooting of nine people in a Christian school by a woman who identified as a man. She kicked off their national day on March 31, 2023, opening fire, killing three children with an "assault-style weapon." The national event scheduled for April 1st was immediately removed from all social media platforms and re-branded as "Trans Day of Visibility" (Crane 2023).

Following the shooting, the Spins went dark; what to do when the suspect was not a cis-gendered, Christian white spermer whom they loathe, with a "weapon of war" they want to be banned. The Progressive Thought Conundrum thus required a "Hail Mary" strategy to deflect blame from the transgender shooter, for whom they pine, and the long gun, which they despise. Hmm, a reverse POPPERS parallel of their own making. What to do? Ah, yes. We will switch POPPERS to intersections via the transgender roundabout that POP us over the intersection of murdered children as victims onto the ramp that deposits us onto transgenders are victims of hate intersection.

It was fourth down, so they attempted a long forward pass, assigning plug-and-play player James Kirchick, from some publication called "Air Mail," to deliver their POPPERS statement on Bill Maher's program. Kirkchick won the coin toss, where play action began.

The desperate pass play fumbled miserably as he attempted a draw play, something about "dead naming and misgendering the shooter." The attempt missed its mark at

CONQUERING THE BONGOS | 467

the feet of Winsome Sears in a Bull Rush maneuver, resulting in a Pick Six that left Mr. Kirkchick with two black eyes. It was EPIC and definitely deserving of a craft beer and popcorn. The turnover was unrecoverable, resulting in the usual silencer being placed over every single newscaster to muffle the blast of hypocrisy (Martin) (Bonchie 2023).

Definitions: Hail Mary

Coined in football. It is a very long forward pass, usually attempted in desperation, with a slim chance of completion. Derived from the Catholic "Hail Mary" prayer, reflecting a low probability of success and the need for strength and help.

Definitions: Pine

To suffer mental decline, or an expression of mental anguish, or a longing or desire for someone or something. All the definitions apply to this story.

Definitions: Dead Name

Coined by Trans activists that describes a person's birth name after transitioning.

Double Jeopardy Question for 800... Using a Transgender person's name as written on their birth certificate.
Answer... What is transphobic?

Trans Day of Vengeance certainly got the notoriety they sought when, on April 6, 2023, Riley Gaines, a collegiate swimmer and twelve-time all-American, dared to share her personal story about competing with a biological male who identified as a woman. While speaking at the University of San Francisco, to which she was invited, she was violently assaulted by a large group of transactivists who stormed the room. Before Ms. Gaines could react, a large man dressed as a woman violently punched her numerous times while yelling obscenities. Fearing for her safety, she was forced to barricade herself in a room for

"When they want you silent, speak louder."
Riley Gaines...

three hours. Silence ensued from the feminist grandstands of pomposity (The Post Millennial 2023) (Blaff 2023).

Then, America's most entrusted truth-teller, Keith Uberhuman, immediately initiated the Progressive's second statute of debate conclusions.

In Review, when losing the argument on its merits, we must pivot to characterize the other as stupid or hateful. Except where Ms. Gaines is concerned, according to the ultimate purveyor of all truth, who was fired from MSNBC, she "sucked at swimming." Yep, according to the Uberhuman, a twelve-time all-American in her sport "sucked at swimming!" Incidentally, it is hard to get fired from MSNBC, which reeks of ESG and DEI spin propaganda. He was also forced out of ESPN and Current TV (Clark 2023).

Ms. Gaines will be suing those responsible at the University of Necropolis by the Bay. No arrests were ever made in a violent attack by a man against a woman half his size. Where is the feminist outrage? It is stunning that it is now acceptable for a man to violently assault a woman standing up for women's rights. Nearly all famous feminist athletes are either siding with transgenders or are silent.

Two acts of vengeance were not enough when, on April 6, 2023, authorities arrested a former middle school trans student in Colorado Springs after allegedly planning a mass shooting at his school. The former student, now nineteen years old, who is a penis proprietor but now identifies as a vagina proprietress, was arrested on suspicion of attempted first-degree murder, among other charges. Investigators found instructions on bomb building, a manifesto and a whiteboard with the school's floor plan in them's bedroom (Dupont 2023).

> *"LGBTQU+ kids are resilient. They are fierce. They fight back. They're not going anywhere. And we have their back. This Administration has their back."*
> *White House Press Secretary Karine Jean-Pierre…*
> *April 6, 2023*

She was amazingly coherent on that statement, wasn't she? (Schwartz 2023)

Then, on June 8th, 2023, The White House was to host an LGBTQ Pride event, "The largest of its kind in the history of the White House." Coincidentally, the "biggest and greatest of its kind event" was postponed due to poor air quality (Associated Press 2023).

"The Big Guy," and the Progressives' anointed King of wokeness, began all this nonsense by choosing his cabinet secretaries and his czars solely based on inclusivity regardless of character or qualifications. Progressives keep careful score. Being the first of everything, virtue signals just how all-inclusive they are. The White House went so far as to proclaim the acquisition of "the very first ever rescue dog, in the White House." Unfortunately, both dogs he chose (German Shepherds), had to be removed from the White House after several biting incidents. One could find a lot of symbolism there (BBC 2021) (Klein 2023) (Linskey 2023).

Checking the Woke Box of Inclusivity

Government vetting is such a pesky exercise for Progressives. It is a formal selection process whereby high-ranking government officials and secretaries are screened before appointments. Among other benefits, you know, like national security, it prevents any embarrassing untoward discoveries that the government used to try and avoid. However, if all an administration aspires to accomplish is to check all those Wokie Woke boxes of all-inclusive firsts, you don't do any vetting. When only choosing from their "all-inclusive woke candidates of distinction list," they have already reduced potential candidates. It is important to note that once you have openly awarded a position of importance to a Wokie Woke character of some critically woke distinction, you can't put that woke genie back in the bottle.

What happens when that DEI hire, can't do the job, or worse, humiliates the administration and the entire country? You can't fire them; otherwise, you face fire and brimstone rioting among your Wokie Woke constituency. It's another conundrum of their own making.

There are so many examples, it is hard to know where to begin. We can start with Da' VEEP in chief, who can't string a sentence together and cackles at the most inappropriate times while prattling ad nauseam about her love of "Venn Diagrams." There was a reason she was forced to be the first candidate to drop out in the Democrat primary. She was awful, lacked speaking and leadership acumen, and had no campaign funds because Democrats refused to donate to her candidacy. However, she did check a crucial integral box of critically woke importance, the very first ever female, Progressive black Vice President (Schwartz 2023) (NPR 2019) (Seitz-Wald 2020).

Then we have the ever-popular White House press secretary, who has a terminal case of "um" and "uh" and cannot speak in complete sentences, which seems like an essential skill for a press secretary. She tends to utter the most inappropriate tone def statements (see above) at exactly the wrong time. From the podium, dishonesty and unintelligible commentary identifies as truth and coherence that even the Spins can recognize. To remedy this problem, the White House intermittently places another press secretary, whose sole purpose is to stand beside her and assist her in speaking intelligibly. Ironically, her intelligible press co-secretary is a white cis-gendered male. Gasp! But she did check that critical box of critical woke importance, the very first-ever Progressive black lesbian press secretary (Nesi 2024) (Moore 2023).

But the pièce de résistance came in the latest reality show episode of "America's Funniest White House Videos." Their latest blooper was hiring a gender non-conformer, the first and only ever openly gender fluid "them," as the waste management director for nuclear waste at The Department of Energy (Viewers).

Deviously, Mr. Gender Bender with a security clearance, was videoed at the Minneapolis-St. Paul airport, stealing expensive designer luggage from the baggage claim turnstile. Expensive designer suitcases generally contain very expensive women's designer clothing, shoes and jewelry, which he definitely identifies with. Following news reports of the Minneapolis theft, Las Vegas authorities reopened a similar theft at Harry Reid International. Both videos recorded Mr. Gender Expansive in the same rainbow-colored atomic symboled shirt as he helped himself to the booty ahead. After lifting his prize, he is shown darting out of each airport, stolen luggage in hand. Lesson number one, never wear your easily identifiable, brightly colored rainbow shirt that proudly displays your near and dear gender-identifying social construct twice, at two different crime scenes (Crane 2022) (Catenacci 2022).

By then, Mr. Non-Binary had already been quietly suspended from the Department of Energy, never to be seen or heard from again. Once the story leaked, no doubt by right-wing conspiracy, insurrectionist newscasters, the White House could no longer hide their gross incompetence. Then Mr. Gender Queer was arrested for felony grand larceny. Now they could justifiably fire him. Thank God!

Wait, hold my craft beer! Photographs posted by our most famous "Gender Flexer" finds him proudly posing in a one-of-a-kind stylish gown previously owned by a successful international fashion designer. However, the last time that dress was ever seen was inside a suitcase, stolen at the Ronald Reagan Washington DC airport in 2018. Mr. Smiling with "pride" has learned yet another vital lesson. Never publicly post photos of yourself in a stylish one-of-a-kind frock, that you stole, that nobody else on the planet owns (Reilly 2023).

A simple internet search could have totally prevented this White House embarrassment. Except with this administration, their wokie first-ever "all-inclusive" hiring spree ignores everything else. This guy was just plain W-E-I-R-D with zero semblance of professionalism or decorum expected of a person as a White House appointee. He describes himself as genderqueer and a self-described LGBTQWTF+ activist. On a site that used to only be found on the dark web, he describes his "kink" as animal sexuality. He gives lectures on sexual play, kink and is a "handler" in puppy play. Internet photos reveal his fellow ladyboys, dressed in leather bondage-type dog costumes, on hands and knees, held on leashes in control by their "handler," Master Ladyboy. Yep, our Department of Defense hired this to oversee nuclear waste in the United States. There is plenty of symbolism there (Cato 2022).

To remain consistent, The White House dug out of the same hole, Dr. Kink Master! Dr. Fetish is known for being escorted on stage by naked men donning bondage gear at your most prestigious kink conventions. To "de-stigmatize" gay orgies and as the White House's MPOX czar, he appeared on MSNBC on June 18, 2023. As the leading government expert in "public sex with anonymous people," he states, "One person's idea of risk is another person's idea of a great Friday night." Yep, this is someone I would take health advice from (RNC Research 2023) (House 2022).

Wow, that one statement resulted in so many POPPERS parallels. One man's joy is another man's death in another Progressive POPPERS of the "my body, my choice" repeater, POPPER'ing transgenderism," which further POPPERS "freedom of expression of your sexual prowess," regardless of who gets hurt or dies from AIDS (Laurene, Give me Joy or Give me Death 2024).

Irony Alert: Dr. Free Sex was previously appointed as the CDC's Director of the Division of HIV/AIDS Prevention in 2020. Except now acquiring AIDS also POPPERS the "my body, my choice" repeater. That "my body, my choice" repeater is a lucrative reinvented Progressive anecdotal dictum within their GULAG.

Definitions: Anecdotal Dictum

An account not necessarily true from a reimagined authoritative source.

Definitions: Reinvention

An action or process through which something is changed so much that it is entirely new.

And they call Conservatives "Weird" (Kinnard 2024).

Military Reinvention

Where Transgenderism now POPPERS the Covid Chronicles, President Ideational and his "reimagined military" seem to be having great difficulty with military recruitment these days. The Navy used to recruit by promoting patriotism, service and teamwork. Now, it's recruiting using "authentically you individualism," with the abstract of "globalist cosmopolitanism and cultural convergence of fairness to conquer others with harmony and reconciliation." To illustrate this abstract, a drag queen influencer within their ranks is the new face of the military. Their "Harpy" ambassador seeks to create a mythological woman who is part bird in a storm with magical winds to inspire more Zoomers to sign up. This abstraction created by our all-inclusive, woke, Progressive government and its "reconceptualized" military is definitely grasping. Using Zoomer language, our Progressive government seeks to motivate a generation of people whom the government engineered to hate our country that they now want them to defend (Clark 2023) (Laurene, Harpy for Harmony 2024).

During the Covid Chronicles, thousands of military personnel were "relieved" of their military participation secondary to their refusal to take the experimental jab. Tens of thousands of National Guard members were sidelined, and 8,000 troops were kicked out for not blindly following orders to inject an un-tested substance into their bodies. Now, the Big Guy and his "redefined" military are seriously groveling, as they smarmily beg all those patriots to return to the military after throwing them out (Niemeyer 2023).

A January 2023 Department of Defense memo rescinded the "military rules" that required them to vaccinate against COVID-19. Evidently, it fell short of its military recruitment goals by a whopping fifty percent and discovered that only twenty-three percent of military-aged individuals between eighteen and twenty-four are physically fit or mentally prepared enough to join the military. Hmm, "beautiful at any size," socially constructed gender non-conforming Zoomers are not physically or mentally fit. Who would have thought? As a result, thousands of military personnel can now request a correction on their military record of service.

Now that our "reframed" military has admitted its mistakes, thousands of military personnel "relieved" from their military posts are lining up in a class-action lawsuit, suing the government for billions of dollars in lost wages, recruitment bonuses and benefits.

So many all-inclusive POPPERS and so little time. Another conundrum of their own making, where transgenderism POPPERS COVID-19 mandates, POPPER'ing the "my-body my choice repeater" that POPPERS American hatred, AKA anti-colonialism, therefore, POPPER'ing *<u>Systemic White Supremacy</u>,"* now crashing head-on with American laws and constitutional rights.

In the land of Regular Normals, when you break down patriotism, you eradicate nationalism, which obliterates love of the homeland. Why would any of these brainwashed youngsters sign up to defend it? Firing thousands of military-ready personnel because of an unconstitutional mandate has gutted our military and our readiness. Then, admitting you are wrong has some very natural consequences. Why would anyone reenlist? And they wonder why recruitment is at historic lows. Geniuses! (Frudd 2023) (Spoor 2022) (Shinkman 2023).

American pride and military readiness have taken a serious back seat to Progressive ideology. It couldn't have happened at a worse time, given global unrest we haven't seen since the 1962 Cuban Missile Crisis. We have developing wars throughout the globe between Ukraine and Russia, and Israel and Iran. We have China threatening Taiwan and we have North Korea's undeterred saber-rattling that is threatening South Korea. We have millions and millions of unvetted young men from third-world countries streaming across our border, and America is terminally divided. It isn't "if" that "Black Swan" event will happen, it is when. Best to prepare your bomb shelter now, but I suggest you not paint it rainbow. Google "camouflage," it might save your life (Engle 2022) (Rodriguez 2024) (W. Clark 2024).

Definitions: Black Swan Event

An event that is rare and unexpected with severe consequences with the potential to cause significant harm that, in hindsight, was completely predictable and preventable.

We have seen this before with the 9/11 attacks. This extremely rare event could very well occur twice in one generation. The first time we were taken by surprise, but now we can all see it coming thanks to our Progressive government, who cannot see beyond their prioritized social molding of our country instead of our safety.

Just when you think it can't get any worse, President Progressive Voter Recruiter has just issued a new memo to all our border security officers: Invaders are no longer addressed unless they first say a universally pleasurable salutation of "good morning or good evening." Next, each invader must be inquired as to what their "preferred pronoun" is. Border officers can no longer use "he, him, she or her" pronouns because they do not appropriately identify an invader's sense of self (gender identity) or sense of attraction (sexual orientation). However, some LGBTQWTFs may define these terms differently (see neopronouns below) (US Customs and Border Protection 2023) (Goldsberry 2023).

According to our Progressive government, in a trans-world construct, sexual trans-identity and trans-attraction override any other concerns that a trans-invader may present as thousands trans-descend illegally across our trans-border at any trans-given time. Additionally, we must trans-courteously address our trans-invaders while offering them a cool trans-beverage. Airline flight attendant schools will be re-branded to that of "Border Trans-Welcoming Agents." Trans-welcoming agents will have their guns confiscated to be replaced with a silver tray to appropriately trans-welcome and trans-serve the trans-invaders their cool beverage. The re-branded United States Department of Trans-Border Hosts will inquire daily which trans-pronoun the trans-invader prefers that day because it can trans-change. We need to be trans-sensitive to the trans-invader's many trans-identities (Arnold 2023) (U.S. Customs and Border Protection 2022) (Solomon 2022) (Laurene, United States Department of Trans World Hosts 2024).

At last count, there were 195 countries across the trans-globe not counting trans-Neo's, that is trans-potentially, at least 390 trans-separate trans-pronouns. Where transgenderism, POPPERS illegal immigration, let's see if I can get this straight: In a "trans-world" within the trans-construct reality, it is trans-incumbent for each trans-border agent to trans-ascertain how to trans-appropriately trans-address using trans-gendered trans-language within each trans-country's trans-gendered trans-dialect. Additionally, using a proper trans-salutation to trans-welcome each trans-invader within their trans-ordered trans-language GULAG, as it POPPERS into trans-anti-colonialism, POPPER'ing "<u>Systemic White Supremacy!</u>"

Our trans-government has mobilized the leading trans-language experts from across the trans-country to trans-compile the trans-dictionary of trans-gendered trans-language in different trans-gendered trans-dialects to comply with this trans-gendered trans-directive. Examples may include Amigo-them or Amiga-they, but our very important ordered language trans-experts are referring to their GULAG as we speak and are researching it now.

Da' VEEPs Beliefs... "I – at some point – you know – we are going to the border. We've been to the border." "So this whole – this whole – this whole thing about the border. We've been to the border. We've been to the border." "I – and I haven't been to Europe. And I mean, I don't – I don't understand the point that you're making."

Such a courageous statement of double border trans-speak. And to think she could very well be our next President.

The Most Courageous "Woman" on Earth

In Progressive land, no woman on the planet is woman enough. As a part of the National Women's Conference and on International Women's Day, the "Woman of Courage Award" was presented to an Argentinian Chest hair grower by First Lady Jill Biden, who we aren't sure is a woman either, because her pronoun has not been publicly confirmed yet (Hall 2023).

The name of the National Women's Conference has been rebranded to that of "The Plurinational Conference of Women and Lesbian, Cross Dressers, Transgenders, Bisexuals, Intersex'ed and Non-Binary Persons" to assure that all "theys" and "thems" are included. Since none of that makes any sense to Normies, let's, as Da' VEEP in chief would say, "unpack all that," shall we? (Peoples Dispatch 2022) (Shoemaker 2015).

Definitions: Plurinational

In this reference, plurinational has been borrowed by "all-inclusiviters" across the globe. It produces all kinds of imagery and symbolism, which, as we all know by now, Progressives covet. Plurinational is a form of government in which a state's nationality breaks free from a "colonialist mentality." Therefore, a plurinational state model eliminates "internalized racial oppression." It recognizes different nations as pluripotent, with their own languages, cultures, and identities historically neglected within governments.

Definitions: Colonialism

Creates imagery of plantation colonies, where members of a white ruling class dressed in white linen lounge on the edge of a cricket field, sipping cocktails served by dark-skinned natives. It is the era that we have been continually lectured upon that defines the elements of _"Systemic White Supremacy."_

Definitions: Pluripotent

The ability to differentiate into many different cell types.

So, let's count all their symbolic POPPERS, shall we? They really outslicked themselves on this one. Where **pluralism** POPPERS transgenderism, that POPPERS "Internalized Racial Oppression," that POPPERS Racism. It double POPPERS Transgenderism as **pluripotent**, POPPER'ing into **pluralnationalism** with an added sprinkle of **anti-colonialism**, AKA "Systemic White Supremacy!" That is a lot of **"plurals"** where I must applaud their POPPERS ingenuity. They were great descriptors added to the White House's political repertoire of all-inclusive **nomenclature**. We have also come to understand that the **"plurality"** of women in the Big Guy's White House staff is only half women. At this point, my father would ask, "what is their other half?" As of yet, there is no confirmation as to what "them" or "they" they or them are. (Bruns 2023).

Definitions: Pluralism

A society in which minority groups maintain their independent cultural traditions.

Definitions: Plurals

A word, symbol or form denoting more than one "diverse" element.

Definitions: Nomenclature

A system of names, terms, or rules of speech to internationally agreed principles and terminology.

Definitions: Plurality

In psychology, it is a dissociative disorder where multiple consciousnesses exist in one body.

Critical pluralistic note: Note that there is not one single parallel to women's rights.

Thanks to the Progressive Party, women are now pluripotent women, which is not fixed as to developmental potentialities but can differentiate into one of many cell types. Meaning, our country no longer identifies within a fixed X or Y chromosomal cell type. There is no longer the "genome" of women, but a new "prototype" of women, within the pluripotent of the plurality of women. It all falls under the new 2020 genomic "social construct of woman." I know, your eyes are glazed over now, but that is the Progressive goal.

Defintions: Genome

Genetic material present in an organism

Definitions: Genomic

The editing of genomes

How will this unfold in an Artificial Intelligence world? We already know that Brandi, the blow-up doll, is considered **"transgressive."** An AI-generated fashion model has already replaced Egger fashion models. I guess modeling agencies are tired of "all-inclusive, whiney, influencer Zoomers" who are costing them more money than they are worth. The first AI-generated model already has 124,000 followers on Instagram and makes $11,000 a month.

Question: With 124,000 followers, is she now considered an AI model influencer? (Laurene, AI Modeling Agency for the Ages 2024) (Bhaimiya 2023)

Definitions: Transgressive

A violation of imposed boundaries.

Da' VEEPs Beliefs: "AI is kind of a fancy thing. First of all, it's two letters. It means Artificial Intelligence."

Yep, this is the expert analysis from the Big Guy's Artificial Intelligence czar and the Democrats newly minted nominee for President of the United States, who is the White House's foremost authority on intelligence that is artificial (Liberatore 2023).

All politicians make public statements and forward actions that make everyone scratch their heads. However, beginning in 2020, Progressives have taken it to new heights. Perhaps it is now a contest to see which party can successfully shatter as many resistance barriers of logic and coherence as possible, which Progressives have indeed mastered. Transformative Language is their art and their science. If you can control the language, you can control the message and, thereby, win the ideological battle. DEI is their vehicle, transporting us onto their virtual super highway of diversionism, which feeds their insatiable appetite for equity superiority while simultaneously diverting attention from known truths to the roundabout of "-isms," "-ists," and "-phobes," leading to diversivolence, which is what DEI is really about.

Definitions…Diversivolence

Desiring strife or difference.

This is something that the state of Illinois is super sharp at. Bill 4409 changes criminal "offenders" to instead be described as "Justice Impacted Individuals." Illinois obviously doesn't have enough to do, even as Chicago had the highest murder rate in 2023 for the twelfth year in a row. Five times higher than New York City, which really is worse for people of color (Illinois House 2024) (Dabrowski 2024).

The public had long accepted trans civil rights, sympathizing with those suffering from dysphoria and accepting that even non-dysphoric trans-identified should be able to live and present as they wished. That is what a free country provides for all its citizens. But the sight of strapping, masculine males taking women's prizes and opportunities went too far. It was, however, a perfect example of the Progressive's simple four-step approach to mainstream absurd notions to that of normalization. You can pick any screwy Progressive notion:

- Shock, awe and anger by Normies, whereby Progressives…
- Shame the normals for the shock, which then…
- Shuts down the discussion, resulting in…
- Artificially shifting the shock to acceptance.

John Cleese's Monty Python's "Loretta" scene in "The Life of Brian" got it correct in 1979. A man wanting to give birth was "symbolic of his struggle against reality" and now personifies the dubiousness of today's realities. It seems that it is apropos that it would be Monty Python that Normies would turn to explain our alternative realities of the 2020s (Monty Python 1979).

If pronouns weren't enough, neopronouns are just another kettle of rancid fish that I can't even begin to process, let alone explain. Evidently, it and "It Identifiers go beyond the nonbinary." Rest assured, you are really down that deep outhouse well, dangling precariously on the outermost edge of reality if you decide to identify as whatever "it" you desire.

In short, neogenders is an umbrella of but not necessarily related to xenogenders. It includes "neurogenders, aesthetigenders, demigenders and other descriptors such as genderfae and genderfaun. I won't even stoop so low as to legitimize this with definitions. Just know it is gender categorizations and hierarchies relating to animals, plants or other creatures and things. Like a five-year-old, one can be any "it" they want to be.

I remember, as a seven-year-old, pretending to be a horse. Using this new **fantastical,** neogendered, fantasized societal construct logic, I was ahead of my time as an "Equigender!" (Andrzejewsk 2023)

Definitions: Fantastical

A departure from any semblance of reality.

Wow, that "Social Construct Committee" is going to be busy now. I can't wait to see which intersectionality axis this will be applied to in the PRIORITISE manual. What is now ten Ax-i will soon be twenty.

Remember those "Furry Conventions" we all heard about on fictional television programming? It is now a social context reality in the 2020s and no longer cloistered within psycho conventions, nor is it isolated to just "Furrys" anymore. Trans activism has binaried deep into neopronoun fantasy hell, taking a battering ram to the "social construct" door. Its concepts are about to be introduced into the California school curriculum of Gavin Newsom, who, incidentally, desperately wants to be President of the United States. How about that? We could all be like California! (Andrzejewsk 2023)

According to the neogenders, "children don't need to understand genderism because they are on a 'gender journey' that will likely change over time." Ahhh, a gender journey which POPPERS every day at any Disney theme park. Pluto's costume is merely a neogendered character for the day. Tomorrow, it will be Donald Duck. None of this horrifying tale of gendered woe is satire. This is what occurs when absurdities are cultivated in a flower garden underneath a decomposing compost pile of inclusivity (Division of Student Affairs 2023) (Schneider 2022).

Trans Activism Will End

Important contextual social context note: This chapter *is not* "Transgenderism Will End." One must always be on one's toes to defensively neutralize the predictable shrieking that ensues once one disrupts the binary cosmos of Progressive postulations. I am talking about trans activism. I will predict right now that this is going to end. It might take a little while, but it will end. Nobody cared before who you were or what you did so long as you kept it to yourself, which is what you used to do. But then you decided you needed to build your ranks and mess with our kids. That was just one trans activist step too far.

They are our children. They are not yours. They have a right to an innocent, emotionally secure childhood, free from the burdens of confusing sexual material. Our little girls have a right to the safety of all girl domains, not government-sponsored predatory traps. With that said, it is now "game over." It is your mental health crisis, not ours. Regular normals could care less what you do in your private lives, but don't pull us and our children into your head space. If you want to pretend to be another sex, creature, plant or cyborg, that is fine, but we are not participating. Take you and your trans-act, back to your trans-bars where it belongs (Fearon 2023).

Parents, I predict, could very well be the epicenter of the next big reset. You can label parents any anti-social, conspiratorial, double-headed, fire-breathing dragon terrorist monster you want. Parents don't care what you call them. They embrace the Progressive description of being "Christo-Fascist, Insurrectionist Agitator terrorists," all because they committed the most heinous crime in society today, interfering in the grooming of their children into cross-gender ideologies (Essex Westward School District 2023).

Societal Consequences of Prioritization

Now that it is 2024, where are we with all the nonsense that began in 2020 when President Re-set and his Progressive comrades took over the country? It is what happens when you normalize deviant behavior, beginning with drag queen story hour. It is what emerges when you legitimize the mutilation of children to recast societal norms and morals. It is what ensues when you destroy all progress in the equality of women and girls while elevating the depraved to platforms and positions of power and authority. It is what evolves when you seek to dismantle the entire moral fabric of our country in the name of "inclusivity." That is when you get videotaped gay sex porn in a Senate hearing room.

Here is something novel that we used to call reality. It has nothing to do with loving whom you want to love or what you do in the privacy of your own home. Those two men and their camera-human are not victims. They symbolize what the United States of America has become, as those in power violate every single acceptable norm that makes up humanity. We counted on our leadership to protect us from forcible assault. Now they are standing there watching, and often cheering, the brutal attack of our laws, our safety, our children and our values. They have become abusers of a country to bring us to our knees and accept their utopic version of socialism.

Definitions Review: Socialism

A "diverse, all-inclusive" system, characterized by social ownership rather than private ownership. **All assets** are subject to social control and distributed to "the community." Per the WEFs: *"We will all own nothing and be happy about it."* The WEFs are a powerful global entity that will be fully characterized later in the book. Their beliefs and goals are completely aligned with our current Progressive government (Stewart 2023).

Prioritization does have its consequences, which Progressives are only just beginning to understand. When people are categorized and prioritized, those who were pre-prioritised become post-prioritised (trendy Euro spelling again), discarded far below their previous ax-i of PRIORITISED importance. It is precisely why they invented POPPERS parallels, the PTSD translation dictionary and their ordered language, GULAG. They may be fictional depictions, but it is a method by which I can demonstrate their doctrine in Normie language so we can understand absurd hidden Progressive principles that we can all be amused by. Once you see it for what it is, can we finally turn the page on all this nonsense and return to normal.

So, what does occur when the prioritised prioritises lower on the prioritisation scale, AKA Ax-i? Or when you bypass your own intersectionality rules and the first law of "oppressionism?"

Progressive Review: Never, ever, ever take over the persona of an oppressed class without recognizing the decades of work and sacrifice of that oppressed class. Their own language flogs all those who commit the offense of "cultural appropriations" and is the basis for their intersectionality priority list of prioritised humans. It is what occurs when social and political movements obliterate one another, which will happen when you attempt to redefine an entire society. It perfectly illustrates the conundrum of opposing parallels (POPPERS) that elevate others at the expense of others. Women, gays, lesbians, blacks and Hispanics, who spent decades fighting for position, are now completely eradicated from that platform by other others. It took less than a year.

Trans activism has erased all gender distinctions. Therefore, gay men, lesbians and women do not meaningfully exist. Women's rights and feminism are so pointless now that they have been discarded in the swirling pissoir of TERFs.

Blacks and Hispanics who have fought against racism for higher education standards, jobs and wages have been effectually cast off as millions of illegals have invaded. The government has re-prioritized resources from black and Hispanic citizens, instead rolling out the red carpet to non-citizens who never had any skin in the game for equal rights (Heck 2022) (Stratton 2023).

The Religiosity of Abortion

Irony Alert! New POPPERS are materializing as we speak. As abortion POPPERS gender, we are all waiting with bated anticipation on where this will land as the abortion debate crashes head-on with the notion of… "What is a woman?"

When you seek to deconstruct fundamental biological truths about gender, all other previous arguments, logic and common sense are destroyed. So, if men can now become pregnant and have an abortion, they indeed have a right to express any opinion they want on abortion. It is no longer an exclusively female issue, as feminists have argued for decades. The pro-choice camp cannot have it both ways. If they want gender re-defined, then men do have a place at the abortion debate table. This will result in some additional ordered language rules in their GULAG. Does anyone else feel the desire for a craft beer about now?

Definitions Review: GULAG

An ordered language manual or **G**eneral **U**niform **L**anguage **A**ssigned **G**uidance.

On June 24, 2022, came a day that will "live in infamy" to some. To some, it was an event that eclipsed that of the attack on Pearl Harbor or 9/11. Uh-huh, tell that to the survivors and families of the victims on both those days. It was the day abortion was overturned as a "constitutional right" by the United States Supreme Court. According to abortion rights activists, it destroyed a woman's right to choose. Except that it didn't. It is simply no longer a federal issue. The individual states, not the federal government, now make the decisions. Yet we all joined others as we watched in amusement and awe as the world again seemingly went insane.

Women "screaming their abortion" with "twerking" exhibitionism, resoundingly exhibited their unhappiness and freedom of sexualization, as well as their lack of dignity. Public spectacles of sexual voyeurism that cross-identified as tantrums were personified by a disgusting display by a Rhode Island state senator, who videoed herself "twerking" on a beach upside down in a bikini, in a pose generally reserved for her gynecologist. She must have made Rhode Islanders very proud (Palmer 2022).

If you know American history and Civics, you will know that abortion should never have been a "constitutional right." The job of the Supreme Court is to rule for or against laws as they pertain to their constitutionality of United States law, as it was written in 1787. All rulings by the United States Supreme Court are to be decided through that lens alone.

Justice Ginsburg knew constitutional design, laws and how American democracy works, AKA, Civics. Her eloquent statement was correct.

Fun fact: Justice Ginsburg and Justice Scalia were fast friends. Although they were on the polar ends of the political spectrum, they still found friendship, respect and camaraderie on the backside of the spectrum. Following Justice Scalia's death, she described him as a "treasured friend." One could find plenty of symbolism there (Cox 2020).

> "The issue of abortion should be decided by the people, not by un-elected Judges."
> *Justice Ruth Bader Ginsburg…*

The reversal of this decision was to restore constitutional design. It did not eliminate a woman's right to an abortion. What it did do was send it back to the individual states for them to decide. If anybody knows an ounce of Civics, which they don't anymore, it is how our country has functionally run, as defined by the Founders since 1787. They are the folks who designed a new nation, The United States of America is a Republic run by the people, not by a kingdom or a dictatorship. Our constitution was explicitly written, according to the Bill of Rights, to protect the people from government tyranny. NOTHING in those documents states "a woman's right to an abortion."

I paraphrase the following crazed, irrational, incoherent rant typical of a Spinner suffering from terminal pseudologia. She is a card-carrying mythomaniacal member for the Spins, spewing mythomaniac rhetoric, which is their number one basic operational strategy they deploy when all other forms of basic coherence fail:

> "We are at war, a war with women. Next, they are getting a national ban on abortion. They are coming for your birth control, taking away LGBT rights, gay marriage, and non-white immigration. They are forcing all women to give birth, especially poor

women and little girls. They are erasing history - black history, holocaust history, and all history about non-white They only worship guns. Assault weapons will flood society and schools to control all people, their voting rights, to marry, and see a drag show. They will subject people to constant risk of death at schools, Walmart, concerts, parades. They don't give a damn how many people die. Anyone who displeases them is on the menu. They want one-party state. They are coming for blue states. A White Christian nationalist hell that they will control. We need to get back to a 'normal party'—the Democratic Party. They are at war with the rest of us. It's Defcon I now. Wake up and take action" (Lipstadt 2011) (Nesbit 2014).

Important contextual Progressive blunder that I am happy to highlight: Actually, stating out loud that the Holocaust is an actual event in history.

That is a lot of blather to absorb. But it is an exceptional representation of a typical rant from a psychotic mythomaniac who masquerades as a journalist. Frankly Sweetie, even though you believe you are visible, you are invisible. Transparent, actually, in your disturbing description of others who disagree with your fanaticism.

Your pronouns are…who/where?

Definitions Review: Pseudologia

A psychiatric syndrome where patients represent specific fantasies as real occurrences.

Definitions Review: Mythomaniac

An abnormal or pathological tendency to exaggerate or tell lies.

Civics Review: Changing the Constitution is not easy. It was not meant to be easy. The Framers of our unique Constitution knew it should never be amended frivolously or haphazardly. The Constitution is a document that protects all citizens, not just a few and not the government. Proud socialist politicians are those who prefer dictatorships, not a republic. Our Constitution has been changed twenty-seven times by our Congress and the people. This is how constitutional change occurs. Congress needs a two-thirds supermajority in the House and the Senate to approve any constitutional amendments. The President of the United States isn't even required to sign off on it, and he cannot veto it. Once passed, it then goes back to the states for approval. Three-fourths of all states need to agree (Longley 2021).

The process is lengthy, time-consuming and a method by which most of our country must agree. It is why our Supreme Court is ruling on so many haphazardly made laws outside of constitutional design (like abortion). It is also the purpose behind the Progressive push to pack the court with like-minded Progressive Judges.

There is only one fundamental difference between Supreme Court justices. They are either constitutional justices or they are not. Constitutionalists believe in the Constitution, as written by the Founders, that protects the rights of all citizens. All United States laws are written and defended based on the Constitution. There are no carve-outs.

Progressives prefer a globalist "living document" or "greater good" viewpoint, which is how they choose their justices. They would prefer that our Constitution accommodate modern beliefs that change over time. Imagine the possibilities if our laws protected Progressive beliefs in lawful gun ownership, climate, gender spectrums, property ownership, land use, income and illegal aliens. Like their PRIORITISE manual, our constitution would be a myriad of carve-out protections for individuals and ideologies, not the nation as a whole. History shows that in 1993 and 1994, President Clinton nominated Justice Ruth Bader Ginsburg and Justice Stephen Breyer. They were the last Constitutional judges ever nominated by the Democrat party (Rutkowski, Open Source).

If partisan politicians can pass a law through the Supreme Court, it becomes the law of the land, bypassing the amendment process. It is much easier to pass partisan amendments to our constitution by judiciary fiat rather than by congressional vote, which is the goal. Progressive politicians work diligently to supplant their own globalist, like-minded justices who have no desire to protect our Constitution. With that said, they undermine each constitutional justice on the court using tried and true strategies to destroy their integrities so they can prevent their appointments or impeach them. The goal is to destroy our Constitution and re-adjust our country into the utopic socialist version they prefer (Kapur 2021).

Da' VEEPs Beliefs: "Well, we are the United States of America because we are united, and we are states."

More Civics Review: States' rights is that section of constitutional design that Justice Ginsburg referred to, where laws must be determined at the state level. The Constitution still protects if state laws undermine our constitutional rights. That is when the Supreme Court intervenes and makes its rulings. It is why unconstitutional state laws regarding gun ownership passed by blue states do not pass constitutional muster and are overturned.

States' Rights are horribly inconvenient to those states with different ideas of how our country "should be" governed, AKA dictatorships. Following the Supreme Court reversal, abortion laws are making their way through state legislatures, as they should be.

Previously fooled in the abortion debate, I believed it when they told us it was rare. It was reasonable that abortion may be necessary to save a woman's life. Then, the debate changed to "a woman's right to choose." It wasn't something I would ever do myself, but who am I to tell another woman what is right or wrong in their own family planning decisions?

Slowly, I heard of infants being aborted alive in late-term gestations, who were then killed by the abortionist's hand. Aborted baby parts were being sold for profit from abortion clinics run by Planned Parenthood.

"The most beautiful things in the world cannot be seen or even touched.
They must be felt with the heart."
Helen Keller…

No matter how hard the Spins tried to divert attention away from these realities, my feelings about abortion began to erode, as did many others. Sold baby parts sound like a lot more than a "clump of cells," abortion advocates describe (The Center for Medical Progress 2020).

CONQUERING THE BONGOS | 491

By the time a fetus is twelve weeks gestation, it is a fully formed living human being with a beating heart, a brain, ten fingers and ten toes. This is when cells are differentiated beyond that "clump" they tell us about. Many factors affect premature infant survival and outcomes. However, neonatologists generally say that by twenty-four weeks gestation, a fetus is viable and has a sixty percent survival rate. Yet it is that gestational age and beyond whose lives are terminated without a moment's thought, unceremoniously disposed of in Kermit Gosnell's or Planned Parenthood's trash bucket (Connor 2013).

Abortion, we were told was "safe, legal and rare," but it involved a secret, more insidious goal: Taxpayer-funded abortion on demand throughout the entire nine months of pregnancy. That is when the cult of abortion activism lost the country. Nobody with a heart, a brain or a conscience would ever accept the thought of aborting a baby close to birth (Prestigiacomo 2019) (Rep. Chu, 2023).

For women who don't want to be mothers, numerous adoption agencies represent one to two million families looking to adopt a child at any given time. Infants are the most sought-after child for couples unable to conceive their own infant (Adoption For My Baby).

Since the Supreme Court decision, abortion activists are now assaulting Supreme Court Justices. They are stalking their homes and running them out of restaurants. They and their families are being harassed and threatened outside their homes by protesters. A "bounty" has been issued by abortion activists to report a Supreme Court Justice or their family in any public venue. As of January 2023, one hundred churches and pregnancy centers have been vandalized and desecrated. Numerous arrests have been made for assaults against clergy, center staff, pro-life supporters and police officers. Celebrities are publicly announcing the acceptability of murdering anybody who is pro-life, and previously respected book authors are ideating new book manuscripts about assassinating Supreme Court justices.

> *"Our nation is founded on the principle that observance of the law is the eternal safeguard of liberty, and defiance of the law is the surest road to tyranny."*
> **President John Fitzgerald Kennedy...**

This is precisely when abortion moved out of the realm of women's rights and into the cult of abortion activism. When it moved beyond a "woman's right to choose," to embracing and practicing those eight criteria described by Dr. Lister (J. Jackson 2023) (Impelli 2022) (Nolfi 2024).

This is truly dangerous. One arrest so far, for an attempted assassination of a Justice by someone once again dangling tenuously on that reality shoestring. A country without laws is not a country. One cannot riot their will to get their way. But again, this is what happens when you fail to teach American history and Civics and where we are being led by government leaders who devalue human life. It cultivates a place of hate and unrest that threatens the safety of all (Lynbrand 2022).

In the United Kingdom, a pro-life woman was arrested for silently praying outside an abortion clinic. She was approached by a British law enforcement officer after an onlooker reported that she "might be praying." The video shows a woman silently standing on a curb across from the abortion clinic. The officer asked her if she was praying, to which she responded, "I might be in my head." She was immediately arrested (Sapper 2022).

Another Civics Review: This is the very country that our constitutional founders escaped and the reason they designed a constitution to protect the people in a new land they called America. There was no such right of freedom of speech in the United Kingdom, notice it says "Kingdom." It is why this right is listed first in our Constitution. If today's government had its way, our freedom of speech would be gone. They are already trying to subvert it through social media and big tech. George Orwell's 1949 **dystopian** novel "1984" was a warning, not a work of fiction (Orwell).

Definitions: Dystopian or Dystopia

Relating to or denoting an imagined state or society where great suffering or injustice exists. It shows us a nightmarish image of the future of the world.

In the United States, they can't eliminate our free speech because it is our Constitutional right, but they have made us afraid to practice it with technological advances that eliminate it, or tried and true methods of ostracism and threats that create fear.

Where abortion now POPPERS trans activism, a national organization called Cordea, is partnering with Planned Parenthood to create a K-12 curriculum. The curriculum is to equip sex educators to avoid using the term "women" in conversations on teen pregnancy (Grossman 2022).

Sacramento City Unified School district (no surprise there) uses a "gender unicorn" to introduce sexuality and gender identity to toddlers. Unicorns are make-believe horses. What an appropriate symbol to represent make-believe women.

Planned Parenthood, the supposed national champion for all women and their abortions, proclaims, "abortion access is now an intersectional issue." Further stating, "Our language needs to acknowledge those intersections." With that, another roundabout has been created to dump women at a random crossroad on some proverbial highway of beings with no actual description of who we are. Per Planned Parenthood, from here, henceforth, and forever, the terms feminine, woman and female have been removed from all definitions within the organization because, wait for it, **"abortion care is really about trans care."** This message was not subliminal. It is clear. Planned Parenthood no longer cares for women. It is all about "thems" (Planned Parenthood 2021).

Wow, I am getting severe "social construct" whiplash here. Wasn't the point of "woman as a construct" so they/them could be pregnant? Then, to comply with their socially constructed world, we change all our language to be "all-inclusive" to that of "menstruators," "egg producers," "chest feeders" and "uterus owners." Except now they want abortions.

Per Planned Parenthood's Propaganda Manual...

- Chapter: Just Say Abortion.
- Category: Abortion Access, Health care Equity
- Section "Abortion isn't just "Women's Health Care"

Per Planned Parenthood, "It is time to retire women's health care and a woman's right to choose. Neither one is a reasonable substitution for the word abortion. These phrases leave out trans and non-binary people. Using that language is transphobic because abortion isn't just for women" (Planned Parenthood 2021).

So where are the feminists? The "fourth wave" of modern feminism has adopted a "more diverse" approach, defined by intersectionality. It's a good thing, otherwise, they would be irrelevant in a social context world (Alfonseca 2023).

What began as 121 genders when I started this book has exploded to 523 genders as a-gendered gender descriptions are being released faster than green grass evacuating through an **agendered** goose. See the previous chapter on "Neopronouns" (youtube.com 2023) (Laurene, Challenge: Collating all the Genders in an A-Gendered Society 2024).

Definitions: Agendered

One whose gender identity and expression do not align with man, woman or any other gender.

Incidentally, where are those stylishly dressed white-garbed Progressive women nowadays in Congress? Your symbolization is lost on us now. Your symbolized gesture of symbolical importance and show of symbolistic unity, that symbolized your symbolist commitment to defend women's rights, has now symboled away. We are all on to your vacuous and meaningless symbologna. You have forfeited women and their spaces to men in your hollowed intersectionality of pandered importance, depending on which direction the political winds are blowing up your faux white skirts. You can **"transplain"** all you want, but we know the truth (Lang 2020).

Historical Definition: Mansplaining

A condescending, overconfident or oversimplified manner of explaining a concept or definition by a man to a woman.

Since there are no men now, this definition has been rebranded in their ordered-language GULAG to substitute trans for man to clarify this new "social construct" of superiority over women. (courses.transplaining.info).

Examples are as follows:

Per the Planned Parenthood's Ordered Language GULAG:

- Women are now… "people with uteruses."
- Feminine hygiene products are now "menstrual products."
- Women's rights are now "human rights."
- Women's choice is now "person choice."
- Women's healthcare is now "reproductive healthcare."

In another "trans-formational" transgender POPPERS parallel to "The Religion of CRT," Planned Parenthood has announced the forthcoming "them's" march. However, white caucasian "Theys" are no longer considered advocates for "person care." Therefore, the annual "uterus owner's march" does not welcome you, so "leave you and your pink pussy-hat at home because you won't be attending" (TikTok 2023) (Grossman 2023).

The Religiosity of COVID-19

Our government, the media, academia and the Reverend led us through every dark tunnel and passageway that harbored new horrors of death, disease and pestilence. We all would surely perish unless we dutifully complied with every single mandate of every chapter and verse of The Covid Chronicles. However, it didn't take long before most of us discovered that those same mandates excluded many folks. Those excluded, included those who were oracles in their own minds and definitely above the peons in society, AKA the American people. Many exceptions were made, and some were profoundly exhibited in full hierarchical display as *"The Elite Chosen Exceptionals"* in our society.

Definition: Hypocrisy

Sanctimonious behavior from elite power-hungry leaders who refused to be ruled by their own rules, otherwise described as "rules for thee but not for me."

In California, Governor Newsom locked down schools for nearly two years yet sent his kids to a private school that remained primarily open. Stating to the residents of California that "he, too, was living through Zoom school and all of the challenges related to it." Unfortunately for him, reporting from Politico and the Los Angeles Times exposed the truth. Only then was he forced to admit that his children were receiving private, in-class instruction (Mays 2021).

Jeopardy Question for 2000: The Democrat's Senate body rules change, requiring every Democrat senator to be present in chambers for any vote even if you were sick with COVID-19.
Answer: What would be the "don't test, don't tell" rules change because, in a 50/50 senate, it is critical to have every single Democrat present in chambers for every single vote, regardless of the rules you set for the rest of the country (Stiles 2022).

One Oracle (in her own mind) was quite the Covid fashionista in our country.

Definitions: Self-Obsessed

Exhibiting an excessively high opinion of one's appearance that produces no useful result.

While presenting herself in public, the Speaker of the House in Congress owns over one hundred masks that match every single dress and pantsuit in her wardrobe, which are clearly custom-made. However, they were unnecessary outside the public eye, especially while visiting her federally-mandated closed beauty salon. Curious because all salons were closed by her and her party to save lives, of course.

Miraculously, Coronavirus was not present inside her own beauty salon. Unfortunately, Queen Pelosi's stylist was a dangerous carrier of a perilously intense contagious variant, as evidenced by her masked face in her Highness' presence. Business security videos are incredibly inconvenient if you are the Democratic Speaker of the House (Dibble 2020).

Soon following the Speaker's hair appointment, it was discovered that the Coronavirus had varying levels of contagiousness, depending on who you were and the circumstances. For some groups and individuals, it was discovered that they were utterly immune:

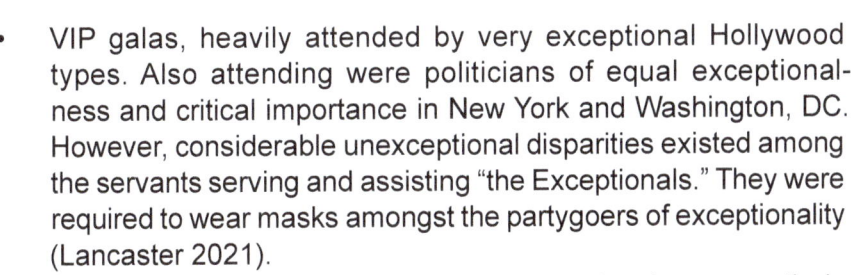

- VIP galas, heavily attended by very exceptional Hollywood types. Also attending were politicians of equal exceptionalness and critical importance in New York and Washington, DC. However, considerable unexceptional disparities existed among the servants serving and assisting "the Exceptionals." They were required to wear masks amongst the partygoers of exceptionality (Lancaster 2021).
- Illegal immigrants crossing the southern border are entirely immune to COVID-19, so much so that Federal officials didn't

even feel the need to test, mask or vaccinate them (United States Office of Inspector General 2021).
- VIP dinner parties by California's exceptionally exceptional Governor and his exponentially exceptional friends of exceptionality (Duffy 2020).
- The California Governor's children and other exceptional children who belong to the oracles of our government hardly lost a day of educational instruction while attending their exceptional private schools.

Fortunately, it was discovered that Coronavirus was highly selective and extremely contagious among BLM and Antifa protesters, as well as swarms of mass shoplifters stealing carts full of items from retailers across the country. I want to personally thank the anarchists for considering our health.

Da' VEEPs Beliefs: "In what they are going to do to reconsider its Covid strategy. It is time for us to do what we have been doing, and that time is every day."

According to data released in February 2022, the death toll of the Coronavirus pandemic reached as high as 919,000 out of 332 million people. This number represents.27 percent of the United States population who supposedly died from COVID-19 as of the above date. Yet to be determined is how much this number is conflated. No distinction was ever made between those who died from COVID-19 or with COVID-19.

Interesting Statistical Note: The CDC 2023 release of the most prevalent causes of death in 2021 had COVID-19 came in as number three. Pneumonia and influenza did not even make the top ten and curiously possessed statistically significant reductions ever recorded in United States history. So amazing, isn't it? Pneumonia and influenza hardly existed during the COVID-19 era (Centers for Disease Control and Prevention 2021).

COVID-19 data can be compared to the Spanish Flu pandemic, where 676,000 people died in the United States out of 103 million, or.65 percent of the population. This statistic is important as you compare pandemics. The Spanish Flu killed 2.5 times more people than COVID-19, even with COVID-19's suspiciously conflated numbers (Centers for Disease Control ongoing) (Lea 2021).

Today's population density is far greater than that of 1918 and is a consequential factor in the spread of killer viruses. Based on census data and figuring the total square miles of the United States plus Washington DC, there was 94.42 people per square mile in 2022. This compared to 15.31 people per square mile in 1919, which illustrates the virility of the Spanish Flu over COVID-19. For my grandfather, what he witnessed and the work he did during the Spanish flu pandemic rivaled anything we saw in 2020. Context matters. This is not minimizing COVID's impact. It is merely an attempt to put the 2020 pandemic in a broader historical context and away from the panic porn propaganda disseminated by our government and their Spinners.

Definitions: Contact Tracing

Quarantining the sick and identifying exposures began in the early 1900s during the Spanish flu pandemic when public health was in its infancy.

Definitions: Preventing the Spread

The act of wearing masks and limiting contact with other people began in the Middle Ages in 476 AD to control the spread of Leprosy.

Definitions: Squandering

Money thrown around in a foolish and reckless manner in the hopes something wonderful will occur.

Billions upon billions of government dollars were freely dispensed throughout the country from the CARES Act, the American Rescue Plan and the Families First Coronavirus Response Act. All that money thrown around produced nothing different from the 1900s. Just as all viruses do, it still spread and killed. It gradually converted into many variants, reducing its virulence to the common flu, dangerous only to the usual immunocompromised populations.

It spread despite all the money, televised expert advice, epidemiologists, government research bodies and committees. Despite all that tumult, the virus behaved as all pandemic viruses behave. Despite all that money, there are still no breakthrough cures. The vaccine they created did not work as promised and can be dangerous to some populations. All in all, the government's efforts were a dismal failure. Nothing new was discovered to prevent the early spread and death toll of COVID-19. Time and money could have been saved with fewer deaths had communities and regions within each state been free to work together with their local resources, just as they did in 1918. Even if one disagrees with all that said, there is one overriding fact we can all learn throughout public health history and all our experiences with killer viruses…Regardless of all that money spent, people still died.

Many studies have now been completed. We can now look back and statistically compare states with stringent lockdown policies to those that did not. Many states, fed up with the government nonsense, broke away and instituted their own directives. They opened schools and businesses and left mask-wearing decisions to individuals and companies. The government and their media repudiated those decisions as dangerous, immoral, evil, uncaring and an "existential threat" to all mankind.

That research (so inconvenient) has now shown that states that continued to remain beholden to all those mandates had higher infection and death rates than states that re-opened with sensible precautions. The micro-managing of 332 million lives did not equate to better outcomes, which should surprise nobody (Swiss Policy Research 2021).

COVID-19 was the mother of all religious attempts ever perpetuated on an entire society that went global. We can all agree that everyone was justifiably frightened at the beginning of the pandemic. It was a brand-new virus that was a killer. Nobody knew if this could be THE PANDEMIC that could wipe out humankind. We know it could be out there someday. The question remains, because this was not "it."

Many in power capitalized on that fear, telling us this was "it." We gave up our constitutional rights to "save lives" from "it." Even as "it" lost its virility as all viruses do, intense media and big tech scrutiny did not wane, even though "it" was waning. Any person, whether you were a scientist or healthcare provider, who did not parrot the preferred narrative was labeled as a "crazed conspiracy theorist" and an "existential threat to society."

Important contextual note: "Existential threat" is another fruitful descriptor in the land of Progressivism. It is a term used liberally for everything from climate change to the Second Amendment to Free Speech to Former President Trump. It was a term used ad nauseam to describe those who chose not to take the experimental jab. It is a popular Progressive term that they use to portray a threat to everyone's existence.

Nothing illustrates this better than the tribalism that occurred in our country with the COVID-19 vaccine. You can apply the concepts to any Progressive ideologies of the 2020s. Tribalism is a branched perception of the world, where the "in-group" is seen as superior, while the other group is dangerous and inferior, creating intense emotional attachment to the "in-group." It evokes strong emotional investment that wholly influences behavior and decision-making, regardless of facts or common sense. Tribalism leads to stereotypes, prejudices, discrimination, division, conflicts and exclusionary attitudes toward others.

Unfortunately for the Covid Religious Tribe, actual science has finally caught up with the lies. It is astonishing how arrogant our government was to believe it wouldn't. History always finds and defines the truth eventually. Perhaps even the most ardent Covidians can learn a few things.

- There is such a thing as natural immunity (Alexander 2021) (Gazit 2021).
- School closure would reduce transmission – There are no such data (Pappas 2020).
- Myocarditis was more prevalent after Covid infection - False. Data proved that the vaccine causes it in both adult and pediatric cases, as well as stroke in adults (National Institutes of Health 2021) (Kracaclik 2022) (Schwab 2022) (Montgomery 2021) (Hoeg 2021) (Aleem 2021) (Elberry n.d.) (Kakovan 2022) (Peckford 2021).
- Lab leak was just a conspiracy theory – False.
- Vaccines and boosters are necessary for young people - False. There is no data or information that a healthy child has died from COVID-19. In fact, vaccines could be dangerous for them (Ph.D. Bardosh 2022).
- COVID-19 vaccines give greater immunity than natural immunity – False. In fact, scientific studies show that boosters could adversely affect the immune response (Yamamoto 2022) (Kulldorff 2022).

The Reverend "expertly" determined that six feet of distance is the minimum distance required to safely socially interact if we MUST interact. Where incompetence identifies as expertise, we later found out...

The Covid Chronicles and their "follow the science" preachers, lectured our lives on a foundation of bad science that took years from our lives. Only after closed-door interviews did the former NIH Director Francis Collins confess that the government's sweeping social distancing guidelines were not backed by any science.

Where Covid POPPERS Transgenderism also POPPER'ing <u>"Systemic White Supremacy."</u> One NIH research paper published titled "Six Feet Apart or Six Feet Under" outlined the impact of the virus on the black community. Another report titled "LGBTQ+ Loss and Grief in a Cis-Heteronormative Pandemic: A Qualitative Evidence Synthesis of the COVID-19 Literature." Yep, this was our tax dollars at work (Kittle 2024).

The Reverend identifies as a Spinner, and our government identifies as propagandists, who both further cross-identify as deceivers. Where "experts" are concerned, we have no government experts. Their expertise is confined to the political messaging they seek to advance. What does that mean? Every single one of us must research everything ourselves and apply our God-given common sense to formulate our own logical strategies.

The Primary Lesson: Always, always be skeptical of ANY government directive that removes our freedoms.

Just In: Project Veritas, the only real investigative journalistic organization that was left in the country, released a sting video. Mr. Jordon Trishton Walker, head of Research and Development at Pfizer, explained in detail Pfizer's own "Gain of Function Research." In his own words, this high-ranking corporate head, illustrated in immense detail, Pfizer's intent to create their own mutated version of the COVID-19 virus. Whereby like "Superthem," they can sweep onto the scene with a one hundred percent effective vaccine, saving us all. Mr. Walker further stated, "COVID-19 and vaccines have become Pfizer's cash cow" (Project Veritas 2023) (Walker 2023) (Twitter.com 2023) (Norton 2023).

In the second installment of the sting video, Mr. Walker further discloses the reported effects on menstrual cycles, a phenomenon Pfizer scientists have been studying for a while. They theorize that the vaccine affects the HPG axis (Hypothalamus, Pituitary Gland and Gonads). Per Mr. Walker, *"it has to be impacting something hormonal to be impacting the menstrual cycle. I will admit, I will say, if it does come back down the line, there is something wrong with the vaccine, then obviously people will criticize the big push. Because there was a lot of social pressure, government pressure and job pressure to get the vaccine. Like, I had to get the vaccine; otherwise, I would have gotten fired. If something were really bad to happen down the road, the scale of that scandal would be enormous."*

This scandal is already enormous. It was a hurried vaccine that among other things, created menstrual irregularities affecting fertility. In all pharmaceutical history, it has been standard practice that: **Any medication, with no long-term studies, especially vaccines under an emergency government authorization, should never be administered to women of reproductive age.** Fertility rates fell to a forty-year low in 2020. Predictably, the Spins blamed it on climate change, er... global warming (Thorp MD 2023).

Lather, Rinse, Repeat...

We have yet to understand what effects the vaccine may have had on vaccine-exposed newborn children across the globe.

Unbeknownst to the country, Pfizer had already recognized a possible link between its vaccine and cardiac anomalies long ago. Since at least 2021, Pfizer's Research and Development Team has investigated and reviewed at least 124 referenced studies and papers. The vaccine never underwent adequate safety and topological testing in accordance with previously established scientific standards. Another study recommends a global moratorium on all modified mRNA products beginning immediately" (Mead M 2024) (Muthukumar 2021) (Mevorach 2021).

Once the sting video hit Twitter, two million hits ensued within two days. A Defcon I emergency was called, whereby all the Spin Room's talking heads immediately conferred in the Department of Defense War Room. Big Tech immediately adjusted its search engine algorithms detrimental to Project Veritas. A Newsweek "fact-checking" story appeared first at the top of every algorithmic list, stating that the *purported* video is "unverified." They immediately instituted the third handle of Progressive debates to destroy the integrity of Project Veritas, labeling them a controversial organization whose stories are "unevidenced" by "other fact-checkers. Oh, he also abused Femmes! So, a video of a high-ranking Pfizer official talking in depth about corrupt experimentation isn't good enough for fact-checkers anymore with an abuse accusation that has yet to find its way to any actual charges or follow-up news reports (Passantino 2023).

Lather, Rinse, Repeat…

Progressive religiosity and tribalism are so engrained that as long as the Stool keeps poisoning the well of truth, it gives their loyal followers all the validation they need, that their pre-conceived notions of what is true remain intact, regardless of facts. With that, Project Veritas and a story exposing the biggest lie of the century magically disappeared into the black depths of the Progressive swamp, never to be spoken of again (Norton 2023).

Once the 2022 elections were over and Republicans controlled investigative directions, we are *coincidentally* hearing from the U.S. Department of Energy and the Director of National Intelligence. Per FBI Director Wray, *"it seems that our national intelligence has confirmed that the Pandemic was started by an 'accidental' laboratory leak at the Wuhan Institute of Virology in Wuhan, China"* (Matza 2023).

> "Rule 39… "There's no such thing as a coincidence."
> *Leroy Jethro Gibbs…*

El' I Be… "Em are Ducks!" All of us stupid, Xenophobic, far-right-wing, clueless, fringe-thinking, uneducated, dimwitted "conspiracy theorists" and an "existential threat" to society were correct all along (Gordon 2023).

You can bet the White House and their collection of spooks within the Department of Defense, CIA and FBI have known this for a long time. Information like this doesn't suddenly materialize; *coincidentally,* at the same time, they lose control of Congress and no longer control the investigations. However, you know this is not the whole story. They only release what they must release, the less, the better (Harmon 2003).

- China, one of our biggest adversaries, has this virology lab in Wuhan, China, *"coincidentally,"* where ground zero of the virus was located (Zilber, 2023) (Ke 2023) (Devine 2023) (Reality Check Team 2021).
- Our government's National Institutes of Health (NIH), run by the Reverend Fauci, helped fund the Wuhan Lab's operation (Diamond 2023).

- Something called "Gain of Function" research was probably taking place in China at the Wuhan Lab (Robertson 2021).

In another made-for-television drama, congressional hearings began, which questioned the Reverend. After much obfuscation, double-speak and an inability to remember anything, like magic, document exposure forced him to suddenly recollect that our government was involved. The United States funded it and ran it under the Reverend's leadership. However, he adamantly denies that "Gain of Function" research was ever conducted at the Wuhan Lab.

Then, in a dramatic turn of events, after years of Reverend denials and dozens of Spinner fact checkers invalidating the obvious, NIH principal deputy director Lawrence Tabak admitted to Congress that US taxpayers funded Gain of Function research at the Wuhan Institute of Virology in China in the months and years before the COVID-19 Pandemic. A controversial unregulated research practice that modifies viruses to make them more infectious. The NIH immediately scrubbed its website of the longstanding definition for gain of function research. Funny how all those Spinner fact-checkers have once again disappeared across the news-feed (Chamberlain 2021) (Christenson 2024).

Definitions: Gain of Function Research

Medical research that genetically alters an organism in a way that enhances the biological functions of gene products. It includes the alteration of pathogenesis, transmissibility or host ranges. It can alter mutations and create variants. Gain of function research is the method by which a biological weapon can be created. The Biden Administration suspended funding for the Wuhan Institute of Virology following a review that determined that the Chinese Institute "is not compliant with federal regulations and is *not presently* responsible" (Diamond 2023).

Important ordered language reveal: The "not presently" in the above statement insinuates that China was compliant and responsible. Progressives and their Spin reporters can't imply in any way that they or their government is corrupt or reveal that they are idiots. Both implications apply here.

It is essential to understand this history to realize why our Progressive government, their Spins and Big Tech buddies sought to control this story. Allowing the truth to be known could usher in a non-progressive government by angry voters, and they can't allow that. Voters must always remain in the dark. It is why they are still inflaming the issue today and why rational thinkers are called every "-ist," "-ism," and "-phobe" in the PTSD translation dictionary. Except, now, after five years, we know what happened:

- Many adults across the age spectrum begin to suddenly get sick. Many died.
- It was quickly determined that this killer virus began in China, which has some of the worst human rights violations across the globe. The same country who has the desire and funding to destroy whole societies if they want to and have in the past. A country that would not think twice about unleashing a biological weapon (Human Rights Watch 2020) (Hansler 2021) (Chang 2021).
- The virus quickly goes global, capable of mutating into perpetuity that the globe will now live with forever.
- The United States ran the lab and funded it in Wuhan, China.

Question: If the United States had not funded and directed the research, would this virus have ever existed? (Miltimore 2023)

Finally, in 2024, Mark Zuckerburg, Facebook's founder and CEO, admitted to Congress that Facebook, under pressure from the Biden/Harris Whitehouse, censored content related to the pandemic (McCullogh 2024).

Newsflash! We, the media, are requesting "Covid Amnesty." We think it is time to move forward from this horrible time in our history. Getting it wrong was "not our fault" and "not a moral failing" because we "just didn't know" (Oster 2022).

Translation: We admit we ignored numerous facts and data, but we were working for "the Greater Good." We protected the government by telling skeptics and questioners that they were brainless, half-wit, moronic fools who were an "existential threat" to society, but we pinky swear that it will never happen again.

Definition: Amnesty:

An official pardon for people who have been convicted of political offenses, not to be confused with an actual apology because it is not.

Per the Atlantic, *"Given the amount of uncertainty, almost every position was taken on every topic. And on every topic, someone was eventually proven right, and someone else was proven wrong. In some instances, the right people were right for the wrong reasons. In other instances, they had a **prescient** understanding of the available information. The people who got it right may want to **gloat**"* (Oster 2022).

Definitions: Prescient

To know beforehand or to use data, history and common sense to predict outcomes that drive strategies and behavior.

Question: What do they mean by "correct people were right for the wrong reasons?"
Answer: In uncertain times, some used their brains to develop logical conclusions based on data and evidence. However, logical conclusions are never a substitute for being right because they are wrong within the context of "the Greater Good."

The "gloat" statement is a preamble to a brand new -ist in the making. Let me pre-empt the cult-defined ordered language GULAG addition that is sure to follow in the PTSD translation dictionary. However, I will create my definition that is certain not to be included.

Definitions: Gloatist

Someone who chooses not to forgive and forget the lies and deceit perpetrated upon the American people. You and your government are responsible for the panic and the inconsistent directives. You and your government conspired to shut down schools, which resulted in a learning loss from which this generation of children may never recover. Because of what you did, our children require counseling and anti-depressants because they missed their teachers and friends. Many committed suicide. You made us prisoners in our homes. We couldn't worship, while you attended parties with your political and celebrity pals. You all conspired to prevent families from visiting their loved ones in nursing homes and hospitals, where they died alone. The same nursing homes that the California, New York and Michigan Governors housed the Covid sick. A viral hellhole where the vulnerable were trapped. Then those Governors lied about death rates in those same nursing homes so they wouldn't be liable financially or to society. They forbid us from saying goodbye or to hug them in a final farewell, then, as we grieved, we couldn't even participate in their funerals (Blankley 2021) (Delie 2021).

Without any evidence, those who refused the experimental jab were labeled lepers and "spreaders." Nobody has yet to admit that their vaccine is responsible for cardiac anomalies in young adults and children. Events that cannot or won't be explained and may have lasting consequences, including death. You and your government are directly responsible for people permanently losing their jobs, their businesses, their livelihoods and their homes. You silenced critical scientific studies during the pandemic that contradicted what it was they were fabricating, a strategy that cost millions of lives.

You and your government dragged Covid around like a dead cat, far longer than it ever should have been. They drove that old dead horse into the ground until it could no longer hold its little Covid head up. When all the data and facts were just too difficult to suppress, they are now telling us to "move on" and forget how they tore our country apart.

You in the media need to understand that you are no longer trusted to protect American interests. You land squarely in the center of the politically correct, woke agenda and are deeply rooted in Progressive politics. You worked with the government at the behest of American dreams and prosperity. Millions of people are victims of your agenda that destroyed their lives. It will never be forgotten or forgiven.

The last peer-reviewed retrospective study before the publication of this book revealed a multitude of significant problems in the previous methods, execution and reports of previous COVID-19 trials, including a re-analysis of Pfizer's trial data. The study was led by The Hoover Institute's former advisor to the White House Coronavirus Task Force, John Hopkins Institute for Global Health, and the University of Chicago's former Chief Economist to the White House Council of Economics. Absolutely none of the findings surprised any of us who thought this through for ourselves. The study identified statistically significant increases in serious adverse events in the vaccine group. These events included death, cancer, cardiac events, and various autoimmune, hematological, reproductive and neurological disorders. It is no wonder that Pfizer and our government sought to sequester that information for seventy-five years (Atlas, et al. March 2024).

"Americans justifiably lost faith in public health institutions. Strict limitations on powers conferred to the executives need time limits and should require legislation to extend. The CDC guidance is strictly advisory and did not have the power to set laws or mandates."

Furthermore, "unless and until key institutions openly acknowledge that lockdowns, school closures and mask/vaccine mandates were catastrophic errors that will not be repeated in the future, the American people will, and should, withhold their trust."

Many other lessons were outlined to include:

- Leaders should calm public fears, not stoke them.
- Lockdowns do not work to reduce deaths or stop viral circulation.
- Lockdowns and social isolation had negative consequences that far outweighed the benefits.
- Government should not pay people more not to work.
- Shutting down schools was a major policy mistake with tragic effects on children, especially the poor.
- Masks were of little or no value and possibly harmful.
- The government should not suppress dissent or police the boundaries of science.
- The real hospital story was underutilization.
- Protect the most vulnerable.
- Warp Speed: Deregulate but don't mandate

"Anti-vaxxer" skeptics were correct. A blanket approach on a population-wide scale had no basis for a global rollout as it had no honest assessment commensurate with a risk-benefit ratio, a process that had never before occurred in the United States. Before the COVID-19 vaccine, previous testing trials underwent investigation for at least four years, which had ALWAYS been the standard of drug approval by the FDA until this vaccine roll-out.

> "A nation that is afraid to let its people judge the truth and falsehood in an open market, is a nation that is afraid of its people."
> **President John Fitzgerald Kennedy...**

The Religiosity of Climate Change

The entire globe has lived with the climate religion and its lies for decades. It was the test subject for the Covid Religion, by which all strategies have been obtained. "Climate change is settled science." Therefore, "climate deniers" are an "existential threat" and will destroy the planet. The globe will be engulfed in an eternal winter, or all the ice sheets will melt. Either way, we will all die. All wind, rain or snow events, are reported as, "unprecedented."

**Definitions:
Unprecedented**

An event or circumstance that has never been done or known before.

*"Snows are less frequent and less deep now.
They are remembered to be formerly frequent, deep, and of long continuance.
The rivers, which then seldom failed to freeze over in the course of the winter, scarcely ever do now.
I remember that when I was a small boy, say 60 years ago, snows were frequent and deep in every winter."
Thomas Jefferson, 1799....*

The Spins have set enough precedence for their precedented exaggerations of unprecedented weather events that only attempt to exaggerate already overstated unprecedented climate circumstances. Where hurricanes are concerned and to quit looking any more foolish, put away your nun chuck and quickly review the history of the aftermath of Hurricane Katrina. Only then will your unprecedented precedence of unprecedented hurricanes be true.

Remember the Mann Curve? Millions of dollars went into that study, which gave us the infamous "hockey stick graph." That study was later determined invalid due to collation errors and unjustifiable extrapolation of source data. It was also fraught with obsolete data, geographical location errors, incorrect calculation of principal components and many other quality control defects (Easterbrook 2011) (NCS Import 2015) (O'Sullivan 2018).

The "humans have caused global warming" position is not settled science, as stated repeatedly by our very important Clima-Czar and others, who characterize climate data as "ninety-seven percent" of Scientists agree…blah, blah, blah." This claim is based on the "Cook et al. and Bedford and Cook studies, which are too comprehensive to add to the content of this book. However, a gentleman named Mr. Mark Bahner went through every single one of the 11,944 abstracts that were the heart of the much-quoted Cook extrapolation of data that stated the supposed, "ninety-seven percent of scientists agree." What Mr. Bahner found was unsurprising when he discovered that the data had been grossly misrepresented. Upon close inspection, Mr. Bahner found that 66.4 percent of the abstracts expressed no position, 32.6 percent endorsed, 0.7 percent rejected it, and 0.3 percent were uncertain about the human-caused theory. A far cry from that "ninety-seven percent agree," but by stating it repeatedly, the view appears mainstream, easily discounting dissenters as cranks or shills of the fossil fuel industry. As we have come to understand, this is the Progressive's Modus Operandi (Hendersen 2014) (Ritchie 2016).

Independent thinkers in our society who think, are not buying what they are selling anymore. They can only restate the impending Clima-apocalypse so many times. They have learned, though, that Clima-disasters must be extended at least thirty years. This way, when the deadline is reached, people forget or die, and the next generation can be brainwashed. I can still remember the 1970s when we were supposedly approaching the second ice age. It was quite cold that decade, so there is that. But then it warmed up, e.g. global warming. To stop looking any more foolish, they changed it then to "climate change."

As fair-minded Americans, we accepted that we ought to care for our planet. We put up with the investment of reusable grocery bags while paying extra for our recycle can at the curb. We pick up after ourselves and others. We recycle and compost, but as all Progressive religions always do, they went too far.

Michael Shellenberger wrote an enlightening book "Apocalypse Never." As a lifelong environmental activist and leading energy expert, he recognized that he needed to speak out to separate science from fiction. Mr. Shellenberger co-created the predecessor to today's "Green New Deal." He states climate change is real, but it will not be the end of the world. He further states that climate change isn't even our most serious environmental problem. Carbon emissions have peaked and have been declining for over a decade due to declining population growth and *"abundant natural gas."* As a past environmental activist, he knows who is behind the apocalyptic message. He describes powerful financial interests and the desire for status and power (Shellenberger 2020).

For decades, the Clima-Progressives have been Clima-peddling various impending Clima-apocalypses with their ever-changing fervent Clima-battle cries: (Ebell 2019) (Perry 2019)

- In the 1970s, it was "global cooling" and an impending ice age
- Then came the 1980s and "acid rain"
- Then came the 1990s and the "destruction of the ozone layer"
- Then came the 2000s and "global warming"
- Then came the 2010s and "climate change"
- Now, in the 2020s, it is "net zero by 2030," or 2050. Both are used interchangeably.

Progressive Clima-fear merchants have been diligently honing in the Clima-apocalyptic message. The next Clima-Armageddon is always "just around the corner." Then we get to the intersection and find yet another roundabout, which deposits us to the next intersection in search of the next "Clima-corner." So, in about 2029, another Clima-horrifying message of Clima-doom will begin the 2030 decade. The climate change agenda has little to do with climate and more to do with global financial equalization by seizing Western wealth and dismantling Western economies and energy systems.

The worldwide spending numbers are gargantuan. Eleven years ago, a progressive group called the Climate Policy Initiative (CPI) issued a study that found that "global investment in climate change" reached $359 billion. However, the CPI also stated that the number "falls far short" of what is needed. In 2013, they Clima-guestimated that the number is closer to five trillion. Now that number is fifty trillion. Yet even when asked, lead Biden Administration officials, who have supposedly gathered the best of the best Clima-Prophets who have been studying this for decades, cannot answer one simple question, **"If we spend $50**

Trillion to become carbon-neutral by 2050 in the United States of America, how much will that reduce world temperatures?" There is no answer to that question from the Biden Clima-Peanut Gallery of Clima-experts (Gillespie 2023) (S. Moore 2018) (Climate Policy Initiatives 2013) (TFTC 2024) (Pladson 2021).

By the climateers' own admission, taxpayers across the globe have made zero progress while only funding decades of hysteria and research. According to them, we have not delayed the apocalypse by a single day (Milman 2021) (Simon 2013).

If it weren't about trillions of dollars of pocket-lining wealth to a few, they would admit that the problem is not human-caused. The globe could move on to sensible solutions, helping all humankind function under a continually changing and fluctuating climate. The globe is hungry for any concrete plan for all that money disappearing into the abyss for decades. Where has all that money gone? It is a money-scheming racket that keeps the Clima-Swindlers and their scientists afloat. How many more decades do we need to prove their postulated man-caused Clima-disaster that never comes?

According to all those Clima experts, melting glaciers will flood the earth. How about if all that money could globally fund the mechanics and methods to capture all that extra seawater, desalinate it and provide clean drinking water to everyone on Earth? It could keep global crops alive in our worldwide state of drought. It would be a tangible legitimate climate strategy that we could all see. They tell us that the desalination process is too expensive. So, let's examine the cost of their wind turbine/solar panel net-zero fantasy land, which is postulated to be the only solution to their Clim-impending Clima-Catastrophe (ThoughtCo. 2019) (Moorhead 2022).

The "dirty" little secret about renewable energy isn't all that secret. The sun doesn't shine when it is dark, and the wind does not blow 24/7. Solar intensity fluctuates and can only power enough energy twenty-five percent of the time. Therefore, some form of energy generation storage (batteries) must step in and seamlessly fill the power gap (Budinger 2019).

In 2019, Clima-activists pushed to close Arizona's Palo Verde nuclear power plant, replacing it with solar panels. The plant generates 4000 megawatts per hour. In one year, Palo Verde generates over thirty million megawatt hours, making it the largest generator of electricity in the U.S. It serves the needs of four million people in Arizona yet only provides about thirty-five percent of Arizona's total power needs. Had they closed the plant, twelve million solar panels would have been required.

Since a five-megawatt solar farm requires twenty-two acres, Palo Verde would have required 17,500 acres and still have provided only thirty-five percent of Arizona's power needs. The current plant sits on 4,000 acres (POWER 2015).

The United States already has within its infrastructure one hundred percent renewable power that does not require banks and banks of battery storage. Yet, Progressives are seeking to destroy a renewable energy infrastructure that has been powering the US for decades. The Biden Administration is actively seeking to breach all four of the lower Snake River Dams in the Pacific Northwest to ultimately destroy hydroelectric power. It is a secretive agreement that will forever alter a system of electric power in place since the 1960s. It is the largest source of renewable power in the nation that electrifies the Pacific Northwest into Montana. It would be that system that invented renewable power. Court battles are brewing as the Clima-administration has rejected all discussions by those who live under hydroelectric power in the West. Progressives seek renewables, but only their kind of renewables (Wiens 2024) (Bonneville Power Administration 2010).

Da' VEEPs Beliefs: We must diversify our water policy…by look at ways…to diversify it.

On March 29, 2023, the U.S. Department of Energy released its comprehensive summary. Its goal is for the United States to be electrically generated by forty-five percent solar energy and thirty-seven percent wind energy by 2050 (Solar Energy Technologies Office 2021).

Really frightening are the Energy Department's wind vision maps to reach their goals by 2050. So evidently, it isn't just solar land acquisition. It also includes turbine land acquisition. Their plan is to take out most of the land mass in Montana, Wyoming, Texas, Kansas, Iowa, Missouri, Arkansas, Oklahoma and Illinois for their turbine farms (Department of Energy).

For comparison purposes: According to the California Energy Commission, the total current energy consumption of Los Angeles County in 2022 was 6.8 billion megawatts. Using the government's numbers, that would equal 3.06 billion megawatts of solar energy and 2.5 billion megawatts of wind turbine energy, giving us 8.2 million acres needed for solar and 3.9 million acres for wind. When discussing only solar panels, the amount of acreage needed **for Los Angeles County alone** is equal to the land mass of New Jersey, Connecticut and Rhode Island combined (California Energy Commission 2023) (The Fact File 2022).

According to the government's survey, they are pursuing "opportunities" to acquire the land mass for their solar panel farm delusion. They say their solar fantasy farm will require 0.5 percent of the land surface area. The United States' total land mass is 2.43 billion acres, therefore, according to the government's own numbers, 121 million acres will be required for the mass inundation of solar panels (Kramer 2022) (Geocaris 2022).

Since approximately fifty percent of the land mass is mountains and forests, nearly all the 121 million acres available will be located within the grasslands, farmlands and deserts of the West, Midwest and Southwest. The land mass required is more than Utah, Montana, Wyoming, Arizona and Idaho combined.

The government owns twenty-seven percent of the land mass across the United States. Even deducting the land that the federal government owns, they still need 88 million acres to be acquired somewhere. This is where "Eminent Domain" will come into play (Congressional Research Service 2020).

Definitions: Eminent Domain

According to the Cornell School of Law, it refers to government powers to take private property and convert it into public use. A taking may be the actual seizure of the property. The Fifth Amendment provides that the government must provide "just compensation."

Translation: That is when your one hundred acres of land worth one million dollars will identify as twenty thousand dollars.

In the case of offshore wind turbines, they have yet to master a monopile foundation structure (tube) that can withstand submersion in a highly corrosive environment that seawater brings. A 2021 Ocean Engineering study by the Department of Naval Architecture, Ocean and Marine Engineering, University of Strathclyde, Glasgow, UK, determined, among other things: An airtight compartment in monopole structures is not feasible. Options to rectify the problem, such as protective coatings, are prohibitively costly. The Danish company Orsted, which Progressives counted on to build offshore wind farms, has pulled out. The projects were scrapped because of the expense (Riggs Larsen 2020) (Rodriguez 2018) (Sunday 2021) (New York Times 2023) (Mathis 2024).

As predicted: Progressives instituted their third order of debate conclusions, "Orsted lacks credibility and competence" (Wildstein 2023) (Nilsen 2023).

The amount of required materials is staggering just to build the infrastructure. Wind turbines and solar panels are only the beginning. Millions of backup batteries and transformers, with thousands of miles of transmission lines sprawling across how many millions and millions of acres. Billions of tons of copper, steel, aluminum, nickel, cobalt, lithium, concrete, rare earth and composite plastics will need to be mined and refined. It will mean billions of additional acreages to mine the trillions of tons of ore that will be necessary. Fossil fuel must be expended to operate the enormous mining equipment, then truck the ore and overlying dirt and rock.

According to the University of Queensland and Wildlife Conservation Society, the mining of those materials will affect more than nineteen million square miles, or thirty-five percent of the earth's land surface, excluding Antarctica. In understandable terms, that is equal to 12.2 billion acres. The entirety of the United States is only two billion acres. Dr. Laura Sonter of the University of Queensland: *"The problem is that renewable energy production is material-intensive—much more so than fossil fuels."* Co-author James Watson: *"The impacts of a pathway to a green energy future on biodiversity are not considered in international climate policies, nor are new mining threats seriously addressed in current global discussions"* (International Energy Agency 2021) (WCS Newsroom 2020).

Cobalt is at the heart of the renewable energy transition and the key mineral component of all lithium-ion batteries in technology devices, especially electric vehicles. It is mined in the Democratic Republic of Congo with child laborers. UNICEF estimates 40,000 children are working in DRC mines, where over half the world's supply of Cobalt is mined (Murray 2022) (CBS News 2018) (L. Boyle 2023).

New York City alone will require 2,000 to 4,000 wind turbines (depending on your source), requiring at least 110 tons of copper, which would require mining, crushing, processing and refining twenty-five million tons of copper ore. Even before they can get to the copper ore, they must excavate and remove some forty million tons of overlying rock and dirt (McKinsey & Company 2022) (Sonter 2020) (University of Queensland 2020).

The Progressives "Inflation Reduction Act" Bill signed into law in 2022, calls for one hundred percent of cars manufactured by 2035 to be one hundred percent electric. EVs require five times more copper than petrol or diesel cars. For EVs alone in their magical world of renewables, the world would need to mine 115 percent more copper than has been mined in all human history. Researchers at the University of Michigan have found it cannot be done. The American vehicle fleet alone would require six new large copper mines brought on annually over the next several decades (Weaver 2024).

What if we were to go all in and accomplish exactly what the Progressives want to do? Do they think all it takes is a wave of their magic wand, and all the infrastructure will simply materialize before our very eyes? What would be the consequences?

Such consequences can be envisioned in one example, and it is in Butte, Montana. Now a toxic waste dump of arsenic and other dangerous chemicals, the Berkeley Pit is also loaded with heavy metals. This very deep cesspool of water cannot be removed. As water seeps into the pit continually throughout the year, the water level must be managed so it doesn't overflow. For forty-two years now and counting, contaminated water is continually pumped out and treated to meet water quality standards. Then, it is discharged into Silver Bow Creek. This is the reality of one single copper mining pit in the United States (Pit Watch Ongoing).

Cancer-causing toxic chemicals in solar panels include cadmium telluride, copper indium selenide, Hexafluoroethane, lead and a host of other wonderful cancer-producing composites are now leaking into the soil in Texas and Nebraska, as all that material is beginning to show up in landfills. Decommissioned panels cannot be buried or burned. One of the most toxic chemicals is silicon tetrachloride. If not properly handled, it causes burns and harmful air pollutants. If exposed to water, it releases hydrochloric acid. According to our government, its cadmium compounds can lead to impaired pulmonary function. Exposure to lead needs no further explanation. There are no salvageable materials on a solar panel that are suitable for recycling, with toxic materials that will contaminate groundwater (Kisela 2022) (Wirtz 2019).

All one needs to do is visit the Columbia River Gorge in Western Oregon. That scene is all anyone needs to witness to realize the visual destruction awaiting us all as our scenic vistas disappear. At least I was able to see for myself the striking grandeur of that once magnificent gorge, which had some of the most breathtaking landscapes of the Pacific Northwest. It is now a complete wasteland, littered with wind turbines that completely distract from the beauty that once existed. The Clima-obsessed cared little about the landscape, water or wildlife in a gorge that windsurfers had been enjoying for years. That once beautiful gorge became the sacrificial lamb to the Clima-Greater-Good (Carvalho 2011).

Dead whales are washing up on shore, decimated by wind turbine exploration and drilling. Interestingly, Marine health was one of the primary principles outlined in: *"Report of the United Nations Conference on the Human Environment,* AKA "The Original Climate Conference." *Stockholm, June 5-16, 1972,* (ANNEXES, "Annex III, Page 73" to wit: "GENERAL PRINCIPLES FOR ASSESSMENT AND CONTROL OF MARINE POLLUTION") *which clearly outlines protections and rules for marine life.* But, that was 50 years ago, well before the Clima-Apocalypse was envisioned, to Clima-scare the Clima-bejesus out of everyone so we can re-Clima-prioritize for the Clima-Greater Good, with a lot of Clima-money. That is an interesting document to read. It talks about fanatical things like "freedom" (United Nations 1972).

To save the planet, we must litter the landscape with millions of solar panels and wind turbines that kill wildlife, migratory birds and marine life. We must increase mining by 10,000 percent. Everyone must own a plug-in electric vehicle where one thirty-minute supercharge uses as much electricity as five average homes in an entire day (Electrly) (Benningfield 2024) (M. Brown 2022).

It is the biggest con ever perpetrated on the population. When coal mining and oil drilling are said to be bad, but mining copper, lithium, cobalt and nickel are good, you know that Johnny Hooker and his hustler friends are in cahoots, and you don't need to watch The Sting to know we have all been stung. This decades-long environmental scheme has left the planet as the biggest loser, as we destroy the environment to protect the environment (Ward 1973).

Where are the Sierra Club, the Nature Conservancy, the Natural Resources Defense Council, the Wildlife Conservation Society, Oceana, Conservation International or the National Audubon Society? Greenpeace and all those owl and eco-tree-huggers have disappeared into the Progressive pit of the "Clima-Greater Good."

We are now officially disgusted with the decades of court battles that environmentalists and Progressive politicians have been waging against fossil fuel production nationwide. They obviously never cared about the wildlife in Alaska's ANWR region because this is fifty billion times worse. Studies have found that the number of wind turbines the U.S. seeks to employ will only increase warming temperatures. It clearly was never about the wildlife or the land. It was only about their war against fossil fuels to strengthen their political power. We already know, where one has power, there is money (Burrows 2018) (Miller 2018).

Since our Clima-President's inauguration, his policies to destroy the fossil fuel industry have only resulted in forty-year high inflation. Their easy excuse was their war in Ukraine and the pandemic. Even if that were true, don't you think their energy war came at a particularly bad time? To a Progressive, time is valuable. Nothing will be certain after the 2024 elections. They had complete control of Congress and the presidency, so now was the time, regardless of whom they hurt.

Da VEEPs Beliefs...We have to address the fact that...we gotta deal with the fact that... folks are pay...paying for gas, paying for groceries...and ... are...are...are...need solutions.

Sweden has officially abandoned its renewable energy quest to be net zero by 2045. Sweden, according to Progressives, has it all together to sustain its population. Yet, they are now ahead of the United States and understand the specifics that such delusions entail. We ought to take a lesson as the Swedish Parliament has come to its senses and is building more nuclear reactors for a sustainable, stable energy system. Sweden's energy projection is far more realistic than the United States' renewable pipe dream train chugging us over the cliff (Mallikka 2023).

Intercontinental Rail Travel

Speaking of trains, intercontinental train commuters are eagerly anticipating President Fantasizer's promised 10,000-mile train system from the Western United States across the Pacific Ocean to the Indian Ocean to Africa. Details are forthcoming, but the White House has employed the most insightful Clima-ideologues to build a solar-powered bullet train capable of supersonic speeds that will deliver international Clima- commuters from Seattle to Johannesburg in less than two hours.

It is expected to completely replace polluting air travel with the prototype to be expanded worldwide 150 years from now (Pope 2023) (Wilson 2023).

Very Clima-Exciting partnerships are being formed following President Bonker's announcement. It has been reported that George Jetson and Cosmo Spacely have visited the White House approximately 45 times since the announcement. Hoverboard masterminds have been brought into the loop. President Spendthrift has approved "over a billion three hundred million trillion three hundred million dollars" to build a 10,000-mile track capable of floating one hundred feet above the ocean. It is another Clima-exciting breakthrough for all the Clima-Fanaticists (sitcom 1962) (The Hole in the Zero 1968, Joseph, M.K.) (Fox 1985) (Abbott 2023) (Laurene, Clima-Commuter's Fantastically Fantastic New Age Commuting 2024).

President Fabricator was immediately shuffled back to bed.

If the Clima-fanaticist's renewable utopia reaches their goal, which they won't, what happens when all that material wears out or breaks? Extreme weather events happen regularly. Events that could fracture any of the 121 million acres of solar panels, which it already has. Researchers estimate that the U.S. will have more than 720,000 tons of blade material to dispose of over the next twenty years. There are no options and no plans to recycle or trash turbine blades, photovoltaic glass or spent batteries for turbine and solar generation (Gosselin 2023) (Stella 2019) (Plainview 2024).

Over $7 billion was signed into law by, you guessed it, "The Inflation Reduction Act," to build tens of thousands (the actual number was never specific) of unreliable EV charger stations that take several hours to charge a vehicle. This one single already-funded mission has been a dismal government failure.

Only eight total stations have been successfully completed. Many excuses have been thrown out by our incompetent Transportation Secretary, but reality seems to be a hard thing for the secretary to swallow (Seligman 2018) (Burrows 2018) (Bikales 2023) (Motavalli 2024).

Simply put, the laws of physics and scale prohibitively make their "net zero pipe dream" unachievable. Even if it could be done, it is decades away. Damage to the environment, not to mention the cost of building, maintaining and disposing of it, is unfathomable. Progressives never thought it out. In the meantime, they are destroying the poor and the middle class with rampant inflation and supply shortages. Yearly salaries of $40,000, now identified as $20,000. As Progressives take us further down their yellow brick renewable road, it will further cross-identify as $10,000. This is a safety issue for the entire country. Yet, they are doubling and tripling down to eliminate fossil fuel energy with nothing to replace it (Sabastian 2022).

Per the White House Spokeshuman:

"These issues are top of mind for the President. He is seriously thinking about the seriousness of the issue. He is laser-focused on these issues to solve these issues as expediently as possible."

So, what exactly are they and their Clima-buddies "laser-focused" on?

Flatulent Perils

"The global dangers of bovine flatulence" is what is "on top of mind." Owning cattle is now equivalent to possessing an oil drill in your backyard. Cow masks and diapers are currently being developed, and billionaire software designer, now Clima-farmer Bill Gates, is seeking to eliminate cattle ranches and instead advocating for genetically engineered synthetic meat. Does anyone recall the dangers of GMOs? (McFall 2023) (Banerjee 2021) (Carnahan 2023)

In a 2017 study, as reported by our most competent news outlet, CNN News, our beloved dogs and cats pose a catastrophic threat to our planet. Evidently, feeding our domestic pets meat by-products results in enough intestinal wind to equal 64 million tons of carbon dioxide in the US annually.

Fido and Muffin farts pollute our planet, comparable to 13.6 million cars. Thank God for all those Clima-scientists who performed such a critical study (Richardson 2022) (Okin 2017).

Fortunately, unlike the justifications of destroying the pre-born to meet climate change objectives, the reporting does not suggest the same with our pets, stating: "Pets provide a host of real and perceived benefits to people, including companionship, increased physical activity, improved mental health and social capital." Phew, that's good because it would be quite a dilemma for Karen, a Progressive, environmental, single, childless, fifty-something, academic Clima-feminist and her beloved kitty, Derpy… who identifies as non-binary because "them" is spayed (Proctor 2022) (Bess 2015) (National Institutes of Health 2018) (The Christian Institute 2017) (Stonestreet 2019) (Laurene, The Derpy Dilemma 2024).

Ah ha! According to the WEFs (coming soon), mealworms are the answer! However, one can't just initiate blanket solutions in a vacuum, as the nation's songbirds will now be in jeopardy. Wild songbirds love to eat all kinds of bugs and add an essential protein during the nesting period. Where are the songbird influencers! It all depends on where the songbird lands on the Clima-fanatics spectrum of the Clima-intersectionality Ax-i of importance. Eagles, including our national bird and other raptors, birds and bats, are being vaporized by solar panels (Laurene, Now Recruiting: Songbird Influencers 2024).

Our country's symbol of freedom, the bald eagle, is now a food staple for illegal invaders flooding across our southern border. It seems apropos, as invaders demolishing our sovereignty, are now eating our national bird. There is definitely symbolism there (Jackson 2020) (Hrala 2016) (Scholl 2021) (Fecht 2015) (J. R. Miller 2023) (Dr. Smith 2023) (Colton 2023).

The real question is, who did this study, and what was the carbon capture method? Can't you see all those Clima-scientists somehow attaching balloons to the business end of the study animals? How much money did that study cost U.S. taxpayers, in some government Clima-subsidized Clima-grant, collected during the last Clima-conference in Clima-reparations that was Clima-confiscated?

Any Great Dane owner would have gladly taken the money to have some Clima-white coat spend one evening with them after feeding time. However, the estimated carbon footprint would have increased to five hundred million tons of emitted carbon instead of just sixty-four (Laurene, Dane Flatulent Perils 2024).

Gas Lighter in Chief

Speaking of gas, our "laser-focused "gas lighter-in-chief, The Clima-President of the United States and ever-vigilant Clima-crusader, launched a public relations trial balloon, stating, "He is contemplating/endorsing banning gas cookstoves." Really and truly, doesn't he have more important things to concentrate on? (Bernstein 2023)

The Clima-White House further announced the 2023 re-cycled version of the 2009 "Cash for Clunkers" program. The new program, now named "Currency for Currents," is part of Congress' 2022 Inflation Reduction Act. Every home can now receive an exciting rebate to remove your "current" gas appliance and replace it with an electric appliance, to save the planet, of course. However, two years later, the Clima-rebates are still not available (Murphy 2009) (Veuger 2014) (Hope 2022) (Energy.gov 2024) (Maruf 2023) (Deppisch 2023).

A wave of backlash occurred, described by The Spins as a "right-wing conservative culture war with no merit." The Clima-President furiously back-peddled, stating, "he had never stated that any gas stove ban was in the works." Later, it was discovered that Da VEEP has her own gas cooking appliance. Warm progressive holiday photographs can be quite revealing when you fail to notice what is in the background of your social media shared photo. Her nun chuck was beside her gas stove on the kitchen counter (Phillips 2023) (Hope 2022) (Vasquez 2023).

Meanwhile, New York and California have changed all building codes to eliminate all gas appliances, including furnaces, for all new buildings in their states. Where Covid POPPERS climate change and their all too familiar "rules for thee but not for me," it was discovered that, like Da' VEEP, the Governor of New York also has a gas stove (Williams 2023).

Make no mistake, the Big Guy's haphazard-appearing policy initiatives have a goal. They are moving in on our gas appliances, which is the first step to converting all our energy to electricity, powered by renewables. Removing gas appliances is a low-hanging fruit to them, as are leaf blowers and lawnmowers. They are starting small and moving up, with tasks assigned to the Big Guy's various progressive gnomes, who are the real maestros behind the scenes of his transformational far-left Progressive agenda. This time, his lead conductor is the energy secretary who was chosen for her job because of her innate ability to speak out of both ends, **"That is so ridiculous, that story. Because it sounds like the government's coming to take your stuff, that is so not true. That is not true."** In perfect concert, she then whips out her baton proposing a new regulation governing home energy consumption, which seeks to diminish the use of, you guessed it, gas stoves in the home. Nothing is as it seems in a progressively led government that continually lies to the American citizens at every juncture to forward their ideology (Blackmon 2023) (Lyman 2021).

So, what does a government need to do when removing gas appliances has become cumbersome and slow? Well, you remove the source. Ahead of the 2023 Labor Day weekend, The Pipeline and Hazardous Materials Safety Administration (PHMSA), AKA another progressive gnome, has eliminated the transport of liquid natural gas via rail. Environmentalists hail the decision as a victory. Well, look at that, they finally showed up. (Pipeline and Hazardous Materials Safety Administration 2023).

Meanwhile, an exploratory study is in progress, led by the White House's **D**epartment **O**f **P**artisans for **E**nvironmental **S**chemes **(DOPES)**, in a program called "Bucks for Bossy." The goal is to virtually eliminate all cow gas (farts and burps, AKA Methane) in the United States. A feasibility study is underway to convince ranchers nationwide to pursue wind and solar farms instead of raising the world's food. It was also noted that they could learn to code. (Laurene, DOPES created "Bucks for Bossy" 2024).

Definitions: Coding

The process of assigning a code to something for classification or identification. It is used to communicate with computers to tell them what to do. Computer coding is used in many applications, such as web development, mobile app development, video game development and medical code billing.

Coding is the Clima-activist's go-to preferred Clima-occupation that produces little to no Clima-disruption. Clima-Coding is the newest and greatest Clima-vocation as the government seeks its own system of Clima-accountability (Kelley 2019).

The CONNIVED System

Announcing! The President's newly formed "**C**ommittee to **O**ptimize **N**on-conformative **N**arratives that are **I**ncompatible and not **V**erifiable, for **E**nvironmental **D**ictates," or the **(CONNIVED)** committee.

In review: Progressive scorekeeping to validate desired Progressive determinations to demonstrate demonstrable deference to Progressive directives.

The CONNIVED committee has directed the Food and Drug Administration to develop the CONNIVED enviro-food labeling system. The label will easily identify the **P**ootus **P**arameter **M**alodorous **s**cale (PPMs) or carbon emissions emitted on each ingested food product and is a part of the government's Clima-accountability directives (Laurene, Enviro-CONNIVED Labeling System 2024) (Laurene, Proper Pootus Parameters 2024).

The U.S. Clima-President's Clima-accountability CONNIVED system has partnered with all banking institutions to track every citizen's grocery and restaurant purchases via their chosen payment card. Once the federal banking system is formed, tracking purchases will be much easier. The CONNIVED system is already forming partnerships with utility companies nationwide to be ready to track energy usage once the banking system is under federal control (Abbruzzese 2022).

By law, one cannot emit over 50,000 PPMs per year of ingested food. If one were to exceed the limit, they will be held directly responsible for the total destruction of the planet. They will be Clima-taxed accordingly because nothing saves the planet more than more money (Laurene, CONNIVED Emmission Standards 2024).

lettuce = 5 PPMs emitted carbon
tomato = 5 PPMs
pickles = 15 PPMs
2 oz slice of cheese = 500 PPMs
soy patty = 50 PPMs
2 slices of Bacon = 1050 PPMs

A beef hamburger with the works = 4815 PPMs of emitted carbon. A delectably juicy one and one half inch, fifteen-ounce Porterhouse steak = 20,000 PPMs

The Clima-President has directed the Clima-accountability office to prepare for Clima-fuel Clima-culpability, whereby all fossil fuel stations will be Clima-retrofitted with a Clima-card slot to measure each person Clima-fossil fuel consumption to be added to their CONNIVED total.

My pronouns are 500,000 PPMs.

Operation "Big Truck"

VEEP Thoughts: "This issue of transportation is fundamentally about just making sure that people have the ability to get where they need to go."

Hmm, we gotta go to where we must go by going there. We are curious, though, where is it that y'all are taking us?

Clima-drivers have a new target now pickup trucks. It seems that my diesel pickup truck is much too big, far too scary and makes too much noise. They are bad for the planet and are responsible for killing more children than any other vehicle on the road. They also "disproportionately affect communities of color."

Lather, Rinse, Repeat…

Additionally, they do unprecedented damage to the roads, and "most people that use them serve no practical purposes." Operation Big Truck further states, "Trucks are merely a status symbol, where vain owners cite their trucks with ruggedness and power." Furthermore, "most of them don't have a trailer hitch anyway!" (Devore 2023)

My pronoun is insurrectionist big truck owner

All one needs to do is wait. Wait for the inevitable qualifying statement that exposes the true goal. *"Big Trucks are not the only problem, SUVs are just as guilty."* There it is! It is not about trucks or diesel. It is about big gas-run vehicles. I guess they are tired of looking up at us from their itty-bitty "Pre-i." It is hard to feel superior when driving a foot off the ground.

A call to action has been announced. We must shift to a weight-based vehicle taxing system to discourage people from driving vehicles that are too big and too dangerous for our streets. Yep, there's the secondary goal, a government-directed entanglement approach to punish those people who drive all those great big vehicles they dislike by taxing them into submission. However, this administration's minions are setting their sights a lot higher than that of trucks or SUVs. This is merely a distraction to introduce:

Transportation equity! Per our illustrious Transportation Secretary Pete Buttigieg, and his barely distinguishably distinguished advisory committee from the most pretentious and distinguished academic backgrounds:

"All cars are bad!" and perpetuate, wait for it… "<u>SYSTEMIC WHITE SUPREMACY!</u>"

> "We need a comprehensive approach to 'reimagine streets' to prioritize equitable, all-inclusive, environmentally sustainable, economically beneficial and diverse transportation modes to repair and heal divided communities and address the damage done by cars" (Hilu 2023).

What in holy blazes are they even talking about? This is what pompous, Progressive, chronically discontented academic elitists perseverate about. Airplanes are falling apart in mid-flight and trains are derailing. It is, therefore, hard for the rest of us to comprehend what the Secretary's imaginary street might look like. I guess we may be returning to the horse and buggy era. It certainly would be safer than their tiny cars, disintegrating airplanes and substandard rail infrastructure. There is always "coding," but the government could also re-train all those in the auto industry to that of "**P**atrollers **O**f **O**diferous **P**iles, or **POOPs**. New business formations could be formed in the environmental recycling of horse chips. All-inclusive food products could be examined. Current transportation engineers could be re-trained in the design and production of another sustainably grown, organic, artisanal,

530 | JO ANNA LAURENE

unrefined, additive-free food source. That would make the Clima-WEFs very happy as an alternative to mealworms. (Yes, I will get to that). There is one problem. Horse hockey's are not gluten-free, and their PPMs are relatively high secondary to horse methane, which my horse Sar has a gracious plenty of. I am sure that the Secretary and his barely distinguishable, highly prestigious, renowned, foremost academics from the most celebrated anti-Semitic institutions of academia are thinking through all this phony horsey boloney as we speak. They are preparing to take their idea to the foremost clima-global experts now convening in Egypt (Laurene, Sar's Patrollers 2024).

VIP Climate Conference

Sharm El Sheikh, Egypt, was the location of the 2022 United Nations Climate Change Conference. Nothing says climate crisis more than six hundred very important Clima-Luminaries and Heads of state, arriving in four hundred Clima-private jets, representing two hundred Clima-countries, AKA The Clima-rulers of the Universe to attend the 27th consecutive year to discuss our critical global climate crisis.

At a ratio of one Clima-jet per 1.5 Clima-rulers, they Clima-strategized the fate of the global population, which at last count was around eight billion people. A number they would prefer to identify as one billion (Vidal 2012).

The highest levels of Clima-speakers were all there, including a young lady with no scientific credentials. Her specialization is caterwauling at global Clima-leaders while Clima-squinting at them angrily for not following her Clima-commands. Her usefulness is measured by how much money she can Clima-requisition from wealthy Western countries (Rosenblatt 2019).

The 2022 theme, "Together4Transparency" aims to unite all the Clima-stakeholders involved in supporting the transition toward an Enhanced Clima-Transparent Framework that emphasizes Clima-transparency as the vehicle for the Clima-framework. It is the "Clima-backbone for better Clima-transparency, in an enhanced Clima-transparent structure.

This will help countries determine their Nationally Determined Contributions (NDCs), AKA Clima-money, for their bottomless Clima-checkbook. The Clima-conference concluded with an agreement for billions more dollars of Clima-reparations to finance their totally Clima-transparent goals globally. Completely exempt of course, is China, the most prolific global polluter. Brilliant on China's part, who can see right through the Clima-con.

Definitions: Reparations

Money is re-distributed from some people who are identified as oppressors to other people who are identified as oppressed. Identities are undefined but can be used in a multitude of circumstances (always political) to coerce the targeted oppressors to pony up more and more money to the oppressed for past oppressions in the Stone Age, or future oppressions as seen through the Progressive's crystal ball.

To fully understand reparations to the oppressed by the unoppressed, beginning May 1, 2023, special Presidential reparations have been awarded to all new mortgagees with poor credit histories. Where economic justice POPPERS home ownership, mortgage reparations now require those with higher scores to pay higher fees to cover the risk that lower scorers no longer must pay. To better understand mortgage reparations, I will use the all-Inclusivists, all-inclusive language (Jacques 2023).

> **"Where there is so much racket, there must be something out of kilter."**
> *Sojourner Truth…*

- Those with credit scores over 700 will now identify as scores under 500.
- Those with credit scores under 500 will now identify as scores over 700.

A little-known Clima-transparent topic was introduced during this conference, which discussed the **dangers** of "climate change adaption."

Climate Change Adaption

Countries and communities across the globe are discovering new opportunities that climate change has presented. Such a dilemma for those activists whose ideological priorities prefer mitigation rather than acclimation, of which mitigative strategies must only include those ideas that are theirs (United Nations Climate Change 2022) (Moor 2024).

We all need to ignore those pesky Greenlanders enjoying a warmer climate with new opportunities for industry and tourism. Greenland is no longer buried in ice, but half of all Danes are not convinced that it is consequential. Melting ice has benefits for navigation and agriculture. The northwest passage is more navigable, benefitting the country's economy and infrastructure. When you no longer live on a glacier, you enjoy green grass, water, and crops and can raise livestock. They are seeking greater access to gas and oil. Gasp! New successes in the fishing industry are occurring.

Question: Does anybody else wonder why this continent is called Greenland?

People in the coldest region on earth are adapting, which was not part of the climate disaster script. Danes are imagining new climate opportunities where none existed before. Danes are more aware of what is happening with the climate than anyone else on the globe, yet they are less inclined to break their banks and livelihoods in a delusional attempt to change it.

In 2022, following an ice melt, environmental DNA was discovered in Northern Greenland. The fragments of a Siberian Mammoth bone were discovered, one million years older than previously recorded DNA samples. The ancient DNA was able to map a two-million-year-old ecosystem that weathered extreme climate change. The results could help predict the long-term environmental impacts of today's naturally occurring climate change phenomena (Kjaer 2022).

DNA has allowed scientists to go back further in time than anyone could have imagined. From sediment, they have determined that in Greenland at the time, temperatures were between ten to seventeen degrees Celsius warmer than Greenland is today. Reindeer, hares, and lemmings were alive and well, as well as birch and poplar trees. Researchers even found a Mastodon roamed as far as Greenland before later becoming extinct. Such inconvenient findings! Who invented DNA anyway?

DNA has proven Greenland and the globe were much warmer than today. It proved that species evolve and adapt to wildly varying temperatures. It proved once again that global climate changes have been unaffected by human activity and have evolved over many millennia. Scientific facts are difficult to challenge but never underestimate the Clima-fanatics who have been using climate as the basis for power, global control and money.

On To Davos

Once the Clima-billions were adequately secured, the Clima-conference ended. Then they all loaded up again on their four hundred Clima-jets and headed to Davos, Switzerland, for the "World Economic Forum" (WEF), which is a ruse. It has little to do with global economies and more to do with obtaining global control using climate change as its vehicle.

Billionaire Clima-WEF's have now concluded that rice is now a dangerous Clima-destroying commodity, responsible for twelve percent of global methane gas emissions. Growing rice is where the WEFs are heading next, seeking to destroy mass agriculture. In another exploding electrifying nano-particle collision, they bolted from climate, destroying the world's food source, to the world's food source, destroying the world. Since rice feeds three billion people worldwide and is the food staple for the global poor, this is perhaps what they really seek to Clima-destroy, human carbon (S. Fleming 2019) (Cho 2018) (Schonhardt 2021).

The WEFs have introduced their plan to use mealworms as food in their bid to reduce meat consumption. Eating bugs, weeds and synthetic meat consumes fewer resources than livestock. The globally superior European Union (Clima-EU's) has ruled that the larval stage of the "Tenebrio Monitor Beetle," AKA, the Mealworm can be eaten whole or in powder form. It is good news for all those who proudly proclaim, "they won't eat anything with eyelashes." Mealworms check all those important boxes as an eco-friendly, humane, artisanal, sustainably grown, handcrafted, free-range, dairy and gluten-free "clima-novel food" (European Union Times 2022) (White 2022).

The discovery is so groundbreaking that Clima-WEFs state

that adding mealworms and other bugs to children's lunches is part of a conditioning campaign to normalize bug eating to save the planet. Shortly after that, US Public Broadcasting (Clima-PUBs) joined the Clima-WEFs, urging Americans to eat "tasty" insects and bugs to help battle global warming, er…climate change. I really fear for the songbird now, at least we may have some selection. One cannot live on horse apples our entire lives.

Question: Are we to believe that Clima-billionaires will be eating mealworms as well?

Important Clima-Note: The total ingested ppm for the mealworm is zero.

The U.S. Clima-President has chosen for his Clima-envoy, Climaczar John Kerry. His job is too Clima-requisition, as much Clima-money he can get his Clima-sleazy hands on. While in Davos, he was sited holding his tin cup in his Clima-grubby hand, making his most Clima-ballsy speech ever, stating: "More money, money, money, money, money, money, money, money, money, money, money, money, money is needed" (Reuters 2023).

Billionaire power-hungry elites across the globe are moving full steam ahead with mind-popping expensive infrastructure, bereft of legitimate ecological realities that WILL destroy the environment. We are decades away (if ever) from building or managing all the Clima-pipedreams they are forcing upon us. Global Progressive politicians throw around billions of dollars as if it is pocket change. Nobody believes money, laws, carbon-neutral money schemes and policies will lower temperatures or create fewer hurricanes.

Finally, using several Progressive POPPERS parallels, we will explore where feminism POPPERS climate, furthering POPPER'ing trans-activism and the new academic construct of the ecoviro femme vs. the neo-ed, the non-binaries and the oppositional dualism of "ecofeminism." In this new academic discipline, feminists who are desperate to stay

CONQUERING THE BONGOS | 537

relevant describe their framework as "each from each other as different but similar in hierarchies exhibited in gender relations through patriarchal social structures within humanity's relationship with nature and humans."

Nope, as ridiculous as that sounds, I did not make that up. Now that feminism has been binarily erased, I guess it is how Femme's parallel now with climate doctrine (Bova 2021).

Cult Religiosity Overview

CNN Reporter: "What do you say to families who cannot afford 5.00/gallon gasoline now?"

Senior spokesman to the President: "This is about the future of the "Liberal World Order," and we need to stand firm" (Karonga 2022).

Definitions: Liberal World Order

A system of cooperation throughout the globe whereby the benefits, inconveniences, shortcomings and encumbrances are all shared equally, with shared values, strategies, and, of course, money. **Also known as… S O C I A L I S M.**

Cult theory has evolved and is no longer limited to small groups, as witnessed in Jonesboro and the Branch Davidian. It is a society-wide attempt to force ideals through that would normally be rejected. Where Covid POPPERS climate, it went global. Where a pandemic failed (for now), climate dogma is continuing down their pathway, as well as transactivism. However, our eyes

> "The battle for this country isn't right or left,
> It is normal vs. crazy."
> Bill Maher January 2023….

are wide open now, as more and more people are beginning to see it for what it is, a ploy that can assert more power over its citizenry to accomplish that "Liberal World Order" they seek. It is evil. Regular normals are smarter than that.

Globalists are painfully discovering we are not the Jonesboro Kool-Aid drinkers they thought we were. We are no longer the silent majority as we have become more civically involved across the country. Many have stopped sitting on their thumbs and are ready to put them on our side of the scale of injustices that have outweighed us for far too long.

Another Civics Review: In our global world, there is only one country with a unique Constitution that protects the freedoms of its people and that is the United States. It is a country comprised of separate states, all with separate laws. It is a decentralized structure that places power in the hands of the people. It is what socialists seek to destroy to centralize power at the federal level and, therefore, all our lives. This is the goal of the Liberal World Order, socialism and shared governance whereby we all live by and for "The Greater Good."

The ultimate goal was actually stated out loud. Those in power of the climate religion seek the destruction of cheap fossil fuels. It includes mass illegal immigration, violent activist causes, CRT doctrine, ANTIFA and Pro-Palestinian occupations. It is about upending police protections and releasing violent criminals through cashless bail. Increases in violence and theft are the direct result of de-criminalizing drugs. Lastly, they have been successful in hopelessly dividing us. A divided country is incapable of logically compromising.

To Progressives, it does not matter that families can't afford gas, groceries, medications or housing, or that neighborhoods and communities have uncontrolled violence, or that drugs are killing more people now than ever in our history. It is all about accomplishing that "liberal world order" of complete control and is rooted in division. Societal damages to them are merely the casualties of their power war, where the end justifies the means. Modern weapons of their division war: Diversity, Equity and Inclusion (DEI), Environmental Social and Governance (ESG) and Critical Race Theory (CRT).

The Goals of the Division Industry

It began with the Obama presidency. There was a great deal of "hope" in the idea of the first black man leading the United States of America. After winning the presidency in 2008, seven in ten Americans believed race relations would improve because of his victory. He had a presence larger than life. He was an eloquent speaker who could have made history, following in the footsteps of President Abraham Lincoln. He was on the world stage as the leader of the free world that could have finally closed that racial curtain of disparities for good in this country and across the globe. Instead, he did the exact opposite, bringing race as the central component in his administration that would become the capstone of the division industry. He and his fellow Progressives were successful in "rubbing racial sores raw," setting race relations back decades. There is no end in sight now, as trans-activism has now joined the race, gender, climate, religious and economic wars (Agiesta 2016) (Investor's Business Daily 2016).

We thought we had escaped seventeenth-century socialist control, but it is returning if we don't act now to change it. Democracy has a life expectancy of around two hundred years.

Every voting cycle, Progressives promise lucrative "fairness" payouts, so people vote for them. Voters continually vote for politicians who promise them free stuff without the need to work for it. Such payouts never equal what their voters expect. Yet, those teaser payouts keep them in office, resulting in record-breaking debt, and crippling inflation that seek to collapse a nation. If it can happen in Rome, it can happen here (Waxman 2019).

> "Democracies only exist until voters discover that they can vote themselves largess from the public treasury."
> *Alexander Tytler, 1747-1813…*

Vote Progressive or democracy is lost: Lately, we have heard a great deal about "protecting democracy." Progressives use this potent phrase to supplant fear in the citizenry. Its goal is to decouple the rest of us from our states for federally centralized power, AKA a fascist state. It is a carefully orchestrated plan (Olander 2022).

More Cultural Bull

As a Westerner who raises their own beef, we have a term that describes the job of one particular bull in the herd. His job is to accomplish the calving success of the entire cow herd. His job is to "settle" any cow that wasn't in the previous go-round. It is his job to ensure the completion of the goal. He is known as "The Cleanup Bull."

So, while we are on the subject of bullsh%!, what, therefore, is the "Cleanup Phrase" Progressive doctrine employs when their ESG, DEI, POPPERS, GULAGS, intersections, roundabouts, their PTSD handbook, their debate conclusions, Transplaining and their PRIORITISE list of prioritized humans fail to convince? Their "Cleanup Phrase" is like parents who can no longer explain the never-ending infinite "but why'" a toddler asks with each passing explanation. It is the last level deployed that is equal to that parent's statement: **"BECAUSE I SAID SO."**

It is the last gown after multiple wardrobe changes to the ultimate upscale design. It is the final rendering of an artist's portrait after many practice sketches. To Progressives, it is the definitive catchphrase that provides legitimacy to an otherwise fabricated invention. It is instrumental in shutting down the discussion of all the Progressive prophetic absolutes in Progressive land. What is it?

"The Greater Good Cleanup Phrase"

It especially appeals to progressive groups or individuals who use it when all other methods fail to "settle" their messaging. Once initiated, it is your undeniable sign that their contradictions begin to outweigh normal logic and understanding. It is the ultimate method employed to divide and conquer a nation to achieve that Liberal World Order. Their goal… Socialism.

Important Note: "The Greater Good Cleanup Phrase" has been added to the post-2009 Debate Conclusions and will be added after "Integrity Conclusions."

DaVEEPs Beliefs: "I think of you in the context of the most recent — now, I guess, it's been a couple of months — report from the United Nations about the significance of this very moment. As you did, I read that, and I — one of the things that really was very obvious about how they articulated the issue and the seriousness of it — the imminence of it and the danger of it — was that they were unambiguous."

After extensive research by the world's best linguists, phoneticians and dialecticians, it has finally been determined that she speaks in non-binary cipher codes taken from their GULAG of multilinguistic polyglots, only understood by the Kryptonians of DC (Wikipedia) (Laurene, Linguistical Ciphers of Coded Bull Hooey, 2024).

For four years we watched President Senility of the United States of America exhibit the obvious classical symptoms of advancing dementia. The Progressive party knew it all along, and they used the pandemic to keep him in his basement and the truth from being exposed to the voting public. While President, they used dementia-improving pharmaceutical cocktails to make him appear capable for as long as they could. He eventually became merely a figurehead that they could easily manipulate to produce their desired results and whom they would periodically parade around to show proof of life.

It was clear to anybody who had a brain that he lacked the mental faculties to drive a vehicle, let alone a country. Only with the debate in 2024, was the con finally exposed for what it was. What is debatable is who has been actually running the country and for how long, because he hasn't been capable for a very long time. You know how bad it is when his state-run media is lamenting that his handlers should better control his infirmities, so he is more presentable (Kornick 2023).

Following that disastrous debate, the power elites of the Progressive party jettisoned his campaign and him into the proverbial trash heap.

It is sad, pitiful and a tragedy. No matter what side of the political aisle you reside in, this was no way to honor an elder statesman in his twilight years (Post Editorial Board 2022).

This latest escapade is further proof of their desire for complete control, and their "Liberal World Order." It is blatant hypocrisy where they themselves subverted the democratic process. If anyone ever accuses you again of destroying democracy, all you need to say is two words, "Joe Biden" (Rigby 2023).

Ripping a page out of their previous playbook, they are hiding Da' VEEP in the basement. Where Biden lacked the mental faculties to effectively campaign, she is just plain stupid. Whenever she opens her mouth, she tests the limits of every Looney Toon cartoon ever produced and party elites know it. Even after a month of being implanted as their nominee, she has refused to give interviews or utter one policy statement. With only two months left before the election, it would seem important for voters to know who it is they are voting for.

Instead, Progressives have been busily studying Memeplexes and the Mimesis of our times. Because their newly minted nominee for President cannot effectively articulate anything comprehensible, they have developed a bright new campaign strategy to appeal to the tech-savvy, low-information, culturally fashionable voter.

To this end, the campaign hired a "Meme-Diversity Manager" in their newly formed "Memetic Unit." The Meme Master will make 85,000.00 a year and, of course, be up to date on their COVID-19 vaccine. Before being selected, all applicants were requested to fill out a diversity meme survey to reveal just how diversely meme-diverse they are.

Important Progressive Meme-Change: Meme Master has been re-evaluated by their Ordered Language committee (a sub-committee of the social construct committee) and thus has been re-branded to that of Meme Chief because Master has been identified in their Intersectionality Prioritized GULAG as misogynistic and is also a blatant example of "*Systemic White Supremacy!*" However, they are still consulting with Native Americans to determine if this change is misappropriated and guilty of "Cultural Appropriations" (Laurene, Culturally Meme-centered Appropriations that are Most Appropriate 2024).

Definitions: Meme

Coined by biologist Richard Dawkins in 1976. They are replicators that are tunes, films, cartoons and catchphrases whose properties influence the chance they will be copied and passed on.

Memeplexes - The study of memes as units of cultural information

Memetic Unit - The propagation of mutating cultural units based on Darwinian Principles that form the subject of memetics.

Mimesis - Plato and Aristotle described it as reflective of the dramas of the period.

There you have it! I'll bet you thought that Meme was just a made-up word! It is loaded with memeaning that has become an essential tool in Da' VEEPs presidential campaign toolbox because actually having her speak is fraught with hazards. It perfectly illustrates this meme-inspiring campaign, which is a meme in and of itself (Biden/Harris Campaign 2024) (Daily Caller 2024) (Niemeyer 2024) (Reinstein 2024).

What are the consequences to a political party when party ghost leaders pre-select nominees ahead of elections? When running mates, cabinet members, secretaries and czars are chosen based only on ideologic and intersectionality principles? The franchise becomes morally bankrupt, and the original players are discarded for "not being liberal enough." The Progressive League has taken a maximalist position on race, abortion, gender, climate and sexuality, which the rest of us are being forced to accept. Positions that even many democrats can't wrap their heads around.

Democrats have been shoved out of their own batter's box. They don't own their league anymore, Progressives do. Over the years, Progressives pitched a slow curve ball far to the left where Democrats are no longer on the team. Democrats are now from a bush league, cast aside in the opposite field as "not left enough."

As a result, the Progressive League has no pool of approved players, and their bench is empty. The last sweet spot was their no-hitter star player, Obama, who delivered several home runs with bases loaded. For eight glorious years, he pitched a perfect Progressive game. He is credited as their iconic **R**enowned **B**olshevik **I**nfluencer (RBI).

Definitions: Bolshevik

A revolutionary socialist associated with the formation of one centralized, cohesive and disciplined party of social revolutionaries focused on overthrowing the existing capitalist system, seizing power and establishing a Leninist-type political structure.

Unfortunately, they committed many errors in later seasons, where Obama's successor never could comprehend the strategy. Now it is the bottom of the ninth, in the final game of the 2024 season. Conservatives are in a scoring position. Las Vegas betters are predicting a shutout. The only strategy left for the Progressive team is their last-minute pitch hitter or cheating their way to victory.

My Pronoun is a "Lying Dog-Faced Pony Soldier!" (Lapin 2020)

In retrospect, all those mean tweets were not bad compared to what we have now. Character flaws were a minuscule problem compared to the Progressive government of today. The Big Guy's bench, who are really playing the game, adopted a maximalist position on race, abortion, gender, climate and sexuality. It is time to change the direction of the game, or the World Series will never play out the same (Arnold 2024).

Immigration policy has been an unmitigated disaster of historic proportions. The disastrous withdrawal from Afghanistan was the defining moment that ushered in global instability. The aftermath of Hamas's terrorist attack on Israel only exposed the true Progressive identity of racism. The Division Industry has been successful in fraying the civic fabric in America with increases in crime and violence. Their war on fossil fuels dumped our economy. Barring extreme deflationary pressures often seen during a severe recession or depression, inflationary prices are now here to stay. The shrinkflation we see in all products will never be reversed. With that said, because of this administration and his party, American families are trapped. There are no good paths to an economic recovery, especially if they remain in power. If that happens, democracy and our republic really are over (Gollom 2021) (Bakst 2017) (Grande 2022) (Kotkin 2021).

Definitions: Shrinkflation

Where manufactured products come in smaller packages, price inflation isn't as noticeable—except with toothpaste, where standard packaging is filled with as much air as toothpaste.

Like a cheating spouse who accuses the other of infidelity, lying and deceit, it is generally the accuser who is the liar, the likes of which we see daily by Progressives and their Spin Masters on every newscast. Satire and truth have become difficult to differentiate, but neither is funny now that we live amid it. Thanks to the Progressive Party, the 2020 decade will go down as the most "trans-formative" time in our country's history in more ways than one. It is something Progressives are very proud of, and they should be. They have made great strides toward their "Liberal World Order."

So what better way to kick off the decade's "trans-formation" than the pride-personified celebration on the White House lawn? The toga party to launch "Pride Month" included a "Full Monty" double-breasted transactivist exhibition of "thems" naked breasts to "Free the Nipple!" It was broadcast in full cinematic televised display for "The Joy of It!" That wasn't enough, so a Progressive staffer broke the back and a table in his poorly edited gay porn flick while a gender expansioner expanded his wardrobe (Pollina 2023) (Robert Carlyle 1997 British Comedy) (Hagstrom 2023).

Meanwhile, alien invaders are settling in nicely amongst millions of others, into every crack, crevice and stoop that can be found, whether there are vacancies or not. During inclement weather, some schools returned to inadequate COVID-inspired distance learning to make room for the invaders to camp out in schools. Neighborhood community centers are now migrant camps. Millions of dollars have been reallocated from the country's homeless citizens and our veterans to house and feed the invaders. Alien invaders are accommodated in luxury hotels courtesy of the US taxpayer while our own homeless are left to fend for themselves. (Frudd 2024) (D. Clark 2024) (Goldstein 2023) (Truitt 2024).

Using the Christmas holiday, the First Lady could not help herself as she unveiled her DEI, ESG all-inclusive Christmas rendition of the Nutcracker Ballet, which was not a ballet, had no nutcrackers and no mice. There seemed to be plenty of fairies, but not of the sugar plum variety. A quick peek into the dance troupe's site calls for urgent action on guns, racism, white privilege, defunding police and gender violence (McBride 2023).

Meanwhile, marijuana and an eight-ball of cocaine have been discovered at the White House, er... "Animal House." The Delta's, er...Secret Service and FBI, with the utmost investigation prowess,

> *"My advice to you is to start drinking heavily."*
> *John Belushi....*

have been dispatched to investigate. They have uncovered more than one "Clue" as to who the doper was who lost track of their Mary Jane and Snow in the most heavily surveilled frat house in the world. President Mental Enfeeblement's ultra-sophisticated domestic intelligence arsenal of investigators has extensively studied the video footage and fingerprints left on the baggie of "blow" and have closed their investigation, concluding that the culprit is Colonel Mustard in the library with the candlestick (Christenson 2023) (Keene 2023) (O'Donnell 2023) (Bowers Bahney 2023) (John Belushi 1978 Comedy) (Popovici 2018) (Laurene, A Delta of a Show Where There are no Clues for the Clueless 2024).

Seeking Strategies

We all know we deserve something infinitely better than eating fake meat or bugs. We shouldn't have to live with electrical blackouts, toxic battery dumps, dead whales, virtual realities, over-run borders, child predators and fortified elections. We are tired of all the hostilities, empty grocery shelves, drugs pouring across our southern border, locked up baby formula, forced school closures, collapsing police forces, toxic jabs and masked kindergarteners. We are done with activist educators who breast-bind our daughters. We are sick of corrupt newscasters, chaotic airports, ignored toxic chemical spills, medication shortages and anarchist rioting. We are fed up with criminal releasing Soros elected district attorneys, Chinese surveillance balloons, and the treasure spent and blood spilled to police the world. We are disgusted with gay porn flicks within our national halls of Congress. We are finished with the indoctrination of our children, where all they know about George Washington is that he owned slaves (Palumbo 2023) (Wendling 2023) (McCausland 2023) (Seligman 2023) (Herb 2023).

It equally applies to all the sacrifices we must endure in the name of climate-saving pipe dreams that will supposedly save the world. It means to draw a red line where abortion is never acceptable. We all want a future where our children are safe at school and not sexualized, politicized or radicalized. A place where we decide that sexual content and expression is not an acceptable form of self-expression in front of children. All of us deserve to be seen as equals, especially our children.

Remember that seven-year-old from Orange County California? A district court Judge has determined that if you are a first grader, you do not have First Amendment rights. Ignoring court precedent in a 1969 ruling (Tinker v. Des Moines Independent Community School District), a Progressive California judge has stated that elementary schools are a totalitarian environment where teachers have a right to punish children for drawing a picture depicting racial tolerance and respect. This is what Progressive politics have done to our country and our people (NTB Staff 2024).

We are done with Progressives. Regular normal Democrats must assume control of their party again because Progressives and their loyals are incapable of applying principled arguments against their political foes. Instead, they execute hyperbolic declarations to destroy the character of their political "enemies." Nobody except Progressives has created a political environment where those dangling on the reality shoestring can be easily manipulated and radicalized to the point of violent actions. If it is any political party seeking to incite those people to do their will, it is Progressives, and that is exactly what happened on July 13, 2024, when a gunman nearly assassinated former President Donald Trump at a campaign rally in Pennsylvania (Karayanis 2024).

> **We're done talking about the debate; it's time to put Trump in a bullseye."**
> *President Joe Biden, July 8, 2024....*

This was not the first time. It occurred on a baseball field in Alexandria, VA on June 17, 2017, when the Republican Congressional baseball team became the victims of a turkey shoot while on the practice field. Six were shot, and Representative Steve Scalice nearly lost his life that day from a crazed socialist gunman, distraught by Trump's presidential victory. The intent was clear. To shoot and kill every single Republican Congressman on that field (Calfas 2017).

Further deliberation of the Brent Kavanaugh assassination attempt needs no further discussion (Fung 2022).

> *"You will pay the price; you won't know what hit you."*
> *Democrat Senator Chuck Schumer...*

This is the same party that applauded antisemitic protests at the nation's campuses. They did nothing during the George Floyd, Antifa and BLM protests that caused billions and billions of damages to our cities. Instead, they go after pro-life advocates and parents who oppose trans-grooming. It isn't just one statement or comment by a politician but the body of violent rhetoric coming from the same direction time after time. Progressives own it; it is only them who are calling for and accepting political violence against their foes (NG 2024).

Our country needs serious introspection, attitude adjustment and a strategy. Thirty percent of this country permanently residing on that shoestring is lost forever. For the rest of us, it is a very simple strategy. This is not difficult. It works when training horses and when disciplining children. It will even work to bring some semblance of sanity back to this country.

In simplest terms, all that needs to occur is to make the wrong thing uncomfortable and the correct thing comfortable. It is really all that simple. As regular normals, we are done being uncomfortable. Our thumbs are firmly placed on our side of the justice scale, and it is time to make some changes.

How to get a stubborn horse to load in a trailer:

- Put the horse in a small corral with a tall fence so he can't jump out.
- Back the trailer up to the corral gate and open the door.
- Drop a mountain lion into the corral.

The result: The horse can't get into the trailer fast enough. It is all about motivations and incentives. The horse was motivated to jump into the trailer, incentivized by avoiding becoming a mountain lion snack. How do we apply this now in the 2020s? (Foundation Reining Training Centre 2009)

> *"Make the right thing easy, and the wrong thing difficult."*
> **Horse Trainer,**
> *Clinton Anderson…*

- What motivates criminals to steal? They don't have to work for money or goods. What is the incentive? No consequences.
- What motivates law-breaking illegal aliens to cross our border? Freedom. What is the incentive? Free government services provide them with a home, food, healthcare, a college education and welfare dollars to fund an American lifestyle. Freedom to run a wide-open fentanyl market with no criminal consequences and free reign to practice human trafficking.

Laws are already on the books and now is the time to re-implement them. Here's an idea…Let's make crime illegal again. Nobody who is not an American citizen should be afforded any welfare dollars, whether it be for food, healthcare, housing or a phone. The only means of transportation they should be given is back to their own country.

What do Progressives, their organizers, their influencers, their non-binaries and anarchists have in common? Their incentives and motivators are nearly identical. It is a coordinated effort to ensnare an entire country to benefit themselves. What motivates them? Power over people. What is the incentive? Money is thrown at them by socialistic billionaires, lobbyists, special interests and duped Americans, who give them more money, exposure and power.

Progressives of all stripes have perfected this into the 2020s with the assistance of being held unaccountable by their state-run media who excoriate Normies for the same offenses. Politically, this has enabled them to supplant like minders within all regulatory and policing agencies and the judiciary.

The June 27, 2024 debate in Atlanta and its aftermath, clearly exposed it for what it is. It is worse than a swamp; it is a slimy, mosquito-infested, boggy morass of thick, fetid, muddy black silt that has exponentially grown in breadth and scope and was useful for throwing their President overboard with cement shoes when he no longer suited them. Former President Trump and the Republican nominee who defeated their first nominee now must beat a second Democrat nominee. A person nobody within their party voted for. It is a staggering betrayal of the democratic process that amazingly, millions of people have accepted. Fortunately, it appears they have gone too far. More and more are seeing it for what it is. So, let's drop that mountain lion into the corral, shall we?

It begins with very simple defined rules, where everyone knows the expectations. Eliminate all those nebulous, confusing diversity, equity or inclusion (DEI) complexities that shut down creativity and thought. All children and young adults need to feel free to share ideas again. I will begin with academia, specifically Progressive universities.

As a parent, you have the power over what and how your kids are educated. Quit sending them to Harvard, UPenn, Columbia, Princeton, Northeastern and other elitist universities that promote antisemitism and indoctrinate weak concepts that will never allow them to function in the real world. Quit donating to their foundations and boosters. Businesses need to stop hiring these graduates. Businesses are hungry for hard-working young people. It is optional to hire graduates of elite Progressive universities who teach lazy, entitled attitudes. They turn out students who live by intolerant DEI principles. Instead of "leaning in" to create opportunities for themselves and the businesses they work for, they seek "quiet quitting" strategies to expend as little effort as possible. They job shop, only lasting a couple of years for any one employer as they seek jobs that only feed their egos and time off. Be especially suspicious of job applicants who present as "their authentic selves." Nobody has time for that or the cost they bring.

Create your own workforce with apprenticeships and hire eager graduates from areas of the country who expect academics and foster positive attitudes. They are easy to find. They are students from colleges who still expect academic performance, attendance and effort. They choose their students based on measurable merits instead of their PRIORITISE classification. Functioning colleges are easy to identify. They focus on academics instead of diversity, performative activism and social impact causes. They don't have tenure, and professors are evaluated on professionalism and expertise, not for their DEI and ESG virtue signals. They behave like universities, not elementary schools. They don't offer "triggered" students cry, kitty, puppy and stuffed animal hugging rooms. They don't have crayon and hot chocolate sipping stations for students disturbed by life. They are universities whose students prioritize their studies instead of antisemitic racist activism and where professors don't give extra credit for activist causes. The are universities and colleges who don't function as an "emergency broadcast station" that warns students of potential "triggers" (Bond 2018).

Definitions: Trigger Warnings

A forewarning that an uncensored statement is about to be loaded that could pick off the snowflaker in a stunning blast of emotional detonation that will obliterate sensitive sensibilities.

It is no wonder that sixty percent of businesses no longer hire based on a college degree. Society has unequivocally stated that we do not need Zoomers and their turmoil. Professors need to act like professors whose job is to nurture our country's next leaders and not the organizing or activism kind.

Businesses and corporations are the backbones of cities. It is you who bring in billions of dollars of tax revenues. Taxes are collected not only from you but from your employees. Violent cities are no place for your employees or your customers. Those cities that condone the violence through defunding police movements, cashless bail, decriminalized drug use and voting in criminal-supporting district attorneys are no place to do business. It is costing you billions of dollars. The answer is very simple. Move your business to a friendlier city and state because it will save you money in the long run. If you are looking to open a new business. Pick a city that actually police's lawless behavior.

Fire employees who embrace "lazy girl" philosophies or incite discontent among other employees. New employee probationary periods should last at least one year. Anybody can fake it for three to six months. This allows enough time for employers to determine if an employee is behaving congruent with the expectations and culture of that business/corporation. Strong employees, build strong businesses and are the foundation of a strong nation.

For companies and corporations duped into dumping money into "inclusion and equity departments," get rid of them. They are costing you useless dollars that should be used for growing your business. We already have laws that protect individuals from discrimination (Raleigh 2023) (Guerette 2023).

Then we have our public school system. School districts need to grow some cojones. All their self-absorbed "education is a social construct," anti-professionalism, overly tatted, pierced, purple-haired teachers who flaunt their near and dear identifiers to children need to be fired. As parents, we are telling those teachers they can leave their gender identity at the door because nobody cares. Your job is to teach our children reading, science, writing and arithmetic, not parade around your preferred sexual identity or preferences. Nobody cares if you want to be called, "they," "them," or "it." Those of us who practice adulting will not call you that, so get over it and yourselves. Here is an extraordinary concept, teaching is not about you. It is about your students. As parents, know that teachers who behave this way do not have your child's best interests at heart. It is all about them, not their students. Remove your child from such classrooms. Only then will school administrators and school boards finally understand. As a regular normal teacher seeking a job, move to areas of the country that practice traditional education standards and codes of conduct. We have a teacher shortage throughout the country. You will find a job and you will be safer in those environments (Jotkoff 2022).

Be an active participant and parent volunteer at your child's school. Attend school board meetings. Become a member of your school's parent-teacher association. Much can be learned about your child's school by simply volunteering your time, skills and expertise. Run to be a member of your school board. Review your school's policies and root out indoctrinating ESG, DEI and CRT programs and practices. Your child should be bringing home homework. Review those assignments. Much can be learned about school policy from those lessons, especially in mathematics.

Important Historical Educational Context: Mathematics is the **inanimate science** of numbers, as it relates to structure, order and relation. It is the elemental practice of counting, measuring and describing the shapes of objects. Amazingly, we have to explain this. It is only

Progressive thought that assigns degrees of subjective philosophy, idealization, abstractions and transformations in mathematics. Our kids need the basics of mathematics before entering any next-level realm of mathematical predictions that objectively calculate future outcomes, for which social constructs have absolutely no application.

Critical Race Theory is where the earliest proposals to abolish algebra originated because for "students of color" it is the single most failed course, preventing students from graduating or advancing on to college. The study of math isn't racist, but it is racist for students of color, who have no other choices, to be continually taught in inferior education settings. Like everything else they do, removing math is a band-aid fix to cover the gaping wound of substandard education quality for students of color (O'Leary 2021) (K. Richardson 2021).

Question: Why do Progressives continue to block school choice initiatives?
Answer: It is a covert method to keep people of color dependent.

Violent students must be permanently expelled in a "one strike, you are out" policy. We are done pandering to violent people who have somehow become "victims" in our "all-inclusive" society. Put their violent, sorry backsides in a detention facility or jail. Let them learn to be productive members of society there and not amongst our children and teachers. Nobody should be a victim of student violence. Parents and the communities within these districts need to demand action. Sue those students, their parents and their school districts if necessary. Only then will schools make the insanity stop (Will 2022) (Kurtz 2022).

We can all agree that the era of "free-range children" is over. Children with unsupervised ranging turn into hoodlums, the gateway behavior to anarchism. Every unsupervised child must be enrolled in after-school tutoring, leadership, clubs, volunteer and sports programs. Legislatures need to shift state money to such programs so they are free.

As an aside; Where could that money be found? $80 billion can be reallocated from guess where... "The Inflation Reduction Act," where 87,000 new IRS agents were hired to collect billions of tax dollars from rich billionaires who don't pay their taxes. Unfortunately, The Wall Street Journal discovered that sixty-three percent of all new audits in 2023 targeted taxpayers with incomes less than $200 thousand. Hmmm, that sure sounds like a middle-class income to me.

What should we do with all those newly hired IRS agents? If they didn't want to learn to code, we could re-train all those agents as **S**pecialized **I**nstructional **T**utors **T**eaching **E**xemplary **R**espectful **S**tudents (**SITTERS**) (K. Taylor 2023) (Carlozo 2024) (Laurene, IRS SITTERS for Enhanced After School Programs 2024).

Sorry, I digressed. Some progress is being made. Legislation is being written by state houses across the nation, making it illegal to expose small children to sexual performances. They are removing sexual content from library shelves and gender guidance-affirming practices in schools. They are banning collegiate competition in any category other than the biological gender of which you were born. Parents are removing their children from public schools, enrolling them in Christian or charter schools, or they are homeschooling. Parents are being elected to school boards across the country and they are suing teachers and school districts for parental interference.

Desperately holding onto their radical beliefs, trans activists are challenging new laws, and they are working their way through the courts. Time will tell how it shakes out, but who knew four years ago that such action would even be necessary? It is chaos, which is the Progressive goal.

If you have the resources, form a 501(c)(3) organization funded for the sole purpose of providing money to litigate in court those victimized by Progressive activist nonsense.

It might be frustrating and slow, but Normies are making a difference. Boycotts have resulted in billions of losses at Anheuser Busch, Target and Disney. Investors have pulled billions out of market funds from companies with "sustainable" agendas amid underperformance and political discontent. In 2020, 165 companies mentioned ESG and DEI within their company's priorities. By 2023, those numbers plummeted to thirty-two. We all must be diligent though, because the Transformative Language team and their WEFs are at it again. Understand that they will never let it go, they will simply transform it. DEI and ESG principles are now being rebranded as "Stakeholder Metrics" to freshen up its image (E. Stewart 2024) (Vanderbilt 2024).

Vote wisely. Don't be duped by buzzwords promising "Social Equity" and Enviro-double-speak in flowery speeches devoid of realistic, tangible and measurable results. Quit voting for or against personas you either like or dislike. Would you choose a cardiologist or neurosurgeon for the same reason? For our health's sake, we would select competence over personality and effectiveness over infirmity. We ought to choose our country's leaders for the same reason. Vote for the policies and the country's health, not because you do or don't like the candidate. It is not a beauty or personality contest. Choosing competence has nothing to do with personage or whether they cheated on their spouse. Nobody is perfect in this world. Always question biased reporting that can ignore navy blue dresses with stains but excoriate the opposite political candidate for the exact same offenses. This includes Presidents absconding with classified materials or running a private server. Unless every single Department of Justice runs apolitically, those offenses will be ignored by the controlling party if criminality affects their party. Congressional hearings and investigations mean nothing if the DOJ doesn't choose to properly investigate and indict classified materials stored in garages or homebrew servers kept in bathrooms. Lastly, the middle class and their success have absolutely nothing to do with global priorities (United Nations 2015) (The Starr Report) (Herridge 2024) (Kristian 2015) (Riechmann 2016).

We can all agree that defunding police, cashless bail and decriminalizing drugs have resulted in entirely predictable outcomes. Oregon is the prime example of what occurs when voters fall for such rhetorical nonsense. Are Western Oregonians really that ignorant? Defunding police wasn't enough when 58 percent of Oregonians voted in favor of ballot measure 110, decriminalizing all hard drugs. Major supporters of the measure included The Wacklanders of Western Oregon, Mark Zuckerberg, and global investor George Soros.

Ole' George from Hungary, with his never-ending bank account, is the sugar daddy of the Progressive party. He is also responsible for funding every election won by all those criminal-supporting, soft-on-crime district attorneys who also target non-progressive leaders who could derail their socialist goals. There is a reason that eastern Oregonians and two-thirds of the land mass are seeking to join Idaho. They are looking to shed themselves from the Wacklands of western Oregon (J. Byrne 2021) (Bland 2016) (Wright 2023).

Astoundingly, measure 110 was supported by the Oregon Nurses' Association, The American College of Physicians, and the Oregon Academy of Family Physicians. I was a member of the ONA once. I had no idea they were that stupid (KGW Staff 2023) (BBC 2020) (AP 2023) (Sabet 2022).

Ultimately, drug-addicted criminals didn't adhere to the Pollyanna approach of trading jail for "drug addiction treatment." Wow, criminals didn't show up to their scheduled counseling session after their drug citation. Who would have thought? The citation was useful, though, to wipe their backsides after defecating on the sidewalk. I guess that's better than using public drinking fountains as a bidet.

Oregon is the poster state of what occurs when DEI, ESG, inclusivity, fairness doctrines, decriminalization of drugs and defunding police are fully operational. Oregon now leads the nation in Fentanyl deaths at thirteen times the number compared to pre-2020 numbers. Eleven times higher than the rest of the country. Again, maybe it is time to make crime illegal again (Thompson 2024).

Jeopardy Question for 50: Illegal environmental contraband that is useful to snort cocaine or methamphetamine in Portland, Oregon's town square.
Answer: What is the plastic straw? (Oregon Revised Statutes 2023)

Consider volunteering at voting precincts, and do not be intimidated by other workers or voters who seek to undermine our elections. This task should no longer be relegated to our communities' sweet little grandmothers and grandfathers. We should be recruiting bouncers at all those non-Bud drinking establishments.

Additionally, there is no excuse for ballot counting to be delayed for days or weeks. This must be addressed at the state level through legislation. We should all be asking why elections in this country suddenly cannot be decided in one day because, before 2018, they sure used to be. Voting day has now evolved into voting month. Following the Progressives' disastrous loss to President Trump, ballot counting suddenly became problematic. "Stuffing the ballot box" has always been a part of election fraud, but ballot harvesting takes that to an entirely new level. It is why voting takes a month because harvesting Progressive-adjacent ballots takes longer than a day. All late ballots that mystically appear out of nowhere must be automatically suspect and removed for further scrutiny. Fully prosecute any instances of voter fraud. Cameras should be in every precinct, dropbox and vote-counting building. Law enforcement needs to be parked in each vote counting area, even at night when counting ceases for the day. Federal law needs to be enacted to make ballot harvesting a criminal offense with fines, jail time and deportation. All voter lists need to be cleaned out every election cycle. If even one illegal or fraudulent registration or ballot is found, fine that county harshly because money drives adherence to rules. Any politician who forwards illegal alien voting and federal IDs to illegal invaders is only in it for one thing, illegal voting. Highly sophisticated electronic voting machines can easily be manipulated or hacked. Our country should never succumb to electronic digital vote-counting machines in a world headed toward Artificial Intelligence.

As regular normals, we need to resurrect all those traits that this country has functioned under that are congruent with our Constitution and the laws of this country. Everyone in America has that right, and we need to fight for them. We have obfuscated the fight to others who cannot do it alone. Now is not the time to sit idly by and expect others to hold up the foundation that has always made our country great. Furthermore, we should never be ashamed of our founding beliefs. It is how we have effectively functioned for 240 years.

Our house is rotting from within, and the foundation is crumbling. The termite infestation has reached maximum capacity, and the swamp is seeping in everywhere. We believe all it will take is the next savior/political leader who will single-handedly save the house. That is not how this is going to work. We all allowed the infestation to happen, so we are all responsible for applying the pesticide and rebuilding. You cannot blame any politician, political party or faceless bureaucrat. We are the ones guilty of allowing it to happen. No one person can patch the holes now because that slimy, muddy, black silt has wholly swamped the house. As voters in this country, only we have the power to change it.

As citizens of the United States, we need to expect a lot more from our elected leaders. We must discard all radical thinking, whether on the right or the left. Moderation and compromise have been the defining strategies that have made this country great. What's more, the geriatric halls of Congress need to close. Nobody should become a permanent fixture in public office for twenty-plus years. We need new blood and ideas. Politicians who seek re-election well into their seventies and eighties are in it for one reason, addiction to power.

Our day of reckoning is not some indefinite someday. It is now. So, what are we as individuals, parents, grandparents, families, churches, clubs, school districts, universities, teachers, Parent Teacher Associations, businesses and corporations, state houses, oversight boards, foundations and organizations going to do about it? Are we ever going to stop ignoring it? Will we ever stop being ruled by propagandized stones, swords and bullets that fly at us to keep us all silent? We all need to ask ourselves if we are one of the stone throwers or one of those firing those bullets? Because if we're firing the bullets we are the problem because in this country everyone is allowed to express opinions.

Violence is not a part of this equation. All we need to do is speak the truth. Stop checking our opinions and language at the door. It is our turn now to speak up. Demand more of your school boards, corporate board rooms and state houses. Run for those seats if you must. Take a stand at your woke corporations, classrooms and financial institutions. Be silent no more.

Check that 401K or IRA portfolio. Whether you are a corporate CEO, a state Governor or an individual, pull out every investment in the plethora of woke agendas financed via your investments. Change your financial fiduciary if you need to. Many governors and corporations have already started.

> *"One person can make a difference, and everyone should try."*
> **President John *Fitzgerald Kennedy…***

Lastly, close the G#@ damn forsaken border. Deport every single illegal alien invader, no matter the cost. Erect that border wall once and for all. The reasons for that are stated throughout this book. A 2019 report stated that illegal immigration has already cost this country $42 billion in cash, Medicaid, food and housing programs, and $68 billion in education costs even before the twelve-plus million invaders crossed our borders. New York is cutting their budget across a range of services to afford the $12 billion cost in services to illegals. Chicago has spent $36 million, and Denver expects to spend $180 million in 2024 alone. All cities are struggling to provide services for the "new arrivals." In contrast, the wall was projected to cost $21 billion. Senate Democrats estimated it to be $70 billion, which is a drop in the bucket now that we have 12 million more and counting (Center for Immigration Studies 2024) (Felbab-Brown 2017).

Turn off cable, satellite or streaming services that advance woke programming. It may be time to turn them all off and dedicate your free time to another activity, one that encourages personal growth. Reconnect with your family and friends and give social media sites a break. All they have done is disconnect us physically, emotionally and spiritually from each other. We have lost the context of feelings, attachment and mutual respect.

I have great faith in the next generation. Generation Alpha is named for the Hebrew and Phoenician first letter of A. It means a sense of "beginning." In astronomy, it is the designation of the brightest star of any constellation. Alpha means strong and powerful. As the children of the millennial generation, they will be the generation who will light the way toward another beginning. Like their parents, they will fight for a simple and sensible existence. However, regular normals need to construct the building blocks to allow it to happen.

It begins with our children. I don't know one engaged parent who gives their young child a mobile device. Children never belong on Facebook, Twitter or TikTok. Send them outside to play. Form neighborhood and after-school programs. Children need to learn to play together once again, not be tied up in the mobile device world of "influencer land" (Riggio PhD 2022) (Klee 2023).

History of Society's Engagement with Technology

Technology has come a long way in a very short period. I often think about Dad when I imagine how far technology has come. There was no Internet in Dad's day, and he used a first-generation computer. It was a 1980s Kaypro computer with the old DOS operating system, learning everything about the complexities of coded typing. Who knew in the 1980s that Ne, Ve, Spivak, Ze/Zie and Hir, Ze/Zie and Zir, Xe, would later become gender pronouns in the 2020s? Dad would have been so amused by that. We are all amid one of those déjà vu moments, as we are pinging around in that infamous pinball machine, as we wizard our way through today's complexities of language and thought. I wish Dad were around today, as he was far more attuned to the mystics of written and spoken symbols that have replaced the English language. Give it another decade, and we will all be speaking in Klingon (R. Brooks 2016).

Times have changed when we only spoke to our grandparents twice a year, on a corded telephone on a "party line." It was a time when we would talk to our sweeties and friends for hours, lying on the floor, tethered to that corded phone. Now, our handy, dandy mobile device is securely positioned in our back pocket to be "connected" at all hours of the day or night, 365 days a year. It is the last thing we look at before bed and the first thing we pick up in the morning.

It is so treasured that some will even venture into the worst caverns of disgustingness on the planet to maintain their possession of it. Nothing illustrates this more than two women in two different states who lost their precious devices at the bottom of an outhouse. It was so catastrophic to their psyche that they tethered down to retrieve them. It takes no imagination to guess what happened next. One landed headfirst (Cagnassola 2022) (Retrops 2023).

People die at the bottom of outhouses depending on their depth. You can't tread water, er…pee in a pile of toilet paper and stool. One could surmise that swimming amongst the stool is like quicksand. An environment where the more one tries to survive, the further one sinks. One cannot live in a swampy stool-infested world forever. I guess it is nearly impossible to let go of such a deeply engrained symbol of one's identity.

Something so embedded within their soul that to lose their smartphone or its connection, is now a phobia, or more specifically, nomophobia (Cherry 2023).

One of the outhouse divers was from California, so there is that. After what seemed like an eternity immersed in stool, she was finally rescued from her swampy Stool cavern of hell. She then refused assistance after occupying the dankest, slimiest, swampiest, most infected, hostile environment known on the planet.

There is plenty of symbolism in a story about outhouses and waste. As in life, a lot of excreta attempting to identify as fertilizer is passed along, seeking to soil our world. "This too shall pass" could very well describe the Stool we seek to unload now.

Our ancestral realities, from which we have benefited in modern society, have nothing to do with technology. It was a time when folks fought man, nature and even himself to survive. It was a time when people could think for themselves, drawing conclusions about life simply by observation and discussion. It was a time when real human interaction defined us as a nation.

This is why the Zoomer generation is so insufferable. What gradually occurred over several generations completely engulfed this generation. They are entirely influenced by only what they see on their devices. So much so that they have become incapable of thinking for themselves. They are so immersed in technology that they have no understanding of how to interact without their mobile device.

Then, Progressives mastered the technology to successfully misappropriate inclusiveness as truth. It was brilliant, really. Unfortunately for the Zoomer generation, society is done with this masquerade. If they don't pivot soon, the nun chuck of veritable truth and justice will beat them over the head.

Laziness kills dreams. The entitled generation does not understand the value of investing in yourself. It includes jobs that build careers if they apply themselves. It is not about sitting at some desk, collecting as much money as you can while doing nothing, waiting for the weekend to arrive. They have serious delusions of grandeur and a personal myth that they are the most relevant. Being bankrolled for a long time, they have overplayed a hand that is one suit short of a full house. With their artificially stacked deck, they bet the bank, arrogantly discarding a Queen to only draw a rag. Normies have run out of patience and have drawn the ace in the hole with an inside straight for the win. Z'ers are out of bluffs, and Normies recognize their tell. We are no longer the underdogs, and they are busted. In a total-sum game, we are cashing in.

Definitions: Rag

Low-value, worthless, or to be severely rebuked. All definitions apply in this instance.

Definitions: Deuce

It is uncountable. It is also a euphemism for "devil." Can be used in expressions of anger and annoyance. All definitions apply.

Their inability to make or save money, buy a home, or land the "correct" job is always somebody else's fault. Adulting is hard work. As the most entitled generation in history, quit your sniveling and your excuses and do something for yourselves, as every generation has done before you (Altus 2023) (Mollman 2023).

My family is an eclectic group with vocational interests that cover the spectrum. We are police officers, nurses, teachers, property managers, real estate developers, heavy equipment operators and contractors. We are marketers, package carriers, horse trainers, farriers, office managers, hospital administrators, school principals, college professors, piano teachers, homemakers, veterinarian technicians, dental assistants and retail clerks. We are private contractors, run or work for non-profits and have owned a mom-and-pop grocery, a salon and craft stores. We are ranchers, nursing assistants, teacher's aides, statisticians, mayors, case managers, youth counselors, dog groomers and computer programmers. Some are self-employed, and some are employed by the government, small businesses, foundations or corporations. Some have college degrees, and some do not.

What it illustrates is that everyone is capable of contributing to society with skills and talents that help America and ourselves grow. No able-bodied person should be sitting on their backsides expecting others to fund them and their dreams from cradle to grave. It is not the government's job to fund dreams. People create their own dreams, based on aspirations and personal desires based on realistic goals. The government's only job is to protect us from domestic and international hostility and to prop those up who physically cannot provide for themselves. To count on government and taxpayer money to support your livelihood chains you and your destiny to somebody else's ideas, destroying dreams. True freedom is only discoverable to those who participate and pay for their life path, which we all create for ourselves.

Why would anybody feel compelled to compare it to others? And worse, be angry about it?

Progressive dividers are good at sowing discontent by comparing different life paths to those who are either oppressors or oppressed. They convince others that oppressors have greater resources, so they have a greater advantage over the oppressed. It is not a fair comparison. Anybody can be successful with the resources that they have at their disposal. It is how we use those resources to define our destiny and success. We all must understand that those who compare life paths do so to create social discontent, resentment and chaos. The division industry does not desire a cohesive society. Their goal is to broaden our differences and fracture communities, which gives them more power. Are we beginning to understand yet?

Our life paths are what we choose for ourselves and define ourselves. Circumstances can derail us for a time, but if we don't look at ourselves as victims of those circumstances, new paths and happiness will be found. Don't be fooled by victimization statements that a socialistic government and its media create. Those statements are merely a method of entrapment to make you dependent on others.

Covering My Backside

Unfortunately, we now live in the land of the vilifiers and finger-pointers. It is a country where ANY real or imagined brutality will be loosely tied to an individual or group that dares to write a book, give a speech, write a column or a blog, broadcast a podcast or program that goes against the preferred agenda, and don't you dare run for any public office. Those who dare dive in understand that the finger pointers who accuse you of some threat or disruption are your undeniable sign that what you have stated, written or broadcast threatens to topple the stool and their deeply held desire to control a nation.

This book was written with the sole purpose of becoming an artifact for my future generations. However, should there be a remote chance that anyone other than my family reads this book, *I unequivocally state that in no way is this book to be construed as a call to violence or cruelty against any named, unnamed, inferred upon, insinuated against a person, persons, groups, entities, clubs, bars, politicians, schools, libraries, healthcare providers, hospitals, clinics, farms, symbols, roads or anyone or anything else.*

So, just in case some mentally perverted individual or group dangling on that proverbial reality shoestring, finds that I may be an effective communicator of political inferences, of which they feel emboldened, triggered, threatened by, or by which they think they can instigate or correlate, some violent act, as an expression of their agreement or disagreement to any portion of this book, neither *I nor this book is responsible. It is always the responsibility of that individual or group's twisted, altered sense of reality who perpetrated the offense.*

WHEW! Do you think that might cover it? Probably not.

Furthermore, this is merely a book of history, stories, anecdotes, satire, news clips and definitions written by an average person seeking to try to define the absurdities happening within our country that we are all trying to understand. Such stories, anecdotes or definitions are therefore written so that perhaps those of us struggling can all laugh about and/or ponder: What in the world on God's green earth is occurring around us?

One more thing, if you cannot smile or ponder during any portion of this book, perhaps you are far too entangled in that progressive web. If so, it is time to crawl out, ungrip your phone, get a grip, and quit griping. Then grip your steering wheel and take a nice drive in the countryside. You will feel better.

Lastly, if one feels compelled to act in some way… GO VOTE!

Despite the insanity of the 2020s, my family and our faith in each other are what ground us. Faith in shared traditional principles that we have always relied on is how we filter out all the misguided messaging forced upon us to derail our peace. It is what all families need to find within themselves, to find their own quietude of an untroubled existence, that we all seek for ourselves and our families.

PART VII

Navigating Our World

Life is too short to constantly accommodate for and understand all the ambiguousness of society around us. We decided long ago not to participate in a world where you must conform speech and actions to somebody else's imaginative definitions. Just like everyone else, we want to live, work, play and raise our families without the absurdities and double standards that harass and plague people every single day. It is how we cope in the 2020s for now. We are waiting for stable, common sense, family-supportive, mainstream ideals to define once again who we are as a country. We still have hope.

As our family began to navigate life after the spring of 2005, we knew we could be kind and accepting of ourselves and our community. We can even do so without losing sight of our identity and beliefs. We do our best to ignore all the nonsense and live our lives as always. We are profoundly grateful for the gift of living in this country. We have always kept sight of the values and morals we were taught by our parents and their parents and grandparents before them. They may be gone now, but their spirit lives within us daily. We live quietly, immersed in our small tribe. It is easier that way, as it allows one to be yourself without accidentally "triggering" someone else's alternative sense of reality.

I have observed from my corner that when you look beyond the ridiculousness, you find a society deeply unhappy and interminably angry about nearly everything in life. For some, you must drive the correct vehicle, which does not include an SUV or a truck. You must recycle, eat organic, use a bicycle for transportation and not eat beef. You must be fit but accepting of all body types. You must be fair but to only those ideas defined by others. No one can ever be thankful for what they have. We can never be proud of our accomplishments or feel satisfied with hard work or dedication to a task. To be able to own a home, get a college education, buy a car or a new blouse, or wish anybody a "Merry Christmas" is pretentious and callous against those less fortunate. It is all a ruse to make you feel endlessly ashamed. It is creating psychic turmoil among us every day. To a Progressive, everyone must be perpetually sad unless everyone across the world is happy. Politics has seeped through every aspect of our lives that has consumed us. The days of carefree whimsical thought without guilt are gone (Harris Rebroadcast 2024).

Hollywood and many entertainers struggling to stay relevant in a social context world bombard us with their subliminal messaging every time we turn on the television or watch a movie. The challenge is identifying the plot or message through their all-inclusive messaging, which is all they are selling in the first place. Programming and commercials are the annoying flies buzzing around our heads that we can't escape. Only then do you get a newspaper or fly swatter to end its miserable life forever. That is what is occurring with the cancellation of satellite and cable subscriptions, opting instead for free streaming services or an old-fashioned antenna (Holzhauer 2023) (Shriber 2022).

Comedic entertainment is dead. Protected tribes cannot be touched because it triggers the woke, humorless sensitivities of Leftyville. Comedians can no longer practice their craft without offending somebody, with the predictable spurn from some subgroup. It is difficult to find anything in the world that they have not ruined for the rest of humanity, of which movies, television, The Boy Scouts, Victoria's Secret, The Olympics, and Sports Illustrated swimsuit models are only a few. Pick anything in the world that Leftyville hasn't left in ruinous ash in their miserable woke world (Hall 2024).

Even gatherings or parties find guests checking their humor at the door for fear of offending someone in the crowd. Humor delivered with no malice intended now results in an overdramatized outburst from a self-obsessed Karen in the crowd that makes everyone uncomfortable. It is about making a scene for a woke belief system of which nobody cares.

At no time can anybody participate in a gathering without some Progressive making some crass remark about Conservatism. I am telling them right now we are sick of it. We are done being nice, so if you continue, prepare yourselves one day for a response you may not expect because here is something enlightening: not everyone thinks the way you do, even in gatherings that appear homogenous in your beliefs. Everyone needs to check their politics at the door (Camosy 2021).

We use our free time in more productive activities other than television. We play with our family. We spend a lot of time outside, listening to the music that nature provides as we hike, horseback ride or snowshoe.

We work hard on home improvement projects. There is always something that needs to be done in the yard or on the farm. We practice our latest fishing techniques while exploring all the various rivers, streams and lakes around us. We read thought-provoking books and concentrate on learning new skills in life. I wrote my first book.

My children are especially wise with the near complete elimination of all devices and screen time from my grandchildren. My grandchildren read piles of books, then spend the day outside riding bicycles and hiking. Activities are created by their parents that cultivate new skills as they grow. They live frugally and work hard within a defined budget, leveraging the modest income they have and never spending beyond their means. They pay off their one credit card every month. They have prioritized their life, their income and their spending so Erica can be home with the children full-time. It is back to basics in their home. They teach core values that begin with love and kindness undistracted from mobile devices or television that prevents proper interpretation of the world around them.

Our Core

Russ and his wife Anita, in their quiet and infinite wisdom, always say that people in your life can be described as an onion. An onion peels off in layers one by one till you are left with the core. Just like the core of that onion, are everyone's core people. Core people are those you share your life and secrets without being scorned or belittled. They are the people who genuinely know and understand you. They are the people who accept you for who you are.

The following rings are family or friends you enjoy spending time with, some more than others. Some are people with whom you may not share intimate details of yourself for fear of being judged. Then there are the people that you are forced to check your language choices to prevent an awkward interaction.

As you peel the onion, people travel between the layers, depending on where your life path takes you. The true test is when you are most vulnerable, sad or afraid. That is when your true core of people presents itself. Fate happens within shifting winds, forming the storms of life that you cannot control. Only when you lose nearly everyone most important to you can you understand that you control nothing in life. In loss comes thankfulness for what you have.

Within death, you discover light. As friends rally around you, special relationships emerge that probably would not have occurred without such a tragedy. Your darkest days can foreshadow a complete change in the trajectory of your life in ways you could have never imagined or foreseen.

In the spring of 2006, my sister married the love of her life and best friend, Steve, on a Hawaiian shore. It was the same island where our family had one of the best vacations we had ever experienced. Justin stepped in for his grandfather, giving away the bride that day. I was her maid of honor. While Kris, Steve, Justin and I stood on that beautiful white sandy beach, with the waves crashing in the background, we were lovingly surrounded by all our core people. All those people who had mobilized around us during the most painful year of our lives. It signified a new beginning for our family. It was the day we finally picked up all the pieces of a shattered year.

We welcomed Steve into our family with love, affection and gratitude. As a good friend, he was there for Kris and our family throughout our year of heartache and loss. He often didn't know what to do or say. He was just there, doing whatever he could, even if it was just bringing a lot of wine and Kentucky Fried Chicken. Steve was my sister's "Knight in Shining Armor," arriving at the most critical time in her life. My sister is as tough as they come. She uses an invisible veneer to protect her most inner vulnerabilities from emotional pain. Yet, that core friendship blossomed into a loving bond. Steve is an ex-bull rider. You can't find anybody tougher or more persistent than that. That persistence broke through Kris' shield of resistance within her spirit at that time. He lifted her up and over anguish so deep that it threatened to bury her soul.

For the entirety of Kris' young adult life, she had been the one to care for everyone. Beginning at the tender age of fifteen, she had many expectations thrown at her. The declining health of our father required more of her than any adolescent in her peer group. She did it, though, with love and honor for the family. That was when that shield of resistance began to form, toughening her exterior that would guide her life path. This is how leaders are made. Only when you love someone or something enough do you rise to the occasion, providing leadership to support those entities you care for so deeply. She did it because she loved our family. She went into law enforcement for the same reason, love of community.

Steve entered our lives following the death of our brother while, at the same time, providing end-of-life care for our mother. I believe he was sent to us at that exact time for a reason. It was then that my sister no longer felt the weight of all the endless, painful responsibilities of caring for a rapidly disappearing family support system. Someone finally arrived who would take care of her for a change. He has fulfilled the role of my new brother in spades. He is an important leader in our family and definitely within the center of our core.

The day after Kris and Steve's wedding, Justin, Kris and I walked out on that beautiful, warm, white sandy beach and into the water. Our core people surrounded us once again that day as Russ led us in prayer. We all poured a glass of wine, toasting our sweet mother's life, blessings and love. We then released her ashes into the surf and told her goodbye. She loved Hawaii. She would have liked that.

Beginning Again

In times of immense heartache, you don't remember much about the sad details like you think you will. I believe it is God's way of healing a broken heart. Kris, Justin and I remember very little of the details surrounding their deaths or funerals. What we remember and talk about today are all the sweet memories.

I have always loved Montana. It is the state where my family first settled, the birthplace of our brother, where our parents met and married and where our entire family is from. However, I had never spent time in the state's northwest region. That is until Mom, Kris and I had an opportunity to tour the state just before Mom's lung cancer diagnosis.

It was a girls' road trip in the fall of 2003 that began in Plentywood. Kris and I had flown in for our uncle's funeral. Mom had been there awhile, helping to care for her brother. It was an opportunity to have some time with her last surviving sibling. Before his passing, he sold his car to her for a price she couldn't refuse. It was a vintage white 1990 Cadillac Deville. It was a classic car, befitting our trip across Montana as we journeyed back to Oregon after his funeral. We stylin' all right, in that white Cadillac with bright red leather interior as we headed out Highway 16, then onto the Highline, otherwise known as Highway 2. Kris was driving while I sat in the passenger seat. Mom was comfortably reclined across the back seat.

Plentywood's state Highway 5 to Highway 2 takes you across the top of the Treasure State on a two-lane highway. It was late fall, and there wasn't much to see except flat, dry farmland. However, it did not curb our joy and enthusiasm, as we talked and laughed throughout our trip. For Mom, it was the first time she had laughed in weeks. Kris and I heard many fun stories that day as we crossed through all the small communities that make up eastern Montana and mother's old stomping grounds.

On the second day of our trip, we dropped down, flanking the east side of Glacier National Park before coming into the Flathead Valley. It was a breathtaking drive of mountain views, glacier vistas and crystal-clear streams and lakes. We stayed the night in Whitefish, at a beautiful hotel overlooking the Whitefish River. We had a wonderful evening on the town, eating dinner at Mackenzie River Pizza that night. Kris introduced us to the best pizza I had ever tasted. A delicious pie made with Alfredo sauce, fajita chicken, smoky bacon, spinach, tomatoes, mushrooms and mozzarella. Mackenzie River calls the pizza "the Flathead." It was a perfect night of good food, locally crafted beer and laughter.

We were not on a schedule, so we decided to stay an extra day and visit downtown Whitefish. We toured the many tourist shops and art galleries. We drove to Big Mountain Ski Resort and marveled at the beautiful views. We visited City Beach at Whitefish Lake.

I wondered why our family hadn't visited this corner of Montana on our many visits to the state. I had never explored a place so beautiful, vibrant and interesting. The Flathead is like the Grande Ronde Valley and La Grande but about ten times larger. It just felt like home. It was then that I knew I would someday return to the state of my family's roots and the Flathead Valley permanently. That someday had suddenly arrived.

Justin had been accepted to the University of Idaho in Moscow. He was well on his way to adulthood and forming his own life. Over half of my family was gone forever. Within two months of Mom's passing, I quit my job, packed everything up, and left the insanities of the State of Oregon for good. With my best friend and soul mate, we headed to the Flathead Valley and the great state of Montana. It was time for me to move on and start over.

The two of us sold our Oregon homes and pooled our money, purchasing a home on twenty acres with a barn and a shop. Over the next twenty years, we worked hard and grew our Montana lifestyle into a sixty-five-acre hobby farm with two homes outside Kalispell. Nestled amongst various species of pine trees and Quaking Aspen, our farm sits at the base of Eagle Mountain. We overlook our beautiful valley and creek, with views of Wild Horse Mountain and the backside of Blacktail Mountain Ski Resort. Our horses and cows blissfully graze in our valley amongst softly waving meadow grasses. The Tamarack, Red Fir and Ponderosa Pines are interspersed among the Quaking Aspen against a mountainous backdrop. In the fall, the Tamarack and Aspens show out, dotting the mountains around us in shades of yellow and gold. Then, the Tamarack fronds fall, covering the road and trails in yellow, where we have a yellow brick road of wonderment and exploration.

We spend our time fishing and boating on numerous lakes within thirty minutes of our house. We have nearly endless trails out our back door to hike, snowshoe and trail ride our Arabian horses. We raise Aberdeen cows for our own organic beef. Our Great Dane and Cocker Spaniel have nearly unlimited space to play, along with our fifteen laying hens and two barn cats. I am living my life now the way Dad had always wanted to, as a "gentleman farmer."

I eventually married my soul mate after eighteen years together. We married on our farm with our families and closest friends. It was a casual stand-up ceremony emphasizing family and friends, coming together with good food, good wine, Nell's home-brewed beer and abundant laughter and thankfulness. It was a great day, and I have never been happier. The greatest part of getting married is not only the cementing of a relationship but the joy that comes from a large extended family, who have adopted me as their own.

Justin attended the University of Idaho before moving back to Oregon to further his education. He, too, eventually left the insanities of Oregon for good, moving to Kalispell for meaningful work. Living in Montana is where he met and married his forever love. Two years later, they were married on the farm in a small ceremony, including family and close friends. It was a beautiful ceremony in our front yard. They stated their vows and promises to each other, overlooking our meadow with gorgeous, timbered mountainous scenery surrounding them.

I thought of Randy often during both celebrations. He was such an expert in creating ceremony and ambiance, and he would have been so impressed with the fashion of both ceremonies.

Justin and Erica are now raising their own family. Erica has been Justin's lighthouse, steering his life path toward happiness and wholeness. For this, I am grateful. She is why I finally see inner peace in Justin's character. Destiny has a way of working everything out. Had Justin not moved to Montana, he would have never met Erica, whom I love as I would a daughter of my own. I have learned a lot from her and seek her input often. She is an intricate part of who we are and has a definite place within our inner core. I thank her parents for raising such a wonderful young lady.

Like my father, Justin is all about making sure his family is happy. He boldly pursues new paths and adventures, and I am incredibly proud of him for this. He is a good man, husband and father. His grandparents would have been very proud of who he has become. They would have adored Erica and delighted with the arrival of their great-grandchildren. I only wish they could have been around to see it themselves.

Kris and Steve have since retired. With Steve's blessing, they left eastern Oregon, the east side of the state was where Steve was born and the only home that Kris knew. They left a state that has left eastern Oregonians behind for senselessness only embraced by Progressive population centers in western Oregon. A place where it doesn't matter where you are, it is scattered with homeless camps and reeks of marijuana smoke. They have a fitting motto on the west side today, *"Make Oregon Weird."*

Oregon had a proud heritage with the arrival of new immigrants who pioneered their way to a beautiful western destination known as the Willamette Valley. A place that one could only dream about. A place where many died along the Oregon Trail to realize that dream. There are only a few remnants of that paradise left in that valley today. The country ought to take a hard look at what unfettered progressivism has done to a once magical place (Eagles 1976).

> "They called it paradise,
> I don't know why...
> You call someplace paradise,
> kiss it goodbye..."
> *The Eagles (1976)*

Like many others leaving Oregon, Kris and Steve were ready to head to a new destination that reflected the family values we were raised in. They couldn't get their Oregon plates off fast enough (Parfitt 2021) (Crombie 2015).

Steve's goal in life is to make sure my sister is happy. He left the state of his family roots, moving my sister to the state of our family's humble beginnings. They are now making their own lives in Big Sky Country on the farm. It is wonderful to have them in Montana with us and be retired together. We all live, play and work together, free of all the absurdities that now define the state of Oregon. A new place where we can smile and shake our heads at each new laughable Oregon headline making the national news. We all felt sad to say goodbye to the state of our youth. So many beautiful memories were made during our lives there, but it was time to move on. Montana espouses all the same values we grew up with in the 1960s, 1970s, and 1980s when Oregon was our home before it became inundated with Californians and their Progressive baggage.

My family and I have found peace in Montana and simple rural living. It is an uncomplicated life that removes the chaos forced upon us. Montanans care for their state, and it shows. Life is good for me and my family right now, which is definitely good enough.

Our Montana

Montana is a special place but is not without its challenges or its realities. The challenges are easy to overcome if you possess certain qualifying traits and are particularly hearty. Otherwise, you may find the realities of Montana disconcerting to some concerting beliefs that are not embraced or even compatible here. So, as a public service, I will outline the realities of living in our state:

- The winters are very long, frigid and most of the time with several feet of snow. Schools rarely close here because of the weather.
- Unless you own a greenhouse, there is no growing season.
- Housing is in shortage, and what you can find is very expensive, created by West Coast escapees. Predictably, this migration has also increased property taxes, pricing out many folks, including Montana natives (Girten 2024).
- Your two-day prime delivery arrives in three to five days, and depending on where one lives, overnight deliveries will never happen.
- The Internet can be spotty and is much slower than most people like to entertain outside Montana. But those of us who live in this state do not live by our Internet connection.
- We play hard in our wide-open spaces. No place on public lands is off limits, and trails are kept maintained and open.
- It's Montana, so everyone here owns at least one gun. Hunting is our favorite pastime. In fact, it is a religion here. Everything stops for six weeks, so plan accordingly.
- We are more relaxed and less scheduled here. Your new home build will take much longer than you anticipate.
- We are a state of Christians, and the Ten Commandments are posted everywhere. Giant statues of crosses and the Virgin Mary are displayed in places you would not expect. We are a patriotic bunch who are proud of our historical heritage and our founding Christian beliefs.
- We manage and log our forests. We endure long, protracted lawsuits from eco-wacko east coasters, but they are logged in the

end. Since we manage our forests, wildfires are less of a problem in our state.
- We have a sense of humor and smile a lot. We shake hands and offer warm embraces. We do not fist-bump here.
- We also embrace big footprints. Like our big vehicles, we have big homes. There is no tiny home industry here.
- Because of our winters, driving can be rugged here. Therefore, we own large diesel-running pickup trucks and SUVs, and we have no emission standards.
- Unless you reside in Missoula or Bozeman, we don't accommodate squatters, nonresident homeless, or illegal invaders.
- We are hostile to Californians who seek to bring their progressive politics here. Even our tourists understand. A photo on social media showed a car touring through Kalispell with a California plate. The tourist taped a big yellow sign above the license plate reading… "It's A Rental" (Acobe 2023).
- We are equally hostile and will run out radical, racist, neo-Nazi, skin-head sympathizers.
- We vote by paper ballot here, resulting in minimal voter fraud.
- We love and respect our military. We have the second largest number of veterans in the United States, second only to Alaska.
- We respect and support our police force and fully fund them to the best of our taxpayers' ability.
- Schoolchildren are expected to be respectful to their teachers.
- Our legislature has removed all radical, woke, indoctrinating school curricula.
- Outside the Missoulian and Boze'Angeles university districts, men are men, and women are women. There is no confusion about that here. We proudly fly the American flag, and outside those university districts, there are no rainbow flags here. We do fly Griz and Bobcat flags, especially during the college football season.
- Places of reverence expect respect, and disruptors will be immediately removed and jailed if they break the law.
- We raise cattle here. It is our livelihood. We are the seventh largest provider of the nation's beef supply. That will never change.
- We do not have formal government-mandated recycling programs with cameras on garbage trucks. Montanans practice recycling independently.
- We embrace the renewable energy industry of biofuels, AKA firewood. Most homes have a biofuel stove, which burns those

- biofuels that eventually identify as heat. Ninety percent of our biofuel burners do not have a catalytic converter.
- Montana is a debt-free state, and we live within our means. As a result, our highways may have potholes. They are a little rough and have no shoulders, but that helps slow people down.
- We do not wear masks unless we want to, and we will never be required to get the COVID-19 vaccine, or close school again over Covid Hysteria.
- We covet our freedom and will fight against a tyrannical federal government.
- Montana is a very red state. Thanks to West Coast refugees, it is getting redder. Trump won the state of Montana by over sixteen points in the 2020 election. Oh my!

Important Public Service Announcement for our tourists:

- Don't always trust your vehicle's GPS when traveling in rural Montana. People have died running themselves over cliffs or freezing to death when they become stranded on unmaintained winter roadways. Under no circumstances should you take a shortcut from September to July.
- It is essential to follow all national park and forest service rules here. They are there for a reason.
- Do not stand on the narrow rock ledges for that all-important duck lip selfie at Glacier Park. The dangers of that are self-explanatory.
- To that end, Darwin awards are alive and well here.

Last of all, Montana is the Wild West. This is not a myth. It is rugged and hostile outside formalized structures, and the weather is not the only reason.

- We possess the largest population of Grizzly Bears in the lower 48. The Grizzly is at the top of the food chain. Their range is… anywhere they want. They are unafraid of humans and will attack if you interrupt them or they feel at all threatened. Keep in mind that they are a particularly grumpy animal (Montana Fish, Wildlife, and Parks).
- The Gray Wolf is abundant in NW Montana, and this is its established range. Montana, Idaho and Wyoming have the largest Gray Wolf populations in the country. In Montana, we hunt them. As such, they are no longer at the top of the food chain here.

Since then, I no longer have wolves in my yard or neighborhood, and our livestock aren't harassed. It's funny how that happens.

Until we were allowed to hunt them, they were unafraid of humans, as evidenced by the spunky group hanging out in my yard. Wolves kill for fun, often decimating an entire band of sheep or elk herd, leaving the remains. They are very threatened by other canine species and will kill your dog without hesitation.

Always carry bear spray in any forested area in Montana. They are effective. Those canisters are available for purchase everywhere in Montana, are expensive, and you can't take them home on an airplane. However, you will be very thankful you have one if needed, so budget for that. Everyone in your group needs to carry one.

No, the state of Montana will not provide bear spray for you. This is not a nanny state. You enter the state and its forested mountainous domains at your own risk. It is survival of the fittest and smartest here. We welcome all people, and we love to share our beautiful state. All we ask of our tourists and new residents is that you respect our land, wildlife, way of life, beliefs and us. Otherwise, go to the beaches in California or Oregon. All you need to dodge there are homeless encampments and their drugged-out zombies. Frankly, I would rather take my chances with the bears and wolves, at least they are predictable.

Announcement: Job Posting by the Federal Administration's Department of the Interior.

"Grizzly Bear Conflict Manager"

Do you want to move to Montana? Do you love bears? Are you a hardy individualist who loves the outdoors and is not dissuaded by harsh climates, swarms of biting insects, wild, dangerous animals or rugged wilderness terrain? Do you hate being behind a desk in a cozy, climate-controlled office environment? Instead, do you embrace prolonged deep wilderness camping all by yourself in the great outdoors? If so, this job is for you.

A successful applicant must expect "substantial field work" utilizing boats, small aircraft, snowmobiles, all-terrain vehicles and on foot. Candidates must also be able to tolerate extremely adverse weather conditions. One needs to be able to carry and properly discharge a firearm. This firearm needs to be adequate enough to protect oneself from large, dangerous, carnivorous wildlife should one threaten. Nope, a .22 pistol will not be big enough. In fact, to have any chance, you will need your Taurus Judge, AKA "the Judge," loaded with .454 Casull rounds (Laurene, Here Come Da' Judge 2024).

Successful applicants must be able to lift fifty pounds easily and accurately lift and aim their 4.5-pound Judge. This also includes prolonged exertion over wet, rough, uneven or rocky surfaces, sometimes in deep snow. Do bring your -40-degree packs.

Definitions: Packs

Boots.

"Applicants only need average strength, agility and skill to accomplish all aspects of this job effectively." Yeah, well, good luck with that.

Important Note: The above language was obviously lifted from Washington, D.C.'s Department of the Interior's official manual of the Americans with Disabilities Act. Bureaucrats who blindly follow "the manual" have ABSOLUTELY no clue what this means in a wilderness complex outside of the all-knowing apparatchiks who make up DC (Federal Administration's Department of the Interior 2022).

The chosen candidate will be required to referee any "cultural conflicts" that arise. Applicants must possess excellent communication skills as they mediate issues that may emerge with our "Carnivore Coexistence Advocates" (CCA's) and all those pesky local inhabitants. Beware of the aggravated rancher who lost his $250,000.00 bull to grizzly predation. He must be considered armed and extremely dangerous (Carnivorecoexistence.org 2023) (Sustainable Business.com 2022) (Laurene, An Aggravated Rancher vs. Grizzly; A Retrospective Analysis 2024).

For a salary between $70,000.00 and $103,000.00, depending on your experience and whether you can lift your Judge and walk in snow-packs, some lucky applicant (with two to three helpers) will have the opportunity to patrol 15.3 million acres of some of the harshest wilderness in the lower 48 within Montana, Idaho, Washington and Wyoming's borders. You will work with the CCA to guard against as well as prevent, any "cultural conflicts" that could occur. But again, only average strength, agility and skill are required of any applicant.

Important Contextual Note: Insert eye roll here.

Definitions: Cultural Conflict

An encounter with a grizzly bear that weighs roughly seven hundred pounds, can run 35 mph, is a carnivore with a jaw strength of 1,200 psi, and possesses four-inch claws capable of ripping apart an adult moose. This bear vs. a human who, unless they are a "Super them," has no chance.

I will further decode this "cultural conflict" for those who still don't quite understand. This I will explain using coded encryption, understandable only to those who live by their GULAG, living within the bastions of the East and West coasts.

**The bear is an "ableist" who by
Progressive definition,
"discriminates against those who are
less able-bodied."
Within the genomic of "bear," this is described
as ripping one into shreds.**

Our Montana Life

As for us, we live peaceably in a conservative state full of Normies. If we didn't read the news, we would have no idea what is happening in the rest of the country. We live an extraordinarily free existence, unencumbered by all the nonsense, with a governor and a legislature, who protects us from all the same nonsense. We have discovered the simplicity of rural living, where we have the blessed opportunity to live and work on a farm. We organically raise our own beef and eggs. Steve's insights into beef cattle production have been enormously helpful. He has now taken over the family's "gentleman farmer" distinction. As the "Chicken Contessa," Kris has become the family's leading egg procurer. Pork is purchased from our ranching friends up the lane, and chicken is supplied locally by the Hutterite community. All embrace hard work, family values, and a genuine organic product at a fair price.

As my great-grandparents discovered, there is solace in life on the family farm. They dedicated their lives to developing freedom-loving beliefs realized through dedication and hard work. The Homestead Act and Farming were the frameworks that defined an America based on faith, strong family values and dreams. Dreams foreshadowed the pilgrimage West of all those seeking that dream and a promise of a better life. Dreams are the seeds of destiny.

What we are witnessing today is another such pilgrimage. One where many are exploring their own "new frontiers," seeking a better life away from the insanities that began with COVID-19 mandates. They are dreamers who are escaping urban centers to open spaces, fewer people and newfound joy. Places of simple common-sense values that blue cities have discarded. Places where people can once again live in harmony with one another and feel safe. Places where we won't find a homeless encampment on the sidewalk in front of our home, or some naked man discarded in a shopping cart. Yep, I saw it myself in a Seattle middle-class neighborhood. I'm pretty sure he was dead.

In Montana, we discovered that there are still places in this country where children can grow amongst the values that once defined a nation.

As children, we have always lived in that world. Our parents were wise when they refused to move us to San Francisco. How much different could our lives have been? Instead, they followed a dream, changing our destiny to that of rural communities and the values inherited within that environment. Our lives changed exponentially when our parents moved us all permanently to La Grande. As a result, we learned all those skills through experience, as my parents taught themselves the commonalities of living a simple life. My mother only home canned after moving to La Grande. Neither of them cultivated a garden or grew a fruit tree. Instead, we learned those skills together as a family. We discovered the value of saving home-grown food for later. Our mother always kept a full pantry. We discovered the value of farm-fresh milk and eggs purchased locally.

We discovered the value of heating with wood to save energy costs. We learned to cut our firewood. We learned the ecological importance of clearing dead trees so live trees and undergrowth can flourish. All our family's free time was used up as we continually worked and played together. It was a life that wasn't built on mobile devices or television. It was a time that built family cohesiveness, which we still practice today.

Having never camped before, Dad had the basics of such through Boy Scouts and ROTC. Our move to La Grande provided wide open spaces and endless entertainment opportunities for families. A place that could build on all those earlier skills in his life while promoting a fun, family-centered activity. Back then, there was little extra money, so camping basics were purchased on a shoestring budget. It was about having fun while learning the basics of survival in a safe environment. It is the fundamental precept of boy scouting and why our brother enjoyed his Camp Silverback experience as much as he did. He would be so sad that Boy Scouting is now dead, having been emasculated beyond all recognition before being swallowed by the DEI shark (Chavez 2024).

I know our parents did not realize at the time what they were ultimately developing back then. All they were doing was creating the conditions for a family-centered universe. A place where families also worked hard together for the betterment and survival of the family. This was our parents' ultimate destiny. Nothing was more valuable than those long-ago lessons they taught us, as they unknowingly prepared us for our world today.

We live a truly sustainable life as we build upon all those skills we learned as kids. We still cut our firewood. We have hunted wild game. We run a hobby farm and keep our pantries full of a steady supply of necessary goods to hold us over in emergencies. Because of our homesteading practices, we are given the derogatory description of being "preppers." I can identify with that description, which is meant to be disparaging. Those living under that banner are proud of it and our accomplishments. We are those who are happy and content. It is the disparagers who are unhappy, angry and bitter who seek to bring us all down to their level of dissatisfaction.

Interestingly, millionaires across the country are building "bunkers." Underground fully contained structures are now the "in thing" among the millionaire elitist class. This is categorized amongst the "prepping class" as next-level prepping, but among the highbrowed, this is merely defined in their ordered language GULAG as "preparedness" (Moench 2023).

Question: Does anybody else wonder why progressive-adjacent millionaires are suddenly preparing for some disaster?

Because of our "racist pantry practices," the infamous toilet paper shortage of 2021 did not take us by surprise. We had plenty to last throughout the crisis. During the Children's Tylenol shortage (which should never happen), Steve used his gun reloading scales to precisely cut and weigh adult Tylenol to a pediatric dose for our very ill grandchild.

I grind wheat berries for fresh flour and bake bread in our sustainable gas stove. Should we run out of propane, we still have an even more sustainable wood cookstove.

Why did we build our sustainable life? The day the Obamas were elected, we readily recognized what was happening to our America. We believed him when he proclaimed, "The fundamental transformation of the United States of America." On that January day in 2009, we knew that one should never count on our government to do what is right to protect America's interests. Over the next fifteen years, we gradually and steadily built our sustainable life.

> *"When someone shows you who they are, believe them the first time."*
> *Maya Angelou…*

As all rural northern families understand, electricity can be unavailable during prolonged winter outages. To that end, we have a hand pump on our well cap and a backup generator. Like Camp Silverback, our generator provides sustained refrigeration, water pumps, livestock water heaters, and allows home water heaters to run. This is the definition of sustainable living. Should an outage last longer than our generator can function, we can still cook and heat our home with firewood, a supply that will last four years. We can always hand pump water from our wells during prolonged electrical outages.

These are the basics of survival. The one thing that Covid taught us is that we are sitting on a great, big, gigantic house of cards. The Covid Chronicles was a warm-up and a warning sign, and those of us who paid attention understand how fragile it is as Progressives fiddle with our energy supplies, our sovereignty and our freedoms. As government debt increases to record levels, inflation runs rampant as they spend more and more money on wars that aren't ours or green energy pipedreams that will never work. $34 trillion in debt cannot have a good outcome. As a result, people across the political spectrum are seeing it for what it is and are preparing for the worst. Close observers have been preparing for a long time.

Who are we? We are concrete thinkers who never dwell on absurd notions of inclusivity. You can only take "fairness" and its abstract notions so far before it begins to override common sense, which it clearly has. Abstract thinkers who live and breathe under their "all-inclusive fairness" doctrine are prevented from seeing a dire reality. Common sense concrete thinkers see all the signs of precarious times that keep building. It is the abstract thinkers primarily in cities who cannot see beyond their noses and are those nowadays who "vote blue, no matter who." It is why common senser's are fleeing the cities to rural domains by the millions (Burnett 2022).

Every decade since the 2000s, Progressives spare no amount of effort to portray how much they dislike us. In 2008, we were "bitter people clinging to our bibles and guns." In 2016, we were the "basket of deplorables." Now, in 2024, we are "angry white rural racist Americans," and the most dangerous "geodemographic" group in America. The book, out this year by the same description, has all the customary Progressive talking head descriptions that include the "existential threat to democracy" as the usual lead-in. To

> "When you see that in order to produce, you need to obtain permission from men who produce nothing. When you see that money is flowing to those who deal not in goods, but in favors. When you see that men get richer by graft and by pull, then by work, and your laws don't protect you against them, but protect them against you. When you see corruption being rewarded and honesty becoming a self-sacrifice You may know that your society is doomed."
> *Ayn Rand, Author Atlas Shrugged, 1957*

Progressives, threats to democracy only exist if they aren't re-elected (K. Reilly 2016) (Pilkington 2008) (Schaller 2024).

In the Progressive game of chess, their king was exposed and vulnerable. Being so cognitively impaired he was incapable of any meaningful counter-offensive. He was then swapped out for a Rook, who can't operate anywhere other than to the left of the chessboard. As the lowly rural pawns against the elite grandmasters, we are creating obstacles, controlling many squares, giving us center control, and blocking their Knights. We have created a "danger zone," and they are afraid. We now have the advantage. We are used to being cast aside by elitist Progressive politicians. They failed to notice that we don't care. Fending for ourselves has made us more resilient.

Common sense tells us that what we are seeing today is the perfect storm building on the horizon. Our Progressive government leaders and their DEI, ESG and intersectional prioritized policies have no desire to ensure a sustainable America. It takes little imagination to realize that an EF5 cyclone is about to hit. Anything can happen, which doesn't mean it will. But if it does, there will be no warning. Everyone has the ability to do something to prepare for such an emergency, and they should.

My pronouns are insurrectionist gloatist, stockpiling, trans-nonconforming TERF, cattle ranching, diesel trucking, pistol-packing, sarcastic, rural, Grammie Barbie.

PART VIII

Today, Tomorrow, and Destinies

While writing this book, I had ample time and opportunity to analyze many formal structures, one of them being my own family structure. Families have built-in leadership that is created over time. It becomes the foundation and the glue that holds the family together. As in any foundation, a family structure with foundational fissures will crumble when the foundation fails. This is what occurred to our extended family when my father died. Dad was the foundation that kept the family standing. Then, a few years later, Dad's sister Pam suddenly passed away from ovarian cancer. With the foundation all but gone, Pam had been the glue that would attempt to hold it together. With her passing, the structure failed. My grandmother was elderly and fragile and incapable of holding it together. Once our grandmother was gone, our family scattered into the wind.

    Moving to Montana helped us reconnect with some of our fractured family. Cousin Jenny, her husband Mike, and their children only live a few hours away. Out of our seven cousins, they are the only family who has stayed close to us. Their children are accomplished football, basketball and baseball athletes on teams that frequently compete against Flathead Valley schools. It has been fun to sit in those bleachers, watching youngsters grow and excel in their chosen sporting activity. Jenny and Mike are talking about retiring someday in the Flathead. I suspect we will have the opportunity to see even more of them in the future, and that is very good.

    Not until I finally penned this book, did I experience a profound discovery. The threads of our lives, seemingly unrelated at the time, intersect in and out again later. I know it is so cliche, but not until I thought about all those distant memories and put them down on paper, did I discover the true meaning of the fabric of our lives. It was a great exercise in understanding the uniqueness of our upbringing and that it wasn't as boring as I thought.

While writing, I also realized how unnecessarily complicated life in the United States has become. Amid all the insanity, I thank my parents daily for the opportunities they gave us as we explored the world around us. As we explored and discovered together, we were taught many lessons as children that have become invaluable today. They did it as all middle-class families used to do. Using the single resource of their time to create strong adults for the future. No amount of money can replace that.

If there is one lesson that I can give my grandchildren, it is the most valuable lesson our parents taught us. Lessons embedded in values are passed down from many generations. They are lessons that taught us that only you are in control of your destiny. If you are unhappy with your direction, do what you need to do to change it. Don't just sit and wallow in misery or discontent and don't expect somebody else to do it for you. Like our pioneer family, decide what you are doing and where you are going. Conceptualize the steps to get there. Write down short and long-term goals to get to that place and that dream. Then do it. It might take a few years, a lot of patience, determination, perseverance and hard work, but as I have stated many times in this book; with that comes strength of character. All dreams are worth accomplishing because they are your dreams. Dreams never stop. They are built throughout a lifetime and can change on a dime. Unforeseen circumstances can force changes in your plan. It is nobody's fault. It is life. As I enter my autumn years, I can't help but marvel at the trajectory of my life as all those dreams either came to fruition or were changed by circumstance. Circumstances that may have crushed previous goals and dreams, only to be re-defined later. Always keep trying and never give up. That is what destiny is all about.

> "This is about life being ahead of you, and you run at it! Because you will never know how far you can go unless you run."
> Penny Chenery,
> *Owner of Secretariat...*

Epilogue

Randy had many plans he was looking forward to. He was finally content with his life. Relieved from the chains of his eating disorder, he was moving forward and beginning again. However, the damage to his body was just too great. Randy died in his sleep that fateful night of a typical sequelae related to obesity, a critical abnormal heart rhythm. For us, none of that matters now.

Fondly recorded in his journal writings and letters to our parents, he always knew that we all loved and supported him. Kris and I struggled for years with what we could have done differently before his death. Were there things that could have been done or words said that could have changed the path that ended his life all too soon? Randy had his own demons, fears and sorrows. He had deep secrets he was afraid to reveal. He could hide all his feelings and fears with his quick wit and funny stories that kept us all amused. While he entertained us, he successfully concealed his torment.

When Justin was an infant, I found Randy one day sitting in a chair, quietly watching Justin as he slept peacefully in his crib. It was one of the only times I found him sorrowful. He looked at me and then at Justin again, marveling at the innocence of children. He mused about how children are so free from all the worry and fears that become such a part of adulthood. I wondered at the time what was occurring in his life that made him make such a remark. In usual Randy fashion, though, he made some humorous light to it, hugging me as he quickly exited the door.

It would be nearly two decades before I would discover what was occurring in his life in front of Justin's crib that day. Only after Randy's death did I find any evidence of those struggles, his anguish and his anger. It would all be revealed later in his personal belongings that I found following his death. Within that discovery were his clinical and journal notes, written while he was in therapy. It revealed something much deeper than what our family realized. Something he didn't want to burden the family with. With this discovery, it became clear that Randy's obesity was a symptom of a much larger issue. What began in childhood was uncontrollably exacerbated as an adult. What we blamed as an extension of a childhood problem had grown into something none of us fully understood.

For others like Randy, who struggle daily with food obsessions, food addictions and obesity, there are people who care and want to help you. As survivors of a loved one's eating disorder, we only wish Randy had shared his struggle with us more than he did. I think we could have helped. Our family was robbed of our brother's companionship due to obesity. We will never know what growing old together would have been like. He would have turned sixty years of age in 2023. We can only dream about what could have been possible.

Unlike my brother, millions of people are out there who still have a chance to change it. I wish every day that Randy was still in our lives. Don't let popular culture and misguided money-making entrepreneurs and "influencers" fool you from exploring your path to health and wellness.

Randy was a great man. He loved unconditionally and would give the shirt off his back to anyone in need. He never said an unkind word or disparaged anyone. His eternal optimism and wit always lit up a room. He was always thoughtful and giving, often giving more of himself than others were willing to give him. His life and loss taught Kris, Justin and I many things. He is remembered today not for what he could have been but for what he was. He taught us that everyone has their own story, whether we choose to share it or not. He taught us that unless we know that story, we shouldn't be quick to judge, dismiss or characterize others. It is something I strive for and continually work on every day.

We sprinkled his ashes into the Lostine River at French camp. It was always our favorite family camping spot in the Wallowa Whitman National Forest. It was a place that brought him joy. It was a special place he always fondly remembered and talked about often. In retrospect, it was a place of fun and delight, free from any adult burdens or responsibilities. It was about the joy and security he once felt, being amongst family.

That sunny summer afternoon, Laura joined Justin, Kris, and me on the Lostine River. We were all a part of Randy's center core. Steve joined us, and we enjoyed a great family picnic at our favorite family camping spot beside the river. His presence was as strong as ever that day as we talked and laughed about good ole' Randy times.

Then, from our old family camping site where we pitched that tent long ago, where we played as children in the quiet cove with our mom where I caught that crawdad. It was where Randy discovered the awe of gray rocks, where Kris found a unique "whistle" on the dirt road, and where we would begin that hike up to the waterfall. It was where Dad cooked our breakfast every morning in the presence of the beauty and the sounds of the Lostine River. Where the three of us would climb up on a driftwood log in the middle of the river to fish, as we could see, smell, and feel the serenity and comfort of our campsite and our parents close by.

Laura, Kris, Steve, Justin and I then waded into that river that held so many beautiful memories for our family. Holding Randy's ashes in our finest crystal stemware, we climbed onto that driftwood log for the last time. We raised our glasses and thanked him for all his contributions to our own lives, which enriched us so much. Then, after saying a small prayer, we poured him into that river, just as we did for our wonderful mother on that beach in Kauai. We then poured a glass of champagne into that fine stemware. We stood out on that driftwood log in the middle of the Wallowa Whitman National Forest. The crystal-clear waters of the Lostine River flowed beneath us. The sunshine warmed our faces as we reached our glasses into the clear blue sky. We then completed a toast, honoring our brother, our best friend and our uncle. He would have liked that.

We have never returned to the Lostine River and French Camp. Thanks to the State of Oregon, it will never be the same. I am not as angry about that as I am sad, not just for me and my family but for other families who will never know what it was or what it could have been for them. French Camp, to me, is a symbol of government overreach and the chinking away of the invaluable freedoms that our country was founded upon. My grandchildren's generation is on the precipice of never experiencing the foundation of freedom and exploration America once enjoyed. Unless we do something about it ourselves, it will soon be gone forever.

In the waning months of Mom's illness, Randy and I had many heart-to-heart conversations in the final two weeks of his life. Those conversations are precious to me now, and I think about them often. Life flies by so fast. It is hard to believe he has been gone for twenty years. I sense his spirit in those conversations, which ultimately helped me through the heartache and the longing for his presence. It has helped me navigate my life today in such a tumultuous time. Randy's loss taught us that life is fragile and fleeting, and we must live every day like it is our last. Kris and I never let a day go by without telling those we care about most that we love them.

In all its unfairness, it became clear to me that despite all his struggles, Randy found that inner peace we all strive for. His destiny was conquering his Bongos with positivity in his heart that affected everyone around him more than he ever knew. He set an example that none of us realized ourselves until he was gone. He was an influencer in kindness, hope and the importance of family, community and country. That is the kind of influencer we all can achieve and share.

Throughout life, we all search for an answer to the question, why exactly are we here. What sort of destiny am I supposed to fulfill? Did I make a difference to those that I love? Dividers, detractors, distractors and the chronically embittered in our society are working overtime to break us down. To them, it is a now-or-never quest for dominance. They use acceptance and "Greater Good" concepts to the exclusion of ourselves. They are the chronically dissatisfied, who seek to bring the rest of us down to their level of discontent. We need to realize that we all have permission to be happy.

Lastly, free belief systems are critical in a free society. It is an environment where one can live, work, share and teach without fear of reprisal. It is a rule of law based on fundamental moral and biological truths that are easily understood, fair and equitably administered.

Bongo means drum, and those of us who love ourselves, our children, and our country, we are beating it hard against the powerful in government and a subculture that is doing its darndest to destroy us from within. They are exploiting us, using the same virtues of fairness against us to destroy the freedoms that have defined our culture and our country for 240 years. The sooner we understand that the sooner this will be over.

Never stop banging that bongo. It is the beat of freedom that will conquer. It won't be easy, but nothing worth it ever is.

"It makes you realize how insignificant man-made objects are in comparison to the creations of a higher power.
It seems to remind us of something easy to forget, that we shouldn't put so much emphasis on the material objects we find around us, they seem so insignificant from such a great height.
We should live on the mountain top all the time, even though we are in the surroundings down below.

My father, circa 1958

Acknowledgments and Heartfelt Thanks

We are grateful to Randy's many friends, who are too numerous to list. Your love and support for our brother meant a lot to him and us. You will never be forgotten.

To our family, Nell, Steve, Anita, and Russ, who is now in heaven. Without your love and support, Kris, Justin and I would never have survived that time.

To my cousin David for his historical family insights and great conversations. Thank you for all the support you gave to our mother and then to us when she died.

To Nell, Steve and Erica, thank you for always holding our hands, even during the most difficult of circumstances.

To my sister Kris, my son Justin and my Aunt Barbara, thank you for sharing your memories and reminding me of some great family stories.

To my sister Leslie for her technical writing counsel. Thank you for your candid advice and for keeping me on the proper path. It wasn't easy, but as you stated, it was worth it.

To my wife, Nell, for her contributions to literary writing, your creative advice and for the final book edit. Hopefully, this book embodies what you tried to teach me.

To my brother and book reviewer Charles. Thank you for your time, effort and forthright advice.

To my cousin, the late Mary Sunderlage. Her book "Sophie," made me proud of my heritage, inspiring me to research further into Sophie's era.

To my great-grandmother Sophia. She endured, regardless of the heartache and the struggles of her time. Throughout her life, Sophie was a pioneer of many things without meaning to be. She created her destiny by pushing boundaries and, in doing so, created new paths for other women to follow. Her determination inspired me as I sought to channel all she stood for in what it means to be a strong woman. It is a potential within all women today that cannot be imitated. It is what defines a woman and is only really understood within the heart of a woman.

My great-grandmother was named after the Holy Patron Saint of Wisdom. In Roman history, St. Sophia had three daughters named after the virtues of Faith, Hope and Love. I know of no other person who has inspired such within me or my family's story. Like my parents, my great-grandmother is my hero.

To my brother Randy, who always saw the best in everybody and interpreted life through rose-colored glasses. Love, laughter and humor were his gifts to everyone he touched. He demonstrated true acceptance by simply living his day-to-day life. He proved that those who practice acceptance do not need to prove it or measure it. He taught us many lessons in the short time he was here. On this twentieth anniversary of his death, hopefully, a piece of Randy lives in all of us.

This book was extra special to me because it was a true family affair. My family helped me gather so many important memories, afforded me such extraordinary talent, and patiently assisted me in becoming a stronger writer.

And finally, many thanks to my good friend Walter from the Appalachians of North Georgia, whose fun illustrations and beautiful portraits brought this book to life. You have an incredible talent. Thank you for sharing it with me and my family.

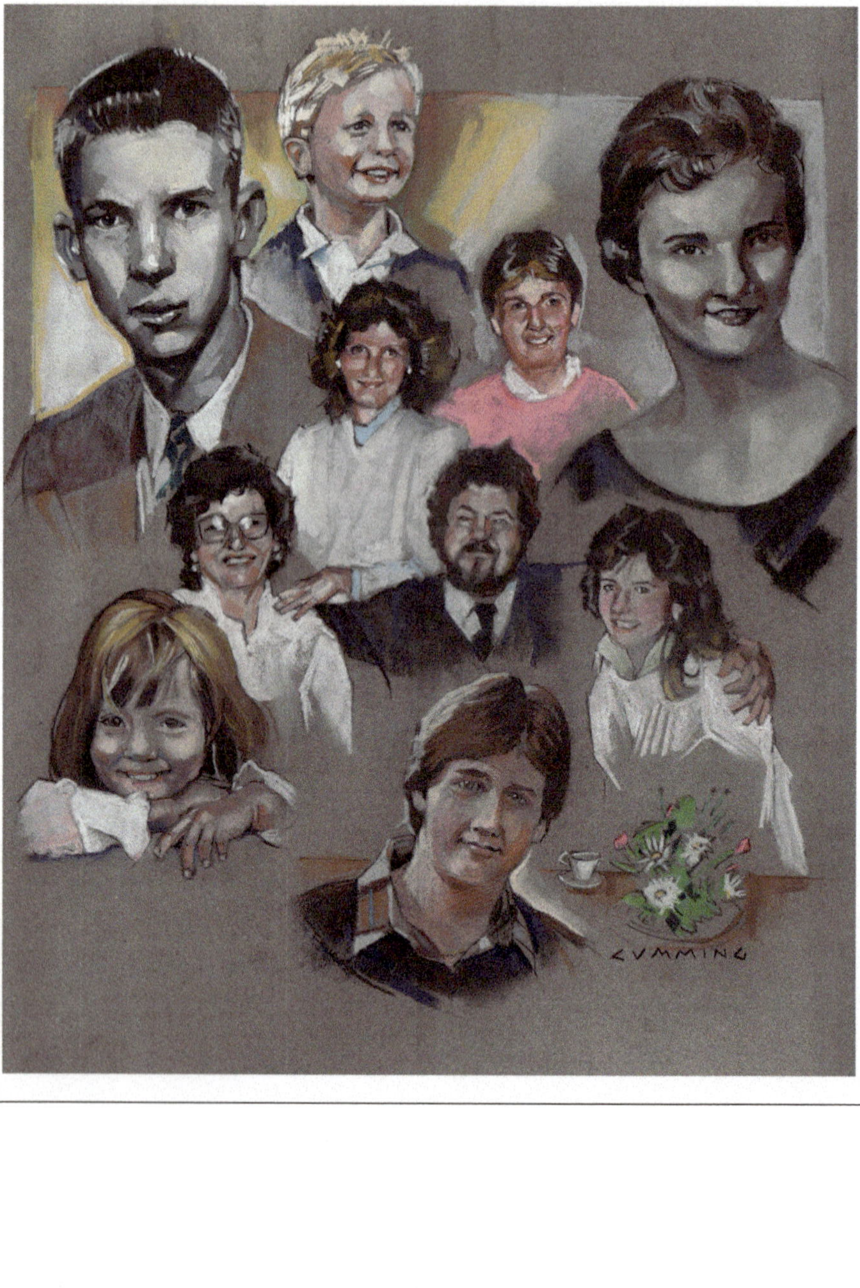
CUMMING

What is Happiness...

It's the simple bits of daily bliss, unrelated to material affluence, that contribute the most to the total happiness of living. If you have a small circle of loved ones, a place to call home, a useful job, and a heart and mind receptive to life's little pleasures, you are as blessed as anyone on earth.

Yours is...

The adoration of youngsters

The majesty of skyscrapers and the blazing panorama of a big city at night

The divine beauty and perfume of flowers

The thrilling glory of a golden sunrise

The sight of silvery frost-painted leaves, lawns and fields on crisp fall mornings

The awe of a single snowflake and the force of a blizzard

The cheerful glow of a fireplace and the snugness of warm garments on cold winter days

The thrill of a good read

The tingle of pride in a task well done

The amazement of vast oceans, endless forests and a bee pollinating a clover.

You are blessed...

If you can watch a schoolyard full of children at play

Smell the aromas of home cooking

Thrill to the majesty of a thunderstorm

Watch fall leaves dance across the landscape on a windswept day

Hear music in crickets, birds and the wind blowing through the trees.

    You have a great deal to be thankful for...

If you can share a laugh with a bosom friend

See romance in a train crawling through the night

Lend a helping hand to someone who needs it, and

Enjoy the peace that settles at the end of the day when families and friends draw close.

    The list is almost endless...

It includes everyone's right to happy thoughts and dreams

It includes the joy when another nick is taken off the mortgage

It is an invitation to a party

The pleasure of a hot bath

Watching a tree grow

The accomplishment of growing your own garden

The pride of hiking to the top of a mountain

The sweet bliss of untroubled sleep, and

The sights one sees on the way to work.

    Besides these things...

Cars, jewels, furs, money, mansions and especially power—pale into insignificance.

Written a century ago by my Great Great Uncle, Dr. W.E. Borgerson. His timeless musings are as relevant today as it was back then...

Source

Aasheim, Magnus. 1970. *Sheridan's Daybreak: A Story of Sheridan County and its Pioneers.* Plentywood: Blue Print and Letter Printers.

Abbott, Joel. 2023. "Have You Seen the New Goat-Horned Demon That Now Stands Atop a New York Courthouse?" *Not The Bee.* January 26.

2023. "Joe On High-Speed Rail Investment Today: "Over a Billion Three Hundred Million Trillion Three Hundred Million Dollars!"." *Not The Bee.* December 8.

Abbruzzese, Jason et al. 2022. "Biden Takes Big Step Toward Government-Backed Digital Currency." *NBC News.* March 10. nbcnews.com.

Acobe, Paulo. 2023. "Rental Car with California Plates Spotted in Kalispell, MT, with Sign Informing Locals They're Not Actually from California." *Tiremeetsroad.com.* February 5. https://tiremeetsroad.com/2023/02/05/rental-car-california-plates-spotted-kalispell-mt-sign-informing-locals-they-re-not-actually-california/.

Adamy, Janet. 2023. "Young Americans are Dying at Alarming Rates, Reversing Years of Progress." *The Wall Street Journal.* May 17. wsj.com.

Adoption for My Baby. n.d. *adoption-for-my-baby.com.*

Agiesta, Jennifer. 2016. "Most Say Race Relations Worsened Under Obama, Poll Finds." *CNN.* October 5. cnn.com.

Aleem, Abdul et al. 2021. "Coronavirus (COVID-19) Vaccine-Inducted Immune Thrombotic Thrombocytopenia (VITT)." *National Library of Medicine; National Center for Biotechnology Information* PMID: 34033367 Bookshelf ID: NBK570605.

Alexander, Paul Elias. 2021. *150 Plus Research Studies Affirm Naturally Acquired Immunity to COVID-19: Documented, Linked, and Quoted.* Compilation of 150 peer-reviewed studies, Brownstone Institute.

Alfonseca, Kiara. 2023. The Feminist Movement Has Changed Drastically. Here's What

the Movement Looks Like Today. *ABC News.* March 11. abc.go.net

Allavena, Rachel. 2019. "Is it Safe for Your Cat or Dog to Eat a Vegan Diet?" *ABC News.* April 6. abc.net.au.

Allen, Blake. 2022. "My High School Punished Me for Saying a Male Shouldn't be Allowed to Watch Me Undress. I Was Taught That Girls Should Speak Up When Something Makes Them Uncomfortable, But the School Didn't Care." *Fox News.* November 17.

Altus, Kristen. 2023. "Millennials, Gen Z go on Tirades Over Jobs Climate: "A Bone to Pick With America."." *Fox Business.* December 13. foxbusiness.com.

Anderson Distillery and Grill. 2022. "Barrel Babes Drag Brunch." *Facebook.* August 28. https://m.facebook.com/events/1273532486725117/?ref=newsfeed.

1985. *Macguyver.* Directed by Created by Lee David Zlotoff. Performed by Richard Dean Anderson.

Andrew Brown, David. 2016. "Living in an 1800s Sod House." *Preppers Will,* January 15.

Andrzejewsk, Adam. 2023. "Substack: Invent Your Own Gender. Governor Gavin Newsom Encourages Youth With Millions in Taxpayer Support." *Open The Books.* September 15.

AP. 2023. "Oregon's Drug Decriminalization Law Faces Growing Pushback Amid Fentanyl Crisis." *New York Post.* November 19. nypost.com.

Armanini, Kate. 2024. "Amid Migrant Crisis, Chicago Food Pantries Experience Unprecendented Demand." *Chicago Tribune.* March 8. msn.com.

Armstrong, Martin. 2022. "The World is Laughing at America." *Armstrong Economics.* April 14. armstrongeconomics.com.

Arnold, Sarah. 2024. "Biden Admin Dishes Out $700,000 Into Another Woke, Radical Transgender Program." *Townhall.* January 13. townhall.com.

2023. "Biden's DHS Forces Border Agents to Use Preferred Pronouns for Illegal Aliens." *Townhall.* November 25. townhall.com.

2024. "Biden DOJ Charges Surgeon for Exposing Trans Surgeries at Hospital; Texas Children's

Hospital Secretly Performing Transgender Surgeries on Minors." *Townhall.* townhall.com. June 8.

2024. "Tyson Foods Fires Hard-Working American Employees and Instead Hires Illegal Immigrants." *Townhall.* March 15. townhall.com.

Asmelash, Leah. 2022. "In 5 Years of #MeToo, Here's What's Changed - And What Hasn't." *CNN.* October 27. cnn.com.

Associated Press. 2024. ""Elderly Man With a Poor Memory": Special Counsel Finds Evidence Biden Willfully Mishandled Classified Info But No Charges Warranted." *Boston Herald.* February 8. bostonherald.com.

2023. "Biden Unveils LGBTQ+ Proposals but Postpones White House Pride Monthe Event Due to Poor Air Quality." *ABC News.* June 8.

2023. "Montana Man Mauled by a Grizzly Bear Has Long Recovery Ahead." *The Flathead Beacon.* September 12. flatheadbeacon.com.

Association, The American Psychiatric. n.d. "What is Gender Dysphoria?" In *DSM-R-TR*, by The American Psychiatric Association.

Atlas, Scott MD, Steve H. Ph.D, Kerpen, Philip, et al. 2024. COVID Lessons Learned;

A Retrospective After Four Years. Committee to Unleash Prosperity, Executive Summary. Report reviews the major policy errors and lessons learned during the COVID-19 pandemic from a balanced perspective. https://www.independent.org/pdf/research_articles/2024_03_15_hanke_tlas_covid%20lessons%20learned_final.pdf March.

Baker, Harry. 2022. "Three People Gored by Bison in a Month at Yellowstone Park. Why Do These Attacks Keep Happening?" *Live Science*, July 2.

Bakst, Daren et al. 2017. "Report: Poverty and Inequity." *The Heritage Foundation*. April 5.

Banerjee, Krishnendu. 2021. "UK Company Develops Masks for Cows to Control Methane Emissions and Fight Climate Change: As Cows Burp Methane, the Smart Mask Breaks it Down and Reduces Greenhouse Gas Emissions to Help in the Fight for Climate Change." *International Business Times: Science.* January 2.

Barber, Harriet. 2023. "Homelessness in the US Soars to Record Level in Blow to Joe Biden; The president's flagship "All In" homlessness, policy, launched a year ago, promised to reduce levels by 25%." *The Telegraph*. December 16. telegraph.co.uk.

Bardosh, PhD. Kevin et al. 2022. "COVID-19 Vaccine Boosters for Young Adults: A Risk-Benefit Assessment and Five Ethical Arguments Against Mandates at Universities." *Journal of Medical Ethics* (SSRN) (https://jme.bmj.com/content/ear).

Barrie, J.M. 1904. *Peter Pan*. Performed by Many. Duke of York.

Bauer, Fred. 2023. "Biden Has Lost the Battle for the Soul of the Nation." *The Telegraph.* December 18.

BBC. 2021. "Major and Champ: Joe Biden's Dogs Moved out of White House." March 9. bbc.com.

2020. "Oregon Becomes First US State to Decriminalize Hard Drugs." *BBC News*. November 4.

Begody, Candace (reviewed by). 2023. "50 Important Welfare Statistics for 2023." *Lexington Law.* April 10. lexingtonlaw.com.

Bennett, Paige. 2023. "East Palestine Trail Derailment Killed More Than 43,000 Fish and Animals Officials Say." *USA Today.* February 24.

Benningfield, Bailey et al. 2024. How Many Watts Does it Take to Run a House? Forbes.com

March 14

Bernstein, Brittany. 2023. "Biden Administration Considers Banning Gas Stoves Over Health Concerns." *National Review.* January 9.

2020. "Biden Says Antifa is "An Idea, Not an Organization" During Presidential Debate." *National Review.* September 29. nationalreview.com.

Berrien, Hank. 2023. "Woke Disney Lost Almost $900 Million on Last 8 Films: Report." *Daily Wire.* June 27.

Berlatsky, Noah. 2018. Judge Rules That Judaism is not a race, but Jewish People can be

Targeted for Racism. Here's Why That Matters; A timely new court ruling is a reminder that human racial differences are based in prejudice, not fact. NBC News. nbcnews.com. August 2.

Bess, Gabby. 2015. "Reuse, Reduce, Reproductive Rights: How Abortion Can Help Save the Planet." *Vice.* October 6. vice.com.

2022. "Whistleblowers: FBI Targeted Parents via Terrorism Tools Despite Garland's Testimony that it Didn't Happen." *Fox News.* May 11. foxnews.com.

Bhaimiya, Sawdah. 2023. "An Agency Created an AI Model Who Earns Up to $11,000 a Month Because it was Tired of Influencers 'Who have Egos'." *Business Insider.* November 24. businessinsider.com.

Bhattacharya, Ankhi. 2022. "What is Child Grooming? How Can Parents Protect Their Kids? How to Deal with Child Grooming." *WONDERSHARE.* August 16.

Biden/Harris Campaign. 2024. Partner Manager, Content and Meme Pages. The Biden

for President Campaign Seeks a Partner Manager to Join the Digital Partnership Team to Engage the Internet's Top Content and Meme Pages. Mobilization-Digital/Full Time/On Site https://jobs.lever.co/BFP/87722c1a-e593-4c2e-a630-50671dea033f/apply.

Bienasz, Gabrielle. 2022. "How Much Do Engineers, Product Managers, And Data Scientists Make At Twitter?" *Entrepreneur.* October 12. entrepreneur.com.

Bikales, James. 2023. Congress Provided $7.5B for Electric Vehicle Chargers. Built so far:

Zero. *Politico.* Politico.com. December 5

Blackmon, David. 2023. "Biden Officials Just Can't Keep Their Hands Off Your Gas Stoves." *Forbes.* February 3. forbes.com.

Blaff, Ari. 2023. "Riley Gaines Assaulted by Trans Activists at San Francisco State University." *National Review.* April 7. news.yahoo.com.

Bland, Scott. 2016. "George Soros' Quiet Overhaul of the U.S. Justice System." *POLITICO.* August. politico.com.

Blankley, Bethany. 2021. "Newsom, State Failed Nursing Home Residents During COVID-19 Outbreak, Reports Find." *The Center Square.* October 18. thecentersquare.com.

Blitzer, Ronn. 2022. "Mom Plans Legal Action After 7-Year-Old Girl Punished by School for BLM Poster That Said "Any Life."." *Fox News.* July 11. foxnews.com.

Bloomfield, Sally F. et al. 2016. "Time to Abandon the Hygiene Hypothesis: New Perspectives on Allergic Disease, the Human Microbiome, Infections Disease Prevention and the role of Targeted Hygiene." *Sage Journals* (RSPH) (https://doi.org/10.1177/1757913916650225).

Bodkin, Henry. 2024. "How the Democrats Finally Ousted Joe Biden." *The Telegraph.*

telegraph.co.uk July 21.

Boeckmann, Catherine. 2024. Kwanzaa 2024: How is Kwanzaa Celebrated? The Origins,

Meaning and Traditions of Kwanzaa. *ALMANAC.* almanac.com. January 17.

Boehm, Eric. 2022. "FDA Finally Admits it Caused the Baby Formula Shortage." *Reason.* July 7.

Bois, Paul. 2019. "Snopes Fact-Checks The Satirical Babylon Bee...Again." *The Daily Wire.* February 20. dailywire.com.

Bonchie. 2023. "Winsome Sears Smacks Down Bill Maher Guest Claiming Nashville Transgender Shooter is Being 'Misgendered.'." *Red State.* April 1. redstate.com.

Bond, Jessica. 2018. "Trigger Warnings are Taking Over Universities, But do They Work?" *New Scientist.* February 21. newscientist.com.

Bonneville Power Administration. 2010. "Fact Sheet: Power Benefits of the Lower Snake River Dams." March. bpa.gov.

Borden, Sam. 2015. "Long Hidden Details Reveal Cruelty of 1972 Munich Attackers." *New York Times.* December 1.

Bova, Tristan. 2021. "Ecofeminism: Where Gender and Climate Change Intersect." *earth.org.* July 19.

Bowers Bahney, Jennifer. 2023. "MSNBC Reports It's "Certainly Notable" That WH Cocaine Was Found Near the Situation Room." *MSNBC News.* July 6.

Boyle, Darren. 2020. "British Government to Compensate People Who Suffer Extreme COVID-19 Vaccine Side Effects With Payments of up to 120,000 Pounds Under the Existing Scheme for Common Jabs." *The Daily Mail.* December 3.

Boyle, Louise. 2023. "'Here it is Better Not to be Born': Cobalt Mining for Big Tech is Driving Child Labor, Deaths in the Congo." *The Independent.* February 23. independent.co.uk.

Brinkley, Collin. 2022. "Test Scores Show Historic COVID-19 Setbacks for Kids Across US." *Associated Press.* October 24. apnews.com.

Britannica. 1876. "Becky Thatcher, a fictional character." *Adventures of Tom Sawyer.* Prod. Mark Twain.

"Vaccine Development of Louis Pasteur." *Britannica.* britannica.com.

British Medical Journal. 2023. "Flawed Body of Research Indicates True "Long Covid" Risk Likely Exaggerated, Says New Study." *Medical Press.* September 25. medicalxpress.com.

Brooks, Jon. 2018. "The Controversial Research on 'Desistance' in Transgender Youth." *KQED.* May 23. kqed.org.

Brooks, Mel. 1987. ""May the Swartz Be With you," A Parady of "May the Force Be with You" from Star Wars." *Spaceballs, Directed by Mel Brooks.*

Brooks, Richard. 2016. "The Top 5 Star Trek Languages." *The Language Blog.* September 14.

Brothers, Warner. Introduced 1937. *Bugs Bunny Cartoon.* Produced by Animated cartoon character by Looney Tunes/Merrie Melodies series. Performed by Elmer Fudd.

Brown, Lee. 2019. ""Eviction" Notices Placed on Doors of Jewish Students at Emory University." *New York Post.* April 5. nypost.com.

2021. "Taliban Has Billions in US Weapons, Including Black Hawks and up to 600 Thousand Rifles." *New York Post.* August 20. nypost.com.

Brown, Mathew. 2022. Wind Energy Company Kills 150 Eagles in US, Pleads Guilty.

Associated Press. apnews.com. April 6.

Bruce, Gregor. 2021. "Definition of Terrorism - Social and Political Effects." *JMVH* (Licensed under a Creative Commons Attribution 4.0 International License) 21 (2): doi-ds.org/doilink/11.2021-37833375/JMVH Vol 21 No 2.

Bruns, Jacob. 2023. "Biden Boasts That More Than Half the Women in His Administration Are Women." *Headline USA.* February 3.

Budinger, Bill. 2019. "Why Wind and Solar Aren't Enough: Both suffer from an intermittency problem. A plausible back-up source is needed-and there's only one." *DEMOCRACY: A Journal of Ideas.* August 9. democracyjournal.org.

Burgess RDN, MacKenzie et al. 2024. "How Many Carbs do you Need in a Day?" *Eating Well.* March 2. eatingwell.com.

Burguiere, Stu. n.d. *Stu Burguiere's VEEP Thoughts - Hilarious Paodies of Kamala Harris.*

Burnett, John. 2022. "Americans are Fleeing to Places Where Political Views Match Their Own." *NPR.* February 18. npr.org.

Burrows, Leah. 2018. " Large-Scale Wind Power Would Require More Land and Cause More Environmental Impact Than Previously Thought." *Harvard School of Engineering and Applied Science.* October 30.

Burt, Greg. 2023. "CA Legislators Pass Bill to Take Children from Parent Who Doesn't Affirm Kid's Gender Identity." *California Family Council.* September 11. californiafamily.org.

Byrne, John. 2021. "Soros-Funded District Attorneys Linked to Increases in Violent Crime." *Capital Research Center.* February 24. capitalresearch.org.

Byrne, Kerry. 2023. "Bud Light Suffers Bloodbath as Longtime and Loyal Consumers Revolt Against Transgender Campaign." *Fox Business.* April 11. foxbusiness.com.

Cagnassola, Mary Ellen. 2022. "Woman Rescued From Washington Outhouse After Dropping Phone and Getting Stuck in Toilet: "A First," Says Fire Chief." *People.* April 25.

Calfas, Jennifer. 2017. "What to Know About Suspected Virginia Shooter James Hodgkinson."

TIME time.com. July 10.

California Energy Commission. 2023. *Electricity Consumption by County.* Table, Los Angeles County: California Energy Commission.

Camosy, Charles. 2021. "Living in the Space Between Bullying and Humorlessness." *ANGELUS.* October 25. angelusnews.com.

Campbell MD, Kevin. 2019. "Don't Believe AMA's Hype, Membership Still Declining Group Focuses More on its Own Finances Than Physicians' Real Concerns." *MedPage Today.* June 19.

Cantor, James M. 2017. "How Many Transgender Kids Grow Up to Stay Trans?" *PsyPost: Mental Health, Social Psychology, Cognitive Science, Psychopharmacology.* December 30. psypost.org.

Carlozo, Lou. 2024. "IRS Most Wanted: Middle-Class Earners Remain the Most Targeted

Group for Audits, Says WSJ Report." *Microsoft Moneywise* msn.com April.

Carnahan, Ashley. 2023. "Farmer Speaks Out Against Forcing Cows to Wear Diapers to Contain Methane Emissions. "Gone to Loony Town."." *Fox News.* January 19.

Carnivorecoexistence.org. 2023. *Vision: A World Where Carnivores Can Peacefull Coexist Alongside Humans.* A Gallery of Multispecies Entanglements; Coexisting With my Wild Neighbors; Environmental Education, Support my PhD Research.

Carrasco, Maria. 2021. "Survey Finds "Openly Jewish" Students Feel Unsafe on Campus." *Inside Higher Ed; Quick Takes.* September 29.

Carvalho, Chris. 2011. "Scenery Stealers: Wind Farms Ruin Views in Columbia River Gorge." *National Wind Watch: Presenting the Facts About Industrial Wind Power.* July 3. wind-watch.org.

Catenacci, Thomas. 2022. "Sam Brinton, Nonbinary Biden Official, Stole Jewelry Worth $1,700.00 in Second Luggage Theft: Police." *Fox News.* December 10. foxnews.com.

Catholicvote. 2023. "Tracker: 298 Attacks on U.S. Catholic Churchs Since May 2020." *Catholic Vote.* March 6. catholicvote.com.

Cato. 2022. "Sam Brinton--The Literal "King of Kink" Just Joined the Biden Administration; So-called tolerance being pushed by the woke leftists is just abject degeneracy; leaving no doubt that America is sliding head-first into moral decay.." *International Family News.* February 27. ifamnew.com.

CBS News. 2018. "CBS News Finds Children Mining Cobalt for Batteries in the Congo." March 5. cbsnews.com.

2023. "Timeline: The Toxic Chemical Train Derailment in Ohio." *CBS News.* February 14.

CNN Staff. 2024. READ: Special Counsel Robert Hur's Report on Biden's Handling of

Classified Documents. *CNN.* cnn.com. February 8

Center for Immigration Studies. 2024. Report: The Cost of Illegal Immigration to Taxpayers.

House Judiciary Committee. Immigration Integrity, Security, and Enforcement Subcommittee.

Centers for Disease Control and Prevention. 2021. "Leading Causes of Death." *National Center for Health Statistics.* cdc.gov.

Centers for Disease Control. ongoing. "COVID-19 Death Data and Resources." *National Center for Health Statistics.* cdc.gov.

Chamberlain, Samuel. 2021. "Fauci Admits "Modest" National Institutes of Health Funding of Wuhan Lab, But Denies "Gain of Function."." *New York Post.* May 25.

Chang, Ailsa et al. 2021. "New Reports Details Firsthand Accounts of Torture From Uyghur Muslims in China." *NPR.* June 10. npr.com.

Chasmar, Jessica. 2023. "Drag Queen Straddles Girl at North Carolina Public School, Video Shows." *Yahoo News.* March 23.

Chavez, Nicole. 2024. Boy Scouts of America Announces Rebrand to "Scouting America"

To Emphasize its Commitment to Inclusion. *CNN.* cnn.com. May 7.

Cherry, MSEd, Kendra. 2023. "Nomophobia: The Fear of Being Without Your Phone." *Very Well Mind.* August 16. verywellmind.com.

Cho, Renee. 2018. "How Climate Change Will Alter Our Food." *Columbia Climate School; State of the Planet.* July 25. news.climate.columbia.edu.

Christenson, Josh. 2024. "Covid "6-feet" Social Distancing "Sort of Just Appeared," Likely Lacked Scientific Basis, Fauci Admits." *The New York Post.* January 10. nypost.com.

2023. "Nearly 6,000 US Public Schools Hide Child's Gender Status From Parents." *New York Post.* March 8.

2024. "NIH Official Finally Admits Taxpayers Funded Gain-of-Function Research in Wuhan -

After Years of Denials." *The New York Post.* nypost.com. May 16.

2023. "Secret Service Admits it Twice Found Marijuana at White House-Months Before Cocaine Discovery." *New York Post.* July 13. nypost.com.

Chung, Frank. 2022. "Pfizer Did Not Know Whether Covid Vaccine Stopped Transmission Before Rollout, Executive Admits." *NEWS.com.au.* October 13. news.com.au.

CiPhr; Center for Innovative Public Health Research. 2023. *"Decoding how Technology Influences Public Health and Developing Technology to Improve It.".* innovativepublichealth.org.

Cillizza, Chris. 2022. "A Brief History of 'Covfefe' *CNN.* cnn.com. April 29.

Clark, Dray. 2024. "NYC Students in Remote Learning due to 2K Migrants in Schools."

NewsNation newsnation.com January 10.

Clark, Jeffrey. 2023. "Keith Olbermann Ripped After Saying "Riley Gaines Sucked at Swimming": Nasty Ignorant Man." *New York Post.* August 31. nypost.com.

2023. "US Navy Platformed "Drag Queen Influencer" to Attract Youth to the Military in Hiring Crisis." *Fox News.* May 3. foxnews.com.

Clark, Ward "Eight Suspected Terrorists with Ties to ISIS Nabbed Nabbed in Three Separate Cities – All were "Fully Vetted." Red State. June 11, 2024. redstate.com

Cleveland, Margot. 2023. "Biden's FTC Punished Twitter for Seceding From the Censorship Complex." *The Federalist.* July 17.

Climate Policy Initiatives. 2013. "Climate Change Investment Totals USD $359 Billion Worldwide." October 22. climatepolicyinitiative.org.

Coaston, Jane. 2019. "The Intersectionality Wars; When Kimberle Crenshaw Coined the Term 30 Years Ago, it was a Relatively Obscure Legal Concept. Then it Went Viral." *VOX.* May 28. vox.com.

College Fix Staff. 2023. "72 Things Higher Ed Declared Racist in 2023." *The College Fix.* December 28. thecollegefix.com.

Colombo, D. 2011. "Cyclosporine in Transplantation--A History of Converging Timelines." *National Library of Medicine* (PubMed) 2011 Oct-Dec;25(4):493-504. (PMID: 22217983). pubmed.ncbi.nim.nih.gov.

Colton, Emma. 2023. "Nebraska Sheriff Stunned as Migrants Allegedly Kill Bald Eagle for Dinner but Feds Pass on Charging Them: Migrants Arrested then Released." March 6.

2020. "Rahm Emanuel Reprises "Never Let a Crisis go to Waste" Catchphrase Amid Coronavirus Pandemic." *The Washington Examiner.* March 24.

Company, Energizer battery. 1988. *The Energizer Bunny.* A parody of the Duracell Bunny.

Congressional Research Service. 2020. *Federal Land Ownership: Overview and Data.* Congressional Research Service.

Connor, Tracy. 2013. "Abortion Doctor Kermit Gosnel Convicted of First-Degree Murder." *NBC News.* May 13. nbcnews.com.

Conroy, Gemma. 2023. "What's Behind China's Mysterious Wafe of Childhood Pneumonia." *NATURE.* November 27. nature.com.

Cook, Nancy, et.al. 2023. "Biden Forgave Billions in Student Debt. Poll Shows It's Not Enough For Gen Z." *Bloomberg.* December 13. bloomberg.com.

courses.transplaining.info. n.d. "Brief Overview of Transplaining for SLPs and Other Clinical Providers."

Cox, Chelsey. 2020. "Fact Check: It's True, Ginsburg and Scalia Were Close Friends Despite Ideological Differences." *USA Today.* September 27. usa-today.com.

CPI Inflation Calculator. 2024. *Inflation Calculator continually updated.* Calculator using official published records by the U.S. Department of Labor. , Consumer Price Index.

Crabtree, Susan. 2024. "Dem Calls for 25th Amendment Against Trump Comes Back to Haunt." *Real Clear Politics.* February 8. realclearpolitics.com.

Crane, Emily. 2019. "Christian Baker in Colorado is Sued for the Third Time After Refusing to make a Cake Celebrating a Gender Transition." *Daily Mail.* June 11. dailymail.com.

2023. "Trans Day of Vengeance Protest to Take Place After Nashville School Shooting." *New York Post.* March 29. nypost.com.

2022. "Who is Sam Brinton, Non-Binary Biden Official Arrested Over Stolen Suitcase?" *The New York Post.* November 30.

Crombie, Noelle. 2015. "Marijuana Odors Bugging You? Annoyed Neighbors have Few Options, Officials Say." *OregonLive.* March 20. oregonlive.com.

Cutica Health. 2021. "Social Impact of Obesity." October 29. cuticahealth.com.

Dabbs, Will. 2023. "Dr. Dabbs - Bella Twin: The Tiny Little Woman and the Really Big Bear." *GUNSAMERICA Digest.* September 15. gunsamerica.com.

Dabrowski, Ted et al. 2024. "Chicago Led Nation in Homicides for 12th Year in a Row in 2023; Murder Rate Still 5 Times Higher than NYC's." *Wirepoints.* wirepoints.org. January 2.

Daily Caller 2023. Stephen Colbert Made a "Skibidi Toilet" Meme of Joe Biden on his Show.

X.https://twitter.com/DailyCaller/status/1793636832481345717?ref_src=twsrc%5Etfw%7Ctwcamp%5Etweetembed%7Ctwterm%5E1793636832481345717%7Ctwgr%5Ee14434c4e3eb79fd7ec980dc3b88afddef443668%7Ctwcon%5Es1_&ref_url=https%3A%2F%2Fredstate.com%2Fnick-arama%2F2024%2F05. May 23.

Daly, Rich. 2022. "Hospitals in Covic-19 Hotspots to Receive 10 Billion More in Federal Aid." *Healthcare Financial Management Association.* July 20. hfma.org.

Damaso, Clarissa. 2022. "Phasing Out Monkeypox: MPOX is the New Name For an Old Disease." *The Lancet.* December 27. thelancet.com.

Davenport, Gabrielle. 2020. "What is Kente Cloth?" *House Beautiful.* August 21. housebeautiful.com.

Davis, Hannah. 2023. "Increased Illegal Immigration Brings Increased Crime: Almost 2/3rds of Federal Arrests Involve Noncitizens." *The Heritage Foundation.* June 20. heritage.org.

Davis, Jack. 2022. "Joe Biden Confirmed to be "The Big Guy" Panicked Messages Revealed: Report." *The Western Journal.* July 28.

Dawson, Shannon. 2023. "Breaking Down the Stereotype: Why the "Black-On-Black Crime" Myth Just Isn't True." *NEWSONE.* August 31. newsone.com.

Debczak, Michele. 2019. "25 Classic Books That Have Been Banned." *Mental Floss.* April 10.

Debtor, Lauren. 2022. "You're Not Imagining It - Stores Are Locking Everything Up." *Forbes.* April 2. forbes.com.

Del Turco, M.A., Arielle. 2023. *Hostility Against Churches.* Issue Brief April 2023/ No. IF23D01 Supplemental Report - First Quarter 2023 , Family Research Council.

Delaney, Matt. 2023. "Bud Light Partners With Transgender Influencer Dylan Mulvaney." *Washington Times.* April 2.

Delie, Steve et al. 2021. "Did Michigan Cover Up Nursing Home Covid Deaths Like New York? Michigan Governor Whitmer May be in the Same Trouble that New York Governor Cuomo is Dealing With.." *USA Today.* March 19. usatoday.com.

Department of Energy. n.d. *Map: Projected Growth of the Wind Industry From Now Until 2050.* See projected growth of the wind industry over the next 35 years, Washington, DC: Department of Energy.

Deppisch, Breanne. 2023. "Gas Stove Bans are Advancing Around the Country - Here's the Rundown." *Washington Examiner.* January 12. washingtonexaminer.com.

Devine, Miranda. 2022. "Hunter Biden's Biz Partner Called Joe Biden "The Big Guy" in Panicked Message After Post's Laptop Story." July 28.

2023. "New Emails Show Dr. Anthony Fauci Commissioned Scientific Paper in February 2020 to Disprove Wuhan Lab Leak Theory." *New York Post.* March 5. nypost.com.

Devore, Chuck. 2023. "The Left Wants to Take Your Truck Because It's Big and Scary." *The Federalist.* January 30. the federalist.com.

Diamond, Jeremy et al. 2023. "Biden Administration Suspends Funding for Wuhan Lab." *CNN.* July 19. cnn.com.

Dias, Joanne et al. 2023. "The Meaning of Allyship & How Leaders Can Show It." *Center for Creative Leadership.* July 19. ccl.org.

Dibble, Madison. 2020. "Nancy Pelosi Had Her Hair Styled in a California Salon That Was Supposed to be Closed, Owner Says." *Washington Examiner.* September 1. washingtonexaminer.com.

Dimuro, Gina. 2019. "The Sturmabteilung: Hitler's Unofficial Army of Thugs." *All That's Interesting.* January 8. allthatsinteresting.com.

Discovering Montana. n.d. "Wolf Point, Montana." discoveringmontana.com.

Division of Studet Affairs, Intercultural Engagement. 2023. "Neopronouns Explained." *Practice here: https://www.minus18.org.au/pronouns-app.* Prod. UNC Greensboro.

Dixon, Bruce A. 2018. "Why I Can't Celebrate Kwanzaa." *JACOBIN.* December 29.

Dobbs. 2023. *Attacks on Churches, Pro-Life Organizations, Property and People Since the Dobbs Leak on May 2, 2022 (As of 5/19/23).* List with links, https://downloads.frc.org/EF/EF22F17.pdf.

Dr. Axe, DC, DNM, CN, Josh. 2018. "Raw Milk Benefits Skin, Allergies and Immunity." *Dr. Axe,* July 19.

Dr. Smith, Jane. 2023. "Can You Eat a Bald Eagle? Legality, Safety, and Implications: Federal Law Prohibits the Hunting, Killing, and Possession of these Birds." *FAUNA ADVICE.* September 7.

Dr. Spock, Benjamin. 1987. *Dr. Spock's Baby and Child Care.* Pocket Books.

Dragos, Adina. 2023. "1 In 5 Millennials & Two-Thirds of Gen Z Struggle to Leave the Nest." *Rent Cafe.* November 6. rentcafe.com.

Dresser, Maggie. 2024. "A Legacy in Wilderness Packing." *The Flathead Beacon* flatheadbeacon.com July 10.

Drucker, Jessie et al. 2020. "Big Hospital Chains Get Covid Aide, and Buy up Competitors." *The New York Times.* May 20. nytimes.com.

drugs.com. n.d. "Medications for Gender-Affirming Hormone Therapy; Medroxyprogesterone." *Know more. Be Sure.*

Duffy, Mike. 2020. "Photos Emerge of Controversial Unmasked Dinner Attended by Gov. Gavin Newsom." *ABC 10.* November 18. abc10.com.

Dumas, Breck. 2024. "Bud Light Sales Down Nearly 30% Year over Year as Rivals Continue to Climb." *Fox News.* February. foxnews.com.

Dupont, Zachary. 2023. "More About the Former Colorado Springs Student Accused of Planning School Shooting." *The Gazette.* April 6.

Eagles. Composed by Glen Fry and Don Henley. The Last Resort. Album Title: Hotel California.

Sony/ATV Music Publishing LLC.

Easterbrook, Don J. 2011. "Geologic Evidence of Recurring Climate Cycles and Their Implications for the Cause of Gloval Climate Changes - The Past is the Key to the Future." *Science Direct, The Medieval Warm Period.*

Eastern Oregon University. n.d. "Our History." eou.edu.

Ebell, Myron and Milloy, Steven J. 2019. "Wrong Again: 50 Years of Failed Eco-Apolcalyptic Predictions." *Competive Enterprise Institute.*

Edge, Sami. 2023. "Oregon Again Says Students Don't need to Prove Mastery of Reading, Writing or Math to Graduate, Citing Harm to Students of Color." *The Oregonian.* October 22. oregonlive.com.

Editors, History.com. 2022. "Homestead Act." *History,* September 13.

Elberry, Mostafa H. et al. n.d. "A System Review of Vaccine-Induced Thrombotic Thrombocytopenia in Individuals Who Received COVID-19 Adenoviral-Vector-Based Vaccines." *National Library of Medicine; National Center for Biotechnology Information* (PMID: 35157188 PMCID: PMC8853120 DOI: 10.1007/s11239-021-02626-w).

Electrly. How Many KWh to Charge a Tesla? https://electrly.com/ev-charging-guide/tesla/model-y/how-many-kwh-to-charge-a-tesla-y.

Energy.gov. 2024. *Application Guidelines for Program Administrators: Program Updates.* Energy.gov.

Engle, Jeremy. 2022. "The Cuban Missile Crisis and Its Relevance Today." *The New York Times.* October 21. nytimes.com.

English, Cameron. 2023. "'Father's Milk': CDC's Science-Free Breastfeeding Advice; The issued guidance related to breastfeeding for "transgender & nonbinary-gendered individuals," may be the most absurd set of recommendations the agency has ever released.." *American Council on Science and Health; Promoting science and debunkig junk since 1978.* July 9. acsh.org.

Epstein, Samuel. 2010. "Hormonal Milk and Meat: A Dangerous Public Health Risk." *HUFFPOST.* June 13. huffpost.com.

Essex Westward School District. 2023. "Paraphrased: To align our curriculum with equity policy, teachers will use gender-inclusive language through our science/health unit.." East Junction, Vermont: https://twitter.com/esanzi/status/1650872259072999435/photo/1 , April 20.

European Union Times. 2022. "Schools in the Netherlands Begin Serving Worms and Bugs to Children to Combat Global Waring." *The European Union Times.* October 16. eutimes.net.

Famous People. n.d. *Famous American Women's Right's Activists.*

Farhi, Paul. 2023. "The Media Navigates a War of Words for Reporting on Gaza and Israel News Outlets and Readers; Debate Terms Such as "Terrorists" vs. "Militants," "Invasion" vs. "Incursion."." *The Washington Post.* October 20.

2023. "For Democrats, Everything is Now a Insurrection." *Washington Examiner.* January 9.

Farmaid Blog. 2016. "Corporate Power and the Food we Eat." *farmaid.org.* March 18. farmaid.org.

Farmaid.com. n.d. "Corporate Control in Agriculture." farmaid.com.

Faust, Katy and Manning Stacy. 22021. "Drag Queen Story Hour Activist Arrest For Child Porn, Still Living With His Adopted Kids." *The Federalist.* March 25.

Fearon, Dylan et al. 2023. "Granby Parents to Meet with School Leaders Over Controversial Pride Video; Shown to third, fourth and fifth-grade students." Granby, Ct, June 7.

Fecht, Sarah. 2015. "Solar Power Towers are "Vaporizing" Birds." *Popular Science.* February 21.

Federal Administration's Department of the Interior. 2022. *Grizzly Bear Conflict Manager.* Job Posting, Department of Forestry.

Felbab-Brown, Vanda. 2017. "The Wall; The Real Costs of a Barrier Between the United States

and Mexico." The wall will not enhance US Security. *Brookings.* brookings.edu. August.

Feminine Me. 2023. "The Ultimate Guide to Inducing Lactation in Med." *Feminine Me.* feminine-me.com.

Fessenden, Maris. 2015. "According to This 1919 Writing Guide, There Are Only 37 Possible Stories." *Smithsonian Magazine.* November 4. smithsonianmag.com.

Find A Grave. n.d. "Charles Edward Conrad." *findagrave.com*.

FindLaw. n.d. "Chemical and Surgical Castration for Sex Offenders." *Depo-Provera; Generic Name: Medroxyprogesterone*.

Flathead Watershed Sourcebook; A Guide to an Extraordinary Place. 2010-2023. "Cultural History." flatheadwatershed.org.

Fleming, Pippa. 2018. "The Gender-Identity Movement Undermines Lesbians." *The Economist*. July 3. economist.com.

Fleming, Sean. 2019. "This is How Rice is Hurting the Plant." *World Economic Forum; Future of the Environment*. June 1. weforum.org.

Fletcher, Jenna. 2021. "Fibromyalgia and Depression: What's the Link? Fibromyagia and

Depression Often Occur Together, and that's Not a Coicidence. *PsychCentral*. psychcentral.com. November 30.

Fonticoba, Gabriel. 2019. "What I Saw at "Drag Queen Story Hour" Shocked Me." *TFP Student Action*. February 21.

Fossum, Sam and Cole, Devan. 2023. "Biden Proposes Rule For Transgender Student Athletes That Allows for some Restrictions, Opposes Categorical Bans." *CNN*. April 6. cnn.com.

Foundation Reining Training Centre. 2009. *Making The RIGHT Thing Easy and the WRONG Thing Difficult*. Prod. http://www.reinersuehorsemanship.com/2009/05/making-right-thing-easy-and-wrong-thing.html.

Fox News. 2015. "Snowboarder Fined For Viral Video of Moose Chase on Montana Mountain." November 21.

Fox, Michael J. 1985. *Back to the Future*. Directed by Robert Zemeckis. Performed by Michael J. Fox.

Frank Thoughts. 2022. "The Voice of Free Speech: Social Credit Score: A Dangerous System." *Frank*. May 3.

Fresh Eggs Daily Blog. n.d. "Can I Claim My Chicken Eggs as Organic?" *fresheggsdaily.blog*. fresheggsdaily.com.

Friedman Ross, Laine. 2022. "COVID-19 Vaccine Refusal and Organ Transplantation." *National Kidney Foundation* (American Journal of Kidney Diseases) 79 (6): DOI:https://doi.org/10.1053/j.ajkd.2022.02.009.

Frishbert, Hannah. 2020. "Glacier National Park Removes Signs Predicting Glaciers Will Be Gone By 2020." *New York Post*, January 9.

Frudd, Timothy. 2024. "NYC Giving $53 Million to Illegal Immigrants in Pre-Paid Debit Cards." *American Military News*. February 5. americanmilitary-news.com.

2023. "US Troops Suing Gov't for Billions in Backpay Over Covid Vaccine Mandate." *American Military News*. December 4. americanmilitarynews.com.

Funaro, Rita. 2015. "Five Reasons Why Government Should be Involved in Raising Kids." *IDEAS MATTER.* October 15. blogs.iadb.org.

Fung, Katherine. 2022. "Video: Schumer Telling Brett Kavanaugh He'll 'Pay the Price' for

Roe Surfaces." *Newsweek* newsweek.com June 8.

Gainor, Dan. 2023. "Mars Shelves M&M Spokes-Candies in Latest Woke Corporate Viasco." *Fox News.* January 26. foxnews.com.

Gandhi Ph.D., Renu et al. 2000. "Consumer Concerns About Hormones in Food." *Cornell University Program on Breast Cancer and Environmental Risk Factors in New York State.*

Garcia, Arturo. 2022. "White House COVID-19 Chief Downplays Mask Use in "Confusing" Interview." *Truth or Fiction.* December 21.

Gazit, Sivan et al. 2021. "Comparing SARS-C-V-2 Natural Immunity to Vaccine-Inducted Immunity: Reinfections Versus Breakthrough Infections." *MedRxiv* (Cold Springs Harbor Laboratory, BMJ, Yale) (doi: https://doi.org/10.1101/2021.08.24.21262415).

GENi. n.d. *Buffalo Calf Road Woman or Brave Woman.*

Geocaris, Madeline. 2022. NREL Releases Comprehensive Databases of Local Ordinances for Siting Wind, Solar Energy Projects. National Renewable Energy Laboratory.

George Lucas, Williard Huyck, Gloria Katz. 1973. *American Graffiti.* Performed by Richard, Howard, Ron, Le Mat, Paul, Ford, Harrison, Martin Smith, Charles, Williams, Cindy, Clark, Candy, Phillips, Mackenzie, Hopkins, Bo, Jack, Wolfman Dreyfuss. Lucas Film.

Gillespie, Brandon. 2023. Watch: Senator John Kennedy Stumps Biden Official on $50 Trillion Cost to Fight Climate Change: "You Don't Know, Do You?". Washington, DC, May 4.

Girten, Nicole. 2024. "Montana Exceeds National Average for Median Home Prices." *KPAX.* January 25. kpax.com.

Glasser, David. 2024. "Oregon University Will no Longer Give D and F Grades." *The College Fix.* January 31. thecollegefix.com.

2022. "Glasspiegel, Ryan." UPenn Transgender Swimmer Lia Thomas Sparks Outrage by Shattering Women's Records. January 20. nypost.com.

Goitein, Elizabeth. 2022. "How the FBI Violated the Privacy of Tens of Thousands of

Americans. *Brennan Center for Justice.* brennancenter.org. October 22.

Gold, Taylor. 2023. "Bombshell Report Reveals What January 6 Committee Did With the Evidence." *American Insider.* September. msn.com.

Golden, Douglas. 2024. "Your Taxes at Work: Biden Admin Spends $700K to Keep "Boys" From Getting Pregnant." *The Western Journal.* January 13.

Golding, Bruce. 2021. "Biden's Gaffe at G-7 Summit Sparks Laughter from World Leaders." *New York Post.* June 15. nypost.com.

Goldsberry, Jenny. 2023. "DHS Issues Order to Border Agents to Use Preferred Pronouns for Migrants." *Washington Examiner.* November 26. washingtonexaminer.com.

Goldstein, Joseph. 2023. "Inside the Manhattan Hotel That is the New Ellis Island."

The New York Times nytimes.com September 21.

Gollom, Mark. 2021. "Why Experts Say the U.S. Withdrawal From Afghanistan Didn't Have to Lead to Chaos." *CBS News.* cbsnews.com.

Gordon, Michael et al. 2023. "Lab Leak Most Likely Origin of COVID-19 Pandemic, Energy Department Now Says U.S. Agency's Revised Assessment is Based on New Intelligence." *Wall Street Journal.* February 26. wallstreetjournal.com.

Gosselin, P. 2023. "Huge Nebraska Solar Park Completely Smashed to Pieces by One Single Hail Storm: 14,000 Solar Panels Reduced to Rubble." *No Tricks Zone.* June 28.

Graef, Aileen. 2023. "Obama Says People Need to Acknowledge Complexity of Israel-Palestinian Conflict to Move Forward." *CNN.* November 4. cnn.com.

Graham, David. 2024. "The Special Counsel's Devastating Description of Biden." *The Atlantic.* February 8. theatlantic.com.

Grammarist. n.d. "Origin and Etymology of "It Takes a Village"." grammarist.com.

Grande, Bette. 2022. "The ESG Movement is Even Worse Than You Think." *Human Events.* April 12. humanevents.com.

Grayson, B. 2023. "Transgender Tennis Coach Undresses Beside Children, Chats Underwear and Menstruation: Welcomed Back to School Despite Concerns of Parents." *The Net Worth Of.* October 2. thenetworthof.com.

Greene, Jenna. 2021. "A "Black Hole for COVID-19 Vaccine Injury Claims." *Reuters.* June 29. reuters.com.

Grimes, Christopher. 2022. "Los Angeles Rethinks "Defunding the Police" as Violent Crime Surges." *Financial Times.* May 25. ft.com.

Grossman MD, Miriam, Child, Adolescent, and Adult Psychiatry, interview by House Energy and Commerce Subcommittee on Health. 2023. *Summary of Testimony* (June 14): https://democrats-energycommerce.house.gov/sites/democrats.energycommerce.house.gov/files/documents/Miriam%20Grossman_Witness%20Testimony_06.14.23.pdf.

Grossman, Hannah. 2022. "California Early Childhood Teacher Admits Using 'Gender Unicorn' to Instruct Kids on Sexual Attraction." *Fox News.* November 16. foxnews.com.

2024. "North Face Offers Discounts for Customers Taking Equity Course That Says Black People Can't Enjoy the Outdoors." *Fox Business.* March 6. foxbusiness.com.

2023. "Planned Parenthood Political Arm Blasts "White Women," Calls for the Elimination of Women in Abortion Advocacy." *Fox News.* February 1. foxnews.com.

2022. "Planned Parenthood Worked on Sex Education Curriculum That Nukes Women From Teen Pregnancy Discussions." *Fox News.* November 22. foxnews.com.

2022. "Rhode Island Official Shares "Extreme View that Using the Wrong Pronoun is an Act of Violence." *Fox News.* November 20. foxnews.com.

Guerette, Sheridan. 2023. "Diversity, Equity, and Inclusion Affected in Massive Lay-Offs." March 3. medium.com.

Guzman, Chad De. 2023. "Southwest Praised for Giving Free Extra Seats: How U.S. Airlines Handle Plus-Sized Passengers." *TIME.* December 15.

Hagstrom, Anders. 2023. "Trans Activists Flaunt Bare Breasts at White House Pride Month Event." *Fox News.* June 13. foxnews.com.

Hall, Alexander. 2023. "Bud Light's Marketing VP Says She Was Inspired to Update, "Fratty, Out of Touch" Branding With Inclusivity." *Fox News.* April 10. foxnews.com.

2023. "Twitter Laughs, Groans as Jill Biden Gives Biological Male Women of Courage Award." *Fox News.* March 8. foxnews.com.

2024. "Olympics Opening Ceremony Sparks Outrage With Drag Queens Parodying Last Supper:

Gone Completely Woke." *Fox News* foxnews.com July 26.

Hammer, Alex. 2022. "Michigan Middle School HIDES Trans Status of Student From Her Parents as Counsellor Warns Teachers to Only Use Child's 'Birth Name' and pronoun 'he' During Parent Teacher Conferences." *Daily Mail.* June 10.

1962. *The Jetsons.* Directed by Hanna-Barbara Productions. Performed by Hanna-Barbera.

Hansler, Jennifer et al. 2021. "US Accuses China of 'Genocide' of Uyghurs and Minority Groups in Xinjiang." *CNN.* January 20. cnn.com.

Harmon, Mark 2003. *NCIS TV Series on CBS.* Performed by Mark Harmon. Agent Gibs followed at least 51 rules to apply to life situations and casework.

Harper, Craig A. et. al. 2021. "Humanizing Pedophilia as Stigma Reduction: A Large-Scale Intervention Study." *National Library of Medicine* (PubMed

Central) doi: 10.1007/s10508-021-02057-x (Arch Sex Behav. 2022; 51(2): 945–960).

Harris, Kamala Rebroadcast Video. 2024. "HOW DARE WE SPEAK MERRY CHRISTMAS!

Because Some Might Not Get to Celebrate." @theblaze twitter.com

Hart, Robert. 2021. "Covid Surges in 4 of 5 Most Vaccinated Countries; Here's Why the U.S. Should be Worried." *Forbes.* May 11. forbes.com.

——. 2021. "Germany, France Restrict Moderna's Covid Vaccine for Under-30s Over Rare Heart Risk-Despite Surging Cases." *Forbes.* November 10. forbes.com.

Hart, Willa. 2023. "3 Key Signs That Someone You Love is Egocentric and Not Just Selfish, According to Behavioral Health Specialists." *Business Insider; Reviews>Health.* January 23. businessinsider.com.

Hartman, Rebecca. n.d. "La Grande." *Oregon Encyclopedia.* oregonencyclopedia.org.

Hayes, Kathleen. 2022. "Gender Ideology's True Believers." *Quillette.* May 19. quillette.com.

Hayward, Nancy. 2018. *Susan B. Anthony (1820 - 1906).* Prod. womenshistory.org.

Heck, Peter. 2022. "It's Happening: "LGB Drops the "T" Keeps Trending on Twitter as Gay Activists Turn on Transgender Activists." *Not The Bee.* August 15.

Helmenstine PhC., Anne Marie. 2019. "Geometric Isomerism: Cis & Trans." *ThoughtCo.* July 25. thoughtco.com.

Hemingway, Mollie. 2024. "Exclusive: Liz Cheney, January 6 Committee Suppressed Exonerating Evidence of Trump's Push for National Guard." *The Federalist.* March 8. thefederalist.com.

Hendersen, David. 2014. "David Friedman on the 97% Concensus on Global Warming." *Econlib.org.* February 27.

Herridge, Catherine et al. "Special Counsel Finds Biden 'Willfully' Disclosed Classified

Documents, But No Criminal Charges Warranted; Classified documents that should have been sent to the National Archives instead of locations in his homes." *CBS News.* cbsnews.com. February 8.

Herb, Jeremy et al. 2023. "US Officials Disclose New Details About the Balloon's Capabilities. Here's What We Know." *CNN.* cnn.com.

Hilu, Charles. 2023. ""All Cars Are Bad": Pete Buttigieg's Equity Advisors Want You to Stop Driving. The Transportation Secretary's Equity Committee Aims to Bring "Diversity and Inclusion" to America's Infrastructure." *Washington Free Beacon.* September 1.

History (updated). 2023. *Spanish Flu.* May 10. history.com.

History. 2023. *Sitting Bull (Updated).* July 10. history.com.

History.com. 2020. "Battle of the Little Bighorn." *HISTORY.* December 21.

History.com Editors. 2022. "Jonestown." *History.* April 19.

History.com Editors. 2009. "Sojourney Truth." *History.* October 29. history.com.

History.com. 2010. *Spanish Flu.* October 12. History.com.

History.com, Editors. 2022. "Oregon Trail." *History.* August 10. history.com.

Hoeg, Tracy Beth et al. 2021. "SARS-CoV-2 mRNA Vaccination Associated Myocarditis in Children Ages 12-17: A Stratified National Database Analysis." *MedRxiv* (European Journal of Clinical Investigation) (doi: https://doi.org/10.1101/2021.08.30.21262866).

Hollingham, Richard. 2020. "The Chilling Experiment Which Created the First Vaccine." *BBC.* September 29. bbc.com.

Hollingsworth, Julia, et al. 2020. "White House Coronavirus Response Coordinator says Masks May Only Provide Partial Protection from COVID-19." *CNN.* June 29. cnn.com.

Holtz-Eakin, Doug. 2019. "How Much Will the Green New Deal Cost? $52 to $93 Trillion." *Aspen Institute.* June 11. aspeninstitute.org.

Holzhauer, Brett. 2023. "Americans Are Cord Cutting in Record Numbers; And it's Not Slowing Down Anytime Soon." *Forbes.* May 26. forbes.com.

Hope, Paul. 2022. "What the Inflation Reduction Act Could Mean for Your Next Appliance Purchase." *Consumer Reports.* August 12. consumerreports.com.

House Judiciary Committee. 2024. "Department of Home Land Security Stonewalls Oversight of Immigration Record of Laken Riley's Murderer." *House Judiciary Commttee.* March 14. judiciary.house.gov.

House, Illinois. 2024. "AMENDMENT TO HOUSE BILL 4409." Section 5.

The Illinois Crime Reduction Act of 2009 is Amended by Changing Section 20. (730ILCS190/20) Sec.20 Adult Redeploy Illinois.

House, The White. 2022. *President Biden Announces Team to Lead Monkeypox Response.* Announcement, The Briefing Room/Statements and Releases.

2023. "Vice President Harris Delivers Remarks on the 50th Commemoration of the Roe v. Wade Decision." *YouTube.* https://www.youtube.com/watch?v=5fv9lSdMv-4.

Howard, Jacqueline. 2022. *Daylight Savings Time Sheds Light on Lack of Sleep's Disproportionate Impact in Communities of Color.* November 25. cnn.com.

Hrala, Josh. 2016. "This Solar Plant Accidentally Incinerates up to 6,000 Birds a Year." *Science Alert.* September 12.

HuffPost. 2013. "All These Local News Anchors Repeat the Exact Same Phrase." December 17. huffpost.com.

Hughes, John. 1989. *Uncle Buck*. American Comedy Film. Directed by John Hughes. Produced by John Hughes. Performed by John Candy and Amy Madigan.

Human Rights Watch. 2020. "China's Global Threat to Human Rights." hrw.org.

Humphrey, Cheyanne. 2022. "ACT Test Scores Drop to the Lowest Levels in 30 Years in Pandemic Slide." *Nation and News World*. October 13.

Hurley, Bevan. n.d. "Biden Slammed for Offering "Insulting" $700 Payments to Maui Wildfire Victims." *The Independent*.

Hutzler, Alexandra. 2024. "Biden Visits East Palestine a Year After Toxic Train Derailment." *ABC News*. February 16. abcnews.go.com.

Huxley, Aldous. n.d. *Brave New World*. Harper Perennial.

2022. *Diet Culture is Based on Oppression; "Good vs. Bad" foods*. Directed by Smarter in Seconds. Performed by Nutritionists Kera Nyemb-Diop and Blair Imani.

Impelli, Matthew. 2022. "Supreme Court Justices Threatened with Murder if Roe Overturned, DHS Warns." *Newsweek*. May 18. newsweek.com.

Interagency. 2014. *Evolution of the Wild and Scenic Rivers Act: A History of Substantive Amendments 1968-2013*. Wild and Scenic Rivers Coordinating Council.

International Energy Agency. 2021. "Mineral Requirement for Clean Energy Transitions." The Role of Critical Minerals in Clean Energy Transitions, https://www.iea.org/reports/the-role-of-critical-minerals-in-clean-energy-transitions, iea.org.

Investor's Business Daily. 2016. "Gallup Poll Reveals Obama Has Turned Back Clock on Race Relations." April 12. investors.com.

Ivanova, Irina. 2022. "Stock Market's Fall Has Wiped Out $3 Trillion in Retirement Savings This Year." *CBS News*. June 17. cbsnews.com.

Jackson, Jon. 2023. "Jane Fonda Floats "Murder" as Response to Abortion Laws." *Newsweek*. March 10. newsweek.com.

Jackson, Kevin. 2020. "Why Do Birds Crash Into Solar Panels?" *SCIENCENODE*. September 14.

Jackson, Sarah. 2023. "Big Money Donors are Slamming Ivy League Universities and Pulling Funding Over Their Responses to the Israel-Hamas War." *Business Insider*. October 17.

Jacobs, Andrew. 2015. "Living a Frontier Dream on the Outskirts of China's Capital." *New York Times*.

Jacobson, Louis. 2023. "The US Freed $6 Billion in Iranian Money. Did it Help Fund Hamas' Attack on Israel?" *Politifact.* October 9. politifact.com.

Jacques, Ingrid. 2023. "Do You Have a Good Credit Score? Biden Wants to Punish You for It." *USA Today.* May 4.

Javaid, Jaham. 2023. "Fall's Favorite Spice Blend Has a Violent History." *The Washington Post.* October 6.

Jeglic Ph.D., Elizabeth L. 2023. "How to Recognize the Sexual Grooming of a Minor." *Psychology Today.* July 7.

Jewett, Christina. 2023. "Drug Shortages Near an All-Time High, Leading to Rationing." *New York Times.* May 17.

Jimenez, Kayla. 2023. "Biden Administration Will Release New Title IX Rules in May. What to Expect." *USA TODAY.* February 8. usatoday.com.

Joe Sachs, Jack Orman, David Zabel et al. 1994. *ER.* Produced by Michael Crichton. Performed by George Clooney, Sherry Stringfield, Noah Wyle, Eriq La Salle Anthony Edwards.

1978 Comedy. *Animal House.* Directed by John Landis. Performed by John Belushi, Tim Matheson, Donald Sutherland, and a host of others.

John Hopkins Bloomberg School of Public Health. 2021. *New Data on COVID-19 Transmission by Vaccinated Individuals.* Data Released by the CDC: Vaccinated people infected with the Delta Variant can carry detectable viral loads similar to those who are unvaccinated., John Hopkins Bloomberg School of Public Health.

Joseph, M.K. 1968. *The Hole in the Zero.* New York, Dutton.

Jotkoff, Eric. 2022. "NEA Survey: Massive Staff Shortages in Schools Leading to Educator Burnout; Alarming Number of Educators Indicating They Plan to Leave Profession." National Education Association.

Jubilee, Diamond. 1987. *Plentywood Portrait: Toil, Soil, Oil.* Herald Printing, Plentywood and Midstates Printing, Inc., Aberdeen S. Dakota.

Just the News. 2023. "Judge Orders FDA to Accelerate Release of COVID-19 Vaccine Trial Data from 23 Years to 2 Years." *Just the News.* May 13.

Justice, Tristan. 2024. "J6 Committee Admits Its Show Trials Were an Election-Year Publicity Stunt; Key Members of the Committee Admit in a PBS Documentary That the Operation was a Publicity Stunt." *The Federalist.* February 1. thefederalist.com.

Kakovan, Maryam et al. 2022. "Stroke Associated with COVID-19 Vaccines." *National Library of Medicine; National Center for Biotechnology Information* (PMID: 35339857 PMCID: PMC8894799 DOI: 10.1016/ j.jstrokecerebrovasdis.2022.106440).

Kapur, Sahil. 2021. "Democrats to Introduce Bill to Expand Supreme Court From 9 to 13 Justices." *NBC News.* April 14. nbcnews.com.

Karayanis, Dean. 2024. "Biden Threat to Put Trump in a Bullseye, Met with Shrugs, in Contrast with Firestorm over Palin Crosshairs." *The New York Sun* nysun.com July 10.

Karonga, Gerrard. 2022. "What is the "Liberal World Order?" Biden Adviser's Remarks Spark Derision." July 1. *Newsweek*. newsweek.com.

2022 – "Video of Joe Biden Making '54 States' Gaffe Goes Viral." *Newsweek*. Newsweek.com October 31.

Kaushik Yeturu, Sai et al. 2023. "Refusal of Transplant Organs for Non-Medical Reasons Including COVID-19 Status." *NIH: National Library of Medicine* (Clinical Ethics) (DOI: 10.1177/14777509221143016). ncbi.nim.nih.gov.

Ke, Bryan. 2023. "The Views Hosts Blame Trump's Xenophobia for People's Dismissal of Covid Lab Leak Theory." *Yahoo*. March 2.

Keene, Houston. 2023. "Not Just Cocaine: Secret Service Reveals Another Banned Substance Was Found in Biden's White House." *Fox News*. July 13. foxnews.com.

Keillor, Garrison. 1974-2016. *A Prairie Home Companion*. Performed by Garrison Keillor. Minnesota Public Radio, Minnesota.

Kekatos, Mary. 2023. "Teen Girls are Experiencing Record-High Levels of Sadness and Violence: CDC." *ABC News*. February 13. abcnews.com.

Kelley, Alexandra. 2019. "Biden Tells Coal Miners to "Learn to Code"." *The Hill*. December 31. thehill.com.

Kelley, Debbie. 2024. Verdict: Colorado Springs Area Resident Found Guilty on all Charges in Capitol Breach Trial in D.C. *The Gazette* gazette.com. May 15.

Kelly, Helena. 2023. "Toe-Curling Moment Drew Barrymore Kneels at the Feet of Biden's Favorite Trans TikToker Dylan Mulvany in Fawning TV Interview." *Daily Mail*. March 14. dailymail.com.

Kelto, Anders. 2014. "Farm Fresh? Natural? Eggs Not Always What They're Cracked Up to Be." *NPR*. December 23. npr.org.

Kennedy, Lesley. 2023. "Inside Jonestown: How Jim Jones Trapped Followers and Forced 'Suicides'." *History*. August 4. history.com.

Keogh, Bryan and Williams, Matt. 2022. "Soaring Energy Costs Fuel Fastest Inflation in 40 Years: 3 Essential Reads." *The Conversation*. April 12. the-conversation.com.

KGW Staff. 2023. "Multnomah County Confirms it Will Distribute Foil and Straws for Fentanyl Smoking." *KGW8*. July 7.

Khan, Chaka. 1986. *Addicted To Love.* Directed by Produced by Bernard Edwards. Performed by Robert Palmer.

Kilgore, Ed. 2024. "It Won't be Easy for Democrats to "Flip" the Border-Security Issue." *Intelligencer.* January. msn.com.

Kinnard, Meg. 2024. "Why Harris and Democratic Allies Keep Calling Republicans Trump

and Vance Weird." *PBS News* pbs.org July 30.

Kjaer, Kurt et al. 2022. "A New Chapter in the History of Evolution; Discovery of World's Oldest DNA Breaks Record by One Million Years." *University of Cambridge.* December 7. cam.ac.uk.

Klee, Miles. 2023. "Elon Musk and Bill Maher Warn Against the "Woke Mind Virus," a.k.a. Historical Facts." *Yahoo News via Rolling Stone.* April 29.

Klein, Betsy. 2023. "Commander Biden Bites Another Secret Service Agent, the 11th Known Incident." *CNN.* September 26. cnn.com.

Klein, Christopher. 2020. "How America Struggled to Bury the Dead During the 1918 Pandemic: Undertakers, gravediggers, and casket makers couldn't keep up with history's deadliest pandemic." *History.* February 12. history.com.

Klompas M.D. M.P.H., Michael, et al. 2020. "Perspective: Universal Masking in Hospitals in the COVID-19 Era." *New England Journal of Medicine* (New England Journal of Medicine) N Engl J Med 2020; 382:e63 (DOI: 10.1056/NEJMp2006372).

Kormos, Jessica. 2022. "Is Myspace Dead?" *Lifewire*, January 21.

Kornick, Lindsay 2023. "MSNBC Host Blames Staff for Biden's Awkward Moments:

He's 80, You Need to be There for Him: Morning Joe hosts angrily attack the Secret Service and President Biden's staff for failing to prevent situations where he falls or looks lost on stage." *Fox News.* foxnews.com July 12.

Kotkin, Joel. 2021. "A Middle Class Rebellion Against Progressives is Gaining Steam." *Newsweek.* June 3. newsweek.com.

Kracaclik, Ph.D., et al. 2022. "Outcomes at Least 90 Days Since Onset of Myocarditis After mRNA COVID-19 Vaccination in Adolescents and Young Adults in the USA; A Follow-up Surveillance Study." *The Lancet* (US Center for Disease Control (CDC)).

Kramer, Jamey. 2022. "How Many Acres is in the United States?" *LAWN Manual.* May 30.

Krauss Whitbourne PhD, ABPP, Susan. 2012. "It's a Fine Line Between Narcissim and Egocentrism." *Psychology Today.* April 7. psychologytoday.com.

Krispenz, Ann et al. 2023. "Understanding Left-Wing Authoritarianism: Relations to the Dark Personality Traits, Altruism, and Social Justice Commitment." *Current Psychology* (https://doi.org/10.1007/s12144-023-04463-x).

Kristian, Bonnie. 2018. "Watch a Surreal Video Compilation of Dozens of Local News Anchors Give the Exact Same Warning about "Fake" News." *The Week.* April 1. theweek.com.

2015. Hillary Clinton's Private Server was Stored in a Bathroom Closet; More than 300

documents contained on that server contained state secrets. The Week. theweek.com. August 18.

Kudlow, Larry. 2024. "Look Under the Hood of Biden's May Jobs Report and You'll See

the Problem: 414,000 Legal and Illegal Job Gains While 663,000 Native-Born Americans Lost Jobs. *Fox Business* foxbusiness.com. June 7.

Kuhfeld, Megan et al. 2022. "The Pandemic Has Had Devastating Impacts on Learning. What Will it Take to Help Students Catch Up?" *Brookings*. March 3. brookings.edu.

Kulldorff, Martin. 2022. "A Review and Autopsy of Two Covid Immunity Studies." *Brownstone Institute.* November 21.

Kupiec, Paul. 2023. "The Migrant and Housing Crises are Colliding With Predictable Results." *The Hill.* October 5. thehill.com.

Kurtz, Holly. 2022. "Threats of Student Violence and Misbehavior Are Rising, Many School Leaders Report." *Education Week; School Climate & Safety.* January 12. edweek.org.

Lakes, Anthony. n.d. *Anthony Lakes: Still Simple. Always Friendly.* anthonylakes.com.

Lalvani, Ajit et al. 2022. "Transmissibility of SARS-CoV-2 Among Fully Vaccinated Individuals." *The Lancet* (The Lancet) (DOI:https://doi.org/10.1016/S1473-3099(21)00761-1).

Lamb, Matt. 2023. "72 Things Higher Ed Declared Racist in 2023." *The College Fix.* December 26. thecollegefix.com.

Lancaster, Jordan. 2021. "Elites Attend Galas and Award Shows Unmasked While Servants Have to Cover Their Faces." *Daily Caller.* September 20. dailycaller.com.

Land, Nikolas. 2023. "Colorado Mass Shooting: Liberal Media Blame Republicans for Tragedy over LGBTQ Rhetoric." *Fox News.* November 23. foxnews.com.

Lane, Brad. 2021. "10 Top-Rated Things to do in Butte, Montana." *Planetware*, June 4.

Lang, Cady. 2020. "Why Democratic Congresswomen Wore White Again to Send a Message at the State of the Union." *TIME.* February 5. time.com.

2023. "Loyola Professor Claims Organized Pantries Are Rooted in "Racist and Sexist" Social Structures." *Fox News.* March 16. foxnews.com.

Lapin, Tamar. 2020. "Student Biden Called "Lying Dog-Faced Pony Soldier," Says She Was Humiliated." *New York Post.* February 10. nypost.com.

Larcombe, Butch. 2022. "Building The East Shore Highway." *The Flathead Beacon.*

Larson, Keely. 2023. "Mysterious Morel Mushrooms at Center of Food Poisoning Outbreak." *The Flathead Beacon.* December 28. flatheadbeacon.com.

Latson, Jennifer. 2015. "A Murder That Shocked the World, at Sea and on Stage." *TIME.* October 7. time.com

Laurene, A Delta of a Show Where There are no Clues for the Clueless 2024

Laurene, AI Modeling Agency for the Ages 2024

Laurene, An Aggravated Rancher vs. Grizzly; A Retrospective Analysis 2024

Laurene, Avian Discrimination 2024

Laurene, Bogus Potential 2024

Laurene, CONNIVED Emmission Standards 2024

Laurene, Challenge: Collating all the Genders in an A-Gendered Society 2024

Laurene, Clima-Commuter's Fantastically Fantastic New Age Commuting 2024

Laurene, Covid Theatre of the Absurd 2024

Laurene, Crossfire Contagion 2024

Laurene, Culturally Meme-centered Appropriations that are Most Appropriate 2024

Laurene, DOPES created "Bucks for Bossy" 2024

Laurene, Da VEEP SPEECH Writer 2024

Laurene, Dane Flatulent Perils 2024

Laurene, Distinguishing Who are Terrorists in an Oppressively Oppressed Society 2024

Laurene, Drivel 2024

Laurene, Enviro-CONNIVED Labeling System 2024

Laurene, Foul Experimentation 2024

Laurene, Gerbil Gender Heterosexist 2024

Laurene, Give me Joy or Give me Death 2024

Laurene, Harpy for Harmony 2024

Laurene, Here Come Da' Judge 2024

Laurene, Here Come Da' VEEP 2024

Laurene, Insurrectionist Barbie 2024

Laurene, IRS SITTERS for Enhanced After School Programs 2024

Laurene, Laryngeal Dog Whistle Implant 2024

Laurene, Linguistical Ciphers of Coded Bull Hooey 2024

Laurene, MSNBC's Election Integrity Team 2024

Laurene, Monkeypox Coming to a Neighborhood Near You 2024

Laurene, New Parallels of Unparalleled Importance 2024

Laurene, Now Recruiting: Songbird Influencers 2024

Laurene, Outline from which to organize all Progressive Narratives 2024

Laurene, PLOT 2024

Laurene, PTSD Translation Dictionary to Institute Obedience Through Coercion 2024

Laurene, Pedi-Planks 2024

Laurene, Progressive Debate Strategies 2024

Laurene, Progressive POPPERS parallels 2024

Laurene, Progressive Rules to Demonstrate Demonstratability 2024

Laurene, Proper Pootus Parameters 2024

Laurene, Rectum Lippers 2024

Laurene, Rice Paralleling Rice 2024

Laurene, Sar's Patrollers 2024

Laurene, Secrets of the Big Board 2024

Laurene, Socially Constructed GULAG of Uniform Language Directives 2024

Laurene, The Acme Air Conditioning Company 2024

Laurene, The Derpy Dilemma 2024

Laurene, The Great Gerbil Invasion of Los Angeles County 2024

Laurene, The PRIORITISE Manual 2024

Laurene, The Reverend Fauci 2024

Laurene, The Spin Room, AKA The Spins, AKA The Spinners 2024

Laurene, The Vagrant Support Commission of Sanctuary Populations 2024

Laurene, Twitter STOP Specialists 2024

Laurene, United States Department of Trans World Hosts 2024

Laurene, Used to be Considered Smut 2024

Laurene, Worldly Abstractions to Diversify Acceptance 2024

Laugh-In, Rowan and Martin's. 1968. *Edith Ann.* Performed by Lily Tomlin. Television variety show by NBC.

Lawler, Colin. 2024. "Biden Pronounces Laken Riley as "Lincoln Riley" During Speech; GOP Response Addresses Murder." *FOX5 Atlanta.* March 7. yahoo.com.

Laycock, Richard. 2023. *U.S. Gas Prices: 2018 to October 2023.* Chart, https://www.in2013dollars.com/ : Finder; Home>Economics.

Lea, Robert. 2021. "How Many Americans Died From Spanish Flu and How did the Pandemic End." *Newsweek.* September 21. newsweek.com

Lee, Alicia. 2020. "Congressional Democrats Criticized for Wearing Kente Cloth at Event Honoring George Floyd." *CNN.* June 8. cnn.com.

Lee, Bruce. 2024. "What is Disease X? The Pandemic Threat Discussed at Davos 2024." *Forbes.* January 27. forbes.com.

Leonard, Meike. 2023. "Half Who Have Bottom Surgery are in so Much Pain They Need Medical Care Years Later, According to a Study of Dozens of Cases; Up to a Third Struggle to Use the Bathroom or Have Sex." *Daily Mail.* January 16. dailymail.com.

Leonhardt, David. 2023. *A Positive Covid Milestone.* CDC Report: Almost one-third of official recent Covid deaths have fallen into the category of another underlying cause of death., The New York Times. nytimes.com.

Lerer, Lisa. 2023. "Obama Urges Americans to Take in "Whole Truth" of Israel-Gaza War; Everyone was "complicit to some degree" in the current bloodshed." *The New York Times.* November 4. nytimes.com.

Levine, Jon. 2022. "Twitter's Top Ranks Riddled with Ex-FBI Employees." *New York Post.* December 17. nypost.com.

Lewis, Dyani. 2022. "Why the WHO Took Two Years to Say COVID-19 is Airborne; Early in the pandemic, the World Health Organization stated that SARS-CoV-2 was not transmitted through the air. That mistake and the prolonged process of correcting it sowed confusion." *NATURE.* April 6. nature.com.

Liberatore, Stacy. 2023. "White House Unveils Crackdown on Artificial Intelligence Amid Fears Tech Could Replace Humanity…But Kamala Harris Will be in Charge of it." *Daily Mail.* May 4. dailymail.co.uk.

Libs of TikTok. 2023. "Minnesota Health Mentor Offers Student Chest Binder for Gender Transition Behind Parents' Backs." *Libs of TikTok.* January 30.

Lifton Dr., Robert Jay. 2014. *Thought Reform and the Psychology of Totalism: A Study of Brainwashing in China.* University of North Carolina Press.

Lindsay, Benjamin. 2023. "Bill Maher Tells Elon Musk Why He Doesn't Tweeet Anymore: The Mob of Mean Girls is Still There." Discuss Cancel Culture, Social Media and the so-called "Woke Mind Virus."." *The Wrap.* April 29. thewrap.com.

Lindsay, James. 2020. "Eight Big Reasons Critical Race Theory is Terrible for Dealing with Racism." *New Discourses; Pursuing the light of objective truth in subjective darkness.* June 12. newdiscourses.com.

Linge, Mary Kay and Levine, Jon. 2022. "Latest Twitter Files Show CIA, FBI Have Spent Years Meddling in Content Moderation." *New York Post.* December 24.

Linskey, Annie. 2023. "How Joe Biden's Kin Profited off the Family Name. "The Big Guy is Calling Me."." *The Wall Street Journal.* September 28. wsj.com.

Lipstadt, Deborah. 2011. "Denying the Holocaust." *BBC.* February 2. bbc.co.uk.

Liss, Samantha. 2020. "Here's How Much For-Profit Hospitals Have Received in Bailout Funding so Far; the nation's largest for-profit hospital chains have received $2.2 billion, money they don't have to pay back." *Healthcare Dive.* May 26. healthcaredive.com.

LIT, TOR CHING. 2017. "Mask Appeal: The Addiction of Surgical Masks in Japan; Wearing surgical masks is a social norm in Japan, but for some, it is turning into an addiction." *The Star.* April 23. pressreader.com.

Lock, Samantha. 2020. ""To Kill a Mockingbird," Other Books Banned From California Schools Over Racism Concerns." *Newsweek.* November 13. newsweek.com.

Loe, Megan. 2022. "Yes, The CDC Changed its Definition of Vaccine to be "More Transparent."." *NewsWest 9.* February 4. newswest9.com.

Longley, Robert. 2021. "How to Amend the Constitution." *ThoughtCo.* September 4.

Lopez, Ian. 2023. "Covid Vaccine Injury Suit May Fuel Federal Overhaul, Litigation." *Bloomberg Law.* November 3.

Lotfinejad MD, Nasim et al. 2021. "Hand Hygiene in Health Care: 20 Years of Ongoing Advances and Perspectives." *The Lancet* (The Lancet) VOLUME 21, ISSUE 8, E209-E221, AUGUST 2021 (DOI:https://doi.org/10.1016/S1473-3099(21)00383-2).

Lou Chen, Vivien. 2022. "7 Reasons Why High Inflation May be Here to Stay, According to Oxford Economics." *Market Watch.* October 27.

Lukianoff, Greg and Haidt, Jonathan. 2015. "The Coddling of the American Mind; In the name of emotional well-being, college students are increasingly demanding protection from words and ideas they don't like.." *The Atlantic.* September. theatlantic.com.

Lungariello, Mark. 2021. "Asian Carp" Rebranded Because Tag is Deemed Racist." *New York Post.* July 19. nypost.com.

Lyman, Brianna. 2021. "Inflation Reduction Act "Has Nothing to do With Inflation," Biden Says." *The Daily Caller.* dailycaller.com.

Lynbrand, Holmes. 2022. "FBI Says Man Accused of Attempting to Kill Brett Kavanaugh, Said He was Shooting for 3 Justices." *CNN.* July 27. cnn.com.

Lynch, James. 2023. "ABC News Reporter Ties Mass Shootings at Christian School by Transgender Former Student to Republican Legislation." *Daily Caller.* March 27. dailycaller.com.

Lynn, K. 2020. "Why We Need to Stop Overusing the Word Unprecedented in 2020; The Word of the Year." *Medium.* November 5. medium.com.

Lynne, Kendra. 2023. "Farm Fresh Eggs vs. Store Bought: Key Differences." *New Life on a Homestead.* October 4. newlifeonahomestead.com.

Macintyre, CR et al. 2015. "A Cluster Randomised Trial of Cloth Masks Compared with Medical Masks in Healthcare Workers." *BMJ Open* (BMJ Journals) BMJ Open 2015;5:e006577. (doi: 10.1136/bmjopen-2014-006577). bmjopen.bmj.com.

Mackay, Hamish. 2021. "Covid: New Omicron Variant Not a Disaster, Says Sage Scientist; some people may be "hugely overstating the situation," a scientist advising the government says." *BBC News.* November 27. bbc.com.

Maki, Kevin. 2023. "Rogers Pass coldest temp record still stands after 69 years." *NBC Montana*, February 5.

Malekinejad, Hasan et al. 2015. "Hormones in Dairy Foods and Their Impact on Public Health;." *Iranian Journal of Public Health* (National Library of Medicine) 44 (6): 742-758.

Mallikka, Miabel. 2023. "Sweden Abandons 100% Renewable Energy Goal." *Nordic News and Business Promotion in Asia.* June 25. Scandasia.

Mamone, Trav. 2015. "What I Mean When I Say "Monosexual Privilege."; Quotes from Shiri Eisner in "Bi-Notes for a Bisexual Revolution.". *Queereka.* July 26.

Mandavilli, Apoorva. 2022. "The CDC Isn't Publishing Large Portions of the Covid Data it Collects." *New York Times.* February 29.

Maren, Jonathon. 2020. "States Working to Help Children Gender Transition Without Parent's Knowledge." December 15. thebridgehead.ca.

Marshall, Lisa. 2023. "Excess Weight, Obesity More Deadly Than Previously Believed." *Colorado University Boulder Today.* February 23.

Martin, Coach. n.d. "50 Football Terms Everyone Must Know (A-Z Glossary)." *Football Advantage.* footballadvantage.com.

Maruf, Ramishah. 2023. "A US Federal Agency is Considering a Ban on Gas Stoves." *CNN.* January 10. cnn.com.

Mary Christie Institute. 2023. *The Mental Health and Wellbeing of Young Professionals.* Survey funded by a gift from the Kellwell Foundation with support from Boston Scientific, American Assoc., of Colleges and Universities, Healthy Minds Network, National Assoc., of Colleges and Employers, and

Morning Consult, Mary Christie Institute with Report Contributors from Mollie Ames et al.

Marzoli, Filippo et al. 2021. "A Systemic Review of Human Coronavirus Survival on Environmental Surfaces." *National Library of Medicine; National Center for Biotechnology Information* (ncbi.nim.nih.gov) Sci Total Environ. 2021 Jul 15; 778: 146191. (Published online 2021 Mar 3. doi: 10.1016/j.scitotenv.2021.146191).

Masters, Jonathan, et al. 2024. "How Much U.S. Aid is Going to Ukraine; As of April 2024 $175 Billion." *Council of Foreign Relations* cfr.org. May 9.

Mathis, Will and Saul, Josh. 2024. "Orsted Withdraws From Contract For Maryland Offshore Wind Farm. Deal to Sell Power was no Longer Viable, Company Says." *bloomberg.com*. January 25.

Matza, Max and Yong, Nicholas. 2023. "FBI Chief Christopher Wray Says China Lab Leak Most Likely." *BBC*. March 1. bbc.com.

Mayer, Grace. 2023. "Bud Light Backlash: How the Fallout From the Dylan Mulvaney Promotion Started, and all the Chaos That Ensued." *Business Insider*. August 18. businessinsider.com.

Mays, MacKenzie. 2021. "Newsom's "Zoom School" Experience Was in the Past, Office Confirms." *Politico*. March 19. politico.com.

McBride, Jessica. 2023. "Jill Biden's White House Christmas Video is Mocked Online, Defended by Others." *Heavy*. December 14. heavy.com.

McCanna, William. 1999. "Outlaws of the Big Muddy." *sites.rootsweb.com*.

1999. "Outlaws of the Big Muddy." sites.rootsweb.com.

McCausland, Phil. 2023. "Map: Here's How Close the Chinese Spy Balloon Flew to the U.S. Nuclear Arsenal; the spy balloon was spotted close to a nuclear missile site, the home of U.S. Strategic Command." *NBC News*. February 7. nbcnews.com.

McCullogh, Colin 2024. "Mark Zuckerberg Says Meta Was Pressured by Biden Administration to Censor Covid-Related Content in 2024." CNN cnn.com August 27.

McFall, Caitlin. 2023. "Bill Gates Says Fake Meat Products Will "Eventually Be Very Good." Gates Says Consuming Meat Alternatives is an Important Step in Reducing Greenhouse Gas Emissions." *Fox Business*. January 14.

McGreal MSc, Scott. 2022. "Who Advocates Political Violence?" *Psychology Today*. June 28. psychologytoday.com.

McKinsey & Company. 2022. "The Raw Materials Challenge: How the Metals and Mining Sector Will be at the Core of Enabling the Energy Transition." *McKinsey & Company*. January 10. mckinsey.com.

McLean, Don. 1971. "American Pie."

McLeod Dr., Saul. 2018. "The Pre-Operational Stage of Cognitive Development." *Simply Psychology.*

McNamara, Chan Tov. 2020. "Misgendering as Misconduct." *UCLA Law Review.* May 11.

McOmie, Grant. 2022. "Anthony Lakes: Oregon's Friendly Little Ski Area." *Travel Oregon*, January 29.

mdt.mt.gov. n.d. *The Rocky Mountain Trench.*

Mead M, Seneff S. Wolfinger R, et al. 2024. "COVID-19 mRNA Vaccines: Lessons Leaarned from the Registrational Trial and Global Vaccination Campaign." *Cureus* Cureus 16(1): e52876. (doi:10.7759/cureus.52876).

Merriam, Ida C. 1955. *Social Welfare Expenditures in the United States.* ssa.gov.

Meston, John. 1952 to 1961. *Gunsmoke.* Television Western Drama. Directed by Norman MacDonnell. Performed by William Conrad and James Arness.

Metzger, Bryan. 2024. "Progressives are Fuming at Biden for Describing a Migrant as an "Illegal" During his State of the Union Address." *Yahoo News.* March 8. news.yahoo.com.

Mevorach, D., Anis E., et al. 2021. "Myocarditis after BNT 162b2 Vaccine Against COVID-19 in Israel." *New England Journal of Medicine* (385 (23), 2140-2149. https://doi.org/10.1056/NEJMoa2109730.).

Meyersohn, Nataniel. 2022. "Why Old Spice, Colgate, and Dawn are Locked Up at Drug Stores." *CNN Business.* August 4. cnnbusiness.com.

Michael Malone, Richard B. Roeder, William L. Lang. 1976. *Montana: A History of Two Centuries.* University of Washington Press.

Miller, Andrew. 2023. "J6 Committee Failed to Preserve Records, Has no Data on Capitol Hill Security Failures, GOP Charges." *Fox News.* February. fox-news.com.

Miller, Harrison. 2023. "Disney Narrows Losses, Subscriber Growth Slows, Iger Addresses Desantis Row." *Investor's Business Daily.* May 11.

Miller, Joshua Rhett and Raff, Franklin. 2023. "Four Whales Die in 4 Days: Wind Farms Creating "Death Zone" at Sea, Says Ex-Greenpeace Boss." *New York Post.* May 8.

Miller, Lee M and Keith, David W. 2018. "Climatic Impacts of Wind Power." *50 Joule* (Joule-Harvard University) (DOI:https://doi.org/10.1016/j.joule.2018.09.009).

Miller, Lee M. and Keith, David W. 2018. "Observation-Based Solar and Wind Power Capacity Factors and Power Densities." *IOP Science* (Environmental Research Letters) 13, Number 10 104008 (DOI 10.1088/1748-9326/aae102).

Milman, Andrew et al. 2021. "The Climate Disaster is Here; Earth is already becoming unlivable. Will governments act to stop this disaster from getting worse?" *The Guardian.* October 14. theguardian.com.

Milner, Richard. 2023. "The Estimated Number of Deaths on The Oregon Trail is Probably More Than You Think." *GRUNGE.* June 1. grunge.com.

Miltimore, Jon. 2023. "It Now Looks Likely That Government Created COVID-19, and Then Tried to Hide the Truth; Even the FBI now concludes the COVID-19 pandemic likely stemmed from a lab incident in Wuhan, China. Here's why that matters." *Foundation for Economic Education.* March 6. fee.org.

Mion, Landon. 2023. "Whole Foods in San Francisco Closing One Year After Opening Due to Safety Concerns." *Fox Business.* April 11. foxbusiness.com.

Moench, Mallory. 2023. "Mark Zuckerberg is Reportedly Building an Underground Bunker

in Hawaii." *TIME* time.com. December 30.

Mollman, Steve. 2023. "I Don't Have Time for Anything": A Gen Z'ers Horror at the 10-Hour Day Required to Commute to an Office for her First Job Goes Viral." *Yahoo Finance.* October 29. finance.yahoo.com.

Montana Connections. 2021. *A Brief History of Butte's Berkeley Pit.* Butte, Montana, January 28.

Montana Fish, Wildlife, and Parks. n.d. "All About Bears." *https://fwp.mt.gov/conservation/wildlife-management/bear/all-about-bears.*

Montana's Historic Landscapes; 35 Years in the Big Sky Country. *"Libby Dam and the*

Transformation of Lincoln County." montanahistoriclandscapes.com

Montana's Missouri River Country. n.d. "Plentywood." *missouririvermt.com.*

Montgomery, Jay, et al. 2021. "Myocarditis Following Immunization with mRNA COVID-19 Vaccines in Members of the US Military." *National Institutes of Health; National Library of Science* (JAMA) (JAMA Cardiol. 2021 Oct 1;6(10):1202-1206. doi: 10.1001/jamacardio.2021.2833 Jay Montgomery et al.).

1979. *Monty Python's "Life of Brian".* British Comedy. Directed by Terry Jones. Produced by Handmade Films. Performed by Graham Chapman, John Cleese, Terry Gilliam, Eric Idle, Terry Jones, Michael Palin Monty Python.

Moor, Joost de. 2024. "How Climate Activists Finally Seized the Issue of Adaption in 2023." *The Conversation.* January 31. conversation.com.

Moore, Mark. 2023. "White House reporters out of patience with Jean-Pierre over Biden docs: report." *New York Post.* January 20. nypost.com.

Moore, Stephen. 2018. "Follow the Climate Change Money." *The Heritage Foundation.* December 18. heritage.org.

Moorhead, Richard. 2022. "California Environmentalists Shut Down Desalination Plant as American West Faces Historic Water Crisis." *The Western Journal.* July 14. westernjournal.com.

Moorwood, Victoria. 2023. "UC Student Says She Failed Assignment for Using Term "Biological Woman"." *Cincinnati Enquirer.* June 5.

Morgan, Ryan. 2022. "Twitter Aided Pentagon on Psyop Operations, Says New Twitter Files Release." *American Military News.* December 20.

Motavalli, Jim.2024. "$7.5 Billion in Federal Funds Yield Only 8 EV Charging Stations."

Auto Week. autoweek.com. May 7.

Murphy, Cait. 2009. "Cash For Clunkers: Did it Work?" *CBS News.* August 31.

Murphy, Colleen. 2023. "What is Cultural Appropriation?" *Health.* October 25. health.com.

Murray, Aphra. 2022. "Cobalt Mining: The Dark Side of the Renewable Energy Transition." *Earth.Org.* September 27.

Musumeci, Natalie. 2023. "Cornell University Students Have Left Campus and Are Afraid to Sleep in Their Rooms After Violent Online Threats Were Made Against Jewish Pupils." *Business Insider.* November 1.

Muthukumar, A and Narasimhan M., et al. 2021. "Myocarditis/Pericarditis After mRNA-COVID-19 Vaccine Administration: Potential Mechanisms and Recommended Future Actions." *Pfizer Confidential* (Pfizer) (Circulation. 2021;144:487-498. doi: 10.1161/CIRCULATIONAHA.121.056038).

My Northwest. 2023. "Minors Seeking Gender-Affirming Treatment Can Shelter Without Parent's Knowledge; Senate Bill 5599, State of Washington." May 9. mynorthwest.com.

Myers, Megan and Raasch, Jon Michael. 2023. "Businesses Setting up Booby Traps to Protect Themselves in this Blue City's Drug Haven: Recovering Addict." *Fox News.* August 16. foxnews.com.

Myers, Megan. 2023. "Philly Cheesecake Landmark Takes Drastic Measures to Protect Shop From Crime." *Fox News.* October 4. foxnews.com.

Natanson, Hannah. 2022. "Loudon Fires Superintendent After Grand Jury Blasts Schools' Handling of Sex Assaults." *The Washington Post.* December 7. washingtonpost.com.

National Institutes of Health. 2021. "Myopericarditis After Messenger RNA Coronavirus Disease 2019 Vaccination in Adolescents 12 to 18 Years of Age." Study Report, All, With the National Library of Medicine; National Center for Biotechnology Information; Surveillance For Safety After Immunization.

2018. "The Power of Pets: Health Benefits of Human-Animal Interactions." *NIH News in Health*, February.

National Park Service. *Yellowstone.* nps.gov

Celebrating 50 Outstanding Remarkable Years! Nps.gov

NCS Import. 2015. "Norm Sauer: Mann's 'Hockey Stick' a Documented Hoax." *The Union.* October 2. theunion.com.

Nelson, Steven and Morphet, Jack. 2023. "Angry Maui Residents Slam Biden, Hold "No Comment" Signs During President's Fire Tour." *New York Post.* August 21.

Nesbit, Jeff. 2014. "Did the Holocaust Exist? Scary Number of People Say 'No' or Not Even Aware." *U.S. News.* May 23. usnews.com.

Nesi, Chris. 2024. "White House at Odds as Feud Reportedly Erupts Between Karine Jean-Pierre and Biden-Favorite John Kirby." *New York Post.* January 5. nypost.com.

New York Times. 2023. "Orsted, Offshore Wind Firm, Cancels M.J. Projects." *New York Times.* November 1. nytimes.com.

NG, David. 2024. "16 Times Hollywood Celebs Fantasized About Violence Against Trump,

Compared Him to Hitler." *Breitbart* breitbart.com July 14.

Niemeyer, Kenneth. 2023. "The US Army is Having a Hard Time Recruiting. Now it's Asking Soldiers Dismissed for Refusing the COVID-19 Shot to Come Back." *Business Insider.* November 18.

2023. "Biden is Hiring a Meme Manager and is Willing to Pay up to $85,000.00."

Business Insider. businessinsider.com. May 23.

Nightingale, Hannah. 2022. "BREAKING: Newsome Signs Bill to Allow Minors From Other States to Receive Medical Gender Transition Without Parental Consent." *News Analysis.* September 30.

2022. "Indiana Parents Lose Custody After Court Rules Not 'Affirming' Child's Gender Identity

is 'Abuse.'." *The Post Millenial.* October 24. thepostmillennial.com.

Nilsen, Ella. 2023. "Energy Company Pulls the Plug on Two Major Offshore Wind Projects on East Coast." *CNN.* November 1. edition.cnn.com.

Nolan, Beatrice. 2022. "Elon Musk Tells Twitter Employees to Return to the Office, or Their Resignations Will be Accepted." *Insider.* November 11.

Nolfi, Joey. 2024. "The View hosts stress 'it's all fiction' as John Grisham says he considered

writing more Supreme Court assassinations; "The current state of the Supreme Court made him consider writing another book about the assassination of justices." *Entertainment Weekly.* msn.com. May.

Norton, Tom. 2023. "Fact Check: Does Project Veritas Video Show Pfizer is Mutating Covid?" *Newsweek.* January 26.

NPR. 2020. "Analysis Finds Big Differences in School Textbooks in States with Differing Politics." January 13. npr.com.

2019. "Citing Lack of Funds, Sen. Kamala Harris Leaves Presidential Race." December 4.

npr.org.

NTB Staff. 2024. "UNREAL: California Judge Says School was Justified in Punishing

7-Year-Old Who Said All Lives Matter Because She's Too Young to Have First Amendment Rights." *Not The Bee* notthebee.com July 19

O' Brien, Cortney. 2021. "Former Biden Covid Advisor Says Cloth Masks Ineffective, Suggests Americans Start Wearing N-95 Masks." *Fox News*. August 3. foxnews.com.

O' Brien, Sarah. 2022. "75% of Middle-Class Households Say Their Income is Falling Behind the Cost of Living." *cnbc.com*. July 18.

O' Donnell, Kelly and Lebowitz, Megan. 2023. "Cocaine Found in the White House Was in a Different Location Than Previously Reported, Sources Say." *NBC News*. July 6. nbcnew.com.

Okin, Gregory S. 2017. "Environmental Impacts of Food Consumption by Dogs and Cats." (PLOS ONE) (https://doi.org/10.1371/journal.pone.0181301).

Olander, Olivia and Cadelago, Christopher. 2022. "Biden: "In Our Bones, We Know Democracy is at Risk." The President's Speech Was a Closing Argument for Democrats Before the Midterms." *Politico*. November 2.

O' Leary, Denyse. 2021. "Yes, There Really is a War on Math in Our Schools." *MIND MATTERS*. February 16. https://mindmatters.ai/2021/02/yes-there-really-is-a-war-on-math-in-our-schools/.

Oliver, Ashley. 2024. "Biden Debate Performance Renews Spotlight on Hur Tapes;

A vindicating moment for former special counsel Robert Hur." *Washington Examiner*. washingtonexaminer.com. June 28.

O' Neill, Natalie. 2023. "Girl Straddled by Drag Queen Sparks Outrage at North Carolina School." *New York Post*. March 23.

Opeka, Theresa. 2024. Senate Dems Block Budd's Laken Riley Act."

The Carolina Journal. carolinajournal.com. March 14.

Open VAERS. 2022. *VAERS COVID-19 Vaccine Adverse Event Reports*. 1,226,312 events through April 8, 2022, https://openvaers.com/covid-data/mortality.

Oregon Revised Statutes. 2023. "ORS 616.892 Single-use plastic straws." *oregon.public.law*.

Oregon State Parks. n.d. "Hilgard Junction State Park." *Oregon State Parks.* stateparks.oregon.gov.

Orwell, George. n.d. *"1984" Summary; "1984" by George Orwell follows Winston Smith, who attempts to fight back against a totalitarian government that rules through fear, surveillance, propaganda, and brainwashing.* Literature Reviews *Summaries* Analysis.

Oster, Emily. 2022. "Let's Declare a Pandemic Amnesty." *The Atlantic.* October 31. theatlantic.com.

2022. "We Need to Forgive One Another For What We Did and Said When We Were in the Dark About Covid." *The Atlantic.* October 31.

O'Sullivan, John, et al. 2018. "What Michael Mann's 'Hockey Stick' Graph Gave to UN Climate Fraud." *Principia Scientific International.* January 5. principia-scientific.com.

Pagans, Stephanie. 2022. "NYC Walgreens Store Keeping Ice Cream in Chained Freezer, Locking up Candy Amid Ongoing Shoplifting Frenzy." *Fox Business.* December 23. foxbusiness.com.

Palmer, Ewan. 2022. "Video of Tiara Mack, R.I. State Senator, Twerking on TikTok Goes Viral." *Newsweek.* July 6. newsweek.com.

Palumbo, Matt. 2023. "George Soros Spent $40 Million Getting Lefty District Attorneys, Officials Elected All Over the Country, Adding to his Vast Political Empire." *New York Post.* January 26. nypost.com.

Pappas, Stephanie. 2020. "Why Are Children 'Missing' From Coronavirus Outbreak Cases? It Seems That Youth Protects Against the Worst Effects of 2019-nCoV." *LIVESCIENCE.* February 10. livescience.com.

Parfitt, Jamie. 2021. "Jackson County Declares State of emergency in Response to Illegal Marijuana Grows." *Newswatch 12.* October 13. kdrv.com.

Parker, Star. 2024. "Liberal Racism Denigrates Black Conservatives." *Rocky Mount Telegram.* March 14. rockymounttelegram.com.

Parks, Kristine. 2024. "Army Vet Says Prepper Food Company Booming as More Americans Plan for Disaster in 2024." *Fox Business.* February 12. foxbusiness.com.

2022. "Study Suggesting Unvaccinated Should Pay Higher Car Insurance Premiums Draw Outrage." *Fox News.* December 14. foxnews.com.

Passantino, Jon. 2023. "James O'Keefe Ousted From Right-Wing Activist Group Project Veritas." *CNN.* February 20. cnn.com.

Pearson, Muriel et. al. 2018. "Who Was David Koresh: Ex-Followers Describe Life Inside Apocalyptic Religious Sect Involved in 1993 Waco Siege." *ABC News.* January 2.

Peckford, Brian. 2021. "Australian Nurses Spill the Beans on Vaccine Injuryies and Deaths - Does Anyone Think This is All Lies, All Made Up?" *Peckford42*. September 28. peckford42wordpress.com.

Pelosi, Nancy, interview by ABC. 2010. *Tea Party is "Astroturf, as Opposed to Grassroots."*, edited by AHFF Geoff. (February 28).

Penley, Taylor. 2023. "California Mom Confronts School District After 11-Year-Old Changed Genders Without Her Knowledge." *Fox News*. April 11. foxnews.com.

2023. "Employers Are Fed Up With College 'Waste,' Opt For Skilled Blue-Collar Workers Instead." *Fox Business*. November 19. foxbusiness.com.

Penn Today. 2021. "Ten Years Later, Examining the Occupy Movement Legacy." https://penntoday.upenn.edu/news/ten-years-later-examining-occupy-movements- legacy

Penzenstadler, Nick. 2023. "Billions from the US is Flowing to Ukraine. Here's Where it Comes From, and How it Adds Up." *USA Today*. September 7. usatoday.com.

People Staff. 2020. "A Sweet Surface Hid a Troubled Soul in the Late Karen Carpenter, Who Would Have Been 70 Today." *People*. March 2.

Peoples Dispatch. 2022. "Latin America is Moving Toward "Plurinational," Slowly But Definitely." *Peoples Dispatch*. February 25.

Pepper, Diarmuid. 2023. "Nobody's Hands Are Clean": Obama Describes the Situation in Gaza as 'Unbearable'. *The Journal*. November 6. thejournal.ie.

Perkins, Tom. 2023. ""It Feels Like an Apocalyptic Movie" Life in East Palestine Six Months After Toxic Train Crash." *The Guardian*. August 4.

Perlstein, Rick. n.d. "Watergate Scandal." *Britannica*. brittannica.com.

Perry, Mark J. 2019. "50 Years of Failed Doomsday, Eco-Apocalyptic Predictions: The So-Called "Experts" are 0 for 50." *American Enterprise Institute*.

PETA. "Animals Are Not Ours." *People for the Ethical Treatment of Animals*. peta.org.

Pflughoeft, Aspen. 2022. "Centuries-Old Warnings Emerge from Riverbed as Europe Faces Historic Drought." *The Miami Herald*.

Philips, Jack. 2023. "Major US City Closing Down Ohio River Intake After Train Derailment." *NTD*. February 17.

Phillips, Aleks. 2023. "Full List of Democrats Who Refused to Condemn Hamas Supporters." *Newsweek*. November 3. newsweek.com.

2023. "Joe Biden Backtracks on Maui Visit After Hawaii Response Receives Backlash." *Newsweek*. August 16.

2023. "Kamala Harris' Thanksgiving Photo Raises Questions." *Newsweek*. November 24. newsweek.com.

Phillips, Amber. 2022. "Analysis; What's Going on With all the Missing J6 Texts?" *The Washington Post*. August 13. washingtonpost.com.

Pilkington, Ed. 2009. "Barack Obama Meets Professor and the Policeman - Over a Beer." *The Guardian*. July 30. the guardian.com.

2008. "Obama Angers Midwest Voters With Guns and Religion Remark." *The Guardian*. April

14. theguardian.com.

Pipeline and Hazardous Materials Safety Administration. 2023. Report: Final Rule;

Suspension of HMR Amendments Authorizing Transportation of Liquid Natural Gas by Rail. *U.S. Department of Transportation. Office of Governmental, International, and Public Affairs, Washington D.C.*

Pit Watch. Ongoing. "The Official Source of Information about the Management Plan to Protect Human Health and the Environment From Berkeley Pit Contamination." *Pit Watch*. pitwatch.org.

Pladson, Kristie. 2021. "Davos: Green Transition is '$50 Trillion Opportunity'." *DW*. January 28. dw.com.

Plainview, Daniel. 2024. "4,000 Acres of Solar Panels Were Destroyed in One Texas Hail

Storm. Locals are Now Worried About Groundwater Poisoning." *Not The Bee*. notthebee.com. March 26.

Planned Parenthood. 2021. *Just Say Abortion*. Trans and Non-binary People Have Abortions; Abortion Isn't Just "Women's Healthcare.", Category: Abortion Access, Healthcare Equity, Planned Parenthood.

2021. "Trans and Non-Binary People Have Abortions. Abortion is't just women's health care."

Planned Parenthood. June 13. plannedparenthoodaction.org.

Poff, Jeremiah. 2022. "NSBA (National School Board Association) Wrote Parents-as-Terrorist Letter at Behest of Education Secretary Miguel Cardona, Emails Show." *Washington Examiner*. January 11. washington-examiner.com.

Pollina, Richard and O'Neill, Jesse. 2023. "Trans Model Rose Montoya Goes Topless During White House Price Party After Meeting Biden." *New York Post*. June 13. nypost.com.

Pomeroy, Ross. 2022. "Why Are Conservatives Happier Than Liberals?" *Real Clear Science*. August 27. realclearscience.com.

Pope, Nick. 2023. "Biden Says He Plans to Build a "Railroad From the Pacific All the Way Across the Indian Ocean."." *Daily Caller*. June 15.

Popovici, Alice. 2018. "The Game Clue Was Borne of Boredom During WWII Air-Raid Blackouts." *History.* August 29.

Post Editorial Board. 2024. "Joe Biden Got Laken Riley's Name Wrong--as he has EVERYTHING in his Border Mess." *New York Post.* March 8. msn.com.

2022. "President Biden Blatantly Disrespected on His Own Turf." *New York Post.* April 6. nypost.com.

2022. "Why Did President Biden Just Endorse the Most Radical Trans Madness?" *New York Post.* October 25. nypost.com.

POWER. 2015. "Top Plants: Palo Verde Nuclear Generating Station, Wintersburg, Arizona." *News & Technology for the Global Energy Industry.* November 1. powermag.com.

Press, Associated. 2023. "Foot Found in Yellowstone Hot Pool, But Case is Still Murky." *Flathead Beacon*, January 4.

Press-Reynolds, Kieran. 2023. "TikTokers Are Warning People Not to Participate in the "Lazy Girl Jobs" Trend and Brag about Their Lax Work Days so They Don't Unintentially Out Themselves and Get Fired." *Business Insider.* July 17. businessinsider.com.

Prestigiacomo, Amanda. 2019. "These 8 States Allow Abortion up to the Moment of Birth." *The Daily Wire.* January 30. dailywire.com.

Proctor, Robert N. and Schiebinger, Londa. 2022. "How Preventing Unwanted Pregnancies Can Help on Climate Change." *Yale Environment 360, Published at the Yale School of the Environment,* July 21.

Programs, Federal Welfare. 2023. "80+ low-income Programs Providing Cash, Food, Housing, Medical Care, and Social Services." *Federal Welfare Programs.* October 26. singlemothersguide.com.

Project Veritas. 2023. "Project Veritas Sting Report." Jordon Trishton Walker of Pfizer on Video.

Prouix, Annie. 2005. *Brokeback Mountain.* Directed by Ang Lee. Produced by Dianna Ossana and James Schamus. Performed by Jake Gyllenhall, Anne Hathaway, Michelle Williams Heath Ledger.

Pruitt, Sarah. 2021. "How Title IX Transformed Women's Sports: The Groundbreaking Gender Equity Law Made a Lasting Impact by Increasing the Participation of Girls and Women in Athletics." *History.* August 16. history.com.

Psychology Today. 2021. "Gender Dysphoria." *Psychology Today.* Diagnostic and Statistical Manual of Mental Health Disorders, Fifth Edition, and National Library of Medicine References: American Psychiatric Association. October 25.

Puhlach, Olha et al. 2022. "Infectious Viral Load in Unvaccinated and Vaccinated Individuals Infected With Ancestral, Delta or Omicron SARS-CoV-2." *Nature Medicine* (Nature Medicine) (https://doi.org/10.1038/s41591-022-01816-0).

Puplava, James. 2023. "The Beginning of the End Part III." *Financial Sense.* October 5. Financialsense.com.

Quote Research. 2014. "We Don't See Things as They Are, We See Them as We Are." March 9. quoteinvestigator.com.

Rahman, Khaleda. August. "Mask Mandates Return: Full List of Places With Restrictions in Place." *Newsweek.* 29 2023. newsweek.com.

Raleigh, Helen. 2023. "DEI Jobs are Drying Up, But Colleges Keep Pushing Diversity Studies." *The Federalist.* July 26.

Ramis, Dan Akroyd and Harold. 1984. *Ghostbusters.* Directed by Ivan Reitman. Produced by Ivan Reitman. Performed by Dan Akroyd and Harold Ramis Bill Murray.

Randall, K. et al. 2021. "How Did We Get Here: What are Droplets and Aerosols and How Far Do They Go? A historical perspective on the transmission of respiratory infectious diseases." *The Royal Society Publishing* (https://doi.org/10.1098/rsfs.2021.0049).

Rantz, Jason. 2024. "Seattle English Students Told It's "White Supremacy" to Love Reading, Writing." *770KTTH.* February 14. mynorthwest.com.

2022. "WA Laws Now Allow Teen Gender Reassignment Surgery Without Parental Consent." *770KTTH.* January 10. mynorthwest.com.

Raymond, Nate. 2023. "Parents Cannot Challenge School Gender Identity Policy, US Court Rules." *Reuters.* August 14. reuters.com.

Reality Check Team. 2021. "Coronavirus: Was US Money Used to Fund Risky Research in China?" *BBC News.* August 2.

Reilly, Katie. 2016. "Read Hillary Clinton's "Basket of Deplorables" Remarks About Donald Trump Supporters." *TIME.* September 10. time.com.

Reilly, Patrick. 2023. "Fashion Designer Claims Sam Brinton Wore Her Clothes That Were Stolen From DC Airport in 2018." *The New York Post.* February 22. nypost.com.

Reinstein, Julia et.al. 2024. "Kamala IS Brat: How Kamala Harris' Campaign is Embracing the Memes." *ABC News* abcnews.go.com. July 22.

Rep. Chu, Judy (D-CA-28). n.d *H.R. 12 - Women's Health Protection Act of 2023.* 118th CONGRESS, House - Energy and Commerce; Judiciary, CONGRESS.GOV, Section 3, paragraph 1. Purpose; To permit people to seek and obtain abortion services, and to permit health care providers to provide abortion services, without harmful or unwarranted limitations or requirements that single out the provision of abortion.

Resnick, Brian et al. 2013. "A Brief History of Terrorism in the United States." *The Atlantic.* April 16.

Retrops, Mister. 2023. "How Does This Keep Happening?" *Not the Bee.* September 22.

Reuters. 2023. "Davos 2023: Key Takeaways From the World Economic Forum." *U.S. News.* January 20.

Reyes, Ronny. 2022. "LA School District is Slammed for Posting Woke Video that Says Calling Junk Food Bad is Wrong and Promotes New Concept of "Food Neutrality" That Claims "Diet Culture is based on Oppression."." *Daily Mail.* September 14. dailymail.com.

Reynolds, David. 2011. "Uncle Tom Revisited: Rescuing the Real Character From the Caricature." *BLACK PAST.* August 9. blackpast.org.

Richardson, Katelynn. 2021. "Kentucky School District to Host Year-Long Anti-Racist Mathematics Training for Teachers." *The College Fix.* July 23. thecollegefix.com.

Richardson, Kimberly. 2022. "Our Pets Are Part of the Climate Problem. These Tips Can Help You Minimize Their Carbon Pawprints." *CNN.* September 27.

Riechmann, Deb. 2016. "IG: Some Emails on Clinton's Server Were Beyond Top Secret." *Associated Press.* January 19. apnews.com.

Rigby, Harris. 2023. "MSNBC Mika Tells Biden Handlers to "Do a Better Job" Covering up Joe's Age: "You can't have these video images of the President tripping or the President, like, going the wrong way!"." *Not the Bee.* July 12. notthebee.com.

2023. "Not Parody: WaPo Wants You to Know Pumpkin Spice Has a "Violent History," and is "Fraught With Colonization."." *Not the Bee.* October 31. https://twitter.com/ByronYork/status/1679106577838612482?cxt=HBwWhIC9gamisc0uAAAA&cn=ZmxleGlibGVfcmVjcw%3D%3D&refsrc=email.

2024. "Viral Throwback: Highlights of the Media and Politicians Shaming People Who Did

Not Get the Jabby jab; Video painful to watch for those of us who were shamed, guilted, despised, and lost their livlihoods because of the vaccine mandates. Never Forget." *Not the Bee.* notthebee.com. May 31.

Riggio PhD, Ronald. 2022. "Social Contagion: How Others Secretly Control Your Behavior; We are often unaware of how others can infuence us." *Psychology Today.* September 24.

Riggs Larsen, Kathy. 2020. "Corrosion Risks and Mitigation Strategies for Offshore Wind Turbine Foundations." *Materials Performance.* May 4.

Ring, Trudy. 2024. "Biden Administration Creates $700K Grant to Create Inclusive Sex Ed for Trans Male Teens." *Yahoo News.* January 26.

Ritchie, Earl. 2016. "Fact-Checking the Claim of 97% Consensus on Anthropogenic Climate Change." *Forbes.* December 14. forbes.com.

RNC Research. 2023. "One Person's Idea of Risk is Another Person's Idea of a Great Festival or Friday Night." *Twitter.com@RNCResearch.* June 18. https://twitter.com/RNCResearch/status/1670433692312018944?ref_src=twsrc%5Etfw%7Ctwcamp%5Etweetembed%7Ctwterm%5E1670

433692312018944%7Ctwgr%5Ec07133ead8ca2b21d81807fd4c4996e01d370653%7Ctwcon%5Es1_&ref_url=https%3A%2F%2Fredstate.com%2Fbonchie%2F2023%2F06%2.

Robb-Dover, Kristina. 2021. "Pathological Lying Can Occur with These Mental Disorders." *FHEHealth.* April 12. https://fherehab.com/learning/pathological-lying-disorders.

1997 British Comedy. *The Full Monty.* Directed by Peter Cattaneo. Performed by Mark Addy, William Snape, and a host of others. Robert Carlyle.

Robertson, Lori. 2021. "The Wuhan Lab and the Gain-of-Function Disagreement." *SciCheck.* July 1. factcheck.org.

Roddenberry, Eugene. 1966 to 1969. *Star Trek.* American Science Fiction Television Series. Directed by Eugene Roddenberry. Produced by Eugene Roddenberry. Performed by William Shatner and Leonard Nimoy.

Rodgers, Henry. 2023. "EXCLUSIVE: Senate Staffer Caught Filming Gay Sex Tape in Senate Hearing Room [GRAPHIC]." *The Daily Caller.* December 15. dailycaller.com.

Rodham Clinton, Hillary. 2006. *It Takes a Village.* Simon & Schuster.

Rodriguez, Andrew. 2024. "CBS Reporter Predicts "Black Swan" Event in 2024: "Fertile Ground for Our Adversaries."." *State of the Union.* January. msn.com.

Rodriguez, Bailey. 2018. "The Effects of Saltwater on Metals." *SCIENCING.* April 27.

Roger Roots, J.D., Ph.D. 2017. "Are The Glaciers in Glacier National Park Growing?" *Watts Up With That*, September 16.

Roos, Dave. 2020. *Why The 1918 Flu Pandemic Never Really Ended.* December 11. history.com.

Roscoe, Matthew. 2021. "FDA Says it Needs 75 Years to Fully Release Pfizer COVID-19 Vaccine Data to the Public." *EuroWeekly News.* December 9.

Rose, Flemming. 2017. "Safe Spaces on College Campuses are Creating Intolerant Students." *HUFFPost.* June 12. huffpost.com.

Rosenblatt, Kalhan. 2019. "Teen Climate Activist Greta Thunberg Delivers Scathing Speech at U.N; "How dare you! You have stolen my dreams and my childhood with your empty words," Thunberg said.." *NBC News.* September 23. nbcnews.com.

Roth, Madeline. 2021. "New York Times Corrects Story After Legal Threat, Admits Babylon Bee is a "Satirical Website" and not "Misinformation"." *Yahoo Entertainment.* June 14. yahoo.com.

Rowland, Christopher. 2022. "The Unintended Consequences of the $178 Billion Bailout to Keep Hospitals and Doctors Afloat. The Pandemic-Driven Provider Relief Fund Widened the Gap Between the Haves and Have-Nots." *The Washington Post.* June 22. washingtonpost.com.

Rubin, April. 2024. "Independent Voters Dominate U.S. While Dems Slip to Record Low: Gallup." *Axios*. January 12. axios.com.

Rufo, Christopher Senior Fellow Manhattan Institute. 2024. "The Real Story Behind Drag Queen Story Hour. A short film exposing the history of this bizarre modern ritual." *Christopher F. Rufo*. January 23. christopherrufo.com.

Ruiz, Michael. 2024. "Illegal Brother of Laken Riley Murder Suspect Linked to Venezuelan Crime Gang: DOJ." *Fox News*. March 7. foxnews.com.

Rumble. 2023. "PBS Documentary Show What J6 Committee was a Show Trial to Destroy President Trump." *One News Page*. onenewspage.com.

Rutkowski, Adam. Open Source. "Constitutional Interpretation Styles of US Supreme Court Justices; A more progressive style of interpretation treats the Constitution as a living document." *Oregon State University*. open.oregonstate.education.

Sabastian, Xavier. 2022. "Gas Shortage and Prices in the United States: A Domino Effect." *WAY*. way.com.

Sabet, Kevin and Kubeisy, Connor. 2024. "How to Address Oregon's Drug Decriminalization Mess; The State's First-in-the-Nation Approach to Decriminalization Has Left Deaths and Overdoses Surging.." *Governing For the People Making Government Work*. January 18. governing.com.

Sabet, Kevin. 2022. "Two Years Later, Oregon's Drug Decriminalization is Not Going Well." *Newsweek*. September 29.

Sahakian, Teny. 2023. "After Colleges Gave Anti-Israel Activists a Pass, Former Penn Trustee Issues Warning to University Admins." *Fox News*. October 28. foxnews.com.

Sahakian, Tiny. 2023. "Illinois Sheriffs Brace for Fallout of "America's Most Dangerous Law" After State Supreme Court Ends Cash Bail." *Fox News*. July 19. foxnews.com.

Salmonsen, Mary. 2022. "5 Reasons Why Rents are Rising at a Record Pace; Inflation, demographic shifts, and supply shortages have created a perfect storm of rent growth, economists say." *Multifamily Dive*. May 10. multifamilydive.com.

Samantha, Lock. 2020. ""To Kill a Mockingbird," Other Books Banned From California Schools Over Racism Concerns." *Newsweek*. November 13. newsweek.com.

Samuel, Robin and Shimada, Michael. 2023. "Employer COVID-19 Mandates: Still Legal, But For How Long?" *Reuters*. April 18. reuters.com.

Sandberg, Sheryl. 2013. *Lean In: Women, Work, and the Will to Lead*. Knopf.

Sapper, Paul. 2022. "Watch Outrage as Woman Praying Silently is Arrested in UK Street - "Taken Away by Police for a Thoughtcrime."." *Britains News Channel*. December 23.

Saul, Derek. 2023. "Disney 'Repeatedly Misled Investors' About Streaming Losses, Lawsuit Alleges." *Forbes.* August 29.

Savage, Rachel. 2020. "With Twitter Pronouns and Victory Speech, Biden-Harris Signal New Era for Trans Rights." *London (Thomson Reuters Foundation).* November 10. reuters.com.

Schaller, Tom and Waldman, Paul. 2024. *White Rural Rage: The Threat to American Democracy.* Random House.

Schilling, Erin. 2024. "Rich Taxpayers in Dark About What IRS Data was Illegally Leaked

including former President Donald Trump." *Bloomberg Tax.* news.bloombergtax.com May 10.

Schneider, Christian. 2022. "Gender Activists Push to Bar Anthropologists from Identifying Human Remains as "male or female"." *The College Fix.* July 18. thecollegefix.com.

Scholl, Eva Marie and Nopp-Mayr, Ursula. 2021. "Impact of Wind Power Plants on Mammalian and Avian Wildlife Species in Shrub and Woodlands." *Biological Conservation: Volume 256* (University of Natural Resources and Life Sciences Vienna, Gregor-Mendel-Straße 33, 1180 Vienna, Austria).

Schonhardt, Sara. 2021. "Wake-Up Call: Climate Change Threatens Rice Farming." *Scientific American.* August 18. scientificamerican.com.

Schooley, Matt et al. 2024. "Pro-Palestinian Student Protest at Northeastern University

Cleared by Police." *CBS News.* CBSnews.com. April 27

Schrag, Jacque. 2023. "Eggs" Make History as Top-Ranked Google Search on Cost in 2023." *Axios.* December 14.

Schwab, Constantin et al. 2022. "Autopsy-Based Histopathological Characterization of Myocarditis After Anti-SARS-CoV-2 Vaccination." (Clinical Research in Cardiology) Original Paper (https://doi.org/10.1007/s00392-022-02129-5).

Schwartz, Ian. 2023. "Watch: VP Kamala Harris Once Again Gets Excited About VENN Diagrams." *RealClear Politics.* February 23. realclearpolitics.com.

2023. "WH's Karine Jean-Pierre: LGBTQI+ Kids Are "Fierce" and "They Fight Back"." *Real Clear Politics.* April 6. realclearpolitics.com.

Scott, Bill. 1959-1964. *The Bullwinkle Show.* Animated television series. Produced by Creator Jay Ward.

Scott, Tristan. 2022. "Gateway to Glacier Trails Gaining Ground." *The Flathead Beacon.* June 10. flatheadbeacon.com.

Scott, Whitlock. 2022. "Students at Expensive New York University Occupy Campus. Demand A-Grades for Everyone." *Fox News.* December 17. foxnews.com.

Searle, George. 1933. *The World's Oldest Industry- Pottery Making.* Performed by George Searle. Lecture featuring Pottery - Old and New, St. Paul Minnesota.

Seitz-Wald, Alex. 2020. "Progressive Group's Analysis Finds Stacey Abrams is Biden's Best

Choice. Here's Why." *NBC News.* nbcnews.com. March 20.

Seligman, Lara et al. 2021. "Electric Vehicles and Biofuel: Pentagon Poised to Go Greener Under Biden. "Where the Military Goes, the Civilian World Often Follows," Says One Influential Player Helping to Shape Policy." *Politico.* March 31. politico.com.

2023. "Timeline: A Chinese Spy Balloon's Trip Across the United States." *Politico.* February 5. politico.com.

Senate RPC. 2021. "A Surge of Drugs Adds to Biden's Border Crisis."

Serling, Rod. 1959. *The Twilight Zone.* Directed by Rod Serling. Performed by Rod Serling. Anthology Television Series.

Services Australia. "COVID-19 Vaccine Claims Scheme; The COVID-19 vaccine claims scheme gives people a way to seek compensation instead of going through legal proceedings." *Australia Government; Department of Health and Aged Care.* servicesaustralia.gov.au.

Settles, Gabrielle. 2021. "Fact Check on George Floyd's Criminal Arrest History." *Politifact.* July 29.

Shapiro, Adam R. 2020. "The Racist Roots of the Dog Whistle; Here's how we came to label the coded language." *The Washington Post.* August 21. washingtonpost.com.

Sharko MD, Marianne et al. 2022. "State-By-State Variability in Adolescent Privacy Laws." *American Academy of Pediatrics* (AAP Publications) 149 (6).

Sharp, David. 2023. "Maine Mom: School Wrong to Help, Hide Gender Transition." *AP.* April 6. apnews.com.

Shaw, Adam. 2023. "Catholic Archdiocese Accuses Walter Reed of Stifling Religious Rights With "Cease and Desist" Order. The Move Came Just Days Before Holy Week.." *Fox News.* April 8. foxnews.com.

Shellenberger, Michael. 2020. *Apocalypse Never: Why Environmental Alarmism Hurts Us All.* Harper.

Shinkman, Paul. 20223. "Pentagon: No Back Pay to Troops Discharged for Refusing COVID-19 Vaccine." *U.S. News.* January 17. usnews.com.

Shirer, William L. 1960. *The Rise and Fall of the Third Reich: A History of Nazi Germany.* Edited by Joseph Barnes. Simon & Schuster.

Shoemaker, Nancy. 2015. "A Typology of Colonialism." *Perspectives on History.* October 1.

Showalter, Brandon. 2021. "We're Now Prey for Men": California Women Inmates Decry Housed with Male Prisoners." *The Christian Post.* July 21.

Shriber, Sara. 2022. "Unplugged: How Digital Detoxing and Device Addiction Impact Job Burnout and Well-Being." *Civic Science.* September 6. civicscience.com.

Sigalos, MacKenzie. 2020. "You Can't Sue Pfizer or Moderna if You Have Severe Covid Vaccine Side Effects. The Government Likely Won't Compensate You for Damages Either." *CNBC.* December 17. https://www.cnbc.com/2020/12/16/covid-vaccine-side-effects-compensation-lawsuit.html.

Simon. 2013. "Australian Climate Madness; Just don't tell me the debate's over..." March 28. australianclimatemadness.com.

Singanayagam PhD, Anika et al. 2021. "Community Transmission and Viral Load Kinetics of the SARS-CoV-2 Delta Variant in Vaccinated and Unvaccinated Individuals in the UK: A Prospective, Longitudinal Cohort Study." *The Lancet* (The Lancet) (doi.org/10.1016/S1473-3099(21)00648-4).

singlemotherguide.com. 2022. *List of 80+ Federal Welfare Programs.* July 16.

Singman, Brooke. 2016. "Coddling Campus Crybabies: Students Take up Toddler Therapy After Trump Win." *Fox News.* November 17. foxnews.com.

2024. "House Jan. 6 Committee Deleted More Than 100 Encrypted Files Days Before GOP Took Majority: Sources." *Yahoo News.* January 22. news.yahoo.com.

Siri, Aaron. 2022. "Why a Judge Ordered FDA to Release COVID-19 Vaccine Data Pronto." *Forbes.* January 18.

1962. *The Jetsons.* Directed by Hanna-Barbara Productions. Performed by George Jetson-animated sitcom.

skynews.com.au. 2021. "The World is Laughing at Joe Biden." September 24. skynews.com.au.

Smith, Emily. 2017. "The Deadly Grizzly Bear Attacks That Changed the National Park Service Forever." *Smithsonian Magazine.* August 10. smithsonianmag.com.

Smith, Zack, et al. 2020. "Little Sisters of the Poor Win Big at Supreme Court, But Fight Isn't Over." *The Heritage Foundation.* July.

Soave, Robby. 2021. "In the Name of Equity, California Will Discourage Students Who Are Gifted at Math; The new framework aims to keep everyone learning at the same level for as long as possible." *reason.* May 4. reason.com.

Solar Energy Technologies Office. 2021. *Solar Futures Study.* Solar Futures Study by the Department of Energy, Office of Energy Efficiency & Renewable Energy.

Solomon, John. 2022. "Already Stretched Thin, Border Agents Must Now Use Politically Correct Pronouns Under New Edict; Changes were Instituted on International Trans Day of Visibility." *Just The News.* April 4. justthenews.com.

Sonter, L.J., Dade, M.C., Watson, J.E.M. et al. 2020. "Renewable Energy Production Will Exacerbate Mining Threats to Biodiversity." *Nature Communications* Nat Commun 11, 4174 (2020) (https://doi.org/10.1038/s41467-020-17928-5).

Sottile, Zoe. 2022. "California Bees Can Legally be Fish and Have the Same Protections, a Court Has Ruled." *CNN.* June 6. cnn.com.

Spector, Nicole. 2023. "These Foods Will Be In Short Supply In 2023, So Stock Up Now." *Yahoo Finance.* August 2. finance.yahoo.com.

Spencer, Saranac Hale. 2023. "Multiple Federal Agencies Supporting East Palestine, Contrary

to Partisan Claims; Do not qualify for direct financial aid from the Federal Emergency Management Agency." Factcheck.org. February.

Spingarn, Adena. 2010. "When 'Uncle Tom' Became an Insult." *THE ROOT.* May 17. theroot.com.

Spoor, Thomas. 2022. "The Rise of Wokeness in the Military." *The Heritage Foundation.* September 30. heritage.org.

Spritzer, Don. 1999. *Roadside History of Montana.* Mountain Press Publishing.

2004. *Documentary: Super Size Me.* Directed by Morgan Spurlock. Performed by Morgan Spurlock.

Stacker. 2022. *See the Most Extreme Temperatures in Montana History.* Stacker.

Stella, Christina. 2019. "Unfurling the Waste Problem Caused by Wind Energy." *NPR.ORG.* September 10.

Stevenson, Peter. 2016. "Hillary Clinton Couldn't Stop Saying Progressive at Thursday's Debate [Video]." *The Washington Post.* February 15. washingtonpost.com.

Stewart, Emily. 2024. "Woke No More; Companies were starting to support political causes,

now are too scared to speak up." *Business Insider.* businessinsider.com. May 9.

Stewart, Richard et al. 2023. "A Future With no Individual Ownership is Not a Happy One: Property Theory Shows Why." 152 (https://doi.org/10.1016/j.futures.2023.103209). sciencedirect.com.

Stiles, Andrew. 2022. "Don't Test, Don't Tell: Democrats Flout Safety Guidelines to Pass Climate Spending Bill Before Summer Recess." *The Washington Free Beacon.* August 5.

Stolberg, Cheryl and Anthes, emily. 2023. "U.S. Considers Vaccinating Millions of Chickens as Bird Flu Kills Millions of Them." *New York Times.* March 17.

Stolberg, Sheryl Gay. 2021. "Biden's Administration May Need More Funds to Fight an Omicron Surge." *New York Times.* December 14.

Stonestreet, John and Morris G. Shane. 2019. "Scientists" Say We Need to Kill More Babies in Abortions to Save the Planet." *LifeNews.com.* November 14.

strangesounds.org. 2019. *Glacier National Park Glaciers Are Growing - Officials Quietly Remove All "Glaciers Will Be Gone By 2020' Signs.* June 8.

Stratton, Allan. 2023. "The Left's Social Contract is Broken. Here's How to Fix It." *Quillette.* July 20. quillette.com.

Sullivan, Becky et al. 2020. "Kenosha Protests, Violence Expose Racial Disparities Among The Worst in the Country." *NPR.* September 2. npr.com.

Sullivan, Kate. 2022. "CNN." *Biden Proposes Strengthening Title IX Protections for Transgender Students.* June 23. CNN.

Sun, Rachel et al. 2022. "Criminology Student Charged with Murder in University of Idaho Killings." *The New York Times.* December 30. nytimes.com.

Sunday, Kingsley and Brennan, Feargal. 2021. "A Review of Offshore Wind Monopiles Structural Design Achievements and Challenges." *Science Direct.*

Sunderlage, Mary. 2007. *Sophie.* Tate Publishing.

Sustainable Business.com. 2022. "Carnivore Co-Existence Advocates." Job Announcement, Earth Island Institute a 503(c) 3 nonprofit.

Swann, Sara. 2024. "Cheap Fake" Videos, and the Phrase Itself, Take 2024 Election's Center Stage." *Politifact.* politifact.com. June 21.

Swiss Policy Research. 2021. *Covid Vaccines: A Reality Check. The Latest Unbiased Facts on Covid Vaccine Safety and Effectiveness.* Swiss Policy Research.

Tabish, Dillon. 2015. "The Man and the Mansion." *Flathead Beacon*, October 7.

Tan, Avianne. 2016. "Why Yellowstone Had to Euthanize a Bison Calf After a Visitor Put it in His Car." *ABC News*, May 18.

Tate, Kristin. 2021. "Coming Soon: America's Own Social Credit System." *The Hill.* August 3. thehill.com.

Taylor, Heather. 2017. "How the Clydesdales Became the Symbols of Budweiser." *HUFFPOST.* December 13.

Taylor, Kelley. 2023. "Are 87,000 New IRS Agents Coming for Your Dollars?" *Kiplinger* kiplinger.com January 10.

Taylor, Penley. 2023. "Employers Are Fed Up With College 'Waste,' Opt For Skilled Blue-Collar Workers Instead." *Fox Business*. November 19. fox-business.com.

Teach, Edward. 2023. "The Biden Administration is Considering Mass Vaccination Campaign for America's Chickens." *Not The Bee*. March 10.

TFTC. 2024. "The United Nations' Whopping $150 Trillion Climate Crisis Bill: An In-Dept Look." January 11. tftc.io.

Thakker, Prem. 2023. "Obama Alumni Call On Former President to "Leverage" Influence For Gaza Ceasefire. Using Obama's own words, recent and past, on Palestine, the former staffers join a rising tide of political operatives opposing unconditional U.S. support for Israel." *The Intercept*. November 14. theintercept.com.

The Center for Medical Progress. 2020. "Planned Parenthood Testimony on Selling Baby Parts Unsealed, New Videos Released." May 26.

The Christian Institute. 2017. US Group: "Abortions Are Good for the Environment." February 9. lifesitenews.com.

The Conversation. 2017. "Explainer: What is Antifa, and Where Did it Come From?" August 29. theconversation.com.

2017. "How Cult Leader Charles Manson Was Able to Manipulate His "Family" to Commit Murder." November 20.

The Daily Journal of the United States Government. 2020. "Declaration Under the Public Readiness and Emergency Preparedness Act for Medical Countermeasures Against COVID-19." *PREP act. Declaration to provide liability immunity against any claim or loss* (Federal Register).

The Fact File. 2022. *50 States Ranked By Size, In Square Miles*. thefactfile.org.

The Gilder Lehrman Institute of American History. Period 5: 1844-1877. "AP US History Study Guide." *Uncle Tom's Cabin and the Matter of Influence*. Edited by Jr., Hollis Robbins, and Henry Louis Gates. Prod. Gilder Lehrman.

The Global BMI Mortality Collaboration. 2016. "Body-Mass Index and All-Cause Mortality: Individual-participant-data meta-analysis of 239 prospective studies in four continents." *The Lancet* (Elsevier Ltd.) Volume 388, Issue 10046, 20–26 August 2016, Pages 776-786 (https://doi.org/10.1016/S0140-6736(16)30175-1).

The Petal Republic Team. "Pink Lotus Flower Meaning and Symbolism." *Petal Republic*.

The Post Millennial. 2023. "Breaking: Riley Gaines Violently Assaulted at SFSU Event." *The Post Millenial News Analysis*. April 7.

The Starr Report. 1998. "Part I: Nature of President Clinton's Relationship with Monica Lewinsky." *The Independent Council*. Washington D.C.

The White House. 2024. A Proclamation on Transgender Day of Visibility, 2024." *Washington DC*

The World Factbook. Ongoing. "Obesity - Adult Prevalence Rate." *The World Factbook.* cia.gov.

The Youth & Gender Media Project. n.d. "Mama Has a Mustache." *The Youth & Gender Media Project.* mamahasamustache.com.

Thomas Jefferson University. 2020. *Philadelphia 1918: The Flu Pandemic Hits Home.* July 7.

Thompson, Brandon. 2024. "Oregon Sees Staggering 41% Increase in Fentanyl Deaths, Highest in the Nation." *KOIN 6 News.* February 19. koin.com.

Thornhill M.D., John et al. 2022. "Monkeypox Virus Infection in Humans across 16 Countries April–June 2022." *The New England Journal of Medicine* N Engl J Med 2022; 387:679-691 (DOI: 10.1056/NEJMoa2207323).

Thorp, M.D. James A. et al. 2023. "Covid-19 Vaccines: The Impact on Pregnancy Outcomes and Menstrual Function." (Journal of American Physicians and Surgeons) 28 (1).

ThoughtCo. 2019. *Can Ocean Desalination Solve the World's Water Shortage?* July 29.

Tierney, John. 2022. "Maskaholics: Wear a mask may still give some a sense of security, but they could breathe more easily if they'd face the facts." *City Journal; Eye on the News.* April 18. city-journal.org.

2023. *"White Women" are not the "right choices" for the annual Women's March. Caption read: "Please leave the pussyhat at home,".* Performed by Vermont Action Fund video on TikTok.

Tober, Kevin. 2023. "Networks Ignore Jan 6 Committee Destroying Evidence Related to

Capitol Riots." MRC *Newsbusters.* newsbusters.org. August 9.

Tooley, Skye. 2021. "5 Ways Teachers Can Support Trans Kids." *We Are Teachers: Ideas and Inspiration for Reaching the Next Generation.* April 1.

Trapasso, Clare. 2023. "The Housing Shortage Hits Crisis Levels: What Homebuyers, Sellers Need to Know Before Making a Move." *Realtor.com.* July 25. realtor.com.

Tremoglie, Christopher. 2022. "Stop Blaming Christianity for the Colorado Springs Shooting." *Washington Examiner.* November 23. washingtonexaminer.com.

Troutman, Elizabeth. 2022. "No Free Lunch: Biden Admin Will Pull Meal Funding for Schools That Don't Comply With Its LGBT Agenda." *Washington Free Beacon.* June 1. freebeacon.com.

1952. *President Truman, Rear Platform Remarks, Eureka, Montana*. Film clip. Directed by Transcript. Produced by the U.S. Army Signal Corps. Performed by President Harry S. Truman. U.S. Army Signal Corp.

Truitt, Brandon. 2024. "Community Groups Forced Out as Roxbury Recreation Center Becomes

Shelter for Migrants." *CBS News* cbsnews.com January 30.

Twitter.com. 2023. "BREAKING: @Pfizer Exploring "Mutating" COVID-19 For New Vaccine." *#DirectedEvolution*. February 2. https://twitter.com/Project_Veritas/status/1618405890612420609?ref_src=twsrc%5Etfw%7Ctwcamp%5Etweetembed%7Ctwterm%5E1618405890612420609%7Ctwgr%5Ee116be9f4e025986dfa0c0bcb4909785ee-044ae2%7Ctwcon%5Es1_&ref_url=https%3A%2F%2Ftownhall.com%2Fcolumnists%2Flarry.

Tyler, Steven. 1975. *Sweet Emotion*. Performed by Aerosmith. Classic Rock.

U.S. Customs and Border Protection. 2022. "Guide to Facilitating Effective Communication With Individuals Who Identify as LGBTQI+." Department of Homeland Security.

U.S. Department of Education. 2023. *Fact Sheet: U.S. Department of Education's Proposed Change to its Title IX Regulations on Students' Eligibility for Athletic Teams*. April 6. https://www.ed.gov/news/press-releases/fact-sheet-us-department-educations-proposed-change-its-title-ix-regulations-students-eligibility-athletic-teams.

United Nations Climate Change. 2022. "At COP27; Scientists Warn Against Limits of Adaption." November 10.

United Nations. 2023. "OHCHR and Terrorism and Violent Extremism." *Office of the High Commissioner, United Nations Human Rights*. ohchr.org.

United Nations. 1972. *Report of the United Nations Conference on the Human Environment*. Conference Report, Stamped: UN Library July 25, 1995, UN/SA Collection.

United Nations. 2015. "Transforming Our World: The 2030 Agenda for Sustainable Development." *17 Goals and 169 targets for a universal agenda to realize human rights for and to achieve gender equity*. Prod. Department of Economy and Social Affairs.

United States Office of Inspector General. 2021. *DHS Needs to Enhance Its COVID-19 Response at the Southern Border*. DHS does not require testing for COVID-19 border crossers; Are instructed to mask wear, but most choose not to. Department of Homeland Security.

University of North Carolina Greensboro. "LGBTQIA Resource Center Glossary, all rights reserved. Not Universal Definitions, nor are they entirely comprehensive." *2023*. The UNC System.

University of Queensland. 2020. "Mining for Renewable Energy Could be Another Threat to the Environment." *PHYS ORG*. September 2. phys.org.

USA FACTS Team 2021. "Which Cities Have the Most People Living in Food Deserts?

USA FACTS usafacts.org June 23.

US Customs and Border Protection. 2023. *Guide to Facilitating Effective Communication with Individuals Who Identify as LGBTQI+*. Memo, Department of Homeland Security.

USGS. 2022. *How Hot Are Yellowstone's Boiling Waters? Some Are Hotter Than Others.* Yellowstone Volcano Observatory.

usgs.gov. 2016. *Status of Glaciers in Glacier National Park.* Northern Rocky Mountain Science Center.

Van Huygen, Meg. 2019. "A Dirty Shame: The Tale of a Vintage Sweater, a Backcountry Bar in Montana, and a Stranger Named Willie." August 11.

Vanderbilt, Commodore. 2024. "Companies Have Rapidly Ditched Woke Terms Over the Past

4 Years, But are Introducing "Stakeholder Metrics." Not the Bee. notthebee.com. May 22.

Vanderhoof, Erin. 2020. "Why Meghan and Harry's Move to California Seemed so Sudden." *Vanity Fair*. March 27. vanityfair.com.

Vanek Smith, Stacey. 2020. "Riots That Followed Anti-Racism Protests Come at Great Cost to Black-Owned Businesses." *npr*. August 12. npr.org.

Vasquez, Maegan. 2023. "Biden Not in Favor of Ban on Gas Stoves, White House Says." *CNN*. January 11. cnn.com.

Vespa, Matt. 2023. "James Carville Delivers a Scathing Observation About Left-Wing Democrats." *Townhall*. September 27.

Veuger, Stan. 2014. "A Clunker of a Program: Obama's Cash for Clunkers Harmed the Industry it Was Meant to Help." *U.S. News*. August 14.

Victor, David, Writer. *Marcus Welby, M.D.* Performed by Robert Young. Produced by

O'Connel David Victor and David J. Universal Television 1969-1976.

Vidal, John. 2012. "Cut World Population and Redistribute Resources, Expert Urges." *The Guardian*. April 26. theguardian.com.

viewers, Homemade videos submitted *America's Funniest Home Videos*. Produced by ABC Television Series. Performed by Bob Saget original host.

Visit NW Montana. n.d. "History of Eureka Montana." visitnwmontana.com.

Visit Ukraine. 2022. "Ukrainian Refugees in the US Will Receive a Pension and Health Insurance: Details." December 25. visitukraine.today.

Vondrich, Clara. 2022. "Reality is Not What it Seems and That Might Just Save the Planet; Cue Quantum Social Change." *Resilience*. August 25. resilience.org.

Walker, Jordon Trishton, interview by Project Veritas. 2023. "Pfizer Director of Research and Development; Strategic Operations and mRNA Scientific Planning." *Sting Video*. (February 2).

Wallace, Danielle. 2023. "St. Louis Prosecutor Kim Gardner Scorched Online After Execution-Style Shooting of a Homeless Man." *Fox News*. March 2. foxnews.com.

Walters, Natalie. 2016. "The Fascinating Story of How Two Brothers Went From Running a Failing Business out of a Van to Building a 100 Million Dollar Company." *Insider*, February 3.

Ward, David S. *"The Sting"* Performed by Paul Newman, Robert Redford, Robert Shaw,

Charles Dunning. Directed by Rob Cohen. Produced by Roy Huggins. 20th Century Fox. December 1973.

Watrobski, Kristina. 2023. "High Schoolers Suspended After "Misgendering" Teacher, California Parents Say." *WCYS News 5; Crisis in the Classroom*. July 7.

Watson, Carlos. 2014. "The Rest of the Story: Paul Harvey, Conservative Talk Radio Pioneer." *NPR*. October 9. npr.org.

Watts, Amanda and Asmelash, Leah. 2021. "6 Dr. Seuss Books Won't Be Published Anymore Because They Portray People in "Hurtful and Wrong" Ways." *CNN*. March 3. cnn.com.

Waxman, Olivia. 2019. "What to Know About the Origins of Fascism's Brutal Ideology." *TIME*. March 22. time.com.

WCS Newsroom. 2020. *Latest Threat to Biodiversity: Mining for Minerals Used in Renewable Energy Production.* News Release, WCSs Zoos, Aquarium and Field Conservation Programs Across the Globe, Study: Nature Communications, Journal: Nature Communications.

Weaver, Tanya. 2024. "The Amount of Copper Needed to Build EVs is Impossible For

Mining Companies to Produce." *Engineering and Technology*. eandt.theiet.org. May 16.

Weis, Julia. 2021. "California Rules in Favor of Sugary Drink Tax, Rejects Penalty Clause of State Preemption Law." *Salud America!* October 21. salud-america.org.

Wen, Leana. 2023. "We Are Overcounting Covid Deaths and Hospitalizations. That's a Problem." *The Washington Post*. January 13. washingtonpost.com.

Wendland, Mike. 2023. "Yellowstone Tourons: The Shocking and Outrageous Behavior of Park Visitors Revealed!" *RV Lifestyle*, July 11.

Wendling, Mike. 2023. "Spy Balloon Sent Data to China in Real Time - Report." *BBC*. April 3. bbc.com.

What's My Spirit Animal. "Goat Symbolism and Meaning: Call in the Goat as Your Power Animal." whatismyspiritanimal.com.

White Wolf Pack. n.d. *Pretty Nose: A Fierce and Uncompromising Woman War Chief You Should Know.*

White, Jamie. 2022. "Eat the Bugs: Netherlands Schools Offer Mealworms and Insects to Children as "Sustainable" Meat Substitute." *Your News*. October 16.

Wiens, Gary. 2024. "Perplexed but not Dispairing." *Rural Montana; Montana Electric Cooperatives' Association Magazine*, February.

Wigington, Patti. 2018. "What Was the Rajneesh Movement?" *Learn Religions*. June 5.

Wikipedia. n.d. "Kryptonian." *From DC Comics Universe, originating from Superman.*

Wildstein, David. 2023. "Statements on Orsted's Cancellation of Offshore Wind. Per Governor Murphy: "Today's decision by Orsted calls into question the company's credibility and competence."." *New Jersey Globe*. October 31. newjerseyglobe.com.

Will, Madeline. 2022. "Violence, Threats, and Harassment are Taking a Toll on Teachers, Survey Shows." *Education Week*. March 17.

Willett, B. J. et al. 2022. "SARS-CoV-2 Omicron is an Immune Escape Variant With an Altered Cell Entry Pathway." *Nature Microbiology* (Nature Microbiology) (https://doi.org/10.1038/s41564-022-01241-6).

Williams, Zach and Campanile, Carl. 2023. "NY Gov. Kathy Hochul Cooks With Gas Stoves While Pushing Ban in New Buildings." *New York Post*. January 22. nypost.com.

Wilson, Ben. 2023. "Watch: Biden Announces Plan to Build Massive Railway Across an Ocean." *Washington Free Beacon*. June 16.

Wirtz, Bill. 2019. "Solar Panels Produce Tons of Toxic Waste - Literally; Non-Recyclable Solar

Panels are Already Showing up in Landfills, Containing Toxic Heavy Metals That Pose Serious Environmental Risks." *Foundation for Economic Education*. fee.org. November 18.

Wisconsin Institute for Law and Liberty, Inc. 2023. "Serious Violate of Girls' Privacy Rights in Sun Prairie East Locker Room." *An 18-year-old stating he was "Trans" entered a 14-year-old girl's locker room, fully undressing.* Sun

Prairie, Wisconsin: Sun Prairie Area School District, Board of Education; shschro@sunprairieschools.org , April 18.

Wise, Talia. 2023. "CA Bill Says Parents Could Lose Their Children if They Don't Affirm Transgender Identity." *CBN NEWS*. June 13. cmsedit.cbn.com.

Wolf, Zachary. 2023. "$113 Billion: Where the US Investment in Ukraine Aid Has Gone." *CNN Politics*. September 21. cnn.com.

Women Are Warriors Too! *Minnie Hollow Wood.*

Wray, FBI Director Christopher, interview by House Committee on Homeland Security (transcript). 2023. *FBI Director Wray Confirms the Border Crisis Poses Major Homeland Security Threat, DHS Secretary Mayorkas Stonewalls.* Washington D.C., (November 15).

Wright, Samantha. 2023. "An Update on the Greater Idaho Movement." NPR - Idaho Matters. boisestatepublicradio.org. September 13.

Xu, Kenny. 2021. "Critical Race Theory Has No Idea What to do With Asian Americans." *Newsweek*. July 13. newsweek.com.

Yamamoto, Kenji. 2022. "Adverse Effects of COVID-19 Vaccines and Measure to Prevent Them." *PubMed.gov* (PubMed.gov) (PMID: 35659687 PMCID: PMC9167431 DOI: 10.1186/s12985-022-01831-0).

Yang, Maya. 2021. "Parents Sue Wisconsin School for Letting Children Change Pronouns Without Their Consent." *The Guardian*. November 22. theguardian.com.

Young, Jacob. "The Body Positivity Movement and its Deadly Consequences." *Political Polls, News, and More*. political.com.

Yurcaba, Jo et al. 2023. "Details About the Nashville Shooter's Gender Identity Sow Confusion and Disinformation; Hours after the shooting, police said the suspect was transgender. As one transactivists says, this is a "disinformation ecosystem."." *NBC News*. March 30. nbcnews.com.

Zilber, Ariel. 2023. " CNN Ex-Boss Jeff Zucker Told Staff Not to Probe "Lab Leak" Theory Because it Was "Trump Talking Point"." March 6.

2023. "Bud Light Sponsors Cincinnati Pride Parade After Dylan Mulvaney Controversy." *New York Post*. May 26.

2023. "CNN Ex-Boss Jeff Zucker Told Staff Not to Probe "Lab Leak" Theory Because it Was a "Trump Talking Point."." *New York Post*. March 6.

2019. "Hunter Biden Was Paid $83,333 a Month by a Ukranian Gas Company to be a "Ceremonial Figure" With a Powerful Name, While his Firm Got a Total of $3.4 Million." *Daily Mail and Reuters*. October 19.

Zimmerman, Paul. 2020. "Librarian-In-Chief Joe Biden Dreams Up Illegal Federal Library Code for Public Schools." *The Federalist*. July 14.

Zolynski, Hallie. 2023. "Digging Montana's Yogo Saphires." *Distinctly Montana*. October 4. distinctlymontana.com.